MARY LOU BURTON

EVENT RESOURCE GUIDE

Portland, Vancouver, Salem and Outlying Areas Edition

The Area's Most Comprehensive Guide to Services for Event Planning

Bravo! PUBLICATIONS, INC.

2 0 0 0

Bravo!® Publications, Inc.
16015 Waluga
Lake Oswego, Oregon 97035
(503) 675-1380, (800) 988-9887; Fax (503) 675-1204
E-mail: bravo7165@aol.com

Visit our Web sites:
www.bravoevent.com & www.bravowedding.com

Copyrighted and registered © 2000 by Bravo!® Publications, Inc. All rights reserved. No part of this work may be reproduced or transmitted in any form or by any means, electronic or mechanical, including photocopying and recording, or by any information storage or retrieval system, without permission in writing from the publisher.

Printed in the United States of America

ISBN 1-884471-23-4

Rental Services continued...

- Event Rental Communications, Inc. 185
- SK Watercraft Rentals, Inc. 186
- A to Z Party Rental 187
- Barbur Blvd. Rentals, Inc. 188
- The Party Pro's at Foster Rentals 189
- Interstate Special Events 190
- The Party Place 191
- Snead's Party Time Rentals & Decorations 192
- Special Events Co. 193
- West Coast Event Productions, Inc. 194

THEMES & PROPS 195–200

- Helpful Hints 196
- Paradym Events 197
- The Prop Shop 198
- West Coast Event Productions, Inc. 199

DECORATIONS, FLORISTS & BALLOONS 201–214

- Helpful Hints 202–203
- Butterfly Magic 204
- Professional Ice Carving 205
- Custom Chair Covers 206
- Bouquets & Balloons 207
- The Final Touch Floral Design & Balloon Decor 208
- M & M Balloon Co. 209
- Crimson & Clover Florist 210
- Crystal Lilies Exquisite Floral Artistry 211
- Flowers by Jacobsen's 212
- Flowers Tommy Luke 213

FORMAL WEAR & TUXEDOS 215–218

- Helpful Hints 216
- Gingiss Formalwear 217
- Mr. Formal 218

INVITATIONS & PAPER SUPPLIES 219–222

- Helpful Hints 220
- PaperPlus® 221
- Towne Papers 222

SPEAKERS & PRESENTATIONS 223–226

- Oregon Speakers Association 224

Speakers & Presentations continued...
Da Verne Bell 225
Jerry Fletcher 225
Linda Greep 225

ENTERTAINERS & PERFORMERS 227–236
Crystal Ball Productions 228
Caricatures by Philip O'Neil 229
Tom McCormack's Legendtelling 230
Tommy Yo-Yo 231
Susan Rice — Comedian 232
Michael John 233
Brainwaves Improvisational Comedy 234
ComedySportz 235

AUDIENCE PARTICIPATION & GAMES 237–256
Helpful Hints 238
Eddie May Murder Mysteries 239
It's a Mystery 240
Wild Bill's 241
Uptown Casino Events 242
A Little Pony & A Little Petting Zoo 243
Wish Upon A Pony 244
All Events & Entertainment Agency 245
Games-To-Go Rentals & MiniGolf-On-Wheels 246
Parties Inc. — A Tommy's Toys Co. 247
Party Outfitters Interactive Games 248
Partyworks Interactive 249
Sonsational Activities, Events & Atmosphere 250
LaserPort 251
Ultrazone 252
Paintball Island at Pat's Acres Karting Complex 253
Virtual Promotions 254
Elway Research, Inc. 255

ENTERTAINMENT CONSULTANTS 257–262
Celebration Music & Events 258
Nonstop Entertainment 259
Northwest Artist Management 260
Pacific Talent, Inc. 261

BANDS 263–276
Helpful Hints 264
Bob Miller's Almost All-Star Band 265

Bands continued...

- Byll Davis & Friends 266
- Cúl an Tí & Tir na Nog 267
- The Essentials 268
- Kim Ralphs & Company 269
- Loose Cannons 270
- Luminos 271
- McQueen 272
- The Moes 273
- Patrick Lamb Productions 274
- Swingline Cubs 275

MUSICIANS 277–282

- Michael Allen Harrison 278
- Harpist Ellen Lindquist 279
- Jo Anna Burns-Miller 280
- Duo con Brio 280
- Tom Grant 281
- Pamela Jordan 281
- System 99 282
- Susy Wolfson 282

DISC JOCKEYS 283–298

- Helpful Hints 284
- AA Two's Company DJ Service 285
- A Dancing Penguin Music Live Music & DJ 286
- All About Music DJ Company 287
- All-Wright Music Co. 288
- Anthony Wedin Productions, Inc. 289
- Complete Music Disc Jockey Service 290
- Decades Mobile Music 291
- DeeJay Entertainment 292
- Encore Studios 293
- Music Express Mobile Disc Jockey Service 294
- Signature Sound Mobile DJ Service 295
- Sound Express Multi Entertainment Inc. 296
- Sunrise Entertainment Services — Mobile DJs & Lighting .. 297
- Ultimate Entertainment Mobile Disc Jockey Service 298

BAKERIES & DESSERTS 299–302

- Baskin Robbins Ice Cream & Yogurt 300
- JaCiva's Bakery & Chocolatier 301

ESPRESSO CATERING 303–306

- Bridgetown Coffee Company 304
- Espresso Volare! Espresso Catering 305

CATERING & ICE CARVINGS 307–348

- Helpful Hints 308–309
- Professional Ice Carving 310
- Rose's Tea Room 311
- A Taste of Holland Bakeries & Catering 312
- Accent on Events 313
- Always Perfect Catering 314
- An Elegant Affair 315
- Authentic Texas BBQ 316
- Baja Grill Restaurant & Catering 317
- Barton Productions Catering 318
- Blimpie 319
- Bruce Goldberg & Co. 320
- Buster's Texas-Style Barbecue 321
- Capers Cafe & Catering Co. 322
- Cassidy's Restaurant & Catering 323
- Catering At Its Best 324
- Chef du Jour 325
- City Grill Catering 326
- Connor's Events & Catering, Inc. 327
- Dale's Catering Service 328
- DeAngelo's Catering & Events 329
- Delilah's Catering 330
- Food in Bloom Catering 331
- Jake's Catering at The Governor Hotel 332
- London Catering 333
- Market Street Catering 334
- Pizzicato Catering & Delivery 335
- Porter's Catering & Woodsmoke Barbecue 336
- Rafati's Elegance in Catering 337
- Red Star Tavern & Roast House 338
- Rheinlander German Restaurant 339
- Salvador Molly's Catering Co. 340
- Sandwich Depot Deli 341
- Tony Roma's Famous for Ribs 342
- Tubby's Deli & Heffernan's Corporate Catering 343
- West Hills Catering Co. 344
- Wilf's Restaurant & Piano Bar 345

Catering & Ice Carvings continued...
   Willaby's Catering 346
   The Wooden Nickel Catering 347

HOTEL ACCOMMODATIONS 349–366

   Helpful Hints 350
   The Benson Hotel 351
   Courtyard by Marriott — Lloyd Center 352
   Embassy Suites Hotel Portland — Washington Square 353
   Embassy Suites Portland — Downtown 354
   Fifth Avenue Suites Hotel 355
   Four Points Hotel Sheraton 356
   The Governor Hotel 357
   Homestead Village 358
   Hotel Vintage Plaza 359
   The Paramount Hotel 360
   Portland Marriott City Center 361
   Quality Inn Hotel & Convention Center 362
   Radisson Hotel Portland 363
   RiverPlace Hotel 364
   Shilo Inn Suites Hotel & Conference Center —
   Portland Airport/I-205 365
   The Sweetbrier Inn 366

RESORT ACCOMMODATIONS 367–386

   Best Western Columbia River Inn 368
   Best Western Oceanview Resort 369
   Eagle Crest Resort 370
   Embarcadero Resort Hotel & Marina 371
   Hallmark Inns & Resorts, Inc. 372
   Holiday Inn Newport at Agate Beach 373
   Hood River Hotel & Pasquale's Ristorante 374
   Hood River Inn 375
   The Inn at Otter Crest 376
   Inn at Spanish Head 377
   Kah-Nee-Ta Resort 378
   Mount Bachelor Village Resort 379
   The Running Y Ranch Resort 380
   Shilo Inn Suites Hotel — Bend 381
   Shilo Inn — Lincoln City Oceanfront Resort & Conference Center ... 382
   Shilo Inn — Newport Oceanfront Resort 383
   Shilo Inn — Seaside Oceanfront Resort 384
   Sunriver Resort 385
   Surfsand Resort 386

TABLE OF CONTENTS

RETREAT ACCOMMODATIONS................ 387–394
The Big K Guest Ranch & Conference Center 388
McMenamins Edgefield 389
McMenamins Kennedy School 390
Namasté Retreat & Conference Center 391
Rock Springs Guest Ranch & Conference Center 392
The Running Y Ranch Resort................................. 393
Silver Falls Conference Center................................. 394

CONVENTION & EXHIBITION SERVICES 395–402
Association & Conference Services (A & CS) 396
ESI — Event Solutions Incorporated 397
Plans & Action... 398
DWA Trade Show & Exposition Services..................... 399
NW Expo Services... 400
West Coast Event Productions, Inc........................... 401

CONVENTION & EXHIBITION FACILITIES..... 403–416
Helpful Hints 404–405
Oregon Convention Center & ARAMARK — GPL 406–407
OMSI — Oregon Museum of Science & Industry............ 408–409
Rose Quarter 410–413
Seaside Civic & Convention Center 414–415
Willamette Events Center at the Linn County Fair & Expo.......... 416

BANQUET, MEETING & EVENT SITES — BOATS, TRAINS & PARKS 417–432
Helpful Hints... 418
Boats... 419–423
Portland Spirit, Willamette Star & Crystal Dolphin............ 419
Sternwheeler "Columbia Gorge" & Marine Park 420
The Sternwheeler Rose 421
"Willamette Queen" Sternwheeler 422
Yachts-O-Fun Cruises, Inc................................... 423
Trains 424–425
Mount Hood Railroad & Dinner Train 424
Vintage Trolley 425
Parks... 426–432
Helpful Hints.. 426
Alderbrook Park Corporation................................. 427
Bridal Veil Lakes... 428
Mt. Hood Skibowl Winter & Summer Resort 429
Oaks Park Historic Dance Pavilion 430

Boats, Trains & Parks Sites continued...
- Oregon State Parks — Portland/Columbia Gorge................431
- Marine Park & Sternwheeler "Columbia Gorge"................432

BANQUET, MEETING & EVENT SITES — SMALLER VENUES..........................433–444

- Avalon Technology Group..............................434
- Buffalo Gap Saloon & Eatery...........................435
- Ernesto's Italian Restaurant..........................436
- Huber's..437
- McMenamins Hotel Oregon...............................438
- Il Fornaio...439
- Kingstad Meeting Centers..............................440
- Morton's of Chicago — The Steakhouse..................441
- Salem Inn..442
- The Screening Room...................................443
- Widmer Gasthaus......................................444

BANQUET, MEETING & EVENT SITES.........445–578

- The Adrianna Hill Grand Ballroom.....................446
- Albertina's at The Old Kerr Nursery..................447
- All Seasons Indoor Golf Club.........................448
- Amadeus at the Fernwood..............................449
- Arnegards..450
- The Atrium...451
- Atwater's Restaurant & Bar...........................452
- BeckenRidge Vineyard.................................453
- The Benson Hotel.....................................454
- Benton County Fairgrounds............................455
- BridgePort Brewing Company...........................456
- Cavanaughs Hillsboro Hotel...........................457
- Celebrate! Catering & Reception Facility.............458
- Central Library......................................459
- CH2M Hill Alumni Center at OSU.......................460
- Charbonneau On The Green.............................461
- Chart House..462
- Chinook Winds Casino & Convention Center.............463
- Chuck E. Cheese's....................................464
- Historic Portland City Hall..........................465
- ClubSport..466
- Columbia Gorge Hotel.................................467
- Courtyard Marriott — Portland North Harbour..........468
- The Crown Ballroom & Garden Court....................469

Banquet, Meeting & Event Sites continued...

Crown Vista Events	470
Crowne Plaza	471
Crystal Ballroom	472
Days Inn City Center	473
DoubleTree Columbia River	474
DoubleTree Hotel • Portland Downtown	475
DoubleTree Hotel Eugene-Springfield	476
DoubleTree Hotel Jantzen Beach	477
DoubleTree Hotel Portland • Lloyd Center	478
Eastmoreland Grill at the Eastmoreland Golf Course	479
Embassy Suites Hotel — Portland Airport	480
Embassy Suites — Portland Downtown	481
End of the Oregon Trail Interpretive Center	482
Fifth Avenue Suites Hotel	483
Florence Events Center	484
The Fountains Ballroom	485
Historic Gentle House	486
Jake's Catering at The Governor Hotel	487
Greek Cusina — Minoan Room	488
The Greenwood Inn	489
Hallmark Inns & Resorts, Inc.	490
The Heathman Hotel	491
The Heathman Lodge	492
Hilton Garden Inn — Portland/Beaverton	493
Hilton Garden Inn — Portland Airport	494
Hilton Portland	495
Holiday Inn Portland Airport Hotel & Trade Center	496
Holiday Inn Select	497
Hood River Hotel & Pasquale's Ristorante	498
Hood River Inn	499
Hunter Creek Farm	500
Typhoon! on Broadway at the Imperial Hotel	501
The Inn at Otter Crest & Flying Dutchman Restaurant & Winery	502
Inn at Spanish Head	503
Kells — Portland's Irish Restaurant & Pub	504
Kingstad Meeting Centers	505
LaserPort	506
Portland Marriott Hotel — Downtown	507
Portland Marriott Hotel — City Center	508
The Marshall House — Officers' Row	509
Marylhurst University Conference & Retreat Center	510
The Melody Ballroom	511

Banquet, Meeting & Event Sites continued...

Mission Mill Museum	512
Montgomery Park	513
Mt. Hood Meadows Ski Resort	514
New Seoul Garden and Salt & Pepper Club	515
North Star Ballroom	516
O'Callahan's Restaurant & Catering at Ramada Inn Portland Airport	517
Oaks Park Historic Dance Pavilion	518
The Old Church Society, Inc.	519
Oregon City Golf Club	520
Oregon Coast Aquarium	521
Oregon Garden	522
The Oregon Golf Club	523
OMSI — Oregon Museum of Science & Industry	524
Oregon Sports Hall of Fame Museum	525
Oregon Zoo	526
Paradigm Conference Center	527
Pazzo Ristorante at Hotel Vintage Plaza	528
Persimmon Country Club	529
Pittock Mansion	530
Port of Portland — Portland International Airport (PDX) Conference Center	531
Portland Art Museum North Wing	532
Portland Center for the Performing Arts	533
Portland Conference Center	534
Portland Spirit, Willamette Star & Crystal Dolphin	535
Pumpkin Ridge Golf Club	536
Red Lion Hotel at the Quay	537
Regal Hall Ballroom at A Night in Shining Amour	538
The Reserve Vineyards & Golf Club	539
The Resort at The Mountain	540
Rheinlander German Restaurant	541
RiverPlace Hotel	542
Rock Bottom Restaurant & Brewery	543
Salty's on the Columbia	544
Sayler's Old Country Kitchen	545
Seven Feathers Hotel & Casino Resort	546
Sheldon's Cafe at the Grant House on Officers' Row	547
Shenanigans' on the Willamette	548
Sheraton Portland Airport Hotel	549
Shilo Inn Suites Hotel Restaurant & Conference Center — Portland Airport/I-205	550
Silver Falls Conference Center	551

Banquet, Meeting & Event Sites continued...

Skamania Lodge 552
Spirit Mountain Casino 553
Sternwheeler "Columbia Gorge" & Marine Park 554
Sunriver Resort 555
The Sweetbrier Inn 556
Sylvia's Italian Restaurant & Class Act Dinner Theatre 557
Tiffany Center 558
Timberline Lodge. 559
Tuality Health Education Center 560
Ultrazone. 561
The Uptown Billiard Club 562
Valley River Inn. 563
Washington County Fair Complex 564
The Westin Portland. 565
The Westin Salishan Lodge & Golf Resort 566
Wilf's Restaurant & Piano Bar 567
Willamette Cafe. 568
Willamette Events Center at the Linn County Fair Expo 569
Willamette Gables Riverside Estate 570
"Willamette Queen" Sternwheeler 571
Willamette Valley Vineyards 572
Wilsonville Family Fun Center & Bullwinkle's Restaurant. 573
Windows Sky Room & Terrace 574
Wittenberg Inn. 575
World Forestry Center 576
World Trade Center Portland 577

BANQUET & EVENT SITE LISTINGS 579–628

Portland Area 579–604
Boats & Yachts, Trains & Trolley 605
Parks 606–608
Oregon Wineries 609–610
Vancouver Area 611–616
Salem Area. 617–623
Coastal Area. 626–627
Central Oregon Area 628
Southern Oregon Area 628

ACKNOWLEDGEMENTS

This Guide would not have been possible without the hard work, dedication, and endless hours from the following people:

Account Managers
Carinne McCulloch
Anne Ryan

Contributing Writer
Dian Lindsay, *EWE-ME & CO.*
See page 55

Public Relations & Marketing
Helen Kern
Amy Waetjen

Trade Show Consultant
Tracy Martin

Copy Writing & Layout Production
Amy Waetjen

Production Support
Amy Burton

Print Production
Kieley Malueg, *idesign*
See page 127

Prepress & Printing
NuWay Printing
Portland, Oregon

COVER

Cover Design
Roz Passion, *Roz & Co.*

Top Photo:
OMSI
See pages 408 & 524

Middle Photos:
Class Act Event Coordinators
See page 51

Class Act Event Coordinators
See page 51

Bottom Photo:
Capers Cafe & Catering Co.
See page 322

TITLE PAGE

Top Photo:
OMSI
See page 524

Middle Photo:
Jak Tanenbaum Photography Associates
See page 146

Bottom Photo:
Vicki Grayland Photographer
See pages 144

Visit our Web sites:
www.bravoevent.com
www.bravowedding.com

ABOUT THE BRAVO! TEAM

Front row: Tracy Martin, Amy Waetjen, Anne Ryan, Quinn Ryan, Jake Ryan, Alex Burton
Back row: Carinne McCulloch, Hailey McCulloch, Mary Lou Burton, Will Burton, Helen Kern, Nick Burton, Amy Burton

© 1999 Moments In Time

Mary Lou Burton

Mary Lou began Bravo! Publications, Inc. in 1989 after planning her own wedding for 550 Italian relatives. On the honeymoon, she and husband, John, realized the hundreds of hours they'd spent researching businesses could be helpful for other brides and grooms doing the same research. Mary Lou and Marion Clifton researched and created the first *Bravo! Bridal Resource Guide* in 1990. In 1994 an additional guide using the same concept and format was created specifically for meeting and event planners — *Bravo! Event Resource Guide*.

Mary Lou graduated from the University of Portland in 1985, with a bachelor's degree in communications management. She has appeared as a guest speaker for Nordstrom and Meier & Frank, as well as appearing on AM Northwest and other local broadcasts. She has written and contributed to several national and local publications. Over the last nine years as Bravo! has grown, so has her family. Mary Lou enjoys volunteering to read and being room parent at Alex and Nick's school and trys to keep up daily with 2-1/2 year old, Will. Husband John and partner for over 10 years has been a constant source of inspiration and has always supported this idea from the very beginning with enthusiasm. It would still just be an idea without his positive "can do" attitude.

Anne Ryan

Anne joined the Bravo! Team in 1994 after planning her wedding. Her excitement and professionalism have brought energy and growth to Bravo! Anne has believed in the Bravo! concept and philosophy and has helped develop several products including the Bravo! Meeting & Event Planners' Trade Show. Anne is a native Oregonian. She is a graduate of University of Portland, with a bachelor's degree in liberal arts, with a minor in psychology, business and history. She and husband Scott keep busy with their three-year-old son, Jake, and 6-month-old daughter, Quinn.

ABOUT THE BRAVO! TEAM

Carinne McCulloch
Carinne worked in the recreation industry for several years and was a client of Bravo! She decided to make a move and Bravo! was fortunate to be the place that she chose. No project is ever impossible with Carinne's "can-do" attitude. Her enthusiasm and easy-going personality has contributed to Bravo's growth while maintaining quality. Carinne graduated from Oregon State University in 1991 with a bachelor's degree in both business and human performance. Carinne and her husband, Derek, are enjoying their new daughter Hailey, as well as maintaining their love for recreation.

Amy Waetjen
Amy joined Bravo! last year as our production manager. With such a small office we wear many hats, and Amy has been able to combine production with Web design and maintenance, graphic design, marketing, plus a variety of other tasks. Amy graduated from Valparaiso University in Indiana with a bachelor's degree in communication. She grew up in Eugene and enjoys running, hiking, snowboarding and writing.

Amy Burton
Amy joined Bravo! this year helping out with production, office management and customer service. She grew up in Indiana and graduated with a BA degree in sports management from Indiana University. Amy and her boyfriend David resided in Portland three years ago to become more involved in the outdoor lifestyle. She loves being outside and enjoys camping, climbing, mountain biking, hiking, running, ultimate Frisbee and her dog Spire.

Tracy Martin
Tracy has worked with Bravo! for three years coordinating and planning the Bravo! Meeting & Event Planners' Trade Show. Tracy comes to us with six years experience from the planning and decorating side of Bravo! She and her husband, Darin, are expecting their first child this November. They enjoy gardening, camping, fishing and spending time with their families.

Helen Kern
Helen, Mary Lou's mother, joined Bravo! last year as well. She is in charge of human relations, always bringing some tasty treat or beautiful flowers to the office. She is our public relations ambassador and helps out with many projects around the office. Her words of wisdom inspire us each day! Helen is the mother of eight children — and her most important accomplishment of all is the faith and hope she gave to all of her children.

Kieley Malueg, idesign
Kieley has worked with Bravo! Publications for four years managing publication print production. She's a Portland native and 1989 graduate of the University of Oregon. Her experience includes marketing, design and print production in the recreation and tourism industries. Her attention to detail and professional expertise has enhanced Bravo!'s efforts to continue to produce affordable, high-quality, user-friendly publications. She and husband Ken have a daughter, Katie, 2-1/2, and new son Timothy, 6 months.

BRAVO! PUBLICATIONS, INC. IS A WINNER OF THE 1999

AWARD FOR PROVIDING A FAMILY-FRIENDLY WORK ENVIRONMENT

Spread The Word!

We need your help. To continue to supply this Guide to you at no charge we rely on you, the reader, to let the businesses and services in this book know that you heard about them through the *Bravo! Event Resource Guide*. Our featured businesses will recognize the Bravo! name.

Pass it on to a friend. Before they walk away with *your* copy, let them know they can fill out the order form on page 21 to receive their own complimentary copy.

The Bravo! Difference

- **Location... Location... Location!**
  This Guide will help you find the perfect spot for your next function, whether it's an overnight retreat for 10 or a company gala for 500—it's all right at your fingertips.

- **All the important details about the sites**
  From cost and terms to what's included and what's extra, the *Bravo! Event Resource Guide* includes descriptions of each facility for easier selection based on what you need. By the time you call a facility, you're thoroughly informed.

- **The ultimate tool for meeting and event planners**
  From listings of over 450 meeting and event sites to attractions, activities and calendars. Choose from exceptional caterers, decorators, rental equipment, and entertainment. You'll find everything for your upcoming event in this one resource guide.

- **This is a book you will rely on**
  Everything has been thoroughly researched to ensure that you have the most current information, updated annually. Everyone we've included is outstanding!

Take A Look At Our Web Site
www.bravoevent.com

If you like our guide... you'll love our Web pages

- **Search by area, capacity, and type of service**
  You'll be able to search our site for the type of product or service you need. Find all downtown facilities that will accommodate more than 500 guests or a gift basket company that will deliver to Beaverton.

- **The Guide is online**
  Every client in the book is listed on the Web site with location, phone number, contact and type of business or service. Client pages can be found online as well, with the same easy-to-read format.

- **Links to event services and facilities**
  Many of our client pages have direct links to their home pages with more details and photos of their facility or service. You can get more detailed information or communicate with many of these services easily online or through e-mail.

- **Guest book and order form**
  We'd love to hear from you. Sign-in to our guest book and let us know what you like about the Bravo! products or services. You can order any of our products online. Check out the new Bravo! online Bridal Shop.

ORDER FORM

Pass this form onto a friend

I would like to order the
Bravo! Event Resource Guide

The Guide is free to pre-qualified meeting planners

❏ Portland • Vancouver • Salem '00 Edition
❏ Greater Puget Sound '00 Edition

To receive your complimentary Guide, please fill out the information below:

Name: _____

Title: _____

Company Name: _____

Address: _____

Mail Stop: _____

City: _____ State: _____ Zip: _____

Phone: _____ Fax: _____

E-mail: _____

Type of business: _____

What type of events do you plan?
(Check all boxes that apply)
❏ Conferences
❏ Conventions
❏ Fundraisers
❏ Golf Tourneys
❏ Holiday Parties
❏ Meetings
❏ Parties
❏ Picnics
❏ Retreats
❏ Seminars
❏ Special Events
❏ Trade Shows
❏ Other: _____

Number of attendees you plan for
(Check all boxes that apply)
❏ 1–50
❏ 51–100
❏ 101–250
❏ 251–500
❏ 501–1,000
❏ Over 1,000

Send order to: **Bravo! Publications, Inc.**
16015 Waluga • Lake Oswego, OR 97035
(503) 675-1380, (800) 988-9887; Fax (503) 675-1204; E-mail: bravo7165@aol.com
Web Sites: www.bravoevent.com & www.bravowedding.com

BRAVO! TRADE SHOW

SAVE THIS DATE!

Bravo!® Publications
6th Annual
Meeting & Event Planners' Trade Show

Come explore new ideas and exciting ways
to make your next event an adventure to remember

**Wednesday, Oct. 25, 2000
1-7 p.m.
Oregon Convention Center**

All your special event & meeting research
can be accomplished in one afternoon!

Over 200 exhibitors
Facilities - Accommodations and Resorts - Florists
Speakers - Musicians - Vocalists - Photographers - Transportation
Audiovisual - Printing and Graphics - Invitations - Formal Wear
Food Sampling from Premier Caterers - Entertainment

PRIZES   PRIZES   PRIZES

Admission is FREE to pre-qualified meeting & event coordinators
Plus pick up your NEW 2001 *Bravo! Event Resource Guide*

Call Bravo! to make sure you are on our corporate list to be invited.
Fill out the form on the right of this page and fax or mail to Bravo!

Register online at: BRAVOPUBS.com

Over 200 booths featuring

Event Sites - Caterers - Entertainers
Decorators - Promotional Items -
Florists - Bands - Speakers
DJs - Resorts - Photographers
And much, much more

Bravo! Presents

2001 Meeting & Event Planners' Trade Show

The largest Trade Show of its kind in the Pacific Northwest

Wednesday, October 25, 2000 - 1-7 p.m.

Plan your events for the entire year in one afternoon!

Oregon Convention Center, Exhibit Hall C

777 N.E. Martin Luther King Jr. Blvd.

Portland, Oregon

While at the show...
pick up your 2001 edition of the Bravo! Event Resource Guide - The area's most comprehensive guide to services for event planning!

To RSVP, return the reservation form below by fax or mail *after* September 1st, 2000.

Name: _____

Title: _____

Company Name: _____

Address: _____

Mail Stop: _____

City: _____ State: _____ Zip: _____

Phone: _____ Fax: _____

E-mail: _____

Type of business: _____

What type of events do you plan?
(Check all boxes that apply)
- ❏ C–Conventions
- ❏ F–Fundraisers
- ❏ G–Golf Tourneys
- ❏ X–Holiday Parties
- ❏ M–Meetings
- ❏ S–Seminars
- ❏ N–Conferences
- ❏ T–Parties
- ❏ P–Picnics
- ❏ W–Trade Shows
- ❏ R–Retreats
- ❏ E–Special Events
- ❏ O–Other Functions

Number of attendees you plan for
(Check all boxes that apply)
- ❏ 1–50
- ❏ 51–100
- ❏ 101–250
- ❏ 251–500
- ❏ 501–1,000
- ❏ Over 1,000

Send RSVP to: **Bravo! Publications, Inc.**
16015 Waluga Drive • Lake Oswego, Oregon 97035
(503) 675-1380, (800) 988-9487; Fax (503) 675-1204; E-mail: bravo7165@aol.com
Web site: www.bravoevent.com

BRAVO! PRODUCT INFORMATION

Bravo!® Organizers

The step-by-step system to track every detail of your event.

Organizers feature:
- Detailed worksheets designed to double as contracts
- Time schedules, checklists and calendars
- Detailed budget worksheets and "who pays for what forms
- "To Do" forms and "Delegating Duties" lists

Bravo!® Wedding Organizer
Suggested Retail: $24.95

Bar/Bat Mitzvah Organizer
Suggested Retail: $22.95

Greater Puget Sound
Bravo!® Event Resource Guide

Venues, Attractions & Activities, Accommodations, Audience Participation, Corporate Gifts & Awards, Food & Beverage Services, and more...

The 2000 Edition features 608 pages
of easy-to-read, résumé-style write-ups on area businesses and service providers, listings of Banquet and Event Sites, how-to's, checklists, and all the helpful hints.

Suggested Retail: $8.95
Complimentary to pre-qualified Meeting and Event Planners... see page 21 for details

Greater Puget Sound
Bravo!® Bridal Resource Guide

Churches, Chapels, Banquet & Reception Sites, Caterers, Florists, Photographers, Videographers, Invitations, Bridal Attire, Tuxedo Rentals, Bridal Registry, Favors, Accessories, Consultants and more...

The 2000 Edition features 544 pages
of easy-to-read, résumé-style write-ups on area businesses and service providers, listings of Banquet and Reception Sites, how-to's, check lists, and all the helpful hints!

Suggested Retail: $9.95

TO ORDER CALL (800) 988-9887

BRAVO!® RESOURCE GUIDES

When You Want Information, Not Glossy Ads—You Want Bravo!

Bravo!® Publications is proud to offer four regional resource guides for planning meetings, events and weddings. Each of the guides featured on this and the following page is filled with important information and details about the area's finest businesses and services providers, and is presented in easy-to-read, résumé style formats, alphabetically, by category. Designed to be user-friendly, each of these guides truly are your planning *Resource*!

Portland • Vancouver • Salem
and outlying areas
Bravo!® Event Resource Guide

Venues, Attractions & Activities, Accommodations, Audience Participation, Gifts & Promotional Items, Food & Beverage, Rental Services, and more...

The 2000 Edition features 640 pages
of easy-to-read, résumé-style write-ups on area businesses and service providers, listings of Banquet and Event Sites, how-to's, checklists, and all the helpful hints.

Suggested Retail: $8.95
Complimentary to pre-qualified Meeting and Event Planners... see page 21 for details

Portland • Vancouver • Salem
and outlying areas
Bravo!® Bridal Resource Guide

Churches, Chapels, Banquet & Reception Sites, Caterers, Florists, Photographers, Videographers, Invitations, Bridal Attire, Tuxedo Rentals, Bridal Registry, and more...

The 2000 Edition features 640 pages
of easy-to-read, resumé-style write-ups on area businesses and service providers, listings of Banquet and Reception Sites, how-to's, check lists, and all the helpful hints!

Suggested Retail: $9.95

Say You Saw It In Bravo!

Every business or service needs to track where their business is coming from. By letting them know you are using one of the *Bravo!® Resource Guides*, you not only ensure that Bravo!® will be available for meeting and event planners or brides in the future, but you also let the businesses or services know where their business is coming from.

TO ORDER CALL (800) 988-9887

BRAVO! ONLINE

IF YOU LOVE THE BRAVO! EVENT RESOURCE GUIDE, WAIT UNTIL YOU BROWSE OUR BRAVO! EVENT WEB SITE!

Check out the Bravo! Publications Web sites at:
www.bravoevent.com *and*
www.bravowedding.com

The Bravo! Web site is:
- **Easy to use!**
- Features all the **detailed information** you're used to seeing in your Bravo! Event Resource Guide!
- Has its own **"search engine"** so you can find things easily by category or location!
- Features **color photographs**!
- Has a comprehensive **Calendar of Events** that will let you know when and where the next Meeting Planning Trade Shows, Seminars or Events will be taking place.

The Bravo! Event and Wedding Web sites will be…
growing and changing weekly, so be sure to browse them often so you can see what's new!

ADD BRAVO! TO YOUR ROLODEX!
(Just cut out the card below and staple or slip it into your Rolodex.)

Bravo! Publications, Inc.
16015 S.W. Waluga
Lake Oswego, OR 97035
Toll Free: (800) 988-9887
Fax: (503) 675-1204
E-mail: bravo7165@aol.com
Web sites: www.bravoevent.com
www.bravowedding.com

INTRODUCTION & HOW TO USE THIS BOOK

The objective of the *Bravo!® Event Resource Guide* is to help planners of any experience level reference information from facilities, caterers, florists, entertainers, etc. Businesses and services are listed in the book based on merit and not just the amount of money they have paid for an advertisement. Small businesses are portrayed in the same light as their counterparts. Information has to be complete, reliable, and factual, including important details like deposits, cancellation terms, and cost.

The *Bravo!® Event Resource Guide* was created by popular demand! Many meeting and event planners were using the *Bravo!® Bridal Guide* as a resource for its many facilities and services. Bravo! Publications published the first Bridal Guide in 1990, and its popularity among brides has made it a number-one seller. Meeting and event planners found the information listed in the Guide invaluable to finding a specific location that met their needs, including information like capacity, price, sleeping rooms, etc.

In creating the *Bravo!® Event Resource Guide,* we worked with professional meeting and event planners and vendors in the industry to offer information and helpful hints based on years of knowledge and experience in the industry. We provide a survey in the front of this Guide and appreciate input from readers like you about what they found useful in the Guide. Please take the time to fill out the survey; your input ensures the success of this publication for future users. Every year the Guide is updated, and we want to know the businesses with whom you had good or bad experiences, or those businesses who you would like to recommend to be in the Guides.

In addition to the Bravo! *Resource Guides* and *Organizers,* we also produce events throughout the year for meeting and event planners to attend, where planners receive information and ideas directly from the businesses and services in the Guides. Your attendance in supporting these events will help us to continue to provide quality products and services! For dates of upcoming Bravo! trade shows and events, check out our web site at: *www.bravoevent.com.*

IMPORTANT NOTE!
It's important to make sure you mention to the businesses or services, that you selected them from the *Bravo!® Event Resource Guide.* This will help us continue to provide this Guide complimentary.

Keeping Up With Technology

More and more meeting planners are accessing information on the World Wide Web. Keeping up with technology, Bravo! has created a web site for meeting and event planners. Now you can access the entire 2000 *Bravo!® Event Resource Guide* on-line. With our own internal search engine, you can find information on businesses and services featured in the following pages by pull-down category lists, key word, capacity, or area! Just go to *www.bravoevent.com* for everything you need to plan your next meeting or event!

Notes

Planning A Meeting Or Event

TYPES OF EVENTS & WHERE TO START

MANY TYPES OF EVENTS

- Conventions
- Holiday Parties
- Seminars
- Tours
- Groundbreakings
- Grand Openings
- Festivals
- Concerts
- Trade Shows
- Sporting Events
- Fund-raisers
- Product Announcements
- Anniversaries
- Picnics
- Sales Meetings
- Carnivals/Fairs

PURPOSE OF EVENTS AND MEETINGS

Corporations are planning more events and special meetings and they have become a big part of the companies overall marketing budget. The reason being that it is more difficult to motivate and attract attention with just a regular in-house memo, announcement or traditional meeting.

BENEFITS OF A WELL-PLANNED EVENT

- More sales, higher profits and employees take ownership of ideas
- Media attention and free publicity
- Target marketing
- Education
- Name recognition
- Good will in the community
- Product loyalty
- Problem-solving
- Networking

PLAN...PLAN...PLAN

Ask professional meeting planners how to ensure a successful event or meeting and they will say, "pay close attention to the logistics and details and plan...plan... plan...ahead so that when the day of the event comes, all the good planning will kick into gear, and you can take care of the 'surprises' that Murphy brings to the event!"

DETAILS

When meeting and event arrangements work well, the attendees have no idea of the details that went into the planning. But, when arrangements aren't right, everyone is aware of the details that needed to be handled and weren't! Whether it's too few chairs or faulty audiovisual equipment, everyone's attention will be focused on the one who planned the event and how things could have been organized and handled better!

ASKING QUESTIONS

Whether it's for yourself, a corporation, a non-profit convention, or other clients, when planning a meeting or an event, you need to start with the basic questions, and from there you will get your event off to a good start. Without the solid foundation of knowing your meeting goals and attendees' expectations, you have no way of determining if your event was successful.

So, before you can get into the nuts and bolts of planning a great meeting or event, you need to ask lots of questions!

On the following pages we offer you the basic questions to ask to start your planning.

DO YOUR HOMEWORK!!!

WHY, WHAT AND WHO

WHY? THE PURPOSE...
Why are you, your client, or your boss wanting to have a meeting or event? Whatever the occasion, you, as the planner, need to know WHY! Ask questions!
- Is it for a celebration?
- An annual convention?
- New product introduction?
- A sales meeting?
- Retirement or anniversary party?
- Employee motivation?
- To educate?
- Allow for networking?

WHAT? THE OBJECTIVE...
Along with the WHY is WHAT are the objectives of the event? Is the objective to thank employees for a hard year at work or to provide recognition for some special people or individuals? Is your objective to promote good feelings within the company or to the general public? Is this an event that has many audiences or just one? How do you want your audience to feel when this event is over? Do you want them to buy your products, feel pride in working for an outstanding company, or learn new techniques to make their jobs more productive?

DETERMINE YOUR OBJECTIVES
The meeting may have multiple objectives...keeping within a budget is one of them, along with keeping the planning time to a minimum. What kind of a retirement party can I realistically plan with $1,000 and two weeks' notice?

WHO? PROFILE THE AUDIENCE...
Determining objectives of your meeting is an important first step because meeting programs are designed from these objectives to bring about the results desired. In order to measure your success, you need to determine goals and objectives, then create a meeting that provides the results you want.

Who will be your attendees, speakers, sponsors, etc? These are all the different audiences with whom you will be working. You need to have a profile of who they are, where they are coming from, and how old they are. Are they couples? Do any have disabilities? Will any attendees be international? Do they speak English? The more you know about your participants, the more success you will have meeting their expectations!

AMERICANS WITH DISABILITIES ACT (ADA)
The Americans with Disabilities Act (ADA), passed into law in 1991, guarantees protection for disabled persons in the area of public accommodations. The meeting planner is legally responsible to make certain all effort has been made to comply with the ADA; know the individual needs of attendees. In compliance with ADA, it is very important to ask your attendees if anyone has disability-related needs. A follow-up call should be made to determine specific needs of attendees, and by clearly communicating these needs to the facility, you have established the intent to comply with ADA. Contact the ADA Portland office or your facility to get detailed regulations.

CHECKLIST, PROFILE & SCHEDULING

PLANNING CHECKLIST

It is helpful to develop a Planning Checklist for your event or meeting; this allows you to jump into the planning and delegating without trying to "re-invent" the wheel with a plain notepad. You can even assign each category to the qualified attendees.

- Profile the audience
- Determine the needs
- Site selection
- Budget
- Publicity plan
- Work plan or work flow
- Registration, invitations, programs
- Staffing
- On-site coordination
- Evaluation and accounting

WHAT ARE YOUR NEEDS FOR THIS EVENT?

Make a list of what you think will be your immediate need. Will you need a facility, or can you do it at your own location, home, or business? Will you need to arrange transportation? Air or ground? Will you include food and hotel lodging for your event guests? Will you need meeting rooms and function space? Will you need audiovisual equipment? Will you need printed materials, signage, extra staff?

SUB-CATEGORY QUESTIONS

These are general questions, but this is the beginning of a needs list. From this general list you will naturally develop your sub-category of questions including: site selection criteria, room rates, bus or shuttle, etc. And then the fun begins….negotiating what you want!!

SCHEDULING

DETERMINING YOUR SCHEDULE OF EVENTS

Determining the "schedule" of an event needs to start in the initial planning stages! Changes and more changes will occur, but having a sense of timing for the various aspects of a two-hour meeting, a one-day seminar, or a five-day conference will help set the groundwork for selecting the site and vendors. Decide what "TYPES" of activities your group will be involved in during your meeting or event. For example: business portions, social portions, recreation free time, exhibits, etc. Begin to map out a schedule of events.

SCHEDULE OF EVENTS (SAMPLE)

DATE: _____

TIME	EVENT	LOCATION	NUMBERS	SETUP
8–9 a.m.	Registration	TBD	300	Flow See Diagram
9–10 a.m.	Breakfast	TBD	300	Rounds
10 a.m.–Noon	General Session	TBD	300	Theatre Style
Noon–1 p.m.	Lunch	Off Property	N/A	N/A
1–3 p.m.	Workshops A B C	TBD TBD TBD TBD	300 100 100 100	Classroom Classroom Classroom Classroom

BUDGET

PREPARING A BUDGET
Preparing a budget is critical to effective meeting or event management. The budget provides you with the control and accountability of all meeting revenues and expenses. Your meeting objectives will influence both the revenues and the expenses of the program. Whatever the goal, it is important to document everything you commit to spending so you know at any time where you stand financially. A well-developed financial plan is a tool to guide the planner in making decisions and identifying priorities throughout the event.

REVENUE
There are two concerns in creating a budget: revenue and expenses. Revenue is determined if you are going to expect income. How will it be generated? Registration fees, exhibitor fees, sponsorships, individual event fees, concession fees, are all ways money is brought in. How much income will you expect to receive in each category?

EXPENSES
After determining your NEEDS PROFILE and your SCHEDULE OF EVENTS, you can develop a list of expenses involved or anticipated with each item. Don't forget the costs of administration, phone, mailings, faxes, staff, and supplies, in other words, your overhead. Experience helps in this process, but if you are a novice, you can do some research with vendors to determine reasonable estimates at this stage.

GOOD PLANNING AND BUDGETING
Good planning results in meeting your objectives. During the budget portion of planning, you need to determine what your financial goals are as well. Determine what the group expects to gain. Should the meeting make money, lose money, or break even? If the group wants to make a profit, the amount or percentage should be determined in this initial stage.

BUDGET WORKSHEET (SAMPLE)

BUDGET WORKSHEET

Meeting Name _____

Meeting Date _____ Division/Cost Center _____

Name of Person Responsible for Meeting_____

HOTEL
Sleeping rooms $ _____
($___/night + ___% tax= $___x___ room nights)
Meeting room rental $ _____
Audiovisual charges $ _____
TOTAL: $ _____

MEALS/FUNCTIONS
Breakfast $ _____
Breaks $ _____
Lunch $ _____
Receptions $ _____
Entertainment $ _____
Recreation $ _____
TOTAL: $ _____

THE PLANNING & TIMELINE PROCESS

MANAGING THE DETAILS

This is what meeting and event planners are famous for and everyone has tools to help them be successful. Everyone develops his or her own style and methods, but generally detail management includes these elements:

- TASKS...determine the tasks needed to be completed to ensure a successful event
- ORDER....determine the order in which these tasks need to be completed
- DEADLINE...determine the time in which they need to be completed
- DELEGATE... determine if, and to whom, they can be delegated

This is where you'll hear those magic words:
TIMETABLES, WORKPLANS AND CHECKLISTS

THREE-PART TIMELINE

One simple way to begin managing your information is to break your timeline into three parts:
1. PRE-EVENT or MEETING
2. ON-SITE
3. POST-EVENT or MEETING

You can then add the functional sub-categories under each part like event design, speaker recruitment, marketing and promotion, registration, site selection, etc. Determine what needs to be accomplished during each phase.

MANAGEMENT TIMELINE
(SAMPLE TIMELINE)

12–18 MONTHS BEFORE THE EVENT

- ❏ Suggest program and "needs" list subjects
- ❏ Define audiences
- ❏ Determine needs
- ❏ Draft theme/title
- ❏ Determine pricing
- ❏ Establish program budget
- ❏ Select dates
- ❏ Conduct site inspections
- ❏ Book meeting, banquet, and sleeping room space

9–12 MONTHS BEFORE THE EVENT

- ❏ Determine speakers
- ❏ Determine agenda: business and social
- ❏ Contact speakers
- ❏ Contract transportation: ground and air
- ❏ Coordinate facility needs
- ❏ Send "save the date" mailings to audiences
- ❏ Solicit exhibits and sponsors

Management Timeline continued...

6–9 MONTHS BEFORE THE EVENT
- ❑ Review program needs
- ❑ Review audiovisual needs
- ❑ Review and refine budget
- ❑ Select catering and event menus and themes
- ❑ Communicate with vendors
- ❑ Establish registration procedure
- ❑ Design registration materials

and so on...

USING A WORKPLAN
Once you have determined the tasks, give them a deadline and delegate. Responsibilities may be assigned to individuals, groups, committees, or suppliers, such as hotels, caterers, etc. Even if you are the ONLY person working on your event, suppliers or vendors do have a place in your delegation timeline. They need to get back to you in a timely way that works for you; you need to get signed contracts and guarantees back to them. Through the WORKPLAN you can manage the details.

WORKPLAN (SAMPLE)

WORK ELEMENT	DEADLINE	ASSIGNED TO
PROGRAM:		
Theme design	Oct. 1	Smith/Jones
Draft agenda	Nov. 5	Staff
Determine speakers	Nov. 15	Smith/Staff
BUDGET:		
Draft budget	Oct. 1	Meyer/Staff
Setup ledgers	Dec. 1	Smith/Accounting

SITE SELECTION

SELECTING THE SITE
Decision time…if you have done your homework, you will be armed with information that will help you make good decisions about your site selection. Once your needs are identified, you must match them with the sites that can handle them. Determine the geographic location that best suits your event…the United States, the West Coast, the Northwest, Oregon, Portland, Downtown Portland. These are all decisions that determine from whom to request proposals.

RESOURCES TO SELECT THE SITE
You can call upon many resources to help you determine the best location for your event. Once you have narrowed the possibilities, you will be ready to make some comparisons and decide. Use the expertise of travel agents, Convention and Visitors Bureaus, Chambers of Commerce, professional planners—anyone that you feel understands your needs. ***This publication gives you a good comparison of over 450 local meeting and event facilities in the Portland, Salem, Vancouver and outlying areas.***

MEETING PROFILE
Develop specifications and requirements for your meeting. This is sometimes referred to as a "Meeting Profile." This will be the natural outcome of your Needs List. It may be as simple as, "I need a room and meals for 30 people on this date, at this time." It might include preferred dates, number of sleeping rooms, meeting rooms, types of food functions, range of acceptable rates, exhibit requirements, and special needs of your group. The more information you can provide, the better chance you have of getting what you want. Many groups provide a detailed history of their event or meeting and the monetary value it has to a property. The profile becomes a request to all sites you choose to bid on your business. Once bids begin to come in, the planner can begin the evaluation and elimination process. After selecting an appropriate number to consider—and that number is up to you—it is recommended that you conduct site inspections.

SITE INSPECTION
A site inspection is the best time to ask questions and get a good look at what each facility has to offer. It will be important for you to identify the property that can best meet your space requirements and the level of service you will need. Request references from groups with similar attendance and requirements, then contact them.

NEGOTIATION

NEGOTIATION AND CONTRACTS
Facility negotiations sound serious, but they don't have to be intimidating. These are important conversations because negotiations build relationships, which will lead to contracts. Contracts are serious business and when you, as a planner, enter into a contract, you want to be sure you have all the knowledge and information you need. Keep in mind that negotiable items and practices vary between areas of the country, so what may be standard procedure on the East Coast is not necessarily the same on the West Coast.

Negotiation continued...

HOMEWORK PAYS OFF!
Before you begin negotiating, you need some tools! If you have done your homework (refer to the first section), you'll be set! You need your meeting profile or prospectus, a history of your meeting or event, the value of your meeting to the facility (your budget), and a profile of your group. If you know your requirements, they will dictate the specific items you can negotiate.

NEGOTIATIONS SHOULD BE WIN-WIN
Don't get bogged down in sleeping room rates! Rates are only one item that can be negotiated. The list of negotiable items may be as long as you want …it never hurts to ask! But, in order to have a successful meeting, negotiations should be a win-win process. For example, if you get the hotel to provide complimentary meeting room space, but in order to afford this, the hotel cuts back on service staff for your meeting…who wins?

CONTRACTS
The most important things to remember are that contracts should be written with an equal amount of risk for both parties, and that all your discussions are put into writing so there will be no confusion when it's time for your event.

VENDOR SELECTION

WORKING WITH VENDORS
Facilities are not the only vendors you will be working with to put on meetings and events. You will communicate with many different suppliers of services. Good planners realize that vendors have their own needs as they relate to your event. You need to select vendors on criteria that you develop for your event. XYZ bus company may have the most modern and comfortable equipment available, but if they are late, or their drivers are rude, they might cause more problems than the shiny buses are worth!

BE SURE TO CHECK REFERENCES
Take every bit as much care in selecting a caterer, transportation company, or a dance band as you do in selecting a site for your event. Unless you have worked with the same vendors over and over again (personnel does change), make sure you check references and ask for bids for their service. Good vendors know how to make planners look good…and good vendors want and deserve repeat business!

USING THE BRAVO EVENT RESOURCE GUIDE
This Resource Guide is an invaluable resource of goods and services. Everything from caterers to musicians is listed in an easy-to-read format that allows you to make informed "apples to apples" comparisons of hundreds of products and services. You can count on reliable information and reliable references, as each business is screened before being listed in the Guide. Also included are helpful hints on checking references, protecting your deposits, securing dates, and more.

ADMINISTRATIVE NEEDS

DAILY TASKS
In conjunction with site and vendor selection, you, as the planner, will also attend to the daily administration tasks necessary to put on an event or meeting. Administration is where communication with your audiences will take place.

COMMUNICATING WITH YOUR AUDIENCE
This is where you will determine appropriate mailing lists and how to handle RSVP's or registrations. How will the mailing happen? Volunteers or mailing houses? Create the graphics and coordinate the printing of all your written materials as early as possible. This is your promotion and publicity for your event. If staff or volunteers are needed, start recruiting them early.

DEVELOPING A SMOOTH SYSTEM
The administration portions of the task list and budget usually include registration, name badges, financial record keeping, database, and computer work. Developing a smooth system that allows checks and balances along the way will help you feel confident that the paperwork is getting handled. A lot of meeting planning is telephone and paper work! The development of clear instructions to the registrants in all your materials will save time and money throughout the meeting process!

GOOD COMMUNICATION
Good communication with your attendees is only half of the successful meeting equation, the other half is good communication with your selected vendors. This means ordering the food and beverages, the room blocks, the room setup, the flowers and the awards! Hopefully, you have selected a great team, and they are supporting you all the way! But they are not mind readers…let them know in writing, in diagrams, charts, and phone calls what you expect—what you are planning, what you need, and when you need it. Lack of information and lack of feeling for the big picture are two of the biggest problems in planning an event. You, as the planner, want to get a timely response from your vendors, and they want to get direction from you.

STAFFING ASSISTANCE
For a large event or trade show, extra staffing and assistance is going to be necessary. There are companies and coordinators that can even deal with the entire registration for your event—handling reservations, organization name badges and staffing. Refer to "Meeting and Event Planners" section of this Guide. Also, there are staffing companies that can offer assistance on a temporary, as needed basis; data entry of names, greeters, setup help. The benefit of these companies is that the company you hire from assumes all the liability of the employee, you just pay an hourly wage. You can find these type of businesses in the "Staffing and Employment Services" section of this Guide.

PROMOTION

SELL THE AUDIENCE ON ATTENDING THE EVENT
Will they come? Even if this is the 100th annual conference, your attendees have to be sold on attending. Even if this is the biggest awards banquet in the history of your company, the employees have to be motivated to come. As the planner, you are in charge of making sure your event is marketed to the right audience. They need to know where, what, when, and how to sign up!

MARKETING TOOLS
You have many tools available to you, and if your kit has a variety of options, you'll have the most success. Some obvious options include direct mail, in-house newsletters, press releases, paid advertising, billboards, bus sides, and word of mouth. Don't rely on what has worked before—things change, people change. Good programs and reasons to attend will always be your best tools.

PUBLIC RELATIONS/PRESS RELEASE
Refer to the "Advertising and Media" section of this Guide for local media (newspapers, radio, and television) addresses and phone numbers. Listed below is information about writing the different types of releases:

MEDIA ALERT (SAMPLE)

WHAT:	Press Conference
WHEN:	Wednesday, December 13, 2001—10:00 a.m.
WHERE:	Convention Center, 455 Grand Ave.
WHO:	Quinn Ryan, President, Meeting Planners
TOPIC:	Oregon's largest convention coming to town

ADDITIONAL INFORMATION: Press pass available. Photo opportunity. Meeting Planners is the largest meeting planner association in the country.

PRESS RELEASE (SAMPLE)

The press release starts the same as the "media alert" on the previous page, then expands upon the what, when, where, who, and topic. Bold the key information throughout the copy.

CALENDAR ITEM (SAMPLE)

WHAT:	Cajun Cooking Seminar
WHEN:	Wednesday, November 8, 2001—10:00 a.m.
WHERE:	Cajun Restaurant, 252 Pacific Road
WHO:	Hailey Rose, Chef, Cajun Restaurant
COST:	$16 per person, senior citizens $8

REGISTRATION: Space limited to 25 people. Pre-registration is required. Registration deadline is November 1, 2001.

ADDITIONAL INFORMATION: Hailey Rose is a world-renowned Cajun Chef, who is sharing her secrets to preparing the hottest food in town.

The calendar continues expanding upon the what, when, where, who and cost. Bold the key information throughout the copy.

ON-SITE & MEETING SURVIVAL SUPPLIES
THE BIG DAY...
BIG AFTERNOON... BIG WEEK...

THE BIG DAY!
Whether your event is a lunch or a major exposition, the Big Day always arrives! Your good planning will determine just how BIG that day will be. If you have met your deadlines, used your timelines, checked off your checklists, verified menus, orders, schedules, and agendas, you will be ready for the last-minute disasters!!

PRE-CONFERENCE MEETINGS
It is a good idea to plan rehearsals, run-throughs, and team meetings. Conference planners often have pre-conference meetings where all the players are in attendance: the food and beverage managers, the audiovisual people, the registration supervisors, the transportation providers, the off-site providers. This is when the last-minute changes are noted, the lines of communication are finalized, and the team is energized for a successful meeting or event!

THE PLANNER IS THE RINGMASTER
On-site is not the place to be determining agenda, policy, or making arrangements. On-site is reacting to the unexpected situations that arise, no matter how good your planning. On-site is maintaining balance as the months, weeks, and days of preparation kick into gear and the event unfolds. The planner is the ringmaster as the acts perform. What happens backstage will most often go unnoticed if good planning has taken place!

TRUST THE TEAM
Delegate as many tasks as possible so you, as the organizer, can attend to the event and troubleshoot. If you are stuck at a registration desk when the lights go out on the main speaker, who's going to get the wheels moving to fix the problems? When the buffet lines are out in the street, who's going to get another serving station set up? Circulate and be everywhere, but don't be in anyone's way. The team has a job to do. They're there to support you and work together to make the event a success. TRUST THE TEAM you have assembled. They are the cast and crew of your production!

MEETING SURVIVAL SUPPLIES

- ❏ File boxes
- ❏ Date and number stamps
- ❏ Stationery and envelopes
- ❏ Computer and computer supplies (disks, etc.)
- ❏ Pens, pencils, markers (multicolor)
- ❏ Staplers and staples
- ❏ Tape (single and double-faced), duct tape
- ❏ Clips, rubber bands, scissors, rulers
- ❏ Toolbox (hammer, screwdriver, assortment of nails)
- ❏ First aid kit
- ❏ Extension cords
- ❏ Colored dots, file folders, labels
- ❏ Flashlight
- ❏ Emergency numbers (messenger services, all-night copy center, etc.)
- ❏ Local telephone book
- ❏ Cash boxes
- ❏ Message pads
- ❏ Extra name badges, place cards, card stock, ribbons
- ❏ Local tourist information, maps, restaurant guides
- ❏ Three-hole and single punches
- ❏ Hand calculator
- ❏ Chalk and eraser, pointer
- ❏ Projector bulb, batteries, carousel tray
- ❏ Cellular phone
- ❏ Packing knife
- ❏ Measuring tape
- ❏ Spot remover
- ❏ Cassette tape and recorder
- ❏ Camera, film
- ❏ Typing whiteout
- ❏ Sewing kit
- ❏ Throat lozenges
- ❏ Stopwatch
- ❏ Other: _____
- ❏ Other: _____
- ❏ Other: _____
- ❏ Other: _____
- ❏ Other: _____

POST MEETING OR EVENT

FINAL WRAP-UP
The event is over, but the work is not. For many meeting and event planners the final wrap-up is the biggest struggle. Not only have you ended months of preparation, now you have to finalize the billings, check the invoices, distribute the monies, etc. The wrap-up may not be fun, but it is crucial.

START THE PROCESS IN THE BEGINNING
Good planners start this final process long before they get on-site. They plan with their vendors how they will verify services during the event, when payments will be due, and what kind of documentation will need to be completed in order to take care of matters in a timely way.

THINGS TO MAKE THIS STEP EASIER
Ask to get all function bills the day of the event so you can verify their accuracy while things are still fresh in your mind. When verifying charges, ask yourself:
- Were you charged for the correct number of people?
- Are there any charges you cannot identify?
- Are there charges you did not anticipate?

DAILY DIARY
Make a daily diary notation of things that worked and didn't work, notes for next year, and things to remember. Write it down or it won't be remembered. Follow-up should include making arrangements in advance to have materials returned or disposed of.

THANK-YOU NOTES
Determine who will receive thank-you notes. Verify addresses, spelling of names, facility, and vendor contacts. Make a note of those people who were especially helpful to you or your attendees!

MEETING WRAP-UP
Schedule a wrap-up meeting in advance with the facility's major department heads, or for small events, your contact. The purpose of this meeting is to find out how well EVERYONE performed, and what could be done differently in the future. This is also a time to ascertain whether you provided the facility and other vendors with appropriate information and instructions. Did you schedule enough time for activities on the agenda? Did you guarantee enough meals within the deadline? Should you have ordered another bar?

FEEDBACK
While you are evaluating, make sure you ask the attendees what they thought of the event, the facility, and the program? Do they have ideas or suggestions for next year? Their feedback can be one of the most important tools to help you plan the next event. Take time before the event to design questions that will solicate answers that will help you plan future events.

REWARD YOURSELF!
Last, but not least…reward yourself! Many planners make this their first task of the meeting or event. They plan what they will do after the BIG DAY. Whether it is a bubble bath or an island cruise, plan something for yourself—you've done a great job and you deserve it!

SPONSORSHIP

HISTORY OF SPONSORSHIP
Sponsorships came about as a good way to finance community events. Large companies were able to generate product awareness, target marketing ad, a good sense in the community as well as receiving a tax break for sponsoring such events. This tradition of philanthropy is one of the oldest forms of corporate social responsibility where companies build stronger communities in which they do business in.

CREATING FINANCE
Almost every event begins with a budget. The shorter you are on budget, the more you must creatively finance. One excellent way to stretch your dollars is to obtain a co-sponsor. When planning your event, seek out another organization or company who is not a competitor, but would likely benefit from exposure to your audience.

SPONSORSHIP PARTICIPATION MAY INCLUDE:
- Share in the cost of the event
- Donate their service
- Advertise the event to their employees or customers
- Include your business at their next event

Terms of co-sponsorship may vary greatly.

YOUR PARTICIPATION MAY INCLUDE:
- Include their name and logo in all event advertising
- Promote them at the event themselves
- Include some of their literature in the next mailing to your customers
- Give them the mailing list from your event
- To follow through on what was promised. Keep samples and photos of sponsor acknowledgements and send a thank-you following the event.

PROMOTIONAL ADVERTISING:
Always ask if there is extra promotional support that can go along with any dollars spent, it can help stretch your budget. For example if a radio schedule is purchased, ask if you can be the sponsor of the morning news broadcast "This message brought to you by…..", then have your commercial run in conjunction with that announcement.

REMEMBER:
- Select your co-sponsors wisely. The affiliation with a sponsor will impact the image of the event.
- Always put your arrangements in writing.
- Promotional coupons at their stores for the event.
- Confirm, confirm, confirm. This is the event planners mantra.

This type of teamwork often leads to very positive, ongoing alliance, making it one of the most exciting aspects of event planning. If the event is a win-win for both and the event is reoccurring, you may have an annual sponsor and funding or promotion for your event.

ORGANIZING A GOLF TOURNAMENT

Planning a golf tournament is a fun way to raise dollars. Golf is also a recreational sport that can promote team building. There are many forms of golf activities:

- Retreat break
- Fund-raiser
- Reunions
- Team building
- Employee motivation
- and pure recreation

There are fun forms of golf for even those with little experience. Scramble golf is where a team of four all play the same ball—each gets a chance to hit. This is a fun, fast way for a large group of experienced and not so experienced golfers to have fun! Try to book golf tournaments early in the morning or late in the day during hot summer months.

Consult your golf courses in "Attractions, Activities & Tours" section of this Guide for more detailed information about coordinating a golf tournament.

ADMINISTRATION/ GOAL SETTING
- Planning, objectives, action plan, budget setting
- Event planning, layout of event
- Tournament calendar
- Mailing list, timelines, committee assignments
- Logo design, brochure design
- Sponsorship packages, sales
- Signage, prizes, auction
- Award Ceremony

COMMITTEE FUNCTIONS/
A GOOD WORKING COMMITTEE IS A MUST
- Securing local clubs for the tournaments
- Developing a calendar for planning the event
- Establishing and obtaining prizes
- Planning additional fund raising activities such as auctions and raffles
- Solicitation of sponsors and "thank you's" after the tournament is held
- Arranging publicity and promotion participation
- Provisions for proper records, including accounting, contestant entries, etc.
- Notifying the committees of all meetings

SPONSORSHIP DEVELOPMENT
- Design packages
- Solicitation, sales, contact list
- Pro/Am packages

SUB-COMMITTEES
- Sponsorship committee: secures sponsors
- Publicity committee: news releases, media exposure
- Prize committee: set and obtain tournament prizes and tee gifts

VOLUNTEERS
- Contact charities to help with parties, day of event registration, etc.

FORMAT FOR DAYS OF PLAY
- Sponsor contests, putting contest, hole-in-ones
- Layout signage
- Tournament play, format of day's play
- Catering services
- Awards, auction

PLANNING A SKI DAY

1. Contact the ski resort and determine the details: dates, times, ski packages available, and prices. (Refer to "Attractions, Activities & Tours" section of this Guide for more information about ski resorts.)
2. Determine if you need transportation. Check with the ski resort to see if they can provide this service. If they do not, refer to the Transportation section of this Guide for transportation ideas.
3. Publicize the ski trip with flyers, posters, and announcements (E-mail, newsletter, etc.). Information should include: dates, package prices, a contact person, transportation pickup points, and where to sign up for the trip.
4. Set a time frame in which to collect all sign-up sheets and fees. It is recommended to get all information at least a few days before the ski trip.
5. After the sign-up sheets and fees are collected, contact the ski resort to place the ticket order. This reservation must be received to confirm the number of lift tickets, lessons and abilities, rental equipment needed, and beginner packages.
6. Arrange to pick up tickets in advance to save the group time waiting in line. Always treat tickets as though they are money.

DAY OF THE SKI EVENT

Arrive early: Schedule your morning departure time early enough to accommodate common delays in boarding the bus and traveling to the mountain. Drive time to Mount Hood from the Portland area is roughly one-and-a-half hours. The best arrival time for a ski day is between 8–8:30 a.m.

The bus: Let all participants know where the bus will be parked and post the group name on the windshield. The bus will be your best base of operation and storage place. Designate a loading and unloading crew and devise a simple system to identify skis.

Safety: Trail maps are available at the ticket office for distribution; familiarize the participants with locations of important facilities (restrooms, ski patrol, guest services desk, etc.). Make sure everyone knows the departure time and have a checklist of all people on the bus to avoid leaving people behind.

PLANNING A COMPANY PICNIC

Planning a company picnic can be easy or difficult depending on several factors: how long you have to plan, how many you are planning for, the type of activities planned, etc. Here are a few things to remember when you begin planning a company picnic:

- **Remember to book your picnic site early!** Spaces are limited, and some companies book their picnic site up to a year in advance.
- **Confirm dates and times in writing.** Don't assume that since you had your picnic somewhere last year that the space is reserved for you this year. Visit the site and look around to make sure it is presentable and what you need for your event.
- **Develop a committee or committees of volunteers to help coordinate the picnic.** Food and beverages, games and prizes, publicity and sign-ups, entertainment, etc. Get feedback from participants on how the event can be improved from the last year.
- **Be sure your contact at the site has a clear picture of what you want.** Be open to suggestions and solutions from the contact at the site—they have experienced all sizes and types of events at their particular site and can be very helpful with what works and what doesn't.
- **Work with the experienced planners on-site** (if one is not available, then check in the Event Planners section of this Guide to find one). The only way you'll find the answer to your questions is by asking someone who has been through it before. You may have never coordinated an event like this, so ask questions to figure out the best solutions. There will always be last-minute problems, such as expecting 700 people and having 1,000 show up. Experienced coordinators and planners can handle even the worst problems. DON'T PANIC! When you work with the professionals, they will not disappoint you.
- **Most importantly**, don't make the picnic so complicated that you drain your volunteers of their energy! This is supposed to be a morale-building event, not a burnout.
- **Prizes and Promotions:** Don't forget to have a keepsake to take home from the picnic like baseball hats with your company's logo, water bottles, Frisbees, etc. (Refer to "Corporate Gifts & Promotional Items" section of this guide for more ideas and information).
- **Games and activities:** Sports-related games and activities can add excitement to your event. Employees would especially love the managers in the dunk tank. There are professional companies that can come and setup games and arrange prizes; they are listed under "Audience Participation" in this guide.
- **Tents and pavilions:** Picnics are planned for summer fun, but we can never count on the sun to shine. A tent or pavilion as a back-up to bad weather at your site can be assurance to a great event come rain or shine.
- **Food for the picnic:** Food choice for a traditional picnic is barbecued hamburgers, ribs, chicken, hot dogs and baked beans and salads. Remember that proper refrigeration can eliminate food spoilage in heat.
- **On-site barbecue trucks:** Special barbecue caterers are using on-site barbecue trucks to store and cook the food right on site. The food is excellent and employees could enjoy the event without cooking and helping to cleanup.

PLANNING A CLASS REUNION

At one time or another in your life you will face the challenge of going to your class reunion. There is nothing more uncomfortable than a poorly planned function, but if you don't lend a hand or ideas, then you can't complain. As the leader or as a team member, class reunions can be fun to coordinate. Here are some helpful hints if you find yourself involved:

- Recruit your team members.
- Track down your classmates and mailing addresses (work with the school to get alumni information).
- Send a questionnaire to classmates to ask what they would like to see happen at the reunion.
- Begin finalizing major details (when, where, what, budget, etc.).
- Finalize lodging accommodations/group rates for out-of-towners.
- Print invitations or flyers. See if the school has a newsletter or booklet that is sent to alumni and can include information about your class reunion in it.
- Have a team party to address and stamp invitations.
- Begin compiling "Where We Are Now" booklet.
- Determine if RSVP response is enough to cover expenses.
- Plan fund raising event (if necessary).
- Call classmates who have not responded.
- Finalize menu and entertainment selections.
- Inform caterers and other vendors of final attendance estimates.
- Think of fun decorating ideas like what was popular during your high school years (Psychedelic '60s, Flower children '70s, etc.).
- Name tags with an old graduation photo on badge (the yearbook is a great source) is a fun way to remember who is who.
- Develop fun ways for spouses to become involved and meet others.
- Ice Breakers: slide show presentations of classmates (contact the school to see if any were kept).
- Make plans to stay in touch with team members. Have a "before the event" congratulations party.
- Decide who will be in charge of the next reunion. Instruct everyone to notify that person if their address changes at any time before the next reunion.

Notes

Meeting & Event Planners

ACCENT EVENT MANAGEMENT

9929 S.W. 48th
Portland, Oregon 97219
(503) 768-3980
Fax (503) 768-3986

We at Accent Event Management are your experts at planning and staging that perfect meeting or event. We specialize in **Convention and Trade Show Planning**, and provide excellent meeting and project management services for our customers. Whether your event is a simple Corporate Meeting or a fully organized Trade Show, we can handle all of the details for you.

Use Your Time Wisely

Let Accent Event Management do all of your planning and on-site requirements for you. We know that your time is very valuable, and that is why we offer a variety of services to meet your needs, so that you may use your time wisely.

Our Services Include:

- Professional Meeting and Planning Services
- Convention and Trade Show Planning
- Site Venue Selection
- Vendor Negotiations and Contracting
- On-Site Event Management
- Employee Events
- Receptions
- Holiday Events
- Theme and Décor Planning
- Entertainment Booking
- Budget Management
- Catering and Menu Planning

Official Event Planner for the
2000 Bravo! Meeting & Event Planners' Trade Show

Full-Service Event Planners
Contact: Susan Adkins, Owner
Portland *(503) 295-7890*
Salem *(503) 371-8904*
Corvallis *(541) 766-2961*
Fax *(503) 589-9166*
E-mail: *classact@open.org*
Web site: *www.open.org/classact/*

Planning a Special Event?
Class Act has been serving the Greater Willamette Valley since 1987, providing quality, creative, flexible, personalized services for corporate clients including:

- Fund-raisers
- Business Meetings
- Company Picnics
- Conventions
- Luncheons
- Seminars
- Open Houses
- Holiday Parties
- Class Reunions

- Ground Breakings
- Grand Openings
- Employee Appreciations
- Golf Tournaments
- Retirements
- Trade Shows
- Anniversaries
- Weddings

Class Act Delivers!
Planning a first-class event requires a full spectrum of management skills and the time to do it right. From budgeting to floor plans to entertainment, event management is a demanding job. It calls for impeccable taste, exacting attention to detail and a thorough knowledge of available resources.

The professional event coordinators at Class Act know the business of event planning. Class Act eliminates the uncertainty and anxiety related to planning meetings and receptions, while assuring a quality presentation that enhances any event.

Class Act has helped dozens of businesses prepare events, from afternoon receptions to five-day conventions. If there is an event in your future, call Susan Adkins today for a free consultation.

References
A sampling of some of our clients:
- Aldrich, Kilbride & Tatone
- Valmont Microflect
- West Coast Bank
- James W. Fowler Company

- Northwest Trailer Parts
- RadiSys
- Rogue Wave Software

Please let this business know that you heard about them from the Bravo! Event Resource Guide.

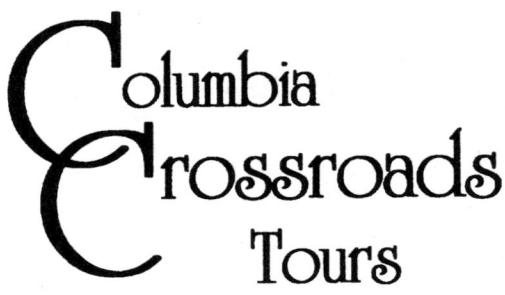

Columbia Crossroads Tours

4800 S.W. Macadam, Suite 255
Portland, Oregon 97201
Contact: Penny Bakefelt
(503) 225-9995; Fax (503) 225-1315
E-mail: cxrds@teleport.com

Detailed oriented people making things happen!

Meetings and Conventions
Planning and Development
Site Selection and Accommodations
Seminars
Registration
On-Site Coordination

Destination Management
Events
Holiday Parties
Picnics
Incentive Programs
Reunions
Gifts
Entertainment
Ice Breakers
Banquets
Tours and Sightseeing
Transportation

Professional Membership/Affiliations
- National Tour Association (NTA)
- Meeting Professionals International (MPI)
- Portland Oregon Visitors Association (POVA)
- Bank Travel
- Convention and Visitors Association of Washington County (CVAWC)
- Oregon Tourism and Travel Task Force (OTTF)
- International Tour Management Institute–Northwest Network
- Better Business Bureau (BBB)
- Cruise Line International Association (CLIA)

ESI EVENT SOLUTIONS
I N C O R P O R A T E D

1298 Elm Street SW • Albany, OR 97321

phone: 541.928.5055   fax: 541.926.3478

e-mail: esi@easyevents.com

website: www.easy events.com

New Technology • Low Prices • High Quality • Fast Delivery

Online Registration Services
Catch the wave of the future and cash in on the savings of new technology in registration services. Let ESI customize an online registration program for your event and enjoy the benefits of instant electronic data exchange.

- ▼ Reduce Overall Costs
- ▼ Communicate Worldwide
- ▼ Increase Accuracy and Efficiency
- ▼ Eliminate Time Zone Barriers

Full Service Event Planning
Special events run smoothly and successfully when our professional meeting planners work behind the scenes. ESI's attentive staff is committed to every aspect of achieving your event objectives.

Enjoy the Professional Touch
ESI provides creative and affordable solutions tailored to fit your unique circumstances. We pay close attention to every detail, making certain everything is in place and on time.

Nationwide Experience
Since 1986 Event Solutions Inc. has provided planning assistance and coordination for conventions, seminars, corporate meetings, conferences, training workshops, and trade shows.

Customized Services
Teaming up with the professionals at ESI enables you to focus on the purpose of the event without sacrificing the needs of your daily routine. You may select individual services or have us do all of the work. Our services include:

- ▼ Registration
- ▼ Site Selection
- ▼ Budgeting
- ▼ Newsletters
- ▼ Marketing
- ▼ Desktop Publishing
- ▼ On-Site Assistance
- ▼ Speaker Coordination
- ▼ Exhibitor Arrangements
- ▼ Contract Negotiation
- ▼ Facilitation of Meetings
- ▼ Lodging Accommodations
- ▼ Association Management
- ▼ Communications Center
- ▼ Bulk Mailing

Planning an Event? Consider it Done...
(541) 928-5055

MEETING & EVENT PLANNERS

Event Planning & Decorating

*P.O. Box 13070
Portland, Oregon 97213
Contact: Debbie Alvarado
(503) 335-6967
Fax (503) 335-5840*

Events Etcetera Specializes In
- Event and Party Planning
- Event Facilitating
- Theme Props
- Table Décor
- Party Decorations
- Entertainment and Live Music
- Menu Planning and Catering
- Marketing and Consulting
- Games and Activities

Call Us for Your Upcoming Event (Any Size, Anywhere!)

Theme Parties	Corporate Events
Holiday Parties	Millennium Events
Unique Grad Parties	Summer Company Picnics
Weddings	Festivals
Fundraisers	Anniversary Celebrations
Formal Galas	Seasonal Office Décor

What Our Customers Say…
- Exceeding expectations!
- Beautiful, elegant events!
- Fun and festive parties!
- Beyond your imagination!
- Excellent personal service!

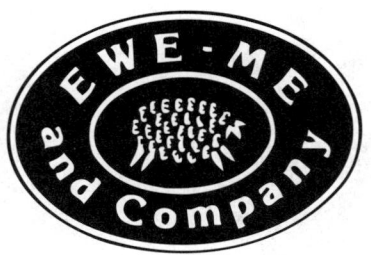

EWE-ME and Company

P.O. Box 25445
Portland, Oregon 97298
Contact: Dian Lindsay (503) 644-1222; Fax (503) 644-1364
E-mail: ewemeco@europa.com

Would "ewe" like someone on your team who
KNOWS THE BEST LOCATIONS
for any kind of event?

Could "ewe" use more
CREATIVITY
PLANNING ASSISTANCE
NEGOTIATION SUPPORT

Whether you have us relieve you of all the work and worry, or simply complement your efforts with our resources and expertise, our meeting and event services will be tailored to your needs.

Meetings, Conferences, and Conventions

- Development and Planning
- Budgeting and Administration
- Marketing and Publicity
- Facilities and Accommodations
- Registration Management
- On-Site Coordination

Management Services

- Hotel/Lodging Contract Negotiation
- Facilities and Catering Consulting and Coordination
- Corporate Events—Creation, Coordination, Management
- Special Events Consulting and Management
- Employee Recognition and Incentive

Destination Management Services

- Receptions
- Themed Events
- Registration
- Shuttles
- Music and Talent
- Picnics
- Speaker Coordination
- Transportation
- VIP Services
- Gifts
- Tours and Sightseeing
- Decorations

Our 20 years of service excellence in Oregon and Washington assure your satisfaction

Professional Affiliations

- Meeting Professionals International
- Portland Oregon Visitors Association
- Washington County Visitors Association

3008 S.W. 1st Avenue
Portland, Oregon 97201
p 503.201.7603
f 503.916-1859
e labevents@aol.com

bringing creative solutions to parties, weddings, meetings

Labyrinth's mission is to provide our clients with elegance, quality, and a unique event experience.

"A mighty maze! But not without a plan." —Alexander Pope

Quality and Creativity
From all-inclusive planning, to event-day facilitation, Labyrinth brings expertise, professionalism, and creativity to every event. We plan successful events by utilizing a network of quality vendors, adding a unique creative edge, and organizing with a keen eye to detail.

Full-Service and More
- Corporate receptions
- Company picnics
- Winery events
- Fund raisers
- Theme parties
- Grand openings
- Meetings
- Auctions
- Weddings
- Executive retreats
- Private parties
- Sales receptions
- Management retreats
- Teambuilding seminars
- Anniversaries

Extended Services
- Graphic design
- Media buying
- Copywriting
- Gift buying (see our page for Queen Bee Gift Baskets)

Giving Back to You
Labyrinth is proud to volunteer event planning services to the 1999 American Diabetes Association's Charity Auction.

Well Connected
Labyrinth is an active member of the Portland Chamber of Commerce.

See Queen Bee, page 165 under Corporate Gifts.

Plans & Action

*A full-service meeting and special event planning firm
dedicated to innovation, service, quality and value.*

*P.O. Box 6807
Aloha, Oregon 97007
Contact: Carolyn B. Wence CMP (Certified Meeting Professional)
(503) 259-0739; Fax (503) 259-0838
Web site: www.plans-action.com
E-mail: wence@cowboyz.com*

Development, Planning and Management
- Budgeting/Needs Analysis
- On-site Coordination
- Vendor Selection/Oversight
- Contract Negotiation
- Registration/Logistics
- Travel and Hotel Accommodations

Destination Management Services
- Speaker/Trainer/Entertainment/Coordination
- VIP Services
- Theme/Activity Development
- Decorations
- Transportation/Shuttles/Tours
- Golf Tournaments
- Hospitality/Gifts

Additional Services
- Seminars
- Association Management
- Travel Management
- Trade Shows
- Incentive Programs
- Staff Management

Professional Affiliations
- Meeting Professionals International
- Portland Oregon Visitors Association
- Oregon Business Travel Association
- Portland Chamber of Commerce
- Executive Women's Golf Association
- Washington County Visitors Association

Serving corporate, small business, association, nonprofit and individual clients on a local, regional and national level.

Please let this business know that you heard about them from the Bravo! Event Resource Guide.

Soirée
special event planning

P.O. Box 5982
Portland, Oregon 97228
Contact: Molli Sisk, Owner
(503) 803-2901
Fax (503) 579-8021
Web site: www.bonsoiree.com

We can plan anything you desire to make your idea of the perfect event a reality!

With over five years experience planning events in the Portland area, we have many contacts and resources to draw from to make your event a success.

Whether it is managing your entire event or concentrating on specific categories that you may need assistance with, Soirée is ready to help.

EVENT MANAGEMENT
- Vendor Research and Coordination
  - Catering
  - Party Supplies
  - Photography
  - Decorations
  - Floral Arrangements
  - Entertainment
- Site Selection and Reservation
- Budget Analysis and Contract Negotiations
- Theme and Creative Development
- Travel and Hotel Accommodations
- On-Site Coordination
- Sponsorships
- Marketing and Promotions
- Administrative Correspondence

EVENT TYPES (Any and all sizes)
- Weddings
- Corporate Gatherings
- Birthdays and Anniversaries
- Bachelorette and Bachelor Parties
- Meetings and Seminars
- Holiday Parties
- Fund Raisers
- Dinner Parties
- Golf Tournaments
- Tours
- Reunions
- Picnics
- Trade Shows
- Grand Openings
- *Any special event*

PROFESSIONAL AFFILIATIONS
- Portland Oregon Visitors Association
- Portland Chamber of Commerce
- Meeting Professionals International

Give us a call to discuss any of your special event ideas, and a proposal for the perfect Soirée will follow…

Meeting & Event Planning Organizations

MEETING PLANNING ORGANIZATIONS

MEETING PROFESSIONALS INTERNATIONAL (MPI)
National phone: (972) 702-3000
MPI now offers its members their own on-line service, called MPINet, based on the CompuServe system. MPI's resource center will do research for members and non-members on just about any subject. MPI can also provide destination information through the Worldview program. The local chapter of MPI is a great education and networking group of local meeting planners and suppliers.
See page 67 in this section about local membership

PORTLAND OREGON VISITOR ASSOCIATION (POVA)
Phone: (503) 275-9750
As a member of POVA, you can obtain the names of who is in charge of most of the convention and tour groups coming to Portland. POVA also publishes four leading visitor guides to the area and has breakfasts every Thursday featuring informative guest speakers.
See page 70 in this section about membership

AMERICAN HOTEL & MOTEL ASSOCIATION (AH&MA)
Phone: (202) 289-3100

AMERICAN SOCIETY OF ASSOCIATION EXECUTIVES (ASAE)
Phone: (202) 626-2723

AMERICAN SOCIETY OF TRAVEL AGENTS (ASTA)
Phone: (703) 739-2782

ASSOCIATION OF CATERING & EVENT PROFESSIONALS (ACEP)
Phone: (503) 299-2237
See page 64

CONVENTION LIAISON COUNCIL (CLC)
Phone: (202) 626-2764

INTERNATIONAL ASSOCIATION OF CONVENTION & VISITOR BUREAUS (IACVB)
Phone: (202) 296-7888

INTERNATIONAL ASSOCIATION OF EXPOSITION MANAGEMENT (IAEM)
Phone: (972) 458-8002

OREGON SOCIETY OF ASSOCIATION MANAGEMENT (OSAM)
Phone: (503) 253-9026

SOCIETY OF GOVERNMENT MEETING PROFESSIONALS (SGMP)
See page 72; E-mail: mmillig@hcs.state.or.us;
National phone: (717) 795-7467
The Oregon chapter of SGMP offers monthly educational meetings and an annual conference with the goal of improving the knowledge, expertise and cost effectiveness for individuals planning and managing government meetings. It is open to planners and suppliers.

Please let these organizations know that you heard about them from the Bravo! Event Resource Guide.

CONVENTION AND VISITORS INFORMATION BUREAUS

Oregon and Southwest Washington

Albany
300 Second Ave., S.W.
Albany, OR 97321
(541) 928-0911
(800) 526-2256

Ashland
P.O. Box 1360
Ashland, OR 97520
(541) 482-3486

Columbia River Gorge Visitors Association (GVA)
404 W. Second St.
The Dalles, OR 97058
(800) 984-6743
See page 65

Convention & Visitors Bureau of Washington County, Oregon
5075 S.W. Griffith Dr., Ste. 120
Beaverton, OR 97005
(503) 644-5555
See page 73

Corvallis
420 N.W. Second
Corvallis, OR 97330
(541) 757-1544

Lane County
P.O. Box 10286
Eugene, OR 97440
(800) 547-5445
See page 66

Lincoln City
801 S.W. Hwy 101, Ste. 1
Lincoln City, OR 97367
(800) 452-2151

Medford
101 E. Eighth St.
Medford, OR 97501
(541) 779-4847

Portland Oregon Visitors Association (POVA)
26 S.W. Salmon
Portland, OR 97204
(503) 275-9750
See page 70

Portland Visitor Information
25 S.W. Salmon St.
Portland, OR 97204
(503) 222-2223
See page 70

Roseburg
P.O. Box 1062
Roseburg, OR 97470
(800) 444-9584

Salem
1313 Mill St., S.E.
Salem, OR 97301
(503) 581-4325
See page 71

Seaside Visitors Bureau
989 Broadway
Seaside, OR 97138
(800) 444-6740

Vancouver
750-C Anderson St.
c/o Howard House
Vancouver, WA 98661
(877) 600-0800

Please let these organizations know that you heard about them from the Bravo! Event Resource Guide.

CHAMBERS OF COMMERCE

Albany
P.O. Box 548
Albany, OR 97321
(541) 926-1517

Beaverton
4800 S.W. Griffith Dr., Ste. 100
Beaverton, OR 97005
(503) 644-0123

Canby
P.O. Box 35
Canby, OR 97013
(503) 266-4600

Cannon Beach
P.O. Box 64
Cannon Beach, OR 97110
(503) 436-2623

Clatskanie
P.O. Box 635
Clatskanie, OR 97016
(503) 728-2502

Cornelius
P.O. Box 681
Cornelius, OR 97113
(503) 359-4037

Estacada
P.O. Box 298
Estacada, OR 97023
(503) 630-3483

Forest Grove
2417 Pacific Ave.
Forest Grove, OR 97116
(503) 357-3006

Gresham
150 W. Powell
Gresham, OR 97030
(503) 665-1131

Hillsboro
334 S.E. Fifth Ave.
Hillsboro, OR 97123
(503) 648-1102

Keizer
3700 River Rd., N., Ste. 8
After Dec.1999:
960 Chemewa Rd. N.E.
Keizer, OR 97303
(503) 393-9111

Lake Oswego
P.O. Box 368
Lake Oswego, OR 97034
(503) 636-3634

Lincoln City
P.O. Box 787
Lincoln City, OR 97367
(503) 994-3070

McMinnville
417 N. Adams St.
McMinnville, OR 97128
(503) 472-6196

Milwaukie
7740 S.E. Harmony Rd.
Milwaukie, OR 97222
(503) 654-7777

Molalla
P.O. Box 578
Molalla, OR 97038
(503) 829-6941

Mount Angel
P.O. Box 221
Mount Angel, OR 97362
(503) 845-9440

Newberg
115 N. Washington St.
Newberg, OR 97132
(503) 538-2014

Newport
555 S.W. Coast Hwy.
Newport, OR 97365
(800) 262-7844
See page 68

Chambers of Commerce continued...

Oregon City
P.O. Box 226
1810 Washington St.
Oregon City, OR 97045
(800) 424-3002

Portland
221 N.W. Second Ave.
Portland, OR 97209
(503) 228-9411
See page 69

Portland African American
P.O. Box 5488
Portland, OR 97228
(800) 880-4040

Salem
1110 Commercial St., N.E.
Salem, OR 97301
(503) 581-1466

Sherwood
25 N. Pine St.
Sherwood, OR 97140
(503) 625-6751

Sunriver
P.O. Box 3246
Sunriver, OR 97707
(541) 593-8149
See page 555

The Dalles
404 W. Second St.
The Dalles, OR 97058
(800) 255-3385

Tigard
12420 S.W. Main St.
Tigard, OR 97223
(503) 639-1656

Troutdale
P.O. Box 245
338 E. Historic Columbia River Hwy.
Troutdale, OR 97060
(503) 669-7473

Tualatin
P.O. Box 701
Tualatin, OR 97062
(503) 692-0780

Vancouver
404 E. 15th St., Ste 11
Vancouver, WA 98663
(360) 694-2588

Vernonia
P.O. Box 7
Vernonia, OR 97064
(503) 429-6364

Welches
P.O. Box 819
Welches, OR 97067
(503) 622-3017

Willamina
105 N.W. Main
Willamina, OR 97396
(503) 876-5777

Wilsonville
29600 S.W. Park Pl.
Wilsonville, OR 97070
(503) 682-0411

For those of you working in the catering and special event industry, this is the association for you!

Our Mission Statement
1. To identify and give status to the catering and event planning industry as a whole and to represent its desires and best interests to the community at large.
2. To promote the exchange of common ideas and problems.
3. To develop a cordial relationship among its members.
4. To present to the members, programs of educational value relating to the catering, event industries and allied businesses.

Our dues are kept low to encourage membership to all sizes of businesses.

Active membership is available to individuals and companies involved in catering and/or event planning and other supporting industries.

Businesses must be licensed, qualified institutional operations.

Student memberships are also available to individuals actively enrolled in an accredited program of study in the fields of food service and/or hospitality management.

We meet on the third Tuesday of each month, except August and December.

**For membership information, call (503) 299-ACEP
E-mail: acep@acep.com; Web site: www.acep.com**

**For more information,
call Royce Mason (503) 283-8828**

COLUMBIA RIVER GORGE VISITORS ASSOCIATION

404 W. Second Street
The Dalles, Oregon 97058
(800) 98-GORGE
E-mail: crgva@gorge.net
Web site: www.gorge.net/crgva

The Columbia Gorge Visitors Association, established in 1990, is a unique volunteer organization of visitor industry members working together to market and promote The Gorge. Representing two states, Washington and Oregon, and the six counties bordering the Columbia Gorge National Scenic Area, our partnership includes both public and private entities.

Convention, Event and Tour Planning

- Our membership offers a wide variety of services, from large full-service conference centers accommodating up to 500 attendees to quaint bed and breakfasts for family retreats.
- Attractions can accommodate groups for activities such as horseback riding, vintage dinner train rides, river cruises, whitewater rafting, museum tours, dam and fish hatchery tours and much more!
- Lodging ranges from rustic campsites to luxury hotels. Whatever your needs are, we have it in the Columbia River Gorge.

GVA Members Working Together

- Our official magazine, *Gorge Guide*, is distributed at many locations and mailed throughout the world. E-mail or call us for a complimentary copy.
- Our Web site includes a calendar of events.
- Cooperative advertising at reduced cost for our members in a variety of publications
- Fulfillment as a result of inquires received upward of 22,000 a year
- Cooperative participation in Travel and Trade Shows
- Motorcoach itinerary and resource guide of member attractions, lodging and services distributed to 500 group tour leaders annually; please call or e-mail us for your copy.

We hope to see you soon in the Columbia River Gorge!

CONVENTION & VISITORS ASSOCIATION OF LANE COUNTY OREGON (CVALCO)

P.O. Box 10286
Eugene, Oregon 97440
(541) 484-5307, (800) 547-5445
Fax (541) 343-6335
E-mail: bconeryly@cvalco.org
Web site: www.cvalco.org/meetoregon.html

CVALCO sales team provides a professional link between the properties, attractions and amenities that will make your meeting or convention a success.

- **CVALCO** is a full-service convention and visitors bureau
- **CVALCO** will obtain bids from hotel properties and facilities, facilitate tours, and provide a broad cross-section of convention services
- **CVALCO** will match the needs of each meeting with community businesses that can best provide assistance

Site Profile
Located in the heart of Oregon, Lane County reaches from the snow-covered tops of Willamette National Forest down along the meandering McKenzie and Willamette rivers out to the shoreline of the Pacific Ocean. Matchless beauty, Northwest hospitality, a wealth of recreation and cultural opportunities plus full-service facilities make Lane County a natural meeting destination.

Accommodations
Lane County has over 4,000 sleeping rooms, with competitive rates, outstanding service standards and hotel meeting rooms ranging in size from 200 to 30,000 square feet. The Lane County Convention Center is over 100,000 square feet and offers complimentary parking.

Cultural Facilities and Activities
Year-round there is something for everyone in Lane County: white water rafting, opera, ballet, symphony, musical theatre, skiing, dune buggy riding, backpacking, golf, mountain biking and more.

Transportation
Eugene Airport is just 15 minutes from downtown Eugene/Springfield and offers air service to and from a variety of destinations. Lane County is easily reached by Amtrak and interstate highways as well. Located one hour and 45 minutes from Portland International Airport makes rental car travel an attractive option.

MPI
MEETING PROFESSIONALS INTERNATIONAL

MEETING PROFESSIONALS INTERNATIONAL
OREGON CHAPTER

(503) 261-9894

The purpose of the Meeting Professionals International Oregon Chapter shall be to provide quality education for its members, to promote professionalism within the meeting industry and to enhance business relationships.

- Open to all professionals in the meeting industry
- Meetings once each month on Tuesday, September through June
- Annual Conference every March

**For membership information call
Nancy Wilson, CMP
Association Manager
(503) 261-9894**

JOIN TODAY AND BECOME PART OF THE ORGANIZATION THAT BENEFITS YOU...

Greater Newport Chamber of Commerce

*555 S.W. Coast Highway
Newport, Oregon 97365-4934
(541) 265-8801, (800) 262-7844
Fax (541) 265-5589
www.newportnet.com/chamber*

Newport awaits your next business meeting, planning session, convention, retreat, or group tour. In Newport you will find a variety of meeting facilities offering full services—comfortable lodging with terrific views, great restaurants with the freshest seafood you'll ever taste, and miles of wide open beaches.

Our coastal community offers a peaceful, yet exciting setting for any traveler. Not only does Newport offer outstanding meeting facilities, but there are also many activities and attractions that can further enhance your visit to the Central Oregon Coast.

Our attractions, ranging from aquariums to historical museums, complement the natural beauty of the area. Recreational opportunities include crabbing, clamming, fishing, whale watching and marine-based tours just to name a few. Whether you incorporate these activities into your agenda, or offer them during free time, they are bound to make a "splash" with your group.

Group tour guide, slides, color photos, itinerary planning assistance, posters, brochure shells, fam/research tours and maps can all be provided by the Greater Newport Chamber of Commerce. We will help to make your next visit to the beach a huge success!

So, give us a call at (800) 262-7844 and find out why we say **"Newport. Preserving the Treasures of the Oregon Coast."**

OUR MISSION

The Greater Newport Chamber of Commerce *is organized to
unite the efforts of the citizens promoting the civic,
commercial, agricultural, tourism, marine and industrial welfare
of the City of Newport and its surrounding economic areas.*

Portland Chamber

Portland Metropolitan Chamber of Commerce
221 N.W. Second Avenue
Portland, Oregon 97209-3999
(503) 228-9411				Fax (503) 228-5126
Business Hours: Mon–Fri 8:30am–5pm

Our Mission
The mission of the Portland Metropolitan Chamber of Commerce is to promote business prosperity within the Portland metropolitan region.

The Portland Chamber is
An association of metropolitan area businesses and individuals working together to promote the interest and welfare of business in our community.

Chamber Membership Benefits and Services
- Business referral
- Small business programs, workshops and resources
- Business publications; timely resource data
- Multiple monthly gatherings for networking and building client relationships
- Legislative advocacy; the Chamber is the voice for business
- Advertising opportunities
- Business exposure through the Chamber Web site

Find out why more than 2,000 Portland area businesses belong to the region's largest business organization. Call **(503) 228-9411** or access our *Completely Portland* newsletter on the Web at **http://www.pdxchamber.org**.

For an Official Calendar of Portland Chamber Events
- Visit our Web site at **http://www.pdxchamber.org** ...*or*
- Call **(503) 228-9411** for information on receiving your annual calendar by mail

Please let this organization know that you heard about them from the Bravo! Event Resource Guide.

PORTLAND OREGON VISITORS ASSOCIATION

the convention and visitors bureau of metropolitan Portland
Three World Trade Center
26 S.W. Salmon St.
Portland, Oregon 97204
(503) 275-9750; Fax (503) 275-9774
Web site: www.pova.com

POVA AT WORK

The mission of the Portland Oregon Visitors Association is to strengthen the region's economy by marketing the metropolitan Portland region as a preferred destination for meetings, conventions and leisure travel.

1,000+ Members and Growing
More than 1,000 businesses in the Portland metropolitan area, the state of Oregon and the Pacific Northwest are members of the Portland Oregon Visitors Association (POVA).

Convention and Tour Business
Members of POVA can market their businesses to the convention/meeting planners and group tour operators visiting Portland and Oregon. The *Portland Oregon Convention & Trade Show Calendar* includes the names, addresses, phone numbers and meeting dates for group meetings in the Portland area.

Thursday Networking and Program Breakfasts
Every Thursday, members can attend an industry breakfast and have the opportunity to network with more than 100 fellow members. Meetings vary in location, giving members the opportunity to experience venues throughout the Portland metropolitan area.

Visitor Information Center
Drop by our busy downtown information and services center and let us help you make decisions about what to see and do in the Portland area. May through October the center is designated an Oregon State Welcome Center with expanded hours of operation and services. Visit the Oregon products gift shop, or purchase tickets to any of the area events at "Ticket Central," POVA's one stop shop ticket center. Member brochures are available for visitors to pick up.

Three Different Publications
POVA produces Portland's award-winning visitor guide magazine, *Portland Oregon: The Official Visitors Guide*, which is mailed to visitors and convention attendees around the world. In addition, members have the opportunity to advertise in two other POVA publications that are applicable to the pursuit of business for members.

Professional Sales Staff
A professional staff of convention sales managers, travel industry sales managers, and marketing experts works for members (and for all of us) to bring visitor business to Portland.

**Join the Portland Oregon Visitors Association and
put the power of POVA to work for you!**

For more information, call the POVA Membership Department, (503) 275-9750.

SALEM CONVENTION & VISITORS ASSOCIATION

your convention planning resource
1313 Mill Street, S.E.
Salem, Oregon 97301
(503) 581-4325, (800) 874-7012; Fax (503) 581-4540
Web site: http://www.scva.org

The Salem Convention and Visitors Association is the official visitor and convention promotion and marketing organization for the City of Salem. Our mission is to enhance the Salem area's economic and social fabric by promoting and selling the area as a leisure travel, and convention and event destination.

Convention and Event Planning

At the Salem Convention and Visitors Association (SCVA) we understand the detail and organization necessary to plan a convention or event. Through the convention program, we work with event planners by providing free professional assistance including bid preparation and presentation, lodging coordination, and site inspections. Salem has more than 1,500 convention-style guest rooms and 250,000-square-feet of flexible meeting and exhibit space to accommodate any event planner's needs. Call (800) 874-7012 to receive a free planning packet.

Convention and Event Services

SCVA is dedicated to providing customized service that will make your experience in Salem memorable. Available services can be as simple as providing free visitor brochures, to providing a staffed display of what to see and do, to as complex as coordinating pre- and post-convention tours. Most importantly, we cater our services to specific event needs.

Professional Services

SCVA members are a valuable resource to the Salem area for any meeting and event planner. Request a *Professional Services Directory* listing businesses ready to serve you or access them via the Internet at *www.scva.org*.

Tour Planning

Salem's rich history, attractions, award-winning wineries, and breathtaking scenery will delight visitors attending Salem activities. Sample tour itineraries highlighting Salem area sites are available to aid in coordinating event delegate activities. For a Salem area tour planner contact SCVA at (800) 874-7012.

Membership Opportunities

More than 400 members have partnered with the SCVA to take advantage of marketing and promotional opportunities and to unite in their support of the tourism industry. Membership highlights include: numerous networking opportunities, free Internet listing, free promotional brochure listings, free newsletter advertising and subscription, visitor center access, leads, referrals and more. Call today for a free membership packet at (800) 874-7012 to see how your business can benefit.

Contact SCVA at (800) 874-7012 for a free
Convention Planning Packet!
www.scva.org

GO-SGMP
Greater Oregon Chapter
Society of Government Meeting Professionals

Who we are!

The Society of Government Meeting Professionals (SGMP) is the only nonprofit professional organization involved in both the planning of government meetings and professionals in the hospitality and convention support industry who supply services to government meeting planners.

Benefits of membership!

- Encourages and improves communication, understanding, and cooperation between meeting planners and suppliers
- Expands knowledge and abilities of planners and suppliers through formal educational conferences, workshops, and monthly meetings
- Aids planners in locating and evaluating commercial meeting facilities and support services
- Provides up to date statistics regarding per diem rates, regulatory policies and legislative issues which effect state and federal government meetings
- Check out our web site at www.jps.net/gosgmp

For membership information call
Cari Stear, Senior Catering Manager
Holiday Inn Select, Wilsonville
(503) 682-2211

Convention & Visitors Bureau of Washington County, Oregon

5075 SW Griffith Drive • Suite 120
Beaverton • OR • 97005-2921
(503) 644-5555 • (800) 537-3149
Fax (503) 644-9784
www.wcva.org

The mission of the Convention & Visitors Bureau of Washington County, Oregon, is to actively promote Washington County as a destination for conventions, business and pleasure travelers.

Located just west of Portland, Washington County is home to some of the largest high-tech and industrial companies in the world, and yet also the home to miles of rivers, parks, trails, bike paths and Oregon's world-famous wine country.

Attractions and events abound in Washington County, including:
- Hot Air Ballooning
- Top Rated Golf Courses
- NW Alpaca Ranch
- World Class Wineries
- Elephant Garlic Festival
- Taste of Beaverton
- Concours d'Elegance Car Show
- Rose Festival Airshow
- Onion Festival
- Crawfish Festival
- Antiques and Boutiques
- Oregon Zoo

Stay and play in Washington County. Our professional staff can assist you with all your convention, group tour, and special event planning needs. Our superior attractions, first-class lodging and meeting facilities, and tax free shopping make Washington County an ideal location for your group. Because we are a full service convention and visitors bureau, you can be sure that your planning process will be trouble free. Plus, our services are completely free.

To assist you in planning your next event we offer many Washington County publications including:
- The Everything Guide
- Wedding Guide
- Parks, Camping & Golf Guide
- Calendar of Events
- 100 Free Things to do in Washington County
- Agri-Tourism Guide
- Convention Services Planning Guide

Call us today at 644-5555 or send an e-mail to info@wcva.org. We look forward to helping you plan your next event!

Notes

Child Care

CHILD CARE

Creative Childcare Solutions, Inc.

Delivering quality childcare to you and your family
*Contact: Michelle Davenport or Deanna Pulford (503) 635-1036
E-mail: michelle@munchkincare.com or deanna@munchkincare.com
Web site: www.munchkincare.com*

You've reserved the hall, the speakers and the band... Now, what are you going to do with the children?

At Creative Childcare Solutions, we believe children should be allowed to be children—not act like "little adults." That's why we offer on-site childcare for your special event.

While your clients are listening to the keynote speaker, their children could be limboing at their very own Calypso Party!

While your guests dine on salmon en croute and sip champagne, their children could be munching on a hotdog and slurping down rootbeer floats at their own Cowboy Hoedown!

Creative Childcare Solutions, Inc. will customize each special event to meet your unique needs and budget. Our qualified, caring CCSI staff will bring with them 25 years of childcare expertise, CPR and First Aid Certification and all the toys, games, arts and crafts the children will need to have a wonderful time!

So, for your next event, let the kids be kids and let the adults relax in the knowledge that their children are nearby in a safe, exciting, loving environment with **Creative Childcare Solutions, Inc.**

COST—Custom designed to meet your specific needs.

TERMS—One contact person required for planning of event. Retainer required for bookings.

Call or e-mail us today to book your next special occasion. Let the children come and have fun while remaining safely near the parents. No more worries about cancelled babysitters—let us take care of the details so you can enjoy yourselves.

Please let this business know that you heard about them from the Bravo! Event Resource Guide.

Event Insurance

EVENT INSURANCE

GALES CREEK INSURANCE SERVICES

800 N.W. Sixth Avenue • Portland, Oregon 97209
(503) 227-0491; Fax (503) 227-0927
Visit our Web site: www.galescreek.com
E-mail: galesins@aol.com

GOOD TIMES. FULLY INSURED.

Gales Creek is the Pacific Northwest's premier insurer of events. We offer coverage for one time events such as concerts, weddings, trade shows, dances, parties, parades, exhibitions, lectures, conventions, meetings and festivals to multiple event coverage for promoters and event planners. If you are a meeting or event planner and you or your clients are in need of customized event insurance — give us a call.

Types of Insurance

Gales Creek has nationwide exclusivity on special event insurance that will save you money. We have a skilled staff that can analyze your exposures and provide a comprehensive insurance package to protect your organization. We can offer tips on risk management and advise you to help avoid accidents. Contact us about: trip and fall premise liability, liquor liability, property damage to leased premise, insurance for rented equipment and other property you own at the event site as well as cancellation/weather insurance. If you host, sponsor or produce events of any kind…call us for a proposal.

Types of Events

- Private Parties
- Corporate Meetings
- Weddings
- Trade Shows
- Concerts
- Festivals
- Conventions
- Dances
- Parades

Events and Organizations We Have Insured

- Art In The Pearl
- Oregon Country Fair
- SOLV
- Earth Day International
- Bumbershoot
- Meals on Wheels
- Double Tee Promotions
- Portland Highland Games
- Bones and Brew
- Whole Life Expo
- Festa Italiana
- Ashland Community Theater

20 Years of Experience

Gales Creek Insurance has been providing service in the Pacific Northwest and nationally for 20 years. We know events. We know your business and how to insure all the risks facing you in producing events large and small. Call us. We would be delighted to do a comprehensive plan for your organization.

Staffing & Employment Services

EMERALD EMPLOYMENT

"Temporary & Permanent Placement"

One Lincoln Center
10300 S.W. Greenburg Road, Suite 485
Portland, Oregon 97223
Contact: John, Jr.
(503) 244-5111; Fax (503) 977-9336
E-mail: greatjobs@emerald-staffing.com
Web site: http://www.emerald-staffing.com

Emerald Temps Offers Professional Staffing to Meet All your Needs

Emerald Temps assists client companies by providing qualified temporary office employees to cover fluctuations in workforce and peak periods. We match your requirements with our employee's special abilities. On each new assignment, our staffing specialist will call to verify the arrival of our temporary employee assigned to you.

Specializing in Temporary Services

- Administrative
- Secretarial
- Data Processing
- Clerical
- Typing
- Communications
- Accounting
- Event Setup

Company Policies and Guarantee

We guarantee your order will be confirmed within 30 minutes from its receipt. If for any reason you are not satisfied with the work of our temporary employee assigned to your company within the first four hours worked, we will replace the employee immediately, and you will not be billed for that period of time

Billing Procedures

Since the temporary employee is on our payroll, we are responsible for all statutory taxes and insurance. Our employees are covered by workers compensation and liability insurance.

Our Commitment

Our entire staff is committed to total client satisfaction. We listen, we respond, and stand behind you. We value your business and know you will be pleased with our performance.

SERVING INDUSTRY SINCE 1978

Members of Oregon Association of Temporary Services, National Association of Temporary and Staffing Services, and Oregon Association of Personnel Consultants.

inn·crowd
hospitality staffing

506 S.W. Sixth Avenue, Suite 406
Portland, Oregon 97204
Contact: Marjorie Surridge
(503) 402-2711; Fax (503) 402-2714

The Petrosky wedding party arrived with 57 more people than expected. The Star Trek Convention would like a separate banquet room for the Klingons. You're already short on housekeepers and the chef just called in sick. When disaster strikes, call the company that specializes in temporary staffing for the hospitality industry.

You know how difficult it is to find temporary help, let alone people with any training or experience in your business. But now, thanks to Inn Crowd, there are qualified, reliable people ready to save the day.

Our Specialty
Inn Crowd specializes in finding and training people for a variety of hotel and restaurant positions. So why waste your time and money running classified ads and dealing with inexperienced people? Call Inn Crowd and we'll send qualified professionals who are ready to get to work.

What Sets Us Apart
- We work with one and only one industry—yours.
- We utilize our proprietary screening process called Hire Standards so only the very best candidates ever become Inn Crowd employees.
- We train every employee to ensure you receive a competent, reliable employee.
- We are there for you with 24-hour access to our Management Team.
- We guarantee every placement through our four-hour guarantee.

Our Specially Trained Staff includes
- Banquet Staff
- Catering Staff
- Door Persons
- Event Set-up/Break-down
- Kitchen Staff
- Front Desk Staff
- Housekeeping Staff
- Parking Attendants
- Receptionists
- Wait Staff
- Middle and Upper level management staff in all hospitality fields

Please let this business know that you heard about them from the Bravo! Event Resource Guide.

Notes

Transportation

Coaches
Buses
Vans
Limousines

HELPFUL HINTS

Airfare Savings: Special negotiated airfares are available for groups of ten or more. To qualify, travelers must share a common destination and be traveling in the same time frames. Travelers need not originate from the same city.

Meeting dates and times for travelers: Planning your meeting dates and times will enable attendees to take advantage of non-refundable excursion airfares which are discounted up to 70%. Schedule meeting dismissal time so attendees can take the last afternoon/evening flight out to avoid the cost of an additional night stay at the hotel.

Bus and Coach Transportation: Buses and coaches come in your basic style of school buses to luxury-Elite Motorcoaches. You'll want to determine your audience and then select the most appropriate transportation.

Livery Service: There are taxi cabs, limousines, and livery service. Livery service is a luxury form of transportation without the recognition of a local cab or limousine. The driver is uniformed and highly skilled with exceptional customer service. This is a VIP form of transportation for important attendees, speakers and special guests.

Valet Service: For your next event or special occasion valet service adds that special touch. Services include: shuttle vans, lot attendants to park your guests' cars, and parking consulting services to help maximize parking space and to monitor the traffic flow. These companies should be properly insured and licensed.

Ground Transportation: Get facts and figures on capacities, capabilities and types of transportation available to and from the meeting site. Talk to planners who have handled groups of your size. Select your transportation on the basis of cost, reputation, degree of service, number, condition and availability of vehicles. Motor-coaches (buses) are the most frequently used vehicle for moving groups. You may need charter buses or shuttle buses. A charter follows a pre-determined route for a specified length of time. A shuttle operates continuously on a regularly established route.

Common questions that should be asked of various transportation companies: Are there minimum rental periods? What is the bus capacity? How is dispatch done? Can disabled passengers be accommodated? Are backups available? Are buses air conditioned? What routes will be used? How comprehensive is their insurance liability? Can the price be negotiated?

VIP Transportation: Pick up speakers, leaders, and guests at the airport or other locations. These people are critical to the success of your event. They deserve special treatment.

Assign staff members as official greeters, select appropriate vehicles, check arrival and departure times and potential customs or immigration problems. Select the best airport location to meet as well as the best drop-off points and the quickest route.

Don't reserve a vehicle over the phone: Go to the transportation company and inspect the vehicle you are considering renting. Be sure you are dealing with an established, reputable company. These businesses will display, or readily make available, important information like their business license and their liability insurance certificate. If you have concerns or questions, ask for references.

TOURS ◆ CHARTERS ◆ SHUTTLES

P. O. Box 17306 • Portland, Oregon 97217
(503) 285-9845 or (800) 422-7042

WE'LL TAKE YOU THERE

Gray Line of Portland is Oregon's largest and most experienced motorcoach company. We've been serving our customers' travel needs since 1913. We've provided more Tours, Charters, and Shuttles than any other motorcoach company in Oregon.

Service
As part of the Gray Line family, we have a strong commitment to quality and service. Our professional staff is truly ready, willing, and especially able to assist you with your transportation needs. Our "Coach Captains" are highly trained, highly skilled, and uniquely qualified to ensure that your group is safe, comfortable, and informed.

Selection
To best suit your needs, we offer a wide variety of vehicles including Elite European-style Motorcoaches, Luxury Motorcoaches, Shuttle Coaches, School Buses, and Vans.

Prices
A charter trip is quoted and priced based on miles or hours, whichever is greater. There is a five-hour minimum on charters. Convention shuttle rates are charged hourly, shop to shop. Please call for specific price quotes.

Reservations
We recommend you make your charter reservations 30 days in advance to ensure availability of the equipment you'll need.

We offer sightseeing tours, convention and corporate shuttles, escorted vacations, custom itineraries, and charters. Whether it's cross-town or cross-country, "we'll take you there!"

Gray Line of Portland Airport Express
- Scheduled service to and from Portland International Airport and downtown Portland hotels and Oregon Convention Center

Please let this business know that you heard about them from the Bravo! Event Resource Guide.

COACH, BUS & VAN RENTALS

RAZ TRANSPORTATION & TOURS

11655 S.W. Pacific Highway
Portland, Oregon 97223-8629
(503) 684-3322, (888) 684-3322; Fax (503) 968-3223, (503) 684-6646
Web site: http://www.raztrans.com

WE GO THE EXTRA MILE

Why deal with *SEVERAL* companies when…
RAZ can service *ALL* your needs?

Motorcoach Charters • Professionally Guided Sightseeing Tours • Meet & Greet Services

Multilingual Guide Services • Airport Transfers • Shuttle Services • Step-on Guides

RAZ Convention Tours and Shuttles

- Mount Hood Loop
- Columbia River Gorge
- Mount St. Helens
- North Oregon Coast
- Portland City Tour
- Oregon Wineries

- A receptive tour operator able to design itineraries and tour packages specific to your needs
- Serving corporate or group travel: both domestic and international
- Employing only professionally trained step-on guides and tour directors
- Fully experienced convention shuttle operator; all equipment with two-way radios
- On-site dispatch with hand-held radios to accommodate flexibility due to traffic, weather, etc.

RAZ Transportation

Providing service since 1937 and offering vehicles for all your ground transportation needs…from *luxury* to *budget*:

Luxury Liner	Deluxe Coach	Transit Coach	School Bus
55 passenger	47 passenger	44 passenger	44 passenger
47 passenger	36 passenger w/lounge		
	24 passenger		

Let us *"Go the extra mile"* for YOU!

Public shuttles to Spirit Mountain Casino EVERY day of the week!

Call (503) 225-5555 ext. 5043 for more information

P.O. Box 2016
Wilsonville, Oregon 97070
(503) 678-7870; Fax (503) 678-7871
E-mail: Funlimobus@aol.com
Web site: funmobile.citysearch.com

TOURS • CHARTERS

The Fun-Mobile is a fun and convenient way to take trips! Our limo-coach seats up to 24 people in high style! The Fun-Mobile organizes day trips and overnight voyages for the perfect getaway, or if you have destinations of your own in mind you can charter the Fun-Mobile for a more personalized journey! The Fun-Mobile is perfect for just about any adventure for you and your friends. Now is the perfect time to sit back, relax, and leave the driving to us!

Create Your Own Trip
- Corporate outings
- Conference/meeting shuttles
- Teambuilding trips
- Special occasions/birthdays
- Wedding service
- Family reunions
- Overnight voyages

Or
Our professional staff will customize a trip specifically for your group.

Capacity
24-passenger, limo coach with luggage compartment.

Availability
Charters and tours are scheduled every day of the week, year-round. Overnight transportation is also available.

Cost and Terms
Trip and tour estimates are based on a flat rate depending upon number of hours and distance of destination; trip quotes differ per request; call for a free quote.

Reservations and Policies
Reservations recommended, first reserved, first served; a nonrefundable deposit is due at the time of a reservation; payments accepted are as follows: major credit cards, cash, checks and purchase orders.

Additional Information
Serving Oregon and Washington.

240 S.E. Yamhill
Portland, Oregon 97214
Reservations (503) 234-2400
(888) TOWNCAR
E-mail: towncar@towncar.com
Web site: www.towncar.com

EXECUTIVE TRANSPORTATION

Experience the Pacific Executive Difference
- Professional Drivers—extensive geographical knowledge, random drug testing, DMV records reviewed
- Computerized Reservations—Y2K compliant dispatch, reservation and flight tracking system
- Office Staffed—seven days a week
- Experienced—dispatchers and customer service representatives
- E-mail Reservations and Itineraries

Portland International Airport (PDX)
- Meet and greet at the flight arrival gate to assist with luggage
- On-sight coordinator to assist in organizing your group arrivals
- Towncars standing by to accommodate last minute changes

Fleet Accommodations
- Luxury Lincoln Towncars—5 passenger capacity
- Luxury Suburbans—7 passenger capacity
- Lincoln Limousines—6, 8, and 10 passenger capacity
- Limousine Coach—15 passenger capacity
- Vans—14 passenger capacity
- Buses/Coaches—24, 47, and 56 passenger capacity

Additional Information
- Major credit cards accepted, cash or approved billable accounts
- Advance reservations recommended

At Pacific Executive Services we look forward to assisting you with all of your transportation needs. Whether it's organizing a large event or personalizing an executive profile, we are ready to make your job easier!

PORTLAND LIMOUSINE COMPANY

730 N.E. 21st Avenue
Portland, Oregon 97232
(503) 235-2221, (800) 826-1431;
Fax (503) 235-2821
Office Hours:
Mon–Fri 8am–7pm; Sat 10am–3pm

PORTLAND LIMOUSINE COMPANY:
YOUR COMPLETE GROUND TRANSPORTATION COMPANY

Portland Limousine Company has
- Sedans
- Limousines (6, 8 and 10 passenger)
- Fifteen passenger vans
- Nineteen passenger buses
- 1961 Bentley S2

Portland Limousine Company has
- Corporate billing
- Uniformed chauffeurs
- Wine, city and special tours
- Shuttle service
- Airport transfers

All of the vehicles from Portland Limousine Company are driven by professionally trained, uniformed chauffeurs. Our limousines have all the amenities including televisions, stereos, CD players, halo lighting, VCRs, cellular phones, moon roofs, champagne flutes, crystal glasses, and are stocked with ice. Our limousines and buses will accommodate from one to 19 people depending on vehicle type.

Additional Information
Portland Limousine Company has provided the finest limousine service since 1983. We pride ourselves on efficient, professional, courteous service.

CALL PORTLAND LIMOUSINE COMPANY FOR
OREGON'S FINEST CHAUFFEURED VEHICLES
(503) 235-2221 OR (800) 826-1431
Web site: http://www.portlandlimousine.com
E-mail: Portlandlimo@juno.com

Notes

Attractions, Activities & Tours

HELPFUL HINTS

The Pacific Northwest is overflowing with attractions: From the Hood to coast, there are endless attractions and activities. The majestic mountains are only an hour-and-a-half away. The miles of beaches are an hour's drive. Award-winning wines at local wineries, and brew pubs are cropping up all over town. The performing arts, museums, scenic and historical sites will keep you busy. Throw in the recreation, sporting events and transportation and there is something for everyone and unique venues for your next event or meeting.

Tours: There are many types of sightseeing tours available, these are fun activities to include spouses. Just some of the tours that are available are: tours of local brew pubs and sampling, Wine Country tours- Oregon is rich with some of the finest wines, and the vineyards are absolutely beautiful to tour. There are shopping tours on antique row, and scenic and historical tours of all Oregon's history.

Destination Management Companies (DMC): These companies are hired by conventions and out-of-state planners. They specialize in packaging group and VIP events. They can customize local activities to fit the planner's need (you will find these companies in the Event Planner section).

Local celebrations and sporting events: Take advantage of local celebrations, sporting events, and theatre schedules to provide "group" activities for free time or for individuals to attend. Sporting activities can be attended as a spectator or local "celebrities" can assist in your programming, offering hands-on windsurfing instruction, rafting trips, or ski excursions for your guests' free time.

Utilize historical sites and attractions as venues for your special events: Have a cocktail reception at an aquarium, or a dinner in a museum. Often the exhibits are interesting "decor" at no additional costs. Docents can serve as greeters, and guests can learn something new.

Audience participation activities: Recreational activities for company events are becoming more and more popular. The company picnic is becoming more interesting. There are corporate-outing events like ski days, paintball tournaments, laser tag for team-building, and mini "Indy car race tracks." The more interesting an event is, the better the attendance.

BREWERY TOURS

Call toll-free 1-888-BIG BREW
www.brewbus.com

Portland, Oregon has more brewpubs per capita than anywhere in the U.S. The Portland BrewBus is a four-hour tour (not a pub crawl) of area breweries and brewpubs. You'll sample up to 20 beers, learn in-depth how each beer is made and see highlights of the Portland scene and scenery. We visit up to four brewery locations from among the following:
- The BridgePort Brewing Co.
- The Lucky Labrador Brewing Co.
- The Nor'Wester Brewing Co.
- The Portland Brewing Co.
- The Tugboat Brewing Co.
- The Widmer Brothers Brewing Co.

Custom Charters: Available year round
Capacity: up to 50 people per bus
Price: $29.95 per person which includes transportation, brewery tours, beer and munchies
Available: Weekday or weekend afternoons. For most evenings, dinner is required at an additional charge of $10 to $15 per person.

We are happy to tailor the charter to meet your needs—pick-up and drop-off locations, times, destinations, meals—just ask!

We can arrange for language translators with 48-hour notice at direct pass-through hourly charges.

We accept checks in advance.

Please note, due to health and safety regulations, we cannot allow sandals or open-toed shoes on the tours. All tours may not be available at all times.

Drink Beer and Learn Something.
It's Like College All Over Again!!

KART RACING AND PAINTBALL

Play Paintball At
PAINTBALL ISLAND

Oregon's Finest Paintball Course & GO Kart Track

Contact: Mike Sinatra (503) 309-9900

PAT'S ACRES KARTING COMPLEX
Racing and Recreation Grounds

6255 S. Arnot Road • Canby, Oregon 97013
Contact: Chris Egger (503) 266-PATS, (503) 519-4392

What is Paintball?
The "sport of paintball" has been in existence since 1982 and caters to players from all walks of life. It's the adult version of "Capture the Flag" and "Tag". Paintball markers are used to mark opponents out of the games with splatters of washable non-toxic paintballs. The sport has demonstrated a great forum for teaching teamwork, good communication skills, leadership, as well as providing aerobic exercise and healthy fun.

Group Information
Paintball provides an exciting activity for you and your group. For groups of 20 or more, we offer private games. Private games are available seven days a week by reservation. Our professional staff is with you throughout the day ensuring that you and your group have a great time. A $200 refundable deposit is required upon the scheduling of your group.

Description
Go racing head to head in our 45 mph racing karts on a half-mile paved road course. Nothing else even comes close! Champagne podium presentation for the Winners…Don't just race the clock—race the boss! Great for team building or employee appreciations.

Excellent For
Corporate parties, family reunions, sales meetings, employee appreciation events, church groups, team building, bachelor parties, or any other group or individual event

Reservations
Reservations are on a first-come, first-served basis; deposit required upon booking. Visa and MasterCard accepted.

Facilities
Pat's Acres features 44 acres of trees and meadows surrounded by the river. We have a secluded private beach and picnic area along with a 2,400 square foot pavilion (barn style) building—great for meetings. Picnic grounds accommodate groups up to 1,500; indoor facility up to 100. Catering is also available.

MT. HOOD MEADOWS SKI RESORT

*Marketing and Sales Department
1975 S.W. First Avenue, Suite M
Portland, Oregon 97201*

Photography by Steve Wanke
Photography by Brian Robb

Contact: Karen Lite
(503) 287-5438
(800) SKI-HOOD
*Business Hours:
Mon–Fri 8am–4:30pm;
evenings by appointment*
E-mail: info@skihood.com

Location
Conveniently located just 65 miles east of Portland, Mt. Hood Meadows has the most diverse skiing terrain in Oregon. Our 10 chairlifts (including four high-speed quads), special programs, three base lodges, and friendly employees make Meadows the kind of place you will want to visit often.

Lifts
- **Four high-speed quad chairlifts**
- Six lighted chairlifts
- Six double chairlifts
- One ropetow

Services
Group rates are available for 25 skiers or more. You receive discounts on lift tickets, ski and snowboard rental equipment, and group lessons. We can also arrange all of your transportation needs.

Mt. Hood Meadows also offers professional catering services. Our friendly staff knows how important the details are to guarantee your event will be a success. We can tailor an event to fit the expectations of your group.

Race Department
Mt. Hood Meadows is a wonderful place to hold a company ski race. From the competitive ski racer to the recreational skier, we have a race to fit your group! Let our professional race department host a race suited to your group. **Race course fee: $300 to $500 (2 hours)**

EXPERIENCE MT. HOOD MEADOWS
Mt. Hood Meadows has a truly magical ambiance. Majestic Mount Hood, framed by snow-covered trees in the winter and green fields with wild flowers in the summer, provides the perfect alpine atmosphere for your next special event.

**Visit us on the Web:
http://www.skihood.com**

See page 514 under Banquet, Meeting & Event Sites.

AQUATIC PARK

400,000 GALLONS OF FUN

7300 S.E. Harmony Road • Milwaukie, Oregon 97222
Contact: Chris Miller or Louise Stangel (503) 557-SURF (7873)
Business Hours: call for information

Capacity: up to 1,000 people
Price Range: conference rooms $15 to $25 hour; private pool $30 to $600 hour
Types of Events: graduation parties, family reunions, business meetings, catered parties, teen parties, sports parties, recreational swimming, wedding receptions

Services and Facility

Our indoor Aquatic Park features five pools, including a wave pool capable of four-feet-high waves, a 200-foot open slide, a 167-foot enclosed slide and a 20-foot-drop slide. We have a large whirlpool for adults, an interactive play area for children, and a wading pool for small children.

We have four conference rooms. Small rooms hold up to 18 people. Large rooms hold 40 people. Our catering specialists would be pleased to cater any of your parties.

Other Amenities

Seating: Spectator area in the pool area holds 100 people comfortably.
Parking: Large parking area available, bus and RV spaces available.
Concessions: Wide range of menu selections at our Surfs Up Cafe and Espresso Bar.

400,000 GALLONS OF FUN

We offer 400,000 gallons of fun for everyone. Convenient location close to the freeway—within a block of Oregon's largest mall. Beautiful picnic area on the grounds and proximity to major hotels make it especially accessible. Since we are totally enclosed, we guarantee "Weather Friendly" fun!

COMPANY PICNICS AT OAKS AMUSEMENT PARK

Portland, Oregon 97202
Contact: Volanne Stephens
(503) 233-5777
Business Hours: Mon–Fri 8am–5pm

Oaks Amusement Park, located along the Willamette River, offers a wide variety of options for your company picnic. Thrill rides, skating, garden golf, and green space picnic areas are just a few options your group will enjoy.

Our in-house catering department will work with you in planning this important day. We can individually design your event to meet your expectations, style, and taste.

NO SURPRISES, JUST FUN AND GOOD TIMES!!!

Join us at our historic riverside park on the Willamette River and let us create a perfect day or evening event for you and your guests. Our facility is ideal for seminars, retreats, corporate dinners, retirement and holiday parties, Children's Christmas parties are a specialty. It is our policy to work with you and offer exemplary step-by-step service all during the event, allowing you to relax and enjoy the party.

See page 430 under Park Sites.

Please let this business know that you heard about them from the Bravo! Event Resource Guide.

FAMILY FUN CENTER

9120 S.E. Powell Blvd.
Portland, Oregon 97266
Contact: Lynne Maginnis
(503) 774-7000; Fax (503) 774-5104
Business Hours: Mon–Thurs 11am–10pm; Fri 11am–11pm;
Sat 10am–11pm; Sun 10am–10pm

Capacity: from two to 600
Price Range: group packages and birthday packages available; call for details
Catering: in-house only; take-out pizza available
Types of Events: staff parties, birthdays, employee incentives, corporate celebrations, school and church events

Availability and Terms
Packages are available. Please make weekend reservations at least two weeks in advance. Midweek parties are preferred for larger groups.

Description of Facility and Services
Seating: up to 600
Servers: provided
Bar facilities: beer and wine
Decorations: birthday setup with package or bring your own
Cleanup: provided at no charge
Parking: ample parking available
ADA: all but one dining platform

Special Services
Interactive video games are available for all age groups.
- New arcade games
- Great prizes to win
- Large meeting area; both professional- and family-based functions welcome
- New expanded menu

A PLACE TO MEET AND HAVE FUN!

WILSONVILLE FAMILY FUN CENTER AND BULLWINKLE'S RESTAURANT

29111 S.W. Town Center Loop, W. • Wilsonville, Oregon 97070
(503) 685-5000; Fax (503) 685-9694
Web site: wffc.citysearch.com
Open year-round
Business Hours: winter: 11am–9pm; summer 9am–11pm

Capacity: amusement park, 2,000 people; Bullwinkle's dining room, 175 people
Price Range: $3–$28 per person
Catering: in-house
Types of Events: corporate picnics, holiday parties, graduation parties, employee incentives, birthday parties, family reunions

Great Food and Entertainment for All Ages
This amazing 6-acre amusement park is located in the city of Wilsonville (I-5, exit 283). The Wilsonville Family Fun Center and Bullwinkle's Restaurant provide a fun and clean atmosphere, safe attractions, great food and entertainment for all ages.

Indoor Attractions
- **LazerXtreme:** laser tag arena
- **Kidopolis:** four-level soft play area for children 5 feet and under
- **Arcade:** two-story arcade with more than 100 games
- **Animation performance:** on stage in Bullwinkle's Family Restaurant

Outdoor Attractions
- **Miniature golf:** two 18-hole courses
- **Go karts:** single and double seater cars available
- **Bumper boats:** enjoy a wild ride on motorized boats
- **Batting cages:** eight batting cages ranging from 40 mph to 70 mph

Availability and Terms
First come, first served. Reservations available during all operating hours. After-hour packages also are available. Deposits are required.

Special Services
Ask about our birthday packages, corporate packages and group discount packages. The Wilsonville Family Fun Center is open year-round, rain or shine.

See page 573 under Banquet, Meeting & Event Sites.

MUSEUM

OREGON MUSEUM OF SCIENCE AND INDUSTRY

1945 S.E. Water Avenue
Portland, Oregon 97214
(503) 797-4000
Science Center Hours:
Memorial Day–Labor Day
Open daily from 9:30am
After Labor Day
Open Tues–Sun from 9:30am
Group reservations:
(503) 797-4501 or (503) 797-4661

Adventure on the Edge of Imagination!

Considered one of the finest science centers in the nation, OMSI is one giant world of wonder, encompassing six major exhibit halls, hundreds of interactive displays, science labs, acclaimed national touring exhibitions, live demonstrations, and unlimited fun.

OMNIMAX® Theater

Experience the world's most advanced film projection system in the OMNIMAX® Theater, where images surround you on a five-story domed screen. See wild animals, far-away places or the depth of the ocean like never before!

Murdock Planetarium

For high inspiration, take a seat in the cosmic Murdock Planetarium and bring the stars down to earth. Enjoy captivating astronomy and laser light productions.

USS Blueback Submarine

Discover a world known only to a few…the undersea world of the submarine. Take a 40-minute tour on board the 219′ USS Blueback.

Motion Simulator

Experience OMSI's new motion simulator ride, a multi-sensory experience that combines a movie-like audiovisual presentation using a high-definition screen and surround-sound with high-speed motion.

A World of Hands-on Fun!

Explore a world of hands-on fun where minds are motivated by computer games, science labs, earthquake simulations, space exploration, cutting-edge technology, and the mysteries of the universe. Wander through the wondrous OMSI Science Store, then relax in our riverfront restaurant. Make it an all-day adventure. Visit OMSI and let the fun begin!

Visit our Web site:
http://www.omsi.edu

See pages 408 under Convention & Exhibition Facilities.

PORTLAND CENTER FOR THE PERFORMING ARTS

1111 S.W. Broadway • Portland, Oregon 97205
(503) 248-4335; Fax (503) 274-7490
Performance Schedule: (503) 796-9293
Web site: www.pcpa.com

Ticket Center—Ticketmaster and Fastixx
PCPA New Theatre Building
S.W. Broadway at Main Street • Portland, Oregon 97205
Hours: Mon–Sat 10am–6pm

PCPA's Resident Performing and Cultural Groups
- Oregon Symphony
- Portland Opera
- Oregon Ballet Theatre
- Portland Center Stage
- Tygres Heart Shakespeare Company
- Oregon Children's Theatre
- Portland Arts & Lectures
- Tears of Joy Theatre
- Portland Youth Philharmonic

These groups perform in the following PCPA venues
- **Arlene Schnitzer Concert Hall**
  S.W. Broadway at Main Street
- **Portland Civic Auditorium**
  S.W. Third between Clay and Market streets
- **Newmark Theatre and Dolores Winningstad Theatre**
  located in the New Theatre Building
  S.W. Broadway at Main Street

See page 533 under Banquet, Meeting & Event Sites.

PORTLAND CENTER STAGE
1999–2000 SEASON

Hamlet: Sept 25–Oct 24
Rosencrantz & Guildenstern Are Dead: Oct 30–Nov 20
A Christmas Carol: Nov 28–Dec 28
Bus Stop: Jan 15–Feb 12
Blues for an Alabama Sky: Feb 19–Mar 18
Gun-shy: Mar 25–Apr 22

Box Office Hours:
Tues–Fri 10am–5pm; Sat 10am–1pm
1111 S.W. Broadway
Portland, Oregon 97205
Web site: www.pcs.org
(503) 274-6588; Fax (503) 228-7058

CELEBRATE AT CENTER STAGE!

What better way to begin a new century…
…than with the thrill of live professional theatre?
From magnificent tragedy to lighthearted comedy, our upcoming season offers rich and varied entertainment. Won't you join us?

"The food was exceptional, the service good, and the evening a complete success. Our people were delighted with such a special holiday event."

—Contact Lumber Company
1998 *A Christmas Carol*

Whatever your entertainment needs, the theatre is a perfect venue for impressive client functions, memorable office parties, and festive social occasions. An event at Portland Center Stage can be simple or lavish—we'll create a unique theatrical experience specifically designed for your group and budget. Our professional staff is available to manage all aspects of your party, from designing the invitations and maintaining the guest list, to coordinating dinner reservations, catering, and parking.

Special benefits for our group clients include:

- **Exceptional Discounts**
  Save up to 30% off the regular single ticket price.

- **Free Tickets**
  Receive one complimentary ticket for every 15 people in your party.

- **Private Event Space**
  Use our lobby in the beautifully designed Newmark Theatre to entertain 50 or more of your guests, either before or after the show.

- **Convenient Location**
  Easily walk to downtown hotels, restaurants, shopping, mass transit, and parking.

To plan your next event at Portland Center Stage,
contact **Kristen Tucker at (503) 274-6598 or kristen@pcs.org**.

Watercraft Rentals, Inc.

↝ Columbia River • Hagg Lake • Wilsonville

3409 N.E. Marine Drive
Portland, Oregon 97211
Contact: Shawn Karambelas
(503) 284-6447; Fax (503) 281-9154
E-mail: SKJSKI@aol.com
Web site: www.quikpage.com/skwaterent

Corporate and Group Events
What better way to show your co-workers a great time at your next picnic, sales meeting, or team building event than a sunny afternoon of fun on the water! Whether it is a group of 15 or 500, we will meet your every need. Our trained staff will deliver the watercraft, set up buoys, speak to your group about safety, and will remain on site for the entire event to ensure everything runs smoothly and safely. Some of the most popular sites we use are: Kelly Point Park, Lake Merwin, Wilsonville Park, Hagg Lake, Rooster Rock and Frenchman's Bar.

Experienced Staff
With experienced staff, our proven success and only the newest, most reliable watercraft, we promise to be the hit of the party! SK Watercraft Rentals is the largest watercraft rental operation in the state of Oregon with three locations and experience in the business since 1993. With everything you are planning, the last thing you have to worry about is the operational details.

Our Watercraft Fleet
We update our entire fleet every year.
- Stand-ups . . . . Yamaha Super Jet (63hp)
- Two-Seaters . . . . Sea-Doo GS (85hp)
- Three-Seaters . . . . . . Sea-Doo GTS (85hp)
- Ski Boats . . . . Bayliner 1850 Capri LS (190hp)

Watercraft Group Tours
We offer staff accompanied tours of many scenic areas including:
- Columbia River Gorge
- Portland Waterfront
- Portland to the Coast
- Oregon City Falls
- Multnomah Falls

**Whatever the Event, SK Watercraft Rentals, Inc.
Can Really Add Some Excitement to Your Next Party!**

Please let this business know that you heard about them from the Bravo! Event Resource Guide.

JETBOAT/TOURS

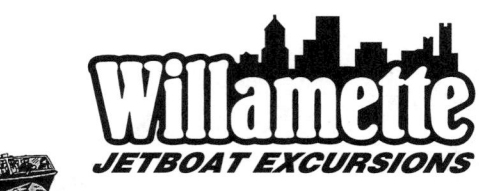

Willamette JETBOAT EXCURSIONS

1945 S.E. Water Avenue
Portland, Oregon 97214
(503) 231-1532, (888) JETBOAT (538-2628)
Web site: www.jetboatpdx.com

Experience fast-paced jetboat action right in the center of Portland. Willamette Jetboat Excursions is the ultimate in river fun! We will take you farther than ever possible, offering thrills, adventure and historic highlights of Portland's waterfront. Our safe, comfortable excursions are guided by USCG certified river pilots who will point out wildlife and maritime history. They will bring the river to life with Native American and early pioneer legends and facts! All this plus the fun found only in a jetboat excursion!

Capacity
Whether you are planning for two or groups up to 83, we will arrange an experience you will never forget! Accommodation for larger groups also can be made. We have daily departures to fit anyone's schedule and can tailor our tours to meet your special needs.

Lunch and Dinner Excursions
In addition to scenic adventures, we also offer lunch and dinner excursions where you can stop at a private park along the river and experience an authentic Northwest Indian Salmon Bake cooked over an open fire. Call for details and plan for an event your group will never forget!

Season
Daily tours scheduled from May through October. Private charters and custom tours also available. Call now for details.

Prices
Excursions start at $22 for adults with lower rates for children and infants. Meal trips start at $40 with lower prices for children. Prices are all inclusive excluding gratuities.

Location
Easily accessible from downtown and convention center! All jetboat excursions depart from OMSI in downtown Portland on the east side of the Willamette River. Boardings at the RiverPlace Marina on the westside, near the Portland Marriott Hotel and RiverPlace Hotel also available. Call for details and easy directions.

Free Parking
Free parking is available at OMSI. Plenty of space for buses and vans too.

CALL TODAY
(503) 231-1532 or
1-888 JETBOAT (538-2628)

Don't forget to visit our "parent" company, *Hellgate Excursions*, the next time you're in southern Oregon.

BREWERIES

Alameda Brew House
4765 N.E. Fremont
Portland, OR 97213
(503) 460-9025

Big Horse Brewery & Pub
115 State St.
Hood River, OR 97031
(541) 386-4411

Big Horn Brewing Co.
515 12th St., S.E.
Salem, OR 97302
(503) 363-1904

BridgePort Brewing Co.
1313 N.W. Marshall St.
Portland, OR 97209
(503) 241-7179
See page 456

Golden Valley Brewery & Pub
980 E. Fourth
McMinnville, OR 97128
(503) 472-2739

John BarleyCorns Brewery
14610 S.W. Sequoia Pkwy.
Tigard, OR 97223
(503) 684-6253

Lucky Labrador Brewing Co.
915 S.E. Hawthorne Blvd.
Portland, OR 97214
(503) 236-3555

McMenamins—Cedar Hills
2927 S.W. Cedar Hills Blvd.
Beaverton, OR 97005
(503) 641-0151

McMenamins—Cornelius Pass Roadhouse & Brewery
4045 N.W. Cornelius Pass Rd.
Hillsboro, OR 97124
(503) 640-6174

McMenamins Edgefield Brewery & Power Station
2126 S.W. Halsey St.
Troutdale, OR 97060
(503) 492-4686
See page 389

McMenamins—Hotel Oregon
310 N.E. Evans St.
McMinnville, OR 97128
(503) 492-2777
See page 438

McMenamins—Kennedy School
5736 N.E. 33rd Ave.
Portland, OR 97211
(503) 249-3983
See page 390

Mt. Angel Brewing Co.
210 Monroe St.
Mt. Angel, OR 97362
(503) 845-9624

Old Market Pub & Brewery
6959 S.W. Multnomah
Portland, OR 97223
(503) 244-0450

Portland BrewBus Tours
(888) BIG-BREW
See page 93

Portland Brewing Co.
2730 N.W. 31st
Portland, OR 97210
(503) 226-7623

Big Horn Brewing Co. & Ram Restaurant
320 Oswego Point Blvd.
Lake Oswego, OR 97034
(503) 697-8818

Rock Bottom Brewery
206 S.W. Morrison St.
Portland, OR 97204
(503) 796-2739
See page 543

Saxer Brewing Co.
5875 S.W. Lakeview Blvd.
Lake Oswego, OR 97035
(503) 699-9524

Widmer Gasthaus
929 N. Russel
Portland, OR 97227
(503) 281-3333
See page 444

Please let these businesses know that you heard about them from the Bravo! Event Resource Guide.

WINERIES

Airlie Winery
15303 Dunn Forest Rd.
Monmouth, OR 97361
(503) 838-6013

Amity Vineyards
18150 Amity Vineyards Rd., S.E.
Amity, OR 97101
(503) 835-2362

Argyle Winery
691 S.W. Hwy. 99W
Dundee, OR 97115
(503) 538-8520

Autumn Wind Vineyard
15225 N.E. North Valley Rd.
Newberg, OR 97132
(503) 538-6931

BeckenRidge Vineyard
300 Reuben-Base Rd.
Dallas, OR 97338
(503) 831-3652
See page 453

Bell Fountain Cellars
25041 Llewllyn Rd.
Corvallis, OR 97333
(541) 929-3162

Bethel Heights Vineyard
6060 Bethel Heights Rd., N.W.
Salem, OR 97304
(503) 581-2262

Champoeg Wine Cellar
10375 Champoeg Rd., N.E.
Aurora, OR 97002
(503) 678-3144

Chateau Benoit
6580 N.E Mineral Springs Rd.
Carlton, OR 97111
(503) 864-2991

Chateau Lorane
27415 Siuslaw River Rd.
Lorane, OR 97451
(541) 942-8028

Chehalem Winery
31190 N.E. Veritas
Newberg, OR 97132
(503) 538-4700

Cristom Vineyards
6905 Spring Valley Rd., N.W.
Salem, OR 97304
(503) 375-3068

Duck Pond Cellars
23145 Hwy. 99W
Dundee, OR 97115
(503) 538-3199

Edgefield Winery
2126 S.W. Halsey St.
Troutdale, OR 97060
(503) 665-2992
See page 389

Elk Cove Vineyards
27751 N.W. Olson Rd.
Gaston, OR 97119
(503) 985-7760

Eola Hills Wine Cellars
501 S. Pacific Hwy. 99W
Rickreall, OR 97371
(503) 623-2405

Erath Vineyards
9049 N.E. Wordon Hill Rd.
Dundee, OR 97115
(800) 539-9463

Flerchinger Vineyards
4200 Post Canyon Dr.
Hood River, OR 97031
(800) 516-8710

Honeywood Winery
1350 Hines St., S.E.
Salem, OR 97301
(503) 362-4111

The Inn at Otter Crest
301 Otter Crest Loop
Otter Rock, OR 97369
(800) 326-5806
See page 376

Kramer Vineyards
26830 N.W. Olson Rd.
Gaston, OR 97119
(503) 662-4545

Laurel Ridge Winery
46350 David Hill Rd.
P.O. Box 456
Forest Grove, OR 97116
(503) 359-5436

Please let these businesses know that you heard about them from the Bravo! Event Resource Guide.

Wineries continued...

Lange Winery
18380 N.E. Buena Vista
Dundee, OR 97115
(503) 538-6476

Marquam Hill Vineyards
35803 S. Hwy. 213
Molalla, OR 97038
(503) 829-6677

Montinore Vineyards
3663 S.W. Dilley Rd.
Forest Grove, OR 97116
(503) 359-5012

Oak Knoll Winery
29700 S.W. Burkhalter Rd.
Hillsboro, OR 97123
(800) OAK-KNOLL

Orchard Heights Winery
6057 Orchard Heights Rd., N.W.
Salem, OR 97304
(503) 363-0375

Ponzi Vineyards
14665 S.W. Winery Lane
Beaverton, OR 97007
(503) 628-1227

Red Hawk Vineyard
2995 Michigan City Ave., N.W.
Salem, OR 97304
(503) 362-1596

Rex Hill Winery
30835 N. Hwy. 99W
Newberg, OR 97132
(503) 538-0666

Serendipity Cellars Winery
15275 Dunn Forest Rd.
Monmouth, OR 97361
(503) 838-4284

Shafer Vineyard Cellars
6200 N.W. Gales Creek Rd.
Forest Grove, OR 97116
(503) 357-6604

Sokol Blosser Winery
5000 NE Sokol Blosser Ln.
Dundee, OR 97115
(503) 864-2282

Spring Hill Cellars
2920 N.W. Scenic Dr.
Albany, OR 97321
(503) 928-1009

St. Innocent
1360 Tandem Ave., N.E.
Salem, OR 97303
(503) 378-1526

Stangeland Vineyards & Winery
8500 Hopewell Rd., N.W.
Salem, OR 97304
(503) 581-0355

St. Josef's Wine Cellars
28836 S. Barlow Rd.
Canby, OR 97013
(503) 651-3190

Torii Mor Wine
905 E. 10th
McMinnville, OR 97128
(503) 434-1439

Tyee Wine Cellars
26335 Greenberry Rd.
Corvallis, OR 97333
(541) 753-8754

Willamette Valley Vineyard
8800 Enchanted Wy., S.E.
Turner, OR 97392
(800) 344-9463
See page 572

Wine Country Farm
6855 Breyman Orchards Rd.
Dayton, OR 97114
(503) 864-3446

Witness Tree Vineyard
7111 Spring Valley Rd., N.E.
Salem, OR 97304
(503) 585-7874

Yamhill Valley Vineyards
16250 Oldsville Rd., off Hwy. 18
McMinnville, OR 97128
(800) 825-4845

Youngberg Hill Vineyard
10660 S.W. Youngberg Hill Rd.
McMinnville, OR 97128
(503) 472-2727

AMUSEMENT CENTERS, RECREATION & SPORTS TEAMS

AMUSEMENT CENTERS

Enchanted Forest
8462 Enchanted Wy., S.E.
Turner, OR 97392
(503) 363-3060

Multnomah Greyhound Park
994 N.E. 223rd Ave.
Wood Village, OR 97060
(503) 667-7700

Oaks Amusement Park
Foot of S.E. Spokane St.
Portland, OR 97202
(503) 233-5777
See page 430

Thrill-Ville U.S.A., Inc.
8372 Enchanted Way, S.E.
Turner, OR 97392
(503) 363-7616

Wildlife Safari
P.O. Box 1600/
1790 Safari Rd.
Winston, OR 97496
(541) 679-6761

Wilsonville Family Fun Center
29111 S.W. Towncenter Lp.
Wilsonville, OR 97070
(503) 685-5000
See page 573

RECREATION

Cascade Soaring
P.O. Box 369
Dayton, OR 97114
(503) 472-8805

ClubSport
18120 S.W. Lower Boones Fry Rd.
Tigard, OR 97224
(503) 968-4500
See page 466

Flying M Ranch
23029 N.W. Flying M Rd.
Yamhill, OR 97148
(503) 662-3222

Fun-Mobile Adventures
P.O. Box 2016
Wilsonville, OR 97070
(503) 678-7870
See page 87

H.O.R.S.E.S., Ltd.
P.O. Box 280
Scotts Mills, OR 97375
(503) 873-3890

The Hoop
3575 Fairview Industrial Dr., S.E.
Salem, OR 97302
(503) 361-7706

Lone Oak Racing, Inc.
P.O. Box 13267
Salem, OR 97309
(503) 370-2627

Multnomah Greyhound Park
N.E. 223rd & Glisan
P.O. Box 9
Fairview, OR 97024
(503) 667-7700

North Clackamas Aquatic Park
7300 S.E. Harmony Rd.
Milwaukie, OR 97222
(503) 557-7873
See page 96

**Paintball Island at
Pat's Acres Karting Complex**
6255 S. Arnot Rd.
Canby, OR 97013
(503) 309-9900, (503) 266-PATS
See page 94

Portland BrewBus
(888) BIG-BREW
See page 93

Portland Meadows Race Track
1001 N. Schmeer Rd.
Portland, OR 97217
(503) 285-9144

LaserPort
10975 S.W. Canyon Rd.
Beaverton, OR 97005
(503) 526-9501
See page 251

Malibu Grand Prix
9405 S.W. Cascade Ave.
Beaverton, OR 97005
(503) 641-8122

Recreation and Sports Teams continued...

Oregon Zoo
4001 S.W. Canyon Rd.
Portland, OR 97221
(503) 220-2789
See page 526

SK Watercraft Rentals Inc.
3409 N.E. Marine Dr.
Portland, OR 97211
(503) 284-6447
See page 103

S.A.L.E.M. Treks Llama Tours
555 Howell Prairie Rd., S.E.
Salem, OR 97309
(503) 362-0873

Skate Palace
1860 Fisher Rd.
Salem, OR 97305
(503) 364-8568

Ultrazone
16074-10 S.E. McLoughlin Blvd.
Milwaukie, OR 97267
(503) 652-1122
See page 252

Uptown Casino
120 N.W. 23rd Ave.
Portland, OR 97210
(503) 226-6909
See page 242

Vancouver-Clark Parks & Recreation
1009 E. McLoughlin Blvd.
Vancouver, WA 98663
(360) 696-8236

Wallace Sports Complex, Inc.
P.O. Box 5722
Salem, OR 97304
(503) 364-1923 ext. 211

Willamette Jetboats
1945 S.E. Water Ave.
Portland, OR 97214
(503) 231-1532
(888) 538-2628
See page 104

SPORTS TEAMS

Portland Forest Dragons (AFL)
9400 S.W. Beaverton-Hillsdale Hwy., Ste. 101
Portland, OR 97005
(503) 297-BALL; Fax (503) 203-2564

Portland Trail Blazers (NBA)
P.O. Box 4448
Portland, OR 97208
(503) 231-8000; Fax (503) 736-2185

Portland Pythons (PSA)
7412 S.W. Beaverton-Hillsdale Hwy., Ste. 110
Portland, OR 97225
(503) 297-BALL; Fax (503) 203-2564

Portland Winter Hawks (WHL)
P.O. Box 3009
Portland, OR 97208
(503) 238-6366; Fax (503) 238-7629
tickets@winterhawks.com

Salem/Keizer Volcanoes (NWLPB)
P.O. Box 20936
Keizer, OR 97307
(503) 390-2225

SKI RESORTS & GAMING CENTERS

SKI RESORTS

Anthony Lakes
47900 Anthony Lakes Hwy.
North Powder, OR 97867
(541) 856-3277

Crystal Mountain Resort
33914 Crystal Mountain Blvd.
Crystal Mountain, WA 98022
(360) 663-2265

Hoodoo
Box 20 Hwy. 20
Sisters, OR 97759
(541) 822-3799

Mt. Ashland Ski Area
P.O. Box 220/
1745 Hwy. 66
Ashland, OR 97520
(541) 482-2897

Mt. Bachelor Ski Resort
P.O. Box 1031
Bend, OR 97709
(541) 382-2442
(800) 829-2442

Mt. Hood Meadows
P.O. Box 470
Mount Hood, OR 97041
(503) 287-5438
See page 95

Mt. Hood Skibowl
87000 E. Hwy. 26
Government Camp, OR 97028
(503) 222-4158
See page 429

Summit Ski Area
East end of Government Camp Loop
P.O. Box 459
Government Camp, OR 97028
(503) 272-0256

Timberline Ski Area
Timberline Lodge, OR 97028
(503) 231-7979
See page 559

GAMING CENTERS

Chinook Winds
1777 N.W. 44th St.
Lincoln City, OR 97367
(541) 996-5852
See page 463

Indian Head Gaming Center
6823 Hwy. 8
Warm Springs, OR 97761
(800) 238-6946
See page 378

The Mill Gaming Center & Resort
3201 Tremont
North Bend, OR 97459
(800) 953-4800

Seven Feathers Hotel & Gaming Resort
146 Chief Miwaleta Ln.
Canyonville, OR 97417
(541) 839-1111
See page 546

Spirit Mountain Casino
27100 Salmon River Hwy.
Grand Ronde, OR 97347
(800) 760-7977
See page 553

Wild Horse Gaming Casino & Resort
72777 Hwy. 331
Pendleton, OR 97801
(541) 278-2274

Please let these businesses know that you heard about them from the Bravo! Event Resource Guide.

SHOPPING

Beaverton Mall
3205 S.W. Cedar Hills Blvd.
Beaverton, OR 97005
(503) 643-6563

Clackamas Town Center
12000 S.E. 82nd Ave.
Portland, OR 97266
(503) 653-6913

Clackamas Promenade
8978-B Sunnyside Rd.
Clackamas, OR 97015
(503) 653-5390

Columbia Gorge Factory Stores
450 N.W. 257th Ave.
Troutdale, OR 97060
(503) 669-8060

Eastport Plaza
3858 S.E. 82nd
Portland, OR 97266
(503) 771-3817

The Galleria
921 S.W. Morrison St.
Portland, OR 97205
(503) 228-2748

Historic Hawthorne District
S.E. 12th to S.E. 52nd
Portland, OR

Jantzen Beach Center
1405 Jantzen Beach Center
Portland, OR 97217
(503) 286-9103

Lancaster Mall
831 Lancaster Dr., N.E.
Salem, OR 97301
(503) 585-1338

Lloyd Center
953 Lloyd Center
Portland, OR 97232-1315
(503) 282-2511

Mall 205
9900 S.E. Washington St.
Portland, OR 97216
(503) 255-5805

Multnomah Village
S.W. Capitol Hwy.
Portland, OR 97219-2437
(503) 244-6055

NIKETOWN
930 S.W. Sixth Ave.
Portland, OR 97204
(503) 221-6453

Nob Hill Shopping District
Burnside to Vaughn, 15th Ave.
to Portland's Northwest Hills

Old Sellwood Antique Row
S.E. 13th north & south of Tacoma St.
8012 S.E. 13th
Portland, OR 97202

Pioneer Place
700 S.W. Fifth Ave.
Portland, OR 97204-2033
(503) 228-5800

Pioneer Place II
385 S.W. Yamhill
Portland, OR 97204
(503) 228-5800

Portland Saturday Market
Old Town — *Under the Burnside Bridge*
108 W. Burnside
Portland, OR 97209
(503) 222-6072

Salem Center
401 Center St., N.E.
Salem, OR 97301
(503) 370-0495

Tanger Factory Outlet
Hwy. 18 at Norton Ln.
McMinnville, OR 97128
(503) 472-5485

Vancouver Mall
8700 N.E. Vancouver Mall Dr.
Vancouver, Washington 98662
(360) 892-6255

Washington Square and Square Too
9585 S.W. Washington Square Rd.
Tigard, OR 97223
(503) 639-8860

The Water Tower at John's Landing
5331 S.W. Macadam Ave.
Portland, OR 97201
(503) 228-9431

Woodburn Company Stores
1001 Arney Rd.
Woodburn, OR 97071
(503) 981-1900

Please let these businesses know that you heard about them from the Bravo! Event Resource Guide.

TRANSPORTATION

TRAINS

Amtrak
800 N.W. Sixth St.
Portland, OR 97209
(800) 872-7245

Lewis & Clark Railroad Co.
2155 Grace St.
P.O. Box 604
Battle Ground, WA 98604
(360) 687-2626

Mt. Hood Railroad
110 Railroad Ave.
Hood River, OR 97031
(541) 386-3556
(800) 872-4661
See page 424

Samtrak
P.O. Box 22548
Milwaukie, OR 97269
(503) 659-5452

TRANSIT

Tri-Met
MAX Light Rail
4012 S.E. 17th Ave.
Portland, OR 97202
(503) 238-RIDE (7433)

Salem Area Transit—Cherriots
3140 Del Webb Ave., N.E.
Salem, OR 97303
(503) 588-2877

Vintage Trolley
115 N.W. First, Ste. 200
Portland, OR 97209
(503) 323-7363
See page 425

BUSES, COACHES & VANS

Fun-Mobile Adventures
Wilsonville, OR 97070
(503) 678-7870
See page 87

Gray Line of Portland
4320 N. Suttle Rd.
Portland, OR 97217
(503) 285-9845
See page 85

Raz Transportation
11655 S.W. Pacific Hwy.
Portland, OR 97223
(503) 684-3322
See page 86

LIMOUSINE & LIVERY

Five Star Limousine Service
P.O. Box 4755
Salem, OR 97302
(503) 585-8533

Hut Airport Shuttle
2990 25th St. S.E.
Salem, OR 97302
(503) 363-8059

Pacific Executive Services
240 S.E. Yamhill St.
Portland, OR 97214
(503) 234-2400
(888) TOWNCAR
Fax (503) 235-5521
See page 88

Portland Limousine Co.
730 N.E. 21st Ave.
Portland, OR 97232
(503) 235-2221 or
(800) 826-1431
See page 89

Valley Shuttle
21499 S.W. 99th
Tualatin, OR 97062
(800) 582-2522
Fax (503) 885-8075

VALET SERVICE

Premiere Valet Service, LLC
4711 S.W. Huber Ste.E5
Portland, OR 97219
(503) 244-7758

Please let these businesses know that you heard about them from the Bravo! Event Resource Guide.

Transportation continued...

BOATS & YACHTS

**Sternwheeler "Columbia Gorge"
& Marine Park**
P.O. Box 307
Cascade Locks, OR 97014
(503) 223-3928
See page 420

**Crystal Dolphin,
Portland Spirit,
& Willamette Star**
110 S.E. Caruthers
Portland, OR 97214
(503) 226-2517
(503) 224-3900
(503) 224-3901
See page 419

The Sternwheeler Rose
6211 N. Ensign
Portland, OR 7217
(503) 286-7673
See page 421

Willamette Jetboats
1945 S.E. Water Ave.
Portland, OR 97214
(503) 231-1532
(888) 538-2628
See page 104

Sternwheeler "Willamette Queen"
P.O. Box 2228
Corvallis, OR 97339
(503) 371-1103, (541) 928-4090
See page 422

Yachts-O-Fun Cruises, Inc.
19345 S. Ferguson Terrace
Oregon City, OR 97045
(503) 234-6665
See page 423

PUBLIC GOLF COURSES
Oregon and Southwest Washington

Broadmoor Golf Course
3509 N.E. Columbia Blvd.
Portland, OR 97211
(503) 281-1337

The Cedars Golf Club
15001 N.E. 181st St.
Brush Prairie, WA 98606
(503) 285-7548 or
(360) 687-4233

Charbonneau Golf Club
32020 S.W. Charbonneau Dr.
Wilsonville, OR 97070
(503) 694-1246
See page 461

Claremont Golf Course
15800 N.W. Country Club Dr.
Portland, OR 97229
(503) 690-4589

Colwood National Golf Club
7313 N.E. Columbia Blvd.
Portland, OR 97218
(503) 254-5515

Creekside Golf Club
6250 Clubhouse Dr., S.E.
Salem, OR 97306
(503) 363-4653

Eagle Crest Golf Course
1522 Cline Falls Rd.
Redmond, OR 97756
(541) 923-2453
See page 370

Eastmoreland Golf Course
2425 S.E. Bybee Blvd.
Portland, OR 97202
(503) 775-2900
See page 479

Fairway Village Golf Club
15509 S.E. Fernwood Dr.
Vancouver, WA 98683
(360) 254-9325

Forest Hills Golf Course
36260 S.W. Tongue Ln.
Cornelius, OR 97113
(503) 357-3347

Glendoveer Golf Club—East
14015 N.E. Glisan St.
Portland, OR 97230
(503) 253-7507

Gresham Golf Course
2155 N.E. Division St.
Gresham, OR 97030
(503) 665-3352

Heron Lakes Golf Course (Gray Blue)
3500 N. Victory Blvd.
Portland, OR 97217
(503) 289-1818

Indian Creek Golf Course
3605 Brookside Dr.
Hood River, OR 97031
(541) 386-7770

Kah-Nee-Ta Resort Course
100 Main St./P.O. Box K
Warm Springs, OR 97761
(541) 553-1112
See page 378

Killarney West Golf Course
1275 N.W. 334th Ave.
Hillsboro, OR 97124
(503) 648-7634

King City Golf Course
15355 S.W. Royalty Pkwy.
King City, OR 97224
(503) 639-7986

Lake Oswego Golf Course
17525 S.W. Stafford Rd.
Lake Oswego, OR 97034
(503) 636-8228

Lakeside Golf & Racquet Club
3245 Clubhouse Dr.
Lincoln City, OR 97367
(541) 994-8442

Langdon Farms Golf Club
24377 N.E. Airport Rd.
Aurora, OR 97002
(503) 678-4653

Golf Courses continued...

Lewis River Golf Course
3209 Old Lewis River Rd.
Woodland, WA 98674
(360) 225-8254

Meriwether National Golf Club
5200 S.W. Rood Bridge Rd.
Hillsboro, OR 97123
(503) 648-4143

Mount Hood Golf Club
68010 E. Fairway Ave.
Welches, OR 97067
(800) 669-4653

Mint Valley Golf Course
4002 Pennsylvania St.
Longview, WA 98632
(360) 577-3395

Mountain View Golf Club
27195 S.E. Kelso Rd.
Boring, OR 97009
(503) 663-4869

Oregon City Golf Club
20124 S. Beavercreek Rd.
Oregon City, OR 97045
(503) 656-2846
See page 520

Orenco Woods Golf Course
22200 N.W. Birch
Hillsboro, OR 97124
(503) 648-1836

Persimmon Country Club
500 S.E. Butler Rd.
Gresham, OR 97080
(503) 661-1800
See page 529

Progress Downs Municipal Golf Course
8200 Scholls Ferry Rd.
Beaverton, OR 97008
(503) 646-5166

Pumpkin Ridge Golf Club
12930 Old Pumpkin Ridge Rd.
North Plains, OR 97113
(503) 647-9977
See page 536

Quail Run Golf Club
16725 Northridge Dr.
La Pine, OR 97739
(541) 536-1303

The Reserve Vineyard and Golf Club
4805 S.W. 229th Ave.
Aloha, OR 97007
(503) 649-2345
See page 539

The Resort at The Mountain
68010 E. Fairway Ave.
Welches, OR 97067
(800) 669-4653
See page 540

Rose City Golf Club
2200 N.E. 71st Ave.
Portland, OR 97213
(503) 253-4744

Skamania Lodge Golf Course
1131 Skamania Lodge Wy.
Stevenson, WA 98648
(509) 427-2540
See page 552

Summerfield Golf Course
10650 S.W. Summerfield Dr.
Tigard, OR 97224
(503) 620-1200

Three Rivers Golf Course
2222 S. River Rd.
Kelso, WA 98626
(360) 423-4653

Top O'Scott Course
12000 S.E. Stevens Rd.
Portland, OR 97266
(503) 654-5050

The Westin Salishan Lodge & Golf Resort
7700 N. Hwy. 101
Gleneden Beach, OR 97388
(541) 764-3632
(800) 890-0387
See page 566

Wildwood Golf Course
21881 N.W. St. Helens Rd.
Portland, OR 97231
(503) 621-3402

MUSEUMS

A.C. Gilbert's Discovery Museum
116 Marion St., N.E.
Salem, OR 97301
(503) 371-3631

American Advertising Museum
5035 S.E. 24th Ave.
Portland, OR 97202
(503) 226-0000

Clackamas Co. Historical Museum
211 Tumwater Dr.
Oregon City, OR 97045
(503) 655-5574

Clark County Historical Museum
1511 Main St.
Vancouver, WA 98668
(360) 695-4681

End of the Oregon Trail Interpretive Center
1726 Washington St.
Oregon City, OR 97045
(503) 557-8542
See page 482

High Desert Museum
59800 S. Hwy. 97
Bend, OR 97702
(541) 382-4754

Marion Country Historical Society Museum
260 12th St., S.E.
Salem, OR 97301
(503) 364-2128

Maryhill Museum of Art
35 Maryhill Museum Dr.
Goldendale, WA 98620
(509) 773-3733

Mission Mill Village
1313 Mill St., S.E.
Salem, OR 97301
(503) 585-7012
See page 512

The Museum at Warm Springs
2189 Hwy. 26
Warm Springs, OR 97761
(541) 553-3331

Museum of Natural History
1680 E. 15th Ave.
Eugene, OR 97403-1224
(541) 346-3024

OMSI—Oregon Museum of Science & Industry
1945 S.E. Water Ave.
Portland, OR 97214-3354
(503) 797-4000
See page 524

Oregon Electric Railway Museum
310 State St.
Lake Oswego, OR 97034
(503) 222-2226

Oregon History Center
1200 S.W Park Ave.
Portland, OR 97205
(503) 222-1741

Oregon Maritime Center & Museum
113 S.W. Natio Parkway
Portland, OR 97204
(503) 224-7724

Oregon Sports Hall of Fame
321 S.W. Salmon St.
Portland, OR 97204
(503) 227-7466
See page 525

Pearson Air Museum
1115 E. Fifth St.
Vancouver, WA 98661
(360) 694-7026

Portland Art Museum
1219 S.W. Park Ave.
Portland, OR 97205
(503) 226-2811
See page 532

Portland Children's Museum
3037 S.W. Second Ave.
Portland, OR 97201-4715
(503) 823-2227

World Forestry Center
4033 S.W. Canyon Rd.
Portland, OR 97221-2760
(503) 228-1367
See page 576

SCENIC SITES

1847 Williams Holmes House
Holmes Lane at Rilance
Oregon City, OR 97045
(503) 656-5146

Adelman Peony Gardens
5690 Brooklake Rd., N.E.
Brooks, OR 97305
(503) 393-6185

Bush Pasture Park Gardens
600 Mission St., S.E.
Salem, OR 97302
(503) 581-2228

The Columbia Gorge Interpretive Center
P.O. Box 396
Stevenson, WA 98648
(509) 427-8211

Cooley's Gardens, Inc.
11553 Silverton Rd., N.E.
Silverton, OR 97381
(503) 873-5463

Crystal Springs Rhododendron Garden
S.E. 28th
North of Woodstock St.
Portland, OR 97286
(503) 771-8386

Elk Rock Garden of the Bishops Close
11800 S.W. Military Ln.
Portland, OR 97219
(503) 636-5613

End of the Oregon Trail Interpretive Center
1726 Washington St.
Oregon City, OR 97045
(503) 657-9336
See page 482

Forest Park
North of W. Burnside
to N.W. Newberry Rd.,
West of N.W. St. Helens Rd.
to S.W. Skyline Rd.
(503) 823-2525

Fort Vancouver National Historic Site
612 E.Reserve St.
Vancouver, WA 98661
(800) 832-3599

Frey's Dahlias
12054 Brick Rd.
Turner, OR 97392
(503) 743-3910

The Grotto
P.O. Box 20008
Portland, OR 97294
(503) 254-7371

Historic Deepwood Gardens
1116 Mission St., S.E.
Salem, OR 97302
(503) 363-1825

The Historic Elsinore Theatre
170 High St., S.E.
Salem, OR 97301
(503) 375-ELSI (3574)

Japanese Garden
611 S.W. Kingston
Portland, OR 97201
(503) 223-1321

McLoughlin House National Historical Site
713 Center St.
Oregon City, OR 97045
(503) 656-5146

Mission Mill Village
1313 Mill St., S.E.
Salem, OR 97301
(503) 370-8855
See page 512

Mount St. Helens Coldwater Ridge Visitors Center
3029 Spirit Lake Hwy.
Castle Rock, WA 98611
(43 miles from Castle Rock)
(360) 274-2103

Oregon Coast Aquarium
2820 S.E. Ferry Slip Rd.
Newport, OR 97365-5259
(541) 867-3474
See page 521

SCENIC SITES

Scenic Sites continued...

Oregon State Capitol & Grounds
Court St., N.E.
Salem, OR 97310

Oregon Garden
P.O. Box 155
879 W. Main St.
Silverton, OR 97381
(503) 874-8100
See page 522

Pioneer Courthouse Square
701 S.W. Sixth St.
Portland, OR 97204
(503) 823-3624

Pittock Mansion
3229 N.W. Pittock Dr.
Portland, OR 97210
(503) 823-3624
See page 530

Powell's City of Books
1005 W. Burnside St.
Portland, OR 97209
(503) 228-4651

Schreiner's Iris Gardens
3625 Quinaby Rd. N.E.
Salem, OR 97303
(503) 393-3232

Sea Lion Caves
91560 Hwy. 101, N.
Florence, OR 97439-8201
(541) 547-3111

Silver Falls State Park
20024 Silver Falls Hwy., S.E.
Sublimity, OR 97385
(503) 873-8681

Tom McCall Waterfront Park
Downtown Portland
end of S.W. Salmon St.
Portland, OR 97209

Washington Park
Rose Garden
400 S.W. Kingston Ave.
Portland, OR 97201
(503) 823-2525

Willamette University Gardens
900 State St.
Salem, OR 97301
(503) 370-6300

Calendar Of Events

CALENDAR OF EVENTS

OREGON CONVENTION CENTER

777 N.E. M.L.K. Jr. Boulevard • P.O. Box 12210 • Portland, Oregon 97212
For Information Contact: Matt Pizzuti, sales and marketing manager
Office (503) 235-7575; Fax (503) 731-7802
Web site: www.oregonocc.org

2000 PUBLIC EVENTS

OREGON INTERNATIONAL SPORTSMEN'S EXPO
January 6–9, 2000

PORTLAND BRIDAL SHOW
January 8–9, 2000

KXL RADIO NW CAREER FAIR
January 29, 2000

PORTLAND INTERNATIONAL AUTO SHOW
February 3–6, 2000

PACIFIC NORTHWEST WEDDING SHOWCASE
February 19–20, 2000

WHOLESALE MARKETPLACE
February 11–13, 2000

2000 YARD, GARDEN & PATIO SHOW
February 25–27, 2000

PORTLAND ROADSTER SHOW
March 2–5, 2000

OFFICE SYSTEMS & BUSINESS EXPO
March 8–9, 2000

SUMMERSHOW 2000–FEATURING CAMPFAIR
April 1–2, 2000

OREGON PUBLIC EDUCATORS FAIR
April 4, 2000

THE MACINTOSH BUSINESS EXPO
April 6, 2000

THE 18TH ANNUAL OPA CERAMIC SHOWCASE 2000
May 5–7, 2000

PORTLAND HANDWEAVERS GUILD, ANNUAL GUILD SALE
May 5–7, 2000

COMPUTER & TECHNOLOGY SHOWCASE
May 17–18, 2000

BEAD & BUTTON SHOW
June 2–4, 2000

EMBELLISHMENT SHOW
July 14–16, 2000

PACIFIC NW WEDDING SHOWCASE
July 23, 2000

PORTLAND GUN & KNIFE SHOW
August 19–20, 2000

2000 OREGON ART & RUBBER STAMP FESTIVAL
September 2–3, 2000

SENIOR EXPO
September 8–9. 2000

NORTHWEST WOMEN'S SHOW
September 29–October 1, 2000

WORKPLACE 2001
September 22–23, 2000

HOME IMPROVEMENT & REMODELING SHOW
October 19–22, 2000

NW CRAFTS ALLIANCE BEST OF THE NORTHWEST
October 27–29, 2000

GOURMET FOOD SHOW
November 3–5, 2000

ITEC EXPO
November 7–8, 2000

ANTIQUE & COLLECTIBLES SHOW
November 17–19, 2000

GEM FAIRE TRADE SHOW
November 24–26, 2000

FESTIVAL OF THE TREES
November 30–December 3, 2000

See page 406 under Convention & Exhibition Facilities.

Please let this business know that you heard about them from the Bravo! Event Resource Guide.

PORTLAND CENTER FOR THE PERFORMING ARTS

1111 S.W. Broadway • Portland, Oregon 97205
Box Office Hours: Mon–Sat 10am–6pm
(503) 248-4335; Fax (503) 274-7490
Event recording (503) 796-9293
E-mail: lorileyba@oregoncc.org; Web site: www.pcpa.com

2000 PERFORMANCE SCHEDULE

TREASURE ISLAND
Civic Auditorium
January 16 and 23

DEFENDING THE CAVEMAN
Civic Auditorium
January 25–30

ROMEO AND JULIET
Dolores Winningstad Theatre
January 13–February 20

BUS STOP
Newmark Theatre
January 15–February 12

DIAVOLO'S CATAPULT
Arlene Schnitzer Concert Hall
January 26

PAGLIACCI/CARMINA BURANA
Civic Auditorium
February 12–19

NORTHWEST AFRIKAN-AMERICAN BALLET–HERITAGE CONCERT
Arlene Schnitzer Concert Hall
February 12

JEKYLL & HYDE
Civic Auditorium
February 22–27

BALLET HISPANICO
Arlene Schnitzer Concert Hall
February 29

BLUES FOR AN ALABAMA SKY
Newmark Theatre
February 19–March 18

SINGING OUR WAY HOME
Dolores Winningstad Theatre
February 25–March 5

DANCE NEAR THE EDGE
Civic Auditorium
March 3–11

PETROUCHKA'S WINTER CARNIVAL
Dolores Winningstad Theatre
March 10–12

GARTH FAGAN DANCE
Arlene Schnitzer Concert Hall
March 15

THUMBELINA
Dolores Winningstad Theatre
March 24–April 2

GUN-SHY
Newmark Theatre
March 25–April 22

THE CUNNING LITTLE VIXEN
Civic Auditorium
March 25–April 1

THE SOUND OF MUSIC
Civic Auditorium
April 4–9

MACBETH
Dolores Winningstad Theatre
April 13–May 21

CHARLOTTE'S WEB
Civic Auditorium
April 16 and 30

MARK MORRIS DANCE GROUP
Arlene Schnitzer Concert Hall
May 2

THE MIKADO
Civic Auditorium
May 13–20

AMERICAN CHOREOGRAPHERS' SHOWCASE
Newmark Theatre
June 2–24

TITANIC
Civic Auditorium
June 7–18

See page 533 under Banquet, Meeting & Event Sites.

Please let this business know that you heard about them from the Bravo! Event Resource Guide.

One Center Court, Suite 200 • Portland, Oregon 97227
Contacts: Cathy Walsh or Rachel Eagleson (503) 235-8771; Fax: (503) 736-2192
Business Hours: Mon–Fri 8:30am–5:30pm
Group Sales: (503) 231-8000; Rose Quarter Event Hotline: (503) 321-3211
E- mail: facilitymarketing@rosequarter.com; Web site: www.rosequarter.com

SCHEDULE OF EVENTS
Come as a group and save—group rates are available for most events.

PORTLAND WINTER HAWKS (WHL)
September 1999–March 2000
Rose Garden, Memorial Coliseum

RINGLING BROTHERS AND BARNUM & BAILEY CIRCUS
September 1999
Rose Garden

PORTLAND TRAIL BLAZERS (NBA)
October 1999–April 2000
Rose Garden

LIVING IN PORTLAND
November 1999
Memorial Coliseum

DISNEY ON ICE—THE LITTLE MERMAID
November 1999
Rose Garden

MOTOR SPORTS
November 1999
Memorial Coliseum

BOSTON POPS
December 1999
Rose Garden

STARS ON ICE
January 2000
Rose Garden

NW REMODELING SHOW
January 2000
Memorial Coliseum

WRANGLER PRORODEO CLASSIC
January 2000
Rose Garden

OREGON CLASSIC WRESTLING
January 2000
Memorial Coliseum

MOTOR SPORTS SPECTACULAR
February 2000
Rose Garden

HARLEM GLOBETROTTERS
February 2000
Rose Garden

DISNEY ON ICE—TOY STORY
March 2000
Rose Garden

OSAA CHEERLEADING COMPETITION
February 2000
Memorial Coliseum

OSAA WRESTLING COMPETITION
February 2000
Memorial Coliseum

NCAA WOMEN'S BASKETBALL REGIONALS
March 2000
Memorial Coliseum

ARENA CROSS
March 2000
Memorial Coliseum

OSAA BOYS 4A BASKETBALL CHAMPIONSHIPS
March 2000
Memorial Coliseum

OSAA DANCE AND DRILL COMPETITION
March 2000
Memorial Coliseum

AL KADER SHRINE CIRCUS
March 2000
Rose Garden

PORTLAND FOREST DRAGONS
May–August 2000
Rose Garden

WNBA EXPANSION TEAM
June–August 2000
Rose Garden

PORTLAND PYTHONS INDOOR SOCCER (WISL)
July–December 2000
Rose Garden

SESAME STREET LIVE
May 2000
Memorial Coliseum

TOUR OF WORLD FIGURE SKATING CHAMPIONS
May 2000
Rose Garden

PORTLAND POLICE ASSN. GATTI CIRCUS
May 2000
Memorial Coliseum

ROSE FESTIVAL GRAND FLORAL PARADE AND SHOWCASE OF FLOATS
June 2000
Memorial Coliseum, Rose Quarter Commons

See page 410 under Convention & Exhibition Facilities.

Desktop Publishing & Signage

HELPFUL HINTS

The many choices of advertising vehicles: There are hundreds of choices of where to spend your advertising dollars if there are any. Radio, direct mail, newsprint, magazines, television, billboards, etc. There may be a proven medium that has always been used by your company, or you may be faced with making the confusing decision yourself. Advertising agencies and consultants can be helpful in exploring the many options available and the results that may be achieved, they can also help in target marketing your customer.

Create the marketing plan and set the goals:
- Critique last year's promotion by reviewing the invitations and brochures.
- Determine your target market in a brainstorming session.
- Gather examples of outstanding ideas and printed pieces you have seen that grab the reader's attention (keep an ongoing library of ideas yearround).

Pick a theme and create a campaign:
- Search for a relevant theme within your organization. Professional companies can help you develop ideas (refer to this section and Event Services in this Guide).
- Decide the key components to your campaign: posters, mailers, teasers, promotional gifts, giveaways, invitations, paid advertising, media contacts, and press releases, etc.

Plan your activity schedule over a six-month period of time:
- Order ad specialties/giveaways, invitations and teasers no later than six weeks before the event.
- Mail teasers four to six weeks prior to event (some meeting planners mail immediately following that year's event, so attendees will save the date)
- Mail invitations three to four weeks prior to event.
- Write a press release at least two weeks prior to the event, and target media alerts for two days prior (after sending a press release, a follow-up phone call to answer any questions can be effective).

Check the design at the post office before printing: Make sure your design is within postal requirements before completing project. Rules are always changing, and it is important to keep up to date.

Bulk Mail: Bulk mail can save dollars when mailing high volume campaigns or invitations. You will need a bulk mail permit or you can buy bulk mail stamps, or the mail house can inkjet the info on your piece. Remember with bulk mail you are not guarateed a quick delivery. Mail that is addressed incorrectly will not be returned to you, unless you type "address correction requested" on the piece. If you plan on sorting your own bulk mail it can be a long process, the post office offers seminars on bulk mail. A mail house is the best investment in this case; it can cost you more in your own time, than if you hired a professional mail house.

Post Card can save you dollars: If printing a post card to save postage dollars, make sure it does not exceed 6″ by 4″ or it will not qualify for the post card rate. Check the post card rates at the post office.

Tracking your results: The best way to know if advertising is working or not for your company is to track results. It can be as simple as asking "how did you hear about this event?". Keep a list at the phone specifying all the ways you received your rsvps or sales. This list should include all forms of advertising: yellow pages, newspaper, direct mail, word-of-mouth.

B · O · E · K Mfg

Banners Of Every Kind

Contact: Steven Boek
(503) 257-5056, (800) 861-1257
Fax (503) 257-5056
E-mail: boek@teleport.com
Web site: www.boeksigns.com

WE SPECIALIZE IN LARGE PROMOTIONAL BANNERS AND EVENT SIGNAGE!

Banners create a festive atmosphere and serve as a cost effective method of communication. The combination of color and movement creates interest and attracts attention to your event.

Indoor/Outdoor Banners For All Occasions
Vinyl or Cloth/Applique, Embroidery, Silk Screen and Large Format Full Color Digital (seamless color up to 10' x 300'!)

- Corporate Logos
- Table Covers
- Backdrops
- Flags
- Truck Banners
- Billboard Banners
- Pennant Strings

- Convention/Trade Show
- Real Estate/Construction
- Street Banners
- Light Pole Banners
- Net Banners
- Airplane Tow Banners
- Changeable Banner Systems

Custom Signs and Pre-Spaced Lettering
- Showcards
- Plastic Signs
- Metal Signs
- Magnetic Signs
- A-Frame Sandwich Signs

- Window Lettering
- Auto and Fleet Graphics
- Custom Decals
- Bumper Stickers

Hardware and Installation
- Banner Poles and Frames
- Brackets
- Custom Hardware

Mention you saw us at the Bravo! Trade Show
And receive 10% off your first order!

DIGITYPE *Imaging & Design, inc.*

your desktop publishing services provider

2355 N.W. Vaughn
Portland, Oregon 97210
(located in the Kobos building)
(503) 224-7903; Fax (503) 224-7908
E-mail: davidk@dtype.com

Digitype Imaging & Design, Inc. is a desktop publishing services provider. Our single focus since 1989 has been to provide our customers with quality, on-time products and service.

We Can Help You with the Following Services

- logo design
- print ads
- directories
- newsletters
- brochures
- corporate ID
- original illustrations
- annual reports
- trade show material/displays
- direct mail marketing
- sales promotion
- spot & four-color printing
- catalogs
- presentation material
- promotional material
- photo scanning
- typesetting
- imagesetting

Digitype can take your ideas to a larger scale with Large Format Color Imaging… digital inkjet printing available on a variety of materials to create solutions for oversize or short-run marketing needs. Easy, quick and competitively priced.

SIGNS SELL: Communicate clearly, identify quickly with SIGNAGE and large format color imaging. One sign or many, more economically than ever.

MAKE A POINT: POINT-OF-PURCHASE displays and full size prototypes of promotions make a professional and lasting impression.

STOP TRAFFIC: Bring more leads to your TRADE SHOW GRAPHICS with color and imagery beyond the ordinary.

BANNERS BUILD AWARENESS: Photo realistic BANNERS on vinyl and other flexible, durable materials for indoor and outdoor use… as many colors as your imagination can visualize.

THE 5th WALL: FLOOR GRAPHICS for a unique angle…temporary and durable with adhesive backing. At the register, in your lobby or booth, identify a new item or lead customers to the sale section!

DECOR IN STORE: Imaged-based or artistic MURALS wrap around corners and cover entire walls to create backgrounds or large scale signage.

ROLLING BILLBOARDS: VEHICLE GRAPHICS advertise when you are on the road, enhance your image and get the most for the miles on your company vehicles. Continuous tone, photographic imagery on durable vinyl or mini-billboards.

YOUR NAME IN LIGHTS: BACKLIT GRAPHICS. Inkjet technology, up to 50" wide by any length.

MAKE IT SPECIAL: Whatever the event, mark it with the special look of big, bold, colorful signage and banners on a variety of substrates for SPECIAL EVENTS.

design & print production

5026 S.W. 39th Drive
Portland, Oregon 97221-3800
(503) 246-1122
Fax (503) 246-4315

Specializing in providing quality full-service typesetting, graphic design and printing.

- announcements — new baby/moving/grand opening
- annual reports
- books/magazines
- brochures
- business cards/forms
- business stationery
- catalogs/manuals
- convention materials
- directional maps
- directories
- fliers
- invitations
- menus
- newsletters
- presentation materials
- price lists
- programs
- proposals
- print ads
- promotional materials
- résumés
- wedding programs

you name it, idesign it!

Call (503) 246-1122

Certified in Oregon as a Women Business Enterprise (WBE)

PRINTING • COPYING • DIGITAL NETWORK

Tigard
12200 S.W. Main Street
Tigard, Oregon 97223
(503) 684-3443; Fax (503) 684-5058
Business Hours: Mon–Fri 8am–5:30pm

Lake Oswego
6302 S.W. Meadows Road
Lake Oswego, Oregon 97035
(503) 620-9454; Fax (503) 620-8192
Mon–Fri 8am–5:15pm

E-mail: ss1016@earthlink.net

We'll Make Sure Your Name Is All Over Town
As fellow business owners and neighbors, we know what it takes to operate a business in this area. And in particular, what it takes to get your business noticed. That's because Sir Speedy has been helping businesses just like yours develop successful communications and images for years.

Here's A Rough Idea Of What We Can Do
We pride ourselves on our ability to help develop your ideas. Whether they're rough ideas on napkins, camera-ready art or computer disks, we'll work with you to make sure you're happy with what you get. And that includes designing, typesetting, printing, collating, trimming, drilling, folding and binding. Because the way we see it, your stationery and other printed materials are more than just office supplies. They're vital links in your business image. And the better they look, the better they make you look—all over town.

Let Us Handle All Your Paperwork
Now that we've told you what we can do, it's time to give you a bill—or a statement, or even a purchase order. In addition to printing everything to build the right impression of your business, we can print everything to help you stay in business. Including multi-part carbonless forms. So go ahead, bury us in your paperwork—we'll do it right. On time. And at a fair price.

Here Are A Few More Selling Points
No matter what you're trying to sell, we can develop a look, message and piece to get the job done. From flyers and mailers to pamphlets and brochures. As well as catalogs, manuals, sales kits, price lists, information sheets, and point-of-purchase materials. And all of it will be done with painstaking attention to detail.

We Can Make You A Company To Watch
Nothing is more important to a business than its appearance. That's why you should trust it to Sir Speedy. We'll print and complete your order with a level of professionalism that will make you the hit of the neighborhood and beyond. Our wide assortment of bindery options will help make your company more presentable than ever before. So give us a call. We'll be right over to pick up the job. Or stop in and let us show you how your neighborhood Sir Speedy can help you spread your name all over town.

Advertising & Media

HELPFUL HINTS

Press Releases are one of your more effective mediums of advertising. Press stories are usually presented in the paper, television, radio or trade publications because of a special interest to the audience. There are a variety of reasons to send out a press release: Grand opening, new office site, an event, new product, exciting news, etc.

Public relations can be like Russian roulette, sometimes you get the coverage and other times you don't. When you do get the story, it can be worth ten times more than advertising. Always send a press release, whether you think there is a story there or not. If the newspaper or television station needs a last-minute story they may publish your release verbatim, or call you to do a story the day of the event.

Timing
- You may want to plan your event when nothing else of significance is happening. Larger, more public events and happenings will always take priority over a smaller event.
- You cannot predict disaster or national news stories, but these can happen and can bump even a story that had been planned and written already.
- In some cases when you send your press release determines if you will receive exposure before or after the event. You may just send info about the event, or invite the press to a press party, or invite the press to cover the actual event.
- Press Releases should be sent out two weeks prior to the event. Call to confirm the release was received and then follow-up with enthusiasm about the event, to see if you can answer any questions or provide any additional information.

Planning
- The more information you collect; facts, figures, interesting points, etc. the better job you can do writing a press release.
- Creative writing is a must.
- Media list: There are hundreds of newspapers, radio stations, television and trade publications. You can choose to send press information to all or just send to a selected list. Then keep this list for future use. Refer to the list of all local media in this chapter. (Note: always update and call-down media list prior to using- updates are recommended every six months)
- During the prior call-down- confirm who the appropriate department and person or editor to send information to. You can develop an ongoing relationship with these persons for future events and happenings.
- When the Press arrives at an event—a fact sheet is helpful for them to take back to their office; fact sheets include details surrounding the event, information about the organization and goals for the event.

Writing and Developing
- Creative angle to press release: Inserting a sample of product, photo. Press releases can be fun in a creative format-using special paper, ink, mounting on foam core, etc. (there are creative firms in this Guide listed under Desktop Publishing and Signage that can help with the entire public relations campaign).
- Try to write the press release in a journalistic manner (no first person). If written well, sometimes the press release will be published word-for-word.
- Keep it brief and to the facts; make sure facts are accurate and specific
- Format for the press release is listed in the front of this Guide (Planning a Meeting or Event, Promotions and Publicity).

The Business Journal

*851 S.W. Sixth Avenue, Suite 500
Portland, Oregon 97204
Contact:
Mike Consol, Publisher
Dan Cook, Editor for press releases
Bryan Lerner, Circulation Manager for subscriptions
Matthew Tolbert, Director of Sales and Marketing for advertising
(503) 274-8733; Fax (503) 227-2650
Web site: www.amcity.com/portland/*

Established in 1984, *The Business Journal* is a weekly newspaper that covers local business news. It is written for business executives and publishes stories about specific industries, trends and people. It is considered a "must read" by professionals, and its award-winning editorial has made *The Business Journal* the best news source for local business in Greater Portland.

Editorial
Editorial sections specifically relating to events and meetings:
- Meetings, Conventions and Hotels
- Business Travel
- Tourism
- Around Oregon
- Hospitality
- Top 25 Hotels and Motels list
- Top 25 Meeting Facilities list

Circulation
- 15,516 total circulation
- 58,500 readers

Readership
- 75% read 4 out of 4 issues
- 63% consider *The Business Journal* their primary source of local business news

Subscriber Information
- 56% in top management
- 69% work in small companies
- Use of local hotels for: meeting rooms—51%; banquet facilities—37%
- 72% male
- Median age—49 years
- 74% college graduates
- Average household income—$184,000

Call for a subscription or advertising information
Sources: ABC, Publisher's Statement 1998, Subscriber Study, 1999

ADVERTISING AND BUSINESS RESOURCE

MEETINGS IN THE WEST

550 Montgomery Street, Suite 750
San Francisco, California 94111
(800) 358-0388, (415) 788-2005; Fax (415) 788-1905
For Advertising Information: *Debbie Richards, Advertising Director*
For Editorial: *Christa Palmer, Editor*
For Subscriptions: *Kim Leonard, Circulation Marketing Director (319) 364-6167*
Web site: www.meetingsweb.com

Meetings in the West delivers in-depth news, features and destination information on the meetings market in the Western United States to a national audience of meeting professionals. Our "beat" includes Alaska, Arizona, California, Colorado, Hawaii, Idaho, Montana, Nevada, New Mexico, Oregon, Utah, Washington, Wyoming, Western Canada and Mexico. We cover the West more thoroughly than any other meetings publication!

The readership of *Meetings in the West* is the most targeted of any meetings industry publication. *Meetings in the West* is well read, because we provide the relevant information planners need to book their next meetings in the West!

- Our readers are 25,000 qualified meeting professionals nationwide who plan and book meetings and events in the Western United States.
- 91% of our readers read every issue or 3 out of 4 issues every month.
- 84% find *Meetings in the West* helpful in making meeting decisions.

Hot Issues for 1999–2000

1999:
November—Portland
December/January—Washington

2000:
March—Summer Mountain Resorts, High-Tech Meetings
April—Convention Centers, Historic Places
May—Small Meetings
June—Oregon, Seattle, Urban Meetings
July—Coastal Meetings
August—Affordable Meetings
September—Winter Mountain Resorts
November—Portland
December/January—Washington

RADIO STATIONS

KBMS Radio
601 Main St., Ste. 400
Vancouver, WA 98661
(503) 222-1491

KBNP Radio
811 S.W. Front Ave., Ste. 430
Portland, OR 97204
(503) 223-6769; Fax (503) 223-4305

KGON Radio/KFXX/KNRK Radio
0700 S.W. Bancroft
Portland, OR 97201
(503) 223-1441; Fax (503) 223-6909

KBOO Radio
20 S.E. Eighth
Portland, OR 97214
(503) 231-8032; Fax (503) 231-7145

KEWS/KKRZ/KEX Radio
4949 S.W. Macadam Ave.
Portland, OR 97201
(503) 225-1190; Fax (503) 224-3216

KINK Radio
1501 S.W. Jefferson
Portland, OR 97201
(503) 226-5168; Fax (503) 226-4578

KISN Radio
888 S.W. Fifth Ave. #790
Portland, OR 97204
(503) 226-9791; Fax (503) 243-3299

KKEY Radio
P.O. Box 5757
Portland, OR 97228
(503) 222-1150; Fax (503) 222-1150

KKRH Radio
888 S.W. Fifth Ave., Ste. 790
Portland, OR 97204
(503) 733-5105; Fax (503) 224-3070

K-LOVE Christian Music Radio
1425 N. Market Blvd., Ste. 9
Sacramento, CA 95823
(800) 525-5683

KMHD Radio
Mt. Hood Community College
26000 S.E. Stark
Gresham, OR 97030
(491) 667-7271; Fax (503) 669-6999

KMUZ Radio/KKBK Radio
24 S. "A" St. Ste.C
Washougal, WA 98671
(503) 227-2156; Fax (360) 835-3400

KOAC Radio
239 Covell Hall
Corvallis, OR 97331
(541) 737-4311

KOPB Radio
7140 S.W. Macadam Ave.
Portland, OR 97219
(503) 244-9900; Fax (503) 293-1919

KOTK Radio
2000 S.W. First Ave., Ste. 300
Portland, OR 97201
(503) 228-4393; Fax (503) 227-3938

KPDQ Radio
5110 S.E. Stark
Portland, OR 97215
(503) 231-7800; Fax (503) 238-7202

KRKT AM/FM Radio
1207 Ninth Ave., S.E.
Albany, OR 97321
(541) 588-0222; Fax (541) 928-9261

KUFO/KBBT Radio
2040 S.W. First Ave.
Portland, OR 97201
(503) 222-1011; Fax (503) 222-2047

KUIK Radio
P.O. Box 566
Hillsboro, OR 97123
(503) 640-1360; Fax (503) 640-6108

KUPL Radio / KKJZ Radio
222 S.W. Columbia, Ste. 350
Portland, OR 97201
(503) 223-0300; Fax (503) 497-2333

KWBY/KCKX Radio
P.O. Box 158
Woodburn, OR 97071
(503) 981-9400; Fax (503) 981-3561

KWJJ Radio
2000 S.W. First Ave., Ste. 300
Portland, OR 97201
(503) 228-4393; Fax (503) 227-3938

KXL Radio
0234 S.W. Bancroft St.
Portland, OR 97201
(503) 243-7595; Fax (503) 417-7660

Please let these businesses know that you heard about them from the Bravo! Event Resource Guide.

TELEVISION STATIONS

KATU-TV
P.O. Box 2
Portland, OR 97207
2153 N.E. Sandy Blvd.
Portland, OR 97232
(503) 231-4222; Fax (503) 231-4626

KGW-TV
1501 S.W. Jefferson
Portland, OR 97201
(503) 226-5111; Fax (503) 226-5059

KNMT-TV
432 N.E. 74th Ave.
Portland, OR 97213
(503) 252-0792; Fax (503) 256-4205

KOIN-TV
222 S.W. Columbia
Portland, OR 97201
(503) 464-0600; Fax (503) 464-0806

KOPB-TV
7140 S.W. Macadam Ave.
Portland, OR 97219
(503) 244-9900; Fax (503) 293-1919

KBXG-TV
4923 Indian School Rd., N.E.
Salem, OR 97305
(503) 390-2202; Fax (503) 390-6829

KPTV-TV
211 S.E. Caruthers
Portland, OR 97214
(503) 230-1200; Fax (503) 230-1065

KWBP-TV
10255 S.W. Arctic Drive
Beaverton, OR 97005
(503) 644-3232; Fax (503) 626-3576

Portland Cable Access
2766 N.E. MLK, Jr. Blvd.
Portland, OR 97212
(503) 288-1515; Fax (503) 288-8173

NEWSPAPERS

The Battleground Reflector
P.O. Box 2020
Battleground, WA 98604
(360) 687-5151; Fax (360) 687-5162
Contact: Marvin Case

The Bee
P.O. Box 82127
Portland, OR 97282
(503) 692-8527; Fax (503) 692-5653
Contact: John Dillan

The Business Journal
P.O. Box 14490
Portland, OR 97293
(503) 274-8733; Fax (503) 227-2650
Contact: Dan Cook
See page 131

The Clackamas County Review
4287 S.E. International Wy., Ste. F
Milwaukie, OR 97222
(503) 786-1996; Fax (503) 786-6977
Contact: Michael Russell

The Columbian
P.O. Box 180
Vancouver, WA 98666
(503) 224-0654; Fax (503) 699-6033
Contact: Dave Jewett

Community Newspapers
P.O. Box 370
Beaverton, OR 97075
(503) 684-0360; Fax (503) 620-3433
Contact: Steve Clark

Corvallis Gazette-Times
P.O. Box 368
Corvallis, OR 97339
(541) 753-2641; Fax (541) 758-9505
Contact: Rob Priewe

Gresham Outlook
1190 N.E. Division St.
P.O. Box 747
Gresham, OR 97030
(503) 665-2181; Fax (503) 665-2187
Contact: Dean Rhodes

Hillsboro Argus
P.O. Box 588
Hillsboro, OR 97123
(503) 648-1131; Fax (503) 648-9191
Contact: Val Hess

Hollywood Star
2000 N.E. 42nd Ave.
Portland, OR 97213
(503) 282-9392
Contact: Nancy Woods

Hospitality News
P.O. Box 21027
Salem, OR 97307
(503) 390-8343; Fax (503) 390-8344
Contact: Brenda Carlos

Just Out
P.O. Box 14400
Portland, OR 97293
(503) 236-1252; Fax (503) 236-1257
Contact: Will O'Brian

Lake Oswego Review
P.O. Box 548
Lake Oswego, OR 97034
(503) 635-8811; Fax (503) 635-8817
Contact: Tom Berridge

Oregon City News
4287 S.E. International Wy., Ste. F
Milwaukie, OR 97222
(503) 786-1996; Fax (503) 786-6977
Contact: Michael Russell

The Oregonian
1320 S.W. Broadway
Portland, OR 97201
(503) 221-8100; Fax (503) 227-5306
Contact: Fred Stickel

Our Town
213 S.W. Ash, Ste. 207
Portland, OR 97204
(503) 224-1774; Fax (503) 224-2080
Contact: Maggie White

Portland Observer
P.O. Box 3137
Portland, OR 97208
(503) 288-0033; Fax (503) 288-0015
Contact: Chuck Washington

The Skanner
P.O. Box 5455
Portland, OR 97228
(503) 287-3562; Fax (503) 285-2900
Contact: Bobbie Foster

**St. Johns Review &
Hayden Island Connection**
8525 N. Lombard
Portland, OR 97203
Tel./Fax (503) 283-5086
Contact: Ty Walker

Statesman Journal
P.O. Box 13009
Salem, OR 97309
(800) 452-2511; Fax (503) 399-6706
Contact: Dick Hughs

West Linn Tidings
P.O. Box 548
Lake Oswego, OR 97034
(503) 635-8811; Fax (503) 635-8817
Contact: Janet Paulson

Willamette Week
822 S.W. 10th Ave.
Portland, OR 97205
(503) 243-2122; Fax (503) 243-1115
Contact: John Schrag

MAGAZINES

Meetings in the West
550 Montgomery St., Ste. 750
San Francisco, CA 94111
(800) 358-0388; Fax (415) 788-1905
See page 132

Oregon Business Magazine
610 S.W. Broadway, Ste. 200
Portland, OR 97205
(503) 223-0304; Fax (503) 221-6544

Notes

Photography Services

HELPFUL HINTS

Why are photographs important? Photographs capture the results of months of hard work after an event is over. Photographs can thank a sponsor. Photographs of a grand opening or award presentation can be used in press releases after the event. Photographs can be a great keepsake and follow-up thank-you for the supporters who attend the function year after year.

Selecting a photographer: Find a photographer whose style you like. Look closely at his or her sample albums, and don't be afraid to ask for references. A contract is important to reserve the date and should confirm that the estimate given will be the actual cost. With over 250 photographers currently listed in the phone book, you want to make sure you select the best photographer to meet your specific needs.

Consulting with your photographer: When you finally select your photographer, sit down together so you can communicate what you envision your photo session or event photos will look like. Be specific about formal and candid photographs. Be sure you let the photographer know what you are expecting.

Assigning a photographer's helper: Save time the day of the event by assigning someone to be the photographer's helper. Submit a list of photographic requests to both the photographer and helper one week before the event so that your helper can guide the photographer to all the right people.

Why hire a video service? Videotaping events is a fairly new concept. There are many reasons for hiring a video service. Videotaping the event or meeting is a great way to re-cap the event for people who were not able to attend. The tape can also be used to evaluate the event for ideas for future meetings, or it can be used as a training tool for future employees. Tapes can be given to sponsors or speakers as a thank-you.

Why hire a professional video service? The professional has the experience, skills, and technical equipment to produce a high-quality video. Check the types of equip-ment the video service has: one-camera, two-camera, or three-camera options. Editing and sound options enhance the video and tailor it to the highlights of the event. Take the time to view samples of their work; it will show you the style and quality. Check the background of the company or individual. Have they been professionally trained or self-taught? If it is important to document your event, don't trust an amateur—you have only one shot to get it right.

Research the different options: There are one-, two-, or three-camera options. Each will provide a different perspective of the event. With only one camera, you cannot tape more than one thing at a time, and there may be several events happening at once that need attention. In this case, two operators may be needed.

Photo Promotions has been the premier promotions and event photographer for many of the Pacific Northwest's major shopping centers, businesses, and schools since 1980.

Our friendly, courteous, professional staff is ready to provide you with colorful, high quality, instant prints, as well as exciting finishing options!

- Take your photos home with you the night of your event!
- Add a fun border for a custom look
  (first "customized" border is free)
- Choose from a wide range of print sizes
  (8x10s, 5x7s, 3¹/²x5s, and wallets)
- You see your photos before they are printed
- Get extra prints while you wait
- Flat rate charges begin at only $5 per sheet!
- Never a setup fee or travel charge
- No extra charges for group shots
- We accept VISA, MasterCard, Discover/Novus, AMEX, checks and cash
- Sepia photos also available
- Excellent references

We also have "real" Santas, Mrs. Claus, Elves and "custom" Easter Bunnies available.

Call us today to look at our samples, border book or schedule your event!

PHOTOGRAPHERS

Adams & Faith Photography

800 N.W. 6th Avenue, Suite 211
Portland Oregon 97209
Contact: Tony or Lori
(503) 227-7850; Fax (503) 227-1863

Adams & Faith Photography is undoubtedly the Northwest's premier photography studio…

Located in the glorious (and convenient) Union Station in downtown Portland since 1976, they have made style and creativity coupled with superb professional service their hallmark.

Tony and his wife, Lori, owners of the prestigious Adams & Faith, are rightfully proud of their successful studio. With a client list that includes many of the major corporations in Oregon and Washington, they continue to supply the business world with a reliable photographic service. Their studio is a state-of-the-art, 2,500-square-foot photographer's dream... fully equipped with all formats of cameras including the availability of digital.

Just recently, Tony received one of the highest honors possible for a photographer. Kodak chose him for their elite International Pro Team and included his story in their book, Promise of Excellence Pro Team.

The recognition of their work has brought national attention, accolades from a state senator and acknowledgment from business leaders throughout the community, but none of that compares to the pride Tony, Lori and their photographers take in capturing images for their clients.

Well-known for their reliability in the coverage of political fund-raisers, dinner dances, reunions, award banquets and seminars, their commitment to get the job done right and to their customer's specifications has become quite obvious. They have photographed hotels and resorts worldwide... cruise ships from the Caribbean to Australia to South Africa... and weddings in Greece.

Whether your needs are a simple business portrait, and extensive brochure for your valued product or even your annual report, Adams & Faith has the expertise to do the job. They have numerous photographers on staff experienced to meet your specific needs.

A reputation of excellence surrounds Adams & Faith Photography and might give businesses the idea that the studio is unattainable. Untrue... and their prices are very competitive!

For the quality and professional service you would expect for a business built on integrity and reliability, call Adams & Faith Photography.

Please visit us at our Web site: www.adamsandfaith.com

Please let this business know that you heard about them from the Bravo! Event Resource Guide.

Keith Aden
PHOTOGRAPHY & VIDEO PRODUCTIONS

1613 SE 7th Avenue • Portland, Oregon 97214

503 230-0325

Web Address: www.adenphoto-video.com
or www.bravoevent.com/pdx00/keithaden
E-Mail • kaphoto@internetcds.com

Style

Since 1968, Keith Aden Photography has been serving the greater Portland metro area. Over the years we have built a solid reputation for a professional, assertive, and unobtrusive style that blends perfectly with your event. From international sales meetings to conventions or political luncheons to company picnics, we can deliver the service that you expect. We are very detail oriented and can tailor our services to fit your budget.

Services

- Commercial Photography   (4x5, Medium Format and 35mm)
- Event Photography
- Video Production   (Industrial 3 Chip S-VHS Multi-Camera Coverage, Media 100xs Non-Linear or A/B Roll Editing Suite)
- Aerial Photography
- Brochures/Post Cards   (Design, Photography, and Printing)
- Digital Imaging Services

SOMEONE WHO CARES

Your choice of a photo or video professional is an important one. It reflects on your reputation as well as your company's reputation. We do not take that lightly! In fact, we put our good reputation on the line every time we take an assignment. And as a former purchasing manager for a national corporation, Keith also understands the needs of business. In short, it is our goal to make everyone look good!

PROFESSIONAL SERVICE
FOR
PROFESSIONAL PEOPLE

1613 S.E. 7th Avenue   •   Portland, Oregon 97214
Studio 503.230.0325 • Fax 503.230.0657 • Toll Free 877.230.0325

Member of

PORTLAND • OREGON VISITORS ASSOCIATION
the convention and visitors bureau of metropolitan Portland

Please let this business know that you heard about them from the Bravo! Event Resource Guide.

PHOTOGRAPHERS

Centrally located in Downtown Portland
*920 S.W. 13th Avenue
Portland, Oregon 97205
(503) 224-4410; Fax (503) 224-4429
Business Hours: Mon–Fri 9:30am–5:30pm;
other hours by appointment
E-mail: ekeene@transport.com*

EDMUND KEENE
photographers

Photographing Portland's important events since 1968.

If you're planning a special event that needs the careful attention and unobtrusive approach of an experienced professional… WE CAN HANDLE THE ASSIGNMENT.

- ❖ Awards Banquets
- ❖ Holiday Parties
- ❖ Seminars
- ❖ Business and Publicity Portraits
- ❖ Annual Reports
- ❖ Bar/Bat Mitzvahs
- ❖ Anniversaries and Reunions

Costs
Competitive bids for any event . . . based on your budget requirements and service needs.

Travel
Metropolitan Portland area at no additional cost. Outside metro area (Oregon or further), prices quoted on request.

THE NEXT STEP . . .
Call us at **224-4410** for our brochure of services and individual price estimates. References upon request.

**Please visit us at our Web site at EKeenephotographers.com
for additional examples of our photography
(503) 224-4410**

ENCORE STUDIOS

Portland, Oregon
(503) 255-8047
E-mail: encore@webcombo.net
Web site: www.bravoevent.com/pdx00/encore–photo

Let our professional photographers photograph your next event! With over 20 years of experience, we pride ourselves on helping you make your next event a success. You are welcome to choose from a wide variety of packages or customize your own package, according to your preferences and budget.

Equipment and Services

The finest and most current cameras are utilized, including medium format and digital cameras. Our state-of-the-art digital cameras are highly advanced, and we are one of the few studios using this innovative technology for your picture perfect event! We are able to shoot in only available light or in studio-type light, and you are welcome to request as many photographs as you wish, indoor or out. Your photographs may be either printed and received usually within two weeks of your event, or you may choose to have them printed immediately on site!

Additional Services

- Black and white photography
- Business photo cards and post cards
- Legal and insurance
- Product photos
- Real estate photos
- Tape transfers
- Press release photos
- Folios, mounts and frames
- Personalized imprinting
- Portraiture in new studio
- Corporate images
- Portfolios
- Seminars
- Annual reports
- Digital services
- Literature photos
- Company logos and overlays
- On-site photo printing

Packages and Prices

With the most comprehensive package selection in the Northwest, you are welcome to choose from our many selections or customize your own package as you'd like. Please call for an appropriate quote. Individual reprints are one of the lowest, and start as low as $3.75 for 2x3 and $12 for 4x5 prints, for example. Volume discounts also available. There is no minimum order required. You are welcome to own your negatives as well. A $100 deposit reserves your date. Visa and MasterCard gladly accepted as well as financing, with no interest payments.

Consultants are available for day or evening appointments.

V I C K I G R A Y L A N D
PHOTOGRAPHER

phOne 5 0 3. 8 7 2. 9 7 0 0

Experience
With 15 years staff experience on a metropolitan newspaper, Vicki Grayland can handle all kinds of shooting situations.

Professionalism
A calm demeanor and a sense of humor make shoots go smoothly and quickly; quick turnaround time on processing and printing.

Quality
An artistic eye and a selection of fine equipment and materials reflect a commitment to quality.

- **Events**
- **Executive Portraits**
- **Annual Reports**
- **Brochures**

Please phone for a written estimate.

503. 872. 9700

E-mail: Grayland@aol.com

HOLLAND STUDIOS

SPECIAL OCCASION PHOTOGRAPHY

Professional • *Relaxed* • *Creative*

134 S.E. Taylor
Portland, Oregon 97214
Contact: Eric Holen (503) 706-5763
Business Hours: By appointment

Whether you are looking for business portraits of your executives, annual report or pictures of your company picnics and holiday parties, Holland Studios will provide you with quality, professional service.

Conveniently Located

We offer a wide range of photographic opportunities. For your convenience, our studio is centrally located in downtown Portland. We will, however, gladly travel to accommodate your needs. Our goal is to capture your images with style and purpose.

Committed to Excellence

For all your photographic needs-seminars, awards banquets, or publicity pictures for catalogues and brochures—Holland Studios is committed to excellence.

**We would appreciate
the opportunity to work with you.**

Professional Memberships:
Kodak's Promise of Excellence program
Portland Metropolitan Photographers Association
Association of Catering and Event Professionals (ACEP)

Please let this business know that you heard about them from the Bravo! Event Resource Guide.

Jak Tanenbaum
PHOTOGRAPHY ASSOCIATES

Philippe Boulot, Chef   The Heathman Restaurant

P. O. Box 82758
Portland, Oregon 97282
Contact: Lynden or Jak Tanenbaum
Phone/Fax (503) 232-1455
Available By Appointment
E-mail: info@photographyassociates.com
Web site:www.photographyassociates.com

We're ready when you are no matter what the event. Be it a black tie gala or a company barbecue, we can help to make it a success.

Conferences or Conventions

We will work with your meeting planners to help design the best possible coverage for each event. Large formal group coverage, individual portraits, and fun candid documentary-style photographs are just a few of the ways we can enrich your event. We tailor each job to your desires, and we listen. We offer sensitive, informed advice gained from years of experience and provide a variety of unique photographic services.

Receptions and Cocktail Parties

We interview each client in advance, discussing the program, locations, and photographic needs for each event, allowing you to enjoy your affair without worry. We often help our clients plan the staging of activities such as award ceremonies and presentations to create memorable photographs instead of candid grab shots. To put it simply, we are professionals. Your guests will appreciate that, and our work will reflect it.

Outdoor Events

We know how to photograph outdoors! Don't worry about those shadows or clouds, we will. We've photographed everything from mountain outings to beach events in every light imaginable, both in color or black and white, and we've got you covered. We can provide you with the high-quality images needed for publications, newsletters, promotional material, or corporate gifts. Let us show you how much we enjoy working with people!

Services and Equipment

We work at any location and are equipped to bring 35mm, $2^{-1/4}$, 4x5, or 8x10 camera equipment to match the job. We use the best portable studio lighting available, and never go on location without carrying backup cameras and lights. We can travel to your event with a complete portable studio including backgrounds, stands, reflectors and all the necessities for high quality photography. We know publication photography—what films work best, what filters work best, how to light each and every subject. In short, we are professionals and our work shows it.

LEO COMMERCIAL PHOTOGRAPHY

1412 S.E. Stark Street
Portland, Oregon 97214
(503) 235-7655

People
Executive portraits, award ceremonies, people at work and play

Places
Interior and exterior photography, hotels, restaurants and architectural detail

Products
Table top to room sets, 2,800-square-foot studio with ground-level access, full kitchen on site—we love to do food photos.

Projects
Convention booths and display transparencies

Design
Service from concept to printed piece; brochures, sales sheets and postcards

Image is Everything.
Portray your business and yourself in "the best light."

17900 S.W. Frances Street
Aloha, Oregon 97006
Contact: Gordy Teifel (503) 642-1251

Professional Photography with Computer Support

Create photographs that fit the specifications. Formats available are 35mm, medium-format Hasselblads, 4x5 and 5x7 view cameras. Mainlight Media is a member of the Kodak Promise of Excellence program. Your satisfaction is assured!

- Groundbreaking events
- Plant dedications
- Architectural facades
- Interiors
- Real estate applications
- Corporate agent principals
- Studio product photos
- Illustrations for computer documents
- Video to computer illustration transfers
- Film to photographic prints
- Video to photographic prints
- News release business portraits
- Employee of the month/year photos
- Photographic copy and restorations
- Computer-enhanced imaging
- Surveillance image optimization
- Archival photography and documentation
- Newsletter photography and halftones

Video Production

Produce corporate video programs for application specific needs. Sony DV source tapes or other formats are artfully edited with Digital Origin Edit DV on a high-end Macintosh PowerPC. This nonlinear system renders a wonderful abundance of special effects and graphics with the video content for terrific results.

- Promotional tapes
- Infomercials
- Corporate milestone events
- Stockholder meetings
- Tape-slide to video transfers
- Conversion: NTSC, PAL, SECAM
- Time-lapse programs
- Golf tournaments
- Funerals/memorial services
- Legal depositions
- Speed analysis
- Court evidence video documenting
- Process recording
- Tape speed conversion
- Weddings and receptions
- Dubbing, labeling and sleeving

Tape-slide Sequences

High impact tape-slide dissolve sequences can powerfully convince your audience on the message you want to get across. Media production at its finest! These substantial programs command extensive visual and aural communication skills with outstanding results. Call Mainlight Media to initiate the process.

Photography by Bob Welsh & Stan Landis
Bob Welsh, Master Photog. Cr., PPA Certified, FP
5035 N.E. Elam Young Parkway Suite 300
Hillsboro, Oregon 97124
(503) 648-0586; Fax (503) 640-1617
E-mail: mitp@teleport.com; Web site: www.mitstudio.com

YOUR FOCUS—OUR FOCUS

It is hard to presume what stage of planning you are at or if you have even begun. Through detailed communication—an eye for the creative—and dependable service, we are able to continually achieve the best for our corporate clients.

- **Corporate Events**—showcasing the atmosphere, location and agenda of your event. From company parties to sales/award banquets, our staff will assist in all areas of photographic planning.
- **Public Relations Portraits**—your professional image is of utmost importance. Detailed attention will result in a business portrait you and your company can be proud of.
- **Commercial Photography**—awareness of your end result and usage are key elements in meeting your creative needs and deadlines.
- **Executive Portraiture**—projecting the image that will translate your personal message to others cannot be compromised. From incorporating architectural design elements to the classic rendition of an heirloom portrait, we will design a portrait that you will enjoy and view with great pride.

Moments In Time Photography has built a reputation on award-winning photography, along with 20 years of communications and excellent service to our clients.

COMMUNICATION

DESIGN

ART

www.mitstudio.com

PHOTOGRAPHERS

(503) 249-7575
www.strongphotography.com

Images that Tell the Story.

Important events are more than mere occasions; they are the fulfillment of a vision. If you want to capture the spirit and vision of your event, and not just the mechanics, turn to an accomplished photojournalist and artist for photographs that are singular in style and beauty.

Strong Photography captures nuances, not just people posing. From the heart-pounding thrill of rafting trips to the spirit and underpinnings of an organization's culture, the joy of graduations to the sweeping elegance of cultural events, photojournalist Craig Strong creates priceless images of people in action. Through his camera lens, everyday moments at your workplace are viewed as extraordinary, while out-of-the-ordinary retreats, sporting events, and holiday celebrations are captured in all their excitement and glory.

You are investing time, money, and even a part of yourself in an event that will benefit the community of people you care about and serve. Complement your efforts with the vision, passion, and unobtrusive style of Craig Strong. An experienced, award-winning photojournalist, Strong will bring a unique, true-life perspective to your well-planned affair.

- Fundraisers/benefits
- Parties/celebrations
- Holiday events
- Conferences
- Sporting events
- Grand openings
- Anniversaries
- Graduations
- Reunions
- Awards banquets
- Publicity events
- Concerts

- Day-in-the-life photo essays
- Retreats
- Trust-building exercises
- Fashion shows
- Corporate events/annual reports
- Company picnics
- Festivals
- Tournaments
- Conventions
- Dances
- Ceremonies
- Receptions

Video Services

ENCORE STUDIOS

Portland, Oregon
(503) 255-8047
E-mail: encore@webcombo.net
Web site: www.bravoevent.com/pdx00/encore–photo

Let our professional videographers videotape your next event! With over 20 years of experience, we pride ourselves on helping you make your next event a success. You are welcome to choose from a wide variety of packages *or* customize your own package, according to your preferences and budget. As professionals, we are as unobtrusive as possible, capturing those special moments on camera.

Equipment and Services

The finest and most current digital video cameras are utilized. These state-of-the-art digital cameras are highly advanced, and we are one of the few studios using this innovative technology for your picture perfect event! We are able to shoot in only available light or in studio-type light. We also use wireless remote microphones for superior sound. Complete editing includes digital effects, music, titling, overlays, logos, and audio dubbing and mixing.

Additional Services

- Broadcast videography
- Betacam, Hi-8, S-VHS formats also
- Multiple camera operators
- Packaging & labeling
- Script writing
- Voice talent
- Wireless microphones
- Multiple cameras
- Conversions: PAL, SECAM, NTSC
- Custom cases and logos
- On and off-camera talent
- Story boards

Events/Purposes

We are experienced, but not limited to, videotaping the following events or purposes:

Industry	Legal	Open Houses	Trade Shows
Bar/Bat Mitzvahs	Receptions	Inventories	Remodeling
Insurance	Advertisements	Training	Seminars
Promotions	Commercials	Corporate Images	Infomercials
Meetings	Funerals	Products/Lines	Auctions
Real Estate	Demos	Transfers	Duplications
Conventions	Music Videos	Conferences	Orientations
Employees	Public Relations	Literature	Executive

Packages and Prices

With the most comprehensive package selection in the Northwest, you are welcome to choose from our many selections or customize your own package as you'd like. Please call for an appropriate quote. A $100 deposit reserves your date. Visa and MasterCard gladly accepted as well as financing, with no interest payments.

Consultants are available for day or evening appointments.

VIDEO PRODUCTIONS

2580 N.W. Upshur Street
Portland, Oregon 97210
Contact: Eric Newland
(503) 295-1991 or (360) 993-1991
Web site: http://www.hybridmoon.com

In this competitive business climate, clear and powerful communication is vital. *Hybrid Moon Video* specializes in helping companies communicate with more impact. Our video productions sparkle with creativity and professionalism. They present your message with crystal clarity. You'll be amazed at the ways you can enhance the power of your communications with customers, employees and the media.

Here are the Types of Video Productions produced by *Hybrid Moon Video*
- Training Tapes
- Promotional Videos
- Seminars and Conferences
- Public Relations Productions
- Music Videos
- Legal Depositions
- Television Commercials

We Also Provide **Pre-Production** and **Production Capabilities**, including
- Script-writing
- Story Boards
- Set Design
- Studio or On-location Shooting
- State-of-the-Art Digital Editing
- S-VHS
- DV
- BetaCam SP
- Computer Graphics and 3D Animation
- VHS Duplication and Fulfillment

Call us today and let us show you samples of our work. Even if you don't need our services today, it still pays to familiarize yourself with our company. We could be a valuable resource to you down the road.

Discover the *Hybrid Moon* advantage
(503) 295-1991 or (360) 993-1991
www.hybridmoon.com

Notes

Corporate Gifts & Promotional Items

CORPORATE GIFTS AND PROMOTIONAL ITEMS

HELPFUL HINTS

Advertising specialties are the items that make an impression and keep your name in the minds of the attendees long after the event is over. These gifts, giveaways, awards, or promotional items feature your meeting name, business logo, or your slogan imprinted on them. Traditional types of imprinted giveaways include pens, coffee mugs, hats, t-shirts, etc. The goal today is that these ad specialties be gifts that will have real meaning and function for the people who receive them.

Get the most from your gift or promotional dollars! Make sure you investigate all the options and come up with the gift or giveaway that has the most importance and value to your audience. Working with a professional company that offers experience and service is important. The experienced company will have a large enough selection available so you won't have to go all over town looking for the perfect gift.

When looking for your gift, promotional item, or giveaway, ask yourself the following questions: How much is the budget? How many pieces will I need? Do I give them to everyone? Do I want a functional or fun item? Is this something I would like to receive? Are the gifts of a quality that reflects your company/meeting standards? What type of imprint is needed on the gifts? What do I want it to say? How much time do I have before I need them?

There is a fine line between a gimmick and a giveaway. A gimmick means you have to do something before you receive the "special gift." Everyone is fed up with scams and phony prizes. A gift or promotional item is given without any strings attached.

Theme and recreational events. There is an idea for every theme or recreational event: golf balls with the company logo imprinted for a golf tournament, imprinted kerchiefs for a western party, water bottles for a run, travel clocks given to meeting planners reminding them it's time to book a meeting, etc.

Giveaways in the new millennium can be sophisticated. Imprinted calculators, watches, duffel bags, golf bags, towels, beach chairs—just about anything is possible. Refer to this section for lots of wonderful ideas.

Favors: Meal time is the perfect time to give a souvenir. Something portable like a lapel pin, an imprinted pen, or small box of chocolates or mints. Favors are often a part of the theme of a gala evening. Make it something convenient to carry, not cumbersome.

HELPFUL HINTS

Gift and fruit baskets: The famous welcome basket of fruit has come a long way! Today meeting planners are pressured to provide "VIP" gifts that are creative, easy to travel with, functional, and even recyclable! The fruit basket has evolved into a theme basket for whatever occasion is at hand. Pick the items and the theme, and the basket can be created. Baskets can be personalized, according to hobbies and season, with food additions (coffee, chocolate, etc.). Refer to this section for professionals who custom-design and deliver to your door.

Thank you gifts: These are most often given to vendors, speakers, and volunteers for doing a good job. After a speaker has presented, many planners send a gift to the speaker's office or hand it to him or her personally. Thanking a vendor or the volunteers who helped create a successful meeting or event is very common. Jewelers and gift stores specialize in gifts like designer pen and pencil sets, crystal or silver pieces, lapel pins, etc.

Room gifts: These are usually light snacks, cheese, wine, crackers, and fruit. Logo chocolates are fun to have for a late-night treat. Other items might be momentos of the city, state, or company. Coffee-table books can be easily packed for the return trip home.

Retirement or acknowledgment gifts: These gifts or awards are usually very nice and more personal—watches, jewelry, crystal or silver pieces. Many of these gifts have a personal message engraved on them or can be an item that fits the person's style and personality.

Annual gifts: The holidays are always busy times for the gift-giving businesses. Thanking clients for their business and thanking vendors for a job well done are reasons to give holiday gifts. Keep in mind these gifts need to be tasteful. A gift given during the year for no particular reason is a nice surprise. Also, a thank-you to a client for a large order or big account is a nice gesture.

Awards: Traditional plaques have little purpose aside from placing them on a wall or desk. Today, many awards have a purpose—an engraved clock or a piece of engraved jewelry. It's nice to receive an award you can proudly use and display throughout the year that reminds you of that special acknowledgment you have earned.

Unique gifts: There are many unique and specialty gifts that are available including gift certificates for Massage Therapy, or bringing in a masseuse to your office as a reward for hitting goals. The masseuse can bring the table or massage chair on-site; set up a private office with music and dim lighting and watch your tensions float away. There are also gift certificates to a day spa, with everything from hair care to six-hour spa treatment packages.

15648 S.E. 114th, Suite 106
Clackamas, Oregon 97015
Contact: Bill Alvastad or Brice Dick
(503) 722-1760, (800) 555-7444
Fax (503) 722-1759

"Your Complete Uniform and Promotional Source"

- Embroidery
- Screen Printing
- Trade Show Traffic Builders
- Custom Apparel Manufacturing
- Uniform Fulfillment Programs
- Golf Tournaments
- Sales Incentives
- Client and Employee Gifts
- Employee Recognition Awards
- Safety Awards
- Corporate Catalog Identity Programs
- Corporate Gifts
- Special Events
- Premiums

Fully Equipped

- Embroidery and Screen Printing In House
- Volume Discounts Enable Us to Offer the Best Value
- Knowledgeable Sales Staff to Meet Your Needs
- Searchable Data Base to Locate Products
- Catalogs and Samples Available
- Large Warehouse to Stock Your Program
- Show Room Access
- Graphic Artists In House

Timing Is Everything

- Rushes and Quick Turnaround Times are Our Specialty
- Large and Small Orders On Time and Within Your Budget

The Choice Is Yours

- Wide Vendor Selections
- Over 500,00 Items to Choose From
- Custom Products

"The Largest Selection of Promotional Products in the Pacific Northwest"

Call
Brice Dick or Bill Alvstad
(503) 722-1760 or (800) 555-7444

Contact: Lynne Elbert, owner
8033 S.W. 166th Place • Aloha, Oregon 97007
(503) 649-4141, (800) 884-8095; Fax (503) 591-1708
E-mail: lynne@lynmar.com
Web site: www.lynmar.com

"We're In Business To Promote Your Event"
Trade Shows • Conferences • Corporate Meetings • Special Events

Promotional Products for Every Event

Awards	Conference Packets	Note Pads
Badges & Buttons	Crystal Ware	Party Favors
Bags (cloth and plastic)	Emblems	Pens
Balloons	Food Gifts	Presentation Folders
Banners	Greeting Cards	Picnic Needs
Bumper Stickers	Jackets (embroidery)	Puzzles
Business Cards	Luggage Tags	Rulers
Calendars	Magnets	T-shirts & Polos
Caps & Hats	Matchbooks	Travel Mugs
Certificates	Menu Covers	Umbrellas
Coffee Mugs	Name Badges	Yardsticks

Fast Service
Whether your event is in four months or four days, our fast service can help you. Some items available in 24 hours. Our in-house graphics department can create any artwork you might need. Custom products are also available. If you've seen it, we can do it!

Buy with Confidence
- Large Selection
- Samples Available
- In-House Graphics
- Rush Jobs Welcome
- Free Catalogs
- VISA/MasterCard Accepted
- Discover/American Express
- Great Customer Service
- Toll-Free Number
- Custom Products
- On-Time Delivery
- E-mail Our Office
- Fast Computer Search

Ordering
Call, fax, e-mail us at lynne@lynmar.com. Having a successful event depends on research, creativity, product selection and a good support team.

Call LYNMAR
a locally owned and woman run company

(503) 649-4141 or (800) 884-8095

Members of
Advertising Specialties Institute
Beaverton and Tualatin Chambers
Promotional Products Association of Oregon & Washington

OREGON SCREEN IMPRESSIONS

SCREENPRINTING & EMBROIDERY

1215 SE 8TH AVE
PORTLAND, OREGON 97214
503-231-0181 • 800-766-5707

Since 1984 Oregon Screen Impressions has served the local and regional market of screen printed and embroidered apparel, and more recently the ad specialty items as well. We are a wholesale company catering to your specific event needs, from uniforms to promotional and souvenir items.

Although you will find us to be very competitive, we do not cut corners. We have a staff of industry veterans and equipment to outperform the competition and exceed your expectations.

Customer Service

We have seven people available to service you and pay attention to your needs. These are knowledgeable individuals well trained in what we can (and cannot) do. We are not commission based; our interest is purely in taking care of your needs, on time and on quality.

Art Department

Our staff of four artists create designs for you, or interpret your vision in the most effective way to maximize your budget. This is a highly qualified group of artists who possess the technical knowledge and equipment to take your image from verbal articulation, sketch, or electronic file, and translate it to the printed medium.

Screen Print

Our screen print department is among the best in the Northwest. There are eight presses ranging from small manual machines for samples and short runs, to large automatic presses capable of printing up to 14 colors.

Embroidery

We create, digitize and embroider apparel in-house, giving us total control on quality and you the ability to make changes, painlessly. We have an award winning embroidery department with over 15 people working multi-shift to meet your needs.

Fulfillment Services

When appropriate, we also have a fulfillment department with the systems and staff in place to warehouse, manage inventory, and production planning in order to cost effectively ship directly to your attendees or distribution points.

The Bottom Line

OSI is not your "corner screen printer". We are a reliable resource for anything with your logo on it. We understand the event business like no other company we know of, as we got our humble start working events almost every weekend. Whether you're planning an event with an attendance of 100,000 or 10, when it comes to logo'd apparel or other merchandise, we would love to work with you.

We are big enough to meet your needs, but small enough to pay attention to them!

Oregon Screen Impressions, Excellence in Screen Printing and Embroidery

910 S.W. Hall
Tigard, Oregon 97223
(next to Circuit City)
(503) 598-1200, (888) 355-4653
Fax (503) 639-9070

2065 N.W. 185th Avenue
Hillsboro, Oregon 97124
(next to Chevys)
(503) 629-8845
Fax (503) 531-9182

11493 S.E. 82nd Avenue • Portland, Oregon 97266
(just north of Clackamas Town Center)
(503) 659-4653 • Fax (503) 659-5004
(800) 618-6020; Web site: www.intlgolf.com

Specializing In
- Tournament Prizes
- Retirement Gifts
- Sales Incentives
- Honorariums
- Tournament Planning
- Custom Imprinting
- Awards
- All your golf retail needs

Who We Are
We are the largest golf supplier in the Portland metro area, serving our community since 1992. We have key account status with all major golf manufacturers to ensure our customers the quickest availability and best prices.

**Contact Denny Taylor at (503) 598-1200
and ask about your complimentary golf balls!**

Celebration!
Gift Basket Company

Contact: Patty Evans, Owner
Phone/Fax (503) 245-1344
Toll Free (877) 245-1344
E-mail: celebrationgift@hotmail.com
Web site: www.celebrationgift.com
Business Hours: Mon–Fri 8:30am–5pm
24 hours by fax, voicemail, e-mail or Web

Elegant, distinctive gift baskets for your clients, guests, VIPs and more!

A Sampling of Our Services

* We offer a fine selection of gourmet food, beverage and gift items, hand-selected for quality and taste.
* Our baskets are elegantly designed in unique baskets and containers, and professionally finished with cellophane and a handmade bow.
* Your gift will be personally delivered in the local Portland metro area, or carefully packaged and shipped to anywhere in the world.
* We accept most major credit cards. We also offer our business clients the convenience of monthly billing.

Customer Service Is Our Priority

Your gift needs to be one-of-a-kind. At Celebration! Gift Basket Company, we understand that, and we will work with you to design a basket to meet your specific gift-giving occasion, and to make it a gift that will be remembered.

Our Satisfaction Guarantee

Our job doesn't end once the basket is delivered or shipped. Give us a try, and you'll discover why our customers keep coming back.

To view many of our basket designs, visit our Web site at
www.celebrationgift.com

To arrange a personal appointment, give us a call at
(503) 245-1344 or toll free (877) 245-1344

5687 S.E. International Way, Suite E
Portland, Oregon 97222
Contact: Grace Gatchell
(503) 654-5000; (888) 366-2323;
Fax (503) 654-5338
Business Hours: Mon–Fri 7am–5pm;
Order 24 Hours A Day
by fax or e-mail

*Designing Success
for 16 years.*

AWARD-WINNING DESIGNS

*Exquisitely arranged and professionally
finished with cellophane and ribbon
by award-winning designer.
Featuring fine gourmet products from
Oregon, The Great Northwest and Beyond!*

We take time to listen and customize each gift to convey your message in a unique and memorable way. Serving the entire Portland metro area with shipping available throughout the U.S.

Order from our **Web site** at http://**www.thecountrybasket.com**.

Ordering is Easy
Call:
Portland metro area (503) 654-5000
Toll Free (888) 366-2323
Fax: (503) 654-5338
E-mail: ctrybskt@juno.com

Member of the following organizations: *1997 Winners of the*

PORTLAND · OREGON VISITORS ASSOCIATION
the convention and visitors bureau of metropolitan Portland

OREGON
BUSINESS TRAVEL ASSOCIATION

Portland Chamber   *award*

*Designing and delivering
extraordinary gift baskets.*

Please let this business know that you heard about them from the Bravo! Event Resource Guide.

GIFT BASKETS

Where all products, "Made, Caught or Grown," in Oregon
5 N.W. Naito Parkway • Portland, Oregon 97209
Corporate Sales Contact:
Carol-Lynn Olsen, Director of Corporate Sales (503) 517-4342
Margaret Earl, Corporate Account Sales Manager (503) 517-4335
Fax (503) 273-8313
Web site: www.madeinoregon.com

We Can Help Make Your Event a Success
- Speakers' Gifts
- Conventioneer Totes
- Spousal Events
- Gifts for Every Occasion
- Salmon
- Wine
- Hazelnuts
- Pendleton Blankets
- Myrtlewood

It's Easy
Our staff of Corporate Specialists can do all the legwork. Tell us the impression you want to make, your budget and timeline—we'll do the rest. We can suggest options, support a company theme, and personalize gifts with your company logo. You can even add your own corporate items to any of our premium gift packs.

It's Reliable
We take care of the details so you won't have to. Give us the information and we'll package and ship your gifts to arrive on time. You'll get an order confirmation, corporate discount and billing. It's our business to make your business look good.

It Always Fits
Whatever thought you want conveyed, whatever occasion to be celebrated—a gift from Made In Oregon always fits. Stunning commemorative gifts like monogrammed Pendleton blankets, myrtlewood or art glass, to gift packs filled with Oregon Delicacies the whole office will love. You'll find even more ideas at our 11 Oregon stores and three annex locations.

Portland, Salem, Eugene, Medford, Newport
Out of Oregon? We ship worldwide.
(800) 828-9673

queen bee
gift baskets

10025 North Smith Street
Portland, Oregon 97203
p 503.515.7645
f 503.916.1859
e qbgifts@aol.com

These ain't your mama's gift baskets.

Hmmmmm... Different?
In short, yes. Queen Bee goes beyond wicker, fruit and bows. A great example—our rustic leather, Indiana Jones-esque bag—perfect for the adventurous sort, or that hip executive you know. Queen Bee does elegant and classic. But Queen Bee does hip and stylish, too.

Flexibility
We build "baskets" to any budget. And we can handle any size order. If you have a wacky idea, just ask us... we will truly bend over backwards to meet your needs. Queen Bee gets a kick from challenges.

Something More
Queen Bee, working with her parent biz, Labyrinth Event Consultants, can plan and orchestrate an entire employee recognition week full of events, gifts, and treats for your oh-so-deserving, loyal, enthusiastic employees. Please see our page for Labyrinth Event Consultants.

No Joking
Queen Bee donates $1 from each basket over $50 to a local breast cancer research program. In addition, in an effort to support local small business owners, the majority of our baskets are created with products from our own bountiful Pacific Northwest. And oh yah, we're active members of the Portland Chamber of Commerce, too.

Call Us
Brochure? Information? Just want to chat? Call Queen Bee.

See page 56 under Meeting & Event Planners.

GIFT BASKETS

Ramona's
BASKETS BEARING GIFTS

205 Commerce Center
11504-K S.E. Mill Plain Boulevard
Vancouver, Washington 98684
Contact: Ramona Lupo
(360) 253-7980, (800) 775-7158;
Fax (360) 253-5728
E-mail: ramonas@pacifier.com
Business Hours:
Mon–Fri 10am–7pm; Sat 10am–5pm

For Over 21 Years...
At Ramona's we take great pleasure in creating baskets bearing gifts of award-winning Northwest wines, microbrews, cheese, sausage, smoked salmon, fresh fruit, pasta, sauces, jams, flowers, plants and the finest chocolate. The offering of gift baskets has a rich heritage in many cultures over thousands of years, and Ramona's continues that tradition. Whether you choose from our Ready To Go, Create Your Own or Custom Design, your gift will be of incomparable quality and style.

A Sampling
- **RTE:** Perfect for a hotel guest or an office, all Ready To Eat, smoked salmon, cheese, fresh fruit, sausage, crackers, sweets, cookies, soda, wine or beer
- **NW Best:** For the executive or the family, a variety of foods from the bounty of the Pacific Northwest. From sweet to savory, this basket is always popular.
- **Smokey the Fish:** You guessed it, smoked salmon, smoked trout, sturgeon, oysters, salmon jerky, paté, crackers, smoked nuts…add a bottle of wine or brew.
- **Basket in Bloom:** Beautiful live green or flowering plants are surrounded with your choice of gourmet products. Or maybe just a plant in a decorated basket.
- **and more:** Fruit Of The Earth, The Brew Basket, Grape Escape, Coffee Lover's Dream, Primo Pasta
  - Wedding and shower baskets
  - Recognition and guest speakers
  - Meeting Snack Paks
  - Trade show display and giveaway baskets
  - Table centerpieces and table favors

Business Gifts
Ramona's offers full-service business gift solutions. We can include your logo on a variety of products for your company gifts, and there are a number of billing options available. Whatever it takes, Ramona's will help enhance your company image. With more than 21 years of "taking care of business" experience, you can trust our expertise in handling business accounts.

Visa, MasterCard, Discover and American Express.
Local delivery and worldwide shipping.

**Visit Ramona's Baskets Bearing Gifts—full service retail store
Cascade Park in Vancouver, just off I-205**

Audiovisual & Communication Services

HELPFUL HINTS

Planning for audiovisual equipment, lighting, and staging for your meeting or event is very important. Exciting new technologies like interactive computer use, live video enhancement of speakers, and teleconferencing have arrived, but the budgets that have arrived with them are steep. The type of audiovisual support you will need for your meeting or event may be simple or more complex. Be sure to review all your options.

Think ahead to what your audiovisual needs will be:
- Get a list of the speakers' needs well in advance of your event and schedule a rehearsal. You will avoid last-minute and rush labor charges this way.
- Give speakers a chance to rehearse with equipment.
- Test equipment immediately prior to beginning of the event.
- Have spare bulbs and extra extension cords on hand.
- Having a technician available to attend to your needs throughout the meeting may be your best insurance policy.
- Many facilities have in-house equipment (check availability and working condition).
- Remember that poor-quality audiovisual equipment can ruin a meeting.

To maximize your audiovisual budget, try the following:
- **Reserve equipment early** so you have what you need from a reputable company. If you have never worked with the company, ask for references and check them. This is an important part of the meeting.
- **Negotiate all costs.** Package deals are good for you and the rental companies. If they know your needs and have your timelines, it will be the cost effective.
- **Put your agreements in writing.** If one company is not able to meet your needs, look at other companies until your needs are met.
- **Write all instructions.** Include agendas and room layouts so your vendors know exactly what you expect. This will eliminate surprises or the need for mind reading.
- **Save yourself headaches.** If you are too busy doing the many other jobs needed for a meeting, seek out and use experienced production managers and technicians to oversee the audiovisual portions of your event.
- **Barter goods and services with your rental companies.** They may want to advertise in your publications, exhibit at your trade show, or acquire leads from your attendees.
- **Guaranteed performance is often a policy of audiovisual companies.** They will compensate clients for rental costs in the event of equipment failure. Even better, many will provide on-site back-up.

Checkout the audiovisual equipment: Many facilities have their own in-house audiovisual department. Ask if any audiovisual equipment is included in your room charge, then be sure to check out the quality and age of the equipment. Most facilities only provide a podium and microphone, so you will need to rent additional equipment from a qualified audiovisual rental company.

BARBUR BLVD. RENTALS

BBR

BARBUR BLVD. RENTALS, INC.

246·4268

8205 S.W. Barbur Blvd. • Portland, Oregon 97219
Fax (503) 246-9375
Business Hours: Mon–Sat 7:30am–6pm; Sun 8am–4pm

Trade Show and Convention Services
- Draped Exhibit Booths
- Exhibitor Support Service
- Electrical and Lighting
- Theme/Prop Design and Development
- Planning and Consultant Service

Party and Event Department
- Tables
- Chairs
- China
- Bars
- Skirts
- Margarita Machine
- Popcorn Machines
- Fencing
- Candles
- Disposable Plates
- Balloons
- Grape Arbur
- Tents and Canopies
- Silver Service
- Serving Trays
- Fountains
- Serving Utensils
- Barbecues
- Poker Tables
- Games
- Candelabras
- Disposable Plates
- Decorations
- Gazebo
- Pillars
- Glassware/Stemware
- Silver and Stainless Flatware
- Linen, Tablecloths and Napkins
- Punch Bowls
- Chafers
- Staging
- Power Taps
- Wedding Arches
- New Express Bars (in colors)
- Napkin Imprinting
- Hacienda Front
- Commercial Food Service Equipment
- New! Luminaries-special occasion designs candelabra 2"–3" centerpieces in a variety of styles and colors-this is a must see!
- And much more, call one of our party consultants for more information…

Homeowner/Contractor Rentals
- Hand Tools
- Tractors
- Pressure Washers
- Fork Lifts
- Power Tools
- Cement Mixers
- Scaffolding
- Chippers
- Garden Equipment
- Paint Sprayers
- Trailers
- Beds/Wheelchairs

Audio/Visual Department
- Projectors
- TV/VCR's
- Big Screen TV
- PA Systems
- Podiums
- Wireless Mics/Lavaliere
- Karaoke
- Stereo Systems

Professional Assistance For 40 Years
Family-owned and operated. Barbur Blvd. Rentals takes pride in providing quality merchandise, equipment and service. Our experienced personnel are available to answer your questions and share their knowledge and ideas. Let Barbur Blvd. Rentals help make your event extra special!

Please let this business know that you heard about them from the Bravo! Event Resource Guide.

AUDIOVISUAL & COMMUNICATION SERVICES

In Portland (503) 235-5009
Nationwide (888) 882-4228
Visit our Web site at:
www.caribinerav.com

Our Most Important Piece of Presentation Equipment?
Peace of Mind.
It Starts with Caribiner Audio Visual.

Being an event planner is tough enough without having to worry if your A/V partner is up to the task. From a boardroom setting to supporting trade shows, coordinating simultaneous breakouts and providing solutions for the largest of general sessions, Caribiner Audio Visual can meet your needs. Across town or across the globe, Caribiner's turn-key approach will give you the peace of mind you deserve.

- Audio Visual Equipment Rental & Sales
- Sound Reinforcement
- Comprehensive Meeting Support
- Hotel & Convention Center Services
- Exhibition & Trade Show Services
- 24-Hour Technical Support
- Latest Audio Visual Technologies

Albuquerque • Anaheim • Atlanta • Austin • Boston • Charleston
• Charlotte • Denver • Ft. Lauderdale • Greenville • Midland, MI
• Minneapolis • New Orleans • New York • Philadelphia • Portland, OR
• Raleigh • San Antonio • San Diego • Seattle • Tampa • Tucson

Essig Entertainment
MORE THAN AN AV COMPANY...

Eugene
Contact: Scott or Kim Essig
(541) 345-7989,
Fax (541) 345-1510

P.O. Box 26409
Eugene, Oregon 97402
(800) 832-7989

Portland
Contact: Christina Fuerst
(503) 296-0441
Fax (503) 296-9286

Essig Entertainment...
for a professional, dynamic, flawless event anywhere in Oregon

Audiovisual Equipment and Services
- Data projectors (up to 1024 x 768)
- Video projectors and monitors
- Projection screens
- Sound systems and microphones
- Video cameras
- Slide and overhead projectors
- Lighting
- Flip charts, whiteboards, and easels
- Technical support (for sound, video, data, etc.)
- Image magnification
- Videography

Special Event Equipment and Services
- Pipe and drapery (stage backdrops to full trade shows)
- Tents
- Tables, chairs, linens
- Staging and dance floors
- Theme events, special effects and decor
- Event planning

Events include
- Meetings, seminars, conferences
- Conventions and trade shows
- Awards presentations, rallies, product launches
- Focus groups and press conferences
- Banquets, auctions, parties, weddings

Essig Entertainment... an *event* company

Technicians on-call 24 hours a day.

Please let this business know that you heard about them from the Bravo! Event Resource Guide.

HOLLYWOOD LIGHTS, INC.

5251 S.E. McLoughlin Boulevard
Portland, Oregon 97202-4836
Production Lighting Contact: Mike Pratt
Electrical Services Contact: Frank Locke
Rentals/Sales Contact: Brian Kameoka
(503) 232-9001, (800) 826-9881; Fax (503) 232-8505
Showroom Hours: Mon–Fri 8am–6pm; Sat 9am–1pm
E-mail: info@hollywoodlights.com; Web site: www.hollywoodlights.com

Services Available

- **Production Lighting:** From corporate meetings and product introductions to special events and rock concerts—the creative team at Hollywood Lights will design and implement a show that will exceed your expectations. The expert Hollywood Lights production teams will set up, focus, operate and tear down your show quickly, safely, and efficiently, keeping your event on time and on budget. Hollywood Lights' complete inventory of state-of-the-art automated lighting equipment will set your event apart. Clients include: Nike, Adidas, Intel, In Focus, Columbia Sportswear, Oregon Ballet Theatre, Rose Festival, Freightliner, Southland Corp., MTV, Dr. Martens, Mt. Hood Festival of Jazz, Fred Meyer Challenge, Nordstrom, Portland Trail Blazers, Mentor Graphics and more.
- **Temporary Electrical Services:** When your event requires power throughout the Northwest, call Hollywood Lights. Whether you are planning a corporate meeting, trade show, outdoor festival, political event, private party, concert, grand opening, wedding/memorial, sporting event, RV rally, or you need an emergency backup system—our professional team of electrical technicians make it happen. Hollywood Lights provides every detail of temporary electrical services from the permit process through all distribution, no matter how remote your location. Additional services include tent lighting to supplemental lighting for warehouse sales.
- **Rentals:** Hollywood Lights offers a complete inventory of equipment you can rent—from mirror balls to fog machines and Christmas lights to deejay-style, dance club effects—all for the creatively inspired do-it-yourselfer. A dazzling addition to your party or event is one call away with Hollywood Lights.
- **Sales:** Where do you go for ideas? Hollywood Lights has a 2,000 square-foot showroom featuring creative applications of lighting and effects for holiday decorations, parade floats, weddings, and unique events. Please visit or call for additional information—our team is full of innovative suggestions.

Why Hollywood Lights?

- Founded in Portland in 1948, Hollywood Lights has a 50 year history of servicing special events in the Northwest. Whatever your vision, Hollywood Lights will make it happen.
- Hollywood Lights offers 24-hour emergency pager service, ensuring that your event runs as planned. Or arrange a standby technician on site at your event.
- With a newly expanded branch office in Seattle, Hollywood Lights covers the Northwest.
- At Hollywood Lights, we believe our people are simply the best. The Hollywood Lights team comprises lighting and electrical professionals who offer technical expertise, creative solutions, and exceptional customer service.
- The lighting and electrical equipment in Hollywood Lights' inventory is extensive. From automated, moving light fixtures to special effect equipment, Hollywood Lights has it!

INTERSTATE *Special Events*
5420 N. Interstate Avenue
Portland, Oregon 97217-4597
(503) 285-6685

At Interstate Special Events, we have everything you need—including the expertise, the attention to detail and the commitment to service—to make your event truly *special*. Our inventory contains a wide variety of items needed for every type of event. From casual to formal, we can supply your needs!

Tables, Chairs and Linens
We offer banquet, round, half-round, umbrella, bistro and stylish serpentine tables. Classic white wood chairs are available, as well as folding Samsonite, white Bistro and black, padded stacking chairs. Our table linens, skirting and napkins are available in a wide array of colors and sizes. And we now offer specialty one-of-a-kind theme linens.

Tents and Canopies
We have one of the largest canopy inventories in the area. Our tents range from 100 square feet to 18,000 square feet. Prices start at $95. We also supply elegant tent liners, pole sleeves, lighting and heating. Site inspections are available.

Tableware, Serviceware and Beverage Service
Our china styles include the classic white, elegant ivory with gold band and clear glass. Whatever the occasion, we have glassware in many styles to meet your needs. Stainless and silver flatware and serving accessories are available. We have many silver plate items such as tea service, punch bowls and chafing dishes as well as vases and bowls in glass, stainless, acrylic and silver. We offer porta-bars, beermeister, beverage fountains, kegtainers, coffeemakers and carafes, pitchers and insulated dispensers.

Additional Items
We carry a large inventory of concession equipment including briquet and propane BBQs, fryers, grills and griddles, gumbo pots and hot boxes. We specialize in staging and carry a large inventory of dance floors. If games are what you are looking for, we have bingo, volleyball, softball, horseshoes and even a Dunk Tank! And don't forget the helium tank. Also available to rent are overhead and slide projectors, screens, PA systems TVs, VCRs and even a bull horn.

Ordering and Delivery
Reservations are highly recommended to ensure availability and assistance in meeting your needs. Delivery is available as well as setup and take-down for a reasonable charge.

**Our Special Events Representatives are eager to assist with your event needs.
Please call us today for more information.**

See page 190 under Rental Services.

PLATINUM RECORDS LIGHTS & SOUND

104 S.W. Second Avenue
Portland, Oregon 97204
(503) 222-9166
Fax (503) 222-9355

915 E. Pike Street
Seattle, Washington 98122
(206) 324-8032
Fax (206) 324-4563

Web site: www.platinum-records.com
E-mail: info@platinum-records.com

Platinum Records, Lights & Sound specializes in lighting and sound reinforcement for small, medium, or large scale events. A full line of lighting and sound products are available for purchase or rental. Check out the following listings for a representation of what is offered, or feel free to visit either showroom for a demonstration!

Lighting

Intelligent Lighting
Par Cans
Theatrical
Fog and Bubble Machines
Stands
Follow Spots
Disco Balls
Nightclub Lighting Effects
Trussing
Controllers

Choose from quality names such as: High End, Martin, Omnisistem and American DJ.

Sound

Speakers
Mixers
P.A. Gear
Turntables
Effects
Amplifiers
Sound Boards
Stands
CD Players
Recorders

Choose from quality names such as: JBL, EAW, EV, Cerwin Vega, Crown and Mackie.

Platinum Lights & Sound Provides Services for your Corporate Event, Holiday Party, Wedding, Reunion, School or Church Function.

Services also available for:
Mobile DJs
Auctions
Bands
Concerts
Public Speaking Events
Musicians
Raves

Delivery and Setup

Delivery, setup, and teardown are available with knowledgeable sound technicians to run your system for optimal results.

At Platinum Records, we help make your event an EVENT!

2515 S.E. Ankeny • Portland, Oregon 97214
(503) 238-6330, (877) 503-ROSE; Fax (503) 238-9872
Business Hours: Mon–Fri 7:30am–6pm; Sat 9am–2pm
(24-hour emergency service)
E-mail: rcs@teleport.com

SINCE 1938

• FULL SERVICE •
• Complete Production Services • Rentals • Sales •
• Service and Repair • Production Coordination • Installations •

• COMPLETE TECHNICAL SUPPORT •
• Sound • Conventional and Intelligent Lighting • Audiovisual •
• Video • Staging and Sets • Data and Multimedia Projection •

• ALL TYPES OF EVENTS •
• Corporate Shows • Conferences • Concerts • Fairs and Festivals •
• Conventions • Sports Events • Fashion Shows • Grand Openings •
• Hotels • Holiday Events • Parties • Company Events • and More! •

• OUR EXPERIENCE COUNTS •
• Whether you're looking for a single piece of equipment or complete technical coordination, our professional staff can assist you in the design, selection, planning, preparation and implementation of all the technical aspects of your next production, meeting or event. From small meetings to full scale productions, our highly experienced planners and designers are ready to handle all of the details or just give some advice. •

"We have the Creative Talent to help you plan the 'Technical Aspects' of your next Event"

• • • • • • • • • • •

ROSE CITY SOUND & LIGHTING
(503) 238-6330
TOLL FREE: (877) 503-ROSE

925 N.W. 19th
Portland, Oregon 97209
(503) 294-7153
Web site:
www.visual-producers.com/visual

THE SCREENING ROOM

This 1930's Private VIP Screening Room Makes the Perfect Impact for any Business or Party Event.

Capacity: 40 seated, 60 standing; with Back Lot accommodates up to 120

Price Range: $350 basic charge for six-hour event; Back Lot area add $200; please call for exact quote of AV equipment

Catering: we work with several licensed caterers and rental companies or select caterer of your choice

Types of Events: client presentations, press conferences, classes, wrap parties, viewing parties for video/film/TV and Pay Per-View sporting events; theme parties like Vegas, '30s Speakeasy Lounge; surprise parties or elegant bachelor/bachelorette parties and perfect for holiday and Christmas parties

Availability and Terms

The Screening Room has flexible room configurations, and an expanded outside area that can be tented in the winter. Most AV equipment in-house; equipment charge is in addition to room. All events are completely customized to your requirements and all technical arrangements are handled for you.

Description of Facility and Terms

Portland's only VIP screening room. Built in the '30s and upgraded with high-end video projection and satellite equipment. The room has been mostly used by the entertainment industry for screenings, auditions, wrap parties, and even for as a shooting location. Ground level in/out access.

Bar facilities: full walkup 12 ft. service bar

Cleanup: $125 fee

Audiovisual and equipment: 15' x 6' x 40" stage with backdrop curtains, spotlight, PA, microphone, and podium; high resolution video projection with 12' x 9' screen—project from computer, laser disk, Beta SP, Pay-Per-View, VHS, Cable, S-VHS

Parking: plenty of street parking and parking lot across street

A LONG AND RICH HISTORY

The Screening Room was once an active part of Portland's historical "Film Row" and has been graced by people such as Jimmy Stewart, Jane Powell, and Walter Bemnen to name a few. Its history, charm, and prime location make it a unique and perfect place for presentations, meetings, small performances, parties and private screenings.

EVENT RENTAL COMMUNICATIONS, INC.

2422 S.E. Hawthorne Street
Portland, Oregon 97214
Contact: Jay Pomeroy or Heather Ware
(503) 232-9031
Business Hours: Mon–Fri 8am–5:30pm
E-mail: Eventcomm@aol.com

Motorola Radio Rentals

Now when you make a snap decision, you can get the word to the people who have to hear it, in a snap.

Rental Equipment

Motorola two-way radios, mobile radios, satellite phones, portable as well as on site repeaters, cellular phones, and pagers.

Specialty Items

Base stations, headsets, speaker microphones, ear pieces, ear microphones, surveillance kits, chest packs, holsters, spare rapid charge batteries, and rapid chargers.

Services Offered

Free multi-channel programming on our UHF/VHF frequencies or yours. Twenty-four hour support service available for emergencies.

Ordering and Delivery

Equipment is available for rent by the day, week, month, or year. Reservations are recommended so that we can guarantee item availability for your event. We ship nationwide. In-town delivery is available; fees vary.

Commitment to Excellence

Accessibility, a qualified staff, prompt responses, and a working knowledge of deadlines have helped us build a successful working relationship with our customers.

At Event Rental Communications, we pride ourselves on working with our customers individually to design temporary communication systems to fit the specific needs of our clientele.

We'll let the results speak for themselves.

**NATIONWIDE TOLL FREE
1-800-283-2666**

Notes

Rental Services

Butterfly Release
Equipment & Accessories
Tables, Chairs & Linens
Tents & Canopies
Communcation Rentals

RENTAL SERVICES

HELPFUL HINTS

Rental stores carry almost everything: You'll find such things as serviceware, portable bars, arches, tents, chairs, tables, and all the tableware, dishes, glassware, and flatware you need. Many shops also carry disposable paper products and a variety of decorations. For meetings, seminars, and conventions, you will find audio visual, lighting, and sound equipment to meet your needs.

Event Rental Coordinator: Event shops can be full-service for your event needs: Decorating, coordinating the caterer, entertainment, etc. They can be a wealth of ideas and knowledge. The details and specifics are what become very tedious at the end of planning a meeting or event, so to have someone on your side to assist with the logistics and coordination can be a life-saver.

Visit a rental store while planning: It's smart to visit a showroom for ideas and to see the types and styles of merchandise and equipment available. Rental stores have brochures that describe all the different items available for rent, including style, colors, sizes, and prices. Rental stores are also terrific places to get ideas for decorations. Meet with the store's consultants and go through your event plans step-by-step. You'll find they will help you select the right items to meet your needs, as well as help determine the correct quantities. You will work very closely with the rental store you choose—make sure you feel confident in the services its staff will provide you. They will be an important extension of your staff.

Decide on formality and budget: Keep in mind the colors and decor of the site. Pick linens or paper products and tableware that will complement the room. Prices will vary depending on the formality you choose.

Table art has become very popular for many events. Your event theme is carried through to the tables—the linens, chair covers, dishware, and centerpiece all have a purpose. This "table art" is the newest buzz among event planners! Visit a rental, specialty linen, or chair cover company today to get lots of incredible ideas!

Deposits, delivery, and setup: Reserve your items as far in advance as possible, especially during the summer months when outdoor events (picnics, fairs, etc.) are popular. A deposit will secure the order for your date. Only a certain number of tents and canopies are available, and every item is reserved on a first-come, first-served basis. There is a charge on most items for delivery, setup, and pickup. Make sure you ask in advance how much those charges are so you can include them in your budget. You can also make arrangements to pick up and return the items yourself.

Returning items: If you don't arrange delivery and pickup services with the rental company, you will want to put someone in charge of picking up and returning the rented items for you. You will be responsible and may forfeit any deposit for items that are damaged, broken, lost, or late.

Specialty event rentals: All kinds of equipment, from cellular phones and pagers to computers and specialty staging and lighting, are available for rent. Because of the sophisticated nature of this type of equipment, it is smart to work with specialized rental companies. They have the technicians on staff to maintain, setup, and operate this equipment.

HELPFUL HINTS

Communications equipment: Almost every large event, meeting, or convention uses some form of communication equipment. Cellular phones are very popular for on-the-go planners. Most planners and event staff operate with some type of immediate communication system. The pager system is affordable, small, and convenient for carrying around, but requires a telephone to respond. Radio phones allow for immediate communication of the message. The staff at a communications company (located in this section) can explain the benefits of each system and help decide what will be the most appropriate equipment for your function.

Computer services are also helpful on-site during the event:
- On-site registration
- Badges
- Computer signage (last-minute changes)
- E-Mail
- Computerized message boards

Computerized accounting systems for meeting and event planners are invaluable and allow the planner to look at the costs by category, function, and income per attendee.

New specialty linens and chair covers to match your theme. These custom linens and chair covers are the new decorating sensation. They fill the room with color and are a great enhancement to your theme. The custom linen styles come in a variety of choices: elegant, festive, creative, classic, seasonal, and more. Refer to this section for the companies that specialize in this service. Custom chair covers are a new look for meetings and events. Chair cover styles can be custom-designed with your business logo or matching theme for your event.

Tent rental: A tent often serves as an ideal back up location for an outdoor event, in case of unsuitable weather conditions. many tents feature transparent vinyl siding that can be raised and lowered as needed. A tent supplier can recommend sources for any portable heating or air conditioning that you might need.

   Important note: Never use canvas tents treated with mineral oil for waterproofing, they are extremely flammable.

Tent capacities: The following are estimated capacities for tents of typical sizes under normal conditions:

Tent Size	Reception	Accommodates Buffet w/ seating	Sit-down Dinner
16' x 16'	45	32	24
20' x 20'	65	56	40
20' x 30'	100	86	60
30' x 30'	180	124	100
40' x 40'	350	280	240

Choosing a tent site: When arranging tents with a single transparent vinyl side, consider the position of the sun during your event; if the clear portion faces due west through an evening event, the sunset may be blinding. Also, be certain that you do not pitch your tent over low or uneven ground that might accumulate water runoff.

Overlooked, but necessary, rental items: Portable restrooms are a very important rental item for a large function or event. Portable restrooms today are much improved from years past. They are attractive and function as a normal restroom. Nothing is more annoying than standing in line for a restroom while the awards are being presented or the speaker is beginning the speech.

Butterfly & Dove Magic

Release Beautiful Live Butterflies or Doves At Your Special Event!

For information or a brochure call (503) 774-9288

Add Fairytale Magic to Your Special Event!
A butterfly release is designed to make your special event enchanting and unforgettable. On that special day, we will deliver the butterflies to your event where you will distribute one box containing a butterfly to each guest. The guests will then release the butterflies at a specially designated moment and read time-honored "fortune cookie-type" passages related to your organization. A butterfly release occasion is great fun for all since it lets your guests participate in your event.

About the Doves
What could be more memorable than the breathtaking sight of 2 to 20 snow white birds circling the horizon and flying off into the heavens in celebration of your special event? Your guests will be awed by their grace and amazed at the unique way you have presented your event! Doves in gorgeous gilded cages can also be placed at the entry way of your event to set your guests a flutter.

About the Butterflies
The butterflies are indoor-bred by the Northwest's most experienced butterfly company. The butterflies are well treated and are fed the day of the event, and there is no need to raise the butterflies yourself.

Butterfly/Dove Combination Package
Now you can experience both butterflies and doves together at a very special price!

Reservations
To best ensure your reservation, it is recommended you order 6–8 weeks before your event. A 50% deposit is required at the time of the order and the balance is due 15 days before the event.

Availability
Butterflies: May–September
Doves: Throughout the year

Custom Chair Covers

The Pacific Northwest's Original Chair Cover Rental Company

(800) 994-1055

AFFORDABLE ELEGANCE FOR ALL YOUR SPECIAL EVENTS!

We can Bring your Decorating Ideas and Theme to Life…

Let us help you bring your ideas and party theme to life with chair covers that will make your special event extraordinary, not ordinary.

- Banquets
- Reunions
- Grand Openings
- Receptions
- Anniversaries
- Special Events
- Holiday Parties
- Award Parties
- Picnics

With Custom Chair Covers Designed to Match…

We work with you to coordinate all of the decor with chair covers as well as all your theme decorations. Our chair covers are available in a variety of assorted colors or fabulous brocades.

Formal or Fun, we Provide the Extra Touches…

At Custom Chair Covers, we provide you with matching or contrasting bows or decorations that will complement and enhance your event colors and theme. Whether you want them to match your flowers or table linens or add a fun note to the occasion, we always coordinate everything to your theme and room decor.

Or Let our Logo Chair Covers and Tops Enhance your Promotional Efforts…

At Custom Chair Covers, we offer an entire division dedicated to manufacturing custom promotional items. You can duplicate your company's logo, feature the guest of honor's name, include the company motto, feature a new product being introduced, or incorporate your event name. Use your imagination; we'll do the rest.

- Chair Covers
- Head Rests
- Chair Backs
- Putter Covers
- Sport Eye Glass Cover
- Bike Helmets

Custom Chair Covers
Making Ordinary Chairs… Extraordinary
For Rental or Sales Information, Please Call
(800) 994-1055

Please let this business know that you heard about them from the Bravo! Event Resource Guide.

ELECTRONIC POLLING

ELWAY RESEARCH, INC.
2101 Ninth Avenue, Suite 211
Seattle, Washington 98121
Contact: Jone Howard
(206) 264-1500; Fax (206) 264-0301
E-mail: egis@elwaypoll.com

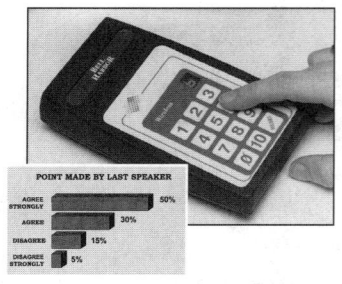

Conduct Fun and Productive Meetings With Electronic Polling

With EGIS, the Electronic Group Interaction System, each meeting participant is able to instantly respond to material being presented through an individual keypad. Participants' responses are continuously recorded on the systems computer. Results can be projected for viewing by all participants or displayed to meeting organizers on a monitor in a separate room. The data is saved—available for statistical analysis.

- **Anonymous response and instantaneous display of group responses** means more productive meetings.
- **EGIS keeps the process moving and on task**. As participants register their opinions, tabulated results are displayed to the group for further consideration.
- **Diverging opinions are revealed**. One group's answers can be instantly compared with another's, and/or with information gathered from a source outside the meeting.
- **Everyone participates, equally and continuously**. Because participants register their responses anonymously, they are included equally—without regard to verbal skills, language barriers, or willingness to speak up in a meeting.

EGIS Enables Participants to
- Remain actively engaged in a meeting
- Feel motivated to participate
- Stay continuously involved

EGIS Enables Meeting Organizers to
- Measure participant attitudes on key questions
- Monitor response as the meeting takes place
- Direct/redirect based on participant response
- Get information to the right people
- Enhance team building

Instant Surveys: What do Participants think about
- Important Issues?
- The points the speaker just made?
- The future of the organization?
- A question from the floor?
- The topic of the next speaker?

Move to Consensus
- Participants see how their views match those of the group.
- Questions can be reformulated as the discussion evolves.

Question On the Fly
- Questions can be added as quickly as you can type.
- Results are displayed within five seconds!

Vote
- EGIS tallies and reports votes instantly.

Elway Research Offers a Complete Range of Meeting Services
- Equipment Rental
- Meeting Facilitation
- Question Design
- Hard Copy Charts
- Polling Facilitation
- Data Analysis and Report

CALL FOR A FREE CONSULTATION ON YOUR NEXT MEETING!

Please let this business know that you heard about them from the Bravo! Event Resource Guide.

EVENT RENTAL COMMUNICATIONS, INC.

2422 S.E. Hawthorne Street
Portland, Oregon 97214
Contact: Jay Pomeroy or Heather Ware
(503) 232-9031
Business Hours: Mon–Fri 8am–5:30pm
E-mail: Eventcomm@aol.com

Motorola Radio Rentals
Now when you make a snap decision, you can get the word to the people who have to hear it, in a snap.

Rental Equipment
Motorola two-way radios, mobile radios, satellite phones, portable as well as on site repeaters, cellular phones, and pagers.

Specialty Items
Base stations, headsets, speaker microphones, ear pieces, ear microphones, surveillance kits, chest packs, holsters, spare rapid charge batteries, and rapid chargers.

Services Offered
Free multi-channel programming on our UHF/VHF frequencies or yours. Twenty-four hour support service available for emergencies.

Ordering and Delivery
Equipment is available for rent by the day, week, month, or year. Reservations are recommended so that we can guarantee item availability for your event. We ship nationwide. In-town delivery is available; fees vary.

Commitment to Excellence
Accessibility, a qualified staff, prompt responses, and a working knowledge of deadlines have helped us build a successful working relationship with our customers.

At Event Rental Communications, we pride ourselves on working with our customers individually to design temporary communication systems to fit the specific needs of our clientele.

We'll let the results speak for themselves.
NATIONWIDE TOLL FREE
1-800-283-2666

Watercraft Rentals, Inc.
Columbia River • Hagg Lake • Wilsonville

3409 N.E. Marine Drive
Portland, Oregon 97211
Contact: Shawn Karambelas
(503) 284-6447; Fax (503) 281-9154
E-mail: SKJSKI@aol.com
Web site: www.quikpage.com/skwaterent

Corporate and Group Events
What better way to show your co-workers a great time at your next picnic, sales meeting, or team building event than a sunny afternoon of fun on the water! Whether it is a group of 15 or 500, we will meet your every need. Our trained staff will deliver the watercraft, set up buoys, speak to your group about safety, and will remain on site for the entire event to ensure everything runs smoothly and safely. Some of the most popular sites we use are: Kelly Point Park, Lake Merwin, Wilsonville Park, Hagg Lake, Rooster Rock and Frenchman's Bar.

Experienced Staff
With experienced staff, our proven success and only the newest, most reliable watercraft, we promise to be the hit of the party! SK Watercraft Rentals is the largest watercraft rental operation in the state of Oregon with three locations and experience in the business since 1993. With everything you are planning, the last thing you have to worry about is the operational details.

Our Watercraft Fleet
We update our entire fleet every year.
- Stand-ups .... Yamaha Super Jet (63hp)
- Two-Seaters .... Sea-Doo GS (85hp)
- Three-Seaters ...... Sea-Doo GTS (85hp)
- Ski Boats .... Bayliner 1850 Capri LS (190hp)

Watercraft Group Tours
We offer staff accompanied tours of many scenic areas including:
- Columbia River Gorge
- Portland Waterfront
- Portland to the Coast
- Oregon City Falls
- Multnomah Falls

**Whatever the Event, SK Watercraft Rentals, Inc.
Can Really Add Some Excitement to Your Next Party!**

A TO Z PARTY RENTAL

995 Commercial Street, S.E.
Salem, Oregon 97302
Business Hours: Mon–Sat 7:30am–5:30pm; Sun noon–4pm
(503) 585-7782; Fax (503) 362-8647

RENTAL SERVICES

A to Z Party Rental is a
full-service, special event supplier.
Our large inventory of equipment and
supplies will ensure a successful event.

Knowledgeable Staff
Our staff will work with you to sort out the details for your event. Years of experience are at your disposal with proven success. You can count on receiving your rentals and purchases as ordered and ready for use with no worries or hassles. Our job is to make you a guest of your own party or event.

Ordering and Delivery
Our delivery rates are determined per zone and amount of time and man-power required.

Equipment and Accessories
- Tables and chairs
- Canopies
- Candelabras and pew abras
- Fencing and panels
- Audiovisuals
- Food preparation equipment
- Barbecues and crab pots
- Silk arrangements
- China and glassware
- Cutlery
- Arches
- Party lighting
- Chafers, trays, salad bars
- Stanchions, traffic cones
- Balloon bouquets
- *Please call for complete list*

Merchandise
- Items available in 23 colors:
  Plates, cups, napkins, cutlery, tablecovers, and tablerolls
- Balloons, balloon bouquets, candles, and arches also available

**We Can Special Order Merchandise For You—
Ask For Details!**

DELIVERY SERVICE AVAILABLE

Please let this business know that you heard about them from the Bravo! Event Resource Guide.

RENTAL SERVICES

BARBUR BLVD. RENTALS

BBR

BARBUR BLVD. RENTALS, INC.

♦ 246·4268 ♦

8205 S.W. Barbur Blvd. • Portland, Oregon 97219
Fax (503) 246-9375
Business Hours: Mon–Sat 7:30am–6pm; Sun 8am–4pm

Trade Show and Convention Services
- Draped Exhibit Booths
- Exhibitor Support Service
- Electrical and Lighting
- Theme/Prop Design and Development
- Planning and Consultant Service

Party and Event Department
- Tables
- Chairs
- China
- Bars
- Skirts
- Margarita Machine
- Popcorn Machines
- Fencing
- Candles
- Disposable Plates
- Balloons
- Grape Arbur
- Tents and Canopies
- Silver Service
- Serving Trays
- Fountains
- Serving Utensils
- Barbecues
- Poker Tables
- Games
- Candelabras
- Disposable Plates
- Decorations
- Gazebo
- Pillars
- Glassware/Stemware
- Silver and Stainless Flatware
- Linen, Tablecloths and Napkins
- Punch Bowls
- Chafers
- Staging
- Power Taps
- Wedding Arches
- New Express Bars (in colors)
- Napkin Imprinting
- Hacienda Front
- Commercial Food Service Equipment
- New! Luminaries-special occasion designs candelabra 2″–3″ centerpieces in a variety of styles and colors-this is a must see!
- And much more, call one of our party consultants for more information…

Homeowner/Contractor Rentals
- Hand Tools
- Tractors
- Pressure Washers
- Fork Lifts
- Power Tools
- Cement Mixers
- Scaffolding
- Chippers
- Garden Equipment
- Paint Sprayers
- Trailers
- Beds/Wheelchairs

Audio/Visual Department
- Projectors
- TV/VCR's
- Big Screen TV
- PA Systems
- Podiums
- Wireless Mics/Lavaliere
- Karaoke
- Stereo Systems

Professional Assistance For 40 Years
Family-owned and operated. Barbur Blvd. Rentals takes pride in providing quality merchandise, equipment and service. Our experienced personnel are available to answer your questions and share their knowledge and ideas. Let Barbur Blvd. Rentals help make your event extra special!

THE PARTY PRO'S AT FOSTER RENTALS

5100 S.E. Foster Road
Portland, Oregon 97206
(503) 774-5508; Fax (503) 774-8563

THE PARTY PRO'S

2460 N.E. Griffin Oaks Street, Suite 1500
Hillsboro, Oregon 97124
(503) 844-9798; Fax (503) 844-2902

Business Hours: Mon–Sat 9am–5:30pm
E-mail: PARTYPRO1@juno.com
Web site: www.THEPARTYPROS.com

Rental Items Available

- **Canopies and tents**, helium tanks, dunk tank, tiki torches, bubble machine, karaoke machine, guest book stands, dance floors, staging, and more!
- **Tables and chairs:** banquet and round, umbrella tables; Samsonite folding chairs and white wood folding chairs
- **Linens:** fine-quality linens available in many different colors; banquet, 90″ round, 120″ round, skirting and napkins
- **Serving pieces:** punch bowls; chafing dishes; acrylic, stainless and silver: bowls, trays, tongs, spoons and servers; silver tea service; stainless flatware
- **Glassware:** champagne, round or fluted, punch, coffee, rocks, wine, pilsner, margarita, water, martini glasses, dessert dishes and Irish coffee mugs
- **China:** sophisticated ivory with gold trim and simple clear glass
- **Beverage service:** champagne fountains, coffee makers, insulated beverage dispensers, carafes, pitchers and beer taps
- **Centerpieces and decorations:** silk flower bouquets in your choice of colors, theme centerpieces, elegant/blacktie centerpieces, many ideas to custom fit your event

Specialty Retail Items

Decorations, centerpieces and ideas galore. Invitations, imprinted napkins, matchbooks and ribbons. Dripless candles available in many colors.

Tableware Retail Items

Paper tableware: floral and solid plates, cups and napkins. Plastic cups, cutlery, tablecloths, skirting, bowls and trays

Full On-site Decorating Service

We will come to your event site, design a decorating plan, provide a written proposal and on the day of the event implement everything. We will handle all setup and takedown. Give us a call to find out what ideas we have for your annual Christmas gala, company summer picnic, or celebration "We-did-it" party. References available upon request.

Ordering and Delivery

Reservations are highly recommended so that we can guarantee item availability for your special event. We are happy to deliver and pick up. Please call our party consultants for an estimate, or set up your free consultation. We'll be happy to come to you.

NO STANDARD IS TOO HIGH!

Our ultimate goal is total customer satisfaction during and after the hustle and bustle of your event planning. Large or small, we can make it happen for you!

INTERSTATE Special Events

5420 N. Interstate Avenue
Portland, Oregon 97217-4597
(503) 285-6685

At Interstate Special Events, we have everything you need—including the expertise, the attention to detail and the commitment to service—to make your event truly *special*. Our inventory contains a wide variety of items needed for every type of event. From casual to formal, we can supply your needs!

Tables, Chairs and Linens
We offer banquet, round, half-round, umbrella, bistro and stylish serpentine tables. Classic white wood chairs are available, as well as folding Samsonite, white Bistro and black, padded stacking chairs. Our table linens, skirting and napkins are available in a wide array of colors and sizes. And we now offer specialty one-of-a-kind theme linens.

Tents and Canopies
We have one of the largest canopy inventories in the area. Our tents range from 100 square feet to 18,000 square feet. Prices start at $95. We also supply elegant tent liners, pole sleeves, lighting and heating. Site inspections are available.

Tableware, Serviceware and Beverage Service
Our china styles include the classic white, elegant ivory with gold band and clear glass. Whatever the occasion, we have glassware in many styles to meet your needs. Stainless and silver flatware and serving accessories are available. We have many silver plate items such as tea service, punch bowls and chafing dishes as well as vases and bowls in glass, stainless, acrylic and silver. We offer porta-bars, beermeister, beverage fountains, kegtainers, coffeemakers and carafes, pitchers and insulated dispensers.

Additional Items
We carry a large inventory of concession equipment including briquet and propane BBQs, fryers, grills and griddles, gumbo pots and hot boxes. We specialize in staging and carry a large inventory of dance floors. If games are what you are looking for, we have bingo, volleyball, softball, horseshoes and even a Dunk Tank! And don't forget the helium tank. Also available to rent are overhead and slide projectors, screens, PA systems TVs, VCRs and even a bull horn.

Ordering and Delivery
Reservations are highly recommended to ensure availability and assistance in meeting your needs. Delivery is available as well as setup and take-down for a reasonable charge.

**Our Special Events Representatives are eager to assist with your event needs.
Please call us today for more information.**

See page 173 under Audiovisual & Communication Services.

The Party Place
A DIVISION OF PORTLAND RENT ALL

Eastside: 10101 S.E. Stark, Portland, Oregon (503) 252-3466
Westside: 8904 S.W. Canyon Road, Portland, Oregon (503) 292-8875

Web site: www.portlandrentall.com

TENTS AND CANOPIES

Sizes range from 10'x10' to our new 60'x160' New Century Tent. Styled with futuristic elegance, this beautiful tent will provide the right atmosphere to your next event. Also available: sidewall, liners, pole covers, lighting, heating, air conditioning and generators. Larger tent sizes available.

STAGING AND DANCE FLOOR
- Staging and stage skirting
- Dance floor available in wood parquet or black and white check.

TABLES AND CHAIRS
- 6' and 8' Banquet Tables
- Conference Tables
- 30", 36", 48", 60", 72" Round Tables
- Card and Serpentine Tables
- Childrens Tables
- White and Black Wood Folding Chairs
- Resin Black and White Bistro Chairs
- Brown, White or Ivory Samsonite Folding Chairs
- Black Stack Chairs (padded)
- Elegant Chivari Chairs
- Childrens Chairs

LINENS AND SERVICEWARE
- 46 colors available
- Banquet Cloths (60"x120")
- 90", 108", 120" Rounds
- Card Table Cloths
- Elegant Gathered Skirting or Box Skirts (prints also available)
- Chafers in Plain Stainless, Brass Trim
- Stainless or Silver Serviceware
- Stainless and Silver Trays (variety of sizes)
- Serving Bowls in Plastic, Glass or Silver
- Other Silver Pieces and Gold Holloware
- Coffee Makers and Insulated Dispensers

CHINA, GLASSWARE AND FLATWARE

Our china styles include Clear Glass, White, Ivory with a Gold Band, White with a Silver Band and Black Octagonal. We also offer a wide variety of glassware options, such as Crystal, Cutglass or Black Stem and our standard glass barware. From Margaritas to Martinis, you'll find the glassware you're looking for. Flatware styles available are plain stainless, hammered stainless or silverplate.

CONCESSION AND FOOD SERVICE EQUIPMENT
- Barbecues (propane or charcoal)
- Sno-cone and popcorn machines
- Hot dog cookers and cotton candy (supplies also available)
- Cambro insulated food pan carriers
- Electric hot boxes
- Portable oven
- Deep fat fryer

EVENT MERCHANDISE

We carry a vast selection of decorations, plastic and paper goods such as napkins, plates, cups and flatware, in over 25 colors. Also available, case pricing, and a large selection of catalogs for special orders. If we don't have the items you're looking for, we will be more than happy to refer you to someone who does.

PERSONALIZED SERVICE, QUALITY PRODUCTS AND PROMPT DELIVERY

141st & Tualatin Valley Highway
Beaverton, Oregon 97005
(503) 641-6778
Mon–Sat 7:30am–6pm; Sun 8am–4:30pm

Rental Items Available *(call for free brochure)*

- **Business Meetings:** Formica conference tables in various sizes. Linens and skirting with a corporate look. Padded folding chairs. Coffee makers and servers. China, glassware, and flatware. Coat racks and hangers.
- **Trade Shows:** Plywood tables in various sizes. Linens and skirting. Samsonite folding chairs. Convention pipe and drapery. Staging and skirting and/or drapery background. Stanchions and carpet runners.
- **Audiovisual Equipment:** Portable and professional sound systems. Wireless micophones. Hand-held tour guides and bull horns. TV sets and VCR players. Big screen video projectors with computer interface. Camcorders, Karaokes. Overhead, movie, and opaque projectors. Slide projectors with carts, stands, and screens. Easels, flip charts, and eraser boards.
- **Convention and Serving Equipment:** Hot dog cookers, popcorn poppers, cotton candy, snow cone, ice shaver, milk shake machines and ice cream cart. Drink dispensers, blenders. Meat slicers, deep fat fryers. Propane cookers, griddles, steam tables, holding ovens, hot plates, and warming trays. Chafers in various styles with pans. Coffee makers.
- **Picnics and Parties:** Bars and beer coolers/taps. Barbecues and accessories. Dance floors. Games: volleyball, horseshoes, softball, tug-o-war, croquet and dunk tank. Round tables with umbrellas.
- **Party Tents:** Free standing from 10'x10' to 30'x60' plus sidewalls, windows, liners, lighting and heaters.
- **Lighting and Special Effects** for parties and shows: beacons, strobe, traffic, black, quartz halogen and color wheel. Mirror ball, bubble and fog machine, confetti cannon, waterfalls, fountains. Grand Opening banners, ground breaking shovel, ribbon cutting scissors. Artificial flowers, plants, and trees.
- **Tables, Chairs and Linens-Skirting:** Many sizes, styles and colors.
- **China, and Flatware:** Ivory, white, black, and clear. Stainless or silverplate
- **Glassware:** Contemporary, lead crystal or utility, stemware, barware, misc.
- **Plastic, Acrylic and Stainless:** Salad bars, bowls, tubs, serving items.
- **Silver and Gold Holloware:** For elegant entertaining: punch bowls, trays, coffee/tea service, candelabra, wine coolers, champagne or punch fountains, floral pieces.
- **Balloons and Helium:** Balloons in 45 colors, 2 sizes, and mylars. Helium tanks in 8 sizes with delivery service and long-term rates.

Snead's Party Time welcomes your inquires and promises top customer service. We are open seven days a week, will take advance reservations and provide delivery service. We offer credit, quantity discounts, and a salesperson to come to your location.

(503) 641-6778

Since 1958
a division of Peter Corvallis Productions, Inc.

SPECIAL EVENTS CO.

79 S.W. Oak Street
Portland, Oregon 97204
Contact: Athena Corvallis
(503) 222-1664
Fax (503) 222-1047
Business Hours: Mon-Sat 8am–7pm

WE PUT THE *SPECIAL* IN *SPECIAL EVENTS*

Imagine going to just one place for all your event and meeting planning needs. There is such a place. The event coordinators at Special Events Co. are experts at turning any occasion into "a special event."

★ Tent and Canopy Rentals
Tents and canopies in sizes ranging from 10'x10' to 100'x500', including the free span Hoecker, tent accessories: clear sidewall, French window wall, pole swags, tent fabric liners, heaters, carpeting, flooring, globe lights and chandeliers.

★ Party Rentals
Tables, chairs, china, silver, flatware, glassware, catering equipment, stages, dance floors, linens and overlays in all colors and patterns.

★ Theme Decorations
Over 100 themes for you to decorate with. Our collection has the most authentic props available to the public. Some of the most well known are Western, Mardi Gras, Fifties, Renaissance, Hollywood, Putting on the Ritz, Central Park, International, Hawaiian, Mexican, Volcano, Safari, Pirates, Carnival and Circus.

★ Audiovisual Services and Rentals
The largest inventory of event meeting and conference equipment that includes video and television systems, projectors, screens, microphones, podiums, sound systems, computers, lighting, and special effects.

★ Convention and Trade Show Services and Rentals
Pipe, drape, and table skirting in all colors. Exhibit booth displays and furnishings, signage, freight, electrical, carpeting and show design.

"We Put It All Together For You"

Our company has 39 years experience in the event industry, providing a level of dedication of service excellence for thousands of companies.

Special Events Co. can offer you planning services, design and consultation, and endless idea possibilities…all part of our service at no added expense to you. Our inventory spans three city blocks of warehouses and offices and our photo library of thousands of our customers' events is always available for your viewing.

RENTAL SERVICES

1400 N.W. 15th Avenue
Portland, Oregon 97209
(503) 294-0412; Fax (503) 294-0616
Business Hours: Mon–Sat 8:30am–6pm
Appointments available any hour

Services
West Coast Event Productions is the Northwest's premier idea center for all events and special occasions. We specialize in the custom planning and design of event staging, lighting, sound, special effects, audiovisual presentations, tabletop décor, and event and theme production. We are able to tailor your event or special occasion to mirror your vision. We are here to help you make all your important event planning decisions. Please feel free to visit our newly designed showroom. Browse for ideas with our Photo Inventory Books. We have many of our specialty props, catering items and equipment displayed to aid in your event planning.

Rental Items Available
Tents and canopies: Sizes range from 10' x 10' to 100' x 200'+ and vary in color from solid white to striped red, green, blue or yellow. Custom tent decorating includes elegant fabric liner, fabric tent pole covers in any color, floral garlands, ambient tent lighting and twinkle lights. French and Cathedral window sidewalls, heaters, air conditioning and flooring are also available.

Wedding accessories: Select from several styles of candelabras, brass and silver table candelabras, brass and contemporary full standing candelabras; wedding aisle and carpet runners; custom chuppah; gazebos and arches; wood, ceramic, marble finish and Grecian columns; table accessories include urns, vases, hurricanes, votives, cherubs and table lamps.

Tables and chairs: Choose from our complete selection of tables and chairs in a variety of sizes and styles: White wood garden chairs, black wood chairs, gold ballroom chairs, folding and stacking chairs. *Ask about our new specialty chair covers.*

China, flatware, glassware and serviceware: Impressive selection of china in 14 different patterns: ivory with gold or silver, white, black octagon and clear octagon. Solid colors in red, yellow, blue and green, formal bone china, contemporary patterns. Stainless, silverplate and goldplate flatware. Glassware for every occasion. Catering items for food service and many other items available.

Sound system, lighting and audiovisual: Complete array of sound equipment from amplifiers, microphone and mixing counsels to high-end data projectors. We offer a variety of unique lighting fixtures and special effects for outdoor receptions.

Stage and dance floor: An assortment of floors from elegant oak parquet to black and white, all white, or colored checks. Elevated foundations for ceremony, head table riser and entertainment—all attractively carpeted and skirted.

Portland now has *Skydancers! Skydancers* are 20-foot tall brightly colored tubular balloon people that dance and sway under a large turbine fan. As seen at the 1998 Super Bowl. Perfect for grand openings and high profile events.

Themes & Props

THEMES AND PROPS

THEMES AND PROPS

HELPFUL HINTS

Why use a theme? A theme provides interest and coherence for the attendees. Planning is more efficient with a theme, creating an automatically organized process. In addition, the key to a successful event is audience participation. The more involved people become in the event they are attending, the more likely they are to enjoy themselves and remember the experience. Attendees may not remember the name of the keynote speaker, but they will remember the "Wacky Olympics" special event!

When is a theme appropriate? Anytime you have an event. When done properly, themes can be used to enhance a business meeting, client appreciation, awards event, and even reunions.

How is a theme chosen? Define the goals of your event first, what you want to accomplish with the event, who is attending, and what you want them to take away with them. Then, you can decide what theme options may work.

Creative Brainstorming: Producing a new idea that ties in with the event can be a great challenge. An effective way of coming up with new and innovative ideas is to work with a group of people to draw synergy out of fun, cooperative teamwork to produce ideas and solutions. Find a meeting space free of distraction: phones, foot traffic, etc. A storyboard can be helpful in this meeting so that all ideas can be captured with an open-mind. Some of the smallest ideas can turn into the best campaigns.

Make sure it is the right theme or concept: The best ideas can end up a failure unless the details of the theme and campaign are thought out. Ask specific questions like: Does it fit within the organizations' image? Will it offend any of our products, customers or employees? Is it one people will remember? Is the message clear, or lost within the creative? Is it an idea to be proud of and put in the portfolio?

Are theme events expensive? They don't have to be. It depends on your budget. Some of your theme ideas can be accomplished with a small budget if you and your committee are willing to spend the time. However, a much better use of your time and money may be to use a meeting planner, prop, or entertainment company.

Decorating tips for theme events: Consider three to four main areas of the facility for theme props. Main focus areas can include the entryway to the event, stage, guest tables, beverage and food stations, to name a few.

Check-out props and displays: A visit to the prop shop or decorator will allow you the opportunity to see the quality, size and color of the prop. While at the warehouse- browse to see what other props and displays they have. This trip may awaken an idea several months later for a future project.

Theme ideas for your next event:

- Casino Night
- M•A•S•H
- Cruise Ship
- Mexican Fiesta
- Western/ Wild West
- International Themes
- Fabulous 50s
- The Jazz Club
- Around the World
- Treasure/Scavenger Hunt
- Indiana Jones Adventure
- Winter Wonderland
- Tropical Island
- Underwater
- Tropical Rain Forest
- Circus! Circus!
- Hawaiian Luau
- The Great Northwest
- State Fair
- Chinese New Year
- Toy Chest
- Futuristic Fantasies
- Murder and Mystery
- South of the Border
- African Jungle
- Mardi Gras
- Medieval Castle
- Nautical
- Great Gatsby Party
- Super Bowl
- Beach Party
- Haunted Halloween
- Hollywood

PARADYM EVENTS

3025 S.W. First Avenue
Portland, Oregon 97201
(503) 219-9290; Fax (503) 525-0675
Web site: www.ParadymEvents.com

- Creative
- Artistic
- Unique
- Style
- Originality
- Imagination
- Elegance
- Visual
- Design
- Expertise
- Color
- Cutting Edge

(503) 219-9290
www.ParadymEvents.com

5406 N. Albina Avenue • Portland, Oregon 97217
(503) 283-8828; Fax (503) 283-3651
Please call for an appointment
E-mail: propsh@aol.com • Web site: www.propshop.com

Full-Service Event Decorating and Design

The Prop Shop team assists you with the development of your theme and transforms it into a full design concept. Custom-designed backdrops, scenery, lighting, and our award-winning staff are just some of the ways we make your event a unique success.

Producing Events of All Sizes

Our internationally recognized team of designers and decorators create your theme using our extensive inventory or will custom-design something new. We create your entire event, including site inspection, design, fabrication, delivery setup and take down.

- **Corporate Events**
  Awards Ceremony, Customer Appreciation, Anniversary Celebration, Holiday Party, Sales Meeting

- **Conventions**
  Welcome Ceremony, Interactive Seminars, Opening Night Party, Awards Ceremony, Closing Night Gala

- **Trade Shows**
  Show Management, Theme Decorations, Interactive Booth Design, Special Product Incorporation

- **Non-Profit Events**
  Auctions, Fund-raisers, Open Houses

- **Festivals and Picnics**
  Company Picnics, Outdoor Festivals, Holiday Celebrations

A few of our more popular themes are: Mardi Gras, Parisian, Art Deco, Latin American, Hollywood, Tropical, Nautical, Western, and Circus.

ACEP Board Member • POVA Member

See M & M Balloons, page 209 under Decorations, Florists & Balloons.

1400 N.W. 15th Avenue
Portland, Oregon 97209
(503) 294-0412; Fax (503) 294-0616
Business Hours: Mon–Sat 8:30am–6pm
Appointments available any hour

Services
West Coast Event Productions is the Northwest's premier idea center for all events and special occasions. We specialize in the custom planning and design of event staging, lighting, sound, special effects, audiovisual presentations, tabletop décor, and event and theme production. We are able to tailor your event or special occasion to mirror your vision. We are here to help you make all your important event planning decisions.

Custom Themes
West Coast Event Production's visual department is deft in the handling and design of props for thematic events. We work with our clients to construct a concept that mirrors the client's vision. The staff at West Coast Event Productions has the experience and creativity to produce events of any size or budget from small gatherings to large corporate events. Please feel free to visit our newly designed showroom. Browse for ideas with our Photo Inventory Books. We have many of our specialty props, catering items and equipment displayed to aid in your event planning.

Rental Items Available
Theme Décor: West Coast designers work in tandem with your project manager to create the perfect environment or individual features, which solve design problems or enhance the mood of your event. Between our Portland, Bend and Las Vegas locations, our collection of sets and props is one of the largest available outside of Hollywood. And what we do not have already, we can build to your specifications. The West Coast reputation is one of total commitment to quality work, creativity and thorough professionalism in everything we do.

Props: We have an extensive inventory of props to support hundreds of themes. Our selection offers columns, statues, waterfalls, oversize rocks, artificial plants, fiberglass animals, architectural shapes and elements, drapery, special effects, games, antiques and memorabilia, and almost anything else from small hand props to giant set pieces.

Table Top: West Coast's unique approach to table top design affords you an unusual selection of ideas. Indoors or out, big or small, with fountains and waterfalls, non-floral theme centerpieces, topiaries, statuary, sculptures, garlands, opulent bouquets and leafy accents, our designers will create a magical focal point for your tables and buffets.

Millennium: Like never before, West Coast offers spectacular ideas for the upcoming New Years celebrations in several categories: Elegant, Futuristic, Theme, and Contemporary. Our collection of special effects equipment will add that needed "wow" at the stroke of midnight. Plan early for the best selection!

Portland now has Skydancers! Skydancers are 20-foot tall brightly colored tubular balloon people that dance and sway under a large turbine fan. As seen at the Olympic Games and Super Bowl. Perfect for grand openings and high profile events.

See page 194 under Rental Services.
See page 401 under Convention & Exhibition Services.

Notes

Decorations, Florists & Balloons

Butterfly Release
Ice Carvings
Chair Covers

HELPFUL HINTS

Kinds of party supplies: Be sure to stop by a party supply store for many great ideas. You will discover fun ways to decorate—from crepe paper to balloons in every color imaginable. A party supply store can help you with special themes and ideas for decorating tables, walls, ceilings, and floors!

Case or bulk discounts: Be sure to inquire about discounts when buying large quantities of items. You may want to consider renting a tank of helium so you can coordinate your own balloon decorations and save money.

Special-occasion decorations: Party shops carry a large selection of party decorations and accessories for theme events, birthdays, anniversaries, etc. Theme-coordinated decorations are very popular—matching plates, napkins, cups, invitations, plus many other accessories. Gift supplies include coordinated wrapping paper, ribbon, gift bags, tissue, cards, and more.

Balloon ideas: Balloons are an inexpensive means of decorating and provide a dramatic visual effect. Balloons often are used to enhance a room and can also be used to hide flaws in walls or ceilings. Balloons can be sculpted in any shape you desire. Arches made with helium balloons enhance entrances, dance floors, and buffet tables. A fun idea is to have a balloon release with special notes inside the balloons. These are certified balloon specialists to help you decide how to decorate with balloons. **NOTE: Some facilities do not allow balloons. Check to be sure they are allowed before you place your balloon order.**

Colors of balloons: Balloons come in a wide variety of colors, sizes, and styles. A special theme color can be created by placing a balloon of one color inside another of a different color.

Imprinted balloons: Balloons can be imprinted with your business logo or event name and date.

Rental decorations: Rental decorations come in a variety of choices—ficus trees with twinkle lights, waterfalls, and fountains. You can create any visual effect you want with the right decorations. An underwater theme is fun with live fish in bowls on the tables as centerpieces. Netting and garland for seaweed hanging from the ceiling creates the illusion of being underwater. Refer to rental companies in this Guide in the Event Rentals section or party supply stores.

HELPFUL HINTS

Selecting a florist: Most florists have a portfolio of their work. Ask for references and see what customers have to say about them. Choose a florist who will spend time with you. If the florist has not been to the site of the event, you may want to take him or her to view the decor. This ensures that they design arrangements that match the surroundings and can be very helpful when you are discussing your ideas and needs. Your florist can also inform you about what flowers will be in season and styles that will appropriately fit your theme and budget.

Develop a plan: Think about your floral design and decorations and write your ideas down. Determine what you will need from the various people involved and have a budget in mind. Ask several florists for formal bids based on your outline, then determine which florist and budget you feel most comfortable with.

Sample Arrangements are a good idea: It might be a good idea to request a sample arrangement prior to your special event, especially if the order placed is very large and if the idea you are trying out is a new one and photos are not available. This way there will be no surprises the day of the event for florist, decorator and coordinator.

Meeting with the florist: You should meet with your florist as soon as possible. A florist can be very helpful in the beginning phases of choosing your theme and can offer decoration ideas that emphasize that theme throughout the event.

Developing rapport with your florist and decorator: After several events with the same vendor you can build a great team of idea generators. They begin thinking of ways to add that extra special touch to your events. Your vendors become your extended staff and will do what it takes to accomplish the job, so treat them well and show your appreciation.

Creative ways of financing flowers and decorations: For a fund raiser, you can auction the centerpieces right off the tables. At an awards function, the winners can bring home flowers with the award, or you can thank those who helped with the function by giving them the table arrangements. Potted plants also make a long-lasting gift.

Delivery and setup of flowers: It is crucial that your flowers be delivered at the right time. They shouldn't arrive earlier than necessary since some facilities are not air conditioned and certain flowers deteriorate rapidly. If your flowers must be in place at a certain time, be sure to tell your florist what time they'll be needed. Always put the location and date on your contract, as well as the desired time of delivery, so there are no questions or last-minute problems. Check to see if the bid includes setup and delivery. If it doesn't, be sure to adjust your budget to include these costs.

Butterfly & Dove Magic

Release Beautiful Live Butterflies or Doves At Your Special Event!

For information or a brochure call (503) 774-9288

Add Fairytale Magic to Your Special Event!
A butterfly release is designed to make your special event enchanting and unforgettable. On that special day, we will deliver the butterflies to your event where you will distribute one box containing a butterfly to each guest. The guests will then release the butterflies at a specially designated moment and read time-honored "fortune cookie-type" passages related to your organization. A butterfly release occasion is great fun for all since it lets your guests participate in your event.

About the Doves
What could be more memorable than the breathtaking sight of 2 to 20 snow white birds circling the horizon and flying off into the heavens in celebration of your special event? Your guests will be awed by their grace and amazed at the unique way you have presented your event! Doves in gorgeous gilded cages can also be placed at the entry way of your event to set your guests a flutter.

About the Butterflies
The butterflies are indoor-bred by the Northwest's most experienced butterfly company. The butterflies are well treated and are fed the day of the event, and there is no need to raise the butterflies yourself.

Butterfly/Dove Combination Package
Now you can experience both butterflies and doves together at a very special price!

Reservations
To best ensure your reservation, it is recommended you order 6–8 weeks before your event. A 50% deposit is required at the time of the order and the balance is due 15 days before the event.

Availability
Butterflies: May–September
Doves: Throughout the year

PROFESSIONAL ICE CARVING
*Sculptor: **Christopher Huessy***
Contact: Dennise Huessy

Warehouse	Office
(503) 557-0650	(503) 654-0075

Traditional Sizes
- Full Size: 20" by 40" • Half Size: 20" by 20" • Individual Table Centerpieces

All sizes are available in clear or with color. Some specialty carvings include roses frozen in the ice. Carving detail generally lasts four to six hours.

Professional Background
Professional Ice Carving is a well-established full-time business. Our sculptor, Christopher Huessy, is a talented ice carver with over 25 years of experience. In addition to private affairs, we are currently servicing over 90 of the finest caterers, clubs, hotels, restaurants and professional organizations within the Portland Metropolitan area. Christopher is a leader in his industry, having custom designed and built his own ice block machine that produces 300-pound clear block ice, thus to ensure the quality of our product.

International Competition Medals and Honors
1999 – Gold medal – Lake Louise, Alberta, Canada
1998 – Competitor – The Nagano Winter Olympics Ice Carving Competition – Karuizawa, Japan
1997 – Sapporo Snow Festival – Sapporo, Japan
1996 – Gold medal – Anchorage, Alaska
1996 – Gold medal – Asahikaiwa, Japan
1994 – Gold medal – Fairbanks, Alaska

Christopher competes internationally to continue to offer "cutting edge" technology and to remain up-to-date on styles and trends.

Corporate Focus
Ice sculptures are a classic expression of prestige. Our ability to create an image in ice is as vast as your imagination. All sculptures are handcarved with artistic flair, and various images can be created for all kinds of events, from the "traditional" to "contemporary." We pride ourselves on our ability to reproduce business logos, complete with color. From practical shapes to extravagant masterpieces, you can rest assured you are in qualified hands.

Services
We take care of the details. What sets us apart is not just our ice carving but our consulting, delivery, safety, setup and expertise. Call for a personal appointment, and we'll be happy to assist you in creating an extraordinary event. We welcome your ideas and work with you to create the perfect affair!

Endorsements

Golf & Country Clubs	Hotels & Inns	Retail Chains
Columbia Edgewater Country Club	Benson Hotel	AT&T Wireless
Multnomah Athletic Club	DoubleTree Hotels	Ben Bridge
Oregon Golf Club	Hilton Hotel	Fred Meyer
Portland Golf Club	Holiday Inns	Meier & Frank
Pumpkin Ridge Golf Club	RiverPlace Hotel	Nordstrom
The Reserve Vineyards & Golf Club	Timberline Lodge	Safeway

INTEL • NIKE • OHSU • OMSI • OREGON CONVENTION CENTER • PSU • ROSE FESTIVAL ASSOC. • US BANK

We invite comparison

Please let this business know that you heard about them from the Bravo! Event Resource Guide.

CUSTOM CHAIR COVERS

Custom Chair Covers
The Pacific Northwest's Original Chair Cover Rental Company
(800) 994-1055

AFFORDABLE ELEGANCE FOR ALL YOUR SPECIAL EVENTS!

We can Bring your Decorating Ideas and Theme to Life...

Let us help you bring your ideas and party theme to life with chair covers that will make your special event extraordinary, not ordinary.

- Banquets
- Reunions
- Grand Openings
- Receptions
- Anniversaries
- Special Events
- Holiday Parties
- Award Parties
- Picnics

With Custom Chair Covers Designed to Match...

We work with you to coordinate all of the decor with chair covers as well as all your theme decorations. Our chair covers are available in a variety of assorted colors or fabulous brocades.

Formal or Fun, we Provide the Extra Touches...

At Custom Chair Covers, we provide you with matching or contrasting bows or decorations that will complement and enhance your event colors and theme. Whether you want them to match your flowers or table linens or add a fun note to the occasion, we always coordinate everything to your theme and room decor.

Or Let our Logo Chair Covers and Tops Enhance your Promotional Efforts...

At Custom Chair Covers, we offer an entire division dedicated to manufacturing custom promotional items. You can duplicate your company's logo, feature the guest of honor's name, include the company motto, feature a new product being introduced, or incorporate your event name. Use your imagination; we'll do the rest.

- Chair Covers
- Head Rests
- Chair Backs
- Putter Covers
- Sport Eye Glass Cover
- Bike Helmets

Custom Chair Covers
Making Ordinary Chairs... Extraordinary
For Rental or Sales Information, Please Call
(800) 994-1055

See page 183 under Rental Services.

1256 N.W. 175th Place • Beaverton, Oregon 97006
Contact: Cheryl Skoric, CBA
(503) 629-5827; Fax (503) 645-9404
Oregon's first Certified Balloon Artist
Business Hours: Day or evening by appointment

Bouquets & Balloons

BALLOON DECOR

More than your ordinary florist
Flowers ❀ Balloons ❀ Theme Creation
We offer beautiful floral arrangements, but we are experts in creating balloon themes.

Corporate Events • Conventions • Trade Shows • Banquets • Theme Parties • Special Events • Company Picnics • Grand Openings • Carnivals & Fairs • Shopping Mall Promotions •

As Corporate Specialists
Bouquets & Balloons offers services designed to simplify your job while providing you with imaginative ideas and unsurpassed service.
• Free consultation at the event site, your location, or ours
• Free delivery and setup in the Portland metropolitan area

Theme Parties
Balloons are the perfect decorating alternative for any occasion or event. Arches, columns, swags, balloon drops and sculptures can highlight the focal points of your event and give the room an air of festivity and elegance. Try Futuristic, Tropical, Fantasy, Carnival, Mardi Gras, Wine Fest, '50s, Under the Sea and Western, just to name a few.

Special Effects
Do you want to create Excitement? Exploding Balloons filled with confetti, balloons, movie tickets or anything else you desire, exploded over the crowd will inspire them. Do you have something that you would like to hide until a specific time? Try the Exploding Wall. Sure to be a crowd pleaser.

Balloon Ideas
Logos • Chinese Lanterns • Cactus • Tumbleweeds • Wagons • Santa Claus • Snowmen • Tin Soldiers • Sea Horses • Octopus • Fish • Waves • Bubbles • Dance Canopies

Floral Ideas
Stage Decor • Buffet Flowers • Centerpieces • Podium Arrangements • Head Table Arrangements • Presentation Bouquets • Corsages • Boutonnieres • Sign-in Table Arrangement

Note: Some facilities do not allow helium-filled balloons. But if you like the looks of balloons, check with us, we specialize in air-filled balloon decorations.

Please let this business know that you heard about them from the Bravo! Event Resource Guide.

BALLOON DECOR

The Final Touch
Floral Design & Balloon Decor
Contact: Wynn and Lindy Bell (503) 579-9499, Shop (503) 579-5999
Web site: www.balloonsandflowers.com

Providing creative and exciting event decor since 1987
Special Rates for Event Planners
Corporate Quantity Discounts

- Holiday Parties
- Trade Shows
- Meetings
- Casino Nights
- Charity Events
- Proms

- Millennium Celebrations
- Banquets
- Theme-Related Events
- Parade Floats
- Conventions
- Bar/Bat Mitzvahs

Balloon and Floral Designs
- Bulk Balloons
- Logos
- Props
- Entrances
- Podiums
- Stage and Photo Backdrops
- Lighted Walls
- Custom Linens and Chaircovers

- Exploding Walls
- Sculptures
- Centerpieces
- Dance Floors
- Florals
- Hanging Lights
- Special Effects
- Dissolving Garland

Wynn and Lindy Bell, Certified Balloon Artists
International Balloon Arts Convention
   1997 Large Sculpture–First Place
   1998 Large Sculpture–First Place

Wynn and Lindy's decor designs have been featured in *Special Event Magazine, Event Solutions Magazine,* The CBS Morning Show, *Modern Bride Magazine, Signature Bride Magazine, Weddings With Style Magazine.*

Visit our Web site to view our full collection of exciting and creative decor ideas and designs:
www.balloonsandflowers.com

BALLOON CO.
A DIVISION OF THE PROP SHOP

5406 N. Albina Avenue
Portland, Oregon 97217
(503) 283-2180
Fax (503) 283-3651
Please call for an appointment
E-mail: M1MBalloon@aol.com
Web site: www.propshop.com

Creative Balloon Imagery For Every Occasion

M & M Balloon Company specializes in custom-designed balloon sculptures and decor for every kind of event, from large corporate parties to company picnics, grand openings to fundraisers for non-profits, small birthday celebrations to elegant weddings. We work with you to create unique results for your special occasion.

Theme Parties

M & M Balloon Company uses centerpieces, sculptures, special effects, and bouquets to make every theme event exciting! A few of our most popular themes are: Tropical, Sports, '50s, Carnival, Mardi Gras, Fiesta, Hollywood, Western and Nautical.

- **Sculptures**—M & M Balloon specializes in designing memorable, eye-catching backdrops of your logo, promotional item or theme. Ask about 3D sculptures, art murals, logos and lighted balloons.

- **Special Effects**—So you want to do something exciting? Try handheld or ground mounted innovative confetti cannons in three different sizes, or fill balloons with smaller balloons and confetti and explode them over the crowd. Other special effects include balloon drops, disappearing walls and lighting effects.

- **Bouquets**—We pride ourselves in unique designs and balloons that are delightfully different, including designer, imprinted, gumballs and shaped balloons.

- **Centerpieces**—We design exciting and colorful centerpieces for your special event. Using a variety of mediums including unique bouquets, sculptures, confetti, and shaped balloons, we custom make each centerpiece to carry out your theme.

ACEP Board Member • POVA Member

See The Prop Shop, page 198 under Themes & Props.

FLORISTS

1507 Broadway
Vancouver, Washington 98663
(877) 3CLOVER, (360) 695-7941
Fax (360) 695-2008
E-mail: Crimson&Clover@yahoo.com

Are you ready for a change? At Crimson & Clover we specialize in unique, artistic designs. Our goal is to visually delight you and to exceed your expectations.

Scheduled Deliveries
Whether it is a weekly lobby or reception enhancement or a pre-scheduled staff recognition, we will assure a prompt delivery.

Personal Recognition
Send a personal thank you to an employee/business associate or delight an out of town guest with a custom gift basket.

Special Events
Your ideas, our expertise—together we will create a look for people to remember.

- Fresh Floral Designs
- Silk Decorations
- Balloons
- Holiday and Theme Décor
- Party Rentals, Plants, Etc.

Place your trust in a florist who truly cares about each order that is placed.

After hours appointments upon request

Please let this business know that you heard about them from the Bravo! Event Resource Guide.

CRYSTAL LILIES
Exquisite Floral Artistry

at Embassy Suites Hotel Downtown
337 S.W. Pine Street
Portland, Oregon 97204
(503) 221-7701

Studio
134 S.E. Taylor Street
Portland, Oregon 97214
(503) 239-4553
Fax (503) 242-2563

Exquisite Floral Artistry
Crystal Lilies is a specialty florist. Our expertise is in providing spectacular floral arrangements and decorations for all events. Using fresh, unusual and beautiful flowers is our hallmark.

Events
- Corporate Events
- Grand Openings
- Weekly Lobby or Reception Arrangements
- Trade Show/Booths
- Holiday Parties

Custom Decorating
- Displays for Office/Home/Shows
- Silk Arrangements for Lobbies and Homes
- Holiday Decorating; Wreaths, Garlands, Christmas Trees
- Extensive Unique Rental Items Available

Special Services
We provide setup and delivery for all events. We always bring a team of professionals to each event to attend to all of the details.

Specialized Floral/Gift Store
Visit our European-style store filled with unique gifts and treasures for all occasions, as well as home decor items that will enhance any home or office. We offer an extensive display of silk arrangements of the finest quality.

**To help you plan your floral and decorating needs,
please call for a personal consultation.
Contact Kimberly Lindsay at (503) 221-7701**

Flowers by

"The Northwest's Family-owned
Wedding Specialist for Over 25 Years"

*435 N.W. Sixth Avenue
Portland, Oregon 97209
(503) 464-1234, (800) 343-1235
Fax (503) 464-1218*

◆ Flowers ◆ Photography ◆ Videography ◆
◆ Music ◆ Open 7 Days a Week ◆

Event Decorations
- Theme decorations in florals, balloons, props, etc.
- Centerpieces and table arrangements
- Balloon arrangements, centerpieces and arches
- Corsages and boutonnieres
- Plant rentals

We are all well known for our international flowers and designs, including European, Oriental, Hawaiian and contemporary.

Specialty Theme Events
Specialty theme items for golfers, fishing and more. Jacobsen's has provided specialty golf centerpieces and decor for the Peter Jacobsen Golf events.

Gourmet Gift Baskets
What better way to say "thank you" than with a wonderful gift basket filled with Oregon and Northwest wines, chocolate truffles, smoked salmon, sausage, Tillamook cheeses and fresh fruit. Each basket can be customized and personalized for your client.

Christmas Decor
Trees, wreaths and garlands custom-designed for any corporate office or event.

Need Flowers? Call Someone Who Cares.
Flowers Tommy Luke is a full-service florist. We can create the perfect floral arrangement for any event. Whether you're looking to decorate a podium, table top, provide centerpieces or simply send an arrangement, we offer a wide range of floral styles that will complement any event. Our staff of designers have extensive experience in creating floral designs to meet all your needs.

A Portland Centerpiece for Over 90 Years
We've been bringing flowers to Portland since 1907. You'll find our arrangements to be full, creative and beautiful. You've probably seen our work at any number of regional, national and international conventions where we were named the official florist.

If there's one thing we're enthusiastic about, it's flowers. Flowers Tommy Luke offers an extensive year-round selection and can provide same day or next day service upon request. To place an order give us a call or visit our new location in the Pearl District.

Notes

Formal Wear & Tuxedos

FORMAL WEAR AND TUXEDOS

HELPFUL HINTS

Formal attire makes any event fun and memorable: Numerous formal wear styles are available. The formal wear shop you decide to work with can offer suggestions for styles and colors that will customize your look for any occasion. Tuxedos do not have to look rented. The thousands of styles and accessories available make everyone look original. Women look great in tuxedos, too.

Final fitting and pickup date: You must instruct each event participant to pick up his/her own tuxedo. Make sure they try on the entire outfit at the store. This will avoid the most common problem with formal wear—fit. If adjustments or replacements need to be made, they can usually be done on the spot or arrangements for substitutions can be made.

Out-of-town guests: If some guests live out of town, the formal wear shop can supply you with measurement cards you can mail back to them. Any clothing or alterations shop should be able to do a complimentary fitting. It is imperative that gentlemen take the time to try on their entire outfit when they go to pick it up!

Group rates and discounts: Many formal wear shops offer special group rates, discounts, or rebates for black-tie or black-tie-optional events. Ask about setting up a special rate for all the guests who will attend the event or function.

Women's formal and evening attire: There are women's rental shops that carry designer formal and evening gowns for special occasions and pageants. These salons carry one-of-a-kind gowns or a limited selection so you won't bump into your gown on someone else at the same event.

Company Parties: Not only will your staff look and feel great in black tie, but renting is more affordable than buying a new suit. **Auctions and Benefits**: Black tie makes any affair an event to remember. People enjoy having a reason to dress up. These events attract guests who don't mind paying a little extra for an unforgettable evening. **Trade Shows**: Formal wear adds that finishing touch to your booth or exhibit; your staff will stand out from the competition. **Awards and Banquets**: There is no better way to honor your esteemed guests than to dress in black tie. Whether presenting or receiving an award, when formally dressed, you are sure to enhance any accomplishment.

Costume theme parties: Tuxedos make great costumes for any theme event. Go avant garde with a black tie and blue jeans, cruise with a white dinner jacket, or stand out at a Hawaiian Luau with the Hawaiian print cummerbund and bow tie.

You chose wisely.

Beaverton Town Square
(503) 643-7022

Clackamas Corner
(503) 653-7668

Vancouver Mall
(360) 256-6424

Web site:
http://www.gingiss.com

Let the world's largest renter of men's formalwear help you make your event or fundraiser "the difference in black and white."

With over 62 years of formalwear experience, your nationwide formalwear specialist can ensure you proper fit, affordable rates and outstanding service. With 275 stores across the United States, we can help you pull together a special event or fundraiser in a few easy steps.

Steps to the Difference in Black and White...

1. Register your special event or fundraiser with our formalwear consultant.

2. Your attendees go to a convenient location, choose high-quality tuxedos at group discounted rates and get measured using our standardized technique. If your attendees are out of town, their measurements can be mailed, phoned or faxed in using our Gingiss Travel Tux Service.

3. Your attendees pick up their tuxedos one to two days before the date of use. Part of Gingiss' service is providing a final fitting to ensure proper fit before they leave the store. They return the day after the event.

Does Gingiss Donate a Portion of Each Tuxedo Rented if Your Event is a Fundraiser or Charity Function?

Yes we do. Our business is caring for others' needs. We help in many ways whether it is by giving money back for a good cause or providing quality service at affordable rates.

FORMAL WEAR & TUXEDOS

24 Years of Excellence

Corporate Office:
1205 S.E. Grand Avenue
Portland, Oregon 97214
Marketing: (800) 284-4889
www.mrformaltuxedos.com
**27 convenient locations—
serving Oregon and the Puget Sound Area**

A Black Tie Event is Unforgettable

Mr. Formal continues to bring a touch of class and sophistication to special events in the Northwest—a tradition for over 24 years. Mr. Formal offers unbeatable rates, quality, and service. With 27 locations in Oregon and Washington, tuxedo fittings and pickups are always convenient. Let Mr. Formal enhance the atmosphere at your next fund raiser or special event.

Fund Raising Opportunities

Mr. Formal proudly works with many local charity fund-raisers, offering a special rental rate with a donation back to your cause with every tuxedo rented. Mr. Formal will design, print, and deliver custom invitation or ticket inserts announcing the group discount for your event.

✦ **$10 donated back to the charity with each full-price rental.**

✦ **$5 donated back to the charity with each discounted rental.**

✦ **10% of each retail purchase for the event donated back.**

Corporate Rental Rates

✦ **12-40 persons from $ 60 per rental**

✦ **41-60 $ 55**

✦ **61 + $ 50**

Tuxedos include coat, pants, shirt, jewelry, and choice of matching cummerbund and tie. Shoes and vests are optional. Designer tuxedos are additional.
* Restrictions may apply May through June

Enhance the Atmosphere of Your Event

✦ **Special events**—Formalwear brings a touch of class and sophistication.

✦ **Fund-raisers**—Black tie makes any affair an event to remember.

✦ **Trade shows**—Formalwear adds that finishing touch to your booth or exhibit.

✦ **Award banquets**—No better way to honor your esteemed guests.

A Few of Our Clients...

- Fred Meyer Jewelers
- Sequent Computers
- Cystic Fibrosis Foundation
- The Boys & Girls Clubs of Portland
- Home Builders Association
- U.S. Bank
- Singing Christmas Tree
- Yoshida Group

www.mrformaltuxedos.com

Invitations
&
Paper Supplies

INVITATIONS AND PAPER SUPPLIES

HELPFUL HINTS

Invitation styles: Thousands of invitation styles are available—traditional, contemporary, custom designs, double envelopes, or a folding invitation sealed with a sticker. When it comes time to select your invitations, pick the one that best suits your tastes, personal style, and budget. This is the first presentation of your event, and it can give your guests their first glimpse of your theme.

Custom invitations: Invitations come in all shapes and styles, but finding the one that is perfect for your event might be difficult. Custom-design and specialty invitation companies can create something tailored to your event. Beautiful spring flowers, ribbons, confetti—anything is possible. Talk to the professionals and brainstorm about the perfect idea.

The art of calligraphy: This art of writing is pleasing to the eye and elegant for an invitation—it gives a one-of-a-kind look to any invitation. Your invitation can also be created in calligraphy and then reproduced (check the services in this section for more information).

Ordering your invitations: Ideally, you should order your invitations three to four months before the event to allow enough time for delivery. Some shops offer quick-print service in one week to one day. Invitations should be sent four to six weeks before the event. Ask if you can get the envelopes in advance for addressing.

Addressing the invitations: There are many new ways of addressing your invitations with new software and laser printing. With all the junk mail people get it's nice to receive an envelope that stands out from the rest of the mail.

Wording the invitation: When you order, be sure to work with a shop that specializes in invitations. These experts can help you fill out the complicated order forms and will help you with correct wording for the invitation. When you order your invitations through a catalogue, there is no one to answer your questions.

Correct spelling of names: Etiquette books cover the proper addressing of envelopes. Before addressing your envelopes, make sure you double-check your master list for the CORRECT spelling of names—no one appreciates his or her name misspelled.

PaperPlus®

TIGARD	PORTLAND	EUGENE
11105 S.W. Greenburg Road	835 E. Burnside	1090 Bailey Hill Road
(503) 684-1892	(503) 238-3607	(503) 345-3223

Business Hours: Mon–Fri 7:30am–5:30pm; Saturdays 9am–2pm

Paper and Presentation Supplies
Paper Plus offers a wide variety of items for people putting on meetings or coordinating events.

- **Ready-to-Print Invitations and Announcements**
  Get selection and uniqueness. Save time and money!

- **Paper**
  The Northwest's largest selection and availability of printing, business, and stationery papers

- **Laser and Inkjet Supplies**
  Including preprinted, four-color, brochures, border paper and cards. Transparencies and labels. Inks, toners, and much more!

- **Computer Supplies**
  Printer paper, disks, tapes and files.

- **Office Supplies**
  Easel to note pads, file folders to presentations binders.

Paper Plus offers only quality products
at low warehouse prices!
20% to 70% off retail, everyday!

TOWNE PAPERS

Social Stationery, Invitations & Gifts

9 N.W. 23rd Place
Portland, Oregon 97210
(503) 224-6156; Fax (503) 224-3616
Business Hours: Mon–Fri 9am–6pm; Sat 10am–5pm; Sun Noon–4pm
E-mail: townepaper@aol.com

Selection and Styles

Traditional or contemporary, Towne Papers has a huge selection of invitations for every event from black tie parties to company picnics in a wide range of pricing. We specialize in finding the perfect invitation for your event. We have access to hundreds of vendors around the world. Paper lines include: Cranes, William Arthur, Regency, Lallie and Elite.

Special Services

We offer in-house printing with same day service available. Towne Papers also has Business Stationery, Holiday Cards, Corporate Gifts and Gift Wrapping Services available. Printed napkins, matches, and ribbon add a special flair to your event. If we do not have it, we'll find it!

Personalized Service

Just let us know what your needs are and one of our experienced sales consultants will take care of it for you. We specialize in the unique. We can help you over the phone, by appointment, or just drop in!

Towne Papers has been in business for over 18 years and is owned and operated by a meeting planner of 10 years who understands the need for flexibility, creativity and interesting time constraints when it comes to planning your event. Conveniently located in Uptown Shopping Center and open seven days a week to serve you!

Speakers & Presentations

MOTIVATIONAL SPEAKERS

Schedule One of These TOP Oregon Professional Speakers for Your Special Event.

They energize, motivate, and educate! And they are all members of the National Speakers Association and the Oregon Speakers Association.

Dr. Eric Allenbaugh—When leadership experience counts, count on Dr. Eric Allenbaugh…a seasoned leadership consultant…a stellar keynote speaker and executive coach. (503) 635-3963; eric@allenbaugh.com

Dick Barnett—Reignite your business with Dick Barnett. What's "stuck"? Eliminate the barriers to your success. Leave your competition in the dust. (503) 629-5210; barnett@ReigniteYourBusiness.com; www.ReigniteYourBusiness.com

Jan Carothers—Spark energy, action and results. Seminars, retreats and speeches. Refreshing keynote: *"Reclaim Your Pioneer Spirit—the Wagon Train Woman Talks, Hiring Champions."* (503) 786-9132; fax (503) 786-1794; SpeakerJan@aol.com

Kathleen Gaibler—Professional speaker and business coach, Kathleen provides leaders with profitable solutions for productivity challenges in the workplace. (503) 762-0611; fax (503) 761-6462; kgaibler@msn.com; www.kgaibler.com

Clayton Lance—Clayton Lance empowers you to achieve personal mastery and excellence in communications and leadership. Learn the life skills to succeed in 2000. (503) 774-8870; (877) POWER77; powerpersuasion@juno.com; www.powerpersuasion.com

Carolyn A. Martin, Ph.D., International Keynoter and Trainer—Schedule this extraordinary speaker to challenge and delight your audiences to become "the employer of choice" with her cutting-edge programs on Generation X. (503) 698-6112; RichMart@SprintMail.com; www.carolynmartin.com

Barbara Lilly—Stand out online and accelerate results with clear, concise communications, technology marketing and the "Eway of Email" with Barbara's high velocity programs. (503) 289-9901; (800) 950 9984; lillywing@aol.com; www.lillywing.com; www.ewayofemail.com

Jean Rupp Murray, National Trainer and Keynoter—Jean's powerful business writing programs teach you "You don't have to work like a dog to write like a pro." Her motivational keynote—"Paws for Thought"—is perfect for any audience! (503) 579-6065; (800) 293-6150; jean@paws4thoughts.com; www.paws4thoughts.com

The Gail Tycer Company—Marketing—Business Development—Strategic Business Writing Consulting—Workshops—Keynotes—Breakout Sessions. www.GailTycer.com; gtycer@coho.net; (503) 292-9681; (888) 634-4875; fax (503) 297-1695

Timothy Williams, Ph.D.—Timothy Williams speaks on the topics of dispute prevention and resolution, building long term business relationships and implementing successful negotiation strategies. (503) 872-9932; (888) 791-9932; Hawthntim@aol.com

Da Verne Bell	**Jerry Fletcher**	**Linda Greep**
Speaker and Trainer	The Networking Ninja	Speaker and Entertainer
(360) 574-7731	(503) 636-4113	(360) 896-0166
Fax (360) 574-7732	*Fax (503) 635-3967*	*Fax (360) 891-1327*

Da Verne Bell, Professional Speaker, Trainer and Consultant

Da Verne Bell is a professional speaker, trainer, and consultant specializing in multicultural/diversity issues, anti-harassment training, motivation, self-esteem, children's and women's issues. Da Verne's mission and commitment are "to make a difference." For over 25 years she has worked to promote better understanding and acceptance among all.

Da Verne's professional career has included: Affirmative Action Officer, Personal Recruiter, Manager of Women's Programs, Member of Human Rights Commissions and Cultural Diversity Programs. She is committed to making a difference for the future and believes in the power of unity and empowerment.

A partial list of clients include American Association of University Women, American Business Women's Association, Clark College, U.S. Forest Service, YMCA, Fort Vancouver Regional Library, Washington State University, U.S. District Court, Tektronix Inc., YWCA, Federal Women's Programs, Seattle University and State of Oregon Children Services.

Jerry Fletcher, The Networking Ninja

Learn how to forge the connections that build businesses, careers and lives of joy! Known as The Networking Ninja, Jerry combines networking and next wave technologies to take sales and marketing to the next level. This former CEO is the author of two books and four audio tape programs. He is an expert at business development and has participated in successful launches of over 200 companies and products.

A partial list of organizations that have profited from Jerry's experience include Digimarc, ADC Kentrox, American Marketing Association, Creative Media, Geffen Mesher, Freightliner, US Bank, Voicestream Wireless, PGE, POVA, Intel and Women Entrepreneurs of Oregon.

For more information visit his Web site at **www.Nextworking.com.**

Linda Greep, Speaker, Trainer and Entertainer

Set sail with Linda Greep—The Lady in Red! For smooth sailing at your next convention, meeting, banquet, seminar or cruise, bring aboard the versatile, multi-talented Linda Greep. Award-winning speaker, trainer and entertainer, she delivers upbeat, humorous and motivating keynotes. Linda makes each event a smashing success, and will even compose and perform a song just for your group. Always energizing, enlightening and entertaining.

Judge Linda by the clients she keeps across North America including: Nordstrom, Benis, Esco Aluminum, Numatech Hanford, Holland/Burgerville Corp., U.S. Veterans Admin., Southwest Washington Med Center Foundation, Gental Dental, Oregon Air National Guard, City of Beaverton, Executive Officers Club and Live! At the Civic.

Notes

Entertainers & Performers

FORTUNE TELLER

CRYSTAL BALL PRODUCTIONS

510 S.W. Third, Suite 418
Portland, Oregon 97204
Contact: Faye Pietrokowsky
(503) 221-2123; Fax (503) 402-1096
E-mail: ide@transport.com
Web site: http://www.transport.com/~ide

INVITE YOUR GUESTS TO PEEK INTO THE FUTURE

Faye Pietrokowsky and Crystal Ball Productions Offer a Unique and Memorable Service

If you would like to create an unforgettable event/party and add novelty to your celebration—you'll want to offer your guests this unique form of entertainment. Hire Faye Pietrokowsky to do fun fortunetelling.

Dressed as a gypsy, Faye sits with each guest at a table adorned with candles, glitter, a crystal ball, jewelry and other props. The guest is invited to ask Faye questions about present and future concerns. Some issues Faye addresses include: career, relationships, travel, family, education, business investments and sporting events.

Faye postures her answers in a positive manner, keeping the session upbeat. She has worked with several entertainment agencies and individuals in the Portland and Vancouver area. She has had the honor of entertaining stockbrokers, attorneys, artists, engineers, business owners, sales people, teachers, children, therapists, etc.

Fee: Reasonable rates. Call for more information.

"It doesn't get any better than Faye Pietrokowsky.. She is the best that there is."
~Carmen Eastman, owner of Eastman Entertainment Agency

"Faye Pietrokowsky has the wonderful gift of intuition. The gift that she gives to others is to let them know they also have this gift."
~Don Wright, speaking coach and president of Don Wright Productions

"Fascinating and fun. Faye's presence at a function guarantees an event worth remembering."   ~Sydney Mead, chief concierge at The Governor Hotel

(503) 234-1857
E-mail: artphil@teleport.com
Web site:
www.teleport.com/~artphil

Let me sketch at your next event…

Your guests will love being the Stars of your party! I can sketch an amazing likeness of your guest in five minutes!

Caricatures create a fun, people-mixing event. It's fascinating to watch and treasured as a souvenir gift! Sketches include improvisational gags, such as guests' favorite sport or hobby themes... Sketch paper is also custom printed with your event title to suit your theme!

Invite me to your…Weddings, Bar/Bat Mitzvahs, Reunions, Graduations and Office Parties.

25 years of experience in the party sketching business. Sketches are "likenesses" rendered in India ink with a brush-pen—which give sketches a surprisingly detailed "finish." Sketch equipment is completely portable for roving around casual standup parties or formal sit-down events...Yes, I can come in tuxedo or tennis shoes!

It's great for conventions, trade shows and picnics too!

It's the perfect party entertainment…because it breaks the ice, creates an upbeat mood and is fun to watch as to receive.

Check out my Web site at:
www.teleport.com/~artphil

TOM MCCORMACK'S LEGENDTELLING

P.O. Box 3138
Wilsonville, Oregon 97070
(503) 402-1823; Fax (503) 585-7848
E-mail: legendteller@hotmail.com

Type of Performance

Tom is a master storyteller who incorporates global indigineos music in his distinctive style. Through unique dialoguing characters and physical animation, Tom brings stories to life. Complementing the tales are live flute music, song segues, sound effects, mime, panto-mime and audience interaction.

Keynotes/Workshops/Seminars

McCormack has keynoted education conferences and presented workshops at conferences for professional organizations across the Western U.S. and Canada. His versatile style and spontanaity enhance his experience as an Emcee. Tom's warm, upbeat flair captivates the audience he addresses, regardless of the event! Imagine your theme presented with glib good-taste…or outrageous out-takes! Keynotes and Emceeing are custom designed to target your needs.

Experience

Through dialoguing multiple characterizations, Tom has entertained different venues across Western North America the past 11 years. Using intense physical movement during his shows, Tom releases the creative imagination into new dimensions. McCormack plays the indigineos flutes of the world with clear precision and rhythm. He has appeared as a featured performer at: Newport Performing Arts Center in Newport, Oregon; Mt. Angel Oktoberfest, Sternwheeler "Columbia Gorge," Oregon Zoo, Oregon State Fair, Northwest Indian Market, Portland, Dreamspeakers International Indigineous Festival, Edmonton, Alberta; Numerous local and national client references available on request.

Cost and Services

Tom works closely with your event producers to ensure a successful experience executed with uncompromising quality. He performs solo, but encourages his performances to be signed (e.g. sign language). The legendteller has multiple booking rates for performances, workshops and speaking engagements. Call for availability and scheduling details.

Business Consulting

Mediation and conflict resolution services bring results for your distressed situation. McCormack skillfully incorporates storytelling tools to diffuse "in-house difficulties." Whether it's bringing two opposing groups together during a business meeting or using his story-wits, Tom will help both parties come to an agreement. Or after the individuals finally arrive at consensus, McCormack will come in and get them all laughing to heal any hard feelings. Let the Story Doctor handle your corporate communication ailments.

"A story may stand on its own, but the teller makes it dance."

YO-YO TOWERS
222 S.W. Harrison 22B
Portland, Oregon 97201
(503) 22-COACH

YO-YO ENTERTAINER

Walk The Dog • Around The World • Rock The Cradle
Entertainer • Coach • Humorist

Call Tommy Yo-Yo for
- Parties
- After Dinner
- Corporate Meetings
- Award Travel
- Picnics
- Grand Openings
- Trade Shows
- Conventions

Everyone Learns Great Yo-Yo Tricks
- Spectacular demonstration: galaxy of two-handed and the most difficult one-handed tricks performed by a world class champion
- Everyone receives a complimentary tournament yo-yo; hands-on instruction
- Yo-yoing made very easy; everyone is successful

Trade Show Superstar!
- Make your exhibit the hottest attraction at the show
- Increase your leads three to 100 times
- Win awards and recognition for your booth

"Thanks for the fabulous yo-yo performances in our booth at the Produce Marketing Association show in Atlanta. Your performances were invaluable to us and put a feather in my cap for hiring you. I will be talking with you soon about performing at next year's show."
~Lindsay Martinez, marketing manager, Boskovich Farms, Oxnard, California

"The National Restaurant Association show in Chicago was a resounding success for us and your participation was a key factor. Do not hesitate to have prospective clients call me. We look forward to working with you again."
~John Hanna, CEO, International Yogurt Co., Portland

Steal the show with Tommy Yo-Yo!
Salesman • Marketer • Closer

**Custom yo-yos, T-shirts and other toys available
Call now...schedule fills fast
(503) 222-6224 • (800) 368-1726**

Please let this business know that you heard about them from the Bravo! Event Resource Guide.

SUSAN RICE
COMEDIAN

Presented by Sterling Talent, Inc.
P.O. Box 231059
Tigard, Oregon 97281
Contact: Becky Stroebel (503) 590-5840
E-mail: Beckysong@aol.com
Web site: www.sterlingtalent.com

Susan Rice's comedic career began in Portland in 1983 and has taken her to every state in the union. Rice's comedy has landed her spots on ABC, CBS, A&E, HBO, FOX Broadcasting and Showtime, as well as Comedy Central. She learned by working with some of the best in the business such as Jerry Seinfeld and Paula Poundstone. Rice's performance style is hilarious and perfectly suited for corporate entertainment and private events.

Rice is know for her wacky, self-revealing routine, complemented by facial twists and contortions not seen since Jerry Lewis. Rice weaves a blend of absurdity and truth into a highly enjoyable comedic presentation for all types of audiences. Rice quotes, "Hey...I couldn't afford therapy, so I got into comedy!"

Recent Clients
Recent clients include Oregon Timber Association, Weyerhauser, Junior Achievement Association, Osteoporosis Foundation, H&R Block, Paper Industry Management Association and many more.

Susan Rice's Past Performances Include
- The MGM Hotel and Casino
- Harvey's Comedy Club... Portland, Oregon
- Giggles... Seattle, Washington
- The Ice House... Pasadena, California
- Catch A Rising Star... Las Vegas
- And Many More!

Call today and find out how Susan Rice can add sparkle and laughter to your special event.

**For pricing and availability call Sterling Talent, Inc.
Promotional video available upon request.**

MICHAEL JOHN
Presented by Sterling Talent, Inc.
P.O. Box 231059
Tigard, Oregon 97281
Contact: Becky Stroebel (503) 590-5840
E-mail: Beckysong@aol.com
Web site: www.sterlingtalent.com

For the last 25 years, Michael John has brought enjoyment to hundreds of thousands of audience participants all over the world. Whether as the opening act for such notables as Jay Leno, Milton Berle, Louise Mandrell, Billy Crystal, David Brenner or Ray Charles, featured entertainer at national venues and resorts or motivational facilitator for corporate, professional and civic events, Michael's ability to captivate and motivate has endeared him to his audiences. Michael's musical talent and unique musical presentation will not only hold your attention but will also touch your heart.

Michael John is one of the hottest one-man shows on tour today! He is adaptable to any situation from colleges to clubs, concerts to banquets, and conventions to resorts.

What Can Michael John Do for Your Event?
Michael's performance is more than a concert…it's an interactive entertainment event! Utilizing his uncanny ability to instantly engage his audience, Michael transforms them into a realm of music and mirth, tugging at their heart strings and tickling their funny bone with a magical blend of music and comedy.

Need and Emcee?
Michael John has emceed all types of events from coast to coast—from corporate parties and festivals, to holiday galas and even talent shows.

Recent Corporate Clients Include
Motorola, Hewlett Packard, Blue Cross Blue Shield, Farmer's Insurance Group, Oregon Association of Chiefs of Police, Continental Airlines, Hilton Head Resort, Vale Resort, Northwest Paper Association and many more.

For booking information and availability, contact Sterling Talent, Inc. Promotional material available upon request.

**Michael John is a total entertainer!
You will love him…your audience will love him…you will want him back!**

62 S.E. 57th Avenue
Portland, Oregon 97215-1221
(503) 796-9550
Web site: http://laugh.at/brainwaves

What is Brainwaves?
Brainwaves Improvisational Comedy is a unique form of entertainment that can make your next event a hilarious success. Made up of professional comic actors, Brainwaves plays corporate functions, colleges, theaters, and comedy clubs all over the country. Brainwaves first formed in 1986, so we have years of experience adapting our performance to fit the needs of you and your audience. Since we are improvisational, we can incorporate anything about your company or event theme into the show. We can also perform for any size group in nearly any venue, including conference rooms, banquet halls, auditoriums, cruise ships, and even outdoor picnics.

What Happens in a Show?
A Brainwaves show consists of scenes based on suggestions from your audience. These may include a live-action soap opera based on the life of a favorite employee, or a fairy tale retold in a variety of literary styles. "Brainwaves TV" uses impressions and characterizations to depict your favorite TV shows, or we can amaze you with the wit and wisdom of our famous two-headed psychic. The show can be any length from 15 to 90 minutes and beyond.

Who's Crazy Enough to Book these Guys?
Corporations that have enjoyed our professional, inoffensive, and consistently funny shows include: Starbucks Coffee Company, Leo Burnett, Hewlett Packard, First Interstate Bank, Safeway, Bonneville Power Administration, Toys R Us, Oregon Medical Association, Pacific Power & Light, Intel, Deloitte & Touche, Oregon Media Production Association, Payless Northwest, Timberline Software, METRO, Vancouver Mall, BRW Consulting, and KPTV-12.

Like to Check Out a Live Show?
Brainwaves performs regularly in Portland-area theaters. Call (503) 796-9550 for dates and passes.

WE *WILL* MAKE YOU LAUGH!

Office:
3308 East Burnside Street
Portland, Oregon 97214
Contact: Patrick Short or
Ruth Jenkins
(503) 236-8888
Fax (503) 235-6291

23 U.S. Cities

15 Years Of Laughs

Regular performances:
Fridays and Saturdays at The ComedySportz Arena
1963 N.W. Kearney Street • Portland
Web site: http://www.comedysportz.com/

What is ComedySportz?

ComedySportz is competitive improvisational comedy—a battle of wits between two teams of professional "actletes" playing a variety of fast-paced scenes and games based on suggestions from your audience. It's funny, topical (your folks make all of the suggestions) and CLEAN! Seeing a ComedySportz match is like seeing a sporting event—energy, excitement, fan involvement—with the additional payoff of laughter. A referee is on-hand to explain games, get suggestions from the fans, time the action, and keep things clean. After the National Anthem, the coin is tossed and the action begins. You might see your boss portrayed as a Shakespearean hero, and an office problem solved as part of a Grand Opera, or a sales goal laid out as a Broadway musical. It could happen!

What are Suitable ComedySportz Events?

Corporate or office parties, picnics, sales promotions, customer conferences, trade shows, project wind-ups, Bar Mitzvahs (seriously)—because we are so portable and flexible, we can play in almost any event or space you dream up. ComedySportz is suitable for all audiences—we're sensitive to your needs and we understand that laughter doesn't have to come at the expense of members of your audience. Because ComedySportz is funny without making fun of who people are, we are the only comedy entertainment truly appropriate for professional settings. Planners from such companies as Tektronix, Coffee People, Mentor Graphics, Intel, Hewlett-Packard, Sears, Epson, Food Services of America, Kaiser-Permanente, Sequent Computer Systems, Starbucks, and Lutheran Family Services have looked like geniuses by choosing ComedySportz.

This Sounds Interesting and Fun—But How Can I Be Sure?

See a regular ComedySportz show! We perform each Friday and Saturday at The Comedy Sportz Arena in Northwest Portland. Make a reservation by calling (503) 236-8888 and bringing this Bravo Resource Guide along. Not only will one of our "actletes" gladly autograph it, but you'll get two free tickets to check us out and have a blast! See for yourself!

Group Unity Training Seminars (G.U.T.S.)

Group Unity Training Seminars are powerful tools for the competitive business landscape. It's one thing to want a strong team that can take advantage of opportunity—it takes G.U.T.S. to make it happen! We've built powerful teams with our clients and customers in hundreds of situations over the past 14 years. The process is fun and the results are real. We tailor half-day, full day and series to meet your objectives, to help you become a focused, improvising organization.

Suitable for companies, not-for-profits, churches, associations and schools—any group that needs to work together and interact with the public.

Notes

Audience Participation & Games

HELPFUL HINTS

Why use a theme and audience participative entertainment? A theme provides interest and coherence for the attendees. Planning is more efficient with a theme, creating an automatically organized process. In addition, the key to successful events is audience participation. The more involved people become in the event they are attending, the more likely they are to enjoy themselves and remember the experience. Attendees may not remember the name of the keynote speaker, but they will remember the "Wacky Olympics" special event!

When is a theme appropriate? Anytime you have an event. When done properly, themes can be used to enhance a business meeting, client appreciation, awards event, and even reunions.

How is a theme chosen? Define the goals of your event first, what you want to accomplish with the event, who is attending, and what you want them to take away with them. Then, you can decide what theme options may work. Brainstorming with a committee or colleague can be a big help.

Are theme events expensive? They don't have to be. It depends on your budget. Some of your theme ideas can be accomplished with a small budget if you and your committee are willing to spend the time. However, a much better use of your time and money may be to use a meeting planner, prop, or entertainment company.

Decorating tips for theme events: Consider three to four main areas of the facility for theme props. Main focus areas can include the entryway to the event, stage, guest tables, beverage and food stations, to name a few.

Interactive and Theme ideas for your next event:

- Casino Night
- Murder Mystery
- Tropical Island
- Cruise Ship
- African Jungle
- Tropical Rain Forest
- Western/ Wild West
- Medieval Castle
- Hawaiian Luau
- Fabulous 50s
- Great Gatsby Party
- Winter Wonderland
- M•A•S•H
- South of the Border
- Underwater
- Mexican Fiesta
- Mardi Gras
- Circus! Circus!
- International Themes
- Nautical
- The Great Northwest
- Learn to yo-yo

Eddie May's Interactive Comedy Murder Mystery Dinner Theater!

Enjoy a night of great food, side-splitting comedy, Mystery, Mayhem and

MURDER
SERVED HOT!

For tickets and information call
(503) 524-4366, Toll Free (877) 2JOIN-IN
Web site: www.eddiemaymysteries.com

Come out and play with the world-traveled, critically acclaimed Portland Cast and experience an evening of first-class, *audience-participation entertainment!* Help the famous Detective Eddie May figure out Whodunit and nail a killer at your *next* party! As you dine with these masters of improv comedy, if a suspect happens to put down an article of clothing, a purse or other personal possession, feel free to pick it up and rifle through it to your heart's content, searching for evidence and clues necessary to nail the guilty fiend or fiends. All evidence is placed on an evidence table for you. You can act individually or as members of a team and cast your ballot at the end of the night! *Can you figure out Whodunit?*

Eddie May Mysteries—The Best Entertainment for

- Breakfast/Brunches
- Company parties
- Out-of-town guests
- Anniversaries
- Sales promotions
- Lunches
- Incentive awards
- Motorcoach tours
- Corporate meetings
- Gift certificates
- Dinners
- Picnics
- Fund Raisers
- Banquets
- Birthdays

Where *are* Eddie May Murder Mystery Dinners?

Public Performances: Every Friday and Saturday night at the Starwood's Days Inn–City Center, conveniently located downtown Portland at 1414 S.W. Sixth and Clay. Complimentary parking is available right at the hotel!

Private Performances: We've performed in tents on the Iraqi border, nightclubs in Iceland, the demilitarization zone between North and South Korea, major hotels, mansions, private homes and at the very best dining establishments! We'll join you wherever and whenever you want to have fun!

How Much is it for the Crime of Your Life?

Public Performances: Only $39.95 pp for a delicious three-course meal of Caesar Salad, warm delicious rolls, a choice of four entrees—Prime Rib, Baked Salmon, Grilled Chicken Breast with a Teriyaki glaze or Pasta Primavera Alfredo—and for dessert, delicious New York Cheesecake and Coffee! *Gratuity is included.*

Private Performances are based on the size of your group, the location you choose and menu choices. Have a private party at the Days Inn—City Center and enjoy a fabulous and exclusive private party at our excellent public prices!

CHOOSE EDDIE MAY'S INTERACTIVE, COMEDY MURDER MYSTERY PARTIES FOR "THE CRIME OF YOUR LIFE!"

Please let this business know that you heard about them from the Bravo! Event Resource Guide.

MURDER MYSTERIES

WE'D KILL FOR YOUR BUSINESS

She was a cold-blooded killer with a pair of icy blues and a heart to match. Now that @#*! cop wants to know why she talked to you all evening. So does your wife.

"Our faces hurt from laughing so much."

Pardon me, is that a knife in your back?

"The president of our association kept asking how we're going to top IT'S A MYSTERY… Well, I honestly don't think we can…"

As soon as I heard the gun, I knew it meant trouble; but who could have imagined this?

"…the entire crew were highly professional, courteous, articulate, incredibly funny, and creative beyond belief."

I'm Detective Richard Sheridan. Don't call me Dick.

"…remarked that this was the most unforgettable and fun event they have ever attended!"

Isn't that Mike's favorite golf club next to the body?

"…the best entertainment we have ever had at a company Christmas party."

CALL ENTCO INTERNATIONAL
Toll Free: (800) 803-0298
Fax: (425) 670-0777
www.entco.com

Since 1982

2318 N.W. Vaughn • Portland, Oregon 97210
Contact: Amy Spatrisano, CMP or Rick Walker
(503) 224-0134; Fax (503) 224-0278 or Toll Free (800) 346-7280
Visit our Web site at: www.wildbills.com

No one just stands around at a Wild Bill's party!
We Provide Exciting Interactive Entertainment For
Company Parties • Reunions • Conventions • Grad Nights
Client Appreciation • Fund Raisers • Holiday Parties • Picnics

Type of Events
- **Casino Parties:** Wild Bill's provides all your favorite casino games and creates an atmosphere of exciting casino action. Whether your theme is a black tie affair, a Roaring '20s speakeasy, or a wild west hoe-down, Wild Bill's brings it to life!

- **Murder Mystery Parties:** Cut-throat negotiations! Dirty politics! Killer deadlines1 Who would have guessed they would be the highlights of your company party? Join our hilarious cast of characters who kill themselves to make sure your guests have an unforgettable experience.

- **Game Shows:** Now you can bring Hollywood style showmanship to your next event with our game show productions. Your guests are the contestants in some of the wackiest games we could think up! They're sensational for educating, entertaining or both.

Here's What Our Clients Have To Say
"The Best Party ever!"   *"...well organized, helpful, FUN!"*
         ~RiverPlace Hotel   ~ Nike
"...exceeded expectations...everyone had a wonderful time."
                                                ~ Elmers

Additional Entertainment Options
- Comical Hypnotist Shows
- Inflatable Games
- Magic Mania
- Mini Auto Racing
- Video Horse Racing
- $10,000 Putting Challenge

**Whatever your reason for having a party,
Wild Bill's can provide the action and excitement
to keep everyone entertained!**

CASINO GAMES

UPTOWN CASINO EVENTS

1888 SW Madison
Porland, OR 97205
Phone: 503-226-8980
Fax: 503-226-6919

www.uptownbilliards.com/casino

Don't gamble...
on your company party, reunion, reception graduation night or private affair...

Play it safe with
Uptown Casino Events!

Experience
The same team that will coordinate your event will host more than 400 activity-oriented company parties this year at The Uptown Billiards Club.

Better Gaming Equipment
Uptown Casino Events has the finest, most elegant gaming equipment in the Portland area.

Lower Prices
We have entrenched competition and we'll do what we must to create the same name for our Uptown Casino Events that we have for the Uptown Billiards Club.

Friendlier People
Although games and activities go a long way in providing atmosphere, only personalities can be "The Life of Your Party." We hire and train a very personable crew.

One Phone Call
is all it takes to plan the food, beverage and entertainment for your event anywhere in the Portland area. Let The Uptown Billiards Club handle the catering and Uptown Casino Events handle the fun and games!

**Call Uptown Casino Events
for an evening you could never forget!**

(503) 226-8980

Please let this business know that you heard about them from the Bravo! Event Resource Guide.

A LITTLE PETTING ZOO

Westside: (503) 222-4509
Eastside: (503) 668-3734
Vancouver: (360) 892-8085
P.O. Box 1299
Sandy, Oregon 97055

20 Years Experience • Rated #1 in the Northwest

Pony Rings and Parties
We provided covered party rings for rainy or sunny weather. Trained, professional and well-groomed ponies; an informed, polite and friendly staff. We will accommodate a one to eight hour event. Over 20 years experience assures your happiness, quality care for your children, and the highest level of safety at all times (fully insured). We also have hourly birthday and special event parties.

Inflatable Castle Jumps
We have them all, the largest selection in the Northwest! We have castles, dragons, Noah's Ark Jump with slides, interactive games, plus Bungee Run, Sumo Wrestling, Velcro Wall, Big Slide and much more. Rental includes setup, tear down and delivery at your site and on time.

Petting Zoos
We feature the following animals for on-site petting zoos:

Alligator	Hamsters	Possums
Bear Cat	Hedgehogs	Prairie Dogs
Bunnies	Huge Turtles	Rabbits
Camel	Lizards	Chicks
Llamas	Sheep	Chinchillas
Mini Cows	Skunk	Ducks
Mini Donkeys	Snakes	Exotic Cats
Mini Pigs	Squirrels	Fallow Deer
Pacman Frog	Four-eyed Possum	Parrots
Sugar Gliders	Goats	Ponies
Tarantulas		

Satisfied Customers

Bones & Brew Festival	Intel Corp.	Pacific Power & Light
Candlelighters Oregon	G.Loomis	Petco
Crawfish Festival	Jantzen Beach Mall	Phoenix Gold
Cross Roads Church	JCPenney	Portland Meadows
Dalles Rodeo	KGON	Portland Trail Blazers
E.C. Co.	KOA	Precision Castparts Corp.
Familian Northwest	KUPL	Protocol Inc.
Family Bargain Centers	Les Schwab Tire Centers	Sequent Computer Systems Inc.
Flying M Ranch	Portland Marriott Hotel	Tanasbourne Mall
Fred Meyer	Mentor Graphics	Tri-Met
Frito-Lay Inc.	New Hope Church	Yoshida's
Harley Davidson	NIKE	Z100
Hewlett Packard	NW Natural Gas	Luis Palau Association

Please let this business know that you heard about them from the Bravo! Event Resource Guide.

26515 S. Hillockburn Road
Estacada, Oregon 97023
Contact: Katie Locke (503) 630-3481
E-mail: WshUpnaPny@aol.com

Pony Ring
Wish Upon A Pony takes great pride in presenting beautiful, well-groomed ponies for all of our events—big or small. Children of all ages can enjoy our ponies, as they range in size. We only need a 20' x 20' area to setup our ring. We are fully self-contained.

Farm Animal Petting Zoo
Our petting zoo includes a variety of goat breeds, as well as sheep, a mini donkey, mini cow, mini horse, bunnies, chickens, ducks, and "Pajama the Llama." You will find our animals to be clean and well-cared for. Most of our animals have been handraised by us, and all have been chosen for their gentle dispositions.

Cost
Wish Upon A Pony is competitively priced. Ask us about package deals and mid-week discounts.

Booking and Delivery
We will provide staffing for all events. We also provide setup and break-down unless other arrangements have been made. A 50% deposit is required to secure your time and date. Early booking is suggested to ensure availability.

Previous Clients We Would Like to Thank
AAA, The Fun Factory, Portland Trail Blazers, Emanual Hospital, Qutama Crossings, The Country Classic, Whip and Spur Ranch, Cherry City Electric, Randall Realty Corp. and everyone who helped to make last year a success.

Wish Upon A Pony is dedicated to providing dependable, on-time, professional services. You will find our staff to be friendly and helpful. Let us help to make your next event a success. Please call anytime. We are available seven days a week.

ALL EVENTS & ENTERTAINMENT AGENCY

P.O. Box 1299 • Sandy, Oregon 97055
Westside: *(503) 222-4509;* **Eastside:** *(503) 668-3734;* **Va**ncouver: *(360) 892-8085*
Fax (503) 668-0284

Rental Items Available

- **Pony Rings**
- **Petting Zoos**
- **Inflatable Play Structures**
- **10-hole Miniature Golf**
- Donkey Basketball
- Carnival Games
- Dunk Tank
- Casino Equipment
- Sumo Wrestling
- Bingo
- Acroflight Bungee Jumper
- Velcro Olympics
- Spin Art
- Slam Dunk Obstacle Course
- Sea of Balls
- Tents
- Balloon Typhoon
- Putting Challenge
- Cash Cube Money Booth
- Paint Ball
- Face Painters
- Human Bowling
- Velcro Wall
- Gladiator Joust
- Bouncy Boxing
- Rodeo Roper
- Bungee Run
- Radical Surf Machine
- Aerotrim Gyro Machine
- Tiger Jungle Bounce
- Sportsgames, Double Shot Basketball, Quarterback Challenge
- Midway Hi-Striker
- Pseudo Golf
- Giant Slide
- Lazer Tag
- Giant Caterpillar
- Church Nativity Animals
- Monster Sports Toss
- Trampoline
- More Items available upon request

Petting Zoo

Fallow deer • goats • sheep • mini pig • mini cows • pony • mini donkey • rabbits • bunnies • chicks • ducks • lizards • hedgehogs • parrots • possums • huge turtles • llama • prairie dogs • hamsters • pacman frog • tarantula • alligator • skunks • snakes • squirrels • sugar gliders • four-eyed possum • chinchillas • bear cat

Satisfied Customers

Satisfied Customers include: Frito-Lay Inc., Fred Meyer, JCPenney, Les Schwab Tire Centers, Family Bargain Centers, Familian Northwest, Crawfish Festival, Portland Meadows, Tanasbourne Mall, Phoenix Gold, Dalles Rodeo, Sequent Computer Systems Inc., CrossRoads Church, E.C. Company, Portland Marriott Hotel, G.Loomis, Precision Castparts Corp., Jantzen Beach Mall, Candlelighters Oregon, Portland Trail Blazers, Harley Davidson, NIKE, Protocol Inc., Yoshida's, Hewlett Packard, Pacific Power & Light, Bones & Brew Festival, Tri-Met, KUPL, KOA, Intel Corp., Petco, KGON, Mentor Graphics, New Hope Church, NW Natural Gas, Z100, Luis Palau Association and Flying M Ranch.

Booking and Delivery

We provide staff, delivery, setup and take down. A 50% deposit is required to reserve any of our equipment; travel charges may vary.

Insurance

All Events & Entertainment Agency carries A Million Dollar Policy on all items.

INTERACTIVE GAMES & SPORTS

"FUN & GAMES" IS OUR BUSINESS

Recreational Fun To Go.
Transform an ordinary party or corporate event into memories of friendly competition and entertainment.

★ **Casino-To-Go**
Fun for all and all for fun! We bring Las Vegas to your event. We'll provide professional dealers…or you deal.
- ★ Blackjack
- ★ Craps
- ★ Roulette
- ★ Wheel-of-Fortune
- ★ Horse Racing Game
- ★ Giant Slot $ Machine

★ **MiniGolf-On-Wheels**
Luck and skill make this a great activity for all ages. Challenging obstacles. Designed for indoor or outdoor events. We deliver, set up, and provide everything you need.
- ★ 9- or 18-hole miniature golf
- ★ Shuffle Golf®
- ★ YOLF®

★ **Games-To-Go-Rentals**
Interactive games for all group sizes and age groups. Our energetic staff will keep your event moving and your guests entertained for hours.
- ★ Ol' Fashion Picnic Game Package
- ★ Animal Kingdom Bounce
- ★ Soak'um Circus
- ★ Dunk Tank
- ★ Balloon Typhoon
- ★ 30+ Carnival Games
- ★ Carnival Booths
- ★ Spin Art
- ★ Powerpull (Tug O' War)
- ★ Sea of Balls,
- ★ "SeaWeed" Obstacle Adventure
- ★ "Candy the 55' Caterpillar'
- ★ Treasure Chest Promotion
- ★ Money Machine
- ★ Electronic Double-Shot Basketball
- ★ Popcorn & Cotton Candy Machines
- ★ Bingo
- ★ Batting Buddy

When quality, dependability, safety and an experienced staff count… hire the GAMES-TO-TO PROS!
(503) 667-7724
www.gamestogorentals.com

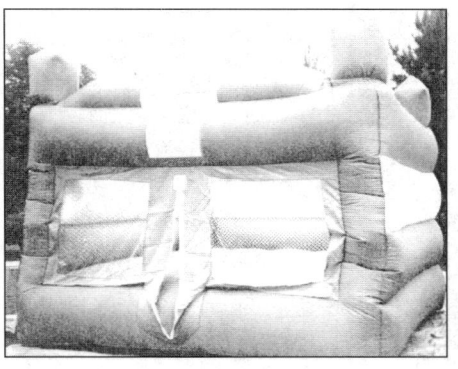

6107 S.W. Murray Boulevard, PMB 153
Beaverton, Oregon 97008
(503) 641-1803, (888) 700-5041
Fax (503) 643-1092
E-mail: ttoys@cyberhighway.net
Web site: www.partiesinc.com

A Tommy's Toys Company

Bring the cutting edge of game technology to your next function or fund raiser! Let **Parties Inc.** bring the excitement of an amusement park to your location. It's portable, affordable fun for your next special event or fund-raiser.

Oregon-based PARTIES INC. can Provide

- **12-foot high Velcro Wall**
- **Rodeo Roper**
- **Sumo Wrestling Suits**
- **Snowboardin' Simulator/ Urban Surfin' Simulator**
- **Miniature Golf Course—9 Holes**
- **Video Interactive Golf**
- **Kiddie Hi Striker—6'**
- **Electronic Chip It On** *miniature golf*
- **Giant Sling Shots**
- **Pinball Machines**
- **Air Hockey**
- **Ping Pong**
- **Human Bowling Ball**
- **Money Grab Machine (Cash Flow)**
- **22' Slide** *inflatable*
- **Inflatable Bouncer** *many types*
- **Electronic Basketball and Football Machines**
- **Pool Tables**
- **Hi Striker**
  Adult and 14' trailered, 8' also
- **Carnival Games and Carnival Booths** *lots*
- **Foosball**
- **Dunk Tanks**

Some of our Satisfied Customers

Intel, Nike, Mentor Graphics, NEC, Skamania Lodge, Portland Rockies, Portland Marriott, Portland Winter Hawks, O'Callahans Catering, Portland Hilton, SunRiver Lodge and Portland Trail Blazers.

Order and Delivery

All items include delivery, setup, and take-down within the Portland Metro area at no charge with a four hour minimum rental. Serving Oregon and Washington.

Have Fun • Will Travel

Fully insured and carry the safety inspection decals for Oregon and Washington

MasterCard & VISA Accepted

Visit our web site at www.partiesinc.com

INTERACTIVE GAMES & SPORTS

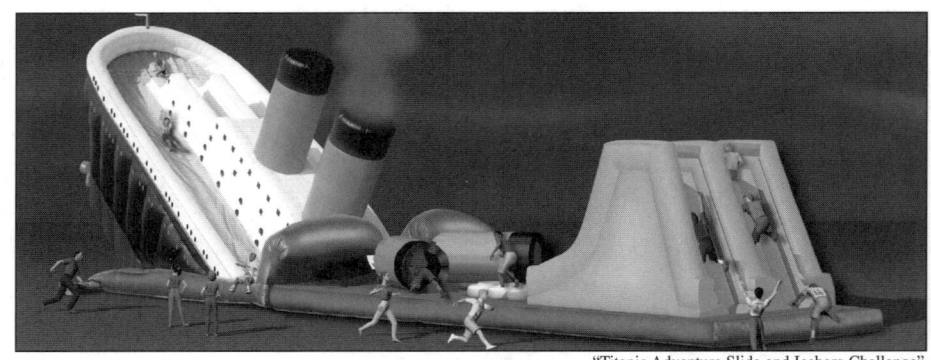

"Titanic Adventure Slide and Iceberg Challenge"

PARTY OUTFITTERS

Contact: Mark Thibodeau
(360) 438-2211
(800) 853-5867
Web site: http://www.partyoutfitters.com/

Parties and Picnics. Over 50 Games.

Big Fun for All Ages
- Velcro Wall
- Human Spheres
- Golf Driving Challenge
- Hurling High Ball
- Wacky Trikes
- 28 ft. Inflatable Rocky Mountain Climber
- Bungee Bull Ride

- Gladiator Jousting
- Big Time Bouncy Boxing
- Hoop'n It Up Basketball
- Human Gyroscope
- Inflatable Obstacle Course
- Miniature Golf
- 22' Tall Inflatable Slide
- Ostrich Riders

- Batting Cage
- Bungee Run
- Off With Your Head
- Sumo Wrestling
- Laser Tag
- Human Foosball
- 26' Tall Inflatable Slide
- Keg Racers

Especially for Kids
- Cameron the Caterpillar
- Noah's Ark Bouncer
- Ellie the Elephant

- Moonjumps
- Giraffe Bouncer

- Splativity—velcro wall, ball pond and rope climb in one!

YOUR ONLY CHOICE FOR INTERACTIVE GAMES

Party Outfitters is the premier interactive entertainment company serving the entire Pacific Northwest. We stand alone as the only choice when it comes to outfitting your special event with fun, creative games. No job is too large or small: team building, company picnics, corporate meetings, conventions, parties or any other special event. When quality, dependability, safety and experience count, don't compromise your event by hiring questionable help. Hire the pros as Party Outfitters.

DELIVERED • INSURED • STAFFED

Call for a FREE fun-filled brochure and RESERVE EARLY:

(360) 438-2211, (800) 853-5867

Visit our on-line brochure at
http://www.partyoutfitters.com/

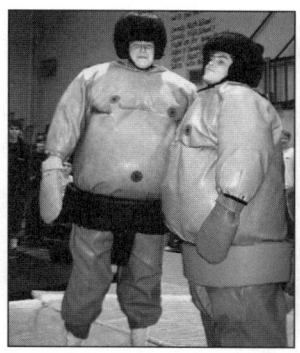

17437 S.E. Kendall Court • Portland, Oregon 97236
Contact: Mike Fazzolari
(503) 665-0260; Fax (503) 665-0472
Business Hours: Mon–Fri 9am–5pm
E-mail: Partywork@aol.com
Web site: www.partyworksnw.com

WE'RE SERIOUS ABOUT FUN!

Sample of Rental Items Available

- Sumo Wrestling
- Mechanical Bull
- Catering
- Event Planning
- Carnival Games
- Casino Games
- Velcro Walls
- Gladiator Joust
- Rodeo Roper
- Inflatable Obstacle Courses (many)
- Bungee Jumpers
- Lazer Tag Productions
- Giant Trikes
- Giant Slides
- Fun Houses
- Mini Nascar Racing
- Video/Pinball Games
- Golf Games (many)
- Dunk Tanks
- Ponies/Petting Zoos
- Bouncy Boxing
- Human Bowling
- Human Gyroscopes
- Air Hockey/Foosball
- Pool Tables
- Cameron Caterpillar
- Inflatable Bouncers
- Propella The Plane
- Water Tag Maze
- 30' Mountain Climber
- Golf Games
- Money Booths
- Human Foosball
- 30' Characters
- Fog Machines
- Black Lights
- Toddler Fun Zone
- First & Goal
- Djs/Live Music
- And Many More!

Satisfied Customers

Satisfied customers include: Portland Trail Blazers, The Halton Company, Fujitsu, Taste of Beaverton, Precision Castparts, Hollywood Entertainment, Portland Forest Dragons, Walt Disney, MGM and many more!

THE NORTHWEST'S MOST EXPERIENCED INTERACTIVE ENTERTAINMENT COMPANY

Put Partyworks' experience to work for you! We've been around longer than any other interactive specialist in the Northwest and have been part of thousands of successful events. We have offices across the country that provide a huge resource for talent and entertainment, so no job is too large or too small. From corporate team building and company picnics to college, church, or school events, Partyworks delivers. When peace of mind matters, choose Partyworks and enjoy the show!

Top Quality • Clean Equipment • Experienced Staff • Dependable • Local

Full Service: Delivered • Staffed • Insured

Please call for a free brochure and video, or visit us at www.partyworksnw.com

Please let this business know that you heard about them from the Bravo! Event Resource Guide.

INTERACTIVE GAMES & SPORTS

Over 100 Inflatables and 200 Games To Choose From!

Sonsational
ACTIVITIES, EVENTS & ATMOSPHERE

S.W. Washington/Oregon Office
514 N.E. 112th Avenue
Vancouver, Washington 98661
(360) 253-4831, (888) 766-7284
www.888SONSATION.com

ALL BRAND-NEW EQUIPMENT EVERY YEAR!

Attention Professional Wholesale Party Planners…we provide a sliding scale of commissions to meet your needs…receive up to 30% Commission/Discount!
Games Available For ALL Ages…Call for a free brochure!

High-Adrenaline Action

- Adrenaline Rush — $962
- Bouncy Boxing — $479
- Bungee Bull — $810
- Bungee Tug-O-War — $479
- Climbndangle — $1,620
- Climbing Mountain — $707–$861
- Gladiator Joust — $479
- Human Foosball — $690
- Human Whirl — $810
- Lazer Maze (enclosed) — $750
- Monster Trikes — $390
- Obstacle Course 40' — $630
- Psycho Swing — $980
- Radar Speed Pitch — $479–$570
- Slides 22' 30' high — $599–$746
- Sticky Wall 14' high — $510
- Stratus Basketball — $450
- Sumo Wrestling — $479
- Trampoline Thing — $899–$1179
- Water Tag — $804
- Word Ball Challenge — $510

Fun For Children

- Carnivals (complete tent packages) — $510+
- Bouncers — $199+
- Cameron the Caterpillar — $479
- Chooch the Train — $479
- Seaweed Sea Monster — $479

Commercial-Grade Gaming

- Air Hockey 8' — $249
- Pool 8' — $249
- Cash Cube — $349
- Electronic Upright Darts — $229
- Giant Twister — $249
- Inflatable Hoop Shot — $559
- Miniature Golf (9-hole) — $779
- Surgery Game — $559
- Ping Pong — $279
- Putting Challenge — $449
- Reaction Attraction — $878
- VR Game Pods (pair) — $1,950

And MUCH MUCH MORE!!

Prices Include Free Local Delivery • Item Attendants • Insurance

Guaranteed Best Pricing, Staffing, and Equipment!

LASERPORT

10975 S.W. Canyon Road
Beaverton, Oregon 97005
Owners: John Gabel and Bill Buhler
(503) 526-9501; Fax (503) 626-6912
Hours: Mon–Thu noon–9pm; Fri noon–midnight; Sat 10am–midnight; Sun 10am–9pm

"THE GAME OF THE GALAXIES"

The 4,000 sq. ft. fully-fogged laser tag arena has been filled with mazes, ultraviolet lighting, strobes, wall-mounted lasers, light displays and upbeat techno music. The total involvement for one game of laser tag is approximately 25 minutes. We supply all the equipment with no additional rental fees.

Capacity: up to 150

Price Range: $7 for the first game and $5 each additional game; special group packages available; please call for current prices

Catering: full-service in-house catering, plus outside catering available upon request

Types of Events: team-building and stress reduction make laser tag the perfect corporate outing; much team and individualized competition is possible using our computer-generated game formats—even a "you're it" option that increases the fun and adds to the excitement; we accommodate; corporate quarterly meetings/parties, birthday parties, youth group outings, school field trips, graduation parties, and other family celebrations!

Availability and Terms

Please make reservations as early as possible, or upon availability. Deposit is required upon reservation. We gladly accept all major credit cards.

Description of Facility and Services

Food: we serve hand-tossed gourmet pizza daily; certain packages will include chicken or vegetarian bento with a variety of sauces, and fresh-tossed salad
Video games: we have over 40 of the latest arcade games; quarter-operated
Seating: tables and chairs provided for up to 80
Servers: host or hostess provided by LaserPort
Bar facilities: for adult groups only; wine and beer available with advance notice
Meeting room: seats 50 for private meetings; TV, VCR and overhead projector
China and glassware: plates, cups and silverware provided
Decorations: no limitations
Audiovisual: provided upon request
Parking: ample free parking
ADA: fully accessible

"LET LASERPORT TURN YOUR GROUP INTO A TEAM!"

Need a little team building? Laser tag is the answer. It's the fastest growing corporate game in America and it's right here in Beaverton. LaserPort's state-of-the-art, futuristic laser sports center will motivate and excite your employees and help develop that camaraderie we all need in the workplace.

ULTRAZONE
"Portland's Best Laser Tag"®

16074 S.E. McLoughlin Boulevard
Milwaukie, Oregon 97267
Contact: Teresa Toole
(503) 652-1122;
Fax (503) 652-5204

ULTRAZONE—THE FUN BUSINESS MEETING

Break the routine and inject a dose of fun and excitement into your business meeting! Ultrazone is a high-tech laser game played in a themed arena where special effects and other players create an exciting adventure. Simply put, it is a futuristic entertainment facility that is fun and safe for all ages. Action takes place in a multi-level arena with 5,000 square feet of fog-filled mazes, electronic wizardry, and computerized obstacles. Teamwork and strategy are key as you locate other teams and score points using our state of the art laser tag system.

ULTRAZONE—THE ULTIMATE TEAM BUILDING ADVENTURE

Blast into success with Ultrazone's team building programs. At Ultrazone:
- Everyone can play regardless of age or physical strength. No running, climbing or strenuous movements are required.
- Employee relations are improved. Teamwork is promoted by removing boundaries and tensions between employees so they work together to reach a common goal.
- Strategy development skills are sharpened. We demonstrate how teams benefit from working together to develop a strategic plan.
- The dramatic environment leaves a lasting impression on each employee.

ULTRAZONE—THE BEST LASER TAG IN PORTLAND

Ultrazone is perfect for business meetings, office parties, birthday parties, morale boosting, sales meetings, or as a fun way to just release some steam. Food is available from all-you-can-eat pizza to a formal sit-down dinner. An excellent selection of video games and simulation rides is also available. Reservations are required.

IS YOUR COMPANY READY TO TAKE THE CHALLENGE?

Join the list of Portland's leading companies that have taken the Ultrazone challenge.

- Hewlett Packard
- Horizon Airlines
- Tektronix
- American Honda
- Burger King
- Commercial Credit
- AT&T Cellular
- Civil Air Patrol
- Boyd Coffee
- Safeco Insurance
- Intel
- Red Lion Hotels
- Shari's Restaurants
- Home Depot
- Sprint
- Adventist Medical
- Ikon
- The Good Guys
- Voicestream Wireless
- Zellerbach
- U.S. Bank
- Western Wireless
- Mentor Graphics
- Standard Insurance
- Phoenix Inn
- Burgerville
- Prestige Care
- Electric Lightwave
- Louisiana Pacific
- Kaiser Permanente

Play Paintball At
PAINTBALL ISLAND

Oregon's Finest Paintball
Course & GO Kart Track
Contact: *Mike Sinatra (503) 309-9900*

PAT'S ACRES KARTING COMPLEX
Racing and Recreation Grounds
6255 S. Arnot Road • Canby, Oregon 97013
Contact: *Chris Egger (503) 266-PATS, (503) 519-4392*

What is Paintball?
The "sport of paintball" has been in existence since 1982 and caters to players from all walks of life. It's the adult version of "Capture the Flag" and "Tag." Paintball markers are used to mark opponents out of the games with splatters of washable non-toxic paintballs. The sport has demonstrated a great forum for teaching teamwork, good communication skills, leadership, as well as providing aerobic exercise and healthy fun.

Group Information
Paintball provides an exciting activity for you and your group. For groups of 20 or more, we offer private games. Private games are available seven days a week by reservation. Our professional staff is with you throughout the day ensuring that you and your group have a great time. A $200 refundable deposit is required upon the scheduling of your group.

Description
Go racing head to head in our 45 mph racing karts on a half-mile paved road course. Nothing else even comes close! Champagne podium presentation for the Winners...Don't just race the clock—race the boss! Great for team building or employee appreciations.

Excellent For
Corporate parties, family reunions, sales meetings, employee appreciation events, church groups, team building, bachelor parties, or any other group or individual event.

Reservations
Reservations are on a first-come, first-served basis; deposit required upon booking. Visa and MasterCard accepted.

Facilities
Pat's Acres features 44 acres of trees and meadows surrounded by the river. We have a secluded private beach and picnic area along with a 2,400 square foot pavilion (barn style) building—great for meetings. Picnic grounds accommodate groups up to 1,500; indoor facility up to 100. Catering is also available.

Please let this business know that you heard about them from the Bravo! Event Resource Guide.

VIRTUAL PROMOTIONS, INC.

1825 N.W. Marshall • Portland, Oregon 97209
Contact: Jason Hedges (503) 916-0331; Fax (503) 227-2513
E-mail: vrzone@hotmail.com

Create a High-Tech Event with Virtual Entertainment

Virtual Reality is the perfect entertainment for these high-tech times. Your guests will experience 360 degrees of total immersive action inside a sensational cyberworld.

- Boxing
- Galactic Showdown
- Missile Command
- Zonehunter
- Dactyl Egg Hunt

The Most Cutting-Edge, High-Speed Racing Action Available

Sit down, put your hands on the steering wheel, your feet on the gas and get ready for the ride of your life!

- Stock-car
- Harley-Davidsons
- Motorcross
- Downhill Ski Racing
- Horse Racing
- Indi-car
- Street Bikes
- Waverunners
- Snowboarding
- And More!

Complete Entertainment Packaging

Make us your one stop for all your entertainment needs:

Rock Climbing Wall	Mini Stock Car Racing	Virtual Fishing
Carnival Rides	Putting Challenge II	Long Driver
Carnival Games	Spinning Gyro	Chip On
Inflatables	Video Games	Talking Robot

Great for

Company picnics, charity events, sales meetings, holiday parties, trade shows, special events, corporate gatherings, teambuilding events, conventions

Valued Customers Include

Intel, Tektronix, Nike, Planar, Oracle, Mentor Graphics, Maletis, State Farm Insurance, Blount, Honda of America, Harley-Davidson, Gunderson, ADP, Napa Auto Parts

Discounts available for multiple entertainment rentals.

ELWAY RESEARCH, INC.
2101 Ninth Avenue, Suite 211
Seattle, Washington 98121
Contact: Jone Howard
(206) 264-1500; Fax (206) 264-0301
E-mail: egis@elwaypoll.com

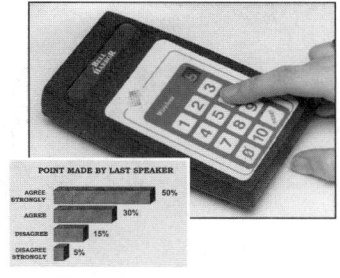

Conduct Fun and Productive Meetings With Electronic Polling

With EGIS, the Electronic Group Interaction System, each meeting participant is able to instantly respond to material being presented through an individual keypad. Participants' responses are continuously recorded on the systems computer. Results can be projected for viewing by all participants or displayed to meeting organizers on a monitor in a separate room. The data is saved—available for statistical analysis.

- **Anonymous response and instantaneous display of group responses** means more productive meetings.
- **EGIS keeps the process moving and on task**. As participants register their opinions, tabulated results are displayed to the group for further consideration.
- **Diverging opinions are revealed**. One group's answers can be instantly compared with another's, and/or with information gathered from a source outside the meeting.
- **Everyone participates, equally and continuously**. Because participants register their responses anonymously, they are included equally—without regard to verbal skills, language barriers, or willingness to speak up in a meeting.

EGIS Enables Participants to
- Remain actively engaged in a meeting
- Feel motivated to participate
- Stay continuously involved

EGIS Enables Meeting Organizers to
- Measure participant attitudes on key questions
- Monitor response as the meeting takes place
- Direct/redirect based on participant response
- Get information to the right people
- Enhance team building

Instant Surveys: What do Participants think about
- Important Issues?
- The points the speaker just made?
- The future of the organization?
- A question from the floor?
- The topic of the next speaker?

Move to Consensus
- Participants see how their views match those of the group.
- Questions can be reformulated as the discussion evolves.

Question On the Fly
- Questions can be added as quickly as you can type.
- Results are displayed within five seconds!

Vote
- EGIS tallies and reports votes instantly.

Elway Research Offers a Complete Range of Meeting Services
- Equipment Rental
- Meeting Facilitation
- Question Design
- Hard Copy Charts
- Polling Facilitation
- Data Analysis and Report

CALL FOR A FREE CONSULTATION ON YOUR NEXT MEETING!
Please let this business know that you heard about them from the Bravo! Event Resource Guide.

Notes

Entertainment Consultants

The Dickens Carolers

Pressure Point

Lily Wilde

CELEBRATION MUSIC & EVENTS

6916 S.E. 17th Avenue
Portland, Oregon 97202
Contact: Peggy or Michael Winkle
(503) 234-2492; Fax (503) 233-0835

E-mail:
cm_michael@yahoo.com
Web site: *www.cmevents.com*

Celebration Music & Events has been providing quality entertainment to the Northwest since 1980. We represent nearly 600 local and regional acts that range from Acrobats to Zydeco bands. Celebration Music & Events provided entertainment for nearly 800 events in 1998 and we are on pace to far exceed that in 1999. We have the resources and the expertise to help you from the initial planning of an event to putting the final touches on what can sometimes be a very challenging undertaking. Let us help you make your event the best that it can be!

Since 1980 we have had the pleasure of working with many fine corporations, clubs and organizations such as these: Nike, Hilton Hotels, Marriott Hotels, United Grocers, Oswego Lake Country Club, OHSU, Muscular Dystrophy Assn., Hewlett Packard, Waverley Country Club, Doernbecher Children's Hospital, Portland Junior League, Assistance League of Portland, Adidas Corporation, The University Club, Intel, OMSI, Mentor Graphics and many more…

Partial Artist Roster

Variety Bands: Pressure Point, Swingline Cubs, Panama, The Power of Ten, The Essentials, Byll Davis & Friends, Design

Big Band/Swing: Lily Wilde & Her Jumpin' Jubilee Orchestra, Art Abrams Swing Machine, Woody Hite, The Let's Dance Band

Blues: Lloyd Jones Struggle, Paul deLay, Linda Hornbuckle, Curtis Salgado

Jazz: Dan Balmer, Tom Grant, Tall Jazz, Rebecca Kilgore, Marilyn Keller

Country: Double Trouble, Cross Country, Joni Harms

Specialty Musical Acts: Body & Soul, Kerosene Dream, Calobo, Johnny Martin, Balafon, Pink Martini, Johnny Limbo & The Lugnuts, Zyda Blue and Rubberneck are but a few of the specialty and original acts that we represent.

Ethnic Musical Acts: Reggae, Greek, Calypso, African Drum, Steel Drum, Mariachi, Klezmer, Salsa, Polka. Create an international affair to remember!

Solo Musical Acts: Piano, Vocalist, Guitar, Organ, Flute. Violin, Harp, Accordion. We offer more solo musical performers than anyone in the area!

Miscellaneous Entertainment Options: Comedians, DJ Service, Karaoke, Casinos, Game Show To Go, Interactive Games, Golf, Magicians, Clowns, Impersonators

If your event needs the added punch that only a national or name act can bring, let us assist you in bringing the excitement of a world-class act to your next convention or fundraiser.

If you would like a complete listing of national acts available for your event, please contact our office at (503) 234-2492.

Dave Anderson
Comedian/M.C.

Greg Moreland
Comic Magician

Joe Stoddard
Comedy and Music

NONSTOP ENTERTAINMENT

Contact: Gerry Durham
(Entertainment Consultant since 1981)
P.O. Box 68480 • Portland, Oregon 97268
(503) 654-1776; Fax (503) 654-5796
E-mail: nse@teleport.com

"Now it's easy to find the right entertainment!"
Bands • Variety Acts • Comics • DJs • Musicians • Theme Events

- **Large talent pool:** a great selection of local, regional and national acts
- **Full service:** concept development, production arrangements and talent supervision
- **Information:** ideas, tips and recommendations for your event

Your one-stop source for meeting, convention and event entertainment is pleased to present three of the Northwest's top entertainers!

Dave Anderson, *Comedian/Master of Ceremonies*
Currently co-host of the "Dave & Dwight Show" on KXL Radio in Portland, he is a veteran of numerous corporate events and conventions, TV shows and comedy clubs across America. Dave cleverly blends clean, intelligent material with audience interactions to create a hilarious comedy routine that is sure to please any group. See for yourself why the *Oregonian* called Dave, "The quickest wit around."

Greg Moreland, *Comic-Magician*
Greg is wonderfully entertaining as the magician who "can't quite get it right." He sets audiences at ease with his personable style and keeps them laughing with his determination to be a "real magician"—which he surprises audiences by proving he really is! Magic wasn't supposed to be this funny!

Joe Stoddard, *High Energy Comedy and Music*
Laugh your lips off comedy and music; standup comedy, crowd participation, satirical impersonations and song parodies. Sing-a-long, clap-a-long, laugh-a-long to a very high energy music and comedy show.

Choice • Service • Experience

NonStop Entertainment (503) 654-1776 • E-mail: nse@teleport.com

Member of: Portland Oregon Visitors Association (POVA), Meeting Professionals International (MPI), and North Clackamas County Chamber of Commerce

ENTERTAINMENT CONSULTANTS

Northwest Artist Management

Musicians, Concerts & Fine Events

6210 S.E. 41st Avenue • Portland, Oregon 97202
Contact: Nancy Anne Tice (503) 774-2511; Fax (503) 774-2511
E-mail: nwartmgt@teleport.com; Web site: www.nwmusicpro.com

Since 1989 Northwest Artist Management has been proud to offer the finest in Classical, Jazz and International music for Concerts, Corporate Entertaining and all fine occasions. From Arias to Zydeco, soloists to elegant dance bands and hot jazz ensembles, we can accommodate just about any entertainment need or musical preference, including assistance with technical details such as sound, set design, lighting and costumes.

Theme Parties are Our Specialty

We are knowledgeable about all music from the Grand Baroque period to the hottest Top 40. We coordinate the musical entertainment, food and decorations to create exciting and memorable events and sizzling nights on the dance floor.

All the artists on our roster are gifted, polished professionals with years of experience helping our clients "custom-design" every detail of their musical needs. We are available to consult with you personally to help you select the perfect ensemble and repertoire that will create and enhance the mood and ambiance of your event and accommodate the needs of your guests. Call for our free promotional literature and tapes.

Western Entertainment

Put the Yahoo into your next Western Night Party! Old Time Fiddlers, Honky-tonk Piano, Singing Cowboys, Bluegrass and Jug Bands, Folk Ensembles with Folk/Square Dance Callers, Country/Rock Bands with Line Dance Instructors, Oregon Trail Speakers and featuring The Trail Band.

Cabaret Theater

Elegant and sparkling after-dinner entertainment highlighting the magical memories of Broadway, Hollywood, the Symphony Pops and the Big Band Era of the '30s, '40s and '50s.

Jazz

Soloists, duos, trios, seven-, nine- or 18-piece Big Bands. Vocalists, Latin, mainstream standards and the finest contemporary jazz for listening, dancing or background.

International Roster

Go ahead, use your imagination! African and Cuban Rhythms, Calypso and Steel Drum bands, Brazilian and Latin, Salsa, Irish, Italian, Mexican, Klezmer and Israeli, Cajun/Zydeco, Reggae, Bagpipes, Flamenco, Medieval and Renaissance, Blues, Mediterranean, Hawaiian, German Oompah, Dixieland, Barbershop Quartets; many acts with dancers, including traditional Chinese performers. Also Native American singers and dancers.

Dance Bands

You name it, we've got it: from Swing to Vintage, Rock-n-Roll, Motown, Funk, R&B, Latin Blues, Country, Folk, Top 40 and Variety. Featuring OPUS 5 and Sambrasil.

Also

Many Classical favorites such as String Quartets, Harps, small chamber ensembles, strolling musicians, DJs, caricature artists, clowns, magicians, comedy and vaudeville shows, and much, much MORE...

Member of:
POVA, Jazz Society of Oregon, Washington County Visitors Association, Weddings of Distinction.

Please let this business know that you heard about them from the Bravo! Event Resource Guide.

PACIFIC TALENT INC.

5410 SW Macadam Avenue, Suite 280
Portland, Oregon 97201-3825 USA
(503) 228-3620; Fax (503) 228-0480
E-mail: inbox@pacifictalent.com
Web site: http://www.pacifictalent.com

ENTERTAINMENT CONSULTANTS

Total Entertainment and Event Planning Services since 1975

ARTIST ROSTER 1999 (Partial List)

- **Northwest Recording Artists:** Pink Martini • Curtis Salgado • Linda Hornbuckle • Five Fingers of Funk • Craig Carothers • Paul deLay • Lloyd Jones • The Countrypolitans • Calobo • Rubberneck • Duffy Bishop • Terry Robb • Kerosene Dream
- **Jazz & World Music:** Tom Grant • Michael Allen Harrison • Boka Marimba • Patrick Lamb • Mary Kadderly • ValGardena • Bobby Torres Ensemble • Ron Steen • Mel Brown • Tall Jazz • Dan Balmer • Balafon • Pa'lante
- **Country:** All Night Cowboys • McKenzie River • Cross Country • Tim Schneider
- **Variety:** Panama • Swingline Cubs • Loose Cannons • Night Flight • Design • The Antics • Opus 5 • The Party Kit • PDX • Wiseguys • Two Much
- **Big Band Swing:** Woody Hite Big Band • Lily Wilde • Art Abrams Swing Machine
- **Special Attractions:** Body & Soul • Steel Breeze • Etouffee • Dick Bright's SRO • The Retros • Pepe & The Bottle Blondes • Hit Explosion • The Beatniks • The Airwaves • Johnny Limbo & The Lugnuts • Riverboat Jazz Band • The Dickens Carolers • Legends In Concert • HB Radke & The Jet City Swingers • Joe Stoddard • The Moes • The Stradivari Strings • Billy's Brass Band • Cascadia Folk Trio • Men In The Making • Lions of Batucada • M-PACT • The Suffering Gaels • The Coats • String of Pearls • The Jefferson Dancers •
- **Miscellaneous:** Comedians • DJ/Karaoke • Family Entertainment • Magicians/Illusionists • Keynote Speakers and Seminars • Murder Mysteries • Dance and Theatre Presentations

NATIONAL ARTISTS *for Conventions and Corporate Events* (Partial List)

Bonnie Raitt	Vince Gill	Alabama	Reba McEntire
The Temptations	The Pointer Sisters	Natalie Cole	James Taylor
Kenny Loggins	Manhattan Transfer	Peter Paul & Mary	Chicago
Jerry Seinfeld	Shania Twain	LeAnn Rimes	Sheryl Crow
George Benson	Roberta Flack	Bruce Hornsby	Randy Travis

SPECIAL EVENTS
Total Event Design and Production, Marketing and Promotion

PARTIAL CLIENT LIST

AT&T Wireless	The Bite of Portland	Blue Cross Blue Shield	Gunderson Inc.
The Heathman Hotel	Hewlett-Packard	Intel Corp.	Merix Corp.
NIKE Inc.	Nordstrom	OMSI	Oregon Arena Corp.
Portland Art Museum	Port of Portland	Sequent	Sysco Food Services
Tektronix Inc.	US West Dex.	US Bancorp	Washington Square

**For more information, call Andy Gilbert at (503) 228-3620
or visit our Web site at www.pacifictalent.com**

Notes

Bands

HELPFUL HINTS

Deciding on a band: Every band should have a music list available for you to review. This will be helpful in deciding on a band. You may want to ask if the band is currently playing somewhere, and then you can listen to their music live and observe their stage presence before you make a final decision.

Reserving a band: Reserve a band or orchestra for your event immediately, especially if the date of your affair falls during peak party seasons like Christmas or New Year's. Popular bands and orchestras are often reserved up to a year in advance.

Written contract: It is advisable to get a written contract stating exactly what you have agreed upon: date, number of hours, the total cost, and so on.

Setup requirements: The formality, facility, and size of your event will determine the type of music that is appropriate. Inquire about whether the site can accommodate dancing and has the area necessary for the musicians to set up and perform. Be very specific about getting the space and electrical requirements from the band so that you can accurately relay the information to your contact person at the facility.

Cutoff hours: When you make all the final arrangements with your facility, be sure to ask if they have any specified time limitations for music. Some facilities require that music be stopped as early as 10pm for the comfort of neighboring homes, businesses, or other guests.

Background music and dancing music: Remember when reserving your music that the first hour of your event is a time for introductions and mingling with guests. If your band begins playing immediately, you'll want to make sure that the music is background-type music that doesn't overwhelm and interfere with conversations. The band can be instructed or signaled to pick up the pace of the music for dancing at a certain time.

NOTE: Make sure your contract is sound, and that your event won't be bumped for a larger engagement. A deposit is usually required.

BOB MILLER'S
Almost All-Star Band

Presented by Sterling Talent, Inc.
P.O. Box 231059
Tigard, Oregon 97281
Contact: Becky Stroebel (503) 590-5840
E-mail: Beckysong@aol.com
Web site: www.sterlingtalent.com

Musical Style
The Bob Miller Almost All-Star Band has established itself as Portland's hottest '60s and '70s review. The band is eight members strong and features two lead vocalists, an outstanding horn section, exciting harmonies and a high energy selection of dance music from the '60s and '70s guaranteed to get the audience on their feet!

Band Philosophy
The Bob Miller Almost All-Star Band began as a promotional vehicle for Bob Miller's popular morning show on KEX radio. The idea for the band emerged from Miller's days as a musician in the '60s and '70s. In the beginning the band played only a few tunes at a time in conjunction with events sponsored by KEX. In time, the demand by fans to play more often and perform at their company events propelled the All-Stars into a full schedule of concerts, festivals, corporate parties and grand openings.

Experience
The Bob Miller Almost All-Star Band has been the band of choice for such clients as Bob Dole, Portland Trail Blazers, the grand opening of the Rose Garden Arena, George Morlan Plumbing, Portland Rose Festival, The Bite, Chittaqua Festival, Taste of Beaverton, Tualatin Crawfish Festival, Lake Oswego Waterfront Concert Series and many more.

Some Quotes from Past Clients
"The band was very hot! They got people who had marched the entire Rose Parade back on their feet dancing...for hours!"
—Richard Ransome, Sheraton Portland Airport Hotel/Portland Rose Festival

"I was blown away! They're tight, professional and obviously love what they're doing. I was so impressed I hired their singers to sing the National Anthem at a Blazer game. They were fantastic!" —Wally Scales, Promotions, Portland Trail Blazers

**For availability, pricing and promotional information,
call Sterling Talent at (503) 590-5840.**

BYLL DAVIS & FRIENDS
(503) 644-3493

Type of Music
Byll Davis & Friends offers complete flexibility in all styles and eras of music, including ethnic, Big Band, good time rock 'n' roll and Top 40.

Instrumentation
Byll Davis can accommodate your needs with one to eight musicians. Dress is usually formal, but we'll dress to suit the occasion. Call for more details.

Experience
Byll Davis has a master's degree in music, has participated in several successful road tours and has led and performed in bands that specialize in Big Band, rock 'n' roll, Top 40 and variety and society musical styles. The Byll Davis & Friends ensemble has performed in literally thousands of engagements locally for a wide variety of events and audiences.

Musical Style and Audience Rapport
The following comments represent the kind of feedback Byll Davis & Friends receives:

"Byll, you were fabulous as always and a delight to work with."

"It was the perfect band for the evening...many, many compliments from our guests."

"Your selections for our event were based on your ability to adjust and come through with what people like."

"Your music was so good it made it difficult to keep the outsiders from crashing in."

Free Consultation
If hiring a band is new to you, or if you want to find out more about Byll Davis & Friends, make an appointment to meet with Byll. The service is free, the information invaluable.

Cost and Terms
Prices, space and electrical requirements will vary depending on the size of the band and location of engagement. Please call for additional information.

RELIABLE
APPROPRIATE
PRICED RIGHT
FUN ! ! ! !

(503) 644-3493

Cúl an Tí & Tir na Nog

505 S.E. 27th Avenue • Portland, Oregon 97214
Contact: Cary Novotny (503) 236-9781
E-mail: culanti@aol.com; Web site: http://members.aol.com/culanti/

ROUSING IRISH AND CONTEMPORARY FOLK MUSIC

Four strong instrumentalists make up this compelling ensemble, which combines the best elements of traditional Irish dance music with exciting, modern Celtic stylings. Bass and acoustic guitars blend with vocals, accordion and red-hot fiddle in fresh arrangements of traditional Irish music, perfect for dancing and celebration. Cúl an Tí—"cool ahn tee"—performs a broad range of music, including slow ballads and waltzes, lightning fast jigs, reels, polkas, bluegrass and American folk music. The band plays throughout the Pacific Northwest; appearances include the 1998 Portland Celtic Festival, the Portland Celtic Minifest, The Bite of Portland as well as countless dates in venues such as Kells and Biddy McGraw's in Portland, and Conor Byrne's Pub and Kells in Seattle.

Tir na Nog

For a captivating Celtic music and dance revue that is sure to make your event a hit, Cúl an Tí can join forces with Tir na Nog, one of the Northwest's most exciting new Irish dance ensembles. This talented group performs a spectacular show of traditional and modern Irish dance forms in the spirit of Riverdance. Adding Tir na Nog to your event with Cúl an Tí will ensure a memorable feast for the senses.

Costs and Terms

Fees are determined on an individual basis, according to length of performance, location, and amplification requirements. All necessary details are included in the contract. Demo tape and references are available upon request.

LIVELY, UPLIFTING DANCE AND MUSIC IN THE SPIRIT OF CELEBRATION

THE ESSENTIALS

6024 S.W. 33rd Place • Portland, Oregon 97201
Contact: Rick Starr (503) 244-5968
E-mail: costar@pacifier.com

Type of Music and Demo
Nowhere in the Northwest will you find another band with the amazing versatility of The Essentials. From Sinatra to Huey Lewis, Glenn Miller to Chicago, the Andrew Sisters to the Pointer Sisters, we have something for everyone! We will work closely with you to ensure a memorable event. Ever have a company talent show or play "Stump the Band"? We can arrange the details. Specialty and audience participation numbers also are featured. Call for a promotional packet including photo, song list and audio demo.

Instruments
The Essentials are an eight-piece dance/show band featuring lead vocalist Jody Money and the Scappoose Horns. Instrumentation consists of guitar, keyboards, bass, drums, trumpet, trombone and tenor/baritone sax.

Experience
Each member of The Essentials has more than 20 years professional experience performing with some of the Northwest's most popular acts.

Music Style and Audience Rapport
No matter what we play, the emphasis is always on fun. We are constantly attentive to our audience's mood and, of course, requests are always welcome.

Special Services
We also offer complete emcee services or, if you prefer, unlimited use of our sound system for presentations, awards, contests or raffles.

Cost and Terms
Quotes are made on an individual basis and are determined by location, length of engagement, season and size of venue. Call for a personal consultation.

"'40s Swing through '90s Rock"

KIM RALPHS & COMPANY

(503) 282-3421

Sinatra, Swing & More!

Imagine the lush soundtrack to *Sleepless in Seattle!* Classic and timeless. Band leader, **Kim Ralphs**, has assembled a fine group of professional musicians that specialize in the elegant and sophisticated music of the 1930s and '40s. They play quiet and tasty jazz instrumentals and the romantic love songs of Tony Bennett, Frank Sinatra, and Glenn Miller. For your dancing pleasure, they offer Big Band Swing and smooth Latin and Bossa Nova favorites.

In a more contemporary vein, they know all of Kenny G's most memorable hits. When you really want to take the temperature up, they can pump out some '50s and '60s rock. Kim Ralphs & Company are polished and versatile professionals who offer a wide variety of musical styles. They are always happy to accommodate your special requests to ensure your event is a success.

Kim plays **piano**, key-bass and various electric keyboard sounds such as **vibes** and **marimbas**. **Sax and flute, drums and vocals** complete the sound. The size of the group can expand to fit your budget. Both male and female vocalists are available, or the band can play only instrumentals, if you prefer.

Since 1985, Kim and his group have performed at the finest hotels and country clubs, and have been recommended by the best event planners and booking agencies. They are always happy to make announcements for you and help coordinate your party. Standard attire is black tuxedos. Let Kim Ralphs & Company create a warm and sparkling atmosphere for your next special event!

LISTEN TO WHAT THE PROFESSIONALS SAY:

"Kim is a fine pianist…and I always enjoy seeing him here."
Dennis Yamnitsky, F&B Manager, **Oswego Lake Country Club**

"Kim plays here often, and always does a great job…highly recommended."
Susan O'Neil, **Waverley Country Club**

"All the music that I have listened to over the years and all the conventions that I have gone to, I can truly say that this band was the best!"
Colleen Greenen, Convention Sales Manager, **Portland Oregon Visitors Association**

"Impeccably professional and experienced… a pleasure to work with."
Nancy Tice, **Northwest Artist Management**

LOOSE CANNONS
Presented by Sterling Talent, Inc.
P.O. Box 231059 • Tigard, Oregon 97281
Contact: Becky Stroebel (503) 590-5840
E-mail: Beckysong@aol.com • Web site: www.sterlingtalent.com

Experience
When it is said that Loose Cannons is made up of some of Portland's finest musicians and vocalists, it is no exaggeration! Band leader, Gene Houck, twice a winner in the male vocalist competition on Star Search defines Loose Cannons' style with the smokey and soulful voice that has made him a favorite performer on many national radio and television commercials including Taco Bell, Quantas Airlines and Budweiser to name a few.

Loose Cannons performs for company parties, concerts, wedding receptions, festivals, schools and much more!

Recent Performances
Loose Cannons has recently been featured at such popular Pacific Northwest events as The Tigard Festival of Balloons, Eugene Celebration, Six to Sunset Concert Series, International Pinot Noir Wine Festival, Camas Days, Keizer Festival and many more.

Past Clients include Nike, Hewlett Packard, KPDX Fox 49, United Grocers, Shriner's Hospital, OHSU, George Morlan Plumbing, Baugh Construction and many others.

Type of Music
Loose Cannons' song list features a wide variety of **high-energy dance** selections from Jazz to contemporary rock and roll. This versatile group will tailor their music to fit your special event.

Loose Cannons performs songs by such artists as Marvin Gaye, Perter Gabriel, Elvis, Tears For Fears, Wild Cherry, Prince, Elton John, The Temptations, Bonnie Raitt, Robert Palmer, The Eagles, The Doors, Garth Brooks, Michael Bolton, CCR, The Beatles and many others too numerous to mention.

Call today for a free estimate and learn how Loose Cannons can add an exciting touch to your event!

Promotional packages furnished upon request.

1035 S.W. Carson Street
Portland, Oregon 97219

Contact: Fritz or Julie Weber (503) 245-5055
E-mail: Julie@luminos.net

Music
Luminos is a musical group consisting of Julie Weber, Peter Moss and Fritz Weber. They have over 18 hours of light jazz and rock in their repertoire. They call their style of music "rhumba-boogie": It's New Orleans-flavored, hipshakin', piano rock and boogie with some zydeco and Jimmy Buffett. A custom song list is created for every engagement after consulting with each client.

Instruments
Julie plays flute, alto flute, piccolo, conga drums and various other percussion instruments. Fritz plays piano, electric keyboards, keyboard bass and rhythm synthesizer. Both are vocalists and Julie also sings in French, Spanish and Portuguese. Peter Moss plays flute, tenor sax, baritone sax and percussion.

They will bring in more musicians if desired, but as a trio they have the sound of a full band. Also, as a trio the space requirements are kept to a minimum. As the sound engineer, Fritz sees that the volume is always matched to the occasion. Their musical instruments, sound system and stage lights are of the best quality and never out of place, even in the most elegant surroundings.

Experience
They have played music professionally since 1973, performing in public clubs and for private parties, wedding services, receptions and many special events. They've played on the West Coast and Hawaii, in the Caribbean and in Europe.

Fee
Their fee ranges from $500 to $800 and is affected by several factors such as date and time, special requests, travel, equipment required and length of engagement.

For more information visit their Web site at www.luminos.net or call for a free consultation.

MCQUEEN

The West Coast's premier country show band
Exclusively represented in the U.S. by Sterling Talent, Inc.
P.O. Box 231059 • Tigard, Oregon 97281
Contact: Becky Stroebel (503) 590-5840
E-mail: Beckysong@aol.com • Web site: www.sterlingtalent.com

McQueen is a hot country show band on the verge of national and international success! Since first appearing on the country music scene in British Columbia, the energy and dynamics of this five-piece band has catapulted them into a whirlwind of major Canadian and American show dates.

Type of Music

McQueen features a well-rounded songlist of popular contemporary country dance tunes sprinkled with comedy and celebrity impressions to captivate audiences of all ages. From hot "Two Stepping" country to hilarious stage antics and heart warming ballads…experience the magic of McQueen

Experience

McQueen has opened for such celebrities as Skip Ewing, Southern Pacific, Shennandoah, Willy Nelson, The Osmonds, Dan Seals, Waylon Jennings, Kathy Mattea and many more!

Veteran entertainers for such clients as the Calgary Stampede, The Albany Timber Carnival, Klondike Days, The National Rodeo Finals and the Chilliwack Country Music Festival in addition to the Ft. Vancouver 4th of July Celebration, Six to Sunset Concert Series and the Lake Oswego Summer Concert Series, this band will have everyone on their feet!

Band Philosophy

It is McQueen's philosophy to "let the audience become part of the show." This continues to be the trademark of this highly polished group of performers. Audience interaction coupled with the incredible comedic talent of band leader Ron Armour has been the key to this band's growing popularity. Armour incorporates hilarious celebrity impersonations into the show featuring such artists as Willie Nelson, Johnny Cash, Elvis, Kermit the Frog, Carol Channing and Elmer Fudd. Call today to find out how McQueen can help make your event the most memorable ever!

THE MOES

The Northwest's hottest show and dance band
Exclusively represented by Sterling Talent, Inc.
P.O. Box 231059 • Tigard, Oregon 97281
Contact: Maria Beatty (503) 230-8812
Web site: www.themoes.com

Rarely in the entertainment industry does a band come along of the caliber of "The Moes." The band's careful attention to detail results in a level of performance and professionalism unequaled in the Pacific Northwest.

From this group's early beginnings as a five-piece band known as "Five Guys Named Moe," it has evolved into one of the most popular show bands in the Pacific Northwest. The 12 entertainers known as "The Moes" mesmerize audiences of all ages with '50s Doo-Woop, Sounds of the '60s, Motown, Swing, Disco and beautiful ballads. The polished harmonies and choreographed dance steps of The Moes' three front singers adds to the band's highly acclaimed show appeal.

Recent Clients Include
The Monarch Hotel. American Express, Chinook Winds Casino, Lake Oswego Sounds of Summer Concert Series, Six To Sunset Concert Series, Eugene Celebration, Vancouver Sausage Festival, Coca Cola and many more

The Moes Performance Consists of
- 12 dynamic entertainers on stage, including a four-piece horn section, powerhouse rhythm section, backup vocalists and three lead singers!
- Colorful costumes and choreography creating visual impact and excitement!
- Complete sound system and lighting reinforcement included in the performance fee!
- A professional business-like attitude toward all aspects of the performance
- A repertoire that is a compilation of music from five decades

The Moes perform for corporate parties and conventions, reunions, fairs, festivals, concerts and wedding receptions.

Let The Moes make your event the most memorable party ever!

544 N.E. Thompson, Suite A
Portland, Oregon 97212
Contact: Amy Maxwell
(503) 335-0790; Fax (503) 335-9074
Sax Line (503) 650-7138
E-mail: lamb@teleport.com

Types of Music and Demo
Imagine the sound of sweet saxophone permeating the atmosphere of your event. Patrick is versatile and plays music appropriate for the occasion including jazz, blues, motown, 70s retro, disco and original music of his own. His recent invitation to play at the White House and appearances at major festivals around the U.S. have given his career momentum. His new release, *For the Love* CD, is commercially available, and recently made "Top 10 in the Northwest" for Northwest bands. Patrick has a funky, versatile group which can tune itself for the needs of almost *any occasion*. From the traditional, relaxed background jazz which is needed for a dinner party, to the '70s party down retro and motown, Patrick's band is a consistent crowd-pleaser. Please call for a promotional package, demo tape and/or more information.

Instrumentation and Personnel
High quality professional musicians including saxophone, vocals, bass, drums, guitar, percussion, piano/organ as appropriate for the size and intimacy of the occasion.

Experience
You might be familiar with Patrick's music from his many appearances which include: The Mount Hood Festival of Jazz, The Bite, The Newport Jazz Festival, Hillsboro Concert in the Park, Lake Oswego Concert Series, Nordstrom, or the private parties he has played including one for FOX49. Or you might have heard his new "Top 10 in the Northwest" release on KKJZ and KINK. Patrick has also toured and recorded with recording artists Tom Grant and Grammy recipient Diane Schuur, opening at festivals for people like Kenny G., Wynton Marseilles, Branford Marseilles, B.B. King, and many others. Patrick has experience in all aspects of the music business form touring, recording, and playing for all kinds of different occasions.

Cost and Terms
Prices are competitive and computed on an individual basis depending on month, day, time, and length of engagement. Our PA and lighting systems are always available for your use. Call for quotations.

Testimonials
"Patrick Lamb's music adds so much to any event or to any venue. He is someone you want to follow and listen to wherever he plays. Any event or venue would greatly benefit from his appearance because of his reputation, his crowd appeal, and the draw that he brings in. Patrick Lamb is simply the greatest!" —Teri Joly, CFI, Portland, OR

"I want to thank you for your beautiful holiday performance at the White House. Your appearance helped to make our 1996 Christmas holiday program truly memorable."
—Ann Stock, social secretary, White House, Washington, D.C.

SWINGLINE CUBS
0755 S.W. Miles Street
Portland, Oregon 97219
Contact: Teddy Deane (503) 246-4739
E-mail: swingcub@teleport.com
Web site: swinglinecubs.com

Showmanship
When the dinner's served, we play in the background. But, when the lights are bright and the show's begun, the "Cubs" keep continuous energy pouring from the stage. The crowd stays comfortably involved and entertained between fast-paced musical selections spontaneously designed to "read" guest energy/fatigue levels and keep the maximum amount of people on the dance floor at all times.

Our Primary Goal: Dance
Our repertoire is based on the music we love combined with years of experience playing the tempos that keep people dancing. We pride ourselves on playing selections that will make experienced and inexperienced dancers seek out the dance floor. We are very much aware of the increase in host success, sponsor satisfaction and guest generosity when people participate by dancing.

Musical Styles
We play all types of swing (especially jump swing), '60s Motown, '70s hits, rhythm & blues, awesome renditions of standards and ballads, and all varieties of rock 'n' roll as well as contemporary pop and jazz. We also have CDs commercially available.

Experience
In the last 15 years, we have played for well over 1,000 events of all kinds. Our client list includes: Portland Trail Blazers, Peter Jacobsen Productions, Oregon Symphony, Hewlett Packard, NIKE, Intel, Jantzen, Boys and Girls Aid Society, American Cancer Society, Doernbecher Children's Hospital, Komen Foundation, University of Oregon, Oregon Health Sciences University, University of Portland, Mayor Vera Katz, Portland Oregon Visitors Association, Reed College, The Bite, Rose Festival, Fort Vancouver Fourth of July, USA network movie, "The Haunting of Sarah Hardy"… and hundreds more.

Personnel and Instrumentation
The "Cubs" are a continuously rehearsed, seven-piece, same-member band. Exceptional vocalist and actress/TV personality Julianne Johnson is featured with prominent lead male and backup vocals. Instrumentation includes piano/synth/Hammond organ, guitar/congas/percussions, trumpet, sax/ clarinet/flute, bass and drums.

Cost and Terms
Prices are always competitive and computed on an individual basis. Variables include event size, site, sound requirements and scheduling (month, day of the week, playing times and duration). Please call for a quotation.

Notes

Musicians

Michael Allen Harrison

P.O. Box 30448
Portland, Oregon 97294
(503) 255-0747
Web site: www.mahrecords.com

Types of Music
Composer/pianist Michael Allen Harrison is an international recording artist who resides in his hometown of Portland, Oregon. Over the last 15 years Michael has released 20 albums of his signature adult contemporary style of new age, classical, pop and jazz. He has also released five Christmas albums and an album dedicated to Gershwin and other artists of that era. His music is heard around the world and locally on KINK FM 102, KKJZ, KMHD, K103, and regularly as the leader of the Good Day Oregon Band on KPTV Channel 12 Good Day Oregon Show. Michael has written and performed his music with orchestras, ballet companies, motion pictures, short films, commercials, and is the featured guest artist for the Celebrity Forum lecture series where he has opened for Walter Cronkite, Jerry Lewis, Collin Powell, Margaret Thatcher, Jerry Spence, Cokie Roberts and James Whitmore.

Experience and Demo
Michael has been performing professionally for 15 years. One of the Northwest's favorite pianists, he regularly plays a rigorous schedule of show and concert dates in the U.S. and abroad. Still he makes time to play weddings, corporate parties, and special events as well as two quite unique and personal services, Fireside Concerts and Dinner with Michael. Fees vary depending on whether he plays piano solo or is joined by part or all of his band. Michael loves to play his original music as well as the favorites and wishes of his clients. He will also write and sing new original music created specifically for a bride and groom or to celebrate a special occasion upon request. We have created several personalized gift packages for wedding parties, corporations and small companies—especially nice for the holidays. Please call for quantity and pricing. Information, demos, photos, and promotional material can be requested over the phone at (503) 255-0747 or though our web site at www.mahrecords.com.

Harpist Ellen Lindquist
(503) 626-4277

DISCOVER THE AMBIANCE AND ELEGANCE OF HARP MUSIC AT YOUR NEXT SPECIAL EVENT

Types of Music
Harp music adds elegance and magic to any event. Ellen's repertoire spans many decades to include Classical, Love Songs, Movie Themes, Show Tunes, Oldies and New Age. Her repertoire ensures each celebration is personal, unique and will create the desired ambiance for any occasion.

Harp Music is Perfect for
- Awards/Recognition Ceremonies
  - Board Functions
    - Sales Milestones
      - Receptions
- Holiday Parties
  - Banquets
    - Retirement Parties
      - Fundraising

Experience
With over 19 years of professional experience, Ellen knows what her clients want and expect. She has played at hundreds of functions in the Portland/Vancouver area and will work with you to blend the music with the type of event. She has played with the Columbia Symphony, Portland Chamber Orchestra, Eugene Symphony, Oregon Festival of American Music, Ernest Bloch Music Fest and Peter Britt. Her experience includes working on cruise ships, hotels in Japan and she has played with celebrities from Kenny Rogers to the Moody Blues. She was trained at the Julliard School of Music in New York and California State University Northridge.

LET HARP MUSIC CREATE THAT EVERLASTING MEMORY

Call for a free brochure, references and prices.

MUSICIANS

PIANIST AND VOCALIST
JO ANNA BURNS-MILLER

P.O. Box 20594 • Portland, Oregon 97294
(503) 254-5776, (800) 893-5776
E-mail: lilpond@internetcds.com

Types of Music
Accomplished on vocals and piano, Jo Anna will give you an occasion to remember. Her song stylings and repertoire are versatile, tasty, powerful, and professional. Often compared to Barbra Streisand and Julie Andrews, her voice is clear and pure. Her renditions are well-selected, polished. Her spontaneous wit and humorous dialogue weave cleverly through her performance to create a fun, rich, positive experience.

Experience
With almost 30 years of experience in the music business, Jo Anna's performances include nightclubs, resorts, concerts and conferences, churches and weddings, fund raisers and corporate events. Receptions, banquets, and parties are fun with Jo Anna, especially for special occasions and at holiday time. She has traveled extensively, and has appeared with a number of artists and on shows, including Lawrence Welk and Grand 'Ol Opry. A prolific songwriter and recording artist, Jo Anna has released 14 albums.

Cost
Jo Anna provides a sound system when necessary, and has a keyboard for rent when one is not available. Her fees are negotiable depending on type and duration of event. Call her for a consultation and demo tape.

VIOLIN & CELLO/STRING QUARTET

Duo con Brio

7455 S.W. Alpine Drive
Beaverton, Oregon 97008
Corey Averill (503) 526-3908; Cell phone (503) 887-4448

Types of Music
Duo con Brio is a professional ensemble consisting of cellist Corey Averill and violinist George Shiolas. The duo may be augmented to a string trio or quartet. We have a large repertoire, from Baroque through Contemporary, as well as seasonal music.

Experience and Cost
Formed in 1989, the duo's members have performed with the Portland Opera, Oregon Ballet, and appeared as soloist with the Oregon Symphony and other orchestras in North America. We have also performed extensively in Europe and the Orient. Duo con Brio supplies a wide range of services, including free consultations and a demo cassette. We look forward to assisting you with your wedding, reception or other special event.
• **Duo** $275 first hour ($125 each additional hour)
• **Trio** $365 first hour ($165 each additional hour)
• **Quartet** $455 first hour ($195 each additional hour)
• **Amplification** $50

P.O. Box 25711 • Portland, Oregon 97225
(503) 244-9547

Types of Music

Tom Grant is an international recording artist who resides in his native Oregon. He has 15 albums to his credit and has toured the world playing his own special blend of pop and jazz. His records have regularly topped the charts in *Billboard* and the other major music industry publications. In Portland, he has his own show on KKJZ and his music is a staple of KKJZ and KMHD radio.

Experience and Demo

Tom has over 20 years experience as a performing musician. He is a pianist, singer, and songwriter. He regularly plays private events. The cost is variable depending on whether Tom plays solo piano or provides a band. He often provides a high quality grand piano and a sound system as part of the package and his repertoire usually includes his own music as well as other favorites as per the client's wishes. Photos, demos, and press packages are available upon request.

"Sensitive, powerful."
Willamette Week

"Sensitive, compelling."
The Oregonian

"Beautiful voice...polished."
The Portland Observer

Introducing Pamela Jordan

Critics call her singing honey-hued, meltingly sensual, arresting. Audiences often compare her vocals to everyone from pop-singers Sade and Des'ree to legendary jazz vocalist Sarah Vaughn. Pamela Jordan has carved out a niche for herself as a jazz-pop chanteuse, working as the featured vocalist for the Woody Hite Band, Dr. T Big Band Orchestra, and with her own duo and trio at coffee houses, clubs, private functions and music festivals…including the Persimmon Country Club Jazz Series, The Reserve Jazz Series, The Cannon Beach Music Series and the Tualatin Summer Music Series.

Jordan was selected as a finalist from more than 700 singer/songwriters to audition for the opening act with the 1999 Lilith Fair tour.

Corporate Events and Parties • Conferences • Receptions
Banquets • Private Parties • Resorts • Festivals • Fundraisers
Holiday Events • Weddings • Concerts • Nightclubs

(503) 833-7379 or pjjordan@aol.com

MUSICIANS

JAZZ AND BOSSA NOVA SOLO GUITAR KEYBOARD/GUITAR DUO
SYSTEM 99

Contact: Andrew Guzie (503) 771-2621

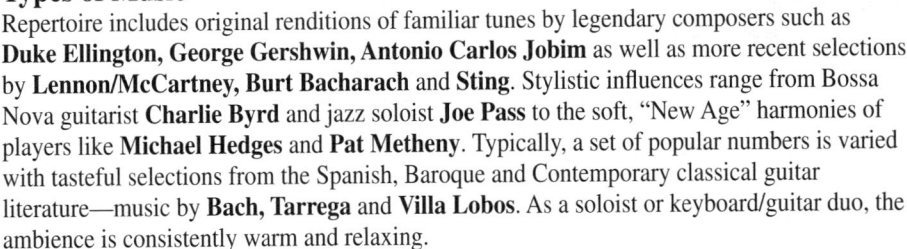

Add a warm and cordial atmosphere to your event with the tasty guitar and keyboard music of System 99.

Types of Music
Repertoire includes original renditions of familiar tunes by legendary composers such as **Duke Ellington, George Gershwin, Antonio Carlos Jobim** as well as more recent selections by **Lennon/McCartney, Burt Bacharach** and **Sting**. Stylistic influences range from Bossa Nova guitarist **Charlie Byrd** and jazz soloist **Joe Pass** to the soft, "New Age" harmonies of players like **Michael Hedges** and **Pat Metheny**. Typically, a set of popular numbers is varied with tasteful selections from the Spanish, Baroque and Contemporary classical guitar literature—music by **Bach, Tarrega** and **Villa Lobos**. As a soloist or keyboard/guitar duo, the ambience is consistently warm and relaxing.

Experience
Andy began studying guitar in his native Minneapolis and earned his Masters of Music degree from the University of Oregon after moving to the Pacific Northwest. He has performed original music on two commercial recordings; *Providence: Ever Sense the Dawn* and *System 99: Soft Fire*. During the past several years he has played solo or with accompaniment at receptions, dinners, and other special occasions in Portland, Salem, and Vancouver. Demo cassette, references and fees are available upon request.

PIANO • KEYBOARDS • VOCALS
SUSY WOLFSON
(503) 244-9607

Solo Background
Susy Wolfson is a musician of uncommon versatility. She is equally comfortable as a solo pianist or accompanying her own vocals, moving smoothly from contemporary styles, jazz standards, rock 'n' roll or rhythm & blues to classical music. Her background includes a magna cum laude performance degree from the prestigious Indiana University School of Music and performances at numerous festivals and engagements including the Spoleto Festival in Italy as well as many years as a freelance musician.

Trio/Quartet/Quintet
Using the classic format of the piano trio plus guitar (with vocals or instrumental only), these musicians are in constant demand for receptions, corporate events, country clubs and winery festivals. From black tie and smooth jazz one night to a kick-off-your shoes rock 'n' roll dance the next, this group will keep 'em dancing! Their song list ranges from Duke Ellington to Sheryl Crow to Stevie Ray Vaughn… and all points in between!

Performance Combinations
- **Solo Piano or Keyboard**
- **Trio/Quartet/Quintet** (vocals, keyboard, guitar, bass, drums—optional saxophone or flute)
- **Vocals and Piano/Keyboard**
- **Flute and Piano Duo** (vocals optional)

Demos, song lists and references for all musical combinations are available upon request.

Disc Jockeys

HELPFUL HINTS

Deciding on a disc jockey: Be sure to meet with disc jockeys in person. Make sure the person you meet is the one you are hiring for your event. Ask to see the equipment and portfolios or presentations of their shows so you know what to expect. If they do more than one show per day, check to make sure they have the appropriate equipment setups for two or more shows. The disc jockey should be able to provide you with a list of music available so that you can pre-select favorites you want played. Be sure there is a good mix of music so that people of all ages can enjoy and participate.

Written contract: It is advisable to get a written contract stating exactly what you have agreed upon: date, number of hours, types of equipment, who will be doing the show, the total cost, what is included, and so on.

Emcee: Be sure to ask whether your disc jockey can act as the emcee at your event. This will help the event flow smoothly.

Volume of music: With your disc jockey, discuss the selection of music you would like, as well as the volume at which it should be played. Keep the volume of music low for the first hour of your event, allowing guests to mingle and ensuring that the sound level is comfortable for older guests. Then when the dancing begins, the volume can be increased.

Setup requirements: Inquire about whether the site can accommodate dancing. Find out whether your disc jockey needs early access to the room and what the space and electrical requirements are. Make sure your facility contact knows about these needs and that they can be met.

Cutoff hours: When you make all the final arrangements with your facility, be sure to ask if they have any specified time limitations for music. Some facilities require that music be stopped as early as 10pm for the comfort of neighboring homes, businesses, or other guests.

Special effects and requests: Most disc jockeys are glad to play special songs if they are requested. Also inquire about any special effects they can supply, such as lighting, strobes, mirror balls, and fog.

AA TWO'S COMPANY DJ SERVICE

P.O. Box 68211 • Portland, Oregon 97268
Contact: Chris Tjaden
(503) 786-9090
E-mail: djtwosco@ptld.uswest.net

Type of Music
We supply your event with a wide range of music. You may choose from the '50s, '60s, '70s and '80s. big band, ballroom, jazz, country and Top 40. Our collection contains over 18,000 title songs, all on compact discs and mini discs. We play to you and your guests.

Demo and Equipment
Our equipment is state-of-the-art with a clean professional look. We will give you a full, high-quality sound at a level you want. Our lighting adds a special effect to your event. Upon request, we will mail you a promotional package, including photo, that will answer all of your questions.

Experience and Attire
With over 25 years experience in the entertainment industry, AA Two's Company knows what it takes to make your event a success. We always dress in appropriate attire for your occasion.

Cost and Terms
We prefer to speak with each client and ask a few questions about their plans for the event. We then describe our service and quote a price. A deposit is required with the signing of the agreement. As always with any special event, it is best to book as early as possible.

Special Services
We will make any special announcements during the event. Our cordless microphone is always available to you and your guests. Special requests are always welcome before and during the event. For the adventurous group, we are happy to get out on the dance floor and teach your guests the "Macarena", "Electric Slide" or even the "Octoberfest Chicken Dance."

QUALITY SERVICE IS OUR GOAL
AA Two's Company is a unique husband-and-wife team who pride themselves on providing quality service. We feel every event deserves our focused attention, so we only book one event per day. Our goal is to make your event a total musical success.

A DANCING PENGUIN MUSIC
LIVE MUSIC & DJ

(503) 282-3421

A Dancing Penguin Music owner, Kim Ralphs, is a professional pianist and DJ with over 15 years of experience entertaining Northwest audiences. His company is very well known and respected in Portland. This outstanding reputation was built with great customer service and attention to detail. He listens to you!

Playing the right song at the right time keeps the dance floor full and your guests happy. Swing, rock, disco, 80s, country, jazz…It's up to you!

You'll have total control of music style and volume.

You'll hear your favorites and special requests.

Master of ceremonies and help coordinating your event are included.

Black tuxedo is standard attire.

LISTEN TO WHAT THE PROFESSIONALS SAY:

"Kim plays here often, and always does a great job…highly recommended."
Susan O'Neil, **Waverley Country Club**

"Kim is a fine pianist…and I always enjoy seeing him here."
Dennis Yamnitsky, F&B Manager, **Oswego Lake Country Club**

"Whenever I need a DJ, A Dancing Penguin Music is the first company I call."
Nancy Tice, **Northwest Artist Management**

"I've recommended Dancing Penguin Music for years. Real professionals."
Diane Parke, event planner, **Occasions Etc. Inc.**

"Kim's piano and DJ combination really adds a touch of class to your event."
Charlotte Seybold, event planner, **Special Occasion Consulting**

Live piano with a DJ will make your event special!

All About Music DJ Company

P.O. Box 20625
Portland, Oregon 97294
(503) 408-7857
E-mail: aamdjcompany@earthlink.net

Type of Music
All About Music DJ Company has a wide variety of music that enables us to play whatever you and your guests request. Our music collection includes everything from Jazz to Country to New Age to Top 40. **We have it all!** We will discuss your event with you in detail so that when your big day arrives, the music will be perfect!

Equipment
Our state-of-the-art digital sound equipment ensures a crisp, clear sound for you and your guests to enjoy. The system is compact and will fit in an 8-foot by 4-foot space easily with a standard electrical outlet. Our system components are manufactured by industry leaders, including: Gemini, Sony, QSC, and American DJ. Lighting and special effects are available for your event upon request.

Experience
We love our job and it shows! Our goal is for you and your guests to have a great time. So sit back, relax, and let us entertain you. We have been disc jockeying for over five years, and know how to get everybody dancing! We are professionals, dressing in appropriate attire for every event.

Cost and Terms
We vary our services to fit your needs, with packages starting at $395 for a 3-hour production. A 50% deposit is due at contract signing in order to hold your date, with the balance due the day of your event.

Special Services
Our staff of professionals will help to coordinate activities during your event and keep them running smoothly. Our DJs act as masters of ceremony, making announcements to notify your guests of special activities throughout your event. Our microphone is always available to you or your guests. We encourage requests throughout the event, and are happy to provide instruction for audience participation dances.

For more information call us or visit our web site. We can send you an information packet, including a list of our most popular songs, or schedule an appointment with you to discuss your plans in detail.

Visit our web site at http://home.earthlink.net/~aamdjcompany.

We look forward to hearing from you soon.

ALL-WRIGHT MUSIC CO.

P.O. Box 3282
Portland, Oregon 97208
Contact: Eric Wright
(503) 452-0040
Web site:
www.bravoevent.com/pdx00/allwrightmusic

All Wright Music!

We love music! AWM DJs mix music from every era—Big Band to '90s top dance hits. Our collection also includes ballroom, disco, club hits, Latin and Top 40. We send out a detailed questionnaire to find YOUR wants and needs because every event is unique. We also encourage all guests to make requests.

Sound and Lighting

Our sound and lighting systems are custom-built in Portland. The systems are compact and detail-finished for professional appearance. Lighting systems are designed for each event and are always included in the total package!

Experience

All Wright Music Disc Jockeys have performed at over 3,500 events. We have experience in many facets of event production. We have also performed at private celebrations for celebrities, including Kevin Costner and Sylvester Stallone. AWM has been flown all over the USA to create festive events. Our resumé speaks for itself.

Cost and Terms

We speak with each client to find out the specific wishes and needs for their event. Please call for a free personal consultation—brochures and information will always be mailed upon request.

Our Guests Have Spoken

"It has been over two years, and people still remember our reception as the best they've ever attended!" —Mrs. R. Roake

"For the fifth year, you've made our annual event a true success! You are our 'Mr. Music!'" —Julie Papen/Special Events, NIKE

"Thanks for the GREAT job! My daughter's night was truly memorable. Best wishes for success!" —Former Governor Neil Goldschmidt

"Sincere thanks for a stupendous job! The party was a glorified triumph—the next party I give you'll be the first one I call!"
—D. Elliott, Con Construction

***For a Sound Event Investment Call Today!
At AWM we know our business—
let us help your next event be outrageously successful!***

Anthony Wedin Productions, Inc.

DJ Entertainment • Slide Show Presentations • Audio/Visual Support

Member of the

1665 Edgewater Court
West Linn, Oregon 97068
Contact: Anthony Wedin (503) 557-8554
Visit our Web sites:
awp.citysearch.com
www.bravoevent.com/pdx00/anthonywedin

WHY HIRE A DISC JOCKEY WHEN YOU CAN HIRE AN ENTERTAINER?

Type of Music
Anthony Wedin Productions provides a wide variety of music from the '40s to the '90s. All music is on compact disc which provides quality sound with a quick request time for you and your guests. We provide all types of music for corporate Christmas parties, theme parties, grand openings, Halloween and retirement parties.

Demo and Equipment
Professional sound equipment not only sounds good but looks good in a large or small boardroom. Anthony Wedin Productions provides equipment ranging from wireless microphones, video cameras, Kodak slide projectors, monitors, Karaoke machines, and quality sound systems.

Experience
Anthony Wedin and his staff are trained to be an interactive part of your special event. We have the music and the music knowledge to make your event exciting and one to remember. We have been creating fun and successful corporate parties since 1988. Dress is always tuxedo, unless you request casual attire. Anthony Wedin and his staff are also members of the Northwest Professional Disc Jockey Association, Gala Events Group, and the Association for Catering and Event Professionals.

Cost and Terms
Prices vary depending on the function and equipment used. Disc jockey and slide show presentation packages also available. Call for details on your event.

Slide Show Presentations
Professional slide show presentations in conjunction with the background audio of your choice is also available. This presentation format can provide important information for your clients, as well as giving them the visual impact of your product or service.

Setting and Requirements
Disc jockey and audio visual services can be provided either indoors or outdoors. All that is needed is a banquet table and a standard outlet.

WHY ANTHONY WEDIN PRODUCTIONS?
Anthony Wedin's professionalism and attention to detail will make your corporate party or business function a great success. He will work closely with your corporate staff to create a successful event your company, clients and employees will enjoy.

COMPLETE MUSIC
DISC JOCKEY SERVICE

**Need a Great DJ?®
Call the Professionals.**

Contact: David Gard
Portland (503) 639-8628 • Salem (503) 378-7975
http://www.cmusic.com

Holiday Events • Picnics • Karaoke • Theme Parties • Reunions

Type of Music
Complete Music takes great pride in being the finest and largest entertainment service in the nation. We are here to please our customers so they can be certain that their event will be memorable for everyone who attends. We bring to every event selections of the most popular music from the Big Band Era through today's Top 40 hits. Every song listed in your music catalog will be brought to your event, including the most recent hits. Call for a FREE catalog and video showing all your entertainment options.

Equipment
Our service includes Complete Music's professional sound system, our entire music library, a wireless microphone and our computerized lighting effects. Your DJ will act as the Master of Ceremonies for all your important events and will perform many audience participation dances at your request.

Experience
Complete Music was established in 1973 and has become the nation's largest due to the personal care taken in tailoring each event to each client's wishes. We customize our service to fit your expectations and guarantee the results to your satisfaction.

Cost and Terms
Complete Music's fees are based on a five-hour program, which includes dinner music, background music and dance music along with a FREE computerized light package, which add to the smooth flow of your event. Call us for our cost and deposit requirements.

Setup
Your DJ will arrive at least one hour prior to your event for setup. This allows the DJ time to prepare for your special event. All that we require is a standard six-foot banquet table and one electrical outlet.

Complete Music's Goals
Our first goal is to ensure that everything runs smoothly and according to your plans. Our second goal is to make certain that all your guests have a good time. Call Complete Music and allow us to find out what your needs are, so that we can combine your ideas with our experience to provide you with a unique event.

Decades Mobile Music

6312 N. Willamette Lane
Portland, Oregon 97203
Contact: Brian Darby or Loretta Korsun
(503) 283-4886; Fax (503) 283-4857

Type of Music
The act of celebration has been associated with dancing since the dawn of time. When you invite Decades Mobile Music to your event, you and your guests can relax and celebrate as we play favorites for everyone— from the youngsters to the young-at-heart! We stock popular dance music and Top 40 for every decade: from the '40s, '50s, '60s, '70s, '80s, and '90s.

We will also act as Master of Ceremonies, if you request, so that every part of your special event flows smoothly.

Song List and Equipment
We provide a song list to help you select your favorite music. Our equipment is the latest professional gear, and all recordings are on compact disk. This assures the clarity that makes music enjoyable at any volume level you and your guests prefer.

Experience and Attire
Others talk… WE LISTEN! Our Event Coordinator is at each engagement to ensure smooth flow and good communication between the host, guests and DJ. We tailor our services to meet your specific needs; your agenda is ours. Our skilled people and people skills make the difference. In addition to drawing on a great depth of knowledge for appropriate music selections, our DJs will play requests (can't remember the name?… hum a few bars!) and dedications. Our Event Coordinator will make announcements, pick up requests, respond to schedule changes, and keep the celebration going! Attire is normally a jacket and tie. We are happy to wear whatever is appropriate for your event.

Cost and Terms
A three-hour show starts at $350. A $100 deposit is required. Additional hours are $75. Lighting and props can be added to make your event more memorable. Special music requests, made in advance, are always free. You are given a written agreement to assure our services will match your expectations.

Setting and Requirements
We arrive at least an hour before the show to setup and test. This allows us ample time to adjust for local conditions. We require two standard 120v outlets, more if lighting is used. A space of 10' x 8' is necessary, indoors or out.

A Party in Every Package

DeeJay Entertainment

503/295-2212 ▪ Toll Free 1-800/963-6968

Visit our Website:
www.deejayentertainment.com

Featuring Portland Radio DJs:

Type of Music
DeeJay Entertainment can play a variety of hit music at your event, including top 40, country, '70s/'80s retro, classic rock and oldies. Every crowd is different and DeeJay Entertainment reacts with the appropriate selections.

Experience
Featuring Portland Radio DJs, DeeJay Entertainment is fortunate to represent some of the most experienced and professional disc jockeys available in the Portland-Metro area.

Demo
Call today and we will mail or fax you a brochure that includes references and a sample song list. Prior to scheduling your event with DeeJay Entertainment, we will discuss the range of music you like, and the presentation style. This will help us create the mood you desire for your event. We set up our own state-of-the-art sound equipment and make all announcements to keep your guests informed.

Costs and Terms
Saturday events scheduled between May 1–September 30, and December 1–31 are $450 (4 hours or less). All other dates are $400 (4 hours or less). Each additional hour is $75.

Thirty percent deposit is required to hold your date with the balance due prior to the start of the event. VISA, MasterCard, and American Express gladly accepted.

PROFESSIONAL...
EXPERIENCED...
RECOMMENDED...

Eighty percent of the events scheduled with DeeJay Entertainment are referrals, so we encourage you to check on availability as soon as you have set a date. We hope to have the opportunity to serve you and invite you to call anytime with questions or to schedule an appointment with one of our representatives.

Find out why so many of our past clients refer other people to DeeJay Entertainment!

ENCORE STUDIOS

Portland, Oregon
(503) 255-8047
E-mail: encore@webcombo.net
Web site: www.bravoevent.com/pdx00/encore–dj

Music sets the mood for any occasion and is particularly important during your private or corporate event. Whether you need disc jockeys or musicians, let us assist you in providing the music you want for your next event.

Type of Music
For your listening pleasure and convenience, we provide music of all styles and have a huge library of music from the '20s to the '90s in all eras: Top 40, Country/Western, Jazz, Classical, Rock 'n' Roll, Motown, Rhythm & Blues, Swing, Ballroom, Big Band, Rap, Reggae, Disco and Ethnic. Your favorites are always welcome!

Equipment and Demo
We have state-of-the-art mobile equipment which sets up quickly in a 6'x6' area with a standard 110-volt outlet. You are welcome to a private or live viewing.

Experience and Attire
With over 20 years of experience, you are assured of knowledgeable service with our professional and *fun* disc jockeys. We are not only disc jockeys but masters of ceremony as well, ensuring your event runs smoothly and successfully. We play the music *you* want to hear, and our packages are designed for every budget and musical preference. Casual or theme attire, tuxedos, or suits and ties are available.

Cost and Terms
Events are customized to your needs and include consultation, professional disc jockey time (additional beyond package at $50), and travel with no extra or hidden costs. Packages start at $275.

Special Services
Special lighting, strobes, spots, mirror balls, ropes, and fog available for special effects.
   Should you prefer live music for your entertainment needs, please ask one of our consultants for assistance.

Music Express

FOR THE PARTY YOU WISH WOULD NEVER END!

Mobile Disc Jockey Service

The Willamette Valley's Premiere Mobile DJ Service
Contact: Eric or Sheila Mousel, husband and wife DJ team
(503) 362-7216, (800) 222-7216
Web site: www.musicexpressdjs.com
E-mail: fun@musicexpressdjs.com
Portland • Salem • Eugene

As the Willamette Valley's premiere mobile disc jockey service, Music Express is dedicated to making your event the one that everyone wishes would never end! Whether you are looking for something light and classy or you want a party that everyone will remember, Music Express has what you're looking for.

Experience and Attire
Music Express DJs are trained event specialists who are familiar with all types of music and are skilled at entertaining for a wide variety of groups. Music Express will provide you with two of the best disc jockeys in the area. Having two experienced professionals means you'll get a much smoother event and it offers the opportunity for novelty dances, line dances and a greater level of guest interaction. The attire will be tuxedos unless otherwise requested.

Types of Music
From big band and country music to classic rock and top 40, we have the music to satisfy almost any request. However, the music played will be customized for your event. Song lists are available and requests are always accepted. All or our music is on CD for the greatest reliability and highest quality sound.

Equipment
We use only professional mobile DJ equipment that looks and sounds great! The equipment is customized to fit the needs of the event and is presented tastefully. Our setup will not detract from your decor. Minimum setup requires one 6' or 8' banquet table and a standard 110-volt outlet. Lights, fog, bubbles and specialty props are available upon request.

Cost and Terms
Our prices are competitive. Packages range from the very basic to the very best and are based on your needs and desires. A minimum $100 deposit is required with signing of a reservation agreement. Credit cards and company checks are accepted.

**Call Music Express for
the party you wish would never end!**

601 Main Street, Suite 210 • P.O. Box 65616
Vancouver, Washington 98665
(800) 903-3830; Fax (800) 328-3930
E-mail: info@ssdj.com
Check out our Web site at: www.ssdj.com

Type of Music
Our high-quality digital music library contains a huge selection of music, enjoyable to all ages. Special requests are always welcome. This will ensure that you and your guests have a great time.

Demo and Equipment
We invite you to call our office for a complimentary consultation. At this time, you can meet your prospective disc jockey, go over our extensive music lists, and arrange any extra details for your special event. You can rest assured that our sound and lighting systems use only the finest professional gear. And our setup appears tasteful, without unsightly cords everywhere.

Experience
Signature Sound disc jockeys have performed from coast to coast, and have an extensive background entertaining all types of people. Our references include the Portland Trail Blazers, the Portland Winterhawks, Intel and more. From low-key to highly interactive, extravagant to simple, we can make your special event one to remember.

Cost and Terms
Our packages range in price from $299 to $999. We offer many options, including exciting lighting packages, bubble machines, extra hours of dance music, and other options like party favors and props. A signed contract is the only requirement to reserve your date.

Setting and Requirements
We can perform at any location, anytime. From the Benson Hotel to your backyard, we've "been there...done that." A typical event requires a normal 110-volt outlet, and a table at least six feet in length, with tablecloth and skirting to match the other tables. If we need to provide our own table, just let us know!

Why Choose Signature Sound?
It's your party, and your group is the center of attention, not us! All DJ advertisements may look alike, but all DJs don't necessarily perform the same. Our full-time office staff, experienced and talented disc jockeys, large music library, and premier sound and lighting equipment make the difference between an extraordinary event and "just another boring company party."

MULTI ENTERTAINMENT INC.

"Entertainment for your Special Event"
4051 S.E. 64th Avenue • Portland, Oregon 97206
Contact: Chris Pearce or Jake Roberts
(503) 235-4924 or Toll Free (800) 9DANCE9
Visit us on the Web: www.expressusa.com

Don't just have a party, have an event! Sound Express will give your event that special feeling that everyone will remember for years. A talented DJ, a great assortment of music and high quality equipment insure an exceptionally great show for all.

Type of Music
Sound Express plays your favorite songs from the '40s through the '90s… from Jazz, Country, to Rock & Roll, R & B, Top 40, and Retro. Special event music is also available for all kinds of functions including weddings, birthdays, and private parties. Song lists are available and music requests are always welcome. Music is updated monthly to always maintain your current favorites.

Experience
As the Northwest's most successful mobile dance company, Sound Express has performed for thousands of events. We have a team of professionals with over ten years experience, providing the best quality mobile dance entertainment available. Sound Express DJs go through an extensive training period and can tastefully M.C. any event. We'll provide the right atmosphere to keep your guests dancing all night.

Equipment
Sound Express maintains complete, state-of-the-art commercial sound systems. Music can be played as soft as a whisper or amplified to create the thunderous setting of a concert. We also have one of the largest selections of lights and special effects available for your individual needs including: fog and bubble machines, spotlights, snow machines, dry ice machines, and more.

Cost and Terms
Sound Express has three different packages to choose from. Prices start at $285 for a three hour performance and are based on your needs. Additional hours are just $50 each. We can also customize a package to fit your needs. Each package includes a free hour of consultation to discuss your event. A $50 deposit reserves the date with the balance due prior to the start of the event. Call for a brochure and song list.

Letters From Our Clients…
"We had a great time…Music was wonderful. Thanks!"
~ Lori & David

"The DJ did a magnificent job, and everyone really had fun with the karaoke."
~ Stacie

"Everyone enjoyed the music & the DJ did a great job of keeping the party going."
~ J.K.

SUNRISE ENTERTAINMENT SERVICES
Mobile DJs & Lighting

2905 18th Avenue • Forest Grove, Oregon 97116
(503) 357-6699, (877) 710-1600
Fax (503) 357-2899, (877) 710-1800
E-mail: joeybdj@sunrisedjs.com
Web site: www.sunrisedjs.com

Nicole and Joe Burruss, owners and proud members of the American Disc Jockey Association. We are also fully insured for your protection!

Type of Music
Wow! Where do we begin? We have every kind of music imaginable! We offer traditional and contemporary ceremony music. We offer ballroom, classical, big band, and swing music—both original and modern. We also offer one of the most complete varieties of music from the '50s, '60s, '70s, '80s and '90s!

We provide a detailed, easy to use directory of all our music for your guests to make requests from. We understand that your guests may range in age from 5 to 105 years old! That's why we believe it is just as important to have a *quality* selection as it is to have a *large* selection.

Equipment
We use nothing but the best! All of our systems are digital, and use only CDs. If you prefer a discrete, high quality system with elevated speakers on stands, we've got them. If you prefer a larger set of speakers with earth shaking bass, we've got them. If you need a sound system big enough to fill a stadium with thousands of people, we've got you covered. We will customize the sound to fit your event.

Our systems are never under-powered or distorted. On the other hand, you won't have to worry about the music being too loud during the times when it shouldn't be! We have wireless microphones available upon request. We use a device called the "Feedback Destroyer Pro," which virtually eliminates all forms of irritating feedback caused by microphones (great if you need us to provide the sound for your singer).

We offer a wonderful selection of special effect lighting including romantic multi-colored mirror balls, high tech effect lighting, intelligent lighting, truss systems spanning 15-foot lasers, fog machines, hazers, and bubble machines. You can choose a standard light package or we will work with you one-on-one to customize a light show to your exact specifications.

Experience
We have over 15 years experience in the entertainment business! Although not all of our DJs are as fortunate to share the extensive experience that we have, we can assure you that we have the best DJs in the trade! The first thing that we look for when we hire our DJs are good people skills. Secondly, we look for DJs with a great love and knowledge of music. Once we've selected our DJs, we put them through an extensive training program to make sure that they arrive properly trained and dressed for your event. Still not enough? Ask us for a list of our references and find out what our previous clients have to say about us!

Submit Everything Online!
You can select and submit your choice of chart topping musical hits, organize the online reception planner to choose your exact order of events, print online contract copies, and much, much more!

**Do Not Hire A DJ
Until You've Been To: www.sunrisedjs.com!**

Please let this business know that you heard about them from the Bravo! Event Resource Guide.

DISC JOCKEYS

Clara's Own
ULTIMATE ENTERTAINMENT
**Portland's Premier
Full Service DJ Company**
*916 S.E. 29th Avenue
Portland, Oregon 97214
(503) 234-3055, (888) 332-6246
E-mail: Claraswe@Sprynet.com*

Find Us On The Web: portlandbridalshow.com/claraswedding

Type of Music
We feel strongly about giving you the right music. Songs that are proven to get your guests up and dancing. That's why we provide you with a catalog of the biggest party songs of all time. Choose from any era…Big Band, Country, '50s & '60s, '70s & '80s, R&B, Top 40, Classic Rock and more! All music is on compact disc to provide clear digital sound. Special requests are always welcome.

Equipment
What's great music without great sound? At Ultimate Entertainment, we use sound systems that contain the finest audio components available. Sound checks are made before guests arrive to ensure excellent sound at every location, both indoors and out. We have a wireless microphone at every event for your convenience. For nighttime functions, a dazzling array of lighting is an option you may choose to enhance your celebration. From the smallest backyard to the largest banquet hall, Ultimate Entertainment has the equipment to handle any situation effectively and efficiently.

Experience
Music and entertainment is the most important factor to the success of any event. When you choose Ultimate Entertainment, you get more than a DJ, you get our experience, quality, and professionalism. We are actively involved before, during, and after your event. This is why we stand by our reputation as "Portland's Premier Full Service DJ Company."

Cost and Terms
Ultimate Entertainment offers two different packages to choose from:
- **Package A includes**: four hours of entertainment, Disc Jockey who gets involved with your planned events, all of your announcements, games and contests.   Our price to you… $299.
- **Package B includes:** All of the above, plus a dazzling light show.
                                                                        Our price to you starts at… $349.

Only a $50 deposit holds your date. Additional entertainment hours are available for only $50 per hour. Please call for your free hour consultation with video presentation.

Special Services
Our disc jockeys are trained event coordinators and will handle your special activities during your event. Whether you are looking for an "interactive host" or a "low key DJ," our DJs can help you with your function. Ultimate Entertainment also has: karaoke, special effect lighting, fog machines, snow machines, and party kits (novelty items… leis, sunglasses, inflatable guitars, saxophones, and beach balls).

THE ULTIMATE ENTERTAINMENT FOR YOUR…

Holiday Party	Company Picnic
Awards Banquet	Convention
Retirement Party	Theme Party
Grand Opening	Trade Show

Bakeries & Desserts

ICE CREAM AND YOGURT TREATS

15994 S.W. Tualatin–Sherwood Road
Sherwood, Oregon 97140
Contact: Richard or Carol Gross
(503) 625-2736
June–August: Seven days a week 10am–11pm;
September–May: Seven days a week 11am–10pm

ON-SITE "BUILD YOUR OWN SUNDAE" PARTY

Make any party or event a sure hit with our Build Your Own Sundae Party. Choose two scoops of ice cream from a choice of four flavors, six toppings, plus our specialty hot fudge, whipped cream, almonds and cherries. We bring everything, clean up, and you have the fun!

Product Offering

- Cones
- Sundaes
- Custom Ice Cream and Cake Creations
- Cappuccino Blasts™
- Waffle Cones
- Shakes and Malts

Baskin-Robbins Express

We offer our Baskin-Robbins Ice Cream Cart for your indoor or small events and our full-service trailer for larger functions. *We'll bring our ice cream and yogurt to your location.*

Event Suggestions

- Office Parties
- Corporate Events
- Carnivals and Fairs
- Company Picnics
- *Your Special Event!*
- Grand Openings
- Birthdays
- Wedding Receptions
- School Functions

Costs

Quantity pricing applies; typical cost: $1.75 to $3.50 per person. Advance scheduling and deposit required.

> Mention the *Bravo! Event Resource Guide* with your booking of $150 or more and receive a $20 in-store certificate.

We Cater to You!

BAKERY & CHOCOLATIER

4733 S.E. Hawthorne
Portland, Oregon 97215
(503) 234-8115; Fax (503) 234-6076
Business Hours: Mon–Sat 6:30am–6pm

United States Pastry Alliance gold medal winner
Winner of the Austin Family Business Award

Chocolate Logos...A Tasteful Business Approach
JaCiva's can take your company logo and turn it into a chocolate gift to be used as client gifts for holiday or promotional items at trade shows. Wrappers for chocolate bars can also be printed with the company name and any message. Everyone loves getting chocolate and will remember your name with logo chocolates.

Cakes and Pastries Available
If you're looking for a beautiful cake for your corporate or social event, that is exquisite looking as well as luscious inside...then JaCiva's is your answer. We are always happy to personalize your cake with company logo or inscriptions.

You can also select from our scrumptious selection of pastries. We offer muffins and danish for your breakfast and brunch meetings. Victorian cookies for that afternoon tea, and European pastries for evening events.

Molded Chocolate Items
For special events or holidays JaCiva's offers special chocolate items such as chess sets, backgammon sets, golf and tennis items, edible chocolate boxes filled with truffles and chocolate life-sized turkeys filled with holiday chocolates and candies. Place your orders early.

Gift Baskets
JaCiva's creates wonderful custom designed gift baskets — the perfect gift for clients, employee incentives, and thank-yous.

Ordering
Early ordering is suggested, especially for large orders.

Gift Shop
Stop in for a cup of coffee and a danish and visit our gift shop.

CALL FOR A CONSULTATION WITH JACIVA'S

Notes

Espresso Catering

ESPRESSO CATERING

*1111 N.W. 16th Avenue
Portland, Oregon 97209
(503) 224-3330; Fax (503) 224-9529
E-mail: java@bridgetowncoffee.com
Web site: http://www.bridgetowncoffee.com*

LET US WIRE UP THE COMPANY BRASS

We cater the finest coffee in the world from the Pacific Northwest's premier micro roaster!

Enhance any Occasion

Bridgetown Coffee Company's hand-sculpted mobile brass and copper espresso machine will add an elegant flourish to any occasion! It has been the centerpiece at galas, political rallies, business gatherings and other high profile events, and it is always the hit of the party!

Service

Our skilled barista will arrive promptly at the venue of your choice to prepare specialty espresso drinks. A standard 110-volt electrical outlet is all you need to wire up our company brass!

Cost

Packages are customized to fit your needs.

Gift Packs from Afar

Bridgetown redefines the spirit of corporate gift giving. When our Master Roaster Don Jensen travels the world, he is always on the lookout for rare and unusual gifts to bring back to his family and friends. As a result, he has assembled unique and beautiful items suitable for your most discriminating clients. Custom create a gift package today.

FOR INFORMATION AND RESERVATIONS, CALL (503) 224-3330 TODAY

ESPRESSO VOLARE!
ESPRESSO CATERING

Contact: Myra Furnish Lee
(503) 246-3398; Fax (503)245-0373
E-mail: EspVolare@aol.com

Description of Service
Personal and professional espresso catering for groups of all sizes and events of all types, from morning meetings to evening occasions. You supply the electrical service, we do the rest. Also available: Italian sodas, iced espresso drinks, teas, juices and pastries.

Types of Events
Including but not limited to:
- Business Seminars
- Employee Appreciation
- Golf Tournaments
- Open Houses
- Trade Shows
- Fund Raisers
- Holiday Parties
- Bar/Bat Mitzvahs
- Grad Night Parties
- Auctions
- Wedding Receptions
- Anniversaries

References
A sampling of some of our clients:
- Portland Teachers Credit Union
- AirTouch Cellular
- Fishel's Furniture
- Congregation Beth Israel
- Portland Marriott
- Louis Dreyfus Property Group
- Portland Hilton
- Riverview Bank
- Target
- The Benson Hotel
- Walsh Construction Co.
- Saks Fifth Avenue

Popular Locations we have Served
- Montgomery Park
- Portland Art Museum
- Jenkins Estate
- Portland Performing Arts Center
- Melody Ballroom
- Oaks Park
- OMSI
- The Pittock Mansion
- Leach Botanical Garden
- Tiffany Center
- Oregon History Center
- Oregon Zoo
- World Trade Center
- Oregon Coast

Our Experience Counts
We are a full-time professional business serving all of Oregon and Southwest Washington. Having been involved in the catering and service industry since 1985, we have chosen to specialize exclusively in espresso catering since 1992. We will gladly work with your selected caterer or location. Please call us for more details **(503) 246-3398**.

A special *thank you* to our wonderful and loyal customers for their eight years of support. We look forward to a continued relationship.

Great coffee and great service are our business.

Notes

Catering & Ice Carvings

CATERING AND ICE CARVINGS

HELPFUL HINTS

Food and beverages can make a major contribution to the success of an event. In addition to breakfast (full or continental), lunch or dinner, food and beverage functions can include theme events, receptions, cocktail parties, and refreshment breaks. Most often at any event or meeting, the food has a lasting impression on your attendees. Whether it was too cold, not enough, or absolutely great, you will hear about it. Include regional or local specialties as often as possible for a memorable touch. Be health conscious and try to offer a variety of foods that are nutritionally balanced and colorful. Avoid heavy sauces and keep lunch light to keep attendees alert! For summer meetings or events, and especially hot days, don't serve alcohol. Don't plan menus with heavy food. Use umbrellas at tables to shade. Provide lots of water, juices and fresh fruit.

You are not limited to printed menu options. Either give the food and beverage providers a budget to come up with options or give them an idea of what you want and ask them to determine the cost.

It is important not to run out of food. Some attendees will have one plate at a buffet, and others will go back for thirds. Customize your menu and quantities based on the types of attendees. Ask your caterer's opinion as to whether served portions or banquet style is the best for your event.

Meal guarantees: Facilities usually require a "guarantee" for the number of guests that will need to be served at each meal function. The guarantee is usually required at least 48 hours in advance of the event. After the guarantee has been given, the facility will allow you to increase the numbers but not decrease.

Catering guidelines: Ask the caterers what their guidelines are and how they figure them. How do they take care of extra people? Some may automatically figure for 10% extra, which will be added to your final bill. Get several estimates if you are using an outside caterer—the price, portions, and what is or isn't included may vary for the same menu. Make sure the prices quoted will be valid the day of your event or have them commit to a percentage cap that can't be increased. For example, the price of beef may rise, but the caterer would guarantee quoted beef prices within 10%.

What a caterer supplies: Caterers can generally supply serviceware, flatware, dishes, cups, and table linens. They also normally provide servers, bartenders, and clean-up crew. Be sure to check what items and services are included.

Delivery of food: If the caterer delivers the food, make sure it is transported in warmers and coolers to ensure that it stays at the appropriate temperature.

Saving dollars: Order bottled beverages served by consumption and at the end of the event count the empty bottles to make certain you are charged the correct amount. Avoid labor intensive foods. Replace a full breakfast with a continental breakfast; it won't be as heavy and people can snack throughout the meeting.

Beverage conversion: One gallon coffee = (20) 8 oz. cups. One bottle of wine= (5) 6 oz. glasses. One full-size beer keg = 15 gallons, or (200) 10 oz. or (160) 12 oz. glasses.

IMPORTANT NOTE: Do not leave food out for long periods of time unless hot food is in chafing dishes and cold food is on ice.

HELPFUL HINTS

Liquor laws and liability: With today's strict liquor laws, it's always smart to check into who assumes the liability for any alcoholic beverage service. Although the event facility and/or the caterer may carry liability insurance, the host or coordinator of the function may still be considered liable. Make sure all parties involved with the event are properly insured and consult with an insurance agent to make sure you have appropriate coverage for yourself.

Oregon and Washington Liquor Control Commission Laws: In Oregon private hosted bars featuring hard alcohol, beer, and wine do not require any special licensing. Private no-host bars may only feature beer and wine and do require a special day license. OLCC does not allow private no-host service of hard alcohol. Only OLCC licensed food and beverage establishments and caterers may sell hard alcohol. **In Washington** private hosted bars featuring hard alcohol, beer, and wine do require a WLCC Banquet Permit. The permit must be obtained one week in advance at any Washington state liquor store. Only WLCC licensed food and beverage establishments may provide no-host bars. For more information regarding these issues, contact: Oregon Liquor Control Commission at (503) 872-5070 or Washington Liquor Control Commission at (360) 260-6115.

Private hosted bars: If you are serving hard liquor (alcohol other than beer or wine) at a hosted bar, you should consider having a state-licensed bartender. Licensed servers have a permit from the Washington State Liquor Control Board.

If you have a no-host bar where money changes hands, it is the law that you must have a server who has a permit from the WSLCB showing that the bartender has completed alcohol-server education.

Advantages of hiring professional beverage servers: Beverage and catering service companies provide professionally trained staff who can handle complete bar services at your event. They take care of the purchasing, bar setup and cleanup, serving, and liability. It costs a little more but may be worth it to ensure the bar will be handled in a professional and legal manner. These people are trained to detect if someone should not be served more, or if someone is underage. This service also allows you to enjoy the event without worrying about your guests.

Oregon Alcohol Service Laws: Any contracted bartender for pay is required to have the OLCC permit to serve alcohol. Volunteer servers do not need a service permit. **Washington Alcohol Service Laws:** Bartenders are not required to have a permit to serve alcohol for a private function.

Beverages in bulk or case discounts: How do you get a good selection of beverages on a budget? Distributors, wine shops, and some stores offer variety and savings when purchasing in bulk. In some instances, unused beverages may be returned for a refund.

Control liquor and keep consumption costs down: Have a no-host bar. Shorten the cocktail reception by 15 minutes. Serve beer, wine, water and soft drinks only; eliminate hard liquor from hosted receptions. Avoid serving salty foods during hosted bars (pretzels, peanuts, etc.). Instruct caterers or waiters to uncork wine bottles only as needed. As a healthy alternative, offer a juice bar or an espresso bar.

PROFESSIONAL ICE CARVING

*Sculptor: **Christopher Huessy***
*Contact: **Dennise Huessy***

Warehouse
(503) 557-0650

Office
(503) 654-0075

Traditional Sizes
- Full Size: 20" by 40" • Half Size: 20" by 20" • Individual Table Centerpieces

All sizes are available in clear or with color. Some specialty carvings include roses frozen in the ice. Carving detail generally lasts four to six hours.

Professional Background
Professional Ice Carving is a well-established full-time business. Our sculptor, Christopher Huessy, is a talented ice carver with over 25 years of experience. In addition to private affairs, we are currently servicing over 90 of the finest caterers, clubs, hotels, restaurants and professional organizations within the Portland Metropolitan area. Christopher is a leader in his industry, having custom designed and built his own ice block machine that produces 300-pound clear block ice, thus to ensure the quality of our product.

International Competition Medals and Honors
1999 – Gold medal – Lake Louise, Alberta, Canada
1998 – Competitor – The Nagano Winter Olympics Ice Carving Competition – Karuizawa, Japan
1997 – Sapporo Snow Festival – Sapporo, Japan
1996 – Gold medal – Anchorage, Alaska
1996 – Gold medal – Asahikaiwa, Japan
1994 – Gold medal – Fairbanks, Alaska

Christopher competes internationally to continue to offer "cutting edge" technology and to remain up-to-date on styles and trends.

Corporate Focus
Ice sculptures are a classic expression of prestige. Our ability to create an image in ice is as vast as your imagination. All sculptures are handcarved with artistic flair, and various images can be created for all kinds of events, from the "traditional" to "contemporary." We pride ourselves on our ability to reproduce business logos, complete with color. From practical shapes to extravagant masterpieces, you can rest assured you are in qualified hands.

Services
We take care of the details. What sets us apart is not just our ice carving but our consulting, delivery, safety, setup and expertise. Call for a personal appointment, and we'll be happy to assist you in creating an extraordinary event. We welcome your ideas and work with you to create the perfect affair!

Endorsements

Golf & Country Clubs	Hotels & Inns	Retail Chains
Columbia Edgewater Country Club	Benson Hotel	AT&T Wireless
Multnomah Athletic Club	DoubleTree Hotels	Ben Bridge
Oregon Golf Club	Hilton Hotel	Fred Meyer
Portland Golf Club	Holiday Inns	Meier & Frank
Pumpkin Ridge Golf Club	RiverPlace Hotel	Nordstrom
The Reserve Vineyards & Golf Club	Timberline Lodge	Safeway

INTEL • NIKE • OHSU • OMSI • OREGON CONVENTION CENTER • PSU • ROSE FESTIVAL ASSOC. • US BANK

We invite comparison
Please let this business know that you heard about them from the Bravo! Event Resource Guide.

Rose's Tea Room

Full Service Event Catering
Business Office: 23501 N.E. 10th Avenue
Ridgefield, Washington 98642
(360) 887-3095
Fax (360) 887-3956
E-mail: rosestroom@aol.com
Web Site: www.rosestearoom.com

Types of Menus and Specialties
Beautiful, elegant and unique, tea events are the ultimate expression of gracious hospitality. Modern tea is comfortable and enticing to the senses, encouraging good conversation and a lively exchange of ideas. Rose's Tea Room full-service catering offers a variety of tea events. Tea Brunches, Afternoon Tea Luncheons, Evening High Teas, Dessert Teas and Theme Teas can be tailored to suit any occasion and group size.

Rose's Tea Room teas are bountiful and satisfying meals. **Sample Menu:**
Cranberry Chicken Salad Puffs ◆ Classic Cucumber Tea Sandwiches
Three Pepper Cream Cheese on Rye ◆ Almond Raspberry Frangipane Tarts
Lemon Madelines ◆ Chocolate Dipped Hazelnut Crisps ◆ Cranberry Orange Poundcake ◆ Chocolate Dipped Strawberries ◆ Fresh Fruit ◆ Mad Hatter Scones
Rose's Wild Blackberry Jam ◆ Blended Black Currant Tea

Rose brings the charm of the tea room to you with china tea cups, exquisite layered table cloths, candles, and fresh flowers. Our Dessert Teas feature tea pastries fresh baked by Rose's Tea Room using only the finest ingredients available.

Cost
Prices range from $9.95 per person for dessert tea, depending upon size of group and menu requested. A 50% deposit is required to reserve your date, with the balance due 72 hours prior to the event. We ask for a guaranteed number of guests three days prior to the event.

Services
Rose's Tea Room caters business lunches, receptions, weddings, bridal showers, anniversary celebrations, and holiday parties such as our Colonial Christmas Tea. Tea, served buffet style, is a refreshing alternative to the cocktail party.

Rose's Tea Room excels in creating an atmosphere of gracious hospitality, where attention to detail and professional, kind service leave guests feeling pampered and happy.

In addition to catering, Rose's Tea Room offers Tea of the Month Club, Tea Time Gift Boxes, Rose's Wild Blackberry Jam, Huckleberry Preserves and our Tea Therapy Tin, available for delivery nationwide. (See our Web site or call for more information.)

"This is the best food I have ever eaten."
— Esther Milligan, Woodland, Washington

"I have been to many teas, and this is the most food ever served to me. I loved it!"
— Becky Neuschwander, Burdoin Mansion, Battle Ground, Washington

(Located inside West Linn Thriftway)
5639 Hood Street • West Linn, Oregon 97068
(503) 656-2981; Fax (503) 650-1230

A "Taste of Holland" Bakeries and Catering

- works with you in creating a one-of-a-kind masterpiece
- allows you to sample several different cakes and fillings
- provides highly skilled color matching from your samples
- creates the finest quality cakes in the nation as judged by National Retail Bakers Association
- provide expanded delivery outside of metro area for a nominal fee
- provide elegant catering for any occasion

Our award-winning bakery team will assist you in selecting from our large assortment of elegant Dutch pastries, gourmet cookies and breads to make your event memorable.

Cost, Ordering and Delivery

We encourage you to come in to order your cake. This allows you to view our portfolio and sample our quality. We request a 20% nonrefundable deposit with your order.

Accent on Events

918 S.W. Yamhill, Second Floor
Portland, Oregon 97205
Contact: Philip Sword or Barbara Abalan
(503) 227-4061
E-mail: accentevnt@aol.com

Full Service Catering and Special Event Production

- Wedding Receptions
- Theme Parties
- Holiday Parties
- Business Meetings
- Corporate Events
- Fundraisers
- Awards Banquets
- Reunions & Proms

Menus
Numerous menus available from which you may select or we will gladly custom design your menu based upon personal requests and budget.

Cost
Cost is dependent on menu and service selected (buffet or sit-down). Prices are per person and inclusive of staff, china, silverware, linens, etc. (except drop-off services). A 50% deposit required to confirm.

Alcohol
Fully licensed to serve all alcoholic beverages with complete liability insurance (hosted, no-host or combination).

Services
Experienced in all locations, from private homes to office buildings and outdoors. We provide only professional and skilled staff.

Accent on Events is the exclusive full-service caterer and event planner for the prestigious Adrianna Hill Grand Ballroom and provide services in the Portland Metro area. You are invited to call for information or schedule an appointment at Portland's most unique location to discuss your next event.

Affordable	Professional
Experienced	Great Food
Innovative	Easy

Special Fully-Inclusive Packages Available
with Rental of The Adrianna Hill Grand Ballroom

Great "Drop-Off" Food Services Available ♠ Parties Ready-To-Go

See page 446 under Banquet, Meeting & Event Sites.

The Cuisine
- Fabulous food is catered to your individualized tastes.
- All dishes are created by our personal chef and made with the finest ingredients.

Specialized Catering
Corporate Events, Holiday Parties, Company Picnics, Business Meetings, Corporate Box lunches, Formal Banquets, Award Banquets, Wedding Receptions, Elaborate Gift Baskets, Silver Platters, and Elegant Hors d'oeuvres Mirrors.

Services
- Professional Chefs, Planners, and Servers prepare for your special event.
- Elegant serving trays, Baskets, and Table Decorations ranging from simple centerpieces to elegant displays are provided.
- Disposable dishware is included with no additional charge.
- Rental coordination of china, linens, silverware, etc., is arranged.
- Our "ALWAYS PERFECT" touch is added to every event.

Gifts
- Impress your clients and friends with an ALWAYS PERFECT Gift Basket filled with fresh food or with an Elegant Hors d'oeuvres Mirror.
- Local Delivery is provided.

Cost and Terms
- We offer free consultations and event planning.
- A 50% deposit is required to confirm the date of your event.
- Corporate accounts and all major credit cards are welcomed.

"Simple to Elegant Catering designed to meet your budget and needs"

Call for your Free Consultation
(503) 465-0400

Distinctive Catering

AN ELEGANT AFFAIR

P.O. Box 80013 • Portland, Oregon 97280
Contact: Melody
(503) 245-2802; Fax (503) 246-4309
E-mail: melodym@spiritone.com

You are cordially invited to experience An Elegant Affair…Your Next Event!

Types of Menus and Specialties

Catering is our only business. An Elegant Affair catering will carefully plan, prepare, and present a tantalizing bill of fare created specifically to fit your budget and needs. Whether it's a business meeting brunch, open house luncheon, holiday hors d'oeuvres cocktail party, or formal board meeting dinner, we are committed to making your affair an elegant one!

Services and Cost

- **Menu planning:** Our seasoned staff can prepare any type of cuisine in our fully licensed catering kitchen, and we are happy to design a menu that will suit your special occasion.
- **Estimating number of guests:** We can help you determine how many guests to expect to ensure accurate food quantities are ordered.
- **Cost:** Our prices are determined on a per-person basis and vary upon menu selection. A 25% deposit is required to reserve your date. The balance is due before the event.
- **Beverage service:** Alcoholic and nonalcoholic beverages are available.
- **Linens and napkins:** Buffet table linen and skirting no charge; paper products no charge; white and colored linen tablecloths and napkins available.
- **Serviceware:** Silver serving trays available no charge; china, glassware, paper, and plastic available.
- **Riverboat receptions and parties:** Available year-round on the Willamette.
- **Servers:** We supply experienced, professional servers and bartenders in formal black and white attire. Setup, serving, and complete cleanup of all food and beverages are always provided at no extra charge.0

For your entertaining ease, let AN ELEGANT AFFAIR handle your next catered event.

(You'll find hosting a special occasion will never be easier or more enjoyable.)

Call today for a complimentary consultation!
(503) 245-2802

AUTHENTIC TEXAS BBQ

20373 S.E. Ridgecrest Drive
Sandy, Oregon 97055
Contact: Richard Boswick (503) 668-8943; Fax (503) 668-8943
E-mail: TexBarbq@aol.com

Types of Menus and Specialty

Barbecue—real BBQ—there's nothing like it! We slow-cook over a wood fire and finish it off to perfection using pecan, mesquite and oak woods. This is the stuff legends are made of! We at Authentic Texas Barbecue take pride in bringing our heritage to the great Northwest. We don't do sushi or bento, so why settle for someone who does a little bit of everything but not enough of either? Make that upcoming event a memorable occasion with the best there is! Our unlimited buffet consists of specialty meats, "homemade" salads, veggie trays, chips, dips, condiments, desserts and anything else you want. You and your guests can help yourselves to as much as you want and come back as many times as you'd like! Our speciality is beef brisket; slow-cooked for 12–14 hours on our custom-made barbecue pit that is on site and guaranteed to be a big hit at every picnic. Our other meats to choose from include smoked ham, smoked turkey, linked sausage, chicken, beef and pork ribs, and of course hamburgers and hot dogs with all the fixins'.

Costs and Services

Now you can treat your guests to the best there is without taking out a loan. Prices are on a per person basis, serving anywhere from 50 to 5,000 guests. With your input and our suggestions we will plan a picnic that is sure to please everyone. Accommodating you and your guests is our top priority, so let us know how we can better serve you! We like special requests—just ask and even vegetarians are tolerated! All paperware and plastic utensils are provided, along with everything else to make your picnic complete. Our crew will set up, service you during the festivities, and clean up afterwards. Relax, let us take care of you!

Experience

Proprietor Richard Boswick, with over 20 years of barbecue expertise, recently relocated to Oregon from the Houston area three years ago. Authentic Texas Barbecue was built on referrals, establishing hundreds of satisfied customers in the Northwest. References are gladly available.

Let us serve your catering needs! We are sure we'll leave you full, satisfied, and asking us to do it again. Remember this ain't Texas *style* barbecue, this **is** Texas Barbecue—the meaning and the definition!

Restaurant and Catering

827 S.W. Second Avenue • Portland, Oregon 97204
Contact: Mark A. Lopez or Judie Lopez, Your Corporate Catering Specialist
Call for our official catering menu: (503) 224-0370; Fax (503) 224-3919
Business Hours: Mon–Fri 7am–4:30pm
Web site: www.bajagrill.citysearch.com

BETTER THAN THE REST MEX!

Baja Grill offers a wonderful variety of freshly prepared traditional Mexican favorites plus a unique assortment of fine eclectic Southwestern-style dishes with a health conscious "no lard" attitude. Choose from our five homemade salsas, finger foods, appetizers, lunches, dinners, vegetarian menu, plus fabulous desserts and beverages.

Just a Sample

Jammin' Jay's Party Platter

- Homemade Tortilla Chips
- Flautitas de Pollo
- Artichoke Quesadillas
- Sweet Cinnamon Buñuelos
- Three Hand-Crafted Salsas
- Black Bean, Chicken, and Beef Taquitos
- Baja-Style Fish Tacos

From $6.75–$8.95 per person

Location

- "Mi Casa Es Su Casa"—Our place…Fiestas up to 100
- Your Place…"the sky's the limit!"

Services

- Custom Menu Planning
- Beer and Wine Service available
- Serving Attendants–from setup, to serving, to clean-up
- Equipment and Rental Coordination for your event "needs"

Cost

We will provide you with the best value…working within your budget. Catering menu charges are based on per person and per item selection.

OUR GOAL

Our goal is to make your special event as wonderful and memorable as possible. We'll bring you the finest and freshest ingredients crafted with striking presentation, served with precision and care.

We love what we do…we think you will too.

PARTIES • FIESTAS • BOX LUNCHES • HOLIDAYS
OFFICE MEETINGS • BREAKFASTS • LUNCHEONS
HECK…ANY OL'REASON!

SPECIALIZING IN CORPORATE CATERING

Barton Productions Catering

1822 N.E. 153rd Street • Vancouver, Washington 98686
(360) 574-7449; Fax (360) 573-9218; E-mail: ebarton@teleport.com

Professional Experience and Classic Style

Barton Productions Catering brings over 20 years experience and professional knowledge to every event it produces. Owner Eric Barton and Chef Greg Retchless have traveled the world studying cuisine and wines as well as gaining several years experience in Portland as Atwater's Dining Room Captain and managing some of the most important events in the city for OMSI, the Portland Art Museum, Nike, Intel, the Portland Spirit cruise ship, Bill Clinton, Vanessa Williams, and Michael Jordan. Barton Productions Catering is the preferred or an approved caterer for the Portland Art Museum, Arnegards, the Crown Ballroom. Hunter Creek Farm, The Northwest Forestry Center, Pearson Air Museum and many others. Whether you are planning an elegant executive dinner for eight, an annual summer picnic on the lake, or the elaborate Christmas event of the year, every event by Barton Productions Catering is presented with the style and special detail afforded the most prestigious events.

Sophisticated, Educated, Appropriate and Personable Staff

Every Barton Productions Catering staff person has several years experience in the finest establishments in the area including the Multnomah Athletic Club, Atwater's, and The Benson Hotel before employment with Barton Productions Catering, along with specialized enological, butler service, and culinary training. The staff is always appropriately attired, whether in classic black tuxedos with white dinner jackets, or starched khaki shorts and white polo shirts, or distinct theme costumes to match your unique event.

Elaborate Decoration and Innovative Presentation

The classic buffets are presented with large slabs of Brazilian marble, gold leaf serving bowls, sterling and gold serving utensils, Greek and Roman architectural elements, palm trees, ferns, gold candles, colored matched linens, coordinated satin swags, and hidden up-lighting and under-lighting, transforming your buffet into a centerpiece of excitement! For your particular theme, Barton Productions Catering always creates a masterpiece incorporating your desired colors, antiques, and glassware and dishware to match the style of your event. Elaborate food displays featuring mountains of salad over four-feet wide and giant waterfalls of fruit cascading from marble cliffs invoke a sense of "WOW" from your guests.

Classic Northwest and Exotic Theme Cuisine

From classic buffet specialties like the Roasted Garlic Encrusted Prime Rib with pan juices, Cabernet, and pearl onions; Poached Copper River Salmon Filets in Riesling tarragon butter sauce; Tijuana Caesar Salad with farm-style French bread and parmesan croutons, to innovative features like the Simmered Risotto with Bing cherries, baby spinach, thyme, and ruby port; Barbecued Pork and Mango Skewers, Sweet Red Pepper Dill Bay Shrimp buttered hors d'oeuvre—Barton Productions Catering has no limits for catered cuisine.

SAME DAY PROPOSALS AND FAXED MENUS

Member of the Association of Catering & Event Professionals

BLIMPIE

Contact: Tiffany Hugo

Westside
1923 S.W. Sixth Avenue
Portland, Oregon 97201
(503) 225-0538
Fax (503) 656-5513

Eastside
4124 82nd Avenue
Portland, Oregon 97266
(503) 771-3719
Fax (503) 656-5513

**If you haven't had your occasion catered by us,
You haven't had the best by Blimpie!**

Menu and Specialties

Blimpie offers a wide variety of sandwiches, salads, fresh baked cookies, and we can also provide ice cream or frozen yogurt cakes for any special occasion. Blimpie specializes in 3-foot and 6-foot Blasts made on homemade bread with your favorite fresh meats and delicious toppings. Blasts may be packaged with its own box and lining.

- 3-foot Blast feeds 15–20 people
- 6-foot Blast feeds 30–40 people

We also have "Blimpie Bites," a tray of our delicious three-inch subs to accommodate your party size with your choice choice of fresh meats and cheeses.

How about a "Blimpie Box"—a six-inch sub with your choice of chips, potato or macaroni salad and a fresh baked cookie, packaged with condiments and utensils in a convenient box. Order 10 "Blimpie Boxes," and the 11th is on us!

Cost and Services

Our cost is based per item. The balance is due upon delivery or pickup, with a 20% deposit due at the time of order. Our catering department would be happy to meet with you for a free consultation and sandwich, so you can experience for yourself how good Blimpie is.

Mention you saw us in the Bravo! Event Guide and receive a 10% discount!

BRUCE GOLDBERG & CO.

8620 N. Lombard
Portland, Oregon 97203
(503) 240-7178; Fax (503) 240-7152
E-mail: bgc@Imagina.com
Web site: http://www.bgcevents.com

Exceptional food, uncompromised service, and over sixteen years of experience define Bruce Goldberg and Co. as one the Northwest's premier resources for catering and event planning. Whether it's a social event, a business function, a fabulous fund-raiser or a talk-of-the-town party…formal or informal, intimate or ultimate… Whether it's to surprise, overwhelm, impress or just entertain your guests, BG&C will turn your next event into a very special occasion. Bruce Goldberg and Co. is full-service custom catering, full-fledged fantasy decor and a creative team of detail driven professionals. We measure our success in the excitement, the satisfaction and relaxed confidence of you and your guests.

Catering
- Individually tailored menus appropriate to the budget and theme of your event.
- A professional and courteous uniformed staff.
- Licensed full beverage service.

Decor
- Signature design service including all floral, tabletop and ambient room decor.
- Custom prop fabrication, lighting and set design.

Event Planning
- Complete implementation of every detail of your event by an experienced event manager.
- "One stop" resource for site selection and availability, rental order, valet parking, audio visual and entertainment needs.

Pricing
Menu pricing is calculated on a per person basis. Labor charges are separate and calculated at an hourly rate. All other services are quoted as itemized costs in each category.

Terms
A 50% deposit of all estimated charges is requested when the contract is generated. The balance is due the day of the event. A final guest count is required 72 hours prior to event date.

Contact Us!
We encourage you to visit our Web site at http://**www.bgcevents.com/** or contact us directly for an appointment.

Portland Area:
Tigard
11419 S.W. Pacific Highway
(503) 452-8384

Milwaukie
17883 S.E. McLoughlin
(503) 652-1076

Gresham
1355 N.E. Burnside
(503) 667-4811

Vancouver Area:
Hazel Dell
1118 N.E. 78th Street
(360) 546-2439

Types of Menus and Specialties

Take it from me, Buster, your next party or picnic should be a festive, Texas-style barbecue. Just give us a call, and we'll bring you a real barbecue, which isn't something you can pour out of a bottle. Our menus feature genuine hardwood smoked barbecue meats cooked in our custom-made pits for up to 12 hours.

Your guests will be happier than a cowboy with a new hat.

Meats available are brisket (beef), chicken, beef ribs, pork ribs, ham, pork loin, turkey, baby-back pork ribs, and link sausages.

Side dishes available are barbecue beans, pinto beans, green salad, potato salad, cole slaw, fresh fruit salad, and corn on the cob.

We have a special children's menu, too.

Experience

We operate several popular Texas-style barbecues in the greater Portland area and have been bringing authentic barbecue to the region since 1982. Catering is all in a day's work for us. We've done numerous functions, serving from 50 to 3,000. If you're looking for a banquet facility, one of our restaurants may be appropriate for your group of 15 to 125.

If you'd like references from our previous catering customers, they're available, of course.

Cost and Services

Cost is on a per-person basis and depends on your choice of one, two, or three-meat dinners. All dinners include Buster's original barbecue sauce, two side dishes, garlic bread, chips, dessert and coffee, iced tea, pop, and lemonade.

We'll provide paper plates, cups, napkins, and plastic knives, forks, and spoons, and the serving people you need.

Service can include beer and wine or a full bar. We're licensed and insured to serve alcoholic beverages.

Call us for a quotation, and we'll help you custom-plan your barbecue.

Web site: www.bustersbarbecue.com

12003 N.E. Ainsworth Circle, Suite A
Portland, Oregon 97220
Contact: Christian or Annette Joly
(503) 252-1718; Fax (503) 252-0178
Business Hours: Mon–Fri 7am–7pm
Web site: www.caperscafe.com

If You're Entertaining Very Important People... We Deliver

When you want to electrify a crowd, nothing causes quite the stir like food prepared by Capers Cafe and Catering Company. Bold, imaginative food... presented with both precision and panache. You've probably got some great ideas. So do we. And together we will plan an event that's destined to be remembered and implemented precisely as planned. All foods are prepared from fresh Northwest products with emphasis on taste and appearance.

Corporate Meeting Room
Capers is able to accommodate private luncheons and meetings for 50–150.

Cost
Cost is based on the food selection and type of event or function. All costs are itemized and on a per-person basis. A 50% deposit is required upon confirmation of event. Cancellations may be made 10 days prior to the event.

Experience
With over 25 years experience in the industry, Christian Joly has prepared international events for 2,000, as well as intimate dinners for two.

Services
Capers Cafe and Catering Company is a fully licensed and insured caterer, capable of providing any style of food and beverage that a customer may require. Seven days a week.

Food Preparation and Equipment
Capers Cafe and Catering Company prepares all foods with flair, putting heavy emphasis on taste and visual appearance.

Serving Attendants
To ensure a successful event, we provide all the necessary professionals to prepare, serve, and clean up. Gratuities are optional.

OUR FOODS AND SERVICES ARE 100% GUARANTEED

Capers Cafe and Catering Company is an extremely successful business because of its employees. Our staff believes in satisfying all the needs of our customers. We never take shortcuts and guarantee our foods and services 100% or we return your money. *We are at your service.*

Restaurant and Catering

1331 S.W. Washington
Portland, Oregon 97205
Contact: Christine, Bob or Mercedes
(503) 223-0054

A Portland Favorite since 1979!

Cassidy's Restaurant is located in a historic building in the heart of downtown Portland. Our exceptional menu features regional cuisine of delicious seafood, premium-cut meats, fresh pastas, seasonal salads and more.

Full-service Catering

Cassidy's offers full service catering tailored to your event. Proprietors Bob and Mercedes Cassidy, manager Christine Hammock and chef Andy Goldstein will help you plan the highest-quality menu, bar and beverage choices and will provide professional staff to meet your needs. Cassidy's is experienced in catering all kinds of events including company picnics, box lunches, fund raisers and formal corporate receptions.

Services

- **Food** — From a sit-down dinner or extensive buffet to appetizers and desserts, we offer our fresh Northwest specialties. We'll help you plan a menu just right for your occasion.

- **Beverage** — Cassidy's offers complete bar service, as well as nonalcoholic drinks and is fully licensed and insured.

- **Staff** — Cassidy's staff of experienced restaurant professionals also services our catered events.

Private Banquet Room and Full-service Restaurant

Cassidy's has a private dining room available for receptions up to 50 people. During the afternoon, Cassidy's offers the entire restaurant facility to private parties for special events up to 300 people.

**FULL-SERVICE CATERING
AT YOUR PLACE OR OURS!**

Contact: Karla or Laura
(503) 238-8889

Seriously Now...
Catering At Its Best takes quality seriously and continuously pushes it to higher levels. Offering unique blends of Northwest native flavors, uncompromised freshness and meticulous organization—our events and galas sparkle. Regardless of the fare—continental breakfasts, boxed or buffet lunches or formal galas—exacting standards, gracious professionalism and a detailed understanding of artful, delicious presentation create wonderful events!

They Say It's All in the Past—We Believe the Best is Yet to Come
Experience has groomed Catering At Its Best. Planning for the unforeseen, preparing for the "what ifs," and asking simple questions set the mark for professionalism. Members of our catering team are proficient, organized and thoughtful. The wait staff offers crisp, groomed service, artistic, bountiful presentation and thorough completion of all tasks. Behind the scenes, the Chefs create works of art with only top grade, fine quality ingredients. Quantities are carefully calculated—unpretentious abundance is the benchmark.

Atmosphere is for the Stars
Regardless of a location's character, the *atmosphere* can be formalized, refined or made to appear fun and festive. Catering At Its Best owns a full line of serviceware, provides color-coordinated linens and is a resource for creative props and decorations. Before each event, we meet at your site and finalize the arrangements to make floorplans flow freely, seating arrangements perfect, and the atmosphere glow. Creativity, ingenuity and experience help transform your ideas into realization, props into ambiance, banquet halls into gala ballrooms, and Mother Nature into paradise.

We Get Around!
Catering At Its Best has partied all over town! From your private home to a public park or corporate setting—we are adaptable to any environment. We are also approved to serve in major locations in and about Portland including the Central Library, Jenkins Estate, The Sternwheeler Rose, Portland Art Museum, Laurelhurst Club, Oregon History Center, Tallina's Garden and The Old Church. Catering At Its Best is the exclusive caterer for Kingstad Meeting Centers.

Welcome One and All
Catering At Its Best is centrally located and is operating in an immaculate, fully licensed and insured commercial kitchen. We welcome you to visit our kitchen, sample our delicious flavors and enjoy our presentation.

Call Now!
As you plan your successful event, call Karla or Laura to learn more about Catering At Its Best's services.

1972 N.W. Flanders
Portland, Oregon 97209

NO THEME TOO EXOTIC; NO CUISINE TOO ESOTERIC

Types of Menus and Specialty

Our fare ranges from New Age/organic to classical decadence. We can design menus for casual or formal dining—from executive breakfasts and boardroom lunches to picnics or theme parties. We offer on- and off-premise catering for celebrations of all kinds.

Think of Us for

LIFE CYCLE EVENTS	*CORPORATE FUNCTIONS*	*SOCIAL EVENTS*
Wedding Receptions	Company Picnics/BBQs	Teas/Brunches
Rehearsal Dinners	Holiday Parties	Cocktail Parties
Bar/Bat Mitzvahs	Grand Openings	Reunions
Birthdays/Anniversaries	Business Meetings	Retirements

Cost

Reasonably priced. Free consultation and planning.

Experience

Chef du Jour Catering has been in business for eight years. We are the exclusive caterer for Congregation Beth Israel in Northwest Portland. We use the freshest available product and classical preparation techniques. Each menu is designed to meet the individual customer's desires and needs.

Service

Chef du Jour is a full-service caterer and can provide linens, glassware, centerpieces or anything else you need for your event. We have a professionally trained staff, attractive and healthy food and innovative food styling. We also offer decorating and florist services and pickup and delivery.

CATERING WITH A DIFFERENCE!

Please let this business know that you heard about them from the Bravo! Event Resource Guide.

Portland
503•665•3894

Vancouver
360•253•8326

At the Briarwood Inn
2752 N.E. Hogan Road • Gresham, Oregon 97030
Portland (503) 665-3894 • Vancouver (360) 253-8326
Fax (503) 492-2638

Experience

City Grill offers full-service catering from experienced restaurant and food service professionals. Our staff can create the event you're looking for. With the help of our skilled event planners, anything is possible, from a glamourous talk-of-the-town black tie affair to a casual come-as-you-are picnic in the park.

You could pay as much as $40 an hour for a professional event planner. At City Grill Catering, the event planner is included—all part of our "full service" catering.

Variety

Whether you like to make all the decisions, or leave the thinking to someone else, our menus are specially designed to make it easy for you. Choose from a variety of already built menus like *The Rustic Italian, The French Provincial* or *The Deli Buffet*. Perhaps the *Build Your Own Taco Bar* or *Baked Potato Bar* would better suit your guests. And for those who like to design their own bill of fare, our A La Carte menu offers a large variety of items to mix and match. Build your own menu tailored to meet your tastes and budget. From standard fare like *Roast Sirloin in Burgundy Mushroom Sauce* or *Bronze Chicken* to upscale entrees like *Rack of Lamb* or *Stuffed Ocean Run Salmon,* we have something to appeal to every palate. Having an appetizer party? Our *Roasted Garlic Chicken Salad Phyllo Cups, Lavosh Spirals* and *Stuffed Artichoke Crowns* would be just the thing to impress your guests. And our desserts...a little slice of heaven on a plate. Choose from our *Marionberry Cobbler, Strawberry Shortcake* or *Praline Pineapple Upside Down Cake*. Think you can't afford desserts on that business luncheon? An assortment of Dessert Bars for $1.50 per person can change that! You'll get a selection of *Lemon, Triple Berry, Chocolate Raspberry and Key Lime Bars*. If you still don't see anything you like, our chefs will customize a menu to fit your needs.

Services

Be a guest at your own party. Our event planners and staff will take care of all the details. We have a whole city of entertainers, musicians, artists and equipment vendors at our disposal. We can even help you find the right venue. City Grill Catering is on the preferred or exclusive list of many local venues, and our event planners are locating new places to have a party every week. Just sit back and relax...enjoy your party for a change.

Please call for a brochure or menu package.
Our picnics and barbecues can't be beat.
We look forward to serving you.

CONNOR'S EVENTS & CATERING, INC.

7598 S.W. Vlahos Drive • Wilsonville, Oregon 97070
Owners/Chefs: Joe and Pat Connor
Phone/Fax (503) 682-6142

Mission Statement
Connor's Events & Catering is dedicated to serving its customers in a friendly, flexible manner, offering the best menus to fit our customers' wants and needs.

Cost
Our cost reflects our flexibility. We have many different menus, with many interchangeable food options. We are at our best when we can change our menu to fit your food and price needs. Our barbecue prices start at $7.95 per person and our elegant dining menus start at $12.25 per person. Give us a call to see what we can work out for you!

Experience
We have over 20 years of experience in the catering industry. Although we specialize in company picnics and weddings, we enjoy catering theme parties, athletic events and open houses. For examples of parties we have catered, please give us a call.

Choices of Food
Again our flexibility is evident when choosing the food for your catered event. We offer a variety of different menus ranging from smoked salmon out of our Southern Pride smoker, to fajitas sauteed on location, to grilled hamburgers, hot dogs and Gardenburgers. We also offer choices of salads, pastas, appetizers and hors d'oeuvres, hot or cold. We cater to your liking.

Facilities
We have catered many locations in the surrounding Portland area and enjoy catering new sites as well. We also have our own in-house facilities. If you are looking for a site to hold your event, we can accommodate your needs.

Staff
Our friendly, helpful staff is what keeps our customers returning to Connor Events & Catering for their catering needs. We are efficient and love the job we are doing. When you choose Connor Events & Catering as your caterer, you will want us to return year after year!

Dale's Catering Service

Always in good taste!

2420 S.E. Belmont Street • Portland, Oregon 97214
(503) 234-9948; Fax (503) 236-9346

*Specialized menus for
each client since 1945*

Experience
Dale's Catering has been serving Portland and the surrounding metropolitan communities since 1945. We pride ourselves on our commitment to our clients.

Types of Menus and Specialty
We will prepare food for any type of event from the most formal of weddings to large company dinners and sporting events. At Dale's Catering we believe each event has its own unique personality and the menu and service should reflect that personality.

Cost and Services
Because we are a full-service catering company, we can provide you with:
- **A menu designed especially for you.**
- **Equipment:** China, glassware, silverware, linens, linen napkins, full silver serving pieces, paper and plastic supplies, tables and chairs, and much more.
- **Beverages:** Assorted alcoholic and nonalcoholic beverages are available. Dale's Catering Service is licensed by the OLCC to serve alcoholic beverages, and all of our bartenders have OLCC service permits.
- **Flowers:** We work with a local florist who can handle all of your floral needs. We will be happy to coordinate all of your floral needs including pickup and delivery.
- **Service personnel:** We have an excellent service staff that is available for any size of function, whether it is a party for 40 or for 4,000.

The cost of catering for your event will be determined by the menu, the number of guests you order for, and the service that is provided. When we supply alcoholic beverages, you will be billed for the amount that is used.

Comments from our Clients
The attention to detail and thoroughness by your company made my job much easier. The feedback from our customers, suppliers and employees was "the shrimp was fabulous"!!

Insulation Supply

We had a wonderful dinner and a wonderful time at the dinner.

Bureau of Land Management

The company and I wish to thank you so very much for the wonderful job you did. The food was outstanding, the fellows serving were terrific, the cakes were beautiful…everything was the best it can be. *Hessel Tractor*

On behalf of myself and TPC/Mercedes-Benz, we would like to express our appreciation and thanks for the wonderful job and impressive catering that Dale's provided for our company.

Truck Project Corporation/Mercedes-Benz Group

Visit us at our Web site: www.citysearch.com/pdx/dales

14297 S.W. Pacific Highway • Tigard, Oregon 97224
Contact: Steve DeAngelo (503) 620-9020
Available for catering seven days a week
Call for store hours

Types of Menus and Specialty
DeAngelo's offers all types of menus from self-serve buffets to full-service formal sit-down affairs. We are well-known for our Gourmet Pizza Feeds, Pasta Bars and Western Barbecues. On-site cooking is always a hit with attendees. Low-fat and vegetarian menus are happily accommodated. A wide range of ethnic menus are available, such as Asian, Italian, Mexican, African, and Caribbean. Give DeAngelo's Catering a call when planning your next fund raiser, social or corporate event, or if you're in need of concession services.

Cost and Experience
Price is based on a per-person basis for full-service events; however, many other options are available. DeAngelo's Catering prides itself on quality food at an affordable price. Delivery service available. Food tasting and references provided upon request.

Services
DeAngelo's is licensed and insured to serve alcoholic beverages. Complete event coordination and site-analysis service available. To complete your event theme, props are available for rent, with all full-service buffets are decorated at no charge. Entertainment packages and interactive games can be arranged.

Presentation and Service Staff
All foods are exquisitely presented using copper chafing dishes along with granite and marble tiles and slabs. Service staff is available for all types of events from formal sit-down dinners to concessions. Attire is always appropriate.

FLEXIBILITY TO MEET YOUR NEEDS
DeAngelo's is always willing to work with clients to find a menu that fits within their budget and menu guidelines. We offer flexibility to adapt to special needs and requests. With our wide range of menus and services, we can accommodate your requests.

Decorations provided FREE
with all full-service buffets!
Visit our Web site: www.cateringbydeangelos.com
E-mail: CaterbyDeA@aol.com; Fax (503) 620-5503

Voted Best Caterer at the 1999 Bravo! Meeting & Event Planners' Trade Show!

A founding member of the Association of Catering & Event Professionals.

833 N.W. 16th Avenue
Portland, Oregon 97209
Contact: Linette True (503) 243-3324
E-mail: delilah@teleport.com
Web site: http://www.teleport.com/~delilah

Classic or Trendy

Your event reflects your style. The food we prepare and the table we set will project this image to your guests.

Cuisine

- **Northwest:** Freshly prepared local seafood, meats, fruits and vegetables, changing with the season.
- **Regional American:** Such as Southwestern, Cajun, Heartland.
- **International:** Authentic ethnic dishes including European, Mediterranean, South American and Asian.
- **Outdoor:** Company picnics and barbecues.

Menus

Buffet or formal table service? Brunch, lunch, cocktails or dinner? Winter, spring, summer or autumn? Cuisine? With this many factors involved in an event, our menus are custom designed to suit the party. We encourage you to mix and match cuisines to include your favorite dishes. Tasty vegetarian options are available.

Services

- **Staff:** Professional waiters, licensed bartenders, chefs for on-site cooking or carving, on-site coordinators.
- **Table settings:** China, linen, silver and crystal are available.
- **Outdoor:** Canopies, tents, dance floors, arches, tables, umbrellas and chairs in many styles.
- **Decoration:** Ice carving, floral design, theme staging.
- **Entertainment:** Musicians, actors, clowns.

Exquisite Presentation

Our luscious food merits a beautiful presentation. Artfully arranged and garnished, our dishes will be a focal point of your event.

OUR GOAL

Is for you to enjoy the event. We take care of details—nothing is forgotten, and you are a star.

Entertaining Portland with Extraordinary Northwest Cuisine

2701 N.W. Vaughn, Suite 205 • Portland, Oregon 97210
(503) 223-6819; Fax (503) 223-0327
E-mail: CharlesStilwell@FoodinBloom.com

Fresh Ideas That Bloom into Brilliant Events

For nearly twenty years, Food in Bloom has brought a beautifully creative Northwest spirit to gatherings of virtually every description. With exceptional cuisine, an exacting caliber of service and an innate sense of what is appropriate for the occasion, we take great pride in doing what is most important: bringing our client's concepts to life.

Whether the event is to be a large-scale thematic opening, a private cocktail gathering, a corporate board meeting, barbecue, light buffet or an important seated dinner, it is our good fortune to have some of Portland's most exceptional talent to carry through for you.

Fresh Northwest Cuisine with a Creative Twist

Having catered some of the most visible events in the City, we know from experience that a successful menu is one that is not only deliciously prepared, but one that is creatively and enticingly served. Our chefs work with only the freshest, finest quality ingredients. Food in Bloom showcases Oregon's bounty with abundance and in doing so, we provide a fresh, contemporary approach to its presentation.

From the Outrageous to the Sublime

Creating the right atmosphere for an event, regardless of location, is an integral part of our service as caterers. Flowers, lighting, entertainment, props and special effects are all a part of our repertoire. Whether the tone of the event is to be beautifully refined, festive, dignified, or downright fun, we know what elements must come together to set the scene in full form.

Always Professionally and Appropriately Orchestrated

To expect the unexpected is what separates the seasoned professionals in this business from the amateurs. The importance of being well organized, supplied and staffed should never be underestimated. Much of our magic is in doing the math. Having enough food and drink for everyone and having enough people to serve are critical, showtime essentials. In our twenty years of catering, we know how to put our systems in order without missing a beat.

Beautifully Conceived to be Abundantly Enjoyed

At Food in Bloom, we know what's on the line when you entertain. Whether hosting a gathering for family, friends, professional colleagues or dignitaries of the highest order, the expectation for the occasion is the same: to be enjoyed by one and all. When planning your event, we recommend that you explore your options and then call us to learn more about Food in Bloom and the catering we do.

Great Party Locations

Food in Bloom is the official caterer at Montgomery Park, with beautiful Atrium-level facilities, and an approved caterer at all major party locations in the City. We are fully licensed by the Oregon Liquor Control Commission.

Call today for a consultation or brochure

JAKE'S CATERING
AT THE
GOVERNOR
HOTEL

611 S.W. 10th Avenue
Portland, Oregon 97205
(503) 241-2125; Fax (503) 220-1849
Web site: http://www.mccormickandschmicks.com

Type of Menus and Specialty

Jake's Catering at The Governor Hotel is a division of McCormick & Schmick Management Group and "Jake's Famous Crawfish." Jake's is one of the most respected dining institutions in the Portland area, and Jake's Catering at The Governor Hotel upholds this prestigious reputation.

Known for offering extensive Pacific Northwest menu selections, including fresh seafood and fish, pasta and poultry dishes and prime cut steaks, Jake's Catering at The Governor Hotel has the flexibility and talent to cater to your needs.

From stand-up cocktail/appetizer receptions to fabulous buffet presentations, to complete sit-down dinners for groups and gatherings of all sizes, Jake's Catering at The Governor Hotel is always poised and ready to serve.

Enjoy delicious hors d'oeuvres and entrees, delectable desserts and specialty theme menus (upon request), all prepared by our talented chefs and served by our friendly and professional staff.

Customers are encouraged to review our catering menus and to tour the elegant banquet facilities at The Governor Hotel to fully appreciate the total scope of menu options, facilities, and full-service capabilities.

Cost

We base our cost on a per-person count and the type of menu developed. We require a 50% deposit to confirm your event and payment in full 72 hours prior to event for estimated charges. We ask for a guaranteed number of guests three business days prior to the event.

Services

Jake's Catering at The Governor Hotel is the exclusive caterer at The Governor Hotel, which features nine exquisite banquet rooms with an Italian Renaissance decor and the capability to host groups from as small as 10 people up to 450 (seated) and 600 (stand-up reception).

Jake's Catering at The Governor Hotel also provides off-premise catering services.

A REPUTATION FOR QUALITY AND A RESPECT FOR TRADITION

This is the motto for Jake's Catering at The Governor Hotel and McCormick & Schmick Management Group. You are guaranteed the finest quality of food and presentation, a friendly and professional staff, and a personalized customer service. Trust your important event to one of Portland's long-time favorites to ensure a truly memorable and successful experience.

See page 487 under Banquet, Meeting & Event Sites.

LONDON CATERING

3220 S.E. Milwaukie
Portland, Oregon 97202
Contact: Charles Barker
(503) 234-1978
Fax (503) 239-7168
Business Hours: 8:30am–5pm

Types of Menus and Specialty
AFFORDABLE! London Catering offers a wide variety of unique and delicious menus designed to meet your personal tastes and budget. Award-winning chef Charles Barker prides himself on preparing only the finest products for your events. All menu items are prepared fresh, including our wonderful homemade breads and desserts. You may choose from one of our established menus or we would be delighted to create the perfect menu for your special affair.

Services
SERVICE! The catering managers of London Catering will assist you every step of the way from initial consultation through to the completion of the event. Our services include:
- Menu planning
- Fully licensed to serve alcoholic beverages
- Gracious and professional service staff
- Rental coordination (including china, silverware, glassware and linens)
- Props and decorations: from simple centerpieces to elaborate theme environments

Location
ACCOMMODATING! London Catering offers a new private conference and adjoining dining room to be used for both personal and professional receptions or conference meetings. Special features include:
- An exquisite central courtyard and fountain surrounded by lush foliage
- Space accommodations: Conference room capacity for sit-down meals is 30 guests and for standing receptions, 50 guests. During summer months, the courtyard can seat or stand 20 additional guests

Reservations for the location can be booked by calling London Catering at (503) 234-1978.

Cost
CALL! You will be delighted at how affordable your event will be when catered by London Catering. The cost of your event will depend upon many factors, including the menu selected, type of service, rentals and decorations. Our catering managers will work diligently to ensure your event is produced within the guidelines of your expectations and budget. Events are priced on a per-person basis including all menu items and services. A deposit of $250 will hold the date for your event.

Food Preparation and Equipment
DELICIOUS! London Catering is known for its famous homemade cuisine often offered among beautiful floral presentations, combining to create an artistic display of your chosen menu items. We can provide all required equipment from a full silver service to French country baskets to unique and colorful linens.

Serving Attendants
COURTEOUS! The staff at London Catering takes great pride in satisfying your guests. We will provide all labor required for your reception, including event setup, service, bartending and cleanup crews.

"We are the preferred caterer to The Crown Ballroom"

1728 S.E. Seventh Avenue • Portland, Oregon 97214
(503) 525-0396 or (503) 232-5757; Fax (503) 232-8557; E-mail: Marketstreetcatering@yahoo.com

Market Street Catering features the very best in Northwest Cuisine. Our unique and innovative menus and presentation are designed to enhance your special event. Whatever the occasion, you may select from one of our varied menus, or allow Chef Mark Rehm to custom-create a menu specifically for you.

Market Street Catering's professional event planners draw upon diverse talents and expertise gleaned from over 30 years combined experience. Let us assist you in every aspect of planning and successfully completing your function, or turn everything over to us. Either way, you will be assured of an extraordinary and memorable occasion.

We offer an array of services including (but not limited to) informal barbecues, corporate functions, business meetings, banquets, fundraisers, weddings, rehearsal dinners, or any occasion where fine food is expected. From appetizers and hors d'oeuvres, to buffet luncheons or dinners, to elegant tableside French service, Market Street's exceptional food, creative presentation and refined service will dazzle and delight you and your guests.

Market Street offers complete beverage service by professional bartenders and is fully licensed by the OLCC.

Join Us For Lunch!
Market Street Cafe, 1728 S.E. Seventh Avenue, serves lunch Monday through Friday from 10:30a.m. to 3p.m. Stop by for an informal lunch and experience one of Southeast Portland's best kept secrets. The Cafe is also available for private parties, breakfast meetings and evening functions.

PIZZICATO Catering & Delivery
274·8855

Pizzicato now offers catering and delivery for meetings, presentations, parties and events. All the ingredients to make your event a success! Our most popular pizzas are listed here. Feel free to order directly from this sample menu, or call us and we will fax you a complete menu including, appetizers, beverages and desserts.

Puttanesca Roma tomatoes, artichoke hearts, Kalamata olives, Feta, Mozzarella, garlic and olive oil. (Anchovies upon request at no charge.)	9.75	13.50	18.00
Cajun Spicy Cajun tomato sauce, Andouille sausage, shrimp, roasted peppers, onions, and smoked Mozzarella.	10.50	14.50	18.75
Wild Mushroom Chanterelle, Shiitake, Portobello and other seasonal mushrooms, Chevre, roasted peppers, red onions, Mozzarella, roasted garlic and olive oil.	10.25	14.25	18.50
Rustica Roasted eggplant, mushrooms, zucchini, Mozzarella, garlic and tomato sauce.	9.00	12.75	17.50
Pomodoro *(cheeseless)* Roma tomatoes, sun-dried tomatoes, artichoke hearts, roasted eggplant, roasted onions, Kalamata olives and tomato sauce.	9.00	12.75	17.50
Genovese Fresh spinach, roasted sweet peppers, sun-dried tomatoes, Feta, Mozzarella, and roasted garlic on a pesto base.	9.75	13.50	17.50
Gamberetto Spicy garlic marinated shrimp, basil, roasted peppers, green onions, Roma tomatoes, Feta, Mozzarella, garlic and olive oil.	10.25	14.25	18.50
Patate e Prosciutto Roasted rosemary red potatoes, Prosciutto ham, smoked Mozzarella, mushrooms and tomato sauce.	9.75	13.50	18.00
Barbecue Chicken Grilled BBQ chicken, onions, Roma tomatoes, roasted peppers, Tillamook Cheddar, Mozzarella and BBQ sauce.	10.00	13.75	18.25
Thai Pizza Spicy peanut sauce, teriyaki chicken, green onions, sweet peppers, Mozzarella, sesame seeds, crushed chili peppers.	10.00	13.75	18.25
Quattro Formaggi with Sausage and Mushrooms Chevre, Fontina, Gorgonzola, Mozzarella, sausage, mushrooms, roasted garlic and olive oil.	10.50	14.50	18.75
Bianca Fresh spinach, sweet Parmesan sausage, Gorgonzola, roasted peppers, walnuts, Mozzarella, garlic and olive oil	10.00	13.75	18.25
Tropicale Canadian bacon, roasted onions, Ricotta, Mozzarella, pineapple and tomato sauce.	9.75	13.50	18.00

Antipasti & Insalate

Roasted Garlic Whole roasted garlics, Gorgonzola cheese and Foccacia.	5.75	
Spinaci Spinach, pine nuts, Roma tomatoes, sliced onions, Feta, with balsamic vinaigrette.	5.25	7.00
Caesar WOW—hope you love garlic.	5.25	7.00
With oven-roasted chicken	6.50	8.25
Greek (ours isn't tossed) Roma tomatoes, cucumbers, Kalamata olives, Feta, Pepperoncini, sliced onions, with balsamic vinaigrette.	5.75	7.25

We deliver all orders of $50 or more, and request 24-hour notice to assure delivery. All orders include paper supplies, setup and pickup of serving dishes. Our staff can help serve your event for a minimal charge.

Please let this business know that you heard about them from the Bravo! Event Resource Guide.

PORTER'S CATERING & WOODSMOKE BARBECUE

1513 S.E. Third
Portland, Oregon 97214
Contact: Hollis Harris
(503) 232-8172; Fax (503) 232-8173
Business Hours: Mon–Fri 10am–4pm

CATERING AT YOUR LOCATION

Types of Menus and Specialty

From corporate catering to Wild West hoe-downs to Star Wars themes…no one loves a great party more than Porter's.

Ever since we've been in business, we've specialized in creating fantasy parties. Everything from the menu right down to the color of the candy mints is handled with precision, planning, and care.

Sample Menus

- **Wild West:** steaks, corn-on-the-cob, potato, biscuits with butter and honey, and assorted tarts
- **Elegant:** woodsmoked salmon, potato with herb butter, Caesar salad, breadstick and garlic butter, and assorted tarts
- **Island:** whole pig, prawns, fruit salad, veggie kabobs, bread and honey butter, pineapple and banana tarts

Services

Porter's is a full-service catering company. We can provide all linens, china, flatware, and alcohol required to make your event a memorable occasion.

Cost

Cost is based on a per-person basis, with price ranging from $10 to $30 per person.

AT PORTER'S…WE CAN DO IT ALL!

Theme Parties • Formal Catering

Wood Smoked, Grilled or Barbecued

Event Planning • Corporate Catering

Gourmet Gift Basket

Northwest and Specialty Cuisine

Elegance in Catering

TIFFANY CENTER
1410 S.W. Morrison, Suite 600 • Portland, Oregon 97205-1930
(503) 248-9305; Fax (503) 243-7147
E-mail: rafatis@vr-net.com; Web site: rafatis.citysearch.com

Types of Menus and Specialty
Rafati's full-service catering staff can assist you with the selection of the perfect menu for your function. From corporate picnics in the park, formal dinner service, the needs of the corporate board, that special holiday celebration or new product introduction to the most unique or casual of corporate meetings and/or receptions, box and buffet luncheons—we've done it all. Our portfolios are filled with pictures of our work—Northwest and other American Regional cuisines to Continental and Ethnic, mirror displays, theme buffet presentations, formal dinner services and elegant hors d'oeuvres passed on silver trays.

Cost
The cost is determined by the menu selection, level of desired service and number of guests.

Experience
Operating under the Rafati's name since 1983, our actual catering and food service experience spans more than 25 years. Experience has made flexibility our hallmark.

Food Preparation and Equipment
Rafati's specializes in delicious, freshly prepared foods set in an elegant, lavish and stylish display. From silver, copper, crystal and mirrors to baskets, china, fresh flowers and theme props—we provide all service equipment needs.

Special Services
Service attendants: trained, professionally uniformed service staff to set up, serve and clean up; OLCC licensed, professionally uniformed and equipped bartenders
Beverages: we offer full liquor, extensive wine and champagne selections, bottled and keg beer (domestic, micro and imported) and a full selection of chilled nonalcoholic beverages; OLCC licensed with liquor liability insurance
Dishes and glassware: china, glassware standard, disposables on request
Napkins and linens: linen cloths, napkins and table skirting in range of colors; paper products in selection of colors
Other: fresh flowers; table, hall and theme decorations; ice carvings—full event services and planning.

WHEN GOOD TASTE AND EXPERIENCE COUNT ...COUNT ON RAFATI'S

Rafati's is the exclusive caterer for the Tiffany Center—a centrally located, historic building featuring event floors and conference space of traditional charm and elegance with gilded mirrors, polished woods and emerald accents. From our fully licensed commercial kitchen we also provide elegant catering services to many other facilities, corporate sites and other venues in the Portland Metro area. Our attention to detail, safe food-handling practices, award-winning chefs, trained professional servers, bartenders and experienced event planners are all dedicated to ensuring your complete satisfaction—guaranteed.

RED STAR TAVERN AND ROAST HOUSE

503 S.W. Alder
Portland, Oregon 97204
Contact: Margie Yager, Director of Catering
(503) 417-3377
E-mail: Margie.yager@redstartavern.com
Business Hours: Mon–Fri 8am–5pm

Types of Menus and Specialty
Executive Chef Rob Pando's "rekindled American classics" feature the freshest and finest Northwest ingredients as he and his staff orchestrate the workings of an aromatic wood-fired brick oven, rotisserie, a smoker and a sizzling grill. Culinary riches include iron skillet cornbread; cedar-planked Rib-eye steak with spring artichoke, cipollini onions and Burgundy essence; citrus-spiced chicken with oven-roasted vegetables, smashed potatoes and natural juices.

Cost
Prices range from $19 to $50 per person.

Experience
Open since May 6, 1996. Portfolio and references available.

Services
Local microbrews, Northwest wines, premium bar, serviceware in house along with white and ivory linens. Catering consultants will work with you every step of the way for your event. Fully OLCC licensed service staff.

Food Preparation and Equipment
We will provide any equipment necessary.

We offer a wide variety of menu options—from wood-grilled baby back ribs with our Tavern nut brown ale barbecue glaze to Skokomish cedar-planked salmon with root vegetable puree and wild mushroom sauce—we can put together a menu that will surprise and delight you and your guests.

Serving Attendants
Servers are included in menu cost. Setup fee varies. Standard 18% gratuity on food and beverage.

EXPERIENCE OUR REKINDLED AMERICAN CLASSICS
We feature the freshest and finest Northwest ingredients with menus to tempt and tantalize the senses. Together we create an event sure to awaken the sleepiest palate and linger in the memory.

See page 355 under Hotel Accommodations.
See page 483 under Banquet, Meeting & Event Sites.

RHEINLANDER

*5035 N.E. Sandy Boulevard
Portland, Oregon 97213
Contact: Candy Stedman
(503) 288-8410
Business Hours: 9am–5pm*

Types of Menus and Specialty
We can do a traditional American menu, an entirely German experience, or a European cuisine base menu. We offer full-service catering and specialize in making each event distinct, whether a unique dinner buffet, an elegant hor d'ouevres reception, or a casual company picnic.

Cost
We charge a per person cost for food based on menu selection. All other costs are charged as applicable.

Experience
The Rheinlander has 36 years of experience behind us, catering functions of any size. We take pride in our tradition of excellence in food preparation and presentation, attention to detail, and the professional orchestration of all events.

Services
To us, full service means that we will take care of all the details for you, from our first meeting to share ideas until we have cleaned up after the function. Our goal is for you to relax in confidence of our ability to coordinate your event so that you may enjoy your function. Tenting, lighting and stages, special props, flowers, and entertainment are just a few of our services.

Food Preparation and Equipment
Our European trained chefs will prepare your meal according to our high standards of quality. We have a vast resource of equipment, linens and other props to make any food buffet presentation fabulous.

Serving Attendants
We will provide a professional and efficient staff for your event.

A TRADITION OF OUTSTANDING QUALITY AND PRESENTATION
We are committed to providing our guests with the finest quality of prepared and presented foods with a friendly, professional staff and personalized customer service from beginning to end.

CATERING

Sample our menu at
Salvador Molly's Sun Stop Cafe
1523 S.W. Sunset Boulevard
in Hillsdale (503) 293-1790

Catering services:
Contact: Rick Sadle
(503) 297-9635; Fax (503) 297-9631
E-mail: catering@salvadormolly.com

Sunny Flavors from the World's Hot Spots

Sample Menu Items
- Wood-smoked Jamaican jerk chicken
- 5 spice teriyaki salmon
- Rosemary lemon pork loin
- Microbrew barbecue beef brisket and ribs
- Vegetarian jambalaya
- South Pacific pu pu platter
- Curry chick peas
- Coconut rice
- Mayan roasted pumpkin seed dip
- Chilled kung pao noodle salad

Type of Menu and Specialties
From the Caribbean to the American South & Southwest, to the Pacific Islands, Latin America, Asia, to the Mediterranean and beyond, sunny climates have fostered much of the world's most interesting and delicious food.

From elegant occasions to tropical celebrations, Salvador Molly's will bring this world of sun-filled flavors to your next event. Salvador Molly's brings its own special blend of exotic flavors to you on heaping platters with colorful presentation, decorations and music. We have many varied menus perfect for a variety of events. We take special joy in custom-designing unique menus for one-of-a-kind celebrations that your guests will never forget.

Salvador Molly's Sun Stop Cafe is recommended by *The Oregonian's A & E*, *Willamette Week*, *Portland's Best*, *Our Town* and thousands of satisfied customers. Salvador Molly's Catering Company has served many top corporations including Mentor Graphics, Adidas, Enterprise Rent-A-Car, AT&T Wireless, Nike, Davis Wright Tremaine, Deloitte & Touche, Ikon Office Products, Intel, Stoel Rives and many more.

Services
From site selections to festive decorations, equipment rentals, live entertainment and more, our experienced catering professionals will help assure the success of every event each step of the way.

Cost
Prices are based on a per person charge that depends on menu, number of guests and service requirements.

THE NORTHWEST'S PREMIER WOODSMOKE BARBEQUE SPECIALIST

Company picnics • Weddings • Corporate meetings • Private parties

From backyards to banquet halls—we make it special!

Sandwich Depot Deli
FINE CATERING

5663 N.E. Glisan
Portland, Oregon 97213
Contact: Esther
(503) 239-4177; Fax (503) 239-4177
Business Hours: Mon–Fri 8am–7pm;
Sat 10am–6pm; Sun 10am–3pm

Corporate Box Lunches
Sandwich Depot Deli can provide light breakfasts, box lunches, self-serve buffets, and hors d'oeuvres for any event.

We specialize in box lunches, which are prepared each day to ensure freshness. Box lunches include a sandwich, fresh fruit cup, homemade pasta/potato salad, brownie or homemade dessert, and mint candy. Try our sandwich specialties such as our Rip City sub with three cheeses and four meats or the Dagwood Club with smoked ham, turkey, salami and provolone.

Sandwich Depot Deli offers an array of vegetarian sandwiches. A variety of breads are available—delivered or picked up.

Holiday Gift Baskets
A perfect corporate gift. Our gift baskets include a variety of Oregon products including wine, specialty candies, cheeses, and fruit.

Services
For that added personalized touch, we will add a company logo or artwork to the lid of each lunch box. We are also happy to assist in making arrangements for tables and chairs. Service staff is available upon request.

Cost
The cost is based on a per-head count. Balance is due upon delivery. Clients can be billed with prior approval.

WE ARE WORTH THE TRIP
Sandwich Depot Deli is a small, low-key deli on the east side of the river. Yet we have customers from all over Portland and Vancouver return to our location because of our great food and service. We always start with fresh ingredients and end with food that not only tastes good but looks good.

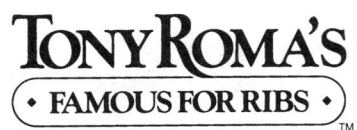

Business Office:
8325 N.E. Airport Way
Portland, Oregon 97220
Contact: Andrew Pollin
(503) 280-8743
Fax (503) 249-7288

Types of Menus and Specialties
Let Tony Roma's Catering staff cook up excitement for your next special event. Dig into our famous Baby Back Ribs, our sweet and sassy Carolina Honey Ribs, barbecued chicken, steaks, seafood and lots more. Everything you'll need is included for just one price.* Catered functions for: company picnics, open houses, holiday parties, conventions, meetings, sales and safety incentives, reunions, wedding receptions.

Cost and Terms
Deposit varies depending on size of party. Please inquire.

Experience
Tony Roma's has served the greater Portland and Vancouver area since 1988. We can please even the most discerning tastes. Some of our satisfied clients include: Intel, Hoffman Construction, Bank of America, OHSU, GTE, Tektronix, and Fred Meyer.

Services
Tony Roma's is a full-service catering company. We can arrange for tents, canopies, tables, chairs, linen-anything you'll need to make your event special and memorable. Full bar, beer and wine service are available. Please inquire.

Food Preparation and Equipment
Tony Roma's provides all the necessary serviceware you will need for your function. All of our food is prepared fresh and hot at the location of your choice, weather permitting. All condiments for hamburgers and hot dogs will be provided.

Serving Attendants
Our amiable staff is always happy to be of assistance.

AWARD-WINNING FAMOUS FOR RIBS
At Tony Roma's we pride ourselves on our ability to create the most incredible summer picnic foods. We make it an event to be remembered.

*Does not include applicable taxes or gratuity.

TUBBY'S DELI & HEFFERNAN'S CORPORATE CATERING

3330 N.W. Yeon
Portland, Oregon 97210
(503) 225-1300; Fax (503) 225-1303

911 S.W. 10th Avenue
Portland, Oregon 97205
(503) 222-5004; Fax (503) 222-5494

Delivery Service

Tubby's Deli has been successfully catering box lunches, warm casseroles, and deli buffets to the Northwest and downtown area for more than eight years. Our box lunches include deli sandwiches, chips, deli salads, fresh baked cookies and beverages. Our service includes labeling each lunch individually to ensure that it reaches the appropriate guest. This works well for a crowded meeting room, when time is limited, conferences, outdoor activities, bus trips and limited budgets. Also included in our delivery service is a build-your-own deli buffet with deli meats, cheeses, and breads. You may add salads, chips, and beverages to customize the menu to your guests' tastes.

If your guests' tastes are heartier, consider one of our casseroles. Our prices include salad, entree, accompaniments, desserts and sodas. All of these choices are attractively garnished on disposable trays, platters and bowls.

Heffernan's Corporate Catering

Heffernan's Corporate Catering was designed to provide customers with a more customized package. Our menu prices include chaffing dishes, utensils, linen, and a buffet line draped with skirting. High quality disposable products are included in the price of our menus. If the occasion requires linens, flatware, china or floral arrangements, we would be happy to provide them at an additional charge. Perfect for formal or in-house celebrations, staff meetings, training meetings, employee functions or hors d' oeuvres parties.

Custom Events

This is the service to select for a really special event or celebration—annual employee barbecues, picnics, or any occasion you want to make memorable. Our customer guidance promotes an atmosphere that is supportive and stress free, from planning and design through completion of the event. Complete customer service includes assistance with finding the ideal location, layout, menu selection and rentals.

Great Food and Friendly Service

So consider the advantages, but most of all the possibilities. Our great food, whether casual or elegant, our warm, friendly service, our ability to be flexible and supportive no matter what the occasion requires, is our unique signature.

**The unpretentious company with a
passion for great service and food.**

West Hills Catering Company

503.228.6822

Visit our Web site:
www.whcc.citysearch.com

Colleen Ann Schultz   Kevin D. Davin
Event Coordinator   *Executive Chef*

Portland's Premier Catering Service
With over 40 years combined experience, Executive Chef Kevin Davin and Event Coordinator Colleen Schultz have teamed up to bring catering excellence to Portland. West Hills Catering Company features praise-winning cuisine and first-rate service.

We also take pride in our service staff. You will not have to worry about the service or the appearance of our staff. Our service and kitchen personnel are experienced and will be in uniform

Concerned About What To Serve?
West Hills Catering Company offers an extensive variety of corporate menu choices including breakfast, luncheons, boxed lunches and dinners. We also offer an assortment of menus appropriate for social functions, company picnics and holiday parties. Or we'll create a customized menu just for you.

We Are Experts at Taking the Show on the Road
Let us transform any site from ordinary to extraordinary! We use only state-of-the art food preparation, handling and transportation equipment. This ensures the safest and highest product quality.

Call for Menus and Compare Our Value
Our per person menu pricing is inclusive of china, flatware, glassware, beautiful silver serving pieces, buffet linens, setup and clean up. There are no delivery fees for the downtown area.

Event Coordinating
Beyond the fine cuisine and outstanding service, West Hills Catering Company also offers complete event coordinating, full liquor license, floral arrangements, entertainment, tents, canopies, equipment rentals and more!

Thank you for considering West Hills Catering Company. We truly believe you will feel very comfortable with us and we look forward to being of service to you. Please take a moment to phone Colleen Schultz. She'll be happy to discuss your plans or answer any questions you may have.

**Put West Hills Catering Company to work for you.
We do the work, and you take the bow.**

WILF'S
Restaurant and Piano Bar at Historic Union Station

N.W. Sixth and Irving
Portland, Oregon 97209
(503) 223-0070;
Fax (503) 223-1386
Web site: www.wilfs.citysearch.com

WILF'S CATERS TO YOU

Since 1975, the Portland area has enjoyed fine food, impeccable service and a warm, relaxed atmosphere at Wilf's. Classic steaks, seafood, seasonal creations, and our renowned jazz and Sinatra-style piano bar lend to make your event perfect! Intel, NIKE, Precision Castparts and PacifiCorp are just a few references who have enjoyed their experiences with Wilf's. Located at historic Union Station in the Pearl District.

Special Services
When your business or personal life requires expert catering, with little work on your part, then *JUST LET US DO IT*. You can trust us down to the last detail for your business entertaining for associates, vendors, employees, or personal entertaining for friends and family. We will plan your event at the restaurant, at your business, or in your home. You can use our private rooms or rent the entire restaurant! We are a "one-stop" catering company offering full coordination of superb menus, beverages, wait-staff, entertainment, decorations, equipment rentals, guest gifts, photography and any other special needs you might have.

Capacity: up to 160 reception-style; 150 seated; private rooms up to 40 people
Price Range: starting at $15 per person; room charge additional; menus available in varying price ranges
Catering: full-service in-house catering plus off-premise catering
Types of Events: sit-down, hors d'oeuvres, buffet; breakfast, lunch, or dinner meetings; corporate or personal; informal or silver service

Availability
Wilf's offers private rooms for up to 35 guests, or our main dining room that accommodates up to 130 guests, all decorated in rich, lush, comfortable colors to complement the historic decor of Union Station. Reserve early for your desired date. Last-minute reservations welcome, as space allows. Advance deposit required; cancellation terms vary.

Description of Facility and Services
Seating: tables and chairs for up to 175 on-site; off-premise, rentals available
Servers: wait-staff provided; off-premise at additional charge
Bar facilities: full-service bar on-site with liquor, wine, beer, nonalcoholic, bartender, and liquor liability; off-site Wilf's or host can provide liquor, liability to be discussed
Dance floor: 30- to 100-person capacity dance floor available at additional charge
Linens: cloth napkins and tablecloths in a variety of colors
China and glassware: ivory china; appropriate glassware
Decorations: special needs may be accommodated; please no tape or nails
Cleanup: included in rental charge
Audiovisual and meeting equipment: arrangements can be made
Parking: free parking at Union Station or valet parking offered
ADA: fully accessible

"Make Your Event The Talk Of The Town!"

8800 Enchanted Way, S.E. • Turner, Oregon 97392
(503) 371-7815, (800) 477-8044; Fax (503) 371-7827

AFFORDABLE • CREATIVE • FRIENDLY • PROFESSIONAL

Menus
Willaby's Catering offers a wide range of menus. Our specialty is our ability to please the client because we can do just about *anything the client requests.* Whether it's a formal cocktail party for 10, or a company picnic for 1,000, Willaby's can cater hors d'oeuvre parties, buffets or formal sit-down dinners.

We Will Work Within Your Budget
We will meet with you to determine your needs and design menus to work within your budget. We are always happy to meet with you for a complimentary consultation.

Services
Willaby's customizes its services to complement any theme, budget or event.

Event planning: we offer the best in event planning to relieve you of the stress of planning an event and keeping track of all the small details—a task that can seem overwhelming

Centerpieces: we have a wide variety of unique centerpieces available to rent that will add a flair to your table decorations

Event decorating: we have decorating, room setup/cleanup services available to you to allow you to be worry-free during your event preparation

Bar services: we can arrange for both alcoholic and nonalcoholic bar services including an espresso bar

Specialty linens: give your table decorations that added touch with our specialty linens

Servers and attendants: *only the best!*; our servers are not only professional but they come with a smile!

Floral: we can provide you with very creative floral pieces for your event

Specialty gift baskets: we now offer gift baskets for any occasion!; if you need gifts for clients, employees or relatives just give us a call and we will create a wonderful gift for you; we can feature any theme you would like or come up with one of our own

Cakes and confections: once you have one of our desserts you will be hooked!; we have a wide variety of delicious cakes, desserts and cookies for any occasion

Try Us For Your Next Event
- Company Picnic—
  featuring a barbecue menu for up to 1,000
- Holiday Event
- Reunion
- Executive Box Lunches
- Appreciation Dinner
- Meeting
- Awards Banquet
- Theme Party

THE WOODEN NICKEL CATERING

P.O. Box 277 • 1610 Pine Street
Silverton, Oregon 97381
Contact: Adrienne or Glen
(503) 873-9979; Fax (503) 873-6830
Web site: www.woodennickel.com

Our Only Limit is Your Imagination!

Experience

For 17 years, the Wooden Nickel Catering Company has been "making the event happen" for clients all over the Willamette Valley. Starting in 1980 with our first slow-smoked Portable BBQ Service, we have grown by the best kind of advertising—the recommendation of our satisfied customers. A reputation for consistently delicious food, prepared from the highest quality ingredients and served with "fun and flare," has been achieved by treating each job with personal attention to every detail.

Menus and Specialty

We offer all types of catering for a variety of events, from barbecue to specialty hors d'oeuvres, box lunches to black tie.

- Company Picnics
- Sports Banquets
- Fairs and Expositions
- Weddings
- Open House Events
- Club Meetings
- Family Reunions
- Wine Tastings

Cost

Our experienced, organized and well-equipped staff can ensure the success of your group's indoor or outdoor buffet for 20 to 2,000 guests at an affordable and realistic price. Cost is based on either a flat fee or on a per person basis. An advance deposit of 50% of the estimated total order is due 15 days prior to the event. This deposit is nonrefundable if cancellation occurs less than seven days before your scheduled event. Any remaining unpaid balances must be paid at the completion of the event by cash or check. Please call for a free estimate.

We love our work…you'll love the results.
Preferred caterer at Oregon Gardens
Information packets are available (503) 873-9979

Notes

Hotel Accommodations

HELPFUL HINTS

Americans With Disabilities Act (ADA): This law passed in 1992 requires public buildings (convention centers, hotels, restaurants, etc.) to meet minimum standards making their facilities accessible to individuals with disabilities. Expect facilities to comply. It is the planner's responsibility to find out what auxiliary aids are available in the facilities they use. Although it may not be readily apparent, nearly every group has at least one person with a disability. Ensuring barrier-free accommodations for disabled people goes beyond inspecting for wheelchair ramps. Keep other attendee needs in mind, such as hearing and visually impaired guests and people with special dietary needs (insulin dependent diabetics may need refrigerators in their rooms).

Room Rates: Rates are available in several categories. Be sure to know which ones you qualify for: commercial rates, corporate rates, government rates. Rack rates are common rates that hotels provide. Rack rate is the facility's standard, pre-established guest room rate and is never considered or accepted by groups.

What determines group rates? Group rates are determined by group size. Definition of the group size might vary or other factors may affect the rate you receive. Rates for sleeping rooms are determined in several ways:

- **Time of year:** "Peak" season, hotels can demand higher rates. Shoulder seasons and off-season rates are usually your best buy.
- **Number of rooms required:** Groups with large numbers are in a better position to negotiate lower room rates.
- **Arrival and departure patterns:** Business hotels tend to have high occupancy mid-week and lower occupancy over the weekend. The opposite is true at resorts.
- **Future business:** If you are, or may be, a repeat customer, you may get more favorable rates.

Be prepared with past history: If the meeting was held at the same place in years past, be sure to know the history and past negotiations. You will be able to negotiate better knowing your previous room block, pickup rate of rooms, and dollars generated by the hotel.

Last minute bookings: Be flexible with the details of the meeting or event to negotiate best rates. You may not be able to get everything you need but by changing the starting or ending time of your meeting to accommodate another meeting, then you may receive a greater concession on rental fees. Also, the hotel is anxious to fill up any last-minute open space.

Off-season can offer great benefits: Most properties offer a 25-50% discount in what they call off-season and shoulder season.

Amenities provided by hotels: Complimentary items provided by a facility for guests may include toilet articles, writing supplies, bathrobes, or fruit baskets. Some planners say that in-room coffee is one of the best amenities. It is reasonable to ask for extra towels for health club use, or for quick delivery of forgotten items, such as razors, toothbrushes, or hair dryers. Find out before if these supplies are available. Concierge services and business centers are valuable to your guests. Don't be afraid to ask for the extras: an extra room for every block of ten rooms, complimentary use of hotel limousine for VIP pickups. Free breakfast for staff.

Tipping: A tip or gratuity is given to an individual at the time the service is provided. Personnel that most frequently receive this type of gratuity are doormen, bell staff, waitstaff, and housemaids or room attendants. If these tips are meeting or event related keep a detailed record, because they need to be accounted for in the budget.

309 S.W. Broadway
Portland, Oregon 97205
For reservations please call
(503) 295-4100
Web site:www.bensonhotel.com

Location
Located in the heart of downtown, The Benson sits majestically in the center of museums, shopping, the Portland Center for the Performing Arts and a bustling nightlife. A historic landmark, the accessibility, style and service of The Benson makes it a favorite for out-of-town guests.

Dining and Entertainment
Unsurpassed food, service and style await you at The Benson. The London Grill has consistently been judged the "Best in the West" by *The Wine Spectator* with one of the premier wine cellars on the West Coast. The Lobby Court Lounge is, for generations of Portlanders, the location for jazz entertainment.

Accommodations
The Benson's 287 guest rooms offer the ultimate in luxury and comfort to enhance each visit. Take advantage of our exclusive Benson Suites or one of our deluxe guest rooms for the finest in accommodations found anywhere!

Convention and Corporate Pricing
Special rates and service are available for groups. Frequent travelers enjoy "**Benson Direct Membership**" programs.

Meeting and Banquet Facilities
The Benson Hotel offers 16,000-square-feet of beautifully appointed meeting and dining spaces. Our professional staff will assist you in creating exceptional special events as well as successful business agendas. More specific information on catering and meeting facilities is available upon request.

Special Features
- Business Center
- Fitness Center
- 24-hour room service
- Fireplaces in Grand Suites
- Les Clefs d'Or Concierge
- In room voice mail, data ports, 2-line phones
- Two lush terry cloth bathrobes
- Choice of complimentary newspaper

See page 454 under Banquet, Meeting & Event Sites.

COURTYARD BY MARRIOTT—LLOYD CENTER

435 N.E. Wasco Street
Portland, Oregon 97232
Contact: Kathy Bayerkohler (503) 234-3200

Description of Hotel
Portland's newest Courtyard by Marriott located in the Lloyd Center district offers 202 comfortable guest rooms. All rooms include coffee maker, iron and ironing board, hairdryer, working desk, two-line, speaker phones with voice mail and dataports, satellite dish network with 25 channels and free HBO.

Location
The Courtyard is located in the heart of the Lloyd Center district. Walking distance to the Convention Center, Max Light-Rail System, Lloyd Center Mall and Restaurants.

Meeting Space
The Courtyard's 1,800 square feet of meeting space accommodates groups of 5 to 40. We offer professional event coordination, complete food and beverage service and setups tailored to your specific needs.

Nearby Attractions
- Rose Garden Arena (six blocks)
- Downtown Portland (one mile)
- OMSI (two miles)
- Oregon Zoo (seven miles)
- Lloyd Center Mall (four blocks)

Amenities
- Complimentary USA Today newspaper delivered to your room daily
- Jacuzzi rooms available
- Secured underground parking
- Large fitness center, indoor pool and spa
- Full-service restaurant and lounge
- 24-hour business center
- Complimentary transportation to and from the airport

EMBASSY SUITES®
Portland—Washington Square

9000 S.W. Washington Square Road
Tigard, Oregon 97223
Contact: Kelli Hall (503) 644-4000

Description of Hotel
The luxurious Embassy Suites Hotel Portland—Washington Square is Oregon's premier all-suite property featuring 354 beautifully appointed suites, each with separate living room and bedroom. Suites overlook the cascading waterfalls of our nine-story tropical atrium and Crossroads Restaurant, which features the finest in Northwest cuisine. The comfort of home awaits your attendees while staying at Embassy Suites; your guests will enjoy our complimentary, full cooked-to-order breakfast and evening Manager's Reception daily. From board meetings to annual conferences, our hotel is perfect for your every occasion.

Location, Location, Location
Location means everything for your special events, and Embassy Suites is right where you need us. Located in the heart of Washington County and surrounded by the continued growth of the high-tech industry, Embassy Suites is where you will want to be. Washington Square Mall is adjacent to the hotel, and we are minutes from Oregon's most prestigious wine country—found right here in Washington County. All highway arterials are easily accessible to our hotel offering you close proximity to downtown Portland, Beaverton, Tigard and Lake Oswego.

Meeting and Banquet Facilities
The conference center at Embassy Suites is ideal for your special occasion; our reputation for attention to detail and customer satisfaction assures you the perfect event. We proudly offer:
- 15,000 square feet of meeting space
- 15 rooms to accommodate groups of 10–1,200 guests
- conference suites: ideal for small board meetings
- in-house audiovisual company available for your every need
- ample free parking for guests and attendees of your event

Suite Accommodations/Amenities
- 354 beautifully furnished suites
- refrigerator, microwave and coffee maker in each suite
- complimentary, full cooked-to-order breakfast
- complimentary Manager's Reception: cocktails, beverages and snacks
- complimentary newspaper delivered to your suite daily
- indoor pool, jacuzzi and sauna open 24 hours
- complimentary use of 24 Hour Fitness health club facility
- dual-line telephones featuring voice mail and data ports
- complimentary parking
- business services available
- hair dryers, irons and ironing boards in all suites
- full-service restaurant and lounge open daily

Please let this business know that you heard about them from the Bravo! Event Resource Guide.

EMBASSY SUITES PORTLAND DOWNTOWN

319 S.W. Pine Street • Portland, Oregon 97204
Contact: Rich Kannapell
(503) 796-5358 or (503) 279-9000; Fax (503) 497-9051

Description of Hotel
Portland's luxury all-suite hotel. On February 8, 1912, Portland enjoyed its first formal look at a hotel that would become the center of social life in the Rose City: The Multnomah Hotel, with its marble stairways, crystal chandeliers and grand ballrooms. The careful restoration in 1997 of this magnificent building has brought the hotel back to its original grandeur, including all modern added touches event planners and travelers expect to find in a great hotel.

Location
The Embassy Suites is located at Third and Pine Streets in the heart of downtown's business and cultural district, just steps from restaurants, nightspots and shopping.

Special Packages
The Embassy Suites has several unique packages including Suite Romance, New Year's Eve, spa and dinner packages.

Other Amenities
All 276 two-room suites have wet bar, microwave, refrigerator, three phone lines with computer jacks and voice mail, video checkout, nightly turndown service, bathrobes, umbrellas, irons, ironing boards and hair dryers. 24-hour room service is available. All guests can enjoy a complimentary full cooked-to-order breakfast and a two-hour manager's reception nightly. The fitness center offers exercise equipment, indoor swimming pool, whirlpool, and sauna. There is a full-service 24-hour Business Center. Adjacent to the lobby is Salon Nyla, an Aveda Concept Salon and Day Spa.

The Embassy Suites has over 22,000 square feet of meeting space including the Queen Marie Ballroom, an elegant restoration of the hotel's original ballroom. The Embassy Suites' dedication to offering unmatched service backed by a 100% satisfaction guarantee assures planners of memorable events at the hotel.

Special Services
There are 350 covered parking spaces in the hotel's private garage just across the street. Valet and self-parking are available. Transportation from the airport to the hotel is available at a charge.

See page 481 under Banquet, Meeting & Event Sites.

5TH AVENUE SUITES HOTEL
"Portland's Masterpiece"
506 S.W. Washington at Fifth Avenue
Portland, Oregon 97204
Reservations: (503) 222-0001, (800) 711-2971
Web site: www.5thavenuesuites.com

Description of Hotel
The 5th Avenue Suites Hotel, a *Mobile Travel Guide* Four-Star Hotel and AAA Four-Diamond Hotel—originally built in 1912 as the historic Lipman, Wolfe & Co. department store—is the picture of comfort and sophistication in downtown Portland. Of the 221 hotel rooms, 135 are spacious one-bedroom suites. The Hotel celebrates Portland's art community through support of local galleries and arts organizations.

Location
Located in the heart of downtown Portland, just two blocks from the light rail system, fabulous restaurants, major department stores and Portland's cultural district

Guest Rooms, Amenities and Services
- 135 one-bedroom suites, 82 deluxe guest rooms, four grand suites
- Evening wine reception in fireside living room
- Guest room rates range from $140–$300
- Fully equipped exercise facility
- Two-line speaker phone with data ports for computer hook-ups
- Personal fax machines located in each room
- 24-hour room service
- Hair dryers, ironing board and iron, bathrobes
- Valet parking
- Concierge
- Business center

Meeting Space
Six conference rooms with a total of 4,500 square feet of flexible meeting space accommodates groups from 10–130. Audiovisual services and event coordinator on site. Banquets catered exclusively by Red Star Tavern & Roast House.

See page 338 under Caterers & Ice Carvings.
See page 483 under Banquet, Meeting & Event Sites.

50 S.W. Morrison Street
Portland, Oregon 97204
Contact: Karol Norris (503) 221-0711
Fax (503) 274-0312
E-mail: riverside@transport.com
Web site: www.teleport.com/~peekpa/riverside.html

Description of Hotel

The Four Points Hotel Sheraton offers gorgeous views of the Willamette River and Portland's downtown skyline. Featuring 140 newly renovated guest rooms, including one suite, we have contemporary accommodations with the warmth and personality of a small European inn. Working with nearby river boats and other facilities, we are the perfect combination for comfort, fun and a successful event.

Location

A downtown waterfront hotel located on the corner of Southwest Naito Parkway and Morrison Street, on the MAX light-rail line, we offer easy accessibility from all the major freeways. Walk to parks, river, marina, shopping, Saturday Market, Pioneer Square, Pioneer Place and the World Trade Center. Cultural attractions in the area include the Portland Art Museum, Portland Center for the Performing Arts, Arlene Schnitzer Concert Hall, Civic Auditorium and the Oregon History Center. A newly located Oregon Museum of Science and Industry (OMSI) with the USS Blueback submarine is just across the Willamette River.

Guest Rooms and Amenities

All our guest rooms are equipped with:
- Color television with remote; pay per view movies and games
- Two telephones, one with a data port
- Coffee maker
- Iron and ironing board

We Also Offer

- On-site parking
- Riverview restaurant and lounge, including room service
- Special floors for nonsmoking guests
- Complimentary use of adjacent health club
- Complimentary USA Today newspaper Monday through Friday

Meeting Space

- **The Riverside Club:** We offer riverview dining in our newly renovated restaurant and bar. Dinner parties and other social gatherings are welcomed into the relaxed atmosphere of Waterfront Park and the Willamette River—all with the finest dining and most reasonable prices in the area.
- **The Hawthorne Room:** 180 square feet in our riverview board room located within The Riverside Club seats ten comfortably for an all-day meeting, lunch or dinner.
- **The Columbia Room:** At 576 square feet, our second-floor meeting room serves as a great gathering place. Whether you're meeting business associates or friends and family, this room will suit your needs. Our Sales and Catering Offices will be happy to assist with any special requests. We are flexible and at your service.

Enjoy The Four Points Hotel Sheraton
"Where downtown meets the river"

THE GOVERNOR HOTEL
S.W. Tenth at Alder • Portland, Oregon 97205
(503) 224-3400 or (800) 554-3456; Fax (503) 224-9426
E-mail: governor@transport.com; Web site: http://www.govhotel.com

Rich in History
Listed on the National Register of Historic Places, The Governor Hotel is an architectural beauty with a striking exterior of terra cotta and white brick. The Hotel, built in 1909, has been completely restored to its original grandeur. With a wood-burning fireplace; hand-painted, sepia-colored murals; and traditional furnishings, the lobby creates a warm Northwest impression.

Location, Location, Location
In the heart of the central city, this turn-of-the-century luxury hotel offers convenience to and from the airport; proximity to the financial, retail, historic and arts districts; ease of access to city attractions; and a safe, quite neighborhood in which to dine, shop, and relax.

Meeting Facilities and Services
Offering 15,000 square feet for meetings and banquets, The Governor Hotel's West Wing is unique in size and presentation. Ten elegantly crafted, historically rich rooms offer space for intimate meetings of six to standing receptions for 600. Rooms such as the Grand Ballroom, the Renaissance Room, and the Library begin to describe the ambiance and feel of the former 1920 Elk's Lodge, which is also found on the National Register of Historic Places.

Event services are provided by Jake's Catering at The Governor. Audiovisual support is available along with a full-service business center for last minute needs. Call Jake's Catering at (503) 241-2125 for information and details.

Guest Rooms and Suites
The Governor features 100 handsomely appointed rooms, including 28 suites. Some suites feature jet spa baths. Several include fireplaces or terraces with dramatic views of the sparkling skyline. The Governor offers the charm and style of a boutique hotel with the utmost in gracious personalized service, including 24-hour room service, twice-daily maid service with turndown, complete concierge services, as well as complimentary shoe shine, newspaper, and morning coffee served in the lobby. There are private bars, voice mail, computer and fax ports, and irons and ironing boards in all rooms. For a nominal fee, fitness-minded guests may enjoy privileges at the hotel's on-site, adult-only athletic club. Group rates are available. Please call the Hotel Sales Office for information and details (503) 241-2106.

See page 487 under Banquet, Meeting & Event Sites.

Please let this business know that you heard about them from the Bravo! Event Resource Guide.

Extended Stay Lodging

Beaverton/Hillsboro	*Tigard/Lake Oswego*
875 S.W. 158th Avenue	*13009 S.W. 68th Parkway*
Beaverton, Oregon 97006	*Tigard, Oregon 97223*
(503) 690-3600	*(503) 670-0555*

Web site: www.stayhsd.com

Looking for an Affordable Alternative?

We are the affordable alternative to traditional hotels with the best price value around. Enjoy all of the comforts of home, perfect for relocation, temporary projects, training assignments or anything requiring an extended stay. All studios offer all the comfort and convenience necessary to make you feel right at home.

Amenities

- Fully-equipped kitchens with cookware, dishes and utensils
- Microwaves, coffeemakers, toasters, stovetop, irons and ironing boards
- Well-lit workstations for dining or projects
- Utilities included and fully air-conditioned
- Data port television with remote-accessible Voice Mail
- Free local calls and personal messaging
- Laundry facilities and weekly housekeeping

Convenient Locations

You can find Homestead in 24 of the top 25 top travel markets in the United States. From the San Francisco Bay area to Boston, Miami to Minneapolis, Homestead carefully selects each location for its convenience to nearby shopping areas, restaurants and entertainment with easy access to major businesses and office parks.

Reservations

For reservations at any Homestead, call our toll free reservations number at (888) STAY-HSD (782-9473) or your travel professional. You may also visit us online at www.stayhsd.com.

**Rent by the week—
No lease to sign, no deposits**

HOTEL VINTAGE PLAZA

"It's a matter of taste"
422 S.W. Broadway
Portland, Oregon 97205
For reservations call:
(503) 228-1212 or (800) 243-0555
Web site: www.vintageplaza.com

Description of Hotel
Hotel Vintage Plaza brings European elegance to downtown Portland. This 4-Star, 4-Diamond Hotel is home of the award-winning Pazzo Ristorante. Selected by *Condé Nast Travel* magazine as one of the best places to stay in the world. With 107 rooms, the Hotel Vintage Plaza includes specialty suites such as two-story townhouse suites, the Starlight Rooms, hospitality and luxury suites.

Location
Hotel Vintage Plaza is conveniently located in the heart of downtown Portland, on the corner of Broadway and Washington.

Guest Rooms, Amenities, and Services
Guest room rates range from $140 to $400. Corporate accounts welcome. For special group rates, please phone the sales office directly at (503) 417-3358.
- Honor bar/refrigerator stocked with emphasis on Oregon-made products
- Fully equipped executive gym
- Two-line speaker telephones with data port for computer plug-in and voice mail
- Personal fax machines in each guest room
- 24-hour room service
- In each room–hair dryer, ironing board and iron, bathrobes
- Valet parking
- Newspaper delivered to each room daily
- Concierge
- Business center
- Evening Northwest wine reception in living room

Meeting Space
Eight conference rooms with a total of 4,800 square feet accommodate from 10 to 100 people reception-style; up to 80 people banquet-style; and 60 classroom-style. Audiovisual services and event coordinator on site. Banquets catered exclusively by Pazzo Ristorante.

EUROPEAN ELEGANCE
"THE LUXURY HOTEL OF DOWNTOWN PORTLAND"
Come enjoy friendly, personalized service and European elegance. Experience surprises such as our complimentary Oregon wines served by the living room fireplace each evening. Explore the friendly atmosphere of our "City of Roses" downtown shopping and restaurants, and the gorgeous landscapes of our Northwest terrain. Of course, a visit to the Hotel Vintage Plaza would not be complete without a sumptuous dining experience at the award-winning Pazzo Ristorante. Call for reservations.

See page 528 under Banquet, Meeting & Event Sites.

The Paramount Hotel
A WESTCOAST HOTEL

808 S.W. Taylor Street
Portland, Oregon 97205
Contact: Sales and Catering (503) 223-9900
Web site: www.westcoasthotels.com

Downtown Portland's Newest Hotel
Opening December 1999

Description of Hotel
European-style, 15-story boutique hotel boasts 154 oversized guestrooms including 46 Executive Kings with whirlpool baths, 20 Deluxe Balcony rooms, and two one-bedroom Grand Suites with whirlpool baths and fireplaces.

Location
Located in the heart of downtown Portland's business, retail and cultural districts, Nordstrom, Pioneer Square Park, Portland Center for the Performing Arts, Arlene Schnitzer Concert Hall, Portland Museum of Art and Portland State University are all within a short stroll.

Accommodations
Deluxe guestrooms feature King or two Queen beds, two telephones with dataport and voicemail, hair dryers, iron and ironing board, refrigerated mini-bar, 25" televisions with internet access, and in-room coffee from Cafe Appasionato, the Northwest coffee experts.

Guest Amenities
- Signature restaurant by the Blowfish Asian Cafe—currently rated one of the top 10 Restaurants in Seattle, opening early 2000
- Includes complimentary morning newspaper Monday through Friday
- Complimentary continental breakfast
- Fully equipped fitness room
- Business Services
- Valet Parking
- Valet Laundry Services
- Room Service; restaurant opening early 2000
- Handicap Accessible

Meeting Space
- Two intimate 750-square-foot function rooms, accommodating up to 70 people

PORTLAND Marriott
CITY CENTER

520 S.W. Broadway
Portland, Oregon 97205
(503) 226-6300; Fax (503) 227-7515

Location
The new Marriott City Center is located in the heart of downtown Portland at the corner of Broadway and Washington. The hotel is just a few blocks from shopping, museums, the Performing Arts Center, restaurants, Pioneer Square and MAX Light Rail.

Hotel Description
Guests enter the Marriott City Center from our main entrance on Broadway. The Grand Staircase with its beautiful wrought iron railing highlights the intimate lobby. The lobby features warm bird's eye maple paneling, rich marble floors and a dramatic chandelier.

Accommodations
The hotel offers 249 guest rooms and suites. All rooms feature the "Room That Works" desk that provides guests exceptional workspace, dual line phones, coffee makers, iron and ironing board. For upgraded accommodations the hotel offers three concierge floors and a beautiful 20th floor concierge lounge with views of the west hills and Mount St. Helens.

Dining
Journey up the Grand Staircase to the second floor restaurant and lounge level. The lounge features a comfortable, quiet setting for a relaxing beverage. The Chinook Grill serves breakfast, lunch and dinner with a Northwest flavor menu in an upscale, bistro-style restaurant.

Meeting and Banquet Facilities
The third floor meeting and banquet facilities feature six rooms for groups of 10 to 120. The Salmon Boardroom features an impressive setting for intimate meetings and the River Ballroom accommodates up to 120 and offers floor to ceiling windows. For last minute copying and computer needs, a Business Center is located on the meeting level.

See page 508 under Banquet, Meeting & Event Sites.

QUALITY INN HOTEL AND CONFERENCE CENTER

3301 Market Street, N.E. • Salem, Oregon 97301
Contact: Sales and Catering
(503) 370-7835 or (800) 248-6273
Web site: www.oregonlink.com/quality_inn

Description of Hotel
The Quality Inn Hotel and Conference Center— all you need to plan an event in one great location. Salem's finest full-service hotel and conference center offering 150 affordable guestrooms and suites provides endless amenities and services with a smile.

Location
We're conveniently located off I-5 at Market street; just minutes from Salem's bustling business district, the State Capitol, colleges, and the Oregon State Fairgrounds. Our friendly front desk staff would be happy to offer information about local events and area attractions.

Meeting and Banquet Facilities
10,000 square feet of flexible meeting space for up to 450 guests; perfect for your next conference, reception, banquet, anniversary, reunion or other special event. Special guestroom rates are available for groups.

Amenities
- 10,000 square feet of flexible meeting space with on-site catering
- O'Callahan's Restaurant and Lounge
- Express room service
- Coffee maker in every room
- Cable TV with premium channels
- Indoor pool, spa, sauna and newly equipped fitness center
- Fax and copy service available
- Ample free parking for cars, buses and trucks
- Bell and portage service available
- Valet and coin laundry
- Designated wheelchair accessible rooms
- Special romance packages available

Radisson
HOTEL PORTLAND

1441 N.E. Second Avenue
Portland, Oregon 97232
Contact: Michelle Long, Director of Sales
(503) 233-2401; Fax (503) 233-0498

Description of Hotel
A touch of class awaits you at the Radisson Hotel—Portland, conveniently located in the heart of the vibrant Lloyd Center Business District. The Radisson made its debut in September of 1999 following a 4 million dollar renovation.

Location
The Radisson has easy access from I-5 and I-84, and is just 20 minutes away from Portland's International Airport. The hotel is four blocks from the Oregon Convention Center and only two blocks from the Rose Quarter Complex and Memorial Coliseum. The Radisson offers complimentary transportation for your guests to and from the airport. A quick ride on the MAX light rail system brings you to the center of downtown Portland. Within easy walking distance of the hotel is the Lloyd Center Mall—one of Oregon's largest indoor shopping malls with several cinemas, indoor ice skating rink and an excellent selection of retail stores.

Accommodations
All 238 spacious guest rooms are beautifully decorated and feature coffee makers, hairdryers, iron and full size ironing boards, cable TV, pay-per-view movies, a large corporate desk, and dataports. The executive level offers added amenities such as micro-fridges and privacy access.

Amenities
The Restaurant and Lounge are located right off the main lobby and feature some of the finest in Northwest cuisine. Room service is available 24 hours a day.

For athletically-minded guests, there is a state-of-the-art exercise facility that includes step machines, life cycles, treadmill and a complete selection of weight machines to get you ready for the day. The health center overlooks the sparking, outdoor swimming pool.

The Radisson features over 3,500 square feet of main level banquet space. The Horizon Ballroom is perfect for a banquet up to 200 guests and offers private entrances, a large foyer and an abundance of complimentary parking.

Come and experience the Radisson—Portland.
The difference is Genuine…

1510 S.W. Harbor Way
Portland, Oregon 97201
Contact: Pamela Graves (503) 423-3100
E-mail: sales@RiverPlaceHotel.com
Web site: http://www.RiverPlaceHotel.com

Description of Hotel
The RiverPlace Hotel is an intimate luxury hotel. Opened in 1985, the hotel's design features include floor-to-ceiling windows so you may take in the views of the city, Tom McCall Waterfront Park and the RiverPlace marina.

Location
The RiverPlace Hotel is in a perfect location for business travelers, meeting and events. Located in downtown Portland along the Willamette River, the hotel's doors open onto a popular riverside jogging area. RiverPlace is within walking distance of shopping, nightlife and office buildings.

Accommodations
- **The Grand Suite:** features include a large living room, dining room, wet bar, marble wood-burning fireplace and a guest bath off the living room. The master bedroom has a king-size bed, walk-in closet and jetted soaking tub.
- **Fireplace Suites (5):** a combination of a private living room and private bedroom with a king-size bed; wood-burning fireplaces, wet bars and oversized whirlpool tubs
- **Parlor Suites (18):** queen or king-size beds and separate living rooms
- **Junior Suites (11):** oversized rooms perfect for business travelers
- **Deluxe Rooms (39):** queen, king or two double beds
- **Condominiums (10):** located adjacent to the hotel, these beautiful condominiums include balconies, wood-burning fireplaces, washers and dryers, separate living and dining rooms, queen-size hide-a-beds and fully equipped kitchens.

Other Amenities
This European-style hotel has 84 elegantly appointed guest rooms. Discounted rates are available for corporate travelers and groups. Guest rooms are spacious and comfortable. Furnishings include a writing desk, armoire and windows open to let in a fresh breeze.

Special Services
- 24-hour room service
- Private dining room for up to 30 people off the Esplanade Restaurant
- Complimentary Continental Breakfast
- Use of RiverPlace Athletic Club
- Business and Concierge service
- Voice mail
- Dual-line phones and computer modems
- Choice of newspapers
- Valet parking

See page 542 under Banquet, Meeting & Event Sites.

Newly Remodeled

Shilo Inn
SUITES HOTEL
*and Conference Center—
Portland Airport/I-205*
11707 N.E. Airport Way
Portland, Oregon 97220-1075
Reservations: www.shiloinns.com;
(503) 252-7500; (800) 222-2244
Sales and Catering Office:
(503) 252-5800
Business Hours: Mon–Fri 8am–5:30pm;
Sat by appointment

Guestroom Accommodations
Two hundred suites; full complimentary breakfast, two complimentary evening beverages, special wedding packages and group rates. Each deluxe suite is equipped with three remote-control TVs, four phones with five lines (2 incoming, hold, voice mail and data port), wet bar microwave, coffee maker, refrigerator, iron and ironing board, two hair dryers, two toweling robes and make-up mirror. We also offer evening turn-down service.

Special Services
Our catering and event-planning staff will assist you with your menu selection and theme planning. A Shilo Inn representative will be on hand at your reception or event to answer questions and to make sure things run smoothly. We offer free airport shuttle.

Capacity: up to 450 people for reception, 400 banquet
Price Range: prices vary
Catering: full-service catering to meet your needs on property
Types of Events: business meetings to formal affairs

Availability and Terms
Call for available dates and terms to be discussed.

Description of Services and Facility
Seating: up to 500
Servers: included in price of catering
Bar facilities: hosted or no-host bar; liquor and bartenders provided
Entertainment: referral service available
Dance floor: available upon request; $75 setup fee
Linens: we have an array of colors available
China and glassware: elegant coordinating china; a variety of glassware
Cleanup: will be provided
Decorations: special theme decorations can be arranged; ask about our ice sculptures
Parking: plenty of convenient free parking
ADA: yes

Reservations
Make reservations for any Shilo Inn by calling our toll-free number: 1-800-222-2244.
CALIFORNIA: Palm Springs, Yosemite/Oakhurst, Mammoth Lakes; UTAH: Kanab/Canyon County; IDAHO: Coeur d'Alene; OREGON COAST and Bend.

Please let this business know that you heard about them from the Bravo! Event Resource Guide.

The Sweetbrier Inn

7125 S.W. Nyberg Road (Exit 289 off I-5)
Tualatin, Oregon 97062
Contact: Sales and Catering Office
(503) 692-5800, (800) 551-9167
Fax (503) 404-1950
Web site: www.Sweetbrier.com
Office Hours:
Mon–Fri 7:30am–5:30pm; Sat 9am–1pm

Location
The Sweetbrier Inn is a two story "country inn" located only 10 minutes south of downtown Portland. Our beautifully landscaped grounds create a true picture of Oregon's beauty. The accessibility style and personalized service of The Sweetbrier Inn makes us an ideal choice for your event.

Accommodations
Our 131 newly remodeled guestrooms and executive suites provide a high level of warmth and comfort. Some of our standard amenities include: complimentary continental breakfast and *USA Today*, free local phone calls, in-room coffee makers, touch tone phones with dataport capabilities, 24-hour fitness center and heated outdoor pool. Our executive suites feature oversized work stations, refrigerator, microwave, separate living room and patio, two televisions and iron with ironing board, making it ideal for an extended stay.

Dining and Entertainment
Award-winning cuisine awaits you at The Sweetbrier Restaurant and Jazz Bar. Open daily for breakfast, lunch and dinner. Our chefs' creations appeal to all tastes. Join us for our Champagne Sunday Brunch or relax Wednesday through Saturday to the live sounds of Portland's premier jazz artists.

Convention and Corporate Pricing
Special rates and services are available for group bookings. Ccontact our sales staff for current prices.

Meeting and Banquet Facilities
The Sweetbrier Inn offers 4,000 square feet of meeting space that can accommodate up to 300 people. Let our professional catering staff help plan your next important meeting, reception or reunion. More specific information on catering and meeting facility is available upon request.

See page 556 under Banquet, Meeting & Event Sites.

Resort
Accommodations

BEST WESTERN COLUMBIA RIVER INN

*735 Wanapa Street • P.O. Box 580
Cascade Locks, Oregon 97014
Contact: Sales Department (541) 374-8777, (800) 595-7108
Web site: www.gorge.net/cri • E-mail: cri@gorge.net*

Description of Hotel
The Best Western Columbia River Inn is located in the heart of the Columbia River Gorge overlooking the historic Bridge of the Gods. The Inn offers 63 deluxe guest rooms with spectacular river and mountain views. All rooms feature refrigerators, microwaves and coffee makers. The Inn also offers spacious suites, romantic rooms with private Jacuzzis as well as rooms with balconies.

Location
In the heart of the Columbia River Gorge! The Best Western Columbia River Inn is located 40 miles east of Portland in Cascade Locks, exit 44 on Interstate 84.

Banquet and Meeting Facilities
The Inn offers meeting and banquet facilities for up to 100 guests. Our experienced staff is happy to organize any event. The Inn features in-house audiovisual equipment, conference service staff and 24 hour fax/copying service. Full catering is available upon request. Mention this ad and your speaker or event planner's guestroom is complimentary.

Additional Amenities
- Indoor pool and spa
- Exercise room
- Complimentary continental breakfast
- Cable television (CNN, HBO, ESPN)
- Microwave, coffee maker and refrigerator in all rooms
- Guest laundry
- Free local calls
- Spa and suite rooms available

Activities
Area activities include golfing at challenging 18-hole courses, sailing and windsurfing, white water rafting, fishing and hiking. The Inn is ideally located near the Cascade Sternwheeler, Columbia Gorge Interpretive Center, Bonneville Dam and Fish Hatchery, Multnomah Falls and Pacific Crest National Scenic Trail.

BEST WESTERN OCEANVIEW RESORT
414 N. Prom • Seaside, Oregon 97138
Contact: Leslie Peterson
(503) 646-0457, (800) 234-8439
E-mail: *sales@oceanviewresort.com*
Web site: *www.oceanviewresort.com*

MORE THAN A PLACE TO STAY, A GREAT GETAWAY

Description of Resort
Oceanview Resort is the North Oregon Coast's largest convention hotel, perfect for group meetings, retreats, conferences and weddings. We pride ourselves on offering first-class accommodations with a "touch of home." The Resort provides 104 beautifully maintained guestrooms, most with a spectacular ocean and/or coastline view. The Resort has a wide variety of guestrooms with unique décor and amenities. Choose from family-style rooms featuring kitchenette, fireplace and oceanfront balcony or our romantic beachfront rooms with oceanview jacuzzi, fireplace, and balcony; additional room types available. All guestrooms at the Resort feature VCR, coffeemaker, and voice mail/dataport.

Location
Situated beachfront, on the Prom in Seaside, we offer our guests an unbeatable combination of outstanding location and scenery. Just 90 minutes from Portland and $3^{1/2}$ hours from Seattle and Eugene, we offer an ideal central location in the Northwest. The Resort is walking distance to downtown Seaside with shops, eateries, arcades, Seaside Civic/Convention Center and more; 12 blocks to Factory Outlet Center. There is an abundance of recreational, historic and tourist attractions in the area.

Other Amenities
Oceanview Resort offers more than 6,000 square feet of functional meeting/banquet space, accommodating up to 340 theater-style, 300 for receptions, 250 for banquets, and 200 classroom-style. Small meeting venues are available as well. Our Chef, Catering/Convention Services Manager, and our other friendly, attentive, seasoned staff are ready to assist you to make your event a productive, memorable success! Oceanview Resort also features an award-winning restaurant, cozy fireplace lounge, indoor heated pool and spa.

Special Services
- Flexibility with catering requests—from custom menus to beach functions
- Group rates available for 10 or more rooms
- Complimentary Resort-owned audiovisual equipment
- Gift certificates—perfect for birthdays, anniversaries and weddings

EAGLE CREST RESORT

P.O. Box 1215
1522 Cline Falls Road
Redmond, Oregon 97756
Contact: Davis Smith (541) 923-2453; (800) 682-4786

Description of Resort
Like a desert oasis, Eagle Crest Resort beckons from the shadow of Central Oregon's magnificent Cascade Mountains. With nearly 300 days of sunshine and just eight inches of rainfall annually, it's a perfect setting for a world-class meeting or vacation. The Inn is located along the 17th fairway and offers 100 rooms and suites. We also offer two- and three-bedroom condominiums, five year-round pools and Jacuzzis, tennis, equestrian center, two fitness centers, a day spa with all the treatments to spoil you and four 18-hole golf courses.

Location
Eagle Crest Resort is just six miles west of Redmond Airport in Central Oregon. Convenient to Bend, Redmond and Sisters.

Packages and Prices
Year-round golf packages, winter ski packages and spa packages. Rack rates range from $67–$135 at the Hotel and $129–$278 in the two- and three-bedroom condominiums. Group rates are available for 10 or more units.

Other Amenities
Besides our two championship golf courses, the Ridge course and the Resort course, we offer a fun and challenging 18-hole putting course. In the fall of 1999, our new 18-hole, 73 par course opened. Our day spa offers an indoor pool and full basketball court along with a picnic area for large groups.

Our 4,600 square-foot conference center can be broken into four separate meeting rooms, and to complement our space we have added a 3,500 square-foot tent located 50 feet from the conference center. Our tent is on a concrete pad, carpeted, heated and air conditioned. In addition to our other meeting space, we can easily accommodate groups of 350 people. With the latest technology and a great staff to serve you, there is no better place to have your business meeting or retreat. Eagle Crest also makes a great place for weddings and family reunions.

Special Services
- Complimentary airport transportation
- Massage and skin treatments
- Children under 17 play golf complimentary after 3 p.m.

RESORT HOTEL & MARINA
EMBARCADERO

1000 S.E. Bay Boulevard
Newport, Oregon 97365
(541) 265-8521 or (800) 547-4779
Web site:
www.embarcadero-resort.com

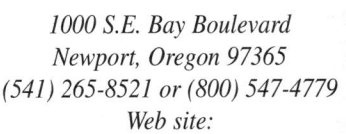

Description of Resort
The Embarcadero Resort Hotel & Marina is located on the central Oregon coast in Newport. Situated on Newport's historic bayfront on the edge of the Yaquina Bay, the Embarcadero offers everything for the vacation traveler and fine facilities for business and group gatherings.

Conference Facilities
Our six banquet and meeting rooms can accommodate groups of 5 to 150 in a casual or formal atmosphere. We offer professional event coordination, complete food and beverage service and facility setups tailored to your specific needs. Three of our meeting rooms offer spectacular views of Yaquina Bay.

Accommodations and Dining
Every room has a view of the Bay and a private deck. Choose from a patio guest room, one-bedroom suite with full kitchen and fireplace, or a two-bedroom townhouse. Our award-winning restaurant overlooks Yaquina Bay and Bridge and offers exceptional Northwest cuisine. Guests may crab or fish from our private dock, and sportfishing and whale excursion services are available on the boardwalk. We also have an indoor swimming pool, sauna, and two outdoor jacuzzis.

Newport Activities
There's more to do in Newport than anywhere on the Oregon coast. Directly across the bay from the Embarcadero is the acclaimed Oregon Coast Aquarium. Just down the road is Newport's historic working bayfront where shops, galleries and restaurants coexist with fishing fleets and canneries. Tennis and five golf courses are nearby. And so are miles of gorgeous beach that front the spectacular Pacific Ocean.

Come see why the Embarcadero is called "The Best of the Coast."
Call 1-800-547-4779 for more information or reservations.

Cannon Beach
1400 S. Hemlock
Cannon Beach, Oregon 97110
Contact: Jenny Brown, Director of Sales
(503) 436-1566, (888) 448-4449

Newport
744 S.W. Elizabeth
Newport, Oregon 97365
Contact: TC Caldwell, Director of Sales
(541) 265-2600, (888) 448-4449

Web site: www.hallmarkinns.com

HALLMARK RESORT AT CANNON BEACH, OREGON

Description of the Resort
This oceanfront Hallmark Resort offers 128 of the most beautifully located guest rooms on the Northern Oregon Coast. Just outside your room is the famous Haystack Rock, and the resort is within walking distance of Cannon Beach attractions and shops. Accommodations range from cozy rooms for two to family-designed two-bedroom suites for six. In addition to guest rooms, there are four oceanfront homes available for beachside retreats and group getaways.

Convention and Meeting Facilities
Perfect for company retreats, banquets and meetings, offering meeting space for up to 150. Audiovisual equipment is available. Please call for group rates and event planning.

Amenities
- Most guest rooms and suites include fireplaces and private decks
- In-room refrigerator, coffee service and morning newspaper
- Recreation Center: indoor heated pool, two whirlpool spas, dry sauna and exercise room

HALLMARK RESORT AT NEWPORT, OREGON

Description of the Resort
Hallmark Resort at Newport offers 158 of the most beautifully accommodated oceanfront guest rooms and luxury suites on the Central Oregon Coast. Close to Newport's attractions, golf courses and shops. All guest rooms and suites overlook the Pacific Ocean. Accommodations range from cozy rooms for two to spacious guest rooms with in-room two-person spa, fireplace and oceanfront balcony.

Convention and Meeting Facilities
Perfect for company retreats, banquets and meetings, the resort offers meeting space for up to 200. Audiovisual equipment is available. Please call for group rates and planning.

Amenities
- Guest rooms and suites include fireplaces, private balconies, mini-galleys, coffee service and morning newspaper
- Recreation Center, complete with indoor pool, whirlpool spa, dry sauna and exercise room

NEWPORT
AT AGATE BEACH

3019 N. Coast Highway
Newport, Oregon 97365
Reservations *(800) 547-3310;* **Group Sales** *(800) 546-5010;* **Local** *(541) 265-9411*

Description of Hotel
Located at Agate Beach, the Holiday Inn Newport offers a spectacular view of the Pacific Ocean and the Yaquina Head Lighthouse. One hundred forty eight tastefully appointed guest rooms feature one king or two queen-sized beds, TV/VCR, microwave, refrigerator, coffee maker, and workspace with telephone and data port.

Location
The Holiday Inn Newport is located north of downtown Newport, within a few hours of Portland, Salem and Eugene, off Highway 101.

Meeting Space
The Cove Room and Agate Ballroom total 5,000 square feet of meeting and convention space and accommodate 10 to 500 people. Our professional catering and banquet staff are eager to serve you for your next meeting.

Other Amenities
- Starfish Grill Restaurant
- Rookies Sports Bar
- Indoor heated swimming pool
- Spa
- Fitness center
- Arcade
- Gift shop
- Movie rentals
- Kids Suites, plus under 12 eat free!

Nearby Attractions
- Oregon Coast Aquarium
- Hatfield Marine Science Center
- Yaquina Bay State Park
- BLM Interpretive Center/Tide pools
- Golf course
- Whale watching
- Fishing and crabbing
- Newport Bay Front attractions and shopping

102 Oak Avenue
Hood River, Oregon
97031

Reservations
(800) 386-1859

Sales
(541) 386-1900

E-mail: HRHotel@gorge.net; Web site: www.hoodriverhotel.com

Description of Hotel
This charming European-style 1913 hotel is listed on the National Register of Historic Places. After complete restoration in 1989, the hotel has retained its turn-of-the-century character, yet offers the conveniences of a modern inn. One might choose from a lace canopy or brass bed, a view of the Columbia River, or one of our larger suites. Amenities include our wine cellar meeting and event space for up to 200+ guests. You will want to make time to visit our fitness, Jacuzzi, and sauna facility. Pasquale's Ristorante offers breakfast, lunch and dinner. We specialize in fine Italian and Pacific Northwest cuisine with menu items from pasta to wild game. After dinner, enjoy a cappuccino or cocktail by the fireplace. Pasquale's is the perfect place to relax after a day's adventure. The Hood River Hotel provides you and your guests a unique establishment, staffed to cater with a personal touch and offering wonderful food to remember us by.

Location
Conveniently located in historic downtown Hood River in the heart of the Columbia River Gorge National Scenic Area, the Hotel offers easy access to movie theaters, restaurants, and shopping. For those looking for outdoor adventure, the area offers windsurfing, white water rafting, skiing, swimming, golfing, and more.

Meeting Space
The banquet room with a total of 2,400 square feet accommodates from 20 to 250 people reception style, up to 150 people banquet style, and up to 100 conference style. Additional areas are available for groups of 20 or fewer. Meeting space is equipped with a wood-burning fireplace, full bar and wine cellar, audio visual services, dance floor, and event coordinator on site. Spa facility adjacent to meeting space for relaxation after a day of meetings.

Other Amenities
- 32 guest rooms; 9 river-view suites with kitchen
- Jacuzzi, sauna, and exercise facility
- Wine cellar
- Full-service restaurant and bar
- Banquet room accommodating 250 people
- Air conditioning

Special Services
For your convenience, the Hood River Hotel offers free transportation to the Hood River Airport. **See page 498 under Banquet, Meeting & Event Sites.**

*1108 East Marina Way
Hood River, Oregon 97031
(541) 386-2200,
(800) 828-7873;
Fax (541) 386-7925
E-mail: hrinn@gorge.net
Web site: www.hoodriverinn.com*

Description of Hotel
The Hood River Inn offers 149 comfortable, well-appointed guest rooms. Most riverview rooms are complemented with private balconies. In-room coffee, clock radios, color television with remote control and room service are among the amenities that we gladly provide. We also offer meeting and banquet rooms for up to 250 people.

Location
The Hood River Inn is located just one hour east of Portland in the heart of the Columbia River Gorge National Scenic Area.

Special Occasion Packages and Prices
Please call for specific price information regarding special packages. Discounts are available for group accommodations.

Other Amenities
The Riverside Grill and Lounge offer indoor and outdoor dining, both with spectacular river and gorge views. A wide range of activities include swimming in our outdoor pool, enjoying our hot tub or strolling our riverside pathway. Nearby are fishing, white water rafting, skiing, mountain biking, hiking, golfing and other outdoor activities.

Special Services
Banquet rooms are available for business meetings, weddings, receptions, luncheons, dinners and family and class reunions. Our professional staff will assist you in planning every detail of your event.

See page 499 under Banquet, Meeting & Event Sites.

The Inn at Otter Crest

301 Otter Crest Loop
Otter Rock, Oregon 97369
Contact: Marilyn Ebe or Ginny Whiffen
(800) 326-5806; Fax (541) 765-2069
Web site: www.ottercrest.com

Description
This resort is unique on any coast. The Inn's 30 rustic buildings are tucked into a wooded hillside overlooking the beaches and tide pools below. The 140 lodging units have all been refurbished and include hotel rooms as well as suites and lofts with fireplaces and kitchens. Each has a private deck with large picture windows. There are covered walkways between the buildings and a hillside cable car connects the levels to the newly remodeled Flying Dutchman Conference Center, Restaurant and Winery. A walk along the Inn's nature trail takes one past old growth Sitka Spruce to the nearby Devil's Punchbowl and six uninterrupted miles of sand beach.

Location
The Inn at Otter Crest is situated in a heavily forested area next to the village of Otter Rock. Located eight miles north of Newport and 15 miles south of Lincoln City on Highway 101.

Banquet and Meeting Facilities
All of our six banquet and meeting rooms have full ocean views and accommodate from five to 300 persons. In addition, our pristine oceanfront lawn and patio area is often utilized for weddings, concerts and social events.

Dining and Wine Tasting
The Flying Dutchman Restaurant and Winery enjoys a reputation for tasty meals and great service. It is a favorite with everyone and now, with the addition or the Oregon Coast's first bonded winery, free wine tasting from our bottles and barrels is a part of every group event.

Packages
The Inn offers many special packages and low season specials. Always popular is our "Adults Eat Free" special. Please call for details.

Amenities
Our 35-acre complex contains nature trails, a private stairway to the beach and tide pools, a heated outdoor pool with spa and saunas, tennis court, basketball court, game room and arcade, gift shop, movie rentals, fitness center, children's playground, whale watching from your room and daily visits by our harbor seal friends on the rocks below. Nearby are golf courses, the Oregon Coast Aquarium, lighthouses, miles of beach, fishing, crabbing, hiking and other outdoor activities.

See page 502 under Banquet, Meeting & Event Sites.

INN AT SPANISH HEAD

4009 S.W. Highway 101
Lincoln City, Oregon 97367
Contact: Group Sales
(541) 996-2161, (800) 452-8127; Fax (541) 996-4089
www.SpanishHead.com

"If you sleep good, you think greater thoughts."   ~J. Schneider

Description of Resort
The Inn At Spanish Head Resort Hotel nestles securely against a bluff on the Oregon Coast and offers 120 ocean front guest rooms. Relax, enjoy the view, and listen to the sound of the sea from your beautifully appointed guest room or suite. Or if you prefer, step outside our backdoor to miles of sandy beach, perfect for a leisurely walk or brisk run. The Inn is complete with a full-service ocean view dining room and lounge, outdoor heated pool, enclosed ocean view spa, saunas, recreation and exercise rooms. Room service is also available. There's nothing like the rhythm of the waves and a fresh ocean breeze to ensure a good night's sleep.

Convention and Meeting Facilities
The Inn is a wonderful place for all kinds of retreats, banquets, meetings or other special events for groups from 10 to 200. All five of the Inn's meeting rooms have floor-to-ceiling windows, so an ocean view is guaranteed. Nothing enhances a meeting more than open space and fresh air. Plus, our experienced staff and in-house catering will put the finishing touches on any event.

Location
The Inn At Spanish Head is located on Highway 101 in Lincoln City, Oregon. It is a scenic two-hour drive from Portland through the lush Van Duzer Corridor of the coastal range. It's just five miles from the Siletz Bay private airport.

Special Packages and Prices
The Inn offers a variety of unique lodging packages. Please call for specific details and pricing. Packages start at $119 per night for two people, including breakfast and champagne in your room upon arrival.

Other Amenities
The Inn offers bedrooms, studios, and one/two bedroom suites. All rooms are ocean front and many come with a balcony and a kitchen/kitchenette. Satellite television is available in all rooms.

Area Activities
Golf, deep-sea fishing, whale watching, hiking, antique stores, art galleries, a factory outlet mall and the Oregon Coast Aquarium are all nearby.

See page 503 under Banquet, Meeting & Event Sites.

Please let this business know that you heard about them from the Bravo! Event Resource Guide.

KAH-NEE-TA RESORT

P.O. Box K
Warm Springs, Oregon 97761
Contact: Tracy Ward, Director of Sales (503) 768-9830

Description of Resort
Located on the Confederated Tribes of Warm Springs Reservation. Paradise to recreation and nature lovers alike, Kah-Nee-Ta Resort shines like a diamond in the rough against Central Oregon's rugged landscape. Located within a two-hour drive of downtown Portland, Kah-Nee-Ta offers a spectacular retreat.

Our accommodations range from village guest rooms, RV Park and teepees to the spectacular Lodge. Designed to capture the landscape of the area, all 170 guest rooms feature a panoramic view of the high desert landscape and are fully equipped for business or pleasure.

Meeting Facilities
Kah-Nee-Ta Resort offers 10,000 square feet of flexible meeting space. From our ballroom to our council room, the conference facilities can accommodate groups up to 700 people. Whether your event is big or small, our staff provides assistance by catering to your specific needs to make your next event a memorable one.

Amenities/Recreation
At the Resort, recreation abounds. Enjoy our 18-hole championship golf course, kayaking on the Warm Springs River, horseback riding, hiking, mountain biking, European-style spa, giant water slide, or relax in the natural hot springs pool. For a cultural experience, the Resort features a traditional Salmon Bake and storytelling with Indian dancers every Saturday, Memorial Day to Labor Day, or let our Director of Culture and Heritage educate you on Native American history by storytelling at dinner or helping with your team-building exercise.

Area Attractions
Visitors may enjoy a trip to the Museum at Warm Springs, located just 11 miles from the Resort on Highway 26. This award-winning museum features a look at the history of the Confederated Tribes of Warm Springs. In addition, you may want to try your luck at the Indian Head Casino adjacent to the Lodge. The casino features hundreds of slot machines, Blackjack and Poker. For additional information on holding meetings or events at Kah-Nee-Ta Resort, please call our Sales Department at (503) 768-9830. For individual reservations, you may call the Resort directly at (800) 554-4786.

MOUNT BACHELOR VILLAGE
RESORT

19717 Mt. Bachelor Drive • Bend, Oregon 97702
Contact: Sales Department
(541) 389-5900, (800) 452-9846; Fax (541) 388-7820
Web site: www.mbvresort.com

Description of Resort
Overlooking the scenic Deschutes River on 170 wooded acres, Mount Bachelor Village Resort provides a distinctly beautiful and tranquil setting where you can truly relax. All of the condominium accommodations are tastefully decorated and include fully equipped kitchens, gas fireplaces, cable TV and daily maid service. River Ridge is our luxury accommodation, which includes indoor and outdoor private spas.

Location
The Village is located on Century Drive in Bend, Oregon. Just minutes from the shopping and great restaurants of Bend, our resort it ideally situated to take advantage of all Central Oregon has to offer.

Convention and Meeting Facilities
With the addition of our new state-of-the-art Conference Center, Mount Bachelor Village Resort has made the commitment to rise above the expected standards of Convention Services. The Village offers 5,700 square feet of flexible meeting space for groups up to 150.

Other Amenities
Mount Bachelor Village Resort offers 130 guest rooms, six tennis courts, swimming, and a 2.2 mile scenic nature trail overlooking the Deschutes River, as well as complimentary access to Bend's finest athletic club, the Athletic Club of Bend.

Area Activities
Activities include golf at over 18 local golf courses, hiking, mountain biking, horseback riding, fishing, whitewater rafting, and much more.

5115 Running Y Road
Running Y, Oregon 97601
(888) 850-0275, (541) 850-5500
Web site: www.runningy.com

THE NEXT GREAT PLACE!

The Resort
The only destination resort in Southern Oregon, The Running Y Ranch Resort has been designed to offer everything you expect of a 3,600-acre residential and recreational development. The resort features a lodge, vacation condominiums, home sites and townhomes, premier golf course designed by Arnold Palmer, sports center, biking, canoeing, horseback riding, and wildlife viewing.

The Lodge
Escape, relax, and enjoy the casual elegance of The Lodge at Running Y Ranch Resort. The lodge is built on a ridge overlooking the golf course, wooded hillside, and Caledonia Wetlands. Each of our 83 guestrooms present the north woods theme in their subtle natural hues and art. Our suites feature walkout balconies, romantic fireplaces and family kitchens. A complimentary breakfast is served each morning.

Area Attractions
There is something here for every taste, mood, whim or desire. Activities include boating, sailing, birdwatching, trout fishing, horseback riding, and golfing.

Meeting Facilities
Let us host your next conference, retreat, workshop, or golf tournament. Our conference rooms have beautiful views of Klamath Lake, wooded hillside, and the golf course.

Location
Located seven miles outside of Klamath Falls, along the shores of Upper Klamath Lake in scenic Southern Oregon.

SHILO INN SUITES HOTEL
BEND

3105 O.B. Riley Road (N. Hwy 97)
Bend, Oregon 97701-7527
(541) 389-9600 or (800) 222-2244
Web site: www.shiloinns.com

NEWLY REMODELED

Accommodations
Shilo Suites Hotel in Bend is nestled on the banks of the scenic Deschutes River, across from the Bend River Mall. Hotel amenities include oversized guest rooms, indoor and outdoor swimming pools, a fitness center and spacious outdoor spa. Choose from a variety of beautifully appointed guest rooms overlooking our peaceful courtyard or the river. In-room amenities include coffee maker, microwave and refrigerator, hair dryer and in-room movies. A complimentary hot breakfast each morning, room service, scrumptious Sunday brunch, fine dining and lounge entertainment enhance your stay at this unique resort.

Special Services
Honeymoon or VIP packages range from $250 (deluxe king suite with a two-person spa) to $270 (suite with two-person jetted tub and round bed), including a $45 restaurant credit. Both packages include a handsome wooden gift box with champagne and two etched Shilo wine glasses.

Capacity: Ballroom: accommodates up to 200 people for sit-down, 250 for receptions; **River Building:** 100 people for receptions, 80 for banquets
Catering: full-service catering tailored to meet your needs
Types of Events: fun theme parties to formal affairs and weddings

Availability and Terms
We suggest making reservations as soon as possible. Two weeks notice is required to cancel catered functions; 48-hour notice to cancel individual sleeping rooms.

Description of Services and Facility
Servers: included with catering
Bar facilities: hosted or no-host bar service available; bartender included
Entertainment: supplier referrals available
Dance floor: available
Linens: linen tablecloths and napkins to complement your colors
China and glassware: included to complement formal and informal themes
Cleanup: setup and cleanup provided by our staff
Decorations: suggestions and referrals available
Complimentary services: shuttle service to Redmond airport and to the Mount Bachelor Super Shuttle location
Sleeping accommodations: 151 newly refurbished spacious guest rooms or suites; special packages and group rates available.

Reservations
Visit our coastal resorts in Warrenton/Astoria, Seaside, Tillamook, Lincoln City or Newport.

RESORT ACCOMMODATIONS

"AFFORDABLE EXCELLENCE"

SHILO INN—LINCOLN CITY OCEANFRONT RESORT AND CONFERENCE CENTER

187 Guest Rooms and 60 deluxe new Suites
1501 N.W. 40th Place • Lincoln City, Oregon 97367

Newly Remodeled

Reservations: (541) 994-3655 or (800) 222-2244
Sales and Catering Office: (541) 994-6275
Business Hours: Mon–Fri 8am-5pm; Sat by appointment
Web site: http://www.shiloinns.com

Our location at the edge of the Pacific Ocean features the panorama of romantic sunsets and the relaxing roar of the tides. Shilo Inn Resort–Lincoln City features 247 guest rooms (oceanfront queen or king bed) including 61 new luxury suites with fireplace, balcony, microwave, refrigerator, wet bar and coffee makers. Relax in our spacious pool, spa or sauna. Nearby activities include a gaming and convention center, shopping, golf courses, stables, racquetball courts and beachcombing. Meeting rooms have ocean views and we can arrange outdoor beach parties.

Price Range: prices vary
Catering: full-service catering to meet all your needs
Types of Events: business meetings to formal affairs

Room	Dimensions	Square Feet	Ceiling Height	Theater	Classroom	Reception	Banquet	Exhibits
ORIGINAL COMPLEX								
Ballroom		6,100	8'5"	450	300	500	400	38
Neptune Room	39'x 28'	1,142	8'5"	50	50	100	50	5
Sandpiper Room	70'x32'	2,229	8'5"	200	100	200	150	13
Whale Room	39'x47'	1,715	8'5"	150	100	150	120	10
Dolphin Room	39'x28'	1,142	8'5"	50	40	75	50	5
SUITES COMPLEX								
Boardroom (10 conference)								
Pacific Rooms–Second Floor								
I & II combined	12'x52'	624	7'9"	40	20	40		
I	12'x26'	312	7'9"	20	15	20		
II	12'x26'	312	7'9"	20	15	20		
Sunset Rooms–Third Floor								
I & II combined	12'x52'	624	7'9"	40	20	40		
I	12'x26'	312	7'9"	20	15	20		
II	12'x26'	312	7'9"	20	15	20		

Special Services

Our catering and event planning staff will assist you with your menu selection and theme planning. A Shilo Inn representative will be on hand at your reception or event to answer questions and make sure your event runs smoothly. Inquire about our special group rates. Honeymoon or VIP packages are available. Call the Sales and Catering Office at (541) 994-6275.

For Reservations at any of our other Shilo Inns call (800) 222-2244

"AFFORDABLE EXCELLENCE"
SHILO INN—NEWPORT OCEANFRONT RESORT

536 S.W. Elizabeth St
Newport, Oregon 97365-5098
(541) 265-7701 or (800) 222-2244
Web site: http://www.shiloinns.com

Amenities

The Newport Shilo—Oceanfront Resort features 179 oceanview guest rooms. Enjoy oceanfront dining at the Shilo Restaurant and Lounge, with fresh seafood prepared daily, or the Shilo Cafe, which features family dining. Leisure activities include two heated indoor pools. Miles of beach for strolling, watching the breathtaking ocean sunsets or just flying a kite in the invigorating beach breezes will keep you refreshed for hours.

All rooms equipped with microwaves, mini refrigerators, coffee makers, irons and ironing boards, phones and remote control TVs. Complimentary fresh fruit, popcorn and USA Today newspaper. Just minutes from the Oregon Coast Aquarium. We provide transportation to and from local airports for out of town guests, free full breakfast and two complimentary beverages each evening.

Capacity: up to 600 for reception, 350 for banquets
Price: from $7 per person
Catering: full-service catering tailored to meet your needs
Types of Events: from casual beach parties to formal affairs and weddings

Availability and Terms

We suggest making reservations as soon as possible. Two weeks notice to cancel catered functions; 48 hours notice to cancel sleeping rooms

Description of Services and Facility

Seating: for groups of up to 350
Servers: included with catering
Bar facilities: hosted or no-host bar service available; bartender and liquor provided
Entertainment: we can help with the arrangements
Dance floor: available
Linens: available in a variety of colors
China: available from caterer
Cleanup: please remove all materials brought in; staff will provide basic cleanup
Decorations: special requests can be arranged
Parking: convenient parking available
ADA: yes

Reservations

Make reservations for any Shilo Inn by calling our toll-free number: 1-800-222-2244.
CALIFORNIA: Palm Springs, Yosemite/Oakhurst, Mammoth Lakes; UTAH: Kanab/Canyon County; IDAHO: Coeur d'Alene; OREGON COAST and Bend.

SHILO INN—SEASIDE OCEANFRONT RESORT

30 North Prom • Seaside, Oregon 97138-5823
(503) 738-9571 or (800) 222-2244
Web site: http://www.shiloinns.com

Situated on the beach at the famous Seaside turnaround, this beautiful resort dominates the area. A variety of room types comprises the 112 guest rooms, and all oceanfront rooms feature fireplace, kitchenette and a viewing balcony. The Shilo Restaurant offers American and Continental cuisine and features a popular Sunday brunch. Guests relax in the lounge dancing to their favorite DJ music or luxuriating in the pool, spa, sauna or steam room. For the exercise-oriented guests, a complete fitness center is available. Reservations can be made for meeting space to accommodate up to 400 people. Golf courses, fishing, clamming, beach volleyball, shopping, arcade browsing and many historical sites are within easy access. You might prefer to go for a horseback ride or simply take a romantic stroll on the beach.

We also have a mini-suites Shilo Inn, which is located a few blocks from the beach. It's an affordable alternative to the oceanfront resort.

Guest Room Amenities
All rooms are equipped with hair dryer, clock radio, coffee maker, iron and ironing board, in-room, first-rate movies, games and entertainment; oceanfront rooms include basic kitchen items (including coffee maker, microwave, and refrigerator).

Capacity: Whale Room: 400 people, receptions; 210, banquets; **Dolphin Room:** 200 people, receptions, 110, banquets
Catering: full-service catering tailored to meet your needs
Types of Events: from coastal beach parties to formal affairs and weddings

Availability and Terms
We suggest making reservations as soon as possible; two weeks' notice to cancel catered functions; 48 hours' notice to cancel sleeping rooms.

Description of Services and Facility
Servers: included with catering
Bar facilities: hosted or no-host bar service available; bartender and liquor provided
Entertainment: we can help with arrangements
Dance floor: available
Linens: available in a variety of colors
China: available from caterer
Decorations: special requests can be arranged
Cleanup: please remove all materials brought in; staff will provide basic cleanup
Parking: convenient parking available
ADA: yes, call for details

Reservations
You can make reservations for any Shilo Inn location by calling our toll-free number (800) 222-2244. Shilo Resorts are in Palm Springs, Yosemite and Mammoth Lakes, California; Yuma, Arizona; Kanab/Canyon area, Utah; Coeur d'Alene, Idaho; the Washington and Oregon coastal resorts and Bend, Oregon.

P.O. Box 3609 • Sunriver, Oregon 97707
Catering Office (541) 593-4605
Fax (541) 593-2742
Web site: www.sunriver-resort.com

Capacity: 14 rooms that can accommodate from 10 to 500 guests
Price Range: starting at $20 per person.; call for more information
Catering: full-service catering for on-premise and off-premise events
Types of Events: breakfast, lunch, dinner, wedding receptions and ceremonies, banquets, parties, meetings and seminars

Availability and Terms
Sunriver Resort is proud of its varied event base with both indoor and outdoor locations, some of which have mountain and golf course views. We recommend that you make your reservations as soon as possible.

Description of Facility and Services
Seating: tables and chairs are provided by the Resort
Servers: staff is included in catering costs
Bar facilities: full beverage services available; Resort provides all alcoholic beverages
Dance floor: complimentary
Linens and napkins: an extensive variety of linen and napkin colors available complimentary
China and glassware: white china; stemmed glassware
Cleanup: provided by Resort staff
Decorations: please consult our catering expert on availability and options
Audiovisual: full-service AV department and Media Specialist Technician
Parking: ample parking available at no extra charge
ADA: ADA compliant

Special Services
Sunriver Resort's location, nestled between the towering Cascade Mountain Range and the high desert is the ideal setting for any event. This, combined with our superior banquet service, our staff's attention to detail, the unparalleled cuisine and our professional catering department, has made Sunriver Resort one of the Northwest's most popular special event locations.

A MEMORABLE DESTINATION THAT HAS IT ALL
In addition to our special event space, Sunriver Resort is a well known destination for the year-round recreational opportunities offered by the area. Located 20 miles from the base of Mount. Bachelor, some of the best skiing in Oregon is at your ski tips! In the warm months, guests will enjoy three renowned golf courses, over 30 minutes of paved bike paths, trails for mountain bike riding, canoeing, kayaking, whitewater rafting, tennis, swimming, horseback riding, hiking, caving, fishing and much, much more! A wide variety of accommodation options, from guestrooms to five-bedroom fully furnished homes, are available for your guests as well. The memories you'll gain are sure to last a lifetime.

SURFSAND RESORT

P.O. Box 219 • Cannon Beach, Oregon 97110
Contact: Jesse Remer Henderson, Director of Events
(800) 797-4666; Fax (503) 436-9116
Web site: www.surfsand.com; E-mail: groupevents@surfsand.com

Total sleeping rooms: 82; **Suites:** 29
Rates: $69 to $319
Special Packages: Sunday–Thursday, October 15–June 15
  Winter Package: Starting at $80 per person (based on double occupancy); includes ocean view room, breakfast, lunch, meeting room and one Surfsand Team Building Activity
Shuttle/transportation: Portland/Cannon beach roundtrip ranges from $28–$80 per person; complimentary Surfsand 14-passenger shuttle within Cannon Beach
Recreation: hiking, biking, horseback riding, kayaking, shopping, tide pool exploration, kite flying, volleyball, golf, crabbing,
Parking: free parking in Cannon Beach

Complimentary Activities

- One complimentary Surfsand Resort Group Activity/Team Building Event (sandcastle building contest, sand sculpture, treasure hunt, scavenger hunt, beach bonfire)
- Additional activities: $50 each or as priced

Complimentary Amenities

- Indoor swimming pool and Jacuzzi therapy spa
- Cannon Beach Athletic Club passes
- In-room coffee and daily newspaper
- Guest services, bell and summer cabana
- Summer Sunday Weenie Roast
- Saturday Ice Cream Social
- Team building events

Description and Location

Nestled between the Coast Mountain Range and Pacific Ocean and just 70 miles from Portland, the oceanfront Surfsand Resort in Cannon Beach is perfect for a rejuvenating retreat, meeting or special event. The ultimate beach resort, the Surfsand welcomes guests with a wide variety of amenities including an indoor pool and Jacuzzi, in-house masseuse, Saturday ice cream social, children's games and crafts, bell service and summer cabana service. Our guests also enjoy complimentary in-room coffee, daily newspaper and free Cannon Beach Athletic Club passes. With over a dozen different room styles and several houses with amenities including panoramic ocean views, Jacuzzis, fireplaces and wet bars, the Surfsand Resort offers a selection perfect for your different needs.

Retreat Accommodations

THE BIG K GUEST RANCH AND CONFERENCE CENTER

20029 Highway 138 West • Elkton, Oregon 97436
Contact: Kathie Williamson (800) 390-2445

Description of Resort
Located on a 2,500-acre beautifully wooded resort, The Big K Guest Ranch is a scenic escape for group and individual activities. The spacious log lodge and 20 luxury cabins are found next to 10 miles of pristine private river frontage on the Umpqua. Fine dining with custom meals, buffets and barbecues are a specialty.

Location
Just one hour south of Eugene, 45 minutes from Roseburg, three hours from Portland and 45 minutes east of Reedsport. Airport transportation between Eugene and Roseburg can be arranged from the ranch.

Special Packages and Prices
Group rates available for conference facilities, cabins and some activities. Cabins can accommodate up to 80.

Other Amenities
Twenty (20) luxury cabins with river access; one meeting room with view; one meeting room/recreation room. Mountain bikes/trails, clay-sporting range, horseback riding, guided fishing trips, birding, float trips, swimming pool and recreation room.

Special Services
Airport service to either Eugene or Roseburg can be arranged for a fee.

Visit our Web site:
www.big-k.com
E-mail: bigk@rosenet.net

RETREAT ACCOMMODATIONS

2126 S.W. Halsey • Troutdale, Oregon 97060; Contact: Sales Office (503) 492-2777
Business Hours: Mon–Fri 9am–5pm; Sat–Sun 10am–5pm, tours by appointment

Capacity: 200 people seated; 250 people reception style
Price Range: $100 to $4,000 food and beverage minimum required; based on size of room and time of day
Catering: in-house catering only; plated, buffet, and hors d'oeuvre; prices vary
Types of Events: meetings, seminars, exhibits, banquets, retreats, holiday parties, reunions, weddings

Availability and Terms

Edgefield has 14,500 square feet throughout 12 function locations, offering a variety of meeting and banquet sites. Several small, private meeting or dining rooms seat between 10 and 40 people, and three large banquet halls seat between 100 and 200 people. Audiovisual equipment available to rent. We suggest you book weekend events at least one year prior, and winter and midweek events year-round three to nine months in advance. Function deposits are 25% of the estimated food and beverage total. Deposit is due 30 days after booking. Over 100 B&B rooms available for lodging.

Description of Facility and Services

Seating: round and rectangular tables for assorted seating; cushioned banquet chairs
Servers: staff included in price; 17% gratuity added to bill
Bar facilities: full-service cocktail bar featuring Edgefield ales and wines
Dance floor: available in two separate banquet rooms
Linens and napkins: assorted tablecloth and napkin colors; no charge
China and glassware: china, glassware, and flatware; no charge
Decorations: responsibility of client
Cleanup: included in price
Audiovisual: equipment available upon request
Equipment: podium, easel, and risers available
Special services: built-in stereo systems in most rooms; 103 bed & breakfast rooms; two on-site restaurants
Parking: free parking and lots of it!
ADA: 11 out of 12 banquet rooms are accessible

EUROPEAN-STYLE VILLAGE

McMenamins Edgefield is the classic gathering place for any group. The historical Main Lodge building is surrounded by specialty buildings with spectacular gardens and landscaping, making the 38-acre property a unique village. Edgefield also has a winery, brewery, movie theater, sports bar, golf course, gift shop, amphitheater, special events, and daily tours.

Please let this business know that you heard about them from the Bravo! Event Resource Guide.

McMENAMINS KENNEDY SCHOOL

5736 N.E. 33rd Avenue
Portland, Oregon 97211
Contact: Group Sales Office
(503) 288-3286
Business Hours:
Mon–Fri 9am–5pm; Sat 10am–5pm; Tours by appointment

Capacity: meeting and banquet facilities ranging from 10- to 250-person capacity
Price Range: food and beverage minimum varies based on size of room and time of day
Catering: in-house catering only
Types of Events: meetings, seminars, retreats, banquets, reunions, holiday parties

Availability and Terms

Kennedy School has several small rooms that seat 10 to 100 people. The theater accommodates up to 250. Reserve your date as early as possible to ensure availability. A deposit equal to 25% of the estimated food and beverage total is required.

Description of Facility and Services

Seating: tables and chairs are arranged to fit your needs
Servers: included in catering cost
Bar facilities: full beverage service available featuring McMenamins wines and ales
Dance floor: our gymnasium's hardwood floor provides a fun dance location
Linens: linens include a wide variety of colors; no charge
China and glassware: all china and glassware included
Decorations: please discuss your decorating ideas with our events coordinator
Audiovisual: a full line of A/V available and every room has chalkboards
Cleanup: included in price
Parking: plenty of free parking
ADA: all banquet facilities are accessible as well as some guest rooms

Special Services

Kennedy School has 35 overnight rooms to accommodate your out-of-town guests. Movies shown nightly in the theater.

HISTORIC BUILDING, GREAT GATHERING SPOT

McMenamins Kennedy School is a unique gathering spot for your group. This historic grade school has been transformed into a wonderful guest facility offering bed and breakfast rooms, restaurant, movie theater, gymnasium, wine tasting, bar, brewery and soaking pool. It is conveniently located minutes from downtown and the Portland airport. Call the Group Sales office for a complete catering packet.

Namasté Retreat and Conference Center

29500 S.W. Grahams Ferry Road • Wilsonville, Oregon 97070
Contact: C. Diane Ragsdale
(503) 682-5683 or (800) 893-1000; Fax (503) 682-4275
E-mail: namaste@lecworld.org
Web site: www.lecworld.org/BookingEvents.htm
Business Hours: Mon–Fri 9am–5pm or leave message 24 hrs.

Capacity: 10 meeting and banquet rooms; largest room seats 1,000 people
Price Range: as low as $52.90; includes three meals and lodging
Catering: in-house catering only; in-house Event Coordinators
Types of Events: retreats, seminars, meetings, conferences, reunions, lectures, exhibits, concerts, weddings

Availability and Terms

Namasté Retreat and Conference Center offers 10 meeting rooms totaling over 29,800 net square feet plus overnight accommodations for as many as 158 people. A 10% deposit is required with the return of your contract and final payment is due upon the receipt of your invoice.

Description of Services and Facilities

Seating: 1,000 person auditorium in addition to 9 meeting and banquet rooms
Servers: included in cost
Dance floor: 15 to 700 person dance floor
China, glassware and linens: included in cost
Decorations: please discuss your decorating ideas with your Event Coordinator
Recreation: state of the art exercise equipment, indoor heated swimming pool, basketball, volleyball, badminton, horseshoes and hiking/meditation trails
Cleanup: included in cost
Audiovisual: full-service, full inventory audio visual department; video conferencing now available
Parking: ample, easy and free
ADA: fully complied, including overnight accommodations

Special Services

Namasté Retreat and Conference Center provides experienced, friendly staff who are service-oriented and assist in making your event successful. All event specifications are planned by our on-site Event Coordinator. Airport shuttle services drive you right to Namasté. Bookstore and gift shop includes greeting cards, jewelry, espresso cart, sundries, candles and a collection of compact discs (CDs) and tapes by internationally renowned musicians and authors.

IT'S MORE THAN A PLACE... IT'S A FEELING

Namasté Retreat and Conference Center is conveniently located just 20 minutes from Portland and 30 minutes from Salem. It is nestled on 95 acres among tall fir trees and beautifully landscaped gardens, offering a haven not often found in such close proximity to metropolitan areas. Namasté Retreat and Conference Center is more than a place, it's a feeling. Information packet and video available.

Please let this business know that you heard about them from the Bravo! Event Resource Guide.

ROCK SPRINGS GUEST RANCH & CONFERENCE CENTER

64201 Tyler Road • Bend, Oregon 97701
Contact: Carole Springer or John Gill
(800) 225-3833; Fax (541) 382-7774; Web site: http://www.rocksprings.com

Description of Ranch

Rock Springs is a beautiful ranch located just northwest of Bend in the foothills of the Cascade Range. As a conference center, our services are especially unique because our policy is to cater to only **one group at a time**. This *exclusive use policy* gives you the opportunity to create the mood and tone you want for your meeting. It also guarantees that you will have the full attention of our professional service staff to ensure that everything runs smoothly and according to plan. Please inquire about our state-of-the-art challenge course.

Capacity: 20 to 50 people—sleeping accommodations; 70—conference capacity; tastefully appointed duplex and triplex cabins; 4,500-square-foot conference building in a warm Western motif; 5,200-square-foot lodge with a massive stone fireplace and comfortable living room ideal for groups large and small

Price Range: prices vary depending on function and group size

Types of Events: meetings, retreats, corporate training and development, seminars, holiday parties, weddings

Activities: horseback riding, hot-tubbing, hiking and jogging trails, trap shooting, tennis, volleyball, swimming, horseshoes, fishing, golf, shopping and sightseeing nearby in the quaint towns of Bend and Sisters

Catering: full service in-house catering

Bar facilities: host/no host beer and wine, featuring regional wineries and breweries

Equipment: on-line capability, phones, fax machine, audio visual

ADA: conference center—yes; cabins—one

Availability and Terms

In the summer we operate as a guest ranch for family vacationers. The remainder of the year, we operate strictly as a conference center for groups of 20 to 70 people. Depending upon the time of year, we suggest you book three to nine months in advance. A 25% deposit on the estimated total is due upon booking and cancellation made 60 days or more prior to arrival will receive a 50% refund.

COMBINING PROFESSIONALISM WITH WARM WESTERN HOSPITALITY

*5115 Running Y Road
Running Y, Oregon 97601
(888) 850-0275, (541) 850-5500
Web site: www.runningy.com*

THE NEXT GREAT PLACE!

The Resort
The only destination resort in Southern Oregon, The Running Y Ranch Resort has been designed to offer everything you expect of a 3,600-acre residential and recreational development. The resort features a lodge, vacation condominiums, home sites and townhomes, premier golf course designed by Arnold Palmer, sports center, biking, canoeing, horseback riding, and wildlife viewing.

The Lodge
Escape, relax, and enjoy the casual elegance of The Lodge at Running Y Ranch Resort. The lodge is built on a ridge overlooking the golf course, wooded hillside, and Caledonia Wetlands. Each of our 83 guestrooms present the north woods theme in their subtle natural hues and art. Our suites feature walkout balconies, romantic fireplaces and family kitchens. A complimentary breakfast is served each morning.

Area Attractions
There is something here for every taste, mood, whim or desire. Activities include boating, sailing, birdwatching, trout fishing, horseback riding, and golfing.

Meeting Facilities
Let us host your next conference, retreat, workshop, or golf tournament. Our conference rooms have beautiful views of Klamath Lake, wooded hillside, and the golf course.

Location
Located seven miles outside of Klamath Falls, along the shores of Upper Klamath Lake in scenic Southern Oregon.

RETREAT ACCOMMODATIONS

SILVER FALLS CONFERENCE CENTER

*20022 Silver Falls Highway, S.E.
Sublimity, Oregon 97385
Contact: Dayna Rich
(503) 873-8875; Fax (503) 873-2937
Business Hours: Mon–Fri 8am–5pm*

Capacity: Smith Creek Meeting Hall, 30 x 40 = 86 persons; Upper Smith Creek Meeting Hall, 20 x 12 = 30 persons; Dining Hall, 20 x 30 = 76 persons
Price Range: $49.20 to $52.25 per person including three meals, one overnight
Catering: Silver Falls Conference Center; in-house only
Types of Events: conferences, retreats, reunions, weddings, picnics

Availability and Terms
Silver Falls Conference Center may be reserved up to one year in advance for groups of 10 or more. A deposit of $15 per person per night is required. Prices subject to change.

Description of Facility and Services
Seating: tables with chairs
Servers: cafeteria-style
Bar facilities: none
Linens: white tablecloths at $5 each
China and glassware: white china; water, wine, champagne glassware; flatware
Decorations: early access available with prior arrangements; please remove all items brought into facility
Cleanup: provided by Silver Falls Conference Center
Audiovisual: TV, VCR, overheads, and slide projectors available at no charge
Equipment: podiums and easels available
Parking: 50-vehicle capacity at Smith Creek; 20-vehicle capacity at Upper Smith
ADA: Alder Lodge (sleeps 12), Smith Creek, Dining Room

Special Services
Silver Falls Conference Center will gladly accommodate any special dietary needs. Specialty meals are available for formal affairs, weddings, and special event banquets.

SECLUDED AND SCENIC LOCATION
Located within Silver Falls State Park (the largest State Park in Oregon), Silver Falls Conference Center surrounds a secluded meadow and is overlooked by tall stands of fir and hemlock trees. The facility is only a short distance from a tranquil trail leading to 10 waterfalls. The park offers a wide variety of outdoor activities such as hiking, biking, swimming, volleyball, and horseshoes.

Convention & Exhibition Services

CONVENTION AND EXHIBITION SERVICES

7140 S.W. Fir Loop #130
Portland, Oregon 97223
(503) 598-0711; Fax (503) 684-6481
Web site: www.a-cs.com
E-mail: a-cs@a-cs.com

Mailing List and Registration Database Support

Your place or ours, we will help you design, customize, and manage your mailing lists, prospect lists, or conference registration lists. Our goal is to help you develop the ability to easily maintain your lists "in house" rather than being dependent on outside agencies for your lists! Using inexpensive, popular and standardized "off-the-shelf" personal computer software, we can put you in control of your important data.

A&CS Can Help You

- ❑ develop and manage your own databases

- ❑ create user-friendly reporting systems… so you can make your information meaningful

- ❑ design and implement your own system for managing conference on-site registration and for tracking exhibitor attendance activity

- ❑ set up you own system for efficiently managing registration to multiple concurrent sessions

- ❑ customize your own production of address labels, confirmation forms, and even personalized name badges

- ❑ package your whole system of use in on-site computerized registration

WE SIMPLY GET IT DONE FOR YOU!
CALL US: (503) 598-0711

In business since 1984

ESI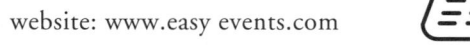

1298 Elm Street SW • Albany, OR 97321
phone: 541.928.5055   fax: 541.926.3478

e-mail: esi@easyevents.com

website: www.easy events.com

New Technology • Low Prices • High Quality • Fast Delivery

Online Registration Services
Catch the wave of the future and cash in on the savings of new technology in registration services. Let ESI customize an online registration program for your event and enjoy the benefits of instant electronic data exchange.
- ▼ Reduce Overall Costs
- ▼ Communicate Worldwide
- ▼ Increase Accuracy and Efficiency
- ▼ Eliminate Time Zone Barriers

Full Service Event Planning
Special events run smoothly and successfully when our professional meeting planners work behind the scenes. ESI's attentive staff is committed to every aspect of achieving your event objectives.

Enjoy the Professional Touch
ESI provides creative and affordable solutions tailored to fit your unique circumstances. We pay close attention to every detail, making certain everything is in place and on time.

Nationwide Experience
Since 1986 Event Solutions Inc. has provided planning assistance and coordination for conventions, seminars, corporate meetings, conferences, training workshops, and trade shows.

Customized Services
Teaming up with the professionals at ESI enables you to focus on the purpose of the event without sacrificing the needs of your daily routine. You may select individual services or have us do all of the work. Our services include:

- ▼ Registration
- ▼ Site Selection
- ▼ Budgeting
- ▼ Newsletters
- ▼ Marketing
- ▼ Desktop Publishing
- ▼ On-Site Assistance
- ▼ Speaker Coordination
- ▼ Exhibitor Arrangements
- ▼ Contract Negotiation
- ▼ Facilitation of Meetings
- ▼ Lodging Accommodations
- ▼ Association Management
- ▼ Communications Center
- ▼ Bulk Mailing

Planning an Event? Consider it Done…
(541) 928-5055

REGISTRATION SERVICES

Plans & Action
Registration Services

A full-service registration provider committed to service, quality and value

P.O. Box 6807
Aloha, Oregon 97007
(503) 259-0739; Fax (503) 259-0838
Web site: www.plans-action.com

Customize registration to meet your needs.

What do you need us to do?
Pre-Registration
- Accept and data enter your registration forms
- Customize registration program
- Travel and housing accommodations
- Accept and account registration fees
- Order supplies and giveaways
- Mailings to attendees and exhibitors
- Secure web site provided for your show and more...

On-Site Registration
- Complete on-site management of registration
- Manage temporary personnel
- Knowledgeable customer service to your exhibitors
- Provide all the laptops, printers and more
- Customize badges and badge holders and more...

Post Show Reports
- Complete attendee database
- Hourly attendee traffic report
- Accommodation report
- Demographic analysis
- Colored graphs and more...

Lead Retrieval System
Choose one of **three** options for your lead retrieval!
- Hand-held, battery operated scanner
- Stationary card swiper
- Manual

Each option can be customized by your exhibitors!

Providing registration services locally and nationwide.

Trade Show & Exposition Services

3720 N.W. Yeon Avenue
Portland, Oregon 97210
(503) 228-6800; Fax (503) 228-6808
E-mail: dwasales@aol.com

DWA Trade Show & Exposition Services is a Full Service Trade Show, Convention and Special Event Contractor.

DWA has been in business since 1977. We are a locally owned and operated company with a very knowledgeable staff that has years of experience in the trade show industry. We have a large inventory of equipment warehoused in our 65,000 square foot facility in Northwest Portland. We are conveniently located just 10 minutes from the Oregon Convention Center, Portland Exposition Center, the Rose Quarter, and many other event facilities, giving us the ability to respond immediately to any emergency that may arise.

DWA Services
- Floor Plans and CAD Design
- Special Events
- Exhibit Installation and Dismantling
- Freight Handling and Storage
- Graphics/Banners
- Rental Exhibits
- Booth Equipment
- Booth Furnishings
- Aisle Carpet

DWA Trade Show and Exhibition Services—
Quality at an affordable price and
where the customer is our number one priority!

☑ **Tradeshows**
☑ **Conventions**
☑ **Expositions**
☑ **Special Events**

8401 S.W. Cedarcrest Street
Portland, Oregon 97223
Contact: Sheri Calaway
(503) 892-3532; Fax (503) 380-1176

NW Expo Services offers a full and complete line of decorating equipment and services

- Tradeshow and convention decorating and services
- Innovative booth design
- State of the art graphics
- Lighting
- Installation and dismantling
- Electrical
- Storage/shipping/tracing
- Logistics
- Event services

Our Network of Clients Include

Adidas	Portland Metro Career Fair
Art of Success	Premier (FTF) Fabric Trim & Fiber
Association of Neuropathologists	Race For The Cure
CFI Pro Services	Salvation Army–Brengel Institute
Commercial Vehicle Safety Alliance	SEIU Convention & Conference
NW High-Tech Career Expo	NW Ski Club Council–Ski Fair
Oregon Style Show	St. Paul Rodeo
Pacific Rim Obedience Association	Tree of Life–Gourmet Awards
PICMET	WCTC Tool Show
Portland Career Fair	West Coast Beauty Supply
Portland Hilton	Vancouver Public Schools
Portland Marriott	Y2K Expo

1400 N.W. 15th Avenue
Portland, Oregon 97209
(503) 294-0412; Fax (503) 294-0616
Business Hours: Mon–Sat 8:30am–6pm
Appointments available any hour

Services
West Coast Event Productions is the Northwest's premier idea center for all events and special occasions. We specialize in the custom planning and design of event staging, lighting, sound, special effects, audio visual presentations, tabletop décor, and event and theme production. We are able to tailor an event or trade show exhibit to mirror your corporate identity or direction.

Convention and Exposition Services
Pipe and drape/skirting/carpeting: Our drape and matching table skirting covers a spectrum of vivid colors creating the ideal backdrop or setting for a booth. Matching table skirting is available for all draping as well as a variety of different styles such as box pleats or straight wraps. Complete selection of pipe and drape for trade show booths, room dividers, stage backdrops, and decorating. Cover drab flooring with a carpeting also available in a variety of colors and styles.

Sound systems, lighting and audio visual: West Coast Event Productions has a complete array of sound equipment from amplifiers, microphone and mixing counsels to CD players. Karaoke machines and high end data projectors. We offer a variety of unique lighting fixtures and special effects including Lycian 2k spotlights, fog machines, image projectors and much more. Our audio visual division includes large screen projection televisions, podiums, and 35mm and overhead projectors with screens for all meeting room events.

Staging and dance floors: An assortment of floors from elegant oak parquet to black and white of color checks. Elevated foundations include meeting room risers, three-tier big band stages-all attractively carpeted and skirted.

New items: Portland now has *Skydancers! Skydancers* are 20-foot tall brightly colored tubular balloon people that dance and sway under a large turbine fan. As seen at the 1998 Super Bowl. Perfect for grand openings and high profile events. We also now carry clear acrylic podiums; perfect for events that require more panache and style than you would have with a simple Oak wood podium.

Event Décor and Rental Items
Themes: Corporate events, fund-raisers, private parties
Props: Accents, photo vignettes and theme occasions
Tents and canopies: Fairs, company parties, weddings, picnics and tent sales
Tables and chairs: Business and personal events

Idea Center
At West Coast Event Productions we pride ourselves in designing exhibit booths that identify an individual company's uniqueness among the competition. We create and produce designs that compel people to take notice of you. West Coast Event Productions has the resources to not only create a winning trade show display, we can provide you with banners, interior and exterior Signage, props and specialty tabletop décor.

West Coast Event Productions
We are dedicated in providing you with a service that is unmatched anywhere else. Our commitment, attention to detail and experience in the event production field has propelled West Coast Event Productions into the one of the most celebrated event companies in the Northwest.

Notes

Convention & Exhibition Facilities

Facilities with over 30,000 square feet

HELPFUL HINTS

Coordinating a trade show is a large task. Your facility coordinator will be your partner for several months. Make sure that you have good communication with your facility and coordinator. It is important for you to find out in the beginning whether the facility can meet your needs. Here is a list of the information that you should get from the facility in advance of booking your trade show:

- Complete floor plan (entrances, loading dock, improvements, etc.)
- Exhibition floor space (total square footage)
- Heights of ceilings (lighting)
- Does the facility meet ADA (Americans with Disabilities Act) requirements?
- Are meeting and banquet rooms available? How far from exhibit space?
- Are there accessible loading and unloading areas?
- Limitations that exhibitors need to be aware of (weight, loading area dimensions, etc.)
- Are there freight elevators and ramps (how many floors to exhibit space, size of elevator, weight limitations)?
- Are there elevators, stairs, and escalators (location, and how many)?
- Are there storage facilities available (if so, cost)?
- What are the insurance requirements?
- Cost of facility (deposit, and terms of payment)
- What services are available? Who is recommended? What are union requirements? (labor rates of electricians, carpenters, decorators, security etc.)
- Additional expenses (telephones, parking, fax machine, press room, utilities, computers, typewriters, show management, desk/office, storage, etc.)
- What are regulations concerning: licenses, liability, fire, building codes, alcohol, cleanup, etc.
- Exhibitors information: shipping address, check-in and checkout procedures, earliest setup time, latest takedown time, inspection dates and times, etc.)
- Types of admission: open/free of charge, badge, charge, etc.
- Key contact for security, theft reporting, off-hour contact

Exhibit Professionals: This is a fast growing industry. There are many professional companies that can help you accomplish your tasks. Exposition service contractors can provide all the services listed here, or you can develop your own team of experts. Exhibit services include: Furniture, floor coverings, accessories, pipe and drape, utilities, floor plans, signage, audio visual equipment, staffing, flower/ plant rentals, cleaning service, security services, exhibit design and construction, lighting, sound, communications, photographic services, business service centers, postal packing services and consulting (you will find most of these services in this guide).

HELPFUL HINTS

Market Analysis: Bringing together the right buyers and sellers. Your success with exhibits will be based on both the interest your attendees have in the exhibitors' products and services, and future sales. If you have had a show before, it is best to survey the attendees to analyze the type of attendee you are attracting. Sample questions include: How did you hear about the show? What is your age? Will you use the products or services presented at the show? What did you like or dislike about the show?

Site Selection: How much exhibit space is available?; How many exhibits will fit?; How accessible is the space for load-in and load-out?; Are professional decorators available? Needed?

Exhibits are becoming more and more an integral part of meetings and conventions. This is often due to the revenue they bring to a meeting from exhibitors' fees. The exhibit program is a complement to the convention and as much time should be spent planning the exhibit portion as the other vital parts of a meeting.

Exhibitor Promotion: Be sure the exhibitors have as much information as they need about your attendees, as well as what needs the exhibitors can expect from the attendees. Also, be sure the exhibitors have all of the detailed information: the size of the booth, the layout of the booths, the exhibit hours, the color of pipe and drape, the booth inclusions, available utilities, and advertising that is available and/or provided.

Communicate often: Exhibitors need to be kept up to date with highlights of the program, list of exhibitors, numbers of attendees. They will also need an exhibitor packet that will give them details on all the official contractors they may order through. For example, forms to order flowers, tables, crate storage, shipping, electricity, etc.

Attendance Promotions: You are obligated to deliver visitors to the exhibitors. You may use direct mail, advertising in newspapers, television, newsletters, and magazines. Be sure to include the name of the event, date, time, location, description of products displayed, fees (if any), and any special attractions.

On-Site: Prepare an operations manual. This will be the exact details of how you want to run the exhibit portion, including the times, dates, location, and who is responsible for what.

Evaluations and Follow-up: A simple questionnaire to gather timely information from your exhibitors will be worth a lot as a planning tool. Find out how the exhibitors did and how you can improve the experience.

OREGON CONVENTION CENTER & ARAMARK—GIACOMETTI PARTNERS, LTD.

777 N.E. Martin Luther King Jr. Blvd.
Portland, Oregon 97232
Contact: OCC Sales
(503) 235-7575

Capacity: Individual Meeting Rooms: 28 combinable meeting rooms totaling nearly 30,000 square feet to accommodate from 10 to 700 people (located directly across from the exhibit area); **Ballroom:** totaling 25,200 square feet divisible into four separate rooms to accommodate from 250 to 1,400 people; **Exhibit Halls:** 30,000 square feet to 150,000 square feet; **Skyview Terrace:** located at the base of the towers, the Skyview Terrace can accommodate from 50 to 200 people for reception style events

Price Range: price determined by event and specific menu

Catering: full-service catering provided exclusively by ARAMARK-GPL; in addition to the wide variety of menu suggestions, the ARAMARK-GPL catering department together with our executive chef can create a special menu to suit your needs

Types of Events: we can accommodate a wide variety of events, from an intimate VIP meeting for 12 to a trade show for 60,000

Availability and Terms
Terms and conditions vary with each event. Events can be guaranteed dates as far as 18 months prior to the event.

Description of Facility and Services
Seating: tables, chairs and head tables provided complimentary
Facility equipment: registration tables, coat racks, water stations, lecterns, podiums, staging and much more available, call for prices and inventory
Audiovisual: large inventory, call for prices and availability
Parking: 830 space parking lot available in addition to off-street city parking
Linens and napkins: wide variety of colors available
China and glassware: white china; stemmed glassware provided complimentary
Decorations: contract decorators available for exhibitors, booths, etc.; ARAMARK-GPL provides water fountains, multi-tiered buffet tables, floral displays, "theme" breaks, and food displays at no additional charge; ice sculptures, floral arrangements, silver service, votive candles available for a fee

BOATS THAT FLY, ALTERNATIVE SOLAR SYSTEMS, SCULPTURES DESIGNED TO ROT...

As meeting attendees approach the Oregon Convention Center (OCC), they're greeted by the harmonious chimes of two massive Asian bronze bells. It's their first clue OCC is no ordinary meeting facility. The feeling grows as they pass sections of our impressive Douglas Fir Nurse Log, whose decomposing centers create new ecosystems. Once inside, an authentic 40-foot dragon boat dangles overhead, ready to breathe fire into any business or social gathering. Not only is our convention center's decor unmatched, but we are confident that our services will surpass any and all expectations.

See page 120 under Calendar of Events.

OREGON CONVENTION CENTER

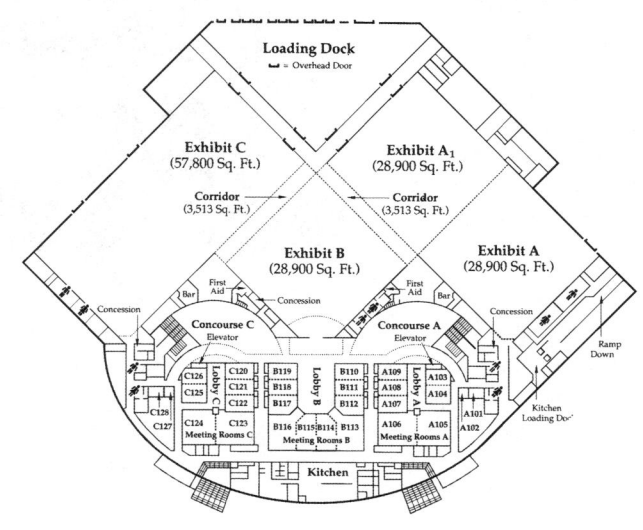

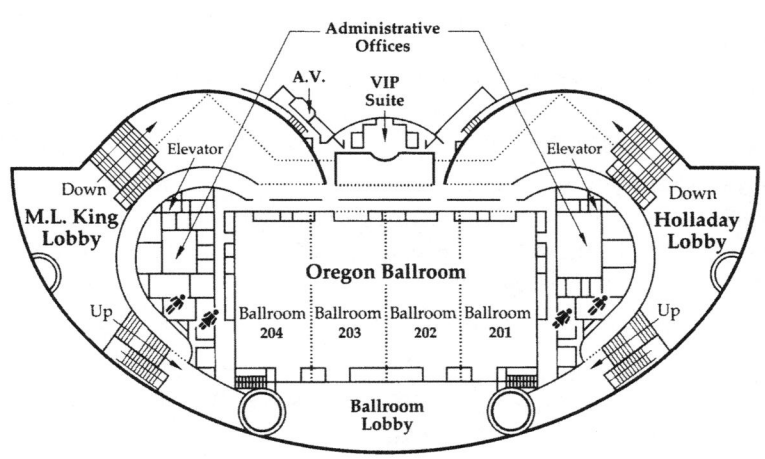

BALLROOM	Square feet	Approx. Dimens.	Ceiling Height	Theater	Classroom	Banquet	10x10' Exhibits
201,202,203,204	6,300	110x58'	25'	675	360	360	30
201-202 or 202-203 or 203-204	12,600	110x116'	25'	1,500	720	720	60
201-203 or 202-204	18,900	110x174'	25'	2,100	1,080	1,170	90
201-204	25,200	110x232'	25'	2,800	1,440	1,530	125

EXHIBIT HALL	Gross Sq. feet	Approx. Dimens.	Ceiling Height	10x10' Exhibits	Theater	Classroom	Banquet
A, A1 or B	30,000	170x170'	30'	145	2,520	1,600	1,600
A-A1 or A1-B or C	60,000	170x340'	30'	330	5,250	3,200	3,200
A, A1, & B or BC	90,000	combined	30'	515	8,000	4,800	4,800
A1, B & C	120,000	combined	30'	680	10,500	6,400	6,400
A, A1, B & C	150,000	combined	30'	830	13,000	8,000	8,000

OREGON MUSEUM OF SCIENCE AND INDUSTRY

1945 S.E. Water Avenue
Portland, Oregon 97214
Contact: Event Sales Office
(503) 797-4671; Fax (503) 797-4566
Event Sales: by appointment
Web site: www.omsi.edu

Capacity: 50 to 4,000
Price Range: call for cost estimates on rental fees and catering
Catering: exclusive, full-service in-house catering available; creative menus are based on budget requirements and/or type of food and beverages requested
Types of Events: conventions, corporate meetings, and social events; receptions set among the exhibits as well as sit-down breakfasts, luncheons and dinners; most areas offer a spectacular view of the downtown city skyline and the river

Availability and Terms
The riverfront science center has five exhibit halls: Turbine Hall, Changing Exhibit Hall, High Tech Hall, Life Science Hall and Earth Science Hall. For additional space and entertainment the Auditorium, Copeland Lumber Dining Room, Outdoor Courtyard, Murdock Planetarium and OMNIMAX® Theater are also available. A 50% nonrefundable deposit of estimated charges is due upon signing an agreement. The balance is due three days prior to your event.

Description of Facility and Services
Seating: tables and chairs in current inventory are available for use at no additional charge. Any equipment that OMSI does not have may be rented for you at an additional cost.
Bar facilities and servers: provided by Fine Host Corporation
Dance floor: may be rented from outside source
Parking: no charge
ADA: meets all ADA requirements
Linens and china: our Event Sales department strives to create events that are visually stunning. We provide a wide variety of specialty linens, china, tableware, and floral arrangements that will make your event at OMSI stand alone.

Special Services
Our experienced event planners will assist you with virtually all planning aspects of your event. Creative menu planning, outstanding service, specialty decor expertise and close attention to detail will provide you with a magnificent event—one your guests will not soon forget.

OMSI'S WORLD CLASS SCIENCE CENTER
OMSI's world class science center is available for private special events and meetings. The museum features interactive hands-on exhibits that will educate, entertain, and amaze your guests. Also featured: an OMNIMAX® Theater that shows educationally rich and thrilling motion pictures on its five-story domed screen; the Murdock Planetarium that features astronomy and laser light shows; and a 219' submarine that is available for tours.

See page 100 under Attractions, Activities & Tours.

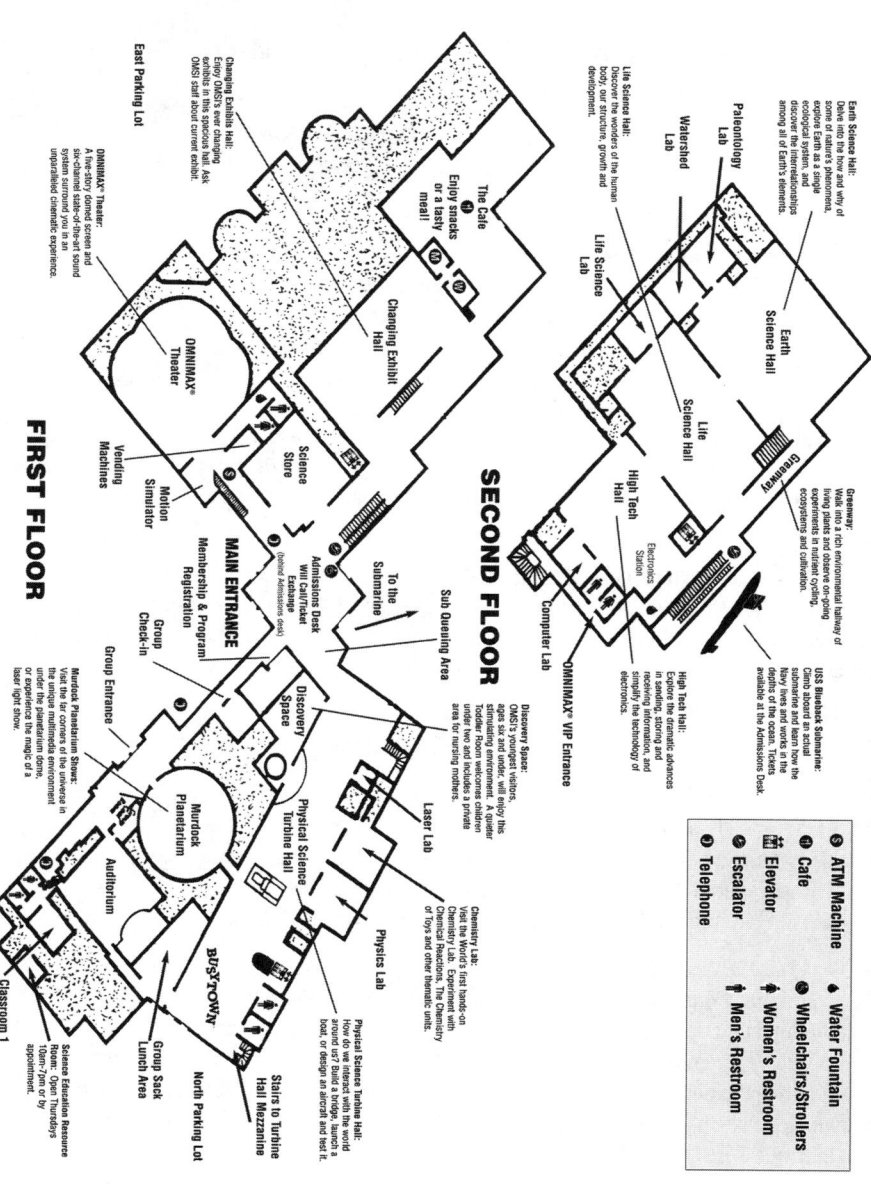

CONVENTION & EXHIBITION FACILITIES

ROSE QUARTER
Memorial Coliseum, Rose Quarter Commons, and Rose Garden

One Center Court, Suite 200 • Portland, Oregon 97227
Contacts: Cathy Walsh or Rachel Eagleson (503) 235-8771; Fax (503) 736-2192
E-mail: facilitymarketing@rosequarter.com
Web site: http://www.rosequarter.com
Business Hours: Mon–Fri 8:30am–5:30pm
Rose Quarter Event Hotline (503) 321-3211

Capacity: up to 21,000; refer to tables on the following pages for specific information
Price Range: please call to receive a comprehensive rate card
Catering: Cutting Edge Concepts is the exclusive caterer and concessionaire for all Rose Quarter events

Types of Conventions/Trade Shows
Memorial Coliseum and its facilities are available for all sizes of association or corporate general sessions as well as trade or consumer shows; a variety of contiguous meeting rooms are available for break-out meetings or small group meetings, banquets and receptions

Availability and Terms
For the date availability, please call!; a nonrefundable deposit is required.

Description of Facility and Services
ADA: completely accessible
Parking: on-site parking is available in the Rose Quarter parking garages; we are adjacent to the Rose Quarter Transit Center which includes a MAX stop
The Rose Quarter is adjacent to the Oregon Convention Center.

Rose Quarter
The Memorial Coliseum, the Rose Quarter Commons and the Rose Garden make up the entertainment complex known as the Rose Quarter. From the only acoustic cloud in the world to *Essential Forces*, a one-of-a-kind water and fire feature, the Rose Quarter offers an entertainment experience that is unparalleled. The Rose Quarter also features on-site restaurants Cucina! Cucina! Italian Cafe and Center Court Cafe & Widmer Brother's Brewing Co., plus the REBOUND Sports Medicine Facility.

Memorial Coliseum
The Memorial Coliseum has the flexibility to host a variety of events in conjunction with the Rose Garden or on its own. Home to the Portland Winter Hawks (WHL), the Memorial Coliseum includes a 12,000$^+$ seat arena, 40,000 square foot Exhibit Hall and seven meeting rooms capable of accommodating groups of up to 500. The Coliseum bowl, all seven meeting rooms, and the 40,000 square foot Exhibit Hall can be utilized for larger show needs.

See page 122 under Calendar of Events.

MEMORIAL COLISEUM

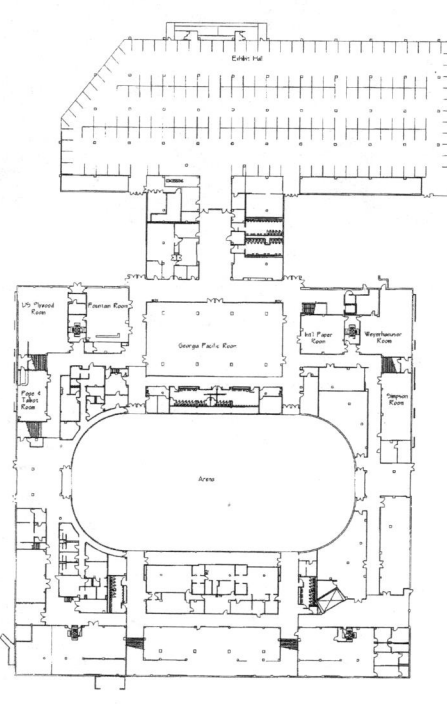

MEMORIAL COLISEUM ARENA			
Rental Rate	**Capacity**	**Banquet Capacity**	**Square Footage**
Ticketed: $6,500 per day or 12% of adjusted gross ticket sales, whichever is greater. **Non-Ticketed:** $6,500 per day defined as five event hours. Event hours above five are billed at an additional $500 per hour. (Event hours are defined as those hours which are open to attendees. Load in/out hours occurring on the same day as event are not counted.)	Center Stage: 13,000 Front of Stage: 10,000 Front and Back of Stage: 12,200	1,800	27,632

COLISEUM CONCOURSE	
Rental Rate	**Square Footage**
$500 per day	25,000

COLISEUM EXHIBIT HALL			
Rental Rate	**Booth Capacity**	**Banquet Capacity**	**Square Footage**
$2,400 per day ($900 per day minimum)	185	2,500	40,000

MEMORIAL COLISEUM MEETING ROOMS				
Rental Rate	**Theater Capacity**	**Banquet Capacity**	**Classroom Capacity**	**Square Footage**
Georgia Pacific—$800 per day	600	350	220	7,470
Weyerhaeuser—$300 per day	180	120	95	2,237
Fountain—$300 per day	110	80	60	1,650
International Paper—$250 per day	90	80	45	1,248
US Plywood—$300 per day	125	80	55	2,590
Simpson—$250 per day	135	80	55	1,537
Pope & Talbot—$250 per day	75	50	20	1,181

Rose Garden

The Rose Garden, a 20,000+ seat arena in Portland's fabulous Rose Quarter, offers a brilliant array of world-class entertainment features. With the largest seating capacity of any arena on the West Coast, the Rose Garden is home to the Portland Trail Blazers (NBA,) an expansion WNBA team, the Portland Forest Dragons (AFL) and the Portland Pythons (WISL) sports franchises along with the hottest concerts, family shows, sporting events and theater productions. We offer a variety of banquet facilities on the Preferred Level for your next function. Player's, Legends Restaurant, the Rose Room, and the Preferred Dining Room are able to accommodate group meetings, banquets and receptions.

Rose Quarter Commons

The Rose Quarter Commons is an outdoor, paved plaza that connects the 20,000+ seat Rose Garden arena, the 12,000+ seat Memorial Coliseum, the Rose Quarter Restaurants and the One Center Court office complex. At over 125,000 square feet (nearly three acres,) the Rose Quarter Commons is Portland's largest outdoor public plaza. The Commons is able to accommodate everything from open-air concerts with seating for 3,000 to outdoor festivals and fairs for up to 8,000 people.

ROSE GARDEN ARENA			
Rental Rate	Capacity	Banquet Capacity	Square Footage
Ticketed: $12,000 per day or 12% of adjusted gross ticket sales, whichever is greater. **Non-Ticketed:** $25,000 per day defined as five event hours. Event hours above five are billed at an additional $500 per hour. (Event hours are defined as those hours which are open to attendees. Load in/out hours occurring on the same day as event are not counted.)	Center Stage: 20,000 Front of Stage: 15,000 Front and Back of Stage: 19,500	2,000	31,725

ROSE GARDEN BANQUET ROOMS		
Rental Rate	Banquet Capacity	Square Footage
Rose Room—$1,000–$1,500 per day	272	6,725
Player's—$750–$1,000 per day	196	9,000
Legends Restaurant—$500–$750 per day	166	5,000
Preferred Dining Room—$250–$300 per day	36	400

ROSE QUARTER COMMONS

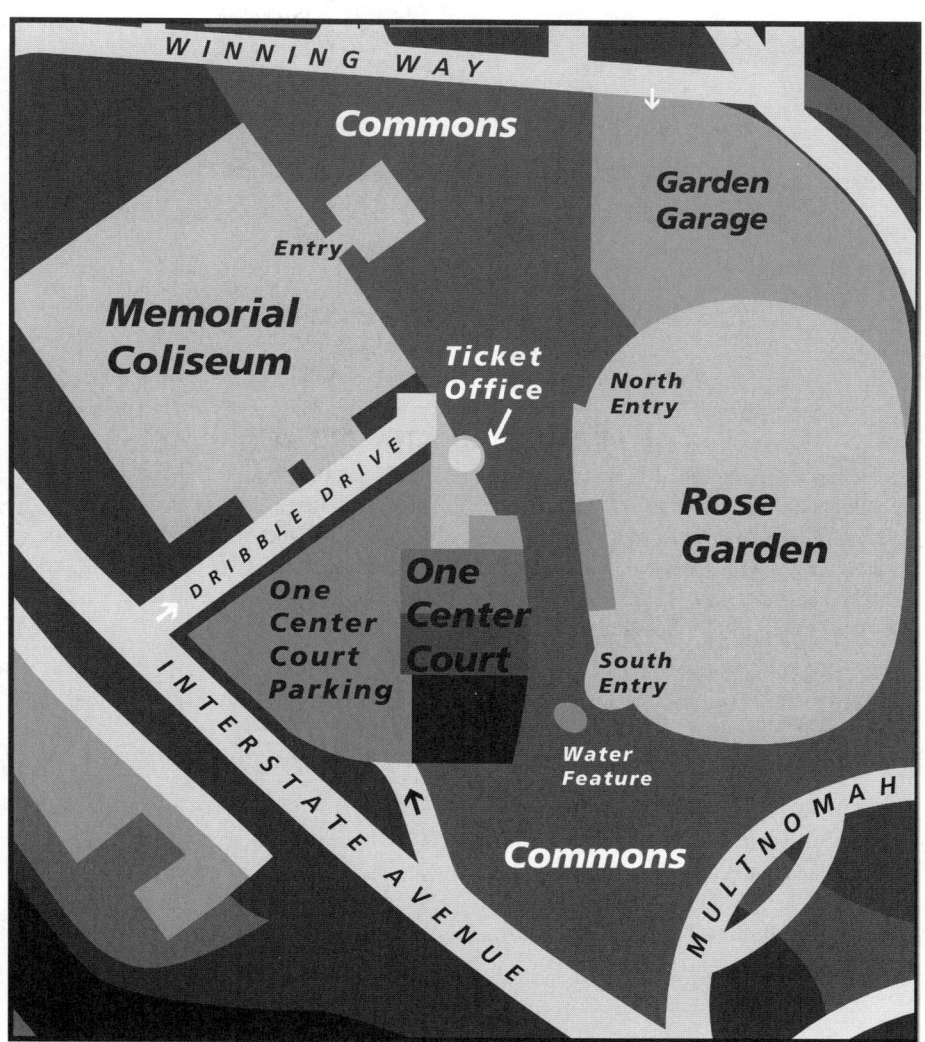

SEASIDE CIVIC AND CONVENTION CENTER

415 First Avenue
Seaside, Oregon 97138
(503) 738-8585 or (800) 394-3303; Fax (503) 738-0198
Office Hours: Mon–Fri 8am–5pm
E-mail: gdarnell@orednet.org; Web site: http://www.clatsop.com/convention

THE PERFECT MEETING PLACE

Seaside has it all! Superb meeting and convention facilities, great food, wonderful accommodations and spectacular coastal scenery. The Convention Center is located within walking distance to downtown and a marvelous variety of 1,200 guest rooms. These include top-notch suites with spectacular oceanviews and cozy bed and breakfast inns complete with fireplaces and sundecks. Recreation and relaxation opportunities abound, as will your delegates enthusiasm for Seaside.

Capacity: from 25 to 2,500 people
Catering: 25 years experience from our in-house caterer "Oregon Fine Foods"; full service bar available
Types of Events: conventions, trade shows, meetings, receptions, banquets

Description of Facility and Services

A professional staff with cumulative experience totaling more than 50 years in convention and meeting planning. Personal attention is our profession. The Convention Center is a nonsmoking facility. For availability and terms, please contact our Director of Sales.
Audiovisual equipment: a full range of audio visual equipment, sound and lighting
Parking: ample free parking available
ADA: fully complies

Seaside Civic and Convention Center—overlooking the scenic Necanicum River and Quatat Marine Park, and just three blocks from the beach and Promenade—affords more than 22,000 total square feet of very flexible meeting space.

LOCATION	Square feet	Approx. Dimens.	Ceiling Height	Theater	Classroom	Reception	Banquet	Exhibits
Main and Exhibit Hall	15,180			1,400	600	1,950	1,300	100
Main Hall	10,500	105'x100'	20'	1,000	500	1,400	1,000	72
Exhibit Hall	4,680	65'x72'	12'	400	250	550	300	28
Riverview	1,944	72'x27'	10'	120	100	130	100	
A/B/C (each)	648	24'x27'	10'	32	24	50	30	
Seaside	1,944	72'x27'	10'	130	100	130	100	
A/B/C (each)	648	24'x27'	10'	40	24	50	30	
Seahorse	1,540	22'x70'	8'	100	65	120	64	
A/B/C/D (each)	385	22'x17'	8'	25	16	30	16	
Haystack	850	17'x50'	8'	75	48	100	50	
A/B/C (each)	283	17'x17'	8'	25	16	30	16	
Seamist	640	20'x32'	8'	40	24	40	30	

SEASIDE CIVIC & CONVENTION CENTER

FIRST FLOOR	
1A	Main Hall
1B	Exhibit Hall
K	Kitchen
6	Sea Mist Room
7	Stages

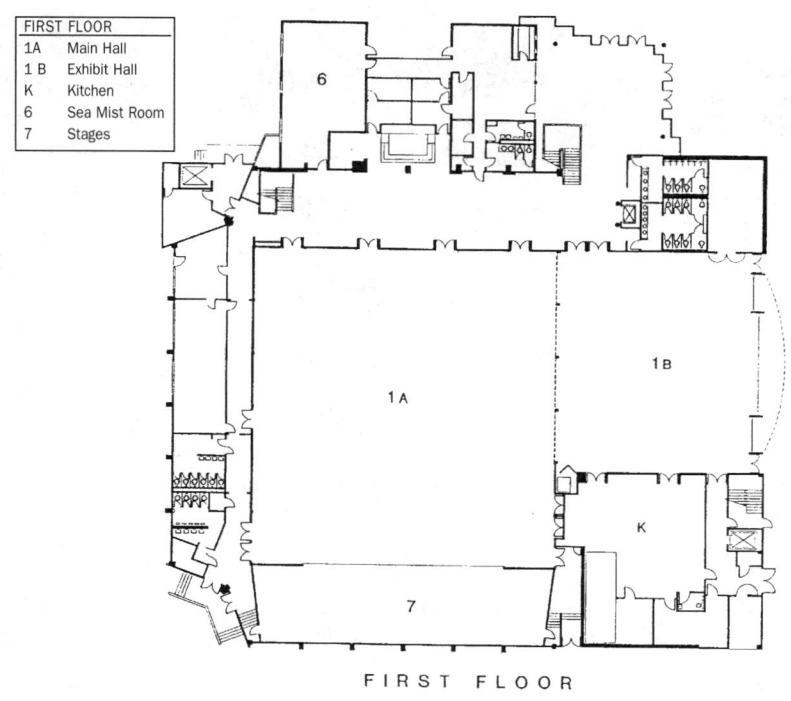

FIRST FLOOR

SECOND FLOOR	
2 ABC	Riverview Rooms
3 ABC	Seaside Rooms
4 ABCD	Seahorse Rooms
5 ABC	Haystack Rooms

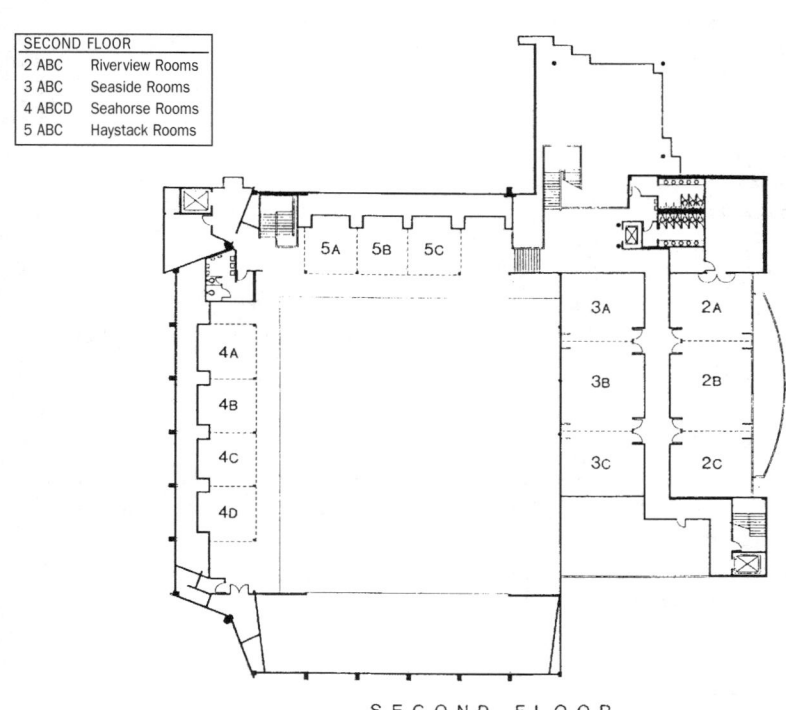

SECOND FLOOR

WILLAMETTE EVENTS CENTER AT THE LINN COUNTY FAIR AND EXPO

I-5 and Knox Butte Road • Albany, Oregon 97321
Contact: Jill Henderson
(541) 926-4314, (800) 858-2005; Fax (541) 926-8630
E-mail: fairexpo@co.linn.or.us
Office Hours: 8:30am–5pm; facility staffed 24 hours

Capacity: Willamette Events Center can accommodate up to 6,000 guests; conferences from 10 to 400 in 48,600 sq. ft.; three additional buildings totalling five acres under cover
Price Range: $40–$1,600
Catering: in-house catering available; contracted and flexible
Types of Events: conventions, conferences, workshops, training seminars, parties, board meetings, expositions, livestock show/sales, horse shows, and more

Availability and Terms
Currently booking into 2005. Please call for availability.

Description of Facility and Services
Seating: provided according to event; up to 3,000
Servers: provided; contracted
Bar facilities: contracted through caterer
Dance floor: available at market rate
Linens: available in a variety of colors
China and glassware: contracted
Decorations: some limitations apply
Audiovisual: slide projector, overhead, TV/VCR
Equipment: A/V carts, cords, podiums, sound; anything can be arranged
Parking: approximately 2,000 public parking spaces available; additional vendor/exhibitor parking; loading dock
ADA: fully accessible

Special Services
Service is extreme here! On-site assistance with local contacts and arrangements. The Linn County Fair and Expo Center is a full-service conference center, exhibit hall, and fairgrounds facility with a professional "can do" staff.

Located near restaurants, lodging, shopping and recreational opportunities. A 10,000 seat amphitheater is adjacent in a wooded park with a lake.

BOAT, TRAIN AND PARK SITES

Banquet, Meeting, & Event Sites

Boats, Trains & Parks

HELPFUL HINTS

- **Begin looking for your banquet or meeting site immediately:** As soon as the event date is decided upon, the first decision that needs to be made is where the event or meeting will be held. Some hotels and facilities will book one to three years in advance, depending on the time of year and size of the event. It is not uncommon for a large convention to be booked five years in advance.

- **Visit the location:** When you narrow down the options of sites available, it is always a good idea to look at the room in person before you reserve it or send the deposit. The look and setup of the room or location will make a difference for the type of event. Also, the room setup will determine the room layout, which is essential to the rest of the planning.

- **Visit your site with vendors:** A site inspection of the facility is important, and you might consider also bringing your vendors for a site visit. These visits can answer questions for caterers, decorators and musicians about parking and unloading, lighting, electrical requirements and permitted work areas.

- **Most common room layouts:**
    - Banquet Seating
    - Classroom Style
    - Conference Style
    - Hollow Square
    - Theatre Style
    - U-Shape

- **Be honest about your budget:** Do not be afraid to tell the facility coordinator or event planner what your budget is. This important information can be used as a guideline that can save time and effort on everyone's part. Make sure to work as a team with your facility staff because they will be the ones that will help create a successful event for you. They can also offer time and budget-saving ideas based on their experience.

- **Deposits are important:** Remember that when you reserve a facility, a deposit is usually required to confirm the date. Do not count on a verbal commitment, everything needs to be confirmed in writing. Facility staff can frequently change, so verbal commitments may be forgotten.

- **Find out what equipment is available at the facility:** (audiovisual, staging, tables and chairs). Find out what you can get at no charge, as well as the quality and quantity of the various equipment. If you are planning to use the equipment, make sure it is reserved in writing. The day of the event, thoroughly check the equipment to make sure it is in working order.

- **In-house audiovisual departments:** Many hotels have their own in-house audiovisual department. Ask if audiovisual equipment in is included in your room charge, then be sure to check out the quality and age of the equipment. If the facility has an in-house specialists they usually know the rooms well, and can help with the most effective room set-up and equipment needs. Most facilities only provide a podium and microphone, so you will need to rent additional equipment from a qualified audiovisual rental company. Remember: poor quality audiovisual equipment can ruin a meeting.

PORTLAND SPIRIT
WILLAMETTE STAR
CRYSTAL DOLPHIN

110 S.E. Caruthers • Portland, Oregon 97213
(503) 224-3900, (800) 224-3901
Web site: http://www.portlandspirit.com
E-mail: sales@portlandspirit.com

From a luncheon meeting for 25 to an elegant sit down dinner cruise for 340, the Portland Spirit will provide you with *Excellence in River Cruise Dining*. The **Portland Spirit, Willamette Star, and Crystal Dolphin** feature first-class sailing, serving Northwest cuisine freshly prepared on board in each ship's galley. Our event planning services ensure that not one detail is overlooked.

Availability, Price and Terms
The Portland Spirit vessels are available year-round from downtown Portland. You may charter the entire **Portland Spirit** vessel or one deck rentals are available. The **Portland Spirit** also offers public cruise schedules. The **Willamette Star** and **Crystal Dolphin** are available for private charter. Prices depend on time of day, season of year and number of guests. NOTE: Capacity recommendations on each vessel depend on time of year, menu selected and type of event planned. Please call for specific recommendations.

Portland Spirit
130 foot, three level yacht, two outside decks
Available for full boat charter, one deck rental
Capacity: up to 540 guests
Seating: tables and chairs for 350, plus outside seating
Dance floor: large marble dance floor

Crystal Dolphin
130 foot, three level yacht, two outside decks
Available for private charter
Capacity: 90 guests
Seating: tables and chairs for 40, plus outside seating

Willamette Star
75 foot, two level yacht, two outside decks
Available for private charter
Capacity: up to 120 guests
Seating: tables and chairs for 80, plus outside seating
Dance floor: available

Description of Vessel Services and Facilities
Enclosed decks are temperature controlled
Linens: linen tablecloths and napkins provided
China: our house china and glassware provided
Servers: included with food and bar service
Bar facilities: full service bar, liquor, bartenders and liability insurance
Equipment: podium and easel available
Audiovisual: equipment available upon request
Cleanup: provided
Parking: commercial and street parking available
ADA: limited with assistance

BOATS

STERNWHEELER "COLUMBIA GORGE" & MARINE PARK

1200 N.W. Front Avenue, Suite 110
Portland, Oregon 97209 • (503) 223-3928
Web site: www.sternwheeler.com
E-mail: sternwheeler@inetarena.com

Owned & operated by the Port of Cascade Locks

Capacity: 450 passengers
Price Range: varies depending on event and length of cruise; two hour minimum; please call
Catering: full range of catering services provided including menu selections for brunch, luncheon, dinner, hors d'oeuvres and theme parties
Types of Events: private charter meal and excursion cruises, company picnics (park only), holiday parties, casino cruises, weddings, fund raisers, meetings, conventions

Availability and Terms
The Sternwheeler "Columbia Gorge" offers two fully enclosed heated decks, providing a comfortable setting for any time of year. Marine Park offers accommodations for groups of 50 to 4,000, as well as a three-acre private island. A 25% nonrefundable deposit is required upon booking; final payment is due 60–120 days prior to scheduled event, depending on season.

Description of Facility and Services
Seating: tables and chairs provided
Servers: provided
Bar facilities: two to three full-service bars with bartenders available
Dance floor: dance area available; full electrical hookup
Linens and napkins: cloth linens and napkins; color coordination available
China and glassware: house china available with our catering service
Decorations: elegant turn-of-the-century motif requires little decoration
Audiovisual: available; please call a sales representative
Cleanup: provided courtesy of the Sternwheeler crews
Parking: *Cascade Locks Marine Park:* free parking; *Portland:* City Center and off-street parking available for a fee
ADA: disabled accessible

Special Services
With two rivers and an abundance of breathtaking views to choose from, the Sternwheeler "Columbia Gorge" and Marine Park continue to provide a unique venue for meetings, banquets, or any event. We can coordinate your event from start to finish, including transportation, catering and entertainment. Please call our sales office for more details.

See page 432 under Park Sites.
See page 554 under Banquet, Meeting & Event Sites.

THE STERNWHEELER ROSE
PORTLAND STEAM NAVIGATION CO.

6211 N. Ensign
Portland, Oregon 97217
Contact: Judy (503) 286-ROSE (7673)
Business Hours: Mon–Fri 8am–5pm

The Sternwheeler Rose

Cruising aboard *The Sternwheeler Rose* is a unique way to make your event special. It's also a festive place to host business meetings, customer appreciations, company picnics, receptions, anniversaries and birthday celebrations. Or, treat your group to a cruise with the Christmas ships for your Christmas party.

Our professional caterer will provide you with breakfast, lunch, dinner or hors d'oeuvre menu suggestions. Of course, you are also welcome to create your own menu. You're limited only by your imagination and budget! Additionally, our staff, crew and captains are available to help you plan every step and execute every detail to make your cruise a wonderful and memorable event.

Capacity: up to 130 people; you may reserve the entire boat for your private cruise
Price Range: prices vary—please inquire
Catering: licensed, in-house catering available; flexible menus
Types of Events: breakfast, lunch, dinner or cocktail cruises, business meetings, corporate parties, receptions, weddings, anniversaries, birthday parties.

Availability and Terms
The Sternwheeler Rose is Portland's finest year-round charter boat. It cruises on the Willamette river. A deposit of 50% is required. Terms are available.

Description of Facility and Services
Boarding location: OMSI; other boarding sites can be scheduled
Seating: tables and chairs provided
Servers: provided
Bar facilities: beer, wine, champagne, soft drinks and bartender standard; full-service bar available
Dance floor: floor for up to 80 people; electrical hookups available
Linens and napkins: all colors of linen tablecloths and cloth napkins available at additional cost; white linens at no charge
China and glassware: glass plates, glasses and barware available
Decorations: No candles, confetti or propane allowed
Equipment: podium, easel, risers available upon request
Cleanup: complete cleanup courtesy of The Sternwheeler Rose with catering
Parking: free at OMSI

Special Services
Be sure to ask about decorations both for ideas and logistics

Please call if you would like more information or a tour.
We at *The Sternwheeler Rose* look forward to serving you.

Visit us at www.sternwheelerrose.com

BOATS

Salem #
371-1103

"WILLAMETTE QUEEN" STERNWHEELER

Located at Riverfront Park—Salem, Oregon
Contact: Irene Solomon
Message phone: (541) 928-4090

WELCOME ABOARD THE 'WILLAMETTE QUEEN,' designed as a scaled down likeness of the former Mississippi and Yukon Territory Riverboats. Relive Oregon's historical past in an elegant dining experience as the ship leisurely glides along the Willamette River.

Capacity: **Dining room:** up to 92; during summer months an additional 15 can be accommodated on outer decks
Price Range: $10; excursions to $35 (dinner with two hour cruise)
Catering: daily lunches, Sunday brunches, dinners, hors d'oeuvres
Types of Events: birthdays, anniversaries, business meetings, banquets, weddings, class reunions, proms, fundraisers—both private and public

Availability and Terms
Reserve seating as soon as possible. Caterers require a 48 hour minimum notice for larger groups; smaller groups may be more flexible.

Description of Facility and Services
Seating: up to 115
Bar facilities: full-service bar
Dance floor: 12' x 12' dance floor available
Linens and napkins: available at no charge
China and glassware: available at no charge
Decorations: flowers, table decorations available, special decorations to be approved
Audiovisual: TV, VCR available at no charge
Equipment: podium, cordless microphone and punch bowels available at no charge
Cleanup: provided; fee for rearrangement of room setup
Parking: available at both Bowman and Salem Riverfront Park
ADA: ADA approved ramps at Bowman and Salem Riverfront Park

Special Services
The captain is a licensed minister and can perform weddings, renewal of vows, live music DJs, melodrama, talent nights and holiday events.

Sternwheeler Excursions, Inc.
P.O. Box 2228
Corvallis, Oregon 97339

YACHTS-O-FUN CRUISES, INC.
A Division of Rose City River Cruises

Contact: Vikki Collie (503) 234-6665
Business Hours: Mon–Fri 9am–5pm, or by appointment

Capacity: 48 guests

Price Range: price will vary according to length of your charter and the services required; summer and winter rates are available; please ask your representative for current price information

Catering: We offer everything from buffet style hors d'oeuvres, special lunch cruises or a seated meal, served by our caterers; either a one-entree brunch menu with champagne or a full-course dinner, with a choice of entrees, including dessert and coffee

Types of Events: business meetings, sales functions, retirement dinners, entertaining clients, Christmas parties, awards to employees for special achievements; any special event or company function can be accommodated and customized to your requirements

Availability and Terms

We will be happy to work with you to create a special cruise for you and your guests. Private Chartering is available 365 days a year. Our lower salon area is totally enclosed for year-round comfort. The upper deck is open to the refreshing river breezes. A deposit is required to hold your date and time, with the final payment due 30 days before the cruise takes place. Cancellation for a private charter is 30 days ahead of the cruise date, for a full refund of deposit amounts. We are able to accommodate most groups on short notice; however, if you have a particular day and time in mind, we suggest making reservations early.

Description of Facility and Services

Seating: tables and chairs are provided if you are catering the event yourself; Yachts-O-Fun will provide all necessary items if using our catering services

Bar facilities: a full-service bar is available for both private chartering and public cruises; a bartender is provided at no charge; liquor, wine, beer and a large selection of nonalcoholic beverages are available

Parking: parking is free at OMSI; river excursion parking in South Lot

Boarding location: next to submarine at OMSI Dock

Special Services

All-day excursions are available for groups of 30 people or more. We offer the only upper Willamette River cruise available, through the Oregon City Locks.

TURN THE ORDINARY INTO THE EXTRAORDINARY!

Celebrate your special event or group function with us. We'll bring you and your guests a cozy, intimate atmosphere of fun and memories to be cherished for a lifetime. Our professional, courteous staff awaits your call, to answer all your questions regarding chartering for group events. A good time will be had by all, so call today to arrange a tour of our vessel or discuss any special requirements you may have for your upcoming event.

RESERVATIONS
(503) 234-6665

TRAINS

MOUNT HOOD RAILROAD & DINNER TRAIN

110 Railroad Avenue • Hood River, Oregon 97031
(541) 386-3556, (800) 872-4661; Fax (541) 386-2140
Business Hours: Mon–Fri 8:30am–5:00pm

Charter the Little Red Caboose, the entire 332-seat Excursion Train or the elegant Mount Hood Railroad Dinner Train for your next special event.

Relax as the unsurpassed view constantly changes before your eyes. Like snowy sentinels, Mount Hood and Mount Adams loom over the landscape. The unspoiled waters of the Hood River tumble along through forested banks where wildlife often appears. Pear and apple orchards stretch to the mountains on either side, showing off seasonal colors from springtime pastels to autumn fire.

Check your cares at the depot. As you step aboard the Mount Hood Railroad Excursion or Dinner Train you enter a different world—an intimate world where time stops and service reigns supreme.

Capacity: Excursion Train: 332 people, Dinner Train: 148 people
Price Range: $18-$75 per person, based on menus and services
Catering: Choose from casual barbecues and picnics on the Excursion Train to elegant dinners and private parties on the Dinner Train.
Types of Events: Special events are offered all year long, from the April Fruit Blossom Festival to the Christmas Tree Trains in December and train robberies, festivals, murder mysteries and events throughout the year. From private parties to corporate dinner meetings, the Mount Hood Railroad Dinner Train offers a "Four-Course Dinner with a Thousand Views."

Description of Facility and Services

Seating: The Excursion Train includes three full-seating cars, one open-air car, one bar car and one caboose. The Dinner Train includes two full-seating cars and one bar car with partial seating and lounge area, complete with karaoke!
Bar facilities: Casual atmosphere and facilities are available on the Excursion Train's Timberline Car. Full-service bar and espresso service are offered on the Dinner Train.
Linens, china and glassware: included in catering fees
Cleanup: included in catering fees
Parking: available on site
ADA: yes; please call for more information

Web site: www.mthoodrr.com

Please let this business know that you heard about them from the Bravo! Event Resource Guide.

VINTAGE TROLLEY

115 N.W. First, Suite 200
Portland, Oregon 97209
Contact: Sarah Fuller, Director of Fun
(503) 323-7363
Business Hours: Mon–Fri 8am-5pm;
call for an appointment

ALL ABOARD!

Take a ride through Portland's history on the Vintage Trolley. The fine craftsmanship and elegant styles of the classic trolley cars provide a charming glimpse of Portland's past. Four hand-crafted streetcars, replicas of the Council Crest trolleys from the turn of the century, serve as both transportation and an attraction in Portland.

For a unique gathering, consider hosting a function on the trolley. Whether you want a catered party on the trolley, a "progressive" event with stops and activities along the way or would rather just go for a ride, Vintage Trolley is prepared to work with you to meet your needs. The trolleys can be used as transportation to and from another facility or as a featured activity during your event.

Capacity: each trolley seats 40 passengers, with standing room for 28 additional passengers. There are many creative ways the trolley can be used with larger groups. Two specially designed serving tables are available for use in the trolley, however use of these will affect available seating. On board is a PA system designed to enhance your event with taped music of your choice, or to provide an efficient system for your announcements. We will be happy to work with you to customize your special event.

Price Range: price varies based on client specifications. A conductor is included in the package and is available to provide a historic perspective on the trolley and sites along the route. Trolley merchandise may be purchased to use as favors for your guests.

Catering: catering and entertainment are not included in the trolley charter cost. You may use the caterer of your choice or provide your own refreshments. Vintage Trolley has no restrictions on the type of food and beverages served on the trolley. Arrangements for catering, entertainment or complete event planning are available for an additional fee.

Charter Ideas *a partial list, limited only by your imagination*

- Art gallery or pub tour
- Casino night or speakeasy
- Sunday brunch, power breakfast or high tea
- Old-fashioned ice cream social, box lunch or picnic
- Rail themes: Take the "A" Train, The Great Train Robbery, Soul Train, Murder on the Orient Express
- Tasting parties
- Shoppers shuttle
- Tailgate party

Charter Availability and Route

The trolleys are available for charter on weekdays from 9:30am to midnight (excluding rush hours from 3pm to 6:30pm) and from 6:30am to midnight on weekends. Charters are scheduled on a first-come, first-served basis. When scheduling, please allow at least 10 days advance notice.

Charters generally operate between N.E. 11th Avenue and S.W. 11th Avenue; however, other routes along the MAX tracks will be approved on a case by case basis.

In early 2001, Vintage Trolley charters will also be available through downtown and N.W. Portland on the new Central City Streetcar route.

HELPFUL HINTS

Planning a company picnic can be easy or difficult depending on several factors: how long you have to plan, how many you are planning for, the type of activities planned, etc. Here are a few things to remember when you begin planning a company picnic:

- **Remember to book your picnic site early!** Spaces are limited, and some companies book their picnic site up to a year in advance.

- **Confirm dates and times in writing.** Don't assume that since you had your picnic somewhere last year that the space is reserved for you this year. Visit the site and look around to make sure it is presentable and what you need for your event.

- **Develop a committee or committees of volunteers** to help coordinate food and beverages, games and prizes, publicity and sign-ups, entertainment, etc. Get feedback from participants on how the event can be improved from the last year.

- **Be sure your contact at the site has a clear picture of what you want.** Be open to suggestions and solutions from the contact at the site—they have experienced all sizes and types of events at their particular site and can be very helpful with what works and what doesn't.

- **Work with the experienced planners on-site** (if one is not available, then check in the "Meeting and Event Planners" section of this Guide to find one). The only way you'll find the answer to your questions is by asking someone who has been through it before. You may have never coordinated an event like this, so ask questions to figure out the best solutions. There will always be last-minute problems, such as expecting 700 people and having 1,000 show up. Experienced coordinators and planners can handle even the worst problems. DON'T PANIC! When you work with the professionals, they will not disappoint you.

- **Most importantly,** don't make the picnic so complicated that you drain your volunteers of their energy! This is supposed to be a morale-building event, not a burnout.

- **Prizes and promotions:** Don't forget to have a keepsake to take home from the picnic like baseball hats with your company's logo, water bottles, Frisbees, etc. (Refer to "Corporate Gifts & Promotional Items" section of this Guide for more ideas and information).

- **Games and activities:** Sports-related games and activities can add excitement to your event. Employees would especially love the managers in the dunk tank. There are professional companies that can come and set-up games and arrange prizes listed under "Audience Participation" in this Guide.

- **Tents and pavilions:** Picnics are planned for summer fun, but you can never count on the sun to always shine. A tent or pavilion at your site as a back-up to bad weather can ensure a great event come rain or shine.

- **Food for the picnic:** Food choice for a traditional picnic is barbecued hamburgers, ribs, chicken, hot dogs and baked beans and salads. Remember that proper refrigeration can eliminate food spoilage in heat.

- **On-site barbecue trucks:** Special barbecue caterers are using on-site barbecue trucks to store and cook the food right on site. The food is excellent and employees enjoy the event without cooking or helping with cleanup.

ALDERBROOK PARK CORPORATION

*Brush Prairie, Washington
Contact: Peter Hessler
(360) 254-3241 or
(503) 283-5152 (phone/fax)
Business Hours:
Mon–Fri 9am–5pm*

Capacity: 200 to 10,000 people
Seasonal: end of May until the first of October; office open all year Monday through Friday
Price Range: to be arranged with facility
Catering: provided by Alderbrook

Types of Events:
- **Corporate Picnics**
- **Corporate Events**
- **Conventions**
- **Chinook Salmon Bake** (for 3,000 people)
- **Western Barbecue** (for 10,000 people)

Availability and Terms
Reservations should be made at least nine months in advance, but shorter notice will be accepted based on availability.

Description of Facility and Services
Seating: tables and benches provided
Servers: appropriate staff provided
Bar facilities: beer, wine or liquor provided by Alderbrook
Dance floor: available
Plates, cups and utensils: provided by Alderbrook
Cleanup: provided by Alderbrook Park
Parking: free parking, accommodations for motor coaches available
ADA: fully accessible

Special Services
Alderbrook, a place in a forest for people, is one of the largest food facilities in the Northwest, assuring the finest food available in the marketplace. Up to 10,000 people can be served at the Western Barbecue, and 3,000 people can be accommodated for a Chinook salmon bake.

NATIONAL WILDERNESS AREA
Alderbrook is a private estate, counted among America's most beautiful private parks. Its vast acreage lies in a natural bowl adjacent to a national wilderness area. Much care has been given to providing first-rate facilities while preserving and promoting the native landscape. Once you've entered Alderbrook, not a car can be seen-only the rare beauty of this natural park.

Please let this business know that you heard about them from the Bravo! Event Resource Guide.

OVERLOOKING THE HISTORIC COLUMBIA RIVER GORGE

P.O. Box 5 • Bridal Veil, Oregon 97010
Contact: Jennifer Miller (503) 981-3695
Web site: www.bridalveillakes.com

Capacity: 1,000 outdoor
Price Range: price varies according to event
Catering: renter may select caterer of choice
Types of Events: picnics, reunions, anniversaries, rehearsal dinners, weddings and receptions

Availability and Terms
We suggest that you book your event one year in advance; we only schedule one event per day Fridays, Saturdays, Sundays and holidays. A $500 refundable deposit is required at booking, with full payment due 30 days before your event. Months of operation are March–October; please inquire for off-season pricing.

Description of Facility and Services
Seating: picnic tables for 100+; please inquire about additional chairs
Servers: provided by caterer
Bar facilities: caterer or renter provides licensed bartender, liquor, and liability insurance
Linens: provided by caterer
China and glassware: provided by caterer
Dance floor: 800 sq. ft. available in pavilion for dancing
Decorations: no rice, paper or metallic confetti; nails, tacks, or staples may not be placed on building surfaces
Cleanup: renter/caterer is responsible for leaving grounds as found
Parking: ample parking available; parking attendants strongly suggested
ADA: accessible

Special Services
Bridal Veil Lakes has a number of RV spaces available.

OUTDOOR ADVENTURE NESTLED IN A PRIVATE SETTING
Bridal Veil Lakes is the perfect setting for your special event. Nestled in the heart of the scenic Columbia River Gorge, just 30 minutes east of Portland, this private recreational area is breathtaking. Forty acres of lush greenery and forest surround our three-acre spring-fed lake. Bridal Veil Lakes offers a custom barbecue facility, covered picnic pavilion, hiking, catch-and-release trout fishing, and canoeing. If an outdoor adventure in a private setting is what you're looking for, you've found the site—Bridal Veil Lakes.

MT. HOOD SKIBOWL
WINTER & SUMMER RESORT

P.O. Box 280 • Government Camp, Oregon 97028
Contact: Karen Norton (503) 222-BOWL (2695) ext. 0
Group Sales Office (503) 272-3206 ext. 100
Business Hours: Mon–Fri 8am–5pm
Web site: http://www.skibowl.com

Capacity: up to 6,000 people
Price Range: starting with a no-charge company discount day up to varied menu and activities
Catering: full-service in-house catering
Types of Events: corporate events, meetings, company picnics, weddings, private parties, concerts

Availability and Terms
Reservations are to be made in advance. A deposit of 25% is required upon reservation.

Description of Facility and Services
Day lodge: 4 day lodges including historic mid-mountain warming hut
Seating: tables and chairs provided under six tented areas in addition to the day lodges
Servers: professional and friendly staff provided
Bar facilities: host/no-host beer and wine available in three full-service bars; six outdoor picnic areas
Plates, cups and utensils: provided with menu at no charge
Decorations: basic decorations provided; theme decorations available for additional charge
Cleanup: provided at no additional charge
Audiovisual and meeting equipment: available upon request
Winter activities: America's Largest Night Ski Area, 65 day runs, 34 night runs, 300 acres of outback gladed terrain, snow tube tow and rentals, snowboard park, sled dogs, sno bikes, indoor sports complex featuring skateboarding, in-line skating and hockey, plus weight room; we also specialize in coordinating events, races and obstacle courses
Summer activities: over 26 attractions where you're in control: 1/2 mile dual alpine slide, three scenic sky chairs servicing nature, interpretive walking trails, mountain bike park with 40 miles of trails plus rentals and tours, horseback, pony rides, indy karts, bungee trampoline, disc and miniature golf, gyroscope, golf blaster, automated batting cages, flytrap, freefall and revenge bungee, kiddy jeeps, adventure river ride, giant inflatable slide, kids fun zone, plus much more…
Parking: ample parking available at no charge; free shuttle between east and west locations
ADA: complied

Services
We can customize any package to fit within your budget, from no-cost to closing the facility down exclusively for your company. Our professional and friendly staff knows just what it takes to make your event an unforgettable one. Our event coordinator arranges all the details from transportation to catering, simple decorations to custom themes and provides promotional support for a successful event.

DISCOVER MT. HOOD SKIBOWL…
Discover this mountain area encompassing over 1,000 acres. Offering a unique setting unlike any other and a view of Mount Hood and six other volcanic peaks. Skibowl offers something for all age groups at affordable prices. Everyone will be able to experience unforgettable fun in the unique alpine environment offered only at Mt. Hood SKIBOWL.

OAKS PARK HISTORIC DANCE PAVILION
at Oaks Park

Portland, Oregon 97202
Contact: Volanne (503) 233-5777
Business Hours: Mon–Fri 8am–5pm

Capacity: dance pavilion with formal seating for 275; festival setup with dancing for 500; outdoor gazebo area for 1,000

Price Range: pavilion rental for a minimum of three hours at $100 per hour, five hours for $450, 10 hours for $700; outdoor gazebo areas are also available

Catering: our in-house catering menus are individually designed to suit your own taste, personality, and style. Our goal is to give you exactly what you want. If you are using an outside caterer, we will charge you a fee of 20% of their final bill

Types of Events: full-line catering, buffet, hors d'oeuvres, and specialty menus

Availability and Terms

Our indoor facility is available for bookings on any day or evening. Our outdoor gazebo and grounds are extremely popular; please don't hesitate to call and inquire. A deposit of $250 is required on the day of booking.

Description of Facility and Services

Seating: we can formally seat 275 people

Servers: we can provide any equipment necessary and the personnel to guarantee your event will run smoothly and at a level of service you expect

Bar facilities: Oaks Park Association provides liquor at the liability of the renter; it is Oaks Park's policy to provide a staff bartender

Dance floor: 99'x54' dance floor with a capacity for 400 people

Linens and napkins: all colors of linen and cloth napkins and tablecloths available for an additional cost

Decorations: we enjoy your personal style—and offer the bonus of fanciful historic carousel horses

Audiovisual: available upon request

Equipment: podium, easel, and risers available

Parking: ample free parking

ADA: fully complies

A PEACEFUL, TRANQUIL SETTING

Join us at our historic riverside park on the Willamette River and let us create a perfect day or evening event for you and your guests. Our facility is ideal for seminars, retreats, corporate dinners, retirement and holiday parties. Children's Christmas parties are a specialty. It is our policy to work with you and offer exemplary step-by-step service all during the event, allowing you to relax and enjoy the party.

See page 97 under Attractions, Activities & Tours.

OREGON STATE PARKS—
PORTLAND/COLUMBIA GORGE

Contact: Reservations (800) 452-5687
Information:
Columbia Gorge/Rooster Rock (503) 695-2261
Champoeg (503) 678-1251
McIver (503) 636-9886
Willamette Mission: (503) 393-1172 ext. 25

For your next picnic or group function, come and enjoy the Great Outdoors just minutes from downtown Portland. The Columbia River Gorge State Parks offer a picnic choice for every taste, from the secluded Talbot State Park, nestled among the towering fir and cedar trees, to Rooster Rock State Park, a water sports paradise on the Columbia River. For those who enjoy the rolling hills or the Willamette River Valley, Champoeg, Milo McIver, and Willamette Mission State Parks offer the ideal picnic spots. The staff at these parks are happy to work with you to make your event a success!

Capacity: 2 to 2,000, depending on facility (groups up to 10,000 at Willamette Mission)
Price Range: $35 for up to 50 people, then 80 cents per person—includes shelter (where available) with electricity, sink, running water, trash bags and receptacles; $6 reservation fee per area
Types of Events: picnics, reunions, receptions and weddings

Availability and Terms
Reservations are accepted up to 11 months in advance. Cancellations must be made at least three days prior to arrival date to receive a refund of the deposit. When cancellations are made less than three days prior to the arrival date, the $6 reservation fee and the deposit will be retained.

Description of Facilities and Services
Cooking facilities: barbecue facilities available at some locations
Cleanup: cleanup is your responsibility; bags and trash receptacles provided
Activities: vary according to park: bicycling, hiking, horse trails, horseshoe pits, volleyball courts, disc golf, swimming, fishing, boating, historical areas
Parking: $3 day use entry fee* per vehicle charged at Rooster Rock, Dabney, Benson, McIver, Champoeg and Willamette Mission
ADA: disabled facilities vary according to park; contact individual park for more information

Special Facilities
Rooster Rock State Park offers three miles of the finest beach on the Columbia River as well as jet ski rentals. Picnic shelters with running water and barbecues are available at Rooster Rock, Benson, and Dabney State Parks. Champoeg also has available for reservation a meeting hall, pavilion, museum meeting room and amphitheater. Camping facilities also available at Champoeg and McIver.

Horse rentals available at McIver and Willamette Mission and boat rentals available at select park locations.

* Annual pass available for entry into any day use fee park.

COME ENJOY THE GREAT OUTDOORS
Call for reservations (800) 452-5687

Please let this business know that you heard about them from the Bravo! Event Resource Guide.

MARINE PARK & STERNWHEELER "COLUMBIA GORGE"

1200 N.W. Front Avenue, Suite 110
Portland, Oregon 97209 • (503) 223-3928
Web site: www.sternwheeler.com
E-mail: sternwheeler@inetarena.com

Owned & operated by the Port of Cascade Locks

Price Range: varies depending on structure, size and length of event; please call
Catering: full range of catering services provided including menu selections for picnics, brunches, buffet dinners, hors d'oeuvres and theme parties
Types of Events: company picnics, weddings, private charters, casino cruises, and public meal and excursion cruises

Availability and Terms
We offer a variety of accommodations for groups up to 4,000. A 25% nonrefundable deposit is required upon booking; final payment is due 60–120 days prior to scheduled event, depending on season.

Description of Facility and Services
Seating: tables and chairs provided with food service; **Pavilion:** seats up to 320 within covered area; **Tent #1:** seats 100 within covered area; **Tent #2:** seats 80
Servers: provided with our catering service
Bar facilities: full-service bars available with bartenders
Dance floor: dance area available; full electrical hookup
Linens and napkins: cloth linens and napkins available with food service in Pavilion and tents only
China and glassware: house china or paper (paper over 200 guests); available with our catering service
Decorations: please call; 110-watt available; PA available at specific locations only
Cleanup: provided courtesy of the Port of Cascade Locks; requires cleaning deposit
Parking: Cascade Locks: free parking; RV parking available for a fee; please call
ADA: disabled accessible

Special Services
Marine Park at Cascade Locks is a spectacular event site located just 45 minutes from Portland. With the added bonus of a cruise aboard the Sternwheeler "Columbia Gorge" from mid-June through September, this unique park offers more than just ample space with breathtaking views. Our customized events include everything from fund-raisers to company picnics. Please call our sales office for more information.

See page 420 under Boat Sites.
See page 554 under Banquet, Meeting & Event Sites.

Banquet, Meeting, & Event Sites

Smaller Venues

SMALLER VENUES

0607 S.W. Idaho Street • Portland, Oregon 97201
Contact: David Mandel, VP of Training
(503) 246-3630; Fax (503) 246-3124
E-mail: dmandel@avalongroup.net
Web site: www.avalongroup.net

Capacity: nine students
Price Range: $600 per day or $300 per half day or evening

Availability and Terms

Make reservations as early as possible. We can accommodate events on short notice if space and time is available. A nonrefundable deposit of 25% of expected expenditures is required one month prior to event. Payment in full is due prior to the day of your function.

Description of Facility and Services

Classroom: Nine student computers and one instructor computer running MS Windows 98 or Linux. All computers are networked and have high-speed internet access. All computers also have access to monochrome and color printers. Other peripherals such as scanners and CD burners are available upon request. The room includes a VGA projector and a white board.

Support staff: A receptionist is available to handle phone calls during the event. Technical staff with experience in Netware, MS Windows, Linuxb and Unix are available if needed. Contract instructors are also available, and may be used to teach an entire class or to team teach with your instructor.

Pre-event/post-event support: Our receptionist will take messages relating to your event. We also provide free e-mail accounts, mailing list support, and space for Web pages on ATG's Web server for advertising and coordinating your event. Web design assistance is available as an optional extra.

Parking: free on-site parking available

BUFFALO GAP SALOON & EATERY

6835 S.W. Macadam (just north of the Sellwood Bridge) • Portland, Oregon 97219
(503) 244-7111; Fax (503) 246-8848
Business Hours: Mon–Fri 7–2:30am, Sat 8–2:30am, Sun 9–2:30am
Office Hours: Mon–Fri 7am–5pm
Web site: www.buffalogap.citysearch.com

Capacity: groups of up to 50 people (depending on event)
Price Range: breakfast $3–$8, lunch $6–$9, dinner $10–$15; room fees range from $35–$100
Catering: full in-house catering exclusively
Types of Events: business meetings, receptions, rehearsal dinners, parties, social events

Availability and Terms
Early reservations strongly encouraged. The Buffalo Gap's "Attic" can be utilized as a completely private space, with full bar, private restrooms, and sundeck (weather permitting). Downstairs dining can accommodate groups of 20 for business or social gatherings.

Description of Facility and Services
Seating: tables and chairs provided
Servers and bartenders: included in price
Bar facilities: two full-service bars, beer and wine
Linens and napkins: white or colored linens can be ordered
China and glassware: provided by Buffalo Gap
Decorations: table decorations are permissible
Cleanup: included at no extra charge
Parking: free on-site and adjacent parking available

Special Services
The Gap has one of the most beautiful and intimate (up to 24 guests) garden patios in the city, an upstairs sundeck, two full-service bars, a game and billiards room, a very accommodating staff, and live music six nights a week.

A GREAT GATHERING PLACE WITH SOMETHING FOR EVERYONE
The Buffalo Gap's building is over 100 years old, and has been used, among other things, as a private residence, rooming house, brothel and saloon. In business for over 25 years, with over 150 menu items to choose from, the gap is conveniently located and a wonderful experience for a diverse group of people.

Please let this business know that you heard about them from the Bravo! Event Resource Guide.

ITALIAN RESTAURANT

8544 S.W. Apple Way
Portland, Oregon 97225
Contact: Gwen Tiemeyer (503) 292-0119; Fax (503) 292-6451
Business Hours: Mon–Thu 11am–10pm; Fri 11am–11pm; Sat 4:30–11pm; Sun 4–10pm

Capacity: seating from 20 to 150, depending on requirements
Price Range: room rental and setup fees may be waived when meal minimums are met; ranges $9.95–$18.95
Catering: full service in-house and on-location catering
Types of Events: conferences, meetings, seminars, luncheons, banquets, wedding rehearsal dinners

Availability and Terms
Advance reservations of two to six months are recommended, however, we will try to accommodate last minute events when possible. A deposit is required to secure the room.

Description of Facility and Services
Seating: variety of seating options available for up to 150
Servers: provided
Bar facilities: host/no-host bars available; restaurant supplies all liquor and bartender
Dance floor: available upon request
Linens: cloth linens available in limited colors at no additional cost; special colors can be ordered for a fee
China and glassware: included in the cost of food and beverage
Decorations: standard decorations including helium balloons acceptable
Audiovisual: in-house sound system, state-of-the-art teleconferencing and video capabilities; wide range of rental equipment available upon request
Parking: ample free parking
ADA: meets all standards; all meeting rooms on ground level

CONVENIENT BEAVERTON LOCATION
Our new restaurant (between Jesuit High School and Zupans on Beaverton-Hillsdale Highway) features spacious dining rooms, a full-service lounge and gorgeous meeting/banquet rooms. Three generations of Italian recipes including fresh pasta, veal, chicken, pizza, calzone and charbroiled steaks. We feature banquet menus that include both Italian and American food, and we know you'll find the service and atmosphere first class. Accessible from both I-5 and Highway 217 and only 10 minutes from downtown Portland.

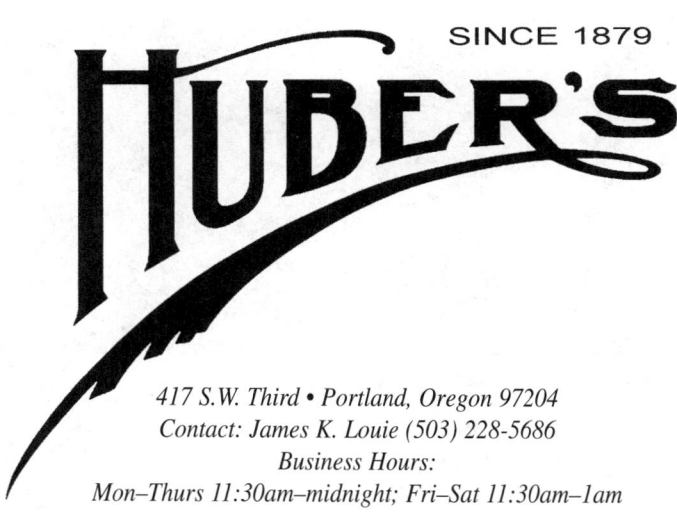

SMALLER VENUES

417 S.W. Third • Portland, Oregon 97204
Contact: James K. Louie (503) 228-5686
Business Hours:
Mon–Thurs 11:30am–midnight; Fri–Sat 11:30am–1am

Capacity: up to 50
Price Range: $13.90 to $26
Catering: on-premise or we can cater at your event site
Types of Events: banquets, buffets, cocktail parties

Availability and Terms
Reservations are recommended three weeks prior to the event. A one-third deposit secures the reservation. There is a $150 room charge if the event goes beyond three hours on Fridays or Saturdays. A 15% gratuity will be added to the total bill.

Description of Facility and Services
Seating: up to 50
Servers: provided by Huber's
Bar facilities: full-service bar; bartenders provided
Linens: cloth linens provided by Huber's
Cleanup: provided by Huber's
Parking: on street available
ADA: fully accessible

Special Services
Fresh turkey roast, a Huber's specialty, is available on request for an additional charge.

PORTLAND'S OLDEST RESTAURANT
Huber's Cafe, Portland oldest bar and restaurant has a new dining room with an exhibition kitchen. The motif is similar to the old dining room; dark mahogany paneling, trimmed with polished brass and crowned with stain glass ceilings. Choose from entrees of poultry, seafood, beef or pasta. We have a wonderful selection of beer, wine and liquor—and of course our signature Spanish Coffee.

MCMENAMINS HOTEL OREGON
310 N.E. Evans Street
McMinnville, Oregon 97128
(503) 492-2777, (877) 492-2777

Capacity: up to 80
Catering: full-service in-house catering
Price Range: $400 to $2,000
Types of Events: banquets, retreats, receptions, conferences and beyond

Availability and Terms
Reservations are recommended at least three months in advance. Deposit required.

Description of Facility and Services
Seating: provided up to 80
Servers: provided
Bar facilities: provided by Hotel Oregon
Linens and napkins: included
China and glassware: included
Audiovisual: available upon request
Equipment: available upon request
Cleanup: provided by Hotel Oregon
Parking: on street parking available
ADA: yes

Special Services
Hotel Oregon features 42 antique-filled guest rooms, a cozy cellar bar, rooftop bar, and a McMenamins pub serving breakfast, lunch and dinner.

RICH IN HISTORY
Hotel Oregon has everything under, and on top of, one roof. Its 42 guest rooms are rich in history spanning back to its opening in 1905. Enjoy breakfast, lunch, or dinner in the spacious McMenamins Pub. Sip regional wines in the Cellar Bar after perusing the hotel's own "gallery" of artwork and historical photographs illustrating every wall. Or take a short elevator ride to the Rooftop Bar and sample craft ales and wines while drinking in the spectacular sights of Yamhill County's orchards and the coastal range.

Il Fornaio

115 N.W. 22nd Avenue
Portland, Oregon 97210
Contact: Faith Chhim, Event Coordinator (503) 248-4324
(503) 248-9400; Fax (503) 248-5678
Business Hours: Mon–Thurs 11:30am–10pm,
Fri–Sat 11:30am–11pm, Sun 10am–10pm
E-mail: fchhim@ilfo.com; Web site: www.ilfornaio.com

Capacity: Private Dining Room up to 28 guests; Piazza (room) up to 55 guests; Piazza and the Private Dining Room combined accommodate up to 80 guests or receptions from 2–5 p.m. up to 130 people; Sala delle Luci (front window room) up to 75 guests

Price Range: varies according to menu selection; no room rental fee; minimum of $16.95 per person for lunch and $27.95 for dinner; a customized menu can be created to meet your specific needs and budget

Types of Events: full sit-down dining is available for business luncheons and dinners, presentations, award programs, parties, receptions, and other special occasions

Availability and Terms

Il Fornaio has an intimate private dining room that can accommodate up to 28 people. In addition, our indoor Piazza garden room with a fireplace and a retractable roof provides a warm setting for groups up to 55 guests. This room is available year-round and can be combined with our Private Dining Room to accommodate 80 guests or receptions from 2–5 p.m. up to 130 people. The Sala delle Luci area is a semi-private room filled with light that pours in from huge windows that look out onto Mount Hood. This room holds a maximum of 50 people for a sit-down dinner and 75 for cocktail parties.

The authentic Italian menu features wood-fired pizzas, rotisserie meats, mesquite grilled local fish, and fresh regional pastas. Each meal includes house-baked breads made fresh throughout the day. We also offer a buffet brunch on Sunday from 10am-1pm.

Description of Facility and Services

Seating: provided to accommodate group size
Servers: provided
Bar facilities: full bar, extensive Northwest and Italian wine selection and full-service café/bar
Linens: white linen
Decorations: flowers, displays and decorative items are welcome
Parking: valet parking
ADA: elevator available

IL FORNAIO OFFERS AUTHENTIC ITALIAN CUISINE

Il Fornaio offers friendly and professional service in a setting that is comfortable and intimate. Bring your next special occasion to Il Fornaio with award-winning authentic Italian food and wine. Our friendly and knowledgeable staff will work with you to create a menu that is befitting to your group. We look forward to helping you plan a memorable occasion.

SMALLER VENUES

Sales Office
3800 S.W. Cedar Hills Blvd.
Beaverton, Oregon 97005
(503) 626-MEET(6338)
Web site: www.kingstad.com

Beaverton
Downtown
Airport

Capacity: largest room accommodates up to 200 people; 24 rooms in three locations; 24,000 net square feet total
Price Range: varies according to event size and menu selection; Complete Meeting Packages available
Catering: full-service catering
Types of Events: meetings, seminars, conventions; luncheons, dinners

Availability and Terms
Kingstad Meeting Centers offers professional meeting rooms, in three locations, accommodating groups of up to 200 people. Reservations should be made as early as possible to ensure availability. A nonrefundable deposit of 25% of expected expenditures is required to confirm your date. Payment in full is due the day of your function. Please inquire about direct-billing application.

Description of Facility and Services
Seating: various seating arrangements offered
Servers: appropriate service staff provided with catering service
Bar facilities: alcoholic beverages allowed; coffee, tea, and beverage service
Linens and napkins: cloth tablecloths and napkins
China and glassware: off-white china; variety of glassware
Cleanup: provided by Kingstad Meeting Centers
Meeting equipment: overhead projectors; VCR and monitor; 35mm projectors; computer projection equipment; ISDN lines; video conferencing; flip charts, pads, markers
Parking: free at Beaverton and Airport locations only
ADA: yes

Special service
Kingstad Meeting Centers offers support services such as copying, faxing, message taking, and free courtesy phones for attendees.

THE CONTEMPORARY WAY TO MEET
Kingstad Meeting Centers offers three full-service facilities that specialize in providing space for small local meetings for groups of 200 or less. Every aspect of our service and facilities have been designed to help make your meetings as productive as possible.

THE STEAKHOUSE
MORTON'S OF CHICAGO

213 S.W. Clay Street • Portland, Oregon 97201
Contact: T. Angelique Leonard (503) 248-2100; Fax (503) 248-2005
Dinner Hours: Mon–Fri 5:30pm–11pm, Sat 5pm–11pm, Sun 5pm–10pm
Lounge opens at 5pm daily

Capacity: Boardroom A: up to 32 (sit-down dinner); **Boardroom B:** up to 40; **A & B combined:** up to 80
Catering: in-house catering only
Price Range: entrees from $18.95 a la carte; $35.95 pre-fixe
Types of Events: corporate meetings, convention groups, wedding rehearsal dinners, birthday and anniversary parties, retirement parties and other celebrations

Availability and Terms
A nonrefundable deposit (10% of estimated dinner total) is required January through Thanksgiving; 30% deposit required Thanksgiving through December; special arrangements may be made for New Year's Eve. Please try to book your event as far in advance as possible.

Description of Facility and Services
Seating: tables and chairs provided; setups include conference style, rounds, hollow square, u-shape, crescent rounds, theatre-style, classroom and cocktail reception
Servers: provided
Bar facilities: full-service bar available with cocktails served butler style
Linens and napkins: white tablecloths and napkins; other colors available for an additional charge
China and glassware: white china with red and white wineglasses set on table; Reidel and decanters available upon request
Audiovisual: P.A. system, hand-held wireless microphone, TV/VCR cart available in-house at no charge; separate sound, lighting, and temperature control in either half of the Boardroom; additional A/V equipment available for rent upon request at cost
Equipment: available upon request; please call
Cleanup: provided at no charge
Parking: valet parking available for $5 on Clay Street; parking lots and garages available on either side of Clay Street entrance
ADA: fully accessible

Special Services
Amid the mahogany and cherry wood interior, subdued lighting and oriental rugs, there are a wide variety of menu items to meet your guests' expectations.

At Morton's of Chicago, we feature USDA Prime, Midwest, grain-fed beef, live Maine lobsters, domestic lamb chops, and a variety of fresh seafood flown in daily! We also offer a premiere wine list and special hors d'oeuvres in our Boardrooms.

Please call Angelique to schedule a time to view the Boardroom's unique setting and atmosphere.

SALEM INN

1775 Freeway Court, N.E. • Salem, Oregon 97303
Contact: Sales Office (503) 588-0515 or (888) 305-0515; Fax (503) 588-1426
Business Hours: Open 7 days a week

Capacity: Capitol Room: 621 sq. ft.; meeting room: 800 sq. ft. (accommodates up to 50 people)
Price Range: $125 per day; 10 or more rooms rented, meeting room is free
Catering: outside catering welcome
Types of Events: seminars, meetings, corporate functions, wedding receptions, reunions

Availability and Terms
No deposit required. Cancellation notice required 48 hours before function. Reservations should be made as early as possible.

Description of Facility and Terms
Seating: tables and chairs provided by Salem Inn
Servers: provided by caterer
Bar facilities: no bar facilities on site
Linens: fee for linens
China and glassware: dishes, flatware and glassware available
Audiovisual: VCR, television, and overhead projector available
Cleanup: provided in rental fee
Parking: ample parking available
ADA: accessible

Special Services
Our friendly staff will strive to make your stay as comfortable and enjoyable as possible. We offer a complimentary continental breakfast each morning. Executive suites available.

CONVENIENT LOCATION
Located at the Market Street exit off I-5, the Salem Inn is close to the State Capitol, State Fairgrounds, Wallace Marine Park, Lancaster Mall and Volcanoes Stadium.
Directions: *I-5 south*, exit 256, turn right and hotel will be on your right. *I-5 north*, turn left, proceed one block and hotel will be on your right.

SMALLER VENUES

925 N.W. 19th
Portland, Oregon 97209
(503) 294-7153
Web site:
www.visual-producers.com/visual

THE SCREENING ROOM

This 1930's Private VIP Screening Room Makes the Perfect Impact for any Business or Party Event.

Capacity: 40 seated, 60 standing; with Back Lot accommodates up to 120

Price Range: $350 basic charge for six-hour event; Back Lot area add $200; please call for exact quote of AV equipment

Catering: we work with several licensed caterers and rental companies or select caterer of your choice

Types of Events: client presentations, press conferences, classes, wrap parties, viewing parties for video/film/TV and Pay Per-View sporting events; theme parties like Vegas, '30s Speakeasy Lounge; surprise parties or elegant bachelor/bachelorette parties and perfect for holiday and Christmas parties

Availability and Terms
The Screening Room has flexible room configurations, and an expanded outside area that can be tented in the winter. Most AV equipment in-house; equipment charge is in addition to room. All events are completely customized to your requirements and all technical arrangements are handled for you.

Description of Facility and Terms
Portland's only VIP screening room. Built in the '30s and upgraded with high-end video projection and satellite equipment. The room has been mostly used by the entertainment industry for screenings, auditions, wrap parties, and even for as a shooting location. Ground level in/out access.

Bar facilities: full walkup 12 ft. service bar
Cleanup: $125 fee
Audiovisual and equipment: 15' x 6' x 40" stage with backdrop curtains, spotlight, PA, microphone, and podium; high resolution video projection with 12' x 9' screen—project from computer, laser disk, Beta SP, Pay-Per-View, VHS, Cable, S-VHS
Parking: plenty of street parking and parking lot across street

A LONG AND RICH HISTORY
The Screening Room was once an active part of Portland's historical "Film Row" and has been graced by people such as Jimmy Stewart, Jane Powell, and Walter Bemnen to name a few. Its history, charm, and prime location make it a unique and perfect place for presentations, meetings, small performances, parties and private screenings.

Please let this business know that you heard about them from the Bravo! Event Resource Guide.

WIDMER GASTHAUS
955 N. Russell • Portland, Oregon 97227
Contact: Gasthaus Managers (503) 281-3333; Fax (503) 331-7242
Business Hours: Mon–Thurs 11am–11pm, Fri–Sat 11am–1am, Sun noon–9pm

Capacity: private room, 20-46 guests; parties of 47–75 require special arrangements
Price Range: $10-$20 per person
Catering: in-house only
Types of Events: rehearsal dinners, birthdays, retirements, holiday parties, business dinners, or any other event where great beer and delicious food will make your party complete

Availability and Terms
All parties require a nonrefundable $100 deposit to secure a date and will be considered tentative until receipt of deposit. A food and beverage minimum of $250 is required Sunday through Thursday; $350 minimum on Friday and Saturday. A 17% gratuity is applied to all food and beverage including no host bar.

Description of Facility and Services
Seating: tables and chairs for up to 46; up to 75 requires special arrangements
Servers: provided
Bar facilities: hand-crafted beers brewed on location as well as a variety of wines and soft drinks available
Dance floor: not available
Linens: white linen is provided on food and beverage tables during banquets with an array of colors available for formal dinners at a nominal fee
Decorations: no nails, tacks or confetti please
Audiovisual: large screen TV, video, DMX sound system
Equipment: overhead and slide projectors and other equipment available at a minimal charge
Cleanup: included
Parking: plenty of on-street parking as well as two parking lots
ADA: yes

FRIENDLY SETTING COUPLED WITH FINE BEER AND WINE
Widmer Gasthaus is a friendly place to enjoy fine food and our excellent handcrafted beers. The Gasthaus is housed in a turn-of-the-century brick building, adjacent to the famous Widmer Brewery. Our chef and staff are experienced in all types of events, from formal dining to Super Bowl parties, so let us make your next celebration one to remember! All information regarding the Gasthaus and its menus can be faxed to you and our managers will be happy to answer any questions you may have regarding availability or menu planning. Until then, PROST!

Banquet, Meeting, & Event Sites

The Adrianna Hill Grand Ballroom
An Enchanting Place of Celebration

918 S.W. Yamhill • Second Floor • Portland, Oregon 97205
Philip Sword or Barbara Abalan (503) 227-6285 • *Shown by appointment only*
E-mail: accentevnt@aol.com

Capacity: up to 300 guests
Price Range: charge varies
Catering: and event planning provided exclusively by Accent on Events
Types of Events: corporate and private celebrations, wedding ceremonies and receptions, concerts, dances, fundraisers, reunions, holiday parties, proms, auctions and more

Availability and Terms
A 50% facility deposit is required to confirm your date at one of the most unique, prestigious and sought-after facilities in the Pacific Northwest. Early reservations suggested.

Description of Facility and Services
Facility rental: includes Victorian ballroom decor, all tables and chairs, dressing room for artists, full service bar area, Roman columns, ambiant lighting, reception tables and coat racks
Event staff: experienced managers, chefs, waitstaff, licensed bartenders and kitchen personnel provided by Accent on Events (included in catering costs)
Bar facilities: all bar services provided by Accent on Events (full bar available)
Dance floor: hardwood floors perfect for dancing; custom stereo sound system available for cassette tapes or CDs; bands and DJs welcome
Silverware, china, glassware and linens: included in catering costs
Parking: across the street at 10th Avenue and Yamhill Street—City Center Parking

TURN-OF-THE-CENTURY GRAND BALLROOM
The Adrianna Hill Grand Ballroom is an elegant 8,000-square-foot Victorian ballroom with a beautiful restored hardwood floor, suspended "U" shaped balcony and 55 foot-long stage backed by a high cathedral-style wall. Built in 1901, this storybook setting with unique architecture is newly remodeled—complete with a 35-foot beamed and vaulted ceiling, large ornate brass chandeliers and elaborate Old World designs along the sculpted balcony. We are proud to offer you a treasured and unforgettable experience in this nonsmoking environment.

*Corporate mid-week specials and
fully inclusive dinner and entertainment packages available*

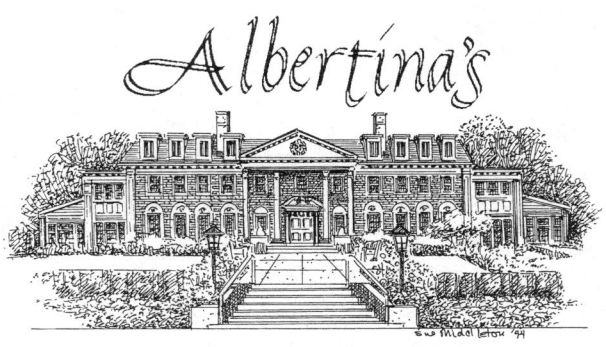

AT THE OLD KERR NURSERY

424 N.E. 22nd Avenue • Portland, Oregon 97232
Contact: Event Coordinator (503) 231-3909
Business Hours: Mon–Fri 9am–5pm

Capacity: up to 75 for luncheons and dinners in main dining rooms; up to 30 for luncheons in private dining room; up to 50 for meetings and seminars in private dining room; up to 250 for receptions
Price Range: price determined by event
Catering: full-service, in-house catering
Types of Events: luncheons, business meetings, seminars, dinners, receptions, retirement parties, special events

Availability and Terms
Reservations should be made as early as possible; deposit to secure your date; terms vary according to event.

Description of Facility and Services
Servers: hostess and servers provided by Albertina's
Bar facilities: champagne, wine, beer
Linens: provided by Albertina's
China, glassware and silver service: provided by Albertina's
Patio: available for summer events; canopy can be added
Special equipment: consult with event coordinator
Decorations: beautiful fresh floral arrangements in colors of your choice
Parking: on-site parking
ADA: fully accessible

GRACIOUS SETTING FOR YOUR SPECIAL EVENT
Only a mile from downtown Portland, near the Convention Center and convenient public transportation stands the stately, three-story Georgian-style Old Kerr Nursery. Erected in 1921 to provide a home for children in need, the building was closed as a nursery in 1967. After careful and loving restoration, the building reopened in 1981 as a beautiful setting for four businesses, the centerpiece of which is Albertina's Restaurant. Guests will appreciate the unique setting, the delicious food and the opportunity to shop in the on-premises gift, antique and resale shops. Albertina's at The Old Kerr Nursery is operated as a nonprofit business with all proceeds donated to Albertina Kerr Centers, whose programs provide services for children and youth at risk, families in need, and individuals with disabilities. The Old Kerr Nursery has been placed on the National Register of Historic Places and is an official Portland Historical Landmark.

All Seasons
INDOOR GOLF CLUB

9665 S.W. Allen Boulevard., Suite 109 • Beaverton, Oregon 97005
Contact: Nick George (503) 644-7676; Fax (503) 646-3550
Winter Hours: Mon–Thurs 10am–10pm; Fri 10am–midnight;
Sat 8am–midnight; Sun 8am–8pm
Summer Hours: Tues–Thurs 10am–8pm; Fri–Sat 10am–10pm;
Closed Sunday and Monday

Capacity: up to 300; 10,500 square feet
Price Range: Winter Rates: $12 for nine holes, $20 for 18 holes; **Summer Rates:** $10 for nine holes, $15 for 18 holes; junior and senior discounts; please call for facility rentals
Catering: full-service in-house catering, or use your own professional caterer
Types of Events: golf tournaments, golf contests, corporate outings and events, birthday, anniversary and retirement parties

Availability and Terms
We at All Seasons have brought the outdoors inside with our beautifully decorated 10,500 square foot facility. To ensure a well planned event, we like to reserve your spot at least four weeks in advance; deposit required.

Description of Facility and Services:
Seating: tables and chairs provided
Servers: provided
Bar facilities: All Seasons provides beer and wine
Dance floor: provided; **capacity:** 100
Linens: provided by caterer, or may be ordered through All Seasons
China: provided by caterer
Decoration limitations: please consult with us prior to decorating
Audiovisual: Stereo system with speakers throughout the facility; other equipment available by request
Parking: ample free parking for any size group
ADA: in full compliance

Special Services:
All Seasons features five golf simulators with ball washers, golf benches, cedar fencing and all the frills of playing golf outdoors. Perfect for that corporate outing, private party or just playing a round of golf at Pebble Beach. All Seasons is Portland's exciting new venue to explore.

VISIT THE WORLD'S FINEST GOLF COURSES
We at All Seasons Indoor Golf have brought some of the world's finest tests of golf to the Portland area and best of all, it's always comfortable and dry! Corporate events can consist of long drive competitions, closet to the pin competitions, putting contests and video tape analysis. Fun for 30 to 300 people—All Seasons is your next destination for a great event!

*Romantic Mansion located on
two wooded acres overlooking the Willamette River*

Amadeus
at the FERNWOOD

*2122 S.E. Sparrow (Off River Road Exit)
Milwaukie, Oregon 97222
Contact: Kristina (503) 659-1735, (503) 353-8948
Business Hours: Seven days a week,
5pm–midnight; Sunday Brunch 10am–2:30pm*

Capacity: 300 people
Price Range: lunches $20; full course sit-down dinners or buffet style $30; plus gratuity
Catering: full-service in-house catering
Types of Events: individual rooms for conferences, seminars, private meetings, large group luncheons, holiday parties, celebration dinners; from small intimate events up to 300, weddings and rehearsal dinners

Availability and Terms
Reservations should be made as soon as possible to ensure availability. A deposit is required at the time of booking. Half the deposit is refundable if cancellations are made at least six months prior to your event. **No** cost for using the facility, bartending services, linens, flowers, and candles.

Description of Facility and Services
Seating: table and chairs provided for up to 300
Servers: provided with catering services
Bar facilities: full-service bar with bartender provided; host/no host; liquor provided according to OLCC regulations
Dance floor: accommodates up to 50 people
Linens: cloth tablecloths and napkins provided in cream color
China and glassware: fine china; variety of glassware
Cleanup: provided by Amadeus at the Fernwood
Decorations: early decorating available; fresh flowers for guest tables provided by Amadeus; please discuss ideas with banquet representative
Parking: ample free parking; valet service
ADA: disabled access available

FACILITY OVERLOOKING WILLAMETTE RIVER
Amadeus at the Fernwood is the perfect setting for an annual, monthly or quarterly function; or dinner for two. You and your guests will enjoy fine continental dining in a wonderful old mansion on two wooded acres, filled with antiques, fireplaces, crystal chandeliers, candlelight and fresh flowers, overlooking the Willamette River. We offer a full bar with a wide variety of Oregon and international wines, outdoor dining and wedding ceremonies on our patio is available. A classical pianist is featured nightly and during Sunday brunch. **SUNSET DINNER SPECIAL:** Daily • 5–6:30pm • $9.95

Arnegards

1510 S.E. Ninth and Hawthorne
Portland, Oregon 97214
Contact: Robin Andersen
(503) 236-2759
Business Hours: Tues–Fri 10am–2pm
After-hour appointments available

Capacity: our entire facility can accommodate up to 450 people; we have two ballrooms and a conference room available

Price Range: prices vary depending on event; please inquire

Catering: catering is supplied by renter, or you may choose from our list of caterers

Types of Events: private parties, corporate parties, cocktail parties, luncheons, dinners, receptions, meetings, all-day seminars, and any other event imaginable

Availability and Terms

Please reserve rooms as early as possible. Short notice reservations depend on availability. A 50% deposit is due at time of booking with the balance due one month prior to event.

Description of Facility and Services

Seating: tables and chairs provided and set up to your satisfaction
Servers: provided by caterer
Bar facilities: caterer or renter provides licensed bartender and liability insurance
Dance floor: large dance floor available; capacity: 100+, electrical: supplied
Linens: provided by caterer or client
China: provided by caterer or client
Decoration limitations: establishment is beautifully decorated; no tape, tacks, or nails on walls; no rice, birdseed, or metal confetti; please consult Event Coordinator prior to decorating
Audiovisual: renter provides, or we can make prior arrangements
Cleanup: renter or caterer is responsible for cleanup; security deposit required
Parking: some off-street parking available; plenty of street parking

Special Services

We have a large stage available with dressing rooms.

NEWLY RESTORED
1920s BALLROOM AND CONFERENCE ROOM

Our newly renovated 1920s ballroom has been open and available to rent since December 1998. We are located conveniently in Southeast Portland. Have your next event in any of our three rooms: ***The Grace Ballroom:*** This maple hardwood-floored ballroom is perfect for company functions, holiday parties, banquets or receptions and can accommodate up to 100 people. ***The Winnington Ballroom:*** This maple hardwood-floored ballroom has a stage, 14-foot high ceilings, lighted ceiling fans and great acoustics. It can accommodate up to 320 people. ***The Conference Room:*** Can accommodate up to 28.

THE ATRIUM

100 S.W. Market Street
Portland, Oregon 97201
Contact: Catering Director
(503) 220-3929
Business Hours: please call
for an appointment

Capacity: up to 300
Price Range: food starting at $16 per person plus room rental
Catering: The Atrium provides all catering services tailored to your special day
Types of Events: hors d'oeuvres, dinner, sit-down, and buffet

Availability and Terms

Our magnificent two-story glass building and convenient location one block from Front Avenue in the heart of downtown Portland make The Atrium a popular facility for special events. To ensure reserving the date you want, plan to make your reservations six months to a year in advance. The $1,200 room-rental fee is required at the time of booking and is also considered the deposit for your event. A 120-day advance cancellation in writing is required for a full refund.

Description of Facility and Services

Seating: tables and chairs for 250+
Servers: full wait staff
Bar facilities: full bar service, bartenders, servers and all alcoholic beverages
Dance floor: 200-person, 1,200-square-foot dance floor with full electrical hookups
Linens and napkins: linen, cloth napkins and tablecloths in assorted colors; included in room rental
China and glassware: provided
Cleanup: included
Decorations: though our policies are fairly liberal, please call for restrictions
Parking: ample free parking
ADA: yes

GET THE FEELING OF BEING OUTDOORS YEAR-AROUND IN OUR MAGNIFICENT TWO-STORY GLASS STRUCTURE

The Atrium's unique structure offers a beautiful setting. Its two-story windows and lush greenery as well as the glass-covered roof along with the back patio and two fountains in a beautiful parklike setting will have a profound impact on all its guests. The Atrium is easily accessible on the corner of First and Market, one block from the Marriott Hotel and Front Street, and only three blocks from the RiverPlace Alexis Hotel. Please call our Catering Director at (503) 220-3929 for information or reservations.

Atwater's Restaurant & Bar

111 S.W. Fifth Avenue, 30th Floor • Portland, Oregon 97204
In-house contacts: Hollie Stafford (503) 275-3662 or Hollie@atwaters.com
Susan Lyon (503) 275-3615 or Susan@atwaters.com
Off-premise contact: Mary McKichan (503) 275-3615
Fax (503) 220-3659; Web site: www.atwaters.com

Office Hours: Mon–Fri 9am–6pm; **Restaurant:** Sun–Thurs 5pm–9pm; Fri–Sat 5pm–10pm
Bar: Sun 5pm–9pm; Mon 4pm–9pm; Tue–Thurs 4pm–11pm; Fri 4pm–1am; Sat 5pm–1am

Capacity: 10 to 300 people
Price Range: $30 per person and up
Catering: full-service in-house; off-premise catering up to 1,000 including food service, equipment, setup and cleanup
Types of Events: full sit-down meals, buffet, cocktails and hors d'oeuvres, theme parties

Availability and Terms

Atwater's has six separate dining rooms that can be used individually for groups of 10 to 60, or in combination to host as many as 300 guests. Atwater's requires a deposit ($100–$500) in advance to reserve space for your event. For cancellations within 180 days of the event, Atwater's will refund the deposit only if another event can be booked in your place. Deposits are credited toward your final bill. Events may be booked up to one year in advance.

Description of Facility and Services

Seating: tables and chairs for 300 available
Servers: included
Bar facilities: fine selection of wines and liquor; liquor liability, bar and bartenders provided courtesy of Atwater's
Linens and napkins: cloth napkins and linens; ask about colors
China and glassware: china is white; many types of glassware
Decorations: please inquire about available table decorations; early decorating possible; decorations must conform to Portland's building and fire codes
Audiovisual: equipment available upon request—video conferencing capability
Equipment: podium, flip charts, TV/VCR, overhead projector and easels available
Parking: garage and street parking available; **ADA:** fully accessible

YOU SHOULD SEE OUR VIEW ON CATERED EVENTS

Our 30th floor private dining suites provide an intimate and elegant setting for groups of 10 to 100. Our 11,000-square-foot banquet room on the 41st floor has a fresh, elegant new look and a breathtaking view of downtown—it can accommodate groups of up to 300 guests. In addition to our in-house catering, Atwater's offers full-service off-premise catering. Amenities include Atwater's cuisine, service staff, equipment, setup and cleanup. Whether it is a grand wedding celebration or an intimate dinner prepared in your kitchen by our chef, Atwater's will put on a flawless performance for you and your guests. Atwater's serves American cuisine featuring the bounty of the Pacific Northwest.

300 Reuben Boise Road • Dallas, Oregon 97338
Contact: Becky Jacroux, Owner/Manager (503) 831-3652
Business Hours: Tue–Sat 10am–5pm;
evenings and weekends by appointment

Capacity: 2,100 sq. ft. event room seats 120, plus 1,200 sq. ft. covered patio
Price Range: $420 to $1,400
Catering: we have a list of preferred caterers; fully equipped kitchen
Types of Events: weddings, receptions, reunions, business meetings and team-building events

Availability and Terms
Located just west of Dallas, 18 miles from Salem. Open year-round; closed in January. A 50% deposit holds your reservation.

Description of Facility and Services
Seating: round tables and chairs for guests; rectangle accessory/serving tables
Servers: provided by caterer
Bar facilities: BeckenRidge and Airlie wines are exclusively served; bottled beer and champagne available upon request; server provided
Dance floor: hardwood floor throughout; stereo sound system available
Linens: ivory cloth tablecloths provided; quality paper napkins available in choice of color
China and glassware: fine china, silver and glassware provided to complement any function
Decorations: silk flower arrangements available at no charge
Audiovisual: AV equipment available
Cleanup: we assist with setup and cleanup
Parking: complimentary parking on site
ADA: fully equipped to accommodate ADA requirements

Special Services
BeckenRidge Vineyard produces five varieties of grapes and our custom-labeled wines are produced by Airlie Winery. Both Airlie and BeckenRidge wines are featured at our events and are also available for individual purchase by attending guests.

CELEBRATE YOUR SPECIAL OCCASION NESTLED IN THE BEAUTY OF THE VINEYARD
You will enjoy our serene, country setting and be delighted with our facility specifically designed for events. BeckenRidge has a warm, friendly lodge-like atmosphere with a commanding view of the vineyard and the Willamette Valley. Special features include a vineyard patio, rock fireplace and grand piano. Personal attention from the owner will help you create a memorable event for you and your special guests.

BANQUET, MEETING & EVENT SITES

HOTEL · PORTLAND

309 S.W. Broadway at Oak Street
Portland, Oregon 97205
Contact: Sales (503) 295-4100;
Fax (503) 226-2709
Office Hours: Mon–Fri 7:30am–6pm;
evenings by appointment
E-mail: belinda@bensonhotel.com
Web site: www.bensonhotel.com

© Dick Busher

Capacity: a number of rooms available that will accommodate 50 to 400
Catering: full-service, in-house catering; will cater outside events
Types of Events: 16,000 square feet of meeting space for lunches, breakouts, receptions, dinners, fundraisers, social functions and meetings

Availability and Terms
Make your reservations as early as possible, especially for the holidays. A deposit may be required on booking. Please call our sales department.

Description of Facility and Services
Seating: variety of seating options available up to 600; tables and chairs provided
Servers: all servers and support staff included as needed
Bar facilities: full bar service; we provide all beverages, bartenders, and servers
Linens and napkins: linens available to match the decor
China and glassware: fine china and glassware available for your use
Decorations: we will be happy to discuss your ideas and needs; plants, candles, chivari chairs
Cleanup: handled by the staff
Audiovisual: complete audiovisual needs arranged by catering department; high-speed internet access available in all meeting rooms
Equipment: podium, easels and risers are available; on-site audiovisual company
Parking: ample parking near the hotel; cost varies according to time of day; valet parking available
ADA: handicap accessibility and facilities in all areas

PORTLAND'S GRAND HOTEL
The Benson has long been known throughout the world for its elegance and fine service. Since 1912 The Benson Hotel has provided excellent service for the business community, entertainers and politicians. We offer traditional hospitality, and we pay attention to every detail to ensure our customers' satisfaction, may your event be for 10 to 600 people.

See page 351 under Hotel Accommodations.

BENTON COUNTY FAIRGROUNDS

110 S.W. 53rd Street
Corvallis, Oregon 97333
Contact: Rayven Davis
(541) 757-1521
Fax (541) 766-6865
Business Hours: Mon–Fri 8am–5pm
Web site: www.corvallis.com/bentoncountyfair

Capacity: 10 to 400 in meeting areas; able to accommodate 1,500 in picnic areas
Price Range: $25 to $700
Catering: no in-house catering available; can assist with selection of local caterer
Types of Events: wedding receptions, company picnics, trade shows, rodeos, horse and livestock activities, seminars and more

Availability and Terms
All bookings are encouraged as soon as possible. Facility is currently booking into 2003; deposit required.

Description of Facility and Services
Seating: tables and chairs provided
Servers: provided by caterer
Bar facilities: provided by caterer
China, glassware and linens: provided by caterer
Audiovisual: TV/VCR, slide projector, overhead screen, PA system available upon request
Cleanup: no cleanup provided
Parking: ample parking available
ADA: facilities accessible

LOCATED IN CORVALLIS
The Benton County Fairgrounds is located in Corvallis—home of Oregon State University. The Fairgrounds are on the outskirts of town with bike lane access, hiking trails to Bald Hill Park, an oak grove for picnicking activities and an 86-foot picnic table. Our friendly staff will assist in making your event a success.

BRIDGEPORT BREWING COMPANY

1313 N.W. Marshall Street • Portland, Oregon 97209
Contact: Manager of Special Events (503) 241-7179 ext. 210; Fax (503) 241-0625
Hours: Mon–Thurs 11:30am–11pm; Fri–Sat 11:30am–midnight; Sun 1pm–9pm
Web site: http://www.firkin.com

Capacity: Heritage Room up to 250; Blue Heron up to 25
Price Range: from $150 to $750, depending on size of group and day of function
Catering: handcrafted pizzas, focaccia bread and fresh salads; outside catering is welcome
Types of Events: holiday parties, business meetings, birthday parties, reunions, wedding rehearsals and receptions; great for luncheons or dinners

Availability and Terms
BridgePort Brew Pub has two unique rooms available every day of the week for private functions. Our Blue Heron conference room accommodates up to 25 people; our Heritage banquet room accommodates up to 250 people. We suggest that you reserve early to ensure availability. An advance deposit is required to hold your reservation, and is applied toward your room rental. The balance for an event is due at the conclusion of the function.

Description of Facility and Services
Seating: tables and chairs provided for your group; arranged as requested
Servers: friendly, professional staff included
Bar facilities: serving up to six handcrafted ales ranging from our bright and hoppy India Pale Ale to our Heritage Blue Heron Ale; local wines, juice, sodas, fine coffee and teas are also available
Dance floor: accommodates DJ or band setup; electrical outlets available
Linens and napkins: napkins provided; linen can be arranged upon guest request
China and glassware: china provided by client; glassware provided by BridgePort
Decorations: please discuss decorating ideas with the Manager of Special Events; early access available with prior arrangement
Cleanup: included in room rental
Audiovisual: equipment available upon request
Equipment: any equipment needs arranged on request
Parking: ample street parking available
ADA: yes, within the limitations of a historic building; elevator accessible

HISTORIC LOCATION—COZY ATMOSPHERE
BridgePort is Oregon's oldest Craft Brewery, located in Portland's historic Pearl District. Exposed brick and timber beams, combined with the fresh aroma of microbrewed ales and homemade pizza, create a cozy pub atmosphere. All of our ales are handcrafted; our kitchen adheres to the same standard of quality that made our beers regionally famous. Uniquely Northwest, BridgePort (an entirely nonsmoking brewpub) is comfortable for meetings, social gatherings, and weddings. View or tour the brewery to see how the famous BridgePort Ales are made.

CAVANAUGHS®
HILLSBORO HOTEL

3500 N.E. Cornell Road
Hillsboro, Oregon 97124
(503) 648-3500
(800) 325-4000

Capacity: up to 150; six meeting rooms totaling 3,100 sq. ft.
Price Range: varies depending on size and length of event; please call
Catering: full range of catering services including sit-down, buffet, cocktails, hors d'oeuvres, picnics, theme or custom parties, meetings, seminars; ideal for conventions, social functions, and retreats; on-premise outdoor events available

Availability and Terms
Groups up to 150 people. A six-month advance reservation is recommended; deposit is required upon booking. Deposit can be refunded with 60–90 day written cancellation notice.

Description of Facility and Services
Seating: tables and chairs provided for any set up
Servers: provided with our catering service
Bar facilities: full-service bars available with bartenders ($75 setup fee required)
Dance space: dance floor available; full electrical hookup
Linens and napkins: cloth linens and napkins available with food service
China and glassware: house china and stemmed glassware available
Decorations: we can assist you; we allow decorations prior to event
Audiovisual: A/V equipment available upon request; fee depends upon item
Equipment: available upon request; fee depends upon item
Cleanup: provided; included in room fee
Parking: plenty of free parking
ADA: complied

HIGH QUALITY SERVICE WITH A PERSONAL TOUCH

Nestled in the heart of the Oregon Silicon Forest, Cavanaughs Hillsboro Hotel offers the perfect location for small to mid-size events. Their specialty is providing high quality service with a personal touch. From cocktail and hors d'oeuvre receptions to formal sit-down buffets—every detail is checked and rechecked to assure our clients that each function becomes a success.

(800) 325-4000

www.cavanaughs.com

CATERING AND RECEPTION FACILITY

Part of the Home Builders Association of Metro Portland
15555 S.W. Bangy Road
Lake Oswego, Oregon 97035
Contact: Barb Chirgwin
(503) 684-1880; Web site: www.hbamp.com
Business Hours: Mon–Fri 8am–5pm

Capacity: 50-200 seated; 50 to 300 reception
Price Range: room rental charge varies per event and season
Catering: in-house or at your location
Types of Events: sit-down, buffet, theme, cocktails and hors d'oeuvres, barbecue, picnic, or special requests

Availability and Terms
Choose between the spacious reception hall/auditorium, featuring a patio, stage, dance floor, and optional bar, or the executive conference room. Audiovisual equipment available. Easy freeway access. Many hotels nearby. Please make your reservations with as much advance notice as possible.

Description of Facility and Services
Seating: round tables, classroom tables, and auditorium-style seating available
Servers: we provide complete staff
Bar facilities: full-service bar and bartender available; host or no-host; liquor, beer, wine, and champagne
Dance floor: dance floor and stage available
Linens and napkins: full array of tablecloths and napkins, ranging from fine linen, cloth, or paper
China and glassware: white china with trim; matching glassware available
Decorations: rooms are accessible for early decorating
Cleanup: cleanup staff provided
Audiovisual: optional media equipment available
Equipment: podium, white boards, easels, and stage available
Parking: plenty of free parking, including disabled parking
ADA: yes, disabled accessible

**CELEBRATE YOUR NEXT EVENT WITH US!
PHONE NOW FOR YOUR PRIVATE CONSULTATION
FOR MEMORIES THAT WILL LAST A LIFETIME!**

We look forward to making your wedding reception, business function, or party a total success. Excellent facilities, friendly staff, easy freeway access, and ample parking.

Central Library

801 S.W. Tenth Avenue
Portland, Oregon 97205
Contact: Events Coordinator
(503) 306-5578
Business Hours: Mon–Fri 9am–5pm
Web site: http://www.multnomah.lib.or.us/lib/rentals/

Capacity: stand-up reception for up to 1,200; seated dining capacity varies; meeting/conference space for up to 100
Price Range: $300-$3,500; please call for specifics
Catering: choose from our list of caterers
Types of Events: receptions, parties, dinners, meetings, weddings and seminars

Availability and Terms
The reading rooms and lobbies are available at the Central Library on Friday and Saturday after 6pm. Meeting rooms are available at all times. Reservations must be confirmed two weeks prior to the event. A 50% deposit is required to hold space.

Description of Facility and Services
Seating: round tables, stacking chairs and banquet tables
Servers: provided by caterer
Bar facilities: provided by caterer; no red wine allowed
Dance floor: provided by caterer
Linens: provided by caterer
China and glassware: provided by caterer
Decorations: no helium balloons, glitter, confetti or fog/bubble machines; all decorations must be approved in advance by Central Library
Audiovisual: some equipment available; please ask for a complete list
Equipment: provided by caterer
Cleanup: provided by caterer
Parking: available on street or in nearby lots
ADA: handicap accessibility and facilities in all areas

THE GARDEN OF KNOWLEDGE
Experience the grandeur of Central Library as never before. After a $24 million, three-year renovation, this historic 1912 building is a masterpiece and an exquisite setting for receptions, parties, dinners, meetings, weddings and concerts. The building's grand lobbies and unique spaces are the perfect backdrop for any event. Enter the building and enter "The Garden of Knowledge," a theme echoed in the building's public art and unique interior detailing. Imagine your event in the Library's reading rooms surrounded by the works of your favorite authors. Your guests will welcome a visit to Central Library's garden paradise.

CH2M HILL ALUMNI CENTER AT OSU

204 CH2M HILL Alumni Center • Corvallis, Oregon 97330
Contact: Lisa Templeton (541) 737-2351; Fax (541) 737-3481
Business Hours: Sun–Thurs 8am–11pm, Fri–Sat 8am–midnight
E-mail: osualum@orst.edu; Web site: www.orst.edu/dept/alumni/ch2m

Capacity: ballroom: 7,000 sq. ft.; **multipurpose room:** 1,600 sq. ft.; **conference rooms:** 680 sq.ft., 940 sq. ft.; **lounge:** 730 sq. ft.; **library:** 550 sq. ft.
Price Range: $100 to $1,000 per room
Catering: list of approved caterers provided
Types of Events: conferences, meetings, banquets, receptions, weddings, and parties

Availability and Terms
We reserve rooms up to three years in advance. A 25% deposit is due at time of booking, with the balance due 30 days prior to the event.

Description of Facility and Services
Seating: tables and chairs included in rental cost
Servers: provided through caterer
Bar facilities: provided through caterer
Linens and napkins: white linens included in rental cost
China and glassware: provided through caterer
Audiovisual: podium, slide projector, overhead projector included in room rental
Equipment: risers and staging provided
Parking: complimentary parking available
ADA: fully accessible

EXPERIENCE THE UNIVERSITY DIFFERENCE

The CH2M HILL Alumni Center in Corvallis, Oregon, is the area's newest Conference and Meeting Center. This beautiful 45,000 square foot facility contains a variety of board and conference rooms, banquet and dining rooms, vendor and display space as well as an elegant lounge and living room area. The facility can host groups up to 1,000. All rooms feature multimedia presentation systems and teleconference capabilities.

The Center has a wide variety of indoor and outdoor spaces to accommodate everything from large regional and national conferences, to smaller local meetings, banquets, and receptions. Located in the heart of the Oregon State University campus, clients have access to the intellectual capital of OSU faculty and a multitude of University resources. Activities abound on campus including PAC-10 sporting events, concerts, world-renowned speakers, art exhibits, theater productions and films. Corvallis and the Alumni Center are centrally located in Oregon and an ideal place to host meetings and conferences. Those seeking quality and affordability need look no further. Call the CH2M HILL Alumni Center and let our event coordinators and staff ensure a successful conference! Mention this ad when booking your event, and receive a complimentary VIP Suite rental (*subject to availability).

Charbonneau
ON THE GREEN

32050 S.W. Charbonneau Drive
Wilsonville, Oregon 97070
Contact: Bob Russell (503) 694-5234
Fax (503) 694-6385
Web site: www.charbonneauonthegreen.citysearch.com

Capacity: 15,000 sq.ft. of banquet space available
Price Range: $5.95 to $22.95 per person
Catering: in-house catering available for up to 200 people; off-site up to 3,000
Types of Events: business meetings, weddings, golf tournaments, cocktail parties

Availability and Terms
Deposit required to hold a room; 30 day notice required for a full refund.

Description of Facility and Services
Seating: tables and chairs provided for up to 180
Servers: provided by Charbonneau
Bar facilities: full-service bar available; portable bar
Dance floor: dance floor available; full electrical hookup
Linens and napkins: a variety of colors available at no charge
China and glassware: provided
Decorations: no limitations
Audiovisual: A/V equipment available upon request
Equipment: available upon request; please inquire
Cleanup: provided by Charbonneau
Parking: 200 spaces available
ADA: handicap accessible

LOCATED ON A GOLF COURSE
Experience casual and fine dining in a country club atmosphere at Charbonneau On The Green. Featuring a view of lakes, trees and fairways, we cater to you the way that we would like to be catered to.

CHART HOUSE

5700 S.W. Terwilliger Boulevard
Portland, Oregon 97201
(503) 246-6963

101 E. Columbia Way
Vancouver, Washington 98661
(360) 693-9211

Business Hours:
Mon–Fri 11:30am–10pm;
Sat 5–10pm; Sun 5–9pm

Capacity: 20–200
Price Range: please call for current prices
Catering: in-house
Types of Events: business meetings, morning seminars, retirement and award dinners, holiday parties, cocktail receptions

Availability and Terms
The entire facility is available for private functions on Saturdays and Sundays until 3:30pm; semi-private dining areas are available during lunch and dinner operating hours. Special event reservations are secured with a deposit. Semi-private area accommodates 60 in Vancouver, 120 in Portland.

Description of Facility and Services
Seating: Portland features view tables upstairs and downstairs; Vancouver features view seating and outside deck, weather permitting
Servers: staff included in price; 14% gratuity on food and beverages
Bar facilities: full or limited bar available
Dance floor: 30-person capacity; electricity available for band or disc jockey
Decorations: schedule early decorating; no limitations if decorations do not harm wood, plants, or paintings; flowers and candles available for arrangements; no confetti please
Equipment: audiovisual equipment and podium available at minimal charge
Parking: complimentary valet parking
ADA: on entrance level; restroom for disabled

Special Services
We offer an extensive wine list and can special order wines and champagnes. A manager will be available to direct staff at all times. We guarantee personalized attention to ensure your event's success.

SPECTACULAR VIEWS!
The Portland Chart House is perched high in the west hills with panoramic views of Mount Hood, Mount St. Helens, the Willamette River and the city lights below. Situated on the banks of the Columbia River, the Vancouver restaurant offers a serene view of the beautiful Northwest and ambiance of a waterfront setting. Both restaurants boast spectacular views coupled with the finest quality food and beverage, and a professionally trained staff that will ensure a memorable dining experience.

& CONVENTION CENTER

1777 N.W. 44th Street
Lincoln City, Oregon 97367
Contact: Pennie Sar-Sangi
(541) 996-5925, (888) CHINOOK
Business Hours: 8am–6pm;
messages taken 24 hours

Capacity: groups from 10–1,000; 20,000 square feet total; main room, 22,000 square feet accommodating 1,270 theater-style and 860 sit-down; six rooms with 3,000+ square feet; three rooms, 600 square feet

Price Range: $70 to $300; call for estimate on room use fee and catering

Types of Events: any type of function: 30 to 1,000 people; dinners, receptions, trade shows, conventions, meetings; breakout rooms available

Availability and Terms
We encourage you to book early to ensure availability.

Description of Facility and Services
Seating: provided by Chinook Winds
Servers: provided by Chinook Winds
Bar facilities: provided by Chinook Winds
Dance floor: in-house floor can be rented; electrical hookups available
Linens: provided; variety of colors to choose from
China: provided; variety to choose from
Decorations: limited themes to choose from
Parking: valet and self parking at no charge
ADA: meets all ADA requirements

Special Services
Our professional staff will work to produce a magnificent event that your company will be proud of.

FLEXIBLE MEETING SPACES
Chinook Winds Casino and Convention Center, overlooking the beautiful Pacific Ocean and offering over 20,000 square feet of meeting space, affords the meeting planner the flexibility to be creative with an event. The main conference area opens up to provide over 20,000 square feet of carpeted meeting space or can be broken down into as many as six rooms with over 3,000 square feet each. To enhance the main area, there are three meeting/breakout rooms with sizes ranging from 550 square feet to 760 square feet.

9120 S.E. Powell Blvd.
Portland, Oregon 97266
Contact: Lynne Maginnis
(503) 774-7000; Fax (503) 774-5104
Business Hours: Mon–Thurs 11am–10pm; Fri 11am–11pm;
Sat 10am–11pm; Sun 10am–10pm

Capacity: from two to 600
Price Range: group packages and birthday packages available; call for details
Catering: in-house only; take-out pizza available
Types of Events: staff parties, birthdays, employee incentives, corporate celebrations, school and church events

Availability and Terms
Packages are available. Please make weekend reservations at least two weeks in advance. Midweek parties are preferred for larger groups.

Description of Facility and Services
Seating: up to 600
Servers: provided
Bar facilities: beer and wine
Decorations: birthday setup with package or bring your own
Cleanup: provided at no charge
Parking: ample parking available
ADA: all but one dining platform

Special Services
Interactive video games are available for all age groups.
- New arcade games
- Great prizes to win
- Large meeting area; both professional- and family-based functions welcome
- New expanded menu

A PLACE TO MEET AND HAVE FUN!

HISTORIC PORTLAND CITY HALL

1221 S.W. Fourth Street
Portland, Oregon 97204
Contact: Faye Musselman,
Bureau of General Services
(503) 823-6947; Fax (503) 823-6924
E-mail: phaye@ci.portland.or.us
Business Hours: 8am–5pm

Capacity and Square Footage: **Council Chambers:** up to 180 and 2725 sq.ft.; **Rose Room:** up to 50 and 960 sq.ft.; **Pettygrove Room:** up to 24 and 778 sq.ft.; **Lovejoy Room:** up to 43 and 892 sq.ft.; **First Floor Public Area:** up to 1,000 and 11,450 sq.ft.; **Full Facility:** 4,000
Price Range: $25–$375 per hour depending on room and type of event
Catering: outside caterers welcome (no on-site cooking facilities)
Types of Events: receptions, parties, "casino night," weddings, business meetings, awards ceremonies, retirement parties, etc.

Availability and Terms
Facility is available after 5 p.m. Monday through Friday, and anytime on weekends. Reservations are confirmed when 50% of full costs are received with reservation form. A fully refundable security deposit (between $500 and $2,500 depending upon event) is required. An information packet with reservation form, rates, policies, procedures and additional photos is available by calling (503) 823-6947.

Description of Facility and Services
Seating: tables and chairs are provided in meeting rooms and Council Chambers
Bar facilities: alcohol permitted; copy of OLCC license required from server
Dance floor: two marble floored light courts (1200 sq.ft.)
China, glassware and linens: not provided
Decoration limitations: no helium balloons, glitter or open flames
Audiovisual and equipment: Council Chambers has a state-of-the-art audiovisual system, including overhead projection screen, hearing impaired devices, etc; all meeting rooms have 12-foot projection screens; variety of meeting room equipment is available for rental
Cleanup: flat $50 charge is assessed for cleanup per event, which includes Event Porter services
Parking: on-street parking or via Smart Park garages
ADA: City Hall is fully handicap accessible

THE HEART OF OUR CITY
City Hall is a 105-year-old, four story building in the 16th Century Manneristic Renaissance architectural style. White and red marble flooring throughout the structure complement the polished oak interior. Two floor-to-ceiling atriums flood the interior with natural light. Private and non-profit organizations as well as private citizens have used City Hall for private events since its recent renovation. A beautiful and unique structure for your special occasion!

18120 S.W. Lower Boones Ferry Road
Tigard, Oregon 97224
Contact: Holly Jensen
(503) 968-4519
Business Hours: Mon–Fri 5:30am–11pm;
Sat–Sun 7am–11pm

Capacity: over 135,000 total square feet (the size of three football fields); we can accommodate up to 400 for special events; conference/banquet room can hold up to 65
Price Range: price varies based on event type, size and menu requirements
Catering: in-house catering by ClubSport Cafe
Types of Events: meetings, parties, seminars, banquets, team-building packages, single or multi-sport activities and birthday parties

Availability and Terms

ClubSport offers a diversity of activities unlike any other meeting facility around. To ensure a well-planned event, reservations need to be made at least four weeks in advance. Payment in full or cancellations are due two weeks prior to the event date (large events require a separate contract).

Description of Facility and Services

Seating: seating from 10 to 800; banquet/conference room seating up to 65
Servers: professional wait staff provided
Bar facilities: ClubSport's bar offers Northwest micro beers, domestic labels, wine, nonalcoholic beverages and a juice bar
Dance floor: available upon request; substantial electrical available
China and linens: available; linens at extra cost
Decorations: available at extra cost; ask us about your specific ideas
Audiovisual: projector and screen, 46" television with VCR, and microphone all located in our conference room
Parking: up to 800 available spaces
ADA: built to comply with all 1996 ADA requirements

Special Services

A variety of sports opportunities including nine basketball and volleyball courts, an indoor arena that offers soccer or inline skating, an unparalleled selection of fitness equipment, a 43-foot climbing wall, and wonderful activities for children. If it is fun or sports activities you want, then we have the facilities to accommodate you! Combine sports activities and team building into your next event.

4000 Westcliff Drive • Hood River, Oregon 97031
Contact: Sales Office
(541) 387-5403, (800) 345-0931
Business Hours: Mon–Fri 8am–5pm

Columbia Gorge Hotel

Capacity: 40 guest rooms; three function rooms, accommodates groups of 10 to 250
Price Range: prices vary according to room type and time of year; call for proposal
Catering: full-service catering; on- or off-premise
Types of Events: specializing in management retreats, banquets, receptions, employee picnics, meetings and seminars

Terms and Description
Early reservations required: advance deposit required to hold space
Seating: River and Garden views; seating for up to 250
Servers: fully staffed; included in price quote
Bar facilities: full liquor service available, plus an extensive selection of award-winning wines and champagnes
Audiovisual equipment: available on request
Dance floor: for up to 50 people; electrical hookups available
Linens and napkins: white linen
China and glassware: traditional patterned
Cleanup: included in service
Flowers and decorations: from Benson's Boutique, our on-site, full-service floral and gift boutique
Parking: ample on-site parking

Special Services
A variety of recreational activities can be arranged for your group including golf, white water rafting, tours of the Maryhill Museum, horseback riding, snow skiing, guided hikes through the Mt. Hood National Forest, Mountain Fly Fishing and much more. The Columbia Gorge Hotel is your gateway to the spectacular Columbia River Gorge.

THE PERFECT MEETING SITE— CONVENIENT, QUIET, UNPARALLELED SERVICE
Meeting planners love the fact that we are only 60 minutes from downtown Portland. No wasting half a day or longer traveling to the meeting site. They find the quiet atmosphere of the hotel to be key to the highly productive sessions that always seem to happen here. And, the quaint size of our hotel allows us to provide unparalleled service to groups of all sizes— service that can't be found at large convention hotels. Put it all together and you have the perfect meeting site.

COURTYARD MARRIOTT–PORTLAND NORTH HARBOUR

1231 North Anchor Way • Portland, Oregon 97217
Contact: Christine Skarphol (503) 735-1818; Fax (503) 735-0888
Business Hours: Mon–Fri 8am–5pm, or by appointment

Capacity: *Indoor:* **North Harbour Room:** 1,100 square feet, seating up to 100; **Boardroom:** 312 square feet, seating up to 18; **Conference Room:** 260 square feet, seating up to 12; *Outdoor:* patio seating up to 250

Price Range: price will vary depending on the type of event and menu selections

Catering: full-service in-house catering

Types of Events: all occasions; wedding receptions, holiday parties, birthdays, anniversaries, business meetings, breakfast, lunch or dinner

Availability and Terms
Advanced reservations of 30 days or more are recommended. Cancellation charges are on a sliding scale and vary with amount of notice given. A minimum deposit of $200 is required, with full payment required 72 hours prior to the event.

Description of Facility and Services
Seating: tables and chairs for up to 250
Servers: staff included in catering costs
Bar facilities: full beverage service available
Dance floor: available at an additional charge
Linens and napkins: all colors available
China and glassware: bone china, assorted glassware
Decorations: responsibility of renter; no tape, staples, or tacks to walls or ceilings
Cleanup: included in price
Audiovisual and equipment: in-house equipment available upon request
Parking: covered parking at no charge
ADA: accessible

Special Services
The Courtyard by Marriott at Portland North Harbour has 133 guestrooms decorated in a palette of colors adopted from those typically found in the French and Italian Riviera. Guestrooms feature amenities including in-room coffee and tea service, 25" televisions, voice mail, data port lines, desks, hair dryers, irons and ironing boards. Jacuzzi and King Suites, as well as a Conference Suite, are also available. A resort-like atmosphere can be enjoyed at the indoor pool, spa and exercise facility, all facing the Columbia River.

MEDITERRANEAN STYLE ON THE COLUMBIA RIVER
The North Harbour Café and Bar have an ambiance of casual elegance and sophistication, overlooking a large seasonally landscaped plaza, complete with gazebo, fountain, and peaceful scenic views. The plaza provides the perfect setting for summer and fall wedding receptions, barbecues, cocktail parties, and celebrations. Our meeting space is designed to accommodate groups of various sizes. The North Harbour Room at 1,100 square feet is ideal for meetings, banquets and receptions of up to 100 people. Our Boardroom and Conference Room are perfect for smaller meetings, ranging from 10 to 18 people.

The Crown Ballroom · *The Crown Stage* · *The Garden Court* · © Goble Studio 1998

THE CROWN BALLROOM & GARDEN COURT
"Where Business Entertains and Celebrates"
918 S.W. Yamhill and Ninth Avenue, 5th floor • Portland, Oregon 97205
(Top floor of the historic Pythian Building, diagonal from the downtown Nordstrom)
Contact: Rayven Davis (503) 227-8440; Fax 227-2654
Business Hours: shown by appointment only

The Crown, proudly atop the historic Pythian Building offers the much celebrated Crown Ballroom—an Italian Renaissance hall built in 1901 in the tradition of a European Grand Salon—with two dance floors, mahogany paneling and a full-curtained stage. And The Garden Court—a stylish reception room with panoramic city views, buffet court and full cocktail bar.

Capacity: **The Crown Ballroom:** 230 guests; **Garden Court:** 100 guests; rooms may be booked separately or together for a facility capacity of 350 banquet or 400 cocktail-style

Price Range: from $300 to $3,500, depending on room, date and size of party

Catering: professional "in-house catering services" to serve from a full-service kitchen and assist in menu/event planning; can work with all party themes and budgets

Types of Events: corporate parties, banquets, business entertaining, lunches, and seminars

Availability and Terms
While only five years old, The Crown is regularly booking Saturdays 6–12 months in advance. Half the rental fee will reserve either or both rooms. Four- to 10-hour time blocks available.

Description of Facility and Services
Banquet seating: tables and double-padded black dining chairs for up to 275 guests
Bar facilities: full bar services—wine, beer, cocktails; host/no-host with experienced bartenders/servers and liquor liability provided by our "preferred in-house caterers"
Dance floors: three hardwood; with spotlights and mirror balls accommodating 2–150 guests
Decorations: richly decorated 10,000-sq. ft. facility, tastefully designed by Goble & Harris with an inspired blend of contemporary and Old World stylings, world-class art collection, large tropical plants and florals, box-beamed and cathedral ceilings, impressive chandeliers, antique bird cages and Baroque mirrors, while tall French-laced curtains on king-sized windows open up to spectacular midtown city views
Convenient parking: 7-level parking structure adjacent to building with economy rates

Special Features
Designer decorated Host/VIP room with city views, comfortable seating, guest phone, TV/VCR and fax; enjoy our popular in-house Black Wing Gallery featuring grand visions by Julian Goble, a gold piano "champagne bar", full-length 20' wide formal-curtained stage for presentations; raised dance floor and complete stereo sound system. Full lounge available to seat 60.

"The Crown is the ultimate destination party showcase!"
—Nancy Joubert, Event Planner, Enterprise Rent-A-Car

Crown Vista Events

19875 N.W. Logie Trail
Portland, Oregon 97231
Contact: Wendy Daniels
(503) 240-6057

Capacity: receptions and dinners from 1 to 150; 350 with outside areas
Price Range: varies depending on type of event and catered service
Catering: full service by Party Princess Catering; guest caterers accepted
Types of Events: weddings, meetings, workshops, retreats, fundraisers, corporate events, pool parties, lunches, cocktail parties, celebrations, theme parties

Availability and Terms
Please contact our sales and catering office for space availability and terms. A 50% deposit is required upon reservation; refundable security deposit.

Description of Facility and Services
Seating: provided as needed
Servers: professional staffing by Party Princess Catering
Bar facilities: full service and bartenders available
Dance floor: available for a fee; electrical outlets available
Linens and napkins: basic colors provided; specialty linens at extra cost
China and glassware: provided by caterer
Decorations: flowers and theme decorations can be arranged
Cleanup: included with site
Parking: ample free parking; valet service available
ADA: accessible

Special Services
Complete event and party planning services from concept to completion, including custom menus, flowers, decorations and entertainment. On-site staff is available to answer questions.

ABOUT CROWN VISTA
Crown Vista is a private, 47-acre estate offering a tranquil setting with a breathtaking, panoramic view of rivers and Cascade peaks. The main facility houses a unique art collection. Only 15 minutes from downtown, guests find serene ponds in the gardens and a creek running through the beautifully landscaped grounds. Lounge by the heated outdoor pool, explore the blackberry-studded forest trails, visit Sauvie Island wildlife refuge or play golf at a nearby course. Professional services and experienced staff make Crown Vista the perfect choice for an outstanding event.

CROWNE PLAZA
HOTELS · RESORTS

14811 Kruse Oaks Boulevard
Lake Oswego, Oregon 97035
For banquet reservations:
Crystal Harrell (503) 624-8400 ext. 253
Sleeping room rates:
Jennifer Snyder (503) 624-8400 ext. 151

Capacity: groups of 20 up to 300
Price Range: inquire about prices
Catering: incredible full-service custom catering
Types of Events: sit-down dinners, buffets, cocktails and hors d'oeuvres, luncheons, business meetings, custom parties, social events

Availability, Terms, and Location
The Crowne Plaza has four private rooms accommodating a variety of group sizes. Early reservations are strongly encouraged. Advance deposits required.

Description of Facility and Services
Seating: tables and chairs for up to 250 people
Servers: included
Bar facilities: full-service bar facilities; bartenders available for private reception
Dance floor: space available for band; large dance floor
Linens and napkins: all colors available (some extra charge)
China and glassware: classic styles
Decorations: inquire about decorations we can provide for an extra cost
Cleanup: handled by The Crowne Plaza
Audiovisual and meeting equipment: all equipment available (ask about charges)
Parking: plenty of free parking, valet parking available
ADA: fully accessible

Special Services
The Crowne Plaza specializes in corporate meetings, seminars, and events as well as social functions including: bridal showers, weddings, anniversaries, bar/bat mitzvahs and family reunions. Special sleeping room rates provided for groups. Mention this ad when booking your event, and your speaker or meeting planner's room will be complimentary.

LUXURIOUS AND ELEGANT
The luxurious and elegant Crowne Plaza features a six-story waterfall in the atrium and 161 tastefully decorated rooms. Other amenities include an indoor-outdoor pool, spa, sauna, exercise facility, gift shop, and concierge level. This hotel is ideal for any corporate or social event.

CRYSTAL BALLROOM

1332 W. Burnside
Portland, Oregon 97209
Contact: Mary Hendrickx
(503) 492-2777
Business Hours: Mon–Fri 9am–5pm;
tours weekends and by appointment

Capacity: 1,000 persons reception-style; 350 seated
Price Range: please contact an event coordinator for price ranges; food and beverage minimum required to waive rental; based on day of week and time of day
Types of Events: meetings, seminars, exhibits, banquets, concerts, dances, holiday parties, reunions, weddings, receptions

Availability and Terms
We suggest that you book your event six months to one year in advance for a weekend date and three to nine months in advance for weekday functions. Function deposits are 50% of room rental cost. Deposit is due 30 days after booking.

Description of Facility and Services
Seating: 16 eight-top round tables available for assorted seating, 130 folding chairs; additional tables and chairs may be rented; fixed seating in the ballroom, including theater seats in the mezzanine and benches surrounding the ballroom, totals 180
Servers: staff included in price; 17% gratuity added to the bill
Bar facilities: full-service cocktail bar featuring McMenamins beer and wine
Dance floor: the Crystal's most remarkable feature is its maple "floating" dance floor; one of the last of its kind, it is said to have the ability to make a good dancer out of anyone
Live music: live music is welcome to complement your event; the cost is the responsibility of the renter, but recommendations will gladly be made
Linens and napkins: assorted linens included in rental fee
China and glassware: silverware and plates included; due to the nature of the "floating" dance floor, some glassware is discouraged
Decorations: responsibility of renter
Cleanup: included in price
Audiovisual: available for rent; technician fee not included in rental
Equipment: podium and risers available; built-in sound system and lighting; sound and light technicians available at additional charge
Parking: street parking is available and several paid parking structures are in close walking distance

BEAUTIFULLY RENOVATED HISTORIC BALLROOM
The historic Crystal Ballroom boasts 7,500 square feet of floating dance floor. Its eclectic and festive decor make it an ideal setting for events ranging from an award banquet to a wedding reception. The Crystal has been a forum for music, dancing, and personalities that have helped define several eras. Extracting inspiration from over 80 years of history, a team of artists have added dimension to the Crystal's walls by painting murals throughout the building and the on-site brewery.

The Best Value Under The Sun.™

DAYS INN CITY CENTER

1414 S.W. Sixth Avenue • Portland, Oregon 97201
Contact: Catering Sales Manager
(503) 221-1611 or (800) 899-0248; Fax (503) 226-0447
E-mail: daysinn@transport.com
Web site: www.daysinn.com

Capacity: we offer three rooms and one suite to accommodate up to 200 people
Catering: in-house catering available
Price Range: varies depending on menu and type of event
Types of Events: breakfast meetings, brunches, lunches, business meetings, seminars, banquets

Availability and Terms

Days Inn City Center recommends that you make your reservation for space as early as possible.

Description of Facility and Services

Seating: tables and chairs provided; banquet, round and classroom tables available
Servers: staff included in catering cost
Bar facilities: full beverage service available
Linens and napkins: an extensive array of colors available at no extra charge
China and glassware: white china and stemmed glassware
Decorations: mirrored tiles, votive candles, bud vases, silk plants, themed decor available
Audiovisual: available upon request
Equipment: podiums, risers and staging available
Cleanup: provided by hotel staff
Parking: free on-site, subject to availability
ADA: accessible

Special Services

Days Inn City Center features 173 newly renovated guest rooms, including one suite. Your guests will enjoy our "heart of downtown" location and other amenities including free parking, complimentary daily newspaper delivered to your door, data ports, and pay-per-view movies and games in each room. Our heated outdoor pool is available seasonally, and Gold's Gym is available complimentary to all guests. Group rates are available for 10 or more rooms.

IN THE HEART OF DOWNTOWN PORTLAND

Plan your event in our flexible meeting space and banquet facilities. We will cater to the needs of your guests while you focus on the business at hand. *We are truly at your service!*

DoubleTree
HOTELS · GUEST SUITES · RESORTS™

COLUMBIA RIVER

1401 N. Hayden Island Drive • Portland, Oregon 97217
Contact: Sales Office (503) 283-2111
E-mail: crsales@teleport.com
Office Hours: Mon–Fri 8am–6pm, Sat 9am–4pm

Capacity: up to 500 people for sit-down events; 15 separate meeting rooms accommodating groups from 5 to 900
Price Range: moderate
Catering: full-service in-house catering provided by the hotel exclusively
Types of Events: from light hors d'oeuvres receptions to elegant luncheon and dinner affairs; small one-day seminars to large corporate meetings

Availability and Terms
Several ballrooms have floor-to-ceiling windows which allow for a dramatic view of the mighty Columbia River and its awesome beauty. Make reservations as soon as possible. A deposit is required at time of booking. Please call the Sales Office for details.

Description of Facility and Services
Seating: tables and chairs provided by hotel
Servers: staff included in catering costs
Bar facilities: full beverage service provided by hotel
Dance floor: available for our guests' use
Linens and napkins: an extensive array of linen colors at no additional charge
China and glassware: white china; stemmed glassware
Decorations: lattice, silk plants, mirror tiles, and votive candles; access for early decoration by prior arrangement
Cleanup: provided by hotel staff
Audiovisual: in-house audiovisual provided by Presentation Services
Equipment: podium, risers, and staging available for our guests
Parking: 750 complimentary parking stalls
ADA: accessible

Special Services
The DoubleTree Columbia River offers 351 deluxe guest rooms with in-room coffee makers, irons and ironing boards. For the business traveler, each room has a large desk with data-port phones and no telephone access charge. Two restaurants give the option of informal or formal dining. Pool, fitness center, and spa also available.

BEAUTIFUL RESORT-LIKE SETTING
We offer 15 flexible meeting rooms, some with floor-to-ceiling windows overlooking the Columbia River. We offer three ballrooms, all approximately 6,000 square feet; two have direct access onto our large Riverdeck, which can be used for receptions, barbecues, or picnics. We also have docking available for all Portland area riverboats. Our location, directly off I-5 and just 10 minutes from downtown, is an ideal location for your next event.

DOUBLETREE HOTEL™
PORTLAND • DOWNTOWN

310 S.W. Lincoln • Portland, Oregon 97201
Contact: Sales Office (503) 221-0450; Fax (503) 225-4303
Business Hours: Mon–Fri 8am–6pm; Sat 9am–1pm

Capacity: seven rooms accommodate from 12 to 400 guests
Price Range: customized menu proposal to fit your budget
Catering: full-service in-house catering exclusively
Types of Events: breakfast, lunch, dinner; meetings, receptions, seminars, parties

Availability and Terms
The DoubleTree Hotel • Portland Downtown's meeting space will accommodate up to 400 guests. We recommend that you make your reservation as soon as possible.

Description of Facility and Services
Seating: tables and chairs provided; banquet, round and classroom tables
Servers: staff included in catering costs
Bar facilities: portable bar; complete bar setup stations; host/no-host; beer, wine, champagne, and soft drinks
Dance floor: complimentary; electrical outlets available
Linens and napkins: variety of colors at no additional charge
China and glassware: white china; stemmed glassware
Decorations: lattice, silk plants, mirror tiles, votive candles, and bud vases available; access for early setup by prior arrangement
Cleanup: provided by hotel staff
Audiovisual: in-house audiovisual services provided by Presentation Services
Equipment: podiums, risers, and staging available
Parking: complimentary on-site parking available
ADA: accessible

Special Services
The DoubleTree Hotel • Portland Downtown has 235 spacious guest rooms, three suites, and a recently renovated lobby. Your guests will enjoy the many "extras" at the DoubleTree, including complimentary parking and airport shuttle, laundry service, in-room coffee makers, irons with full-size boards, in-room hair dryers, complimentary access charge for long distant credit card calls, heated outdoor pool and exercise room. Special group rates are available for ten or more rooms per night.

A MEMORABLE OCCASION
The DoubleTree Hotel • Portland Downtown is conveniently located on the southwest side of downtown, directly off major Interstate access. We will do everything possible to make your stay special. You and your guests are our main focus!

DoubleTree
HOTELS · GUEST SUITES · RESORTS™
EUGENE–SPRINGFIELD

3280 Gateway Road
Springfield, Oregon 97477
Contact: Kim Barbisan (541) 988-4019
Business Hours: Mon–Fri 8am–6pm

Capacity: DoubleTree Ballroom: up to 2,000 people; over 12,000 sq. ft. of meeting space, may be divided into 12 separate meeting rooms
Catering: full-service in-house catering
Price Range: price varies depending on event and menu selection
Types of Events: business meetings, seminars, banquets, weddings and reunions

Availability and Terms
Reservations are recommended as early as possible. Contact the catering and sales department for more information

Description of Facility and Services
Seating: tables and chairs provided
Servers: provided by Hotel
Bar facilities: full-service bar provided by Hotel
Linens and napkins: large selection of linens available
China and glassware: white china and stemmed glassware
Decorations: fountains, ice sculptures, lattice, greenery, candles, mirror tiles
Audiovisual: available upon request
Equipment: all equipment needs available upon request
Cleanup: provided by Hotel staff
Parking: ample free parking available; large lot ideal for car shows or other outside events
ADA: yes

Special Services
- Group room discounts available
- Two restaurants
- Fitness room, pool and spa
- Room service

SPACIOUS ROOMS AND CONVENIENT LOCATION
DoubleTree Hotel Eugene–Springfield is a large property featuring two beautiful courtyards. Our spacious rooms include balconies overlooking both poolside and a park-like setting. Our excellent staff puts your satisfaction at the top of their list. We are conveniently located off I-5 and Beltline Road.

DoubleTree Hotel
Portland • Jantzen Beach

909 N. Hayden Island Drive • Portland, Oregon 97217
Contact: Sales Office (503) 283-4466
E-mail: jbsales@teleport.com
Office Hours: Mon–Fri 8am–6pm; Sat 8am–5pm

Capacity: up to 1,400 people for sit-down events; 16 separate meeting rooms accommodating groups from 5 to 2,000
Price Range: moderate; price varies on individual budget and season
Catering: full-service in-house catering provided by the hotel exclusively
Types of Events: from light hors d'oeuvres receptions to elegant luncheon and dinner events; small one-day seminars to large corporate meetings

Availability and Terms
Make reservations as soon as possible. Please call the Sales Office for details.

Description of Facility and Services
Seating: tables and chairs provided by hotel
Servers: staff included in catering costs
Bar facilities: full beverage service provided by hotel
Dance floor: available at no additional charge
Linens and napkins: an extensive array of linen colors at no additional charge
China and glassware: white china; stemmed glassware
Decorations: lattice, silk plants, mirror tiles, votive candles, and bud vases available; access for early decoration by prior arrangement
Cleanup: provided by hotel staff
Audiovisual: in-house audiovisual provided by Presentation Services
Equipment: podium, risers, and staging provided at no additional cost
Parking: 750 complimentary parking stalls
ADA: accessible

Special Services
The DoubleTree Hotel Jantzen Beach offers 320 deluxe guest rooms with in-room coffee makers, irons and ironing boards. For the business traveler, each room has a large desk with data port phones and no telephone access charge. Two restaurants give the option of informal or formal dining. Fitness room, business center, tennis courts, pool, and spa also available.

BEAUTIFUL RESORT-LIKE SETTING
We offer 16 flexible meeting rooms, most with floor-to-ceiling windows overlooking the Columbia River. At the heart of our hotel is Portland's largest hotel ballroom. With 18,000 square feet, it offers a wonderful view of the river and surrounding area. We have large patio areas for receptions, picnics, or barbecues. We also have docking available for all the Portland area riverboats. Our location, directly off I-5 and just 10 minutes from downtown, is an ideal location for your next event.

DOUBLETREE HOTEL
PORTLAND • LLOYD CENTER

1000 N.E. Multnomah • Portland, Oregon 97232
Contact: Catering Office (503) 249-3130
Business Hours: Mon–Fri 8am–6pm; Sat 9am–noon

Capacity: four ballrooms seating up to 1,100; 17,000-square-foot exhibit hall accommodates 120 8'x10' exhibit booths
Price Range: price will vary depending on type of event and menu selection
Catering: full-service in-house catering provided by the hotel exclusively
Types of Events: light hors d'oeuvre receptions to elegant luncheon and dinner affairs, meetings, seminars, conventions, or any other type of event

Availability and Terms
The DoubleTree Hotel Portland • Lloyd Center offers <u>four</u> separate ballrooms to accommodate any size event. The Pacific Northwest Ballroom, our newest addition, offers floor-to-ceiling windows that overlook the pool and outside patio. Reservations are suggested six to nine months in advance with a deposit. Please call the catering office for details.

Description of Facility and Services
Seating: your choice of banquet rounds or informal cabaret style
Servers: staff included in catering costs
Bar facilities: full beverage service available; DoubleTree Hotel Portland • Lloyd Center to provide all beer, wine, and liquor
Dance floor: available at no additional charge
Linens and napkins: an extensive array of linen colors at no additional charge
China and glassware: white china; stemmed glassware
Cleanup: included in price
Audiovisual and meeting equipment: in-house audiovisual company; podium, risers and staging available
Parking: parking for over 750 cars
ADA: accessible

Special Services
The DoubleTree Hotel Portland • Lloyd Center offers 24-hour concierge services as well as a full-service business center to meet all your business and meeting needs. We offer special group rates on our 476 beautifully appointed guest rooms.

RELAX AND ENJOY THE MOMENT
Choose the DoubleTree Hotel Portland • Lloyd Center. Our professional catering coordinators can accommodate all your planning needs. From menu planning to room decor and design, our experienced and friendly staff are specially trained to take the stress and pressure out of planning your event. Our convenient location and ample parking make attending your special event easy for your guests. Our new Northwest Ballroom, with beautiful window-views of the outdoor pool and patio area, provides the perfect setting to make your event memorable.

EASTMORELAND GRILL AT THE EASTMORELAND GOLF COURSE

2425 S.E. Bybee Boulevard
Portland, Oregon 97202
Contact: Jerilyn Walker
(503) 775-5910; Fax (503) 775-6349
Office Hours: 9am–5pm

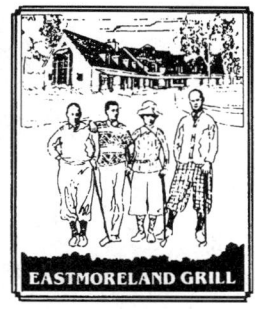

Capacity: 125 for a sit-down dinner; 175 for a reception
Price Range: $250 to $500 room-rental charge, depending upon size of event; $10 to $30 per person; the menu will be created especially for you by our staff
Catering: full-service catering available in-house
Types of Events: cocktails and hors d'oeuvres, buffet, sit-down dinners, luncheons, breakfast, barbecues and business meetings

Availability and Terms
The Eastmoreland Grill encourages your reservations up to one year in advance. A deposit is required and is nonrefundable. Half-payment is required 30 days in advance, with the remaining half payable on the day of the event.

Description of Facility and Services
Seating: tables and chairs provided for up to 125 sit-down guests
Servers: full staff available; a gratuity will be added to food and beverage purchases
Bar facilities: full-service bar and staff bartender provided upon request; host/no-host; liquor, beer, and wine
Dance floor: we can provide a dance floor on a rental basis
Linens and napkins: cloth tablecloths and napkins available in some colors
China and glassware: white china; glassware in plastic or glass, as required
Decorations: our catering manager will discuss with you and help develop your decoration plans
Cleanup: cleanup provided
Audiovisual and meeting equipment: arrangements can be made to accommodate
Parking: large parking lot with overflow area
ADA: fully complies

Special Services
The Eastmoreland Grill will cater to your every need to ensure your event is perfect.

GRACIOUS STYLE OVERLOOKING LUSH GREENS
The lush, beautiful greens of the Eastmoreland Golf Course are the setting for our gorgeous new Tudor-style clubhouse. The banquet room overlooks the tenth tee and has a large, gracious veranda for outdoor entertaining. Winter events are equally blessed with a handsome fireplace where guests love to gather. Our staff has extensive experience in corporate events, anniversaries, weddings, birthdays, and reunions, and we will create a personal menu exactly to your specifications. A telephone call to our staff will start you on your way to a carefree and beautiful event.

EMBASSY SUITES

EMBASSY SUITES HOTEL— PORTLAND AIRPORT

7900 N.E. 82nd Avenue
Portland, Oregon 97220
Contact: Sales and Catering Offices
(503) 460-3000; Fax (503) 460-3030
Business Hours: Mon–Fri 7am–6pm; Sat 9am–1pm

Capacity: Portland Grand Ballroom: 8,450 sq. ft. accommodates 563 in rounds of 10, 994 theatre-style; Cedars Conference Room: 2,144 sq. ft. accommodates 143 in rounds of 10, 252 theatre-style; two dedicated boardrooms and convention office—14,000+-sq. ft. total
Price Range: negotiable—dependent upon guestroom block and meal/catering function
Catering: full-service in-house catering, with off-site capabilities; flexible menus
Types of Events: all corporate, exhibit and social events including weddings and receptions, parties for all occasions, ballroom and atrium availability, seasonal outdoor

Availability and Terms
Reservations can be made up to six months in advance; 30–60 day sliding scale cancellation fee. Minimum deposits required with full payment in full 72 hours prior to all events.

Description of Facility and Services
Seating: 563 round tables with 16' ceiling height in Grand Ballroom; 143 round tables with 12' ceiling height in Cedars Ballroom
Servers: one server per 20 guests; one bartender per 75 guests
Bar facilities: in-house; one lobby bar and portables available
Dance floor: two 30' x 30' dance floors (900 sq.ft. each)
Linens: in-house linen (white, burgundy, cream) optional colors available at additional cost
China: in-house white hotel china and dress plates; other options available at additional cost
Equipment: in-house audiovisual and banquet equipment; additional theme decor available
Cleanup: provided by hotel
Parking: complimentary; 24-hour airport shuttle
ADA: nine fully accessible suites; facility meets ADA requirements
100% Satisfaction Guarantee!

BREATHTAKING VIEWS
COMBINED WITH LUXURY AND CONVENIENCE

Bring the outdoors in with the eight-story, open-air, skylit atrium lobby. Sparkling waterfalls and streams flow throughout the lobby from the central glass elevators. Towering trees and lush foliage with a colorful array of flowering plants contribute to the garden atmosphere, topped off with the gentle strains of a baby grand piano in the lobby bar.

Located at the corner of Airport Way and 82nd Avenue—only one mile form the terminal, two miles from the golf course, minutes from downtown and 45 miles from skiing on Mount Hood. All 251 suites include breathtaking views of Mount Hood, Mount St. Helens and the Columbia River. We offer creative and magical packages for your special evening.

EMBASSY SUITES PORTLAND DOWNTOWN

319 S.W. Pine Street • Portland, Oregon 97204
Contact: Denise Fredlund (503) 279-9000 ext. 6166; Fax (503) 497-9051

EMBASSY SUITES

Capacity: Colonel Lindberg: 2,905 square feet, 220 banquet, 300 meeting; Queen Marie: 2,240 square feet, 150 banquet, 234 meeting
Price Range: please inquire
Catering: in-house catering
Types of Events: meetings, banquets, wedding receptions, trade shows

Availability and Terms
Two elegant ballrooms, seven smaller rooms and 20 conference suites. Most rooms have windows and are decorated in the classic style of the Multnomah Hotel with all the amenities of an Embassy Suites. Direct billing with approved credit application.

Description of Facility and Services
Seating: tables and chairs for up to 220 in largest room
Servers: professional service staff available
Bar facilities: hotel provides liquor and bartenders; corkage charge of $7.50 per bottle of wine brought in
Dance floor: available with electrical hookups
Linens and napkins: several colors available at no charge
Decorations: check with hotel staff representative
Cleanup: provided by hotel
Audiovisual: on-site
Equipment: staging, podiums, risers and flip charts on site
Parking: 404 covered parking spaces; valet and self parking available
ADA: all facilities handicapped accessible

Special Services
276 guest suites, full cooked-to-order breakfast, manager's reception. 100% satisfaction guarantee. Full sales and catering staff to assist in event arrangements.

FLEXIBLE MEETING SPACE IN MAGNIFICENT SURROUNDINGS
The Multnomah Hotel, originally built in 1912, has been restored to its original grandeur and is now the Embassy Suites Portland Downtown. The original grand ballroom of the hotel has been magnificently restored and is part of over 22,000 square feet of flexible meeting and banquet space. The largest room can do banquets up to 220, meetings up to 300 and 25 exhibit booths. The hotel's 20 conference suites are perfect for small board meetings or hospitality suites. **See page 354 under Hotel Accommodations.**

END OF THE OREGON TRAIL INTERPRETIVE CENTER

1726 Washington Street • Oregon City, Oregon 97045
Contact: Event Coordinator (503) 557-8547; Fax (503) 557-8590
Business Hours: Mon–Fri 9am–5pm
Web site: http://www.endoftheoregontrail.com

Capacity: indoor up to 300 people for stand-up receptions, seated capacity varies; outdoor 200–800
Price Range: $150 to $850
Catering: you may use the caterer of your choice; caterer referral list available
Types of Events: receptions, parties, fund-raisers, lectures, dinners, meetings, brunches, reunions, presentations, weddings, company picnics, concerts

Availability and Terms

The Center is available for your special event and after business hour needs. A variety of outdoor terraces and indoor rooms with historical displays are available for rent. A 50% rental deposit and signed contract reserve space. Event planning services are also available.

Description of Facility and Services

Seating: some bench seating provided; limited number of banquet tables and chairs
Servers: provided by caterer or client
Bar facilities: provided by licensed caterer
Dance floor: not available; please inquire further
Linens and napkins: provided by caterer or client
China and glassware: provided by caterer or client
Decorations: historical background provides the setting; limitations on decorations apply
Audiovisual: available for rent
Equipment: stage, podium, small canopy, tent
Setup and cleanup: provided by caterer or client
Parking: ample parking for cars and motorcoaches
ADA: fully accessible

Special Services

Our living history interpreters are available to provide your event with historical presentations and pioneer life demonstrations. Period musical entertainment is also available.

The site for the End of the Oregon Trail Interpretive Center is Abernethy Green, the main arrival area for the emigrants and the true end of the Oregon National Historic Trail. The 8.5-acre site features three 50-foot-high covered wagon-shaped buildings, an outdoor amphitheater and heritage gardens. We invite you and your group to experience the history, heritage and spirit of the people at the End of the Oregon Trail.

FIFTH AVENUE SUITES HOTEL
Red Star Tavern and Roast House

506 S.W. Washington • Portland, Oregon 97204
Contact: Margie Yager, Director of Catering
(503) 417-3377
Business Hours: Mon–Fri 8am–5pm

Capacity: 6,000 square feet of meeting/private dining space; intimate parties of 16; receptions up to 200
Price Range: $19 to $50 per person
Catering: enjoy "re-kindled American classics" in-house catering from Red Star Tavern and Roast House's Executive Chef Rob Pando
Types of Events: meetings, dinners, receptions, luncheons, breakfasts

Availability and Terms
Space should be reserved as soon as possible—minimum of 72 hours notice. A deposit equal to one half the estimated expense is required. Cancellation terms apply.

Description of Facility and Services
Seating: tables and chairs provided
Servers: provided
Bar facilities: bartender provided; Red Star provides all beverages
Dance floor: will be rented
Linens: white and ivory provided; other types will be rented
China: in-house china available; other patterns will be rented
Decorations: no decorations to be attached to walls or ceilings
Audiovisual: provided by Fifth Avenue Suites Hotel
Equipment: podium, microphone, flip chart, laser pointer, screen, overhead and slide projectors
Cleanup: fees vary
Parking: valet parking available at Fifth Avenue Suites Hotel, 24 hours
ADA: yes

Special Services
Complimentary evening wine tasting in our fireside lobby, complimentary coffee service, fitness center, 24-hour room service, concierge, Aveda spa. Our catering consultants are available and happy to assist you in making your event successful and memorable.

THE PICTURE OF COMFORT AND SOPHISTICATION
Historic 10-story 1912 building, formerly a distinguished department store, is the picture of comfort and sophistication. Of the hotel's 221 rooms, 135 are spacious 550-square-foot suites. As part of a $25 million renovation, the hotel has the residential feel of a turn-of-the-century American country home.

Our banquet rooms are located on the main, second and third floors of the hotel. Within these rooms, you will find a decor filled with classic lines and warm ambiance.

See page 338 under Caterers & Ice Carvings.
See page 355 under Hotel Accommodations.

Please let this business know that you heard about them from the Bravo! Event Resource Guide.

P.O. Box 175 • 715 Quince Street
Florence, Oregon 97439
Contact: Jim Willers, General Manager,
Barbara Gulias, Marketing Director
Kevin Rhodes, Operations Director
(541) 997-1994; Fax (541) 902-0991

E-mail: barb@eventcenter.org • Web site: www.eventcenter.org

Capacity: accommodating groups of up to 500, we offer 6,000 square feet of flat floor meeting space with five easily partitioned breakout areas, plus a 2,000 square foot lobby; Events Center also has a tiered, 482-seat proscenium theater with wheelchair access, a full fly loft, excellent acoustics, stage lighting and dressing rooms

Price Range: call for cost estimates on rental fees and catering; multi-room and multi-day discounts are available

Catering: full meal and beverage service is supplied by L&M Catering, the Florence Events Center's on-site caterer; creative and flexible, L&M can create unique menus to suit all your meal function needs; call (541) 997–8385 for more information

Types of Events: conventions, conferences, corporate retreats, seminars and workshops, trade shows, art shows, banquets, parties, wedding receptions, concerts, plays and more

Availability and Terms
Terms and conditions vary with each event. Deposits are required.

Description of Facility and Services
Seating: tables, chairs, and head tables provided
Servers: provided by caterer
Bar facilities: full bar service available
Linens and napkins: wide variety of colors available
China and glassware: white china and stemmed glassware provided
Cleanup: custodial services provided
Equipment: variety of booth sizes plus piping and drape
Audiovisual: complete audiovisual inventory for flat floor area and theater; many standard items included in room rental fee; any equipment not currently in-stock may be rented for you at an additional cost
Parking: free off-street parking available
ADA: fully accessible

WHERE THE RIVER MEETS THE OCEAN...
WHERE THE SAND DUNES MEET THE MOUNTAINS...
THE FLORENCE EVENTS CENTER IS THE RIGHT MEETING PLACE FOR YOUR NEXT EVENT

Our goal is to make your meeting as successful as you envision it by combining professional service with a personal touch. Our reputation is built not only on the amenities of our facility, but on the attention and hospitality you will receive by our experienced staff and gracious community. From suites with ocean or river views to superb dining and shopping, Florence will welcome you with style and charm. Don't miss the incredible coastal experience of holding your next event at the Florence Events Center.

The Fountains Ballroom
223 S.E. 122nd Avenue • Portland, Oregon 97233
(503) 261-9424; Fax (503) 261-2989 • Web site: www.lum.com/fountainsballroom
Business Hours: Tues–Thurs 9am–9pm or by appointment

Capacity: up to 300 with outside garden patio
Price Range: $75 to $1,500 depending on day, time, package deal etc.
Catering: in-house catering and beverage services
Types of Events: company parties, banquets, dances, meetings and seminars, etc.

Availability and Terms
Four rooms (one large ballroom) are available. A nonrefundable deposit and 50% down payment are required; the remaining 50% of the cost is due 10 days prior to event.

Description of Facility and Services
Seating: 15 round tables and 200 white chairs
Servers: professional staff in formal attire
Bar facilities: available; liquor and liability insurance provided by the Fountains Ballroom
Dance floor: three optional dance floors
Linens and napkins: linen available as well as personalized napkins; all colors
Glassware: included
Cleanup: included in package
Parking: free parking available

Special Services
Table decorations and valet parking available. Rooms are accessible for early decorating if room is available.

We can take care of any service you need: copies, faxing, entertainment, fine food, affordable lunches, corporate photographs, press release photos. Free parking. One block from MAX light-rail.

THE HISTORIC GENTLE HOUSE

855 N. Monmouth Avenue • Monmouth, Oregon 97361
Contact: Jeanette Crosby-Kruljac (503) 838-8673
E-mail: gentlehouse@wou.edu
Web site: www.wou.edu/President/University/Advancement/gentle/gentle.html

Capacity: Reception style: **Indoor:** up to 200; **Outdoor:** up to 500
Catering: you are welcome to bring in your own caterer or provide the food yourself; full kitchen facility on premises
Price Range: varies according to event; please call for information
Types of Events: meetings, seminars, banquets, receptions, and wedding ceremonies

Availability and Terms
Reservations should be made as early as possible. Bookings are made on a first-come, first serve basis. A $200 deposit will secure your date.

Description of Facility and Services
Seating: Meeting for 120; Banquet for 75
Servers: provided by caterer
Bar facilities: provided by caterer
Linens and napkins: table linens available for a fee
China and glassware: provided by caterer
Audiovisual: piano, pump organ, sound system and speakers available upon request
Equipment: microphone, podium, dry-erase board and projector available
Cleanup: you must remove all materials you bring in; some or all of your deposit may be kept for damage or extra labor for clean up
Parking: 22 parking spaces; additional parking available
ADA: yes

VICTORIAN CHARM AND GRACE

The Historic Gentle House is geared towards bringing people for special events, conferences, meetings, and retreats. Gentle House is a renovated Victorian country home nestled around romantic landscaped grounds. Accented by a charming gazebo and nestled in rural Monmouth (just 20 minutes from downtown Salem and adjacent to Western Oregon University). Gentle House is guaranteed to make your event special.

WESTERN OREGON UNIVERSITY

JAKE'S CATERING
AT THE
GOVERNOR
HOTEL

611 S.W. 10th Street
Portland, Oregon 97205
(503) 241-2125; Fax (503) 220-1849
Web site: http://www.mccormickandschmicks.com

Capacity: 600 reception; 450 sit-down dinner
Price Range: $28 to $50
Catering: Jake's Catering is the exclusive caterer for The Governor Hotel; off-premise catering available
Types of Events: from stand-up cocktail/appetizer receptions to fabulous buffet presentations to complete sit-down dinners for groups and gatherings of all sizes

Availability and Terms

Our Italian Renaissance style rooms offer variety and flexibility for groups of 20 to 600. The majestic Ballroom, Renaissance Room, Fireside Room, Library, and five additional rooms gracefully complement the charm of The Governor Hotel. We require a 50% deposit to confirm your event and payment in full 72 hours prior to event for estimated charges.

Description of Facility and Services

Seating: tables and chairs for up to 450
Servers: all servers included as hotel service
Bar facilities: full-service bar and bartender
Linens and napkins: cloth napkins and linens provided in a variety of colors
China and glassware: fine china and glassware provided
Decorations: please inquire about specific decoration ideas and needs
Audiovisual and meeting equipment: available upon request
Parking and ADA: ample parking available near hotel; full ADA compliance

Jake's Catering...A Tradition

Jake's Catering at The Governor Hotel is a division of McCormick & Schmick Management Group and "Jake's Famous Crawfish." Jake's is one of the most respected dining institutions in the Portland area, and Jake's Catering at The Governor Hotel upholds this prestigious reputation.

Known for offering extensive Pacific Northwest menu selection, including fresh seafood and fish, pasta and poultry dishes, and prime cut steaks, Jake's Catering at The Governor Hotel has the flexibility and talent to cater to your needs.

CLASSIC ELEGANCE AND SERVICE

Listed on the National Register of Historic Places, The Governor Hotel is an architectural beauty. Built in 1909 and renovated in 1992, the hotel has been completely restored to its original grandeur. The original design and ornate craftsmanship of the grand banquet space area were preserved in the original Italian Renaissance styling. The room's chandeliers, high vaulted ceilings, marble floors, and black-walnut woodwork and walls are truly unique.

See page 332 under Caterers & Ice Carvings.

Please let this business know that you heard about them from the Bravo! Event Resource Guide.

404 S.W. Washington
Portland, Oregon 97204
Contact: Ted Papas (503) 224-2288
Business Hours: Mon–Thurs 7am–midnight;
Fri and Sat 7am–2:30am

Capacity: up to 500
Price Range: varies by number of persons and menu selection
Catering: in-house catering only; off-premise catering always available
Types of Events: meetings, seminars, banquets, holiday parties, reunions, weddings; you may choose from sit-down dinners, buffets, cocktails and hors d'oeuvres

Availability and Terms
Please make reservations as soon as possible. Short-notice reservations gladly accepted upon space availability.

Description of Facility and Services
Seating: tables and chairs for up to 500
Servers: provided
Bar facilities: provided by Greek Cusina
Dance floor: available; with electrical hookups
Linens: available upon request
China: fine china available at no charge
Decorations: we can decorate or client can
Audiovisual: PA system, big-screen TV
Equipment: available by request
Cleanup: provided by Greek Cusina
Parking: available on street or in adjacent parking structure
ADA: accessible

Special Services
Music—come see what's making the Greek Cusina *the* place for entertainment. Live Greek performances at no charge!
Off-premise catering—let us cater your next event, whatever the occasion, whatever the location. Have your event Sunday through Thursday and get the band for yourself at no charge!

A TOUCH OF GREECE IN THE HEART OF PORTLAND
Authentic Greek decor in hues of blue, aromas of freshly prepared ethnic dishes and pleasant folk music greet your senses and invite you to enjoy a truly unique dining experience. Our upstairs event facility is perfectly suited for all your special occasions. From small business meetings, complete with fresh pastries and coffee, to large receptions, parties or banquets, let the Greek Cusina dazzle you with our exceptional food as you enter a world of Mediterranean charm and flavor.

Our new Minoan Room
"A Must See Event Facility"
No Room Charge

The Greenwood Inn

S.W. Allen Boulevard at Highway 217
Beaverton, Oregon
Contact: Catering
(503) 643-7444 ext 726 or 727
Office Hours: Mon–Fri 8am–5pm
Web site: www.greenwoodinn.com

Capacity: 10 to 800 people
Price Range: room rentals and setup fees may be waived when meal minimums are met.
  Ranges: Breakfast $8 to $12; Lunch $10 to $16; Dinner $18 to $32; Reception $10 to $30
Catering: full service in-house catering
Types of Events: conferences, seminars, conventions, award luncheons and dinners, receptions and retreats

Availability and Terms
The Greenwood Inn has nine private rooms accommodating a variety of group sizes. Advance reservations of two to six months are recommended. Also available is our Grand Suite for your special VIP events.

Description of Facility and Services
Seating: various setup styles available
Servers: setup, full service, tear down
Bar facilities: host/no-host bars available; hotel supplies all liquor and bartender
Dance floor: spacious dance floor available
Linens and napkins: cloth linens available in a wide variety of colors at no additional cost
China and glassware: included in the cost of food and beverage
Decorations: limited decorative items provided at no additional charge. Elaborate theme events can also be arranged by our professional staff.
Cleanup: handled by The Greenwood Inn at no additional cost with normal usage
Audiovisual: complete in-house sound system; remote controlled, programmable lighting, state-of-the-art teleconferencing and video capabilities; wide range of rental equipment available upon request
Equipment: lectern, whiteboards, easels, and risers available at no charge
Parking: ample free parking
ADA: meets all standards; all meeting rooms on ground level

OVER 20 YEARS OF EXCELLENT SERVICE

The Greenwood Inn offers a resort-like atmosphere with a convenient location for you and your attendees. From rooms for your out-of-town guests to complete event and meeting planning services, we are here for you. It is our pleasure to be a part of your special event.

A Heathman Management Group Property

HALLMARK INNS & RESORTS, INC.

Cannon Beach
1400 S. Hemlock
Contact: Jenny Brown, Director of Sales
Cannon Beach, Oregon 97110
(503) 436-1566, (888) 448-4449

Newport
744 S.W. Elizabeth
Contact: TC Caldwell, Director of Sales
Newport, Oregon 97365
(541) 265-2600, (888) 448-4449

Web site: www.hallmarkinns.com

Capacity: *Cannon Beach:* up to 150 reception; *Newport:* up to 200 reception
Price Range: varies depending on size and length of event; please call
Catering: full range of catering services on premise; outdoor events available with tent
Types of Events: business meetings, company retreats, seminars, banquets

Availability and Terms
A six-month advance reservation is recommended; deposit is required upon booking. Deposit can be refunded with 30-day written cancellation notice.

Description of Facility and Services
Seating: tables and chairs provided
Servers: provided with our catering service
Bar facilities: full-service bars available with bartenders ($30 setup fee required)
Dance floor: dance floor available, full electrical hookup
Linens and napkins: cloth linens and napkins available with food service
Decorations: we can assist you, and we allow decorations prior to event with special arrangement
Audiovisual: PA and other audiovisual available upon request
Cleanup: provided and included in catering cost
Parking: ample free parking available

A GREAT PLACE TO MIX BUSINESS WITH PLEASURE

Cannon Beach, Oregon
This oceanfront Hallmark Resort offers 128 of the most beautifully located guest rooms on the Northern Oregon Coast. Just outside your room is the famous Haystack Rock, and the resort is within walking distance of Cannon Beach attractions and shops. Accommodations range from cozy rooms for two to family-designed two-bedroom suites for six. In addition to guest rooms, there are four oceanfront homes available for beachside retreats and group getaways.

Newport, Oregon
Hallmark Resort at Newport offers 158 of the most beautifully accommodated oceanfront guest rooms and luxury suites on the Central Oregon Coast. Close to Newport's attractions, golf courses and shops. All guest rooms and suites overlook the Pacific Ocean. Accommodations range from cozy rooms for two to spacious guest rooms with in-room two-person spa, fireplace and oceanfront balcony.

See page 372 under Resort Accommodations.

HEATHMAN PRIVATE DINING

1001 S.W. Broadway at Salmon Street • Portland, Oregon 97205
Contact: Catering (503) 790-7126

Capacity: 220 people reception; 120 people seated
Price Range: varies depending on type of event and menu selection
Catering: full-service in-house and off-premise catering available
Types of Events: sit-down meals, buffets, receptions

Availability and Terms
Please contact the catering office for details. Advance deposits are required.

Description of Facility and Services
Seating: tables and chairs provided
Servers: provided, with 19% service charge
Bar facilities: full-service bar with bartenders available for your event; The Heathman supplies the liquor, beer, and wine
Dance floor: available
Linens and napkins: variety of linen selections available
China and glassware: fine china, silver, and crystal supplied
Decorations: candles available; no nails, tacks or tape permitted
Cleanup: included in price
Audiovisual: audiovisual and computer hookups available with advance notice
Parking: parking available; price varies
ADA: fully accessible

Accommodations
Walk through the doors into the most elegant and enchanting atmosphere in Portland. Located in the heart of the arts and culture district of downtown Portland, the historic Heathman Hotel will exceed your highest expectations. Enjoy the stylish, warm ambiance of one of our eight private dining rooms. Adorned with silk wall coverings, classic wood shutters, topiary plants or even a fire-lit room adjacent to the Heathman Library, each room has its' own distinct character. The ambiance is perfectly matched by our staff. Dedicated personally to your event, our goal is to spoil you rotten! And that's exactly how you will feel after you've enjoyed the cuisine of Chef Philippe Boulout. Nominated for the James Beard Award as the Best Chef in the Northwest, Chef Boulout maintains his reputation as one of the culinary stars of the nineties. Perfect for your meeting, holiday party, corporate or social event—relax and let The Heathman worry about the details.

A Heathman Management Group restaurant

THE HEATHMAN LODGE

7801 N.E. Greenwood Drive • Vancouver, Washington 98662
Contact: Sales & Catering Office (360) 254-3100 or (888) 475-3100
Business Hours: Mon–Fri 8am–5pm

Capacity: up to 300 people; 4,500 total square feet of meeting/private dining space
Price Range: please inquire
Catering: full-service, upscale catering
Types of Events: business meetings, seminars, retreats, award luncheons, dinners, receptions and trade shows

Availability and Terms

The Lodge offers 4,500 square feet of meeting and private dining space. The ballroom is divisible into three rooms, each with pre-function space. Two additional meeting rooms are available as well. The Lodge also offers a 1,230 plus-square-foot Presidential Suite and three large conference suites.

Description of Facility and Services

Seating: various setup styles available
Bar facilities: host/no-host bars available; hotel supplies all liquor and bartender
Dance floor: available
Linens: available
China and glassware: included in cost of food and beverage
Decorations: limited decorative items available at no additional charge; creative theme events can be arranged
Audiovisual: state-of-the-art audiovisual capabilities
Cleanup: handled by hotel at no additional charge
Parking: ample free parking
ADA: meets all standards; all meeting rooms are on ground level; any special needs are the responsibility of the meeting planner

Special Services

A night in one of the 121 guest rooms or 22 suites is a truly memorable experience. Old-world craftsmanship is evident in stretched leather lampshades and hand-crafted mirrors and frames. Hickory and pine furnishings lend comfort to the surroundings.

The Heathman Lodge is Vancouver, Washington's newest full-service upscale hotel. An unexpected urban retreat, the Lodge offers travelers and locals from the Portland/Vancouver area a blend of heart-felt service, business amenities and rustic, mountain lodge comfort. Inspired by authentic Pacific Northwest decor and cuisine, the Lodge provides each guest a calm refuge and a memorable experience.

HAND-HEWN HOSPITALITY

We invite you to take a virtual tour at www.heathmanlodge.com

Hilton Garden Inn®
Portland/Beaverton

*15520 N.W. Gateway Court
Beaverton, Oregon 97006
Contact: Lisa Brown (503) 466-2604; Fax (503) 439-1818
Business Hours: 7:30am–6pm
Web site: www.hilton.com*

Capacity: **Multnomah/Rose Garden:** up to 100; 1,236 sq.ft.; **Mt. Hood:** up to 30; 612 sq.ft.; **Two Boardrooms:** up to 12; 450 sq.ft.
Catering: full-service in-house catering
Price Range: $100–$400
Types of Events: banquets, receptions, meetings, seminars, conferences

Availability and Terms
Reservations should be made as early as possible; credit card deposit required.

Description of Facility and Services
Seating: tables and chairs provided
Servers: provided
Bar facilities: full-service bar service available
Linens and napkins: provided
China and glassware: provided
Audiovisual: on-site A/V equipment
Cleanup: provided by Hilton Garden Inn staff
Parking: ample free parking available
ADA: yes

BEAUTIFUL FOUR-STORY HIGH-RISE
A beautiful four-story high-rise with 150 guestrooms, The Hilton Garden Inn—Portland/Beaverton includes 14 two-room suites and four Jacuzzi suites. The Garden Inn has all the amenities that the business traveler expects including two-line phones with data ports, a refrigerator, microwave and coffee service in each room as well as an iron and ironing board, hair dryer and complimentary USA Today daily. The Great American Grill offers a deluxe breakfast buffet or a cooked-to-order breakfast. Some of our lunch and dinner specials include pasta, sandwiches, seafood, steak, and other classic American favorites.

Conveniently located 12 miles west of downtown Portland and 20 miles west of the Portland International Airport.

Hilton Garden Inn®
Portland Airport

12048 N.E. Airport Way • Portland, Oregon 97220
Contact: Liz Charbonneau (503) 255-8600; Fax (503) 255-8998
Business Hours: Mon–Fri 8am–5pm

Capacity: three meeting rooms totaling 1,900 square feet accommodating 10 to 100
Catering: full-service catering provided exclusively by hotel
Price Range: price will be determined by event and menu selection
Types of Events: business meetings, seminars, receptions, breakfast, lunch and dinner

Availability and Terms
Reservations should be made as early as possible to ensure availability. A $200 deposit is required upon booking with remainder due in full 72 hours prior to event (unless credit has been established). Cancellation of 30 days notice is required.

Description of Facility and Services
Seating: tables and chairs provided
Servers: included in price
Bar facilities: full beverage service available; provided by hotel only
Linens and napkins: wide selection available at no charge
China and glassware: provided
Audiovisual: full range available at additional cost
Equipment: additional equipment available for an extra charge
Cleanup: provided by staff
Parking: complimentary parking available
ADA: yes

Special Services
We offer a special group rate with a booking of 10 or more guest rooms per night.

FOUR STAR SERVICE AT A THREE STAR PRICE
Our professional and courteous sales staff can handle all facets of your business meeting or special event, from guest accommodations, meeting room/banquet space and catering services. The Hilton Garden Inn—Portland Airport is a beautiful four-story hotel that provides all the amenities you need. Our signature pavilion provides a bright and welcome feeling to all guests. Our staff is trained to give personal, courteous and timely service to all guests, from a business meeting of 10 to that special dinner of 100. Make your next event a memorable one at the Hilton Garden Inn—Portland Airport, where we provide four star service at a three star price!

Hilton Portland

921 S.W. Sixth Avenue
Portland, Oregon 97204
Contact: Sales/Catering
(503) 226-1611; Fax (503) 220-2293
Business Hours: Mon–Fri 8:30am–5:30pm
Web site: www.portland.hilton.com

Capacity: 10 to 1,200 people; 24 meeting rooms—30,000 total square footage
Price Range: customized menus at varying prices
Catering: full-service catering
Types of Events: conventions, corporate meetings, sit-down dinners, theme events, black tie galas, trade shows

Availability and Terms
The Hilton Portland has many different reception rooms of varying sizes to accommodate any event from small sit-down dinners, board meetings to large black tie galas. We feature our elegantly appointed Pavilion Ballroom, ideal for 250 to 350 guests. Our Broadway Room is suited for groups between 75 and 200. The Grand Ballroom can accommodate up to 1,200.

Description of Facility and Services
Seating: your choice of banquet rounds or informal cabarets
Servers: included in catering cost
Bar facilities: hosted or no-host bar; beer, wine, and champagne service; we provide all beverages, bartender, and servers.
Dance floor: appropriately sized inlaid parquet dance floor
Linens and napkins: fine linens in coordinating colors; specialty linens also available
China and glassware: white china and stemmed glassware; ornate silver chafing dishes and urns
Decorations: lattice, plants, theme decorations, candles
Lodging: 455 guest rooms with six suites
Cleanup: included in catering charges
Audiovisual: Hilton Portland has our own in-house full service audiovisual department
Business Center: full-service business center with computers photo copying, faxing and transparencies
Parking: parking available; costs vary
ADA: fully equipped to accommodate ADA requirements

WE ACCOMMODATE ALL YOUR NEEDS
The Hilton Portland is a full-service hotel, conveniently located in the heart of downtown Portland. The Hilton Portland is equipped to handle all of your conference and convention needs. Also, we have an in-house athletic club. Memberships are available too. Our reputation for superior service is built on 36 years of excellent experience.

Four Diamond

**Portland Airport
Hotel and Trade Center**
*8439 N.E. Columbia Boulevard
Portland, Oregon 97220
(503) 256-5000; Fax (503) 256-5631
E-mail: HIPDXSALES@aol.com*

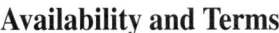

Capacity: maximum of 1,200 guests
Price Range: customized to meet your needs
Catering: full-service catering on or off premise
Type of events: meetings, conventions, trade shows and social events

Availability and Terms
We offer a wide selection of rooms to fit your needs. Advance reservations are strongly encouraged. Deposits are required and are refundable with 60 days written notice.

Description of Facility and Services
Seating: all types of tables and chairs
Servers: staff included in catering cost
Bar facilities: full beverage service available; Holiday Inn Portland Airport to provide all beer, wine and liquor
Dance floor: cost varies per size of dance floor
Linens and napkins: variety of colors available
China and glassware: white china and stemmed glassware
Decorations: silk plants, mirror tiles, votive candles, ficus trees and bud vases
Audiovisual: in-house audiovisual
Equipment: podium, risers and specialty props
Cleanup: included in price
Sleeping accommodations: 286 modern guest rooms with 17 suites
Parking: free parking for 900 cars
ADA: accessible

Special Services
Our professional sales and catering staff are ready to assist with all your needs. Allow Holiday Inn Portland Airport to take the stress out of your next event. The success of your event is our ultimate goal.

STAY WITH EXCELLENCE!
The Holiday Inn Portland Airport is part of the John Q. Hammons Hotel Corp., one of the nation's largest. It has 286 modern guest rooms with the largest meeting facility five minutes from the airport. In addition to the 12 meeting and banquet rooms totaling 33,607 square feet of flexible meeting space we have the ability to fulfill any client's needs or challenges. We welcome the opportunity to give you 100% guest satisfaction.

25425 S.W. 95th Avenue • Wilsonville, Oregon 97070
Contact: Catering Department (503) 682-2211
Business Hours: Mon–Fri 8am–5:30pm; Sat 9am–noon

Capacity: 10 to 900; 10,150 square feet of meeting space
Price Range: please ask our catering specialists for current menu prices
Catering: full-service in-house catering
Types of Events: meetings, reunions, conventions, receptions

Availability and Terms
Reservations should be made as early as possible. Our catering specialists will be happy to assist with our current event policies.

Description of Facility and Services
Seating: tables and chairs for 600
Servers: staff included in catering costs; gratuity will be added to final bill
Bar facilities: full-service bar available
Dance floor: available at minimum charge
Linens and napkins: white linen tablecloths and napkins; special colors additional charge
China and glassware: white china and stemmed glassware
Decorations: silk flower arrangements, mirrors, oil candles, ficus trees
Audiovisual: available upon request
Equipment: available upon request
Cleanup: provided by the Holiday Inn
Parking: ample free parking available
ADA: banquet rooms and Atrium fully accessible; elevator to guest rooms; nine ADA compliant guestrooms

Special Services
The Holiday Inn Select Portland South offers 169 spacious comfortable guestrooms, including Executive Level accommodations. Other amenities include a full-service business center, indoor pool, whirlpool, fitness center, and on-site dining at the South City Diner and South City NightClub.

A "SELECT" BRAND OF EXCELLENCE
The **Holiday Inn Select Portland South** is the first "Select" brand of Holiday Inns in Oregon. Conveniently located off Interstate 5, only 15 minutes form downtown Portland, 26 miles from the airport, and 30 miles from Salem. Our professional catering staff "caters to your every need," from initial planning stages until the last guest leaves. "Let us take the stress off you!"

"STAY WITH SOMEONE YOU KNOW"

102 Oak Avenue
Hood River, Oregon
97031

Reservations
(800) 386-1859

Sales
(541) 386-1900

E-mail: HRHotel@gorge.net; Web site: www.hoodriverhotel.com

Capacity: 5 to 250 guests
Price Range: price varies according to room and time of year; call for proposal
Catering: full-service in-house catering and off-premise catering
Types of Events: banquets, receptions, parties, retreats, meetings, and seminars

Availability and Terms
Hood River Hotel's banquet room can accommodate up to 200+ people. Additional areas are available for groups of 20 or fewer. We suggest that you book early to ensure availability. A deposit is required at time of booking to secure your date with the balance due the day of your event. **See page 374 under Accommodations, Resorts & Retreats.**

Description of Facility and Services
Seating: tables and chairs for up to 200 people
Servers and cleanup: included in catering cost
Bar facilities: full liquor service from Pasquale's Ristorante and Wine Cellar Bar; bartender included in price quote; extensive selection of wines and champagnes
Dance floor: accommodates up to 55 people
Linens and napkins: cloth linens available in a variety of colors
China and glassware: traditional pattern; assorted glassware
Decorations: floral supplies available upon request; early decorating by prior arrangement; some restrictions apply
Audiovisual and meeting equipment: arrangements can be made to accommodate
Parking: on-street and designated off-site parking
ADA: fully accessible

Special Services
Pasquale's Ristorante, offers breakfast, lunch, and dinner, specializes in fine Italian and Pacific Northwest cuisine with menu items from pasta to wild game. After dinner, enjoy a cappuccino or cocktail by the fireplace. Pasquale's is the perfect place to relax after a day's adventure.

EUROPEAN-STYLE CHARM
This charming European-style 1913 hotel offers 41 rooms and is listed on the National Register of Historic Places. Conveniently located in the heart of historic downtown Hood River and the Columbia River Gorge National Scenic Area, our banquet facility offers a unique location for your special event. Decorated in a wine cellar theme, our banquet room offers a full bar and the finest Italian and Northwest cuisine in the Columbia Gorge. Our warm European charm and friendly staff will ensure an event you and your guests will remember forever.

1108 East Marina Way
Hood River, Oregon 97031
Contact: Sales and Catering
(541) 386-2200 or (800) 828-7873
Business Hours: Mon–Sat 8am–5pm;
Sundays and evenings by appointment
E-mail: hrinn@gorge.net
Web site: www.hoodriverinn.com

Capacity: seven banquet rooms can accommodate up to 300 for reception; 225 for sit-down; 149 guest rooms
Price Range: prices vary depending on menu selection and size of event
Catering: in-house and off-site
Types of Events: meetings, seminars, receptions, sit-down, buffets, barbecues, or any custom event

Availability and Terms
Hood River Inn has seven banquet rooms and outdoor space that will accommodate up to 300 people. We suggest that you book as far in advance as possible to ensure availability. A 10% deposit is due at time of booking with the balance due the day of your event. Deposit is refundable if cancellation is made 30 days prior to date.

Description of Facility and Services
Seating: tables and chairs for up to 300 people
Servers: included in catering cost
Bar facilities: full-service bar and liability provided by Hood River Inn
Dance floor: 24'x24' dance floor; electrical hookups available
Linens and napkins: cloth linens available in many colors at no additional charge
China and glassware: bone china; assorted glassware
Decorations: limited supplies available; early decorating allowed
Cleanup: included in catering costs
Audiovisual: all audiovisual needs will be accommodated
Equipment: all meeting equipment requirements will be accommodated
Parking: ample free parking
ADA: fully accessible

Special Services
- The Best Western Hood River Inn has 142 guest rooms and 7 suites available.
- Our professional staff is prepared to assist you in every detail of your event.

FUN AND ADVENTURE AWAIT
The Hood River Inn combines excellent service and hospitality with one of America's most scenic locations—the Columbia River Gorge. Situated on the shores of the majestic Columbia River, our professional staff will ensure you a successful and enjoyable event.

See page 375 under Resort Accommodations.

Hunter Creek Farm

14441 S.W. Wilsonville Road
Wilsonville, Oregon 97070
Contact: Angela or Marilyn
(503) 625-3424
Business Hours: 8am–8pm, 7 days a week

Capacity: 400 outdoor, 125 indoor
Price Range: $15 per person
Catering: outside catering welcome
Types of Events: meetings, retreats, reunions, parties, weddings, and horse shows

Availability and Terms
A 50% deposit is due at time of registration.

Description of Facility and Services
Seating: 40 indoor, 100 outdoor
Servers: provided by caterer
Bar facilities: provided by caterer
Linens and napkins: white linen provided at no extra cost
China and glassware: provided by caterer
Audiovisual: none provided
Equipment: none supplied
Cleanup: included in price
Parking: ample parking available
ADA: no handicap facilities to main house

Special Services
Five guestrooms with private bathrooms are available.

PREMIERE EVENT LOCATION
Located on the Willamette River in Wilsonville, Hunter Creek Farm is a bed and breakfast and premiere event location on a 120-acre equestrian park. The home is 6,000 square feet and beautifully decorated in "Ralph Lauren" equestrian fabrics. Resembling an old English fox hunting lodge, the farm is complete with English gardens, a swimming pool, and pool house. Events of 400+ can be held outdoors at the pool and event area.

IMPERIAL HOTEL

On Broadway

400 S.W. Broadway at Stark
Portland, Oregon 97205
Contact: Typhoon! (503) 224-8285; Fax (503) 224-1894
Business Hours: Mon–Fri 9am–5pm

Capacity: 15 to 150 people
Catering: full-service through Typhoon! catering
Types of Events: receptions, reunions, office parties, business meetings, buffets, breakfasts, sit-down dinners, lunches and many other functions

Availability and Terms
Room rates are $150–$1,000. Advance deposit required with full payment due the date of the event. Please add 18% service charge to all food and beverage service.

Description of Facility and Services
Setup: tables and chairs for 150; reception and buffet tables provided; wide array of setups
Servers: included
Bar facilities: host or no-host services and bartenders available; Typhoon! by law is to supply alcoholic beverages
Linens and napkins: table linens and napkins available
China and glassware: china, silver, glassware and stemware provided
Decorations: candles available; early decorating permitted; please no nails, tacks or tape
Cleanup: cleanup services provided
Audiovisual: equipment available upon request
Equipment: podium, flags, and easels available
Parking: several major lots within one block; rates vary
ADA: fully accessible

Special Services
You can concentrate on your agenda, because we're concentrating on ours—making sure your event is a complete success.

TYPHOON! IN THE IMPERIAL HOTEL
Featured as one of the five top ethnic restaurants in America in *Bon Appetit* (September, 1998), Typhoon! has expanded to its new location in the Imperial Hotel, in the heart of downtown Portland. Typhoon! is the creation of Bo Lohasawat Kline, lauded by *Bon Appetit* magazine as one of "the most innovative chefs in America." Bo draws her dishes from the pushcarts of the peasants to the palaces of Asia, earning recognition and recommendations from *Sunset, Esquire, National Geographic, Traveler* magazines, as well as *Zagat, Northwest Best Places, Mobil Travel Guide, Fodor's* and virtually all the local media.

BANQUET, MEETING & EVENT SITES

The Inn at Otter Crest

AND FLYING DUTCHMAN RESTAURANT & WINERY

301 Otter Crest Loop
Otter Rock, Oregon 97369

Contact: Marilyn Ebe or Ginny Whiffen (800) 326-5806; Fax (541) 765-2069
Web site: www.ottercrest.com

Capacity: each of our six conference rooms has a full ocean view; banquet and meeting rooms can accommodate from 10 to 300 people for any type of event

Price Range: prices vary depending upon the event; free wine tasting from our bottles and barrels is always included

Catering: full-service catering on premises including front lawn and in-room dining

Types of Events: meetings, retreats, receptions, reunions, formal and informal banquets, sit-down dinners, buffets, custom and theme parties, weddings and anniversaries

Availability and Terms

Then Inn is a popular place—early reservations are recommended. The room sizes vary from the 22-person cliff house (perched above the ocean in its own building), to the ballroom with a sit-down capacity of 250 persons. Deposits are required upon booking the space and can be refunded with written notice of cancellation. Call for details.

Description of Facility and Services:

Seating: various setup styles available; tables and chairs for up to 300 people
Servers: provided; all well-trained and with smiles
Bar facilities: full-service bar with professional staff; host or no-host services
Dance Floor: any size available
Linens and napkins: cloth linens available in many colors at no additional charge
China and glassware: ivory china, silver, clear glassware and stemware provided
Decorations: early decorating allowed
Audiovisual and other equipment: available upon request
Cleanup: always included
Parking: adjacent parking is free; complimentary shuttle to remote lot parking for large events
ADA: fully accessible

Special Services

The food at the Flying Dutchman has been described as the tastiest on the coast. And the service is great, too. Housed in the Flying Dutchman building is the new Flying Dutchman Winery with its first vintage winning a medal at the 1999 Oregon State Fair. The winery can be a part of your group event with special barrel tasting—professional tasting where food and wine is matched. Free wine seminars for your group are also available.

The Inn offers 140 oceanfront rooms.

See page 376 under Resort Accommodations.

INN AT SPANISH HEAD
4009 S.W. Highway 101 • Lincoln City, Oregon 97367
Contact: Group Sales
(541) 996-2161, (800) 452-8127; Fax (541) 996-4089
www.SpanishHead.com

"A clear head is more receptive to fresh ideas." ~*J. Schneider*

The Inn At Spanish Head is located right on the beach in Lincoln City. All five of the Inn's meeting rooms and each guest room comes complete with an ocean view. There's nothing better than open space and the fresh sea air to clear your head for new inspiration and ideas.

Capacity: groups from 10 to 200
Price Range: each group is individually priced to meet your specific needs
Catering: full-service, in-house catering offers a wide variety of choices for breakfast, lunch, dinner or mid-morning or afternoon snacks; be sure to ask about our Afternoon Motivator, unique box lunches or beach barbecues
Types of Events: all types of meetings and social functions, retreats, banquets, buffets, cocktails and hors d'oeuvres, desserts, custom parties and team building activities

Availability, Terms and Location
Plan in advance or call at the last minute. We'll work hard to take care of your needs. Direct billing is available with approved credit. Advance deposits may be requested.

Description of Facility and Services
Accommodations: five meeting and reception rooms with floor-to-ceiling windows offer a breathtaking view of the Pacific Ocean; two beach level rooms have access to the pool deck for outdoor gatherings
Seating: tables and chairs for up to 150
Servers: friendly and helpful servers are automatically included
Bar facilities: full-service bar with bartenders; the Inn supplies the liquor, beer and wine and can accommodate most special needs; ask about our hand shaken, fresh-squeezed cocktails
Decorations: let's talk; we're full of ideas and are ready to help you with yours
Audiovisual and meeting equipment: we're well-equipped, including one of the few LCD video projectors (low to no light) on the Oregon Coast
Parking: parking is free; valet parking and shuttle service is provided to the upper parking lot
ADA: yes

Special Services
The Inn works with you to plan every detail of your event, whether it's for business or fun. We can arrange special beach barbecues, hikes to Cascade Head, whale watching tours, golf, tennis, horseback riding and shopping at the nearby Factory Outlet Stores. Ask about our team building activities, too.

If your meeting requires an overnight stay, the Inn's 120 guest rooms are all ocean front. Many have balconies and kitchens or kitchenettes. Guests have unlimited use of our outdoor heated pool, oceanview enclosed spa, recreation and exercise room and saunas.

Come to the Inn and open your mind to fresh ideas.

Please let this business know that you heard about them from the Bravo! Event Resource Guide.

112 S.W. Second Avenue
Portland, Oregon 97204
Contact: Brad Yoast
(503) 227-4057; Fax (503) 227-5931

PORTLAND'S IRISH RESTAURANT & PUB

E-mail: portland@kellsirish.com • Web site: www.kellsirish.com

Capacity: private banquet facilities located on second floor; capacities range from 15–150 and up to 300 reception-style

Price Range: varies according to room and services

Catering: full-service in-house and off-premise catering

Types of Events: We provide buffet and formal sit-down service for receptions, rehearsal dinners, business luncheons, cocktail and hors d' oeuvre parties, holiday and surprise parties, fund raisers and gala events

Availability and Terms

The K Club is located on the second floor of the historic Kells building near the waterfront in downtown Portland. With the Irish ambiance, excellent service and outstanding food you've come to expect from Kells, the elegant K Club invites your guests to celebrate in the stately ballroom and mingle in the intimate Ulster and Cigar Rooms.

Description of Facility and Services

Seating: variety of seating customized to meet your needs from 15–150

Servers: included in service

Bar facilities: host/no host bar; largest single malt selection in the northwest, full range of micro beers, extensive wine list; fine cigars also available

Dance floor: we offer two separate locations for bands, a long list of our most popular local acts, electrical hook-ups available

Linens and napkins: included in service; inquire about our color selection

China and glassware: white china with glassware to complement

Cleanup: included with full-service catering

Decorations: discussion of your ideas and needs welcomed

Parking: parking for events may be made in advance, garages within close proximity

ADA: Kells first floor is ADA accessible; parties may be arranged for this space as well

PORTLAND'S FAVORITE IRISH RESTAURANT & PUB

Kells has become a Portland landmark since its opening in 1990. One of Portland's favorite nightspots, Kells offers a great menu of New World Irish cuisine mixing traditional favorites with fresh, northwest seafoods, produce, and all-natural ingredients. Kells also features live Irish music seven nights a week, a grand stone fireplace and comfortable cigar room. All this and the warm, friendly service and atmosphere of a genuine Irish Pub.

Sales Office
3800 S.W. Cedar Hills Blvd.
Beaverton, Oregon 97005
(503) 626-MEET(6338)
Web site: www.kingstad.com

Beaverton
Downtown
Airport

Capacity: largest room accommodates up to 200 people; 24 rooms in three locations; 24,000 net square feet total
Price Range: varies according to event size and menu selection; Complete Meeting Packages available
Catering: full-service catering
Types of Events: meetings, seminars, conventions; luncheons, dinners

Availability and Terms
Kingstad Meeting Centers offers professional meeting rooms, in three locations, accommodating groups of up to 200 people. Reservations should be made as early as possible to ensure availability. A nonrefundable deposit of 25% of expected expenditures is required to confirm your date. Payment in full is due the day of your function. Please inquire about direct-billing application.

Description of Facility and Services
Seating: various seating arrangements offered
Servers: appropriate service staff provided with catering service
Bar facilities: alcoholic beverages allowed; coffee, tea, and beverage service
Linens and napkins: cloth tablecloths and napkins
China and glassware: off-white china; variety of glassware
Cleanup: provided by Kingstad Meeting Centers
Meeting equipment: overhead projectors; VCR and monitor; 35mm projectors; computer projection equipment; ISDN lines; video conferencing; flip charts, pads, markers
Parking: free at Beaverton and Airport locations only
ADA: yes

Special service
Kingstad Meeting Centers offers support services such as copying, faxing, message taking, and free courtesy phones for attendees.

THE CONTEMPORARY WAY TO MEET
Kingstad Meeting Centers offers three full-service facilities that specialize in providing space for small local meetings for groups of 200 or less. Every aspect of our service and facilities have been designed to help make your meetings as productive as possible.

LASERPORT

10975 S.W. Canyon Road
Beaverton, Oregon 97005
Owners: John Gabel and Bill Buhler
(503) 526-9501; Fax (503) 626-6912
Hours: Mon–Thu noon–9pm; Fri noon–midnight; Sat 10am–midnight; Sun 10am–9pm

"THE GAME OF THE GALAXIES"

The 4,000 sq. ft. fully-fogged laser tag arena has been filled with mazes, ultraviolet lighting, strobes, wall-mounted lasers, light displays and upbeat techno music. The total involvement for one game of laser tag is approximately 25 minutes. We supply all the equipment with no additional rental fees.

Capacity: up to 150

Price Range: $7 for the first game and $5 each additional game; special group packages available; please call for current prices

Catering: full-service in-house catering, plus outside catering available upon request

Types of Events: team-building and stress reduction make laser tag the perfect corporate outing; much team and individualized competition is possible using our computer-generated game formats—even a "you're it" option that increases the fun and adds to the excitement; we accommodate; corporate quarterly meetings/parties, birthday parties, youth group outings, school field trips, graduation parties, and other family celebrations!

Availability and Terms

Please make reservations as early as possible, or upon availability. Deposit is required upon reservation. We gladly accept all major credit cards.

Description of Facility and Services

Food: we serve hand-tossed gourmet pizza daily; certain packages will include chicken or vegetarian bento with a variety of sauces, and fresh-tossed salad

Video games: we have over 40 of the latest arcade games; quarter-operated

Seating: tables and chairs provided for up to 80

Servers: host or hostess provided by LaserPort

Bar facilities: for adult groups only; wine and beer available with advance notice

Meeting room: seats 50 for private meetings; TV, VCR and overhead projector

China and glassware: plates, cups and silverware provided

Decorations: no limitations

Audiovisual: provided upon request

Parking: ample free parking

ADA: fully accessible

"LET LASERPORT TURN YOUR GROUP INTO A TEAM!"

Need a little team building? Laser tag is the answer. It's the fastest growing corporate game in America and it's right here in Beaverton. LaserPort's state-of-the-art, futuristic laser sports center will motivate and excite your employees and help develop that camaraderie we all need in the workplace.

PORTLAND Marriott DOWNTOWN

1401 S.W. Naito Parkway
Portland, Oregon 97201
Contact: Sales and Catering Department
(503) 499-6360; Fax (503) 226-1209
Business Hours: Mon–Fri 7am–6pm; Sat 9am–4pm

Capacity: up to 1,000 people
Price Range: price will be determined by event and specific menu
Catering: provided by the hotel exclusively
Types of Events: business meetings, seminars, breakfasts, luncheons, dinners

Availability and Terms
The Portland Marriott Hotel offers a wide selection of rooms to fit your specific needs. The addition of the beautiful Mt. Hood Room offers a new view of Portland. Overlooking the Willamette River and Mount Hood, it's the perfect room for any special event. We suggest reserving your date as soon as possible to ensure availability.

Description of Facility and Services
Seating: tables, chairs, and head tables provided
Servers: included in price
Bar facilities: full beverage service available; Portland Marriott Hotel to provide all beer, wine, liquor, and bartenders
Dance floor: available at no charge
Linens and napkins: extensive linen selections at no charge
China and glassware: Marriott Hotel uses only fine china, crystal, and silverplated flatware
Cleanup: included in price
Parking: limited valet parking available in hotel; plenty of public parking adjacent to hotel
ADA: yes

Special Services
The Portland Marriott Hotel has 504 guest rooms to accommodate your out-of-town guests.

A TRADITION OF CARE, CONCERN, AND SERVICE
At Marriott, we bring something extra to every event—a tradition of care, concern, and service that assures peace of mind for you and a memorable occasion for your guests. After playing host to hundreds of special events, Marriott has the art of event planning down to a science. Let us assist you in planning a successful and memorable event.

PORTLAND Marriott
CITY CENTER

520 S.W. Broadway
Portland, Oregon 97205
(503) 226-6300; Fax (503) 227-7515

Capacity: six banquet and meeting rooms accommodating groups from 10 to 120 attendees
Price Range: varies depending on size and type of event
Catering: full service in-house catering; groups may chose to offer attendees "off the menu" selections or complete meeting packages
Types of Events: we specialize in servicing the needs of small to medium size events; we can accommodate business meetings, board meetings, breakfast, luncheons, receptions and dinners

Availability and Terms
The Marriott City Center on Broadway offers six meeting rooms for a variety of events up to 120 people. We suggest reserving your date as soon as possible. Contact our event staff to discuss terms and conditions.

Description of Facility and Services
Seating: tables and chairs provided, seating up to 120
Servers: all servers and support staff included at no additional charge; an 18% gratuity is added to all food and beverage functions
Bar facilities: full-service bar, beer and wine; hotel must provide and serve all beverages
Linens and napkins: numerous colors to choose from at no additional charge; specialty colors may be secured for a nominal fee
China and glassware: provided at no additional charge
Dance floor: available at no additional fee
Cleanup: included in event cost
Audiovisual: available for an additional fee
Parking: valet parking available at a cost; numerous self-parking facilities are nearby
ADA: accessible

Special Services
The new Portland Marriott City Center offers 249 rooms including 11 suites and three concierge floors. Special weekend rates and packages are available.

A NEW MARRIOTT HOTEL... ON BROADWAY

Hold your next event at the new Marriott City Center located in the very center of Portland, on Broadway. Our specialty is small to medium size events for up to 120 people. For simplicity, we offer complete packages that include select meals, coffee breaks, audiovisual and setup fees, all presented with "per person" pricing. For added flexibility and individual choice, group attendees may individually order their entrees from our special banquet menus.

See page 361 under Hotel Accommodations.

THE MARSHALL HOUSE

1301 Officers Row
Vancouver National Historic Reserve
Vancouver, Washington 98661
Contact: Frances Anderson (360) 693-3103
Business Hours: Mon–Fri 9am–5pm; Sat by appointment

Capacity: 25 to 225 inside; more if verandas or gardens are used
Price Range: $100 to $850
Catering: caterers from Marshall House's approved list only; caterers required for any food, beverage, or cake service
Types of Events: sit-down, buffet, hors d'oeuvres, cake and punch, or garden

Availability and Terms

You may rent as many rooms as you need (up to 4) to accommodate from 25 to 350 guests for as many hours as you need. Standard weekend rental periods are from 11am to 6pm, and from 6pm to 1am. Reservations should be made as soon as possible—six months to one year in advance for the busy summer months. A $100 deposit is required to hold your date.

Description of Facility and Services

Seating: antique tables and chairs
Servers: must be provided by caterer; one per every 50 guests/minimum of two
Bar facilities: champagne, white wine, and bottled or canned beer only (no hard liquor or kegs); must be served by an approved bartender; no self-serve alcohol
Dance floor: 20'x30' hardwood dance floor; electrical hookup available
Linens: linen rental available
Serviceware: coffee urns, and punch bowls available for rent
China and glassware: your caterer provides
Decorations: no tape, tacks, staples, or wire; you carry liability for damage
Cleanup: we provide; extra charge for extra cleanup
Audiovisual: rear screen slide equipment
Equipment: podium and easels available
Parking: 60 spaces adjacent to building, additional parking one block away
ADA: fully complied

Special Services

The Marshall House encourages the unique and will be happy to help you create the perfect event. With four spacious rooms, verandas, and lawn, the house accommodates business meetings to large receptions and parties. Call for a tour and an information packet. Our staff will assist you from planning through party.

IN THE ELEGANT VICTORIAN STYLE

Picturesque Officers Row on the Vancouver National Historic Reserve features 21 grand houses on 21 acres of lawn, trees, and gardens. The George C. Marshall House stands as a centerpiece on the Row in the historic Queen Anne-style. With wide verandas, rich colors and textures, 11-foot ceilings, and a magnificent central staircase, the Marshall House is sure to provide a most elegant backdrop for your event.

Please let this business know that you heard about them from the Bravo! Event Resource Guide.

MARYLHURST UNIVERSITY CONFERENCE AND RETREAT CENTER

P.O. Box 261
Marylhurst, Oregon 97036-0261
Contact: Conference Office
(503) 699-6250; Fax (503) 697-5592
Business Hours: Mon–Fri 9am–4pm
E-mail: conf@marylhurst.edu

Capacity: 10-200 guests; overnight lodging for up to 54
Price Range: please call for current prices
Food Service/Catering: cafeteria-style in the college commons or catering available for special events
Types of Events: seminars, conferences, retreats, meetings

Availability and Terms

Marylhurst University Conference and Retreat Center has 11 meeting rooms of various sizes and capacities for up to 200 guests. Overnight lodging is available in dorm-style manner for 54 guests. The Conference and Retreat Center is pleased to host events that are compatible with the mission and goals of Marylhurst University and are educational in nature. Please call for detailed information.

Description of Facility and Services

Public transportation: Tri-Met Public Transportation (busline) to main campus entrance. Shuttle service available from airport and major points of interest.
Lodging: clean, simple, dorm-style guest rooms that include sink, towels and bedding (no private restrooms)
Seating: various styles to include classroom, theater, conference, etc.
Servers: wait staff is available for catered events
Linens: available for an additional cost
China, silver and glassware: available for an additional cost
Cleanup: provided by Marylhurst staff
Audiovisual: whiteboards, overhead projectors, slide projectors at no additional rental fee; please call for current prices on additional AV equipment
Office equipment: fax and copy machine
Parking: ample free parking available; no RV overnight parking
ADA: fully accessible

MARYLHURST UNIVERSITY CONFERENCE AND RETREAT CENTER

Marylhurst University is situated on a century-old campus of 63 acres of rolling lawns, surrounded by deep-wooded ravines and nestled in a bend of the Willamette River. The College is located 15 minutes from downtown Portland, 20 minutes from the Portland Airport, 1.5 hours from beautiful Oregon beaches and majestic Mount Hood. Within 5 minutes drive time, the area offers many fine restaurants, shopping and special events. The Conference and Retreat Center is the perfect setting for an out-of-the-way conference or retreat that is minutes from a major metropolitan area.

THE MELODY BALLROOM

615 S.E. Alder • Portland, Oregon 97214
Contact: Kathleen Kaad (503) 232-2759; Fax (503) 232-0702
E-mail: melody.ballroom@mci2000.com
Business Hours: Tue–Fri 10am–2pm or by appointment

Capacity: two rooms, up to 1,100 people; used separately, 300 and 800 people
Price Range: varies, please call
Catering: in-house catering and beverage services only
Types of Events: sit-down, buffet, theme, cocktails and hors d'oeuvres

Availability and Terms
The Melody Ballroom requires a room rental fee as a deposit to reserve your date. Reservations are accepted one year or more in advance. Catering cost must be paid one week prior to the event.

Description of Facility and Services
Seating: tables and chairs provided as needed
Servers: staff included in catering costs; gratuity on food and beverage
Bar facilities: full-service bar provided; host/no-host; liquor, beer, and wine
Dance floor: 30'x30'; 300 capacity; two large stages; can accommodate full touring bands
Linens and napkins: cloth and linen tablecloths and napkins; limited colors
China and glassware: china and clear glassware
Decorations: no limitations; we can provide fresh flowers and limited decorating accessories
Cleanup: included in catering cost
Audiovisual: equipment available upon request
Equipment: podium, easels, and risers available; all other by prior arrangement
Parking: free street parking

Special Services
The Melody Ballroom rents on a per day basis, giving our clients the flexibility for decorating and music set up at your convenience. Our event coordinators will be happy to help you plan and execute your event to perfection...just ask.

EXTRAORDINARY FOOD AND FRIENDLY SERVICE WILL MAKE YOUR EVENT A SUCCESS!
The Melody Ballroom is a unique, historic facility, owned and operated by a professional chef. Our philosophy is to say "Yes!" and to make your event truly individual. We work with diverse menus and styles—even your favorite recipes! Our caring staff provides friendly service that will make your guests feel as if they were in your own home.

MISSION MILL MUSEUM

1313 Mill Street S.E.
Salem, Oregon 97301
Contact: Cheryl Clark
(503) 585-7012; Fax (503) 588-9902
E-mail: missionm@teleport.com
Business Hours: Mon–Fri 9am–4:30pm

Capacity: 10 to 500 inside; some outside facilities available; five meeting rooms available, ranging from 888 to 6,384 sq. ft.
Price Range: prices vary according to time frame, room size, and day of week
Catering: Mission Mill has a restaurant on-site that can cater your event, or you may use the caterer of your choice
Types of Events: banquets, receptions, parties, meetings and seminars, special business package lunch available with room rental

Availability and Terms
Terms and conditions vary with each event.

Description of Facility and Services
Seating: tables and chairs included with all rentals.
Bar facilities: Mission Mill allows alcohol to be served; conditions vary; bartender service available through local reference
Dance floor: flooring in larger rooms suitable for dancing; capacity up to 350
Electrical: adequate for a variety of functions
Linens: provided by caterer or local references available
China and glassware: provided by caterer or local references available
Decorations: early decorating by prior arrangement; some restrictions apply
Audiovisual: limited equipment available upon request; local references provided
Equipment: podium, risers, tables, chairs, and kitchens available
Parking: more than 140 spaces are available on-site
ADA: all facilities are handicap accessible, with the exception of Pleasant Grove Church

LIKE NO OTHER PLACE

Mission Mill is like no other place. Located in downtown Salem, just three blocks from the state Capitol at 13th and Mill Street, Mission Mill offers a startling combination...the convenience of a city location with the pleasurable experience of a charming, five-acre historic site. Mission Mill houses 16 historic buildings and homes, including the Thomas Kay Woolen Mill, all on the National Register of Historic Places. Enjoy the natural lighting and lovely views of the trees and grounds from our five meeting and banquet rooms: the Card Room, Finishing Room, Dye House, Spinning Room, and Pleasant Grove Church. Mission Mill offers a quiet, picturesque atmosphere where you can enjoy a variety of retail shops, dine at the café, picnic along the millrace, or savor our sweetly scented herb garden. Step back in time and feel what life was like at Mission Mill, while satisfying your business needs.

MONTGOMERY PARK

2701 N.W. Vaughn Street
Portland, Oregon 97210
Contact: Paula Person, event director (503) 228-7275
Office Hours: Mon–Fri 8:30am–5pm

Capacity: 15 to 1,200 people (up to 400 seated, 1,200 standing); 15,400 square feet
Price Range: $80 to $2,800
Catering: inside catering contracted to Food in Bloom; outside catering through one of four approved caterers: Jake's, The Best of Everything, Briggs & Crampton, or Eat Your Heart Out
Types of Events: meetings, receptions, trade shows, buffets, corporate events, business parties

Availability and Terms
Montgomery Park has a large banquet facility, a beautiful atrium and two meeting rooms. Deposits or reservation fees may be required. Book up to one year in advance. Available hours are flexible.

Description of Facility and Services
Seating: tables and chairs provided (one setup included in room cost)
Servers: provided by caterer
Bar facilities: bar services and liquor provided by caterer
Dance floor: dance floor in the Atrium accommodates 500+ people with electrical hookup for bands or disc jockeys available
Linens, china and glassware: caterer provides
Decorations: no helium balloons or tape; table decorations must be obtained from caterer, florist, or other source
Cleanup: you must remove all materials you bring in; some or all of your deposit may be kept for damage or extra labor for cleanup
Equipment: podium, easel, table cloths, flip chart, whiteboard, overhead projector, phone service, and full audiovisual service available
Parking: 2,200 free spaces available on weekends and evenings

Special Services
An event coordinator, security or maintenance personnel will be available depending on the time of the event.

SOARING ATRIUM AND MODERN DECOR
Montgomery Park, a beautifully renovated historic building, features a 135-foot soaring atrium, a light airy atmosphere, and a contemporary black-and-white decor. It is an impressive site for your function. Montgomery Park is located in Northwest Portland at the bottom of the northwest hills, providing a beautiful setting for your special event.

Please let this business know that you heard about them from the Bravo! Event Resource Guide.

BANQUET, MEETING & EVENT SITES

MT. HOOD MEADOWS SKI RESORT

*Marketing and Sales Department
1975 S.W. First Avenue, Suite M
Portland, Oregon 97201*

Photography by Steve Wanke

Photography by Brian Robb

Contact: Karen Lite
(503) 287-5438, (800) SKI-HOOD
Business Hours:
Mon–Fri 8am–4:30pm;
evenings by appointment
E-mail: info@skihood.com

Capacity: up to 400 people; on-hill capacity much greater
Price Range: $200 to $1,200 room-rental charge; discounts available with catering
Catering: full-service catering available
Types of Events: meetings, conferences, sit-down, buffet, cocktails and hors d'oeuvres, receptions, hillside picnics, summer or winter outdoor barbecues, ski events

Availability and Terms

With our reputation for superb skiing, many people overlook our meeting and banquet services for winter and summer events. Whether your event takes place in one of our meeting rooms, the slopeside sun deck, or out on the slopes, you're sure to have a truly memorable event. A deposit is required upon booking your reservation, with the remaining balance due ten days prior to the event. Please make reservations as early as possible; however, we will make every effort to accommodate reservations on short notice.

Description of Facility and Services

Seating: tables and chairs provided
Servers: friendly staff included
Bar facilities: full-service bars available
Decorations: by prior arrangement; table pieces at additional cost
Cleanup: provided by Meadows
Audiovisual: equipment available upon request; please inquire for pricing
Activities: skiing, snowboarding, cross-country skiing, snowshoeing, hiking, horse shoes and volleyball
Parking: ample parking available; Sno-Park permit required during the winter months
ADA: fully complied

Special Services

You'll find our friendly and professional staff knows just how important the details are for a wonderful special event. We can tailor your event with audiovisual support, business amenities, catering services, entertainment, meeting planners, tour guides as well as great ski packages.

EXPERIENCE MAGIC ON THE MOUNTAIN AT MEADOWS

Mt. Hood Meadows has a truly magical ambiance all year round. The natural beauty of majestic Mount Hood, framed by snow-covered trees in the winter and green fields with wild flowers in the summer, provides the perfect alpine atmosphere for your next special event.

Visit us on the Web: www.skihood.com
See page 95 under Attractions, Activities & Tours.

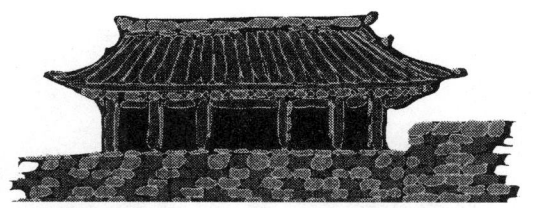

NEW SEOUL GARDEN YAKINIKU KOREAN B.B.Q. KOREAN RESTAURANT AND SALT & PEPPER CLUB

10860 S.W. Beaverton-Hillsdale Highway
Beaverton, Oregon 97005
Contact: Paul Rouse (503) 643-8818; Fax (503) 256-8800
Business Hours: 11am–2am

Capacity: up to 180

Price Range: from $10 to $30 per person depending upon menu and type of event; we have a price to fit any budget while maintaining the high quality expected; room rates also available

Catering: Asian/American cuisine catered in-house; dedicated to high standards, we deliver a menu ranging from convenient hors d'oeuvres to full banquet settings

Types of Events: from the most intimate business meetings and wedding receptions to full-blown car shows, we welcome the challenge to satisfy your needs and demands

Availability and Terms

The room should be reserved as far in advance as possible. A 50% deposit is required upon contract signing and all other terms will be explained at that time.

Description of Facility and Services

Seating: tables and chairs provided
Servers: provided; 18% gratuity requested
Bar facilities: full no-host bar available
Dance floor: large dance floor and stage are available with plenty of electrical outlets; music can be provided by our house DJ at a reasonable cost or you may hire your own DJ; large selection of international music available
Linens and napkins: white tablecloths with peach napkins; other colors available at cost
China and glassware: provided
Decorations: no limitations set; please allow plenty of time to set up prior to the event
Cleanup: provided
Audiovisual: audiovisual aids and podiums can be provided at cost
Parking: large parking lot located in rear of building
ADA: we are completely handicap accessible

EXCELLENCE IN SERVICE AND QUALITY

With a reputation for excellence in service and quality, a friendly staff, and a very competitive price range, you can rest assured that your experience at the New Seoul Garden and Salt & Pepper Lounge will be one of satisfaction and repeated comfort seven days a week. Everything goes better with a little Salt & Pepper.

NORTH STAR BALLROOM

635 N. Killingsworth Court
Portland, Oregon 97217
Contact: Harriet Fasenfest
(503) 240-6088; Fax (503) 240-8229
Business Hours: Mon–Fri 10am–2pm;
or call for an appointment
E-mail: northstar@teleport.com
Web site: www.northstarballroom.com

Capacity: 2400 sq. ft. ballroom, 250 standing, 150 seated; 250 sq. ft. salon/bar accommodates 20; 540 sq. ft. dining room, capacity 50; 350 sq. ft. meeting/reception area, capacity 30; 200 sq. ft. private dressing/meeting room, capacity 10
Price Range: $75–$1,500
Catering: on-site available; outside caterers welcome
Types of Events: private parties, receptions, meetings, retreats, reunions, community events and more

Availability and Terms
A 50% facility deposit is required at the time of reservation. Refundable cleaning/damage deposit required. Deposits are refundable under terms. Rooms may be reserved up to two years in advance.

Description of Facility and Services
Seating: tables and chairs provided for up to 300
Servers: caterer to provide
Bar facilities: bar available; caterer or bar service to provide liquor and liability
Dance floor: large maple floors up to 250; up to 220 volt
Linens and napkins: caterer to provide
China and glassware: caterer to provide
Cleanup: responsibility of caterer
Decorations: upon approval
Audiovisual: arranged for an additional cost
Equipment: stage, piano, podium, easel with large tablet; sound and lighting equipment available
Parking: free off-street parking available; valet parking can be arranged at an additional cost
ADA: handicap ramp to lower level; one handicap accessible bathroom

Special Services
Discounts available to non-profit groups—Sunday through Thursday.

URBAN SOPHISTICATION AND ECLECTIC MEDITERRANEAN STYLE

Looking for a unique place for your next special event? Then discover the hidden treasures of Portland's only "neighborhood villa." Conveniently located just off I-5, less than 10 minutes from downtown, the North Star Ballroom offers a variety of rooms that capture the spirit of its Italian Renaissance architecture.

O'CALLAHAN'S
RESTAURANT & CATERING

at RAMADA INN PORTLAND AIRPORT

6221 N.E. 82nd Avenue
Portland, Oregon 97220
Contact: Ann Conger
(503) 253-2400; Fax (503) 253-1635
Business Hours: Mon–Sat 8am–6pm

BANQUET, MEETING & EVENT SITES

Capacity: Executive Ballroom: 4,200 square feet (divides into 3 rooms); Upstairs Ballroom: 2,820 square feet (divides into 3 rooms); 1 boardroom: 180 square feet
Price Range: each room rents for $195; boardroom $50
Catering: full-service in-house and off-premise catering; references available
Types of Events: meetings, conventions, conferences, trade shows, dinners, banquets, lunches, wedding receptions, company picnics

Availability and Terms
O'Callahan's offers two ballrooms, the Executive Ballroom and the Upstairs Ballroom. Reservations for meetings should be made 30 to 90 days in advance; other events six months to a year in advance. A 25% deposit is required to secure your date with the balance due the day of your event. Credit is available with prior approval. A 60-day cancellation notice is required for deposit refund.

Description of Facility and Services
Seating: chairs for up to 600 guests
Servers: appropriate service staff available
Bar facilities: full-service bar with bartender; portable bar available; liquor liability provided by O'Callahan's
Dance floor: portable dance floor with 550 capacity; 110 and 220 outlet available
Linens and napkins: linen tablecloths and napkins available in a variety of colors
China and glassware: white china; variety of glassware
Decorations: early decorating (two hours prior) available; decorations to match our room colors available; please no scotch tape or thumb tacks
Cleanup: provided by O'Callahan's staff
Audiovisual: available upon request
Equipment: podium, risers, house microphones
Parking: ample free parking
ADA: access to restrooms, elevators and guest rooms

Hotel Accommodations
- **108 Mini Suites:** queen bed, sofa, remote control TV, wet bar, microwave, refrigerator, free HBO, CNN and ESPN
- **94 Deluxe Guest rooms**: two double beds, queen bed or king bed; four parlors

CONVENIENTLY LOCATED
O'Callahan's is located five minutes from Portland International Airport and only ten minutes from downtown Portland (easy access to Interstate 205 and 84).

Please let this business know that you heard about them from the Bravo! Event Resource Guide.

OAKS PARK
HISTORIC DANCE PAVILION
at Oaks Park

Portland, Oregon 97202
Contact: Volanne (503) 233-5777
Business Hours: Mon–Fri 8am–5pm

Capacity: dance pavilion with formal seating for 275; festival setup with dancing for 500; outdoor gazebo area for 1,000

Price Range: pavilion rental for a minimum of three hours at $100 per hour, five hours for $450, 10 hours for $700; outdoor gazebo areas are also available

Catering: our in-house catering menus are individually designed to suit your own taste, personality, and style. Our goal is to give you exactly what you want. If you are using an outside caterer, we will charge you a fee of 20% of their final bill

Types of Events: full-line catering, buffet, hors d'oeuvres, and specialty menus

Availability and Terms
Our indoor facility is available for bookings on any day or evening. Our outdoor gazebo and grounds are extremely popular; please don't hesitate to call and inquire. A deposit of $250 is required on the day of booking.

Description of Facility and Services
Seating: we can formally seat 275 people

Servers: we can provide any equipment necessary and the personnel to guarantee your event will run smoothly and at a level of service you expect

Bar facilities: Oaks Park Association provides liquor at the liability of the renter; it is Oaks Park's policy to provide a staff bartender

Dance floor: 99'x54' dance floor with a capacity for 400 people

Linens and napkins: all colors of linen and cloth napkins and tablecloths available for an additional cost

Decorations: we enjoy your personal style—and offer the bonus of fanciful historic carousel horses

Audiovisual: available upon request

Equipment: podium, easel, and risers available

Parking: ample free parking

ADA: fully complies

A PEACEFUL, TRANQUIL SETTING
Join us at our historic riverside park on the Willamette River and let us create a perfect day or evening event for you and your guests. Our facility is ideal for seminars, retreats, corporate dinners, retirement and holiday parties. Children's Christmas parties are a specialty. It is our policy to work with you and offer exemplary step-by-step service all during the event, allowing you to relax and enjoy the party.

See page 97 under Attractions, Activities & Tours.

THE OLD CHURCH SOCIETY, INC.

1422 S.W. 11th Avenue • Portland, Oregon 97201
Contact: Trish Augustin
(503) 222-2031; Fax (503) 222-2981
Web site: www.oldchurch.org
Business Hours: Mon–Fri 11am–3pm; Sat by appointment

Capacity: up to 300 people
Price Range: price varies according to type and time; call for specific price
Catering: no in-house catering; warming kitchen available; caterer referral list
Types of Events: seminars, business meetings, workshops, concerts, luncheons, teas, weddings, receptions and more

Availability and Terms
Make reservations as early as possible. We can accommodate events on short notice if space and time are available. A 50% rental deposit is expected on booking with the balance payable one month prior to event.

Description of Facility and Services
Seating: pew type seating in auditorium; tables and chairs set up to your specifications for Kinsman Hall, Lannie Hurst Parlour and Jackson Hall
Servers: referrals available
Bar facilities: renter provides bartender and liquor liability; OLCC permit required; please call for detailed alcohol policies
Stage: auditorium features 12'x25' stage with podium, lighting, concert quality grand piano, and beautiful antique Hook and Hastings tracker organ
Dance floor: available on request
Linens and napkins: available from caterer or you provide
China and glassware: available from your caterer or you provide; two large coffee urns and two large punch bowls available
Decorations: please inquire about restrictions and early decorating
Setup and cleanup: provided by The Old Church
Audiovisual: we offer some audiovisual equipment; call for details
Equipment: podium and easel available; overhead projector, slide projector
Parking: street parking, City Center and U-Park lots nearby; lots can be reserved
ADA: wheelchair ramp available

Special Services
Our goal is to assist you in planning a successful and memorable event. We will be happy to refer you to other services such as caterers, musicians, florist, etc. An Old Church staff person is on-site to offer assistance during your entire event.

A UNIQUE GATHERING PLACE
The Old Church has been a Portland landmark since its completion in 1883. On the National Register of Historic Places since 1972, it no longer is a dedicated church, but serves Portland as a unique community facility. Concerts, conferences, seminars, workshops and weddings are but a few of the activities it houses. Our professional staff is dedicated to assure you a successful event. Call to arrange for a tour and discuss your upcoming event.

OREGON CITY GOLF CLUB

20124 S. Beavercreek Road • Oregon City, Oregon 97045
Contact: Event Coordinator
(503) 656-2846
Business Hours: Mon–Sun 8am–6pm
E-mail: OCGCI@aol.com

Capacity: 125 seated; 160 standing; can accommodate additional guests depending on season
Price Range: $200 to $1,000
Catering: we work with an approved list of caterers
Types of Events: meetings, seminars, retirements, private parties, tournaments, birthdays, graduations, wedding receptions, bridal showers, baby showers

Availability and Terms
We suggest that you reserve as early as possible but we are sometimes able to accommodate parties on short notice. A deposit is required to secure your date.

Description of Facility and Services
Seating: round or adjustable tables with double padded white chairs for 125+ guests
Servers: appropriate staff will be provided
Bar facilities: host or no-host; beer, wine, champagne available; bartenders provided; compliance with all local and state liquor laws; liquor liability provided
Dance floor: available; CD player provided; electrical available
Linens: linens available; a variety of colors available from caterer for an additional cost
China and glassware: clear glass china available; variety of crystal glassware available
Cleanup: provided by Oregon City Golf Club
Decorations: no staples, nails, tacks or tape; artist's putty may be used
Parking: free parking
ADA: yes

Special Services
Our event coordinator will work with you in planning and executing all details, to make your event a total success.

SOCIAL EVENTS TO TOURNAMENTS
Oregon City Golf Club was built in 1922 and is the third oldest public golf course in the State of Oregon still in operation. With our newly remodeled clubhouse and banquet facility, we can handle all of your social events and tournament needs.

2820 S.E. Ferry Slip Road
Newport, Oregon 97365
Contact: Events Office
(541) 867-3474 ext. 5221
Fax (541) 867-6846
Business Hours:
summer 9am–6pm; winter 10am–5pm
E-mail: cem@aquarium.org
Web site: http://www.aquarium.org

OREGON COAST AQUARIUM

Capacity: 15-100 seated, 30-500 reception/dinner throughout exhibit galleries
Price Range: please call for specific price and catering information
Catering: exclusive full-service, in-house catering available
Types of Events: elegant sit-down dinners, progressive dinners throughout the galleries, barbecues, buffets, wedding receptions, holiday parties, corporate functions, etc.

Availability and Terms

The lobby, overlooking an estuary (2,140 square feet) with vaulted ceilings and bay windows, is perfect for elegant sit-down dinners and receptions. Four indoor galleries provide opportunities for strolling buffets and cocktail parties. The Sandy Shores gallery (1,360 square feet) features exhibits including leopard sharks, skates and sea pens. A touch pool in the Rocky Shores gallery (1,051 square feet) permits guests to gently handle tide pool animals. The Coastal Waters gallery (1,125 square feet) features our largest indoor exhibit, a wall-to-wall salmon and sturgeon display. Moon jellies and sea nettles are also focal points in the Coastal Waters gallery. The Wetlands and New Currents gallery features educational traveling exhibits. Slide presentations or lectures can be held in the US West Whale Theater (1,037 square feet).

The Oregon Coast Aquarium is available for booking year-round. All exhibits are open for after-hours events. A 20% deposit is required upon booking, with balance due within two weeks of event.

Description of Facility and Services

Seating: tables and chairs provided
Servers: provided by in-house caterer
Bar facilities: full-service bar available/OLCC regulated
Dance floor: provided upon request; 110-volt hookups available
Linens: linen tablecloths and napkins available in assorted colors at no cost
China and glassware: white china and stemmed glassware provided
Decorations: all decorations must be approved in advance
Audiovisual and equipment: available upon request
Cleanup: provided
Parking: ample free parking
ADA: yes

NEVER THE SAME PLACE TWICE— OREGON COAST AQUARIUM

Named one of the top 10 aquariums in the nation by *Parade* Magazine, the Oregon Coast Aquarium offers the perfect setting for your special event. In June 2000 you'll experience an underwater adventure leading you on a journey through shark infested waters—all in the safety of a 200-foot acrylic walkway nestled deep beneath our simulated sea. Adjacent to the exhibit is an elegant banquet space with a large viewing window that looks back into the spectacular exhibit, and a viewing deck overlooking the picturesque Yaquina Bay.

SILVERTON, OREGON

879 W. Main Street • P.O. Box 155
Silverton, Oregon 97381
Contact: Tamara Muldoon
(503) 874-8100; Fax (503) 874-8200
Office Hours: Mon–Fri 8am–5pm
Web site: www.oregongarden.org

Capacity: J. Frank Schmidt Jr. Pavilion: banquets to 600; receptions to 1,200;
  Event Lawn: outdoor banquet seating to 1,000, picnics/receptions to 2,000;
  Teufel Amphitheater: outdoor concert amphitheater, lawn seating to 2,500
Price Range: rental rates vary; please call for a quote
Catering: full-service catering is available; custom menus on request
Types of Events: banquets, receptions, meetings, seminars, retreats, reunions, trade shows, company picnics, parties, fund raisers, dances, concerts

Availability and Terms
The Pavilion's indoor halls and outdoor event spaces are available independently or in conjunction. A deposit is required to guarantee a space reservation.

Description of Facility and Services
Seating: tables and chairs for up to 400; additional seating can be rented
Servers: provided by caterer
Bar facilities: full bar service available; minimum sales or fee required
Dance floor: use existing floor surface, or rent portable wooden dance floor
China and glassware: provided by caterer
Linens and napkins: provided by caterer
Decorations: some restrictions; please discuss with event coordinator
Audiovisual and equipment: available on request for additional charge
Cleanup: provided by facility; included in rental fee
Parking: free on-site parking; subject to availability and parking capacity
ADA: all event spaces are accessible

Special Services
We are happy to provide a presentation and/or guided tour of the Oregon Garden as a part of your event at no charge.

OREGON'S NEWEST GARDEN ATTRACTION
The Oregon Garden is a world-class botanical display garden currently under construction in Silverton, just 15 miles northeast of Salem. The Garden will showcase Oregon's rich botanical heritage and serve as an education and research resource for the region. Although the Garden will not officially open until 2001, its unique event venues are now complete and open for business. Let us help you plan your next event at the Oregon Garden!

25700 S.W. Pete's Mountain Road
West Linn, Oregon 97068
Contact: Catering Department (503) 650-6900
Business Hours: 8:30am–5pm
Web site: www.oregongolfclub.com

Capacity: meeting rooms to accommodate 12 to 500 people
Price Range: price varies depending on room, day and menu
Catering: full-service, in-house catering
Types of Events: sit-down, buffet, cocktail and hors d'oeuvres, breakfast and lunch meetings, corporate parties, corporate golf tournaments, reunions

Availability and Terms
Please make reservations as early as possible. Four rooms are available to meet your specific needs. A deposit is required; payment is due seven days in advance.

Description of Facility and Services
Seating: tables and chairs provided for up to 500
Bar facilities: full-bar service provided
Dance floor: 18' X 18' floor; electrical available
Linens and napkins: provided; in all colors
China: fine white china provided
Decorations: we will be happy to discuss your specific needs
Audiovisual: available; please inquire
Equipment: podium, stage, easel, flip chart, dry erase board; please inquire about charges
Cleanup: provided by The Oregon Golf Club
Parking: free parking
ADA: disabled accessible

Nestled in the Willamette Valley against a backdrop of the majestic Cascade Mountain Range, The Oregon Golf Club boasts an exceptional reputation. Inspired by the Scottish traditions of golf's birthplace and enlivened by the beauty of the Pacific Northwest, our spectacular facility is an ideal location for your business meeting, golf tournament or corporate party. Treat your business associates to a party they'll remember for years to come. If you want to present a new product or just congratulate your staff for a job well done, you will find our private country club setting, the natural beauty and charm, the exceptional service and attention to detail will allow you to have a first-class event that you and your guests will thoroughly enjoy.

OREGON MUSEUM OF SCIENCE AND INDUSTRY

*1945 S.E. Water Avenue
Portland, Oregon 97214
Contact: Event Sales Office
(503) 797-4671; Fax (503) 797-4566
Event Sales: by appointment*

Capacity: 50 to 4,000
Price Range: call for cost estimates on rental fees and catering
Catering: exclusive, full-service in-house catering available; creative menus are based on budget requirements and/or type of food and beverages requested
Types of Events: social events; receptions set among the exhibits as well as sit-down breakfasts, luncheons and dinners; most areas offer a spectacular view of the downtown city skyline and the river

Availability and Terms
The riverfront science center has five exhibit halls: Turbine Hall, Changing Exhibit Hall, High Tech Hall, Life Science Hall and Earth Science Hall. For additional space and entertainment the Auditorium, Copeland Lumber Dining Room, Outdoor Courtyard, Murdock Planetarium and OMNIMAX® Theater are also available. A 50% nonrefundable deposit of estimated charges is due upon signing an agreement. The balance is due three days prior to your event.

Description of Facility and Services
Seating: tables and chairs in current inventory are available for use at no additional charge. Any equipment that OMSI does not have may be rented for you at an additional cost.
Bar facilities and servers: provided by Fine Host Corporation
Dance floor: may be rented from outside source
Linens and china: our Event Sales department strives to create events that are visually stunning. We provide a wide variety of specialty linens, china, tableware, and floral arrangements that will make your event at OMSI stand alone.
Parking: no charge
ADA: meets all ADA requirements

Special Services
Our experienced event planners will assist you with virtually all planning aspects of your event. Creative menu planning, outstanding service, specialty decor expertise and close attention to detail will provide you with a magnificent event—one your guests will not soon forget.

OMSI'S WORLD CLASS SCIENCE CENTER
OMSI's world class science center is available for private special events and meetings. The museum features interactive hands-on exhibits that will educate, entertain, and amaze your guests. Also featured: an OMNIMAX® Theater that shows educationally rich and thrilling motion pictures on its five-story domed screen; the Murdock Planetarium that features astronomy and laser light shows; and a 219' submarine that is available for tours.

**Visit our Web site:
www.omsi.edu/geninfo/eventsales**

Please let this business know that you heard about them from the Bravo! Event Resource Guide.

OREGON SPORTS HALL OF FAME MUSEUM

321 S.W. Salmon Street
Portland, Oregon 97204
Contact: Janice Carter, Operations Director
(503) 227-7466 ext. 10
Business Hours: 10am–6pm Tue–Sun

Capacity: up to 300 for stand-up receptions; seated capacity varies
Price Range: price varies based on event type and size
Catering: preferred list of caterers available
Type of Events: receptions, fund raisers, dinners, parties, retirement, holiday events, award ceremonies

Availability and Terms

The museum is available for special events after normal business hours. A 50% rental deposit and signed contract reserves the space.

Description of Facility and Services

Seating: 10 eight-foot tables; 75 chairs
Servers: provided by caterer
Bar facilities: provided by caterer
Dance floor: please inquire with event coordinator
Linens: provided by caterer
China: provided by caterer
Decorations: limitations apply; we welcome your ideas
Cleanup: provided by caterer and museum staff
Audiovisual: please call to discuss needs
Equipment: please call to discuss needs
Parking: after-hours parking available in the Standard Insurance Center parking garage or in several other conveniently located garages; located three blocks from MAX
ADA: fully accessible

MAKE YOUR NEXT PARTY ONE THEY'LL ALWAYS REMEMBER

The Oregon Sports Hall of Fame and Museum is an exciting, world-class museum located in the heart of downtown Portland. The colorful, energetic decor captivates every visitor. The highly interactive and emotional exhibitry entertains and educates guests on the fabulous history of Oregon sports. Museum exhibits range from the Oregon Sports Timeline to Terry Baker's Heisman Trophy to catching a fastball. The museum has been designed specifically to accommodate private use. Two highly adaptable multi-media theater screens anchor the 3,000-square-foot Grand Hall. The 17-foot ceiling lends to the visual drama and excitement that this conveniently located venue offers.

Please call our operations director at (503) 227-7466 extension 10 to arrange a tour to see for yourself the possibilities of this exciting venue.

OREGON ZOO

4001 S.W. Canyon Road
Portland, Oregon 97221
Contact: Gary Wilson or Lisa Schur
(503) 220-2789; Fax (503) 220-3689
E-mail: zoocatering@metro.dst.or.us
Business Hours: Mon–Fri 8:30am–5pm

The Oregon Zoo has always been a unique place for special events. Our banquet center is a venue that is sure to please everyone. Big, bold, high-tech, yet intimate in Cascadian-style, the room will accommodate up to 500 people for banquets or up to 800 reception guests. Warm colors, rich textures, and thick, plush carpets will ensure the comfort of your clients and guests. High-tech compatibility will help you make your presentations shine.

Join the people who have discovered the Zoo as Portland's ideal event site. With plenty of space for statewide or regional functions, our banquet center will give you the feel of a Northwest lodge, delicious cuisine, and a walk on the wild side. The Oregon Zoo is located on the MAX light rail only five minutes from downtown. A portion of all event fees is used in endangered species research and protection.

Capacity: indoor up to 800; outdoor up to 6,000
Price Range: price varies according to menu selections
Catering: in-house catering
Types of Events: reunions, corporate events, meetings, trade shows, seminars, outdoor barbecues, indoor banquets, theme parties… anything is possible!

Availability and Terms

Our banquet center can accommodate up to 800 people. Our outdoor site can accommodate groups up to 6,000. A deposit is required to confirm reservations. Book early, as our facilities are very popular.

Description of Facility and Services

Seating: tables and chairs provided for up to 500 guests
Servers: provided by the zoo
Bar facilities: host or no-host bars available
Dance floor: we can rent one for your event for an additional fee
Linens and napkins: assorted colors of tablecloths and napkins
China and glassware: provided for indoor events; can be rented for outdoor events
Cleanup: included in catering cost
Audiovisual: equipment available upon request
Equipment: podiums, risers, and easels available
Parking: large lot adjacent to the entrance
ADA: fully complied
Lightrail station: 50 yards from zoo entrance

Special Services

The Oregon Zoo offers complete special event planning services. Animals and zoo program staff can visit your event for an extra charge. Train rides can be arranged.

PARADIGM CONFERENCE CENTER

3009 S.E. Chestnut St. • Milwaukie, Oregon 97267
Contact: Clem or Mark
(503) 654-6426; Fax (503) 654-3929
Business Hours: 9:30am–6pm daily

Capacity: up to 290 seated
Price Range: varies depending on time of event and services
Catering: in-house full-service catering; sit-down meals, buffet or hors d'oeuvres
Types of Events: conferences, seminars, retreats, trade shows, banquets, auctions and parties

Availability and Terms
A deposit is required. Please call our sales office for more information; corporate accounts welcomed.

Description of Facility and Services
Seating: tables and chairs provided for up to 290
Servers: provided by Paradigm
Bar facilities: host/no host bar provided by Paradigm
Dance floor: available at no charge
China and glassware: provided by Paradigm
Linens and napkins: provided by Paradigm
Decorations: please ask about limitations
Audiovisual: state-of-the-art capabilities
Equipment: podium, risers and staging available
Cleanup: provided by Paradigm staff
Parking: ample free parking available
ADA: yes

SHIFT TO EXCELLENCE
Our elegant and functional ballroom can be divided into three self-contained meeting rooms. A total of five rooms are available. Our relaxing, park-like refuge enhances creativity and productivity. Paradigm Conference Center is a unique setting on nearly two beautifully landscaped acres accented with ponds, waterfalls and gardens. The Paradigm is located only ten minutes from downtown Portland. Our staff will make your next meeting memorable and stress-free. Call today for a tour!

BANQUET, MEETING & EVENT SITES

HOTEL VINTAGE PLAZA

422 S.W. Broadway • Portland, Oregon 97205
Contact: Private Dining (503) 412-6316
Business Hours: Mon–Fri 9am–5pm

Capacity: 200 people reception; 140 people seated
Price Range: prices vary; call for details
Catering: full-service in-house and off-premise catering from Pazzo Ristorante
Types of Events: sit-down, buffet, hors d'oeuvres, receptions, corporate meetings

Availability and Terms
The Hotel Vintage Plaza has banquet rooms available to accommodate functions of many sizes. These rooms are located on the second floor of the hotel and display the same European decor seen throughout the hotel lobby, restaurant, and guest rooms. Also available is the Pazzo Cellar which has the capacity for seating up to 72 guests, 80 for a reception The Pazzoria bakery can accommodate up to 25 people for an evening event. We encourage you to reserve as soon as possible to secure your desired date. A nonrefundable deposit is required to confirm your space.

Description of Facility and Services
Seating: up to 80
Servers: serving attendants available; 18% gratuity
Bar facilities: full-service bar with liquor, beer, and wine provided
Linens: tablecloths and napkins available in ivory, specialty colors available upon request
China and glassware: ivory china; sheer-rim wine glasses
Decorations: no tape or nails may be placed in wall covering or ceiling
Cleanup: included in catering charges
Audiovisual and meeting equipment: available upon request
Parking: valet parking available; $5 per car for short-term parking; $15 per call for all day; parking garage located across the street for self-park
ADA: fully complied

Guest Rooms
Hotel Vintage Plaza has 107 guest rooms and suites. Each evening the hotel serves an Oregon Wine Reception in the lobby. Call (503) 412-6312 for details.

Meeting Space
Eight conference rooms with a total of 4,800 square feet accommodate from 10 to 100 people reception-style; up to 80 people banquet-style; and 60 classroom-style. Audiovisual services and event coordinator on site and a fully equipped executive gym.

NORTHERN ITALIAN IN SUMPTUOUS STYLE
From the warm and friendly greetings of the doorman to the pampering from our wait staff, our guests experience cozy European elegance and personalized service. Pazzo Ristorante offers exquisite food that embraces the warmth of Northern Italian cuisine with artistic presentation and quality services. We will be happy to assist you in custom designing a menu to meet the needs of your function.

See page 359 under Hotel Accommodations.

PERSIMMON COUNTRY CLUB

500 S.E. Butler Road • Gresham, Oregon 97080
Contact: Events Coordinator (503) 667-7500
Business Hours: Mon–Fri 8am–5pm
Web site: http://www.persimmongolf.com

Capacity: Conference Room up to 12; Restaurant up to 110; Banquet Room up to 300
Price Range: varies
Catering: in-house by Persimmon Grille
Types of Events: golf outings/tournaments, business meetings, trade shows, conventions, seminars, holiday parties, barbecues, retreats, weddings

Availability and Terms
We suggest that you reserve space up to one year in advance; however, we can accommodate on shorter notice when space allows. A deposit is required to reserve space.

Description of Facility and Services
Seating: tables and chairs provided for up to 300 for meals; 500 lounge-style
Servers: included in catering cost
Bar facilities: Persimmon has alcoholic beverages and bartender available
Dance floor: accommodations available; electrical outlets available
China and glassware: white china; glass or plastic beverage ware available
Linens and napkins: white tablecloths and napkins; colors available at additional charge
Decorations: please inquire with events coordinator
Cleanup: courtesy of Persimmon
Audiovisual: available at additional charge
Parking: free on-site parking
ADA: fully complied

Special Services
Persimmon provides impeccable attention to all the details of your special-event needs.

THE PERFECT SETTING FOR ANY EVENT
Persimmon can accommodate a variety of functions in a relaxed, elegant environment set on over 375 pristine acres with spectacular views of Mount Hood. At Persimmon, you will find quality service and outstanding cuisine.

Pittock Mansion

3229 N.W. Pittock Drive
Portland, Oregon 97210
(503) 823-3623

Capacity: reception 200; seated dining for 50
Price Range: very reasonable; please call to discuss your needs
Catering: a list of recommended caterers is offered
Types of Events: receptions, dinners, and presentations for businesses and non-profit organizations

Availability and Terms
The Mansion is available only in the evenings and only to organized community or business groups. A $200 deposit will hold your date.

Description of Facility and Services
Seating: tables and chairs for up to 50
Servers: provided by caterer
Bar facilities: provided by caterer
Linens: provided by caterer
China and glassware: provided by caterer
Decorations: Pittock Mansion is fully decorated with beautiful antiques and offers interesting self-guided tours
Audiovisual: slide projector, laser pointer, table, screen, TV, and VCR available for additional fee
Equipment: podium
Parking: ample free parking
ADA: largely compliant

Special Services
An experienced event coordinator is available throughout the evening to help your event run smoothly. A grand piano is available in the beautiful French Renaissance drawing room.

AN INCOMPARABLE EXPERIENCE AWAITS

Enjoy the magnificent splendor of Portland's Pittock Mansion during your next evening event. Located five minutes from downtown, this beautifully restored 16,000-square-foot French chateauesque mansion offers an incomparable experience of architectural delight, beautiful antiques, fine art and natural beauty with truly inspiring views.

Imagine enjoying the truly unique blend of history, beauty and romance Pittock Mansion offers for your entertaining pleasure.

PORTLAND INTERNATIONAL AIRPORT CONFERENCE CENTER
PORT OF PORTLAND

7000 N.E. Airport Way
Portland, Oregon 97218
Contact: Paula Sorensen, manager (503) 460-4051
Business Hours: Mon–Fri 8am–5pm
Web site: http://www.portlandairportpdx.com

Capacity: PDX Conference Center has five conference rooms varying in size from 173 square feet to 1,061 square feet; accommodates up to 100 people
Price Range: day and hourly rates available; please call for details
Catering: in-house catering only
Types of Events: meetings, seminars, receptions, small banquets

Availability and Terms
Advance notice is recommended. No deposits are required. Credit cards are accepted; invoicing available. A 48-hour cancellation notice is required to avoid a $25 fee.

Description of Facility and Services
Seating: various setup styles available
Servers: appropriate staff for event
Bar facilities: liquor available; fee charged for bartender
China and glassware: white china and glassware provided at no extra charge
Audiovisual: TV/VCR, slide projector, overhead projectors, computer projection, microphones, in-house sound and lighting system, In Focus, Laptops
Equipment: podium, lecterns, easels at no extra charge
Parking: short-term, economy, or parking garage
ADA: complies with ADA standards

Special Servicesx
On-site staffed business center, notary service, private workstations, data ports, office supplies, computer rental and Internet access available

JUST MINUTES FROM AIRLINE GATES

The PDX Conference Center is conveniently located in the airport terminal, on the mezzanine level, just minutes from airline gates. The conference center offers architecturally stunning and contemporary furnished meeting rooms. Rooms include speaker phones, data ports, whiteboards and electronic screens. Business services are conveniently located on-site to meet your office needs. Knowledgeable and customer service oriented staff is available to assist with planning your catering and meeting needs and business services whether you need faxing, photocopying or last-minute word processing.

PORTLAND ART MUSEUM
NORTH WING

1119 S.W. Park Avenue
Portland, Oregon 97205-2486
Contact: Food and Beverage Manager
(503) 226-2811 Ext. 4291
Business Hours: Mon–Thurs 10am–4pm;
Call for an appointment

The Portland Art Museum's North Wing Building offers unique and magnificent rooms for any kind of gathering. Situated in the heart of Portland's Park Blocks, this architectural beauty features two large ballrooms, one banquet room and several meeting rooms—each with a gracious and distinctive style. Arrangements can be made to view the current exhibition or tour galleries in conjunction with your event.

Capacity: 15 to 1,000 with very flexible configurations; or the entire building for up to 1,500

Price Range: varies according to room; please call for specific information

Catering: choose from list of preferred caterers

Types of Events: every imaginable possibility, from business meetings, seminars, training sessions and fund raisers, to holiday parties, elegant receptions, full dress balls, weddings, and more.

Availability and Terms
Reserve your room up to one year in advance. A deposit confirms your reservation. Liability insurance and nominal security fee are required.

Description of Facility and Services
Seating: tables and chairs available; choose from a variety of floor plans
Dance floor: hardwood dance floors in all ballrooms
Bar service: available through caterer
Decorations: elegant facilities need little decoration
Parking: available on street or in several nearby lots
ADA: accessible

**Reserve the Portland Art Museum
for a truly artful affair!**

PORTLAND CENTER FOR THE PERFORMING ARTS

1111 S.W. Broadway • Portland, Oregon 97205
Contact: Booking & Sales Department (503) 248-4335
E-mail: lorileyba@oregoncc.org; Web site: www.pcpa.com

Capacity: Arlene Schnitzer Concert Hall: theater—2,776 seats, lobby—up to 400; Portland Civic Auditorium: theater—2,992 seats, lobby—up to 500; Newmark Theatre—880 seats; Dolores Winningstad Theatre—292 seats; New Theatre Building lobby—up to 800
Price Range: determined by event
Catering: on-site: Aramark Corporation and several others; list of approved caterers available upon request
Types of Events: performances, meetings, conferences, seminars, lectures, receptions, sit-down dinners, weddings, galas, trade shows

Availability and Terms
Terms and conditions vary with each event.

Description of Facility and Services
Seating: 250 banquet chairs available at $2.50 each; caterer provides tables
Bar facilities: caterer provides bar and liquor
Linens: caterer provides
China: caterer provides
Decorations: no helium balloons, nails, tape, glue, open flames
Audiovisual: available from local providers
Equipment: lectern, risers, staging available as needed
Cleanup: provided at no additional charge
Parking: available in one of several adjacent parking lots and garages
ADA: meets ADA requirements; infrared listening systems in all theaters as well as handicapped seating

Special Services
A professional staff, excellent in-house and approved caterers, all four theaters complete with both light and sound equipment, as well as dressing rooms and backstage areas.

DISTINCTIVE VENUES FOR BUSINESS AND SOCIAL EVENTS
Located in the heart of downtown Portland and the Cultural District, PCPA's four distinctive performance venues and three beautifully-designed lobby spaces are equipped to meet the needs of business and social events alike. With fully-equipped stages and professional IATSE stage crew, PCPA staff will guarantee a successful event every time! The Arlene Schnitzer Concert Hall's elegant and ornate Rococo-style Grand Lobby is the perfect setting for weddings, dinner parties and galas; in the New Theatre Building's Rotunda Lobby, situated beneath the beautiful and sparkling Spectral Light Dome, any social event will fit perfectly. With Main Street Plaza and its unique ornamental paving situated between the concert hall and New Theatre Building, a special "courtyard" can be created for guests to wander through—a delightful treat on a summer evening.

See page 121 under Calendar of Events.

Please let this business know that you heard about them from the Bravo! Event Resource Guide.

PORTLAND CONFERENCE CENTER

300 N.E. Multnomah Street • Portland, Oregon 97232
Contact: Sales Coordinator (503) 239-9921
Business Hours: Mon–Fri 8am–5pm or by appointment
E-mail: info@portlandcc.com
Web site: www.portlandcc.com

Capacity: 700 reception, 400 banquet, 630 auditorium, 440 classroom; 12 rooms ranging from 475 to 4,600 square feet; 15,000 net square feet total
Price Range: price varies depending on room, day and menu
Catering: full range of in-house catering services; off-site catering available; we will customize a menu with you or you may choose one of our Chef's suggested menus.
Types of Events: business meetings, seminars, conferences, trainings, trade shows, special celebrations, parties, receptions, proms, corporate functions

Availability and Terms
Reserve early for your desired date. We can accommodate events on short notice if space is available. A 50% room deposit is expected upon booking.

Description of Facility and Services
Seating: tables and chairs provided
Servers: provided
Bar facilities: host/no-host bar(s); non-alcoholic beverages available; liability provided
Dance floor: built in and portable dance floor; electrical hookups for band or DJ
Linens and napkins: variety of colors available included with catering
China and glassware: white china and glassware provided with catering
Equipment: complete line of audiovisual equipment available; large stage available in our Bridges Ballroom
Parking: ample parking available and MAX light-rail stops at our door
ADA: main and lower level fully comply

"YOUR EVENT IS AS IMPORTANT TO US AS IT IS TO YOU"
WHAT OUR CLIENTS ARE SAYING...

"We liked the fact that we could trust you to do a professional job."
~ Wedding Reception

"I heard nothing but wonderful reviews about the quality and quantity of food. This was the most enjoyable part of organizing the festival—working with you folks. I will recommend you highly when we return to Portland."
~ N.W. Music Educators

"Excellent service. Everyone responded most promptly and courteously."
~ Bonneville Power Administration

"Your facilities give a touch of class. We were proud to invite and host Kiwanis from all over the Northwest."
~ Kiwanis Club of Portland

PORTLAND SPIRIT
WILLAMETTE STAR
CRYSTAL DOLPHIN

110 S.E. Caruthers • Portland, Oregon 97213
(503) 224-3900, (800) 224-3901
E-mail: sales@portlandspirit.com
Web site: http://www.portlandspirit.com

From a luncheon meeting for 25 to an elegant sit down dinner cruise for 340, the Portland Spirit will provide you with *Excellence in River Cruise Dining*. The **Portland Spirit, Willamette Star, and Crystal Dolphin** feature first-class sailing, serving Northwest cuisine freshly prepared on board in each ship's galley. Our event planning services ensure that not one detail is overlooked.

Availability, Price and Terms
The Portland Spirit vessels are available year-round from downtown Portland. You may charter the entire **Portland Spirit** vessel or one deck rentals are available. The **Portland Spirit** also offers public cruise schedules. The **Willamette Star** and **Crystal Dolphin** are available for private charter. Prices depend on time of day, season of year and number of guests. NOTE: Capacity recommendations on each vessel depend on time of year, menu selected and type of event planned. Please call for specific recommendations.

Portland Spirit
130 foot, three level yacht, two outside decks
Available for full boat charter, one deck rental
Capacity: up to 540 guests
Seating: tables and chairs for 350, plus outside seating
Dance floor: large marble dance floor

Crystal Dolphin
130 foot, three level yacht, two outside decks
Available for private charter
Capacity: 90 guests
Seating: tables and chairs for 40, plus outside seating

Willamette Star
75 foot, two level yacht, two outside decks
Available for private charter
Capacity: up to 120 guests
Seating: tables and chairs for 80, plus outside seating
Dance floor: available

Description of Vessel Services and Facilities
Enclosed decks are temperature controlled
Linens: linen tablecloths and napkins provided
China: our house china and glassware provided
Servers: included with food and bar service
Bar facilities: full service bar, liquor, bartenders and liability insurance
Equipment: podium and easel available
Audiovisual: equipment available upon request
Cleanup: provided
Parking: commercial and street parking available
ADA: limited with assistance

12930 Old Pumpkin Ridge Road
North Plains, Oregon 97133
Contact: Catering Director
(503) 647-4747; Fax (503) 647-2002
Business Hours: 8:30am–5pm
Web site: www.pumpkinridge.com

Ghost Creek Golf Course at Pumpkin Ridge, where...*the rest of the world can wait.*
Set on the edge of the beautiful Willamette Valley, yet convenient to downtown Portland, Ghost Creek offers a stunning setting for your special event. The gracious 18,000 sq. ft. clubhouse features dramatic architecture and an old Portland flavor. Ghost Creek Sunset Room, with open beam ceilings, skylights and a generous deck, is a spacious banquet facility offering a panoramic view of our championship courses. Our catering department offers professional event planning and culinary expertise. Every meeting, tournament, and banquet will be made memorable by its unique artistry and style. Our mission is to provide the utmost in customer service with a knowledgeable staff dedicated to fulfilling your every need.

Capacity: accommodates up to 200 guests; 250 with use of adjoining outdoor deck
Price Range: price varies according to menu selection
Catering: full-service, in-house catering
Types of Events: formal and casual sit-down, buffet, cocktail and hors d'oeuvres; breakfast and lunch meetings, corporate parties, corporate golf tournaments, reunions, receptions, holiday parties and all special occasions

Availability and Terms
Please inquire. A deposit is required; payment is due on or before the day of your event.

Descriptions of Facilities and Services
Seating: tables and chairs provided for up to 250 guests
Servers: service staff included in catering cost; 20% service charge is added to all food and beverage selections
Bar facilities: full-service bar provided
Dance floor: parquet dance floor available in a variety of sizes
Linens and napkins: provided; available in a variety of colors
China and glassware: provided
Decorations: please inquire; we look forward to discussing your specific needs
Audiovisual: available; please inquire
Equipment: podium, flip charts, microphone, overhead projector, fax machine available
Cleanup: provided by Pumpkin Ridge Golf Club
Parking: convenient free parking
ADA: wheelchair access to all rooms

Special Services
Complete golf outings, tournament packages, and golf schools for groups of all sizes available at Ghost Creek Golf Course, named the Best New Public Course of 1992 by *Golf Digest*.

RED LION HOTEL®
VANCOUVER (At the Quay)
100 Columbia Street • Vancouver, WA 98660
360-694-8341 • Fax: 360-694-2023
www.redlion.com

Capacity: 14 meeting rooms; largest room, 7,500 square feet, will seat up to 450 guests classroom style and 700 guests theater style
Price Range: varies depending on type of event and meal service
Catering: full-service in-house catering exclusively
Types of Events: full array of meeting and social functions, including small conferences and state-wide conventions

Availability and Terms
Please contact the sales and catering office to discuss space availability and terms.

Description of Facility and Services
Seating: tables and chairs provided
Servers: staff included in catering costs
Bar facilities: full beverage service; hotel provides all alcoholic beverages
Dance floor: complimentary; electrical outlets available
Linens and napkins: linen tablecloths and napkins in a variety of colors at no additional charge
China and glassware: white china; stemmed glassware
Decorations: lattice, silk plants, votive candles, and bud vases available; access for early decorating by prior arrangement
Cleanup: provided by hotel staff
Audiovisual: in-house services provided by Presentation Services
Equipment: podiums, risers, and staging available at no charge
Parking: complimentary
ADA: all meeting rooms are accessible

Special Services
The Red Lion Hotel at the Quay offers 160 guest rooms and 3 suites. Your guests will enjoy the many "extras," including coffee, coffee maker, iron and ironing board available in each room, no access charge for calling card calls and upgraded terrycloth towels. Special group rates are available for ten or more rooms per night.

EXPERIENCE THE DIFFERENCE
By selecting the Red Lion at the Quay, you will benefit from our unique and dramatic setting on the Columbia River, as well as our professional meeting coordinators, who will assist you with all your planning needs. From menu planning to room decor and design, our experienced and friendly staff are trained to ensure a memorable and worry-free event. Our convenient location at the Washington/Oregon border situates us perfectly to draw attendees from both states. Experience the difference of the Red Lion at the Quay and your success is assured!

Regal Hall Ballroom
at
A Night in Shining Amour

115 W. Ninth Street
Vancouver, Washington 98660
Contact: Joe and Pam Thielman
(360) 750-7891
E-mail: jthielm@pacifier.com
Web site: www.shining-amour.com

Capacity: theatre style: 120; reception: 175; meetings and other events depend on type of setup required
Price Range: varies depending on event and length of time needed; please call
Catering: full range of catering services can be provided or you can self cater your event with a deposit
Types of Events: specializing in weddings and receptions, management retreats, banquets, employee parties, meetings, seminars, and privately catered family gatherings

Availability and Terms
Call for availability. A 50% deposit is required at time of booking based on the time required at a rate of $150 per hour for the first four hours and $90 per hour after the initial four hours. Balance is due one week prior to event. Lower prices are available during the week.

Description of Facility and Services
Seating: all-white wooden chairs with padded seats, rectangular or round tables available and seating arranged as requested
Servers: provided, or as you desire
Bar facilities: arranged on request
Dance floor: beautiful hardwood flooring makes the entire ballroom-area a wonderful place to dance
Linen: provided
China: available for rent or you provide
Decorations: beautiful white and gold decor accommodates a wide variety of color schemes
Cleanup: provided or extra charge, depending on package
Parking: street side and several parking lots and garages nearby
Audiovisual: available
ADA: complied

About Us
We are Pam and Joe Thielman and will serve as the host/hostess of your function, attending to every detail, if you wish. We endeavor to remain as flexible as possible regarding our service to you. We have many resources available to make your event the best it can be and will work with you to control your costs.

Built in 1910, the building has been remodeled, giving it an ambiance and charm of style and grace. You will find the ballroom a wonderful place for your special event.

THE RESERVE
VINEYARDS AND GOLF CLUB
4805 S.W. 229th Avenue
Aloha, Oregon 97007

Contact: Sarah Smith or Nancy Marshall
(503) 649-2345 • Web site: www.reservegolf.com
Business Hours: Mon–Tues 8am–4pm; Wed–Thurs 8am–9pm; Fri–Sat 6am–10pm

Capacity: Harvest Room, 175; private dining room, 20; Vintage Room deck, 80 (limited availability; three possible tent sites
Catering: in-house catering only
Types of Events: golf tournament functions, meetings, weddings, receptions, banquets

Availability and Terms
A $1,000 deposit is required and will be applied to the final bill. Deposit is fully refundable with 90-day notice of cancellation; $500 will be refunded with a 45-day notice.

Description of Facility and Services
Seating: tables and chairs provided as needed
Servers: provided as needed
Bar facilities: The Reserve provides liquor; outside liquor can be brought in with a corkage fee
Dance floor: 12' x 12' floor accommodates 20–25
Linens: white provided; other colors must be rented by guest
China and glassware: all china and glassware provided
Decorations: please inquire about club specifications; no rice, birdseed, confetti, etc.
Audiovisual: TV/VCR combo, overhead projector and screen, podium
Equipment: all must be rented by guest with Reserve approval
Cleanup: provided by The Reserve
Parking: available for 375
ADA: all ADA accessible

Special Services
Nestled amongst the grapevines of Oregon's fabulous wine country is a magnificent new celebration of golf and pleasure. Our championship courses are ready to host your tournament, as well as provide the utmost "challenge" to the avid golfer. In our spectacular 40,000-square-foot clubhouse, where no detail has been overlooked, we have numerous locations to host your variety of events. The Vintage Room restaurant features the finest in Northwest cuisine inspired from our regionally influenced wine list. Just as a "reserve" label distinguishes a premium wine, The Reserve Vineyards and Golf Club provides the premium event experience.

THE RESORT AT THE MOUNTAIN
68010 East Fairway Avenue
Welches, Oregon 97067 (at the western base of Mount Hood)
(503) 622-2220 from the Portland area
(800) 733-0800 from outside the Portland area

Capacity: 15,000 square feet; groups of up to 700 in any one of our 12 meeting rooms
Price Range: moderate to customized events; please inquire
Catering: in-house catering only
Types of Events: business meetings, themed galas, banquets, retreats and golf outings

Availability and Terms
Advance bookings are encouraged. Deposits required with payment due in full upon arrival.

Description of Facility and Services
Seating: provided to accommodate group size
Servers: provided
Bar facilities: liquor and liability provided by The Resort
Dance floor: provided; accommodates up to 200; electrical hookups provided
Linens: provided at no charge
China: fine china and all glassware provided
Decorations: prior approval must be obtained by Convention Services
Audiovisual: well-equipped with in-house audiovisual; equipment and technicians.
Equipment: all necessary meeting/convention equipment provided.
Parking: ample complimentary parking
ADA: fully complies

Special Services
The Resort at The Mountain offers 160 luxury guest rooms.

GET AWAY FROM IT ALL AT THE RESORT
The Resort at The Mountain offers the spirit of Scotland in the Highlands of Mount Hood just an hour from Portland. It's the perfect location for events, meetings or conferences. In addition to one of the most beautiful 27-hole golf courses in the Northwest, The Resort at The Mountain offers restaurants, lounges, shops, Scottish artifacts and decor, croquet and lawn bowling, a fitness center, Jacuzzi, pool (seasonal), tennis courts, and a mountain of other activities such as fly fishing on the Salmon River, miles of nearby hiking trails and skiing on Mount Hood just 20 minutes away.

For more information on events or meetings at
The Resort at The Mountain, please call our sales department.

Visit our Web site: http://www.theresort.com

RHEINLANDER

5035 N.E. Sandy Blvd.
Portland, Oregon 97213
Contact: Banquet Staff
(503) 288-8410
Business Hours: Mon–Fri 9am–5pm

Capacity: 20 to 85 people; 100 people for stand-up
Price Range: please call for current prices, customized menus available
Catering: full in-house catering; call for information regarding outside catering
Types of Events: sit-down dinners, hors d'oeuvres, rehearsal dinners, wedding receptions, anniversaries, birthdays, holiday parties, retirements, luncheons, meetings, seminars and corporate functions

Availability and Terms

Our beautiful banquet rooms can accommodate up to 100 people. We recommend reserving a room as soon as possible, but welcome you on short notice—space permitting! We require a deposit which is applied to the balance.

Description of Facility and Services

Seating: round or rectangular tables available depending on your size and needs
Servers: staff included
Bar facilities: host or no-host bars with a minimum setup fee; bartender included; cocktail service provided at no charge
Linens and napkins: linen tablecloths and napkins; color coordination available
China and glassware: beautiful, traditional china and glassware provided
Cleanup: provided by Rheinlander
Decorations: pre-approved by the banquet staff; tape only; early access for decorating. Ask about our additional decorating services!
Parking: free parking; private banquet entrance
ADA: Rheinlander is entirely handicap accessible

Special Services

We specialize in corporate functions. We want your event to be perfect and exactly how you imagined it to be. Our experienced banquet staff will work with you on every detail. Please call for an appointment to view rooms, look at samples or even taste the food!

BEAUTIFUL BANQUET ROOMS ENHANCED BY DELIGHTFUL ENTERTAINMENT!

The Rheinlander is proudly celebrating 36 years in Portland. We offer authentic German cuisine and fresh continental specialties including poultry, beef, seafood and pork. Strolling accordionists and singers complement your evening with their beautiful music.

Please let this business know that you heard about them from the Bravo! Event Resource Guide.

BANQUET, MEETING & EVENT SITES

1510 S.W. Harbor Way
Portland, Oregon 97201
Contact: Sales & Catering (503) 423-3112
E-mail: sales@RiverPlaceHotel.com
Web site: http://www.RiverPlaceHotel.com

Capacity: 10 to 400 attendees; 200 sit-down meal
Price Range: varies according to room and services
Catering: meal prices starting at $15 per person for lunch and $24–$50 for dinner
Types of Events: sit-down and buffet meals, hors d'oeuvre receptions, business meetings, catered affairs in Tom McCall Waterfront Park

Availability and Terms
The hotel's three meeting rooms as well as its waterfront Esplanade Restaurant, Grand Suite, Private Dining Room, and Courtyard are available for corporate and special events. Each provides a unique space whether for 10 or 400 attendees. Direct billing may be arranged with approved credit.

Description of Facility and Services
Seating: variety of seating customized to meet your needs up to 200; receptions for 400 persons with seating for 150
Servers: professional servers and bartenders provided
Bar facilities: host/no-host bar; alcohol and nonalcoholic beverages; liability provided; full lounge available for your convenience following your event
Dance floor: complimentary dance floor; electrical hookups available
Linens and napkins: white napkins and cloths; inquire about color selections
China and glassware: ivory china with wine-colored border and gold band; crystal glassware; only silver chafing dishes and flatware are used
Decorations: discussion of your ideas and needs welcomed
Cleanup: included in full-service catering
Audiovisual: can arrange for audiovisual needs
Parking: Master Account Parking may be arranged; garages within walking distance
ADA: fully accessible

Special Services
Specialized menus are easily created by Executive Chef of the Esplande Restaurant. Inquire about corporate and group discounted room rates.

A WATERFRONT LOCATION IN DOWNTOWN PORTLAND
The RiverPlace Hotel overlooks the marina on the Willamette River, a perfect setting for any corporate function. The hotel has 84 elegant guest rooms that create a warm impression consistent throughout the hotel. The RiverPlace Hotel is sure to live up to all your expectations.

See page 364 under Hotel Accommodations.

ROCK BOTTOM RESTAURANT & BREWERY

210 S.W. Morrison
Portland, Oregon 97204
Contact: (503) 796-2739; Fax (503) 796-1051
Business Hours: Mon–Thur 11am–1am; Fri–Sat 11am–2am; Sun 11am–11pm

Capacity: Mill Room–up to 30, window area–up to 65, Pool Room–up to 100
Price Range: Pool Room rental fee before 4 p.m. is $35, after 6 p.m. $64 per hour; food charges vary; custom banquet or packages for parties of 20 or more
Catering: eclectic comfort food; in-house catering only
Types of Events: meetings, parties, reunions, events

Availability and Terms

We welcome all types of events. Pool Room is not available on Fridays and Saturdays after 6pm. Parties of 20 or more should make reservations at least one week in advance. A $100 deposit is required at time of booking for parties of 50 or more; deposit will be applied toward food and beverage bill. A gratuity of 18% is applied to parties of eight or more.

Description of Facility and Services

Seating: tables and chairs provided
Servers: provided
Bar facilities: full bar in separate area
Dance floor: not available
Linens: white available at no charge
China and glassware: fiesta ware provided
Decorations: okay to decorate appropriately
Audiovisual: big screen monitors with VHS in pool room
Cleanup: provided by Rock Bottom Brewery

Special Services

Rock Bottom is a brew house with five local microbrews and seasonal in-house specialties in the heart of downtown. The entire restaurant has a capacity of 460 so we can accommodate most business meetings or celebrations. The Pool Room located on the second floor is semi-private including six championship Billiard tables and large screen televisions. Handcrafted microbrews are available in kegs for outside events.

"BEERVANA" SERVED WITH A SMILE

Rock Bottom is light and airy with vaulted ceilings, tall windows and fans—architecture reminiscent of the French Quarter in New Orleans. Come in for banquet dining, "comfort food," pool tables, live music and, of course, our handcrafted ales. Our motto is, "We don't just want to make good beer, we want to make good beer drinkers." Diners are welcome to take in-house brew tours while waiting for their food.

ON THE COLUMBIA

3839 N.E. Marine Drive
Portland, Oregon 97211
Contact: Dorothy Lane
(503) 288-4444
Web site: http://www.saltys.com

Restaurant Hours:
Lunch Mon–Sat 11:15am–3pm; Dinner Mon–Thur 5–10pm, Fri–Sat 5–10:30pm;
Sunday Brunch 9:30am–2pm; Sunday Dinner 4:30–9:30pm; winter hours vary

Capacity: Private **Wine Room**: 10-30 seated and 40 reception-style; **North Shore View Room**: 10-100 seated and 200 reception-style
Price Range: call for current prices
Catering: full-service catering; in-house or off-premise
Types of Events: all-day meetings, board meetings, seminars, employee recognition events, retirement and holiday parties, rehearsal dinners, wedding receptions and other special events, business breakfasts, sit-down dinners and luncheons, seafood and brunch buffets, cocktails and hors d'oeuvres

Availability and Terms
We recommend reserving your space three to six months in advance. But if you need assistance with last minute planning—we can help! A deposit is required to reserve your date. Room fees are waived with a minimum purchase of food and beverage.

Description of Facility and Services
Seating: a variety of table sizes and seating options
Servers: after a specified minimum gratuity or 18%, servers provided at no additional charge
Bar facilities: full-service bar provided courtesy of Salty's; host/no-host; liquor, beer and wine
Linens: house colors available at no extra cost
China and glassware: restaurant silver, china and glassware available
Audiovisual: overhead and slide projector with screen; TV, VCR, flip charts available for rent
Cleanup: handled by Salty's staff
Parking: plenty of free parking; complimentary valet service available Mon–Sat nights
ADA: first floor accessible for handicapped; Wine Room and North Shore View Room are on second floor

Special Services
Our catering director works closely with you to ensure your event's success. We print a personalized menu for you and your guests. We are happy to refer you to florists, DJs and musicians. At Salty's, we pride ourselves on catering to your every whim.

GIVE YOUR NEXT EVENT A BETTER POINT OF VIEW
Located on the riverfront only 15 minutes from downtown Portland, Salty's provides the perfect recipe for successful business meetings and social events for up to 200 guests. Salty's exceptional Northwest cuisine, warm hospitality, and spectacular views of the mighty Columbia River and majestic Mount Hood will make *your* event a special occasion! We're easy to get to, and ready to serve you the very best seafood, steaks, Sunday Brunch, and riverfront view in Portland.

Sayler's OLD COUNTRY KITCHEN

4655 S.W. Griffith Drive
Beaverton, Oregon 97005

10519 S.E. Stark
Portland, Oregon 97216

Contact: Sally Kanan (503) 252-4171 or (503) 644-1492

Capacity: West: restaurant, up to 500 for reception; five rooms 50–100, 500–1,200 square feet; **East:** restaurant, up to 500 for reception; six rooms 50–125, 500–2,000 square feet
Price Range: $7-$20
Catering: in-house
Types of Events: receptions, meetings, banquets, rehearsal dinners

Availability and Terms
Flexible terms and reservation policies; deposit required.

Description of Facility and Services
Seating: 50 tables; 300 chairs
Servers: provided by Sayler's
Bar facilities: bartenders, cocktail waitresses, liability provided
Dance floor: 12' x 12' floor can be rented; electrical available
Linens: white available for no charge; colored linens available at extra charge
China and glassware: white china and glassware provided
Decorations: flexible; please inquire
Audiovisual: full inventory available for rent
Equipment: can be rented
Cleanup: provided by Sayler's staff
Parking: plenty of free parking
ADA: ADA approved

WE SERVE A GREAT AMERICAN MEAL

The Old Country Kitchen is perfect for small daytime meetings, Monday through Friday, large daytime receptions and small banquets or rehearsal dinners in the evening. We specialize in great, affordable, American food. Try our prime beef, exceptional seafood and home-style chicken. Buffets, sit-down or food stations, are our specialty. You get all the amenities of a restaurant but lots of privacy for your meetings.

SEVEN FEATHERS HOTEL AND CASINO RESORT

146 Chief Miwaleta Lane • Canyonville, Oregon 97417
Contact: Diane Lawson (800) 548-8461 ext. 7186; Fax (541) 839-4222
E-mail: sales@sevenfeathers.com; Web site: www.sevenfeathers.com

Capacity: Umpqua Grand Ballroom: 21,000 sq. ft. (1,500 person capacity); eight conference rooms ranging from 225 to 2,200 sq. ft.

Price Range: contact sales and catering staff for pricing information

Catering: full-service in-house for meetings, conventions and receptions

Types of Events: buffet or sit-down banquets, live entertainment and boxing events, conferences, conventions, trade shows, weddings and holiday parties

Availability and Terms
Contact the sales and catering department at (800) 548-8461 ext.1386 for more information.

Description of Facility and Services
Seating: tables and chairs for up to 1,500
Servers: full staff available
Bar facilities: full-service bar available
Dance floor: in-house 60' x 60' dance floor available
Linens and napkins: provided; variety of colors may be special ordered
China and glassware: provided
Cleanup: provided
Decorations: allowed with prior approval
Audiovisual: LCD projector, overhead, screens, TV, VCR, variety of microphones available
Equipment: podiums, risers and staging
Parking: valet and self-parking available at no charge
ADA: meets ADA requirements

Special Services
Seven Feathers offers a variety of gaming entertainment including 550 slots, live Keno, high stakes Bingo, Roulette, Craps, Let it Ride, Big Six, Poker Room, Blackjack Tables, Player Services and special events. For an elegant experience in fine dining, The Camas Room features Northwest and Mediterranean cuisine. Cow Creek Restaurant is open 24 hours and offers an extensive menu and buffet. Scoops Ice Cream Parlor specializes in a variety of desserts, espresso, and deli sandwiches.

FULL SERVICE HOTEL
Seven Feathers Hotel and Casino Resort boasts a full service, 147 room hotel with complimentary 24-hour valet parking, shuttle and concierge service. Extended amenities include a full-service RV park, indoor/outdoor pool, fitness center, sauna, spa and video arcade.

SHELDON'S CAFE
at the Grant House on Officers' Row

1101 Officers' Row
Vancouver, Washington 98661
Contact: Gary
(360) 699-1213
Business Hours:
Tues–Sat 11am–2pm, 5pm-8pm

Capacity: a variety of rooms are available for groups of 10 to 50 people; total capacity 100+

Price Range: continental breakfast $5, lunch $6.50, dinner $11.95 to $17.95

Catering: full-service catering available in-house or off premise

Types of Events: meetings, conferences, seminars, luncheons, dinners, weddings and receptions, anniversaries, birthdays, retirements, etc.

Availability and Terms
Reservations gladly accepted, however we strive to satisfy short-notice requests. All-day events are available including continental breakfast, lunch and afternoon cookies. A nonrefundable deposit/room charge of $150 full day/$75 one-half day is required to confirm your date.

Description of Facility and Services
Seating: a variety of seating options is available
Servers: our professional staff will serve you
Bar facilities: regional beers and wines available
Dance floor: outdoor patio only; accommodates 40+ people
Linens: burgundy no charge; specialty linens available for $1.50 per tablecloth
China: fine china and glassware available
Decorations: please call to discuss your needs
Audiovisual: equipment can be provided with advance notice (fee charged)
Cleanup: provided by our staff
Parking: plenty of free parking; easy access to I-5
ADA: yes

Special Services
Our facility is conveniently located near downtown Vancouver and is less than 10 miles from downtown Portland and the Portland International Airport.

Sheldon's Cafe is located in the historic and elegant Grant House on Officers' Row in Vancouver. Built in 1850 and listed on the National Register of Historic Places, the Grant House features wrap-around verandas, a main dining room with two fireplaces, a private dining room, and a sunroom that looks upon our herb and flower garden patio. Our sylvan setting will help to make your meeting or event a relaxed and effective gathering.

ON THE WILLAMETTE

4575 N. Channel • Portland, Oregon 97217
Contact: Michael Baker (503) 289-1597
Business Hours: Mon–Fri 8am–6pm;
Sat 9am–5pm; or by appointment
Web site: www.shenanigansrestaurant.com

Capacity: ballroom seats 400, 560 in entire facility; 800+ reception
Price Range: our complete menu packages start at $9.95 (lunch) and $14.95 (dinner)
Catering: full service, in-house Northwest specialty, custom tailored to your needs
Types of Events: We offer a variety of sit-down breakfast, lunch or dinner, along with buffets and hors d'oeuvres packages for business meetings, seminars, reunions, fund raisers, training classes—we do it all!

Availability and Terms

The entire facility includes four tastefully appointed rooms available for your use. Reservations should be made as soon as possible to ensure availability. A nonrefundable, nontransferable deposit is required within 30 days of confirming reservations. Credit applications are available for groups requesting direct billing.

Description of Facility and Services

Seating: all tables and chairs provided and set to your specifications
Servers: our professional staff is provided with a customary service charge
Bar facilities: full service, host/no-host bars include large oak bar for ballroom, variety of portable bars for smaller rooms
Dance floor: 1,200-square-foot oak dance floor located in ballroom with electrical hook ups
Linens and napkins: available in a variety of colors at no additional charge
China and glassware: white china and stemmed glassware at no additional charge
Cleanup: included in service
Decorations: Shenanigans' picturesque view requires little decoration. Table candles, mirror tiles, bud vases and punch fountain are provided at no charge. You are welcome to bring your own decorations.
Audiovisual: equipment rental available through Shenanigans'
Equipment: podiums, microphones, risers and easels provided by us at no charge
Parking and ADA: ample free parking; disabled access available

Special Services

Shenanigans' offers flexibility coupled with 50 years of combined experience. These two qualities along with our assurance of our undivided attention will guarantee your event will be easy for you and successful for your guests.

SPECTACULAR RIVERSIDE SETTING

Shenanigans' is conveniently located on the scenic banks of the Willamette River, in the bungalow-style Ports O' Call complex, only minutes from downtown Portland. Please come in and see for yourself the exquisite panoramic view and impressive hospitality that makes Shenanigans' one of Portland's premier places to entertain. Exit 303 off I-5, follow the signs to Swan Island, left on N. Port Center, take immediate right and we're just to your left.

Sheraton Portland Airport
HOTEL

8235 N.E. Airport Way
Portland, Oregon 97220-1398
Contact: Janet Eichner
(503) 249-7642
E-mail: jeichner@sheratonpdx.com

Capacity: 14,400 total square feet accommodating 10 to 700 seated, 750 standing
Price Range: $6.50 to $25 per person for meals; $75 to $1,200 rental
Catering: full-service in-house and off-premise available
Types of Events: corporate meetings, conventions, symposiums, trade shows, banquets, receptions

Availability and Terms
Schedule early to ensure availability. Rental is based on a sliding scale dependent on food and beverage and/or guestrooms required. The cancellation policy varies according to type of event; $500 advance deposit required.

Description of Facility and Services
Seating: tables and chairs for 700
Servers: included as hotel service
Bar facilities: full-service with bartenders; hotel must provide all beverages
Dance floor: complimentary
Linens and napkins: large selection available at no charge
China and glassware: white china; all types of glassware
Decorations: standard decorations including helium balloons acceptable
Cleanup: included in price
Audiovisual: meeting rooms are internet ready; videoconferencing available; large selection of rental equipment available in-house
Equipment: podiums, risers, whiteboards, and easels provided at no charge
Parking: complimentary
ADA: fully complied

Special Services
Sheraton Portland Airport Hotel offers 214 superior guestrooms including nine suites with honor bar and voice mail, Club Level and Corporate Club rooms, complete Business Center, video conferencing, Concierge Service, two restaurants and lounges, fitness center with therapy pool, and 24-hour airport shuttle service.

SUITES HOTEL

Restaurant and Convention Center—
Portland Airport/I-205
11707 N.E. Airport Way
Portland, Oregon 97220-1075
Contact: Sales/Catering Office
(503) 252-7500, ext 270
Business Hours:
Mon–Fri 8am–5:30pm;
Sat by appointment

Capacity: banquet rooms to accommodate up to 350 guests
Price Range: packages to fit most budgets
Catering: full-service at our deluxe hotel or your special location
Types of Events: business meetings to formal affairs

Availability and Terms
You are invited to visit our facility to discuss your needs.

Description of Facility and Services
Seating: banquets of up to 350 guests
Servers: professional, full-service staff for all events
Bar facilities: hosted or no-host bars and table service
Entertainment: musician and DJ referrals available
Dance floor: beautiful wood floor at $50 setup fee
Linens: included to complement your colors
China and glassware: included; styled to complement formal and informal themes
Cleanup: setup and cleanup by our staff
Decorations: chandeliers, mirrored walls, table and buffet decorations included
Guestroom accommodations: 4-Diamond/AAA rated; 200 Junior Suites; special wedding packages and group rates available; kitchenette and two full dressing vanities in every room
Parking: free parking available on-site
ADA: banquet rooms and guest suites

Special Services
Our professional catering coordinators will assist you in planning your event. We offer the convenience of a full-service banquet facility, restaurant and deluxe hotel on one property.

OUR TRADITION OF AFFORDABLE EXCELLENCE CONTINUES
Newly Remodeled

SILVER FALLS CONFERENCE CENTER

20022 Silver Falls Highway, S.E.
Sublimity, Oregon 97385
Contact: Dayna Rich
(503) 873-8875; Fax (503) 873-2937
Business Hours: Mon–Fri 8am–5pm

Capacity: Smith Creek Meeting Hall, 30 x 40 = 86 persons;
Upper Smith Creek Meeting Hall, 20 x 12 = 30 persons;
Dining Hall, 20 x 30 = 76 persons
Price Range: $49.20 to $52.25 per person including three meals, one overnight
Catering: Silver Falls Conference Center; in-house only
Types of Events: conferences, retreats, reunions, weddings, picnics

Availability and Terms
Silver Falls Conference Center may be reserved up to one year in advance for groups of 10 or more. A deposit of $15 per person per night is required. Prices subject to change.

Description of Facility and Services
Seating: tables with chairs
Servers: cafeteria-style
Bar facilities: none
Linens: white tablecloths at $5 each
China and glassware: white china; water, wine, champagne glassware; flatware
Decorations: early access available with prior arrangements; please remove all items brought into facility
Cleanup: provided by Silver Falls Conference Center
Audiovisual: TV, VCR, overheads, and slide projectors available at no charge
Equipment: podiums and easels available
Parking: 50-vehicle capacity at Smith Creek; 20-vehicle capacity at Upper Smith
ADA: Alder Lodge (sleeps 12), Smith Creek, Dining Room

Special Services
Silver Falls Conference Center will gladly accommodate any special dietary needs. Specialty meals are available for formal affairs, weddings, and special event banquets.

SECLUDED AND SCENIC LOCATION
Located within Silver Falls State Park (the largest State Park in Oregon), Silver Falls Conference Center surrounds a secluded meadow and is overlooked by tall stands of fir and hemlock trees. The facility is only a short distance from a tranquil trail leading to 10 waterfalls. The park offers a wide variety of outdoor activities such as hiking, biking, swimming, volleyball, and horseshoes.

Skamania Lodge
In The Columbia River Gorge

1131 Skamania Lodge Way • Stevenson, Washington 98648
Sales Office: (509) 427-2503 or (800) 376-9116
Reservations: (800) 221-7117
E-mail: lodge@Gorge.net; Web site: http://www.dolce.com
Business Hours: Mon–Fri 8am–5pm

Capacity: 450 to 500 people
Price Range: $20 to $45
Catering: Our Catering Coordinator will coordinate all your catering needs
Types of Events: conventions, retreats, meetings, banquets and parties

Availability and Terms
Our Conference Center consists of two large ballrooms, each divisible into four smaller spaces by state-of-the-art acoustic walls. The ballrooms are accessible to vehicles through large outside doors. Each ballroom is attractively decorated with wainscoting, handsome acoustic panels, and open wood-beamed ceiling. The large ballroom features a fireplace for a special dinner or cozy event. Two comfortable open areas provide flexible reception or breakout options. A moderately-sized board room is located off the main lobby for executive sessions.

Description of Facility and Services
Seating: tables and chairs for up to 500
Servers: appropriate service staff provided
Bar facilities: full-service bar, portable bars, and bartender; all beverages and liquor liability provided by Skamania Lodge
Dance floor: 21'x30' dance floor; electrical outlets available
Linens and napkins: available in all colors at additional charge
China and glassware: house china; variety of glassware
Cleanup: provided by Skamania Lodge staff
Decorations: please discuss decorating ideas with event coordinator
Parking: 500 parking spaces
ADA: meets ADA requirements

IDEAL EVENT FACILITY FOR GROUPS OF ALL SIZES
Skamania Lodge is a full-service resort and conference center consisting of 195 guest rooms, 18-hole golf course, pro shop and snack bar, fitness center with indoor swimming pool, indoor and outdoor spas, tennis courts, hiking trails, volleyball court, dining room, gift shop, and game room. The location is convenient and absolutely beautiful; the mood is comfortable and relaxing; and the breadth of activities and sights cannot be matched anywhere else.

SPIRIT MOUNTAIN CASINO

P.O. Box 39
Grand Ronde, Oregon 97347
Contact: Group Sales
(800) 760-7977
Business Hours: Mon–Fri 8am–5pm
Casino Hours: 24 hours
E-mail: groupsales@spiritmtn.com
Web site: www.spirit-mountain.com

Capacity: 3,000 sq. ft. banquet room that divides into two sections accommodating groups of 25 to 200; 2,300 sq. ft. meeting room that divides into two sections accommodating groups of 10 to 150
Price Range: room is complimentary with a $150 minimum purchase
Catering: full-service, in-house
Types of Events: meetings, seminars, conventions, luncheons, dinners, receptions, gatherings, parties

Availability and Terms
Contact Group Sales at (800) 760-7977 for terms and availability.

Description of Facility and Services
Seating: provided for 25-200 at rounds, 300 theater-style
Servers: provided
Dance floor: complimentary with advance notice
Linens and China: provided
Decorations: allowed with prior approval
Audiovisual: overhead, slide projector, LCD projector, TV, VCR, flip charts, podium, cordless hand-held and lavaliere microphones
Cleanup: provided
Parking: ample free and valet parking available
ADA: fully complies

Special Services
Entertainment: At Oregon's most popular attraction, you'll find 1,100 slots machines, blackjack, poker, roulette, craps, Pai Gow and Let It Ride poker, live Keno, a Big 6 Wheel, off-track betting, and a 850 seat bingo hall which also hosts live headline entertainment.
Dining: *Legends* restaurant features Northwest cuisine including steak, seafood and pastas. *Coyote's*, a buffet-style restaurant, presents a rotating menu with over 300 dishes. Other options include *Spirit Mountain Cafe*, proudly brewing Starbucks Coffee, and *Rock Creek Court*, featuring an American Grill, a New York-style deli and traditional Asian cuisine.
Lodging: Spirit Mountain Lodge has 100 guest rooms and suites featuring Northwest-style furnishings and original cultural art. A hospitality suite accommodating groups of up to 25 is also available. Group rates available. Please call group sales for more information.
We're located about an hour from Portland and a half hour from Salem. Groups may be eligible for free luxury motorcoach transportation.

Please let this business know that you heard about them from the Bravo! Event Resource Guide.

STERNWHEELER "COLUMBIA GORGE" & MARINE PARK

1200 N.W. Front Avenue, Suite 110
Portland, Oregon 97209 • (503) 223-3928
Web site: www.sternwheeler.com
E-mail: sternwheeler@inetarena.com

Owned & operated by the Port of Cascade Locks

Capacity: 450 passengers
Price Range: varies depending on event and length of cruise; two hour minimum; please call
Catering: full range of catering services provided including menu selections for brunch, luncheon, dinner, hors d'oeuvres and theme parties
Types of Events: private charter meal and excursion cruises, company picnics (park only), holiday parties, casino cruises, weddings, fund raisers, meetings, conventions

Availability and Terms

The Sternwheeler "Columbia Gorge" offers two fully enclosed heated decks, providing a comfortable setting for any time of year. Marine Park offers accommodations for groups of 50 to 4,000, as well as a three-acre private island. A 25% nonrefundable deposit is required upon booking; final payment is due 60–120 days prior to scheduled event, depending on season.

Description of Facility and Services

Seating: tables and chairs provided
Servers: provided
Bar facilities: two to three full-service bars with bartenders available
Dance floor: dance area available; full electrical hookup
Linens and napkins: cloth linens and napkins; color coordination available
China and glassware: house china available with our catering service
Decorations: elegant turn-of-the-century motif requires little decoration
Audiovisual: available; please call a sales representative
Cleanup: provided courtesy of the Sternwheeler crews
Parking: *Cascade Locks Marine Park:* free parking; *Portland:* City Center and off-street parking available for a fee
ADA: disabled accessible

Special Services

With two rivers and an abundance of breathtaking views to choose from, the Sternwheeler "Columbia Gorge" and Marine Park continue to provide a unique venue for meetings, banquets, or any event. We can coordinate your event from start to finish, including transportation, catering and entertainment. Please call our sales office for more details.

R E S O R T
Sunriver, Oregon

P.O. Box 3609 • Sunriver, Oregon 97707
Catering Office (541) 593-4605
Fax (541) 593-2742
Web site: www.sunriver-resort.com

Capacity: 14 rooms that can accommodate from 10 to 500 guests
Price Range: starting at $20 per person.; call for more information
Catering: full-service catering for on-premise and off-premise events
Types of Events: breakfast, lunch, dinner, wedding receptions and ceremonies, banquets, parties, meetings and seminars

Availability and Terms

Sunriver Resort is proud of its varied event base with both indoor and outdoor locations, some of which have mountain and golf course views. We recommend that you make your reservations as soon as possible.

Description of Facility and Services

Seating: tables and chairs are provided by the Resort
Servers: staff is included in catering costs
Bar facilities: full beverage services available; Resort provides all alcoholic beverages
Dance floor: complimentary
Linens and napkins: an extensive variety of linen and napkin colors available complimentary
China and glassware: white china; stemmed glassware
Cleanup: provided by Resort staff
Decorations: please consult our catering expert on availability and options
Audiovisual: full-service AV department and Media Specialist Technician
Parking: ample parking available at no extra charge
ADA: ADA compliant

Special Services

Sunriver Resort's location, nestled between the towering Cascade Mountain Range and the high desert is the ideal setting for any event. This, combined with our superior banquet service, our staff's attention to detail, the unparalleled cuisine and our professional catering department, has made Sunriver Resort one of the Northwest's most popular special event locations.

A MEMORABLE DESTINATION THAT HAS IT ALL

In addition to our special event space, Sunriver Resort is a well known destination for the year-round recreational opportunities offered by the area. Located 20 miles from the base of Mount. Bachelor, some of the best skiing in Oregon is at your ski tips! In the warm months, guests will enjoy three renowned golf courses, over 30 minutes of paved bike paths, trails for mountain bike riding, canoeing, kayaking, whitewater rafting, tennis, swimming, horseback riding, hiking, caving, fishing and much, much more! A wide variety of accommodation options, from guestrooms to five-bedroom fully furnished homes, are available for your guests as well. The memories you'll gain are sure to last a lifetime.

7125 S.W. Nyberg Road (Exit 289 off I-5)
Tualatin, Oregon 97062
Contact: Sales & Catering Office
(503) 692-5800, (800) 551-9167; Fax (503) 404-1950
Web site: www.Sweetbrier.com
Office Hours: Mon–Fri 7:30am–5:30pm; Sat 9am–1pm

The Sweetbrier Inn

Capacity: from 5 to 300 people; 4,000 square feet of meeting space
Price Range: please call for current prices; individual and custom menus available
Catering: full-service in-house catering
Types of Events: meetings, breakfast, lunch and dinner receptions, sit-down or buffet

Availability and Terms
Four separate rooms are available; we can seat 250 for dinner or host 300 for a reception. Please contact the sales and catering office to discuss space availability.

Description of Facility and Services
Seating: tables and chairs provided
Servers: included in price
Bar facilities: full-service bar available
Dance floor: 225-square-foot dance floor; PA systems and risers available
Linens: white linen tablecloths and colored napkins; white skirting
China and glassware: white china; variety of glassware
Decorations: creative catering staff to assist you
Cleanup: provided by hotel
Audiovisual: available upon request
Equipment: all meeting equipment available upon request
Parking: ample free parking
ADA: fully accessible

Hotel Features
The Sweetbrier Inn is a two-story "country inn" located only 10 minutes south of downtown Portland. Offering 131 tastefully decorated guest rooms including 32 executive suites that provide a high level of warmth and comfort. Our beautifully landscaped grounds create a true picture of Oregon's beauty. Some of our standard amenities include free local phone calls, touch-tone phones with data port capabilities, and in-room coffeemakers. Our executive suites have two televisions, oversized workstations, two-line phones, microwaves, refrigerators, and private patios. Our hotel features a newly renovated full-service bistro and jazz bar with some of Portland's finest jazz artists playing four nights a week, a 24-hour fitness center, heated outdoor swimming pool, room service, ample free parking, valet and laundry service. Special group rates available. AAA rated–Three Diamond.

SYLVIA'S ITALIAN RESTAURANT & CLASS ACT DINNER THEATRE

5115 N.E. Sandy Blvd. • Portland, Oregon 97213
Contact: Norm Stone (503) 288-6828
Dinner: Sun 3–9pm; Mon–Thurs 4–10pm; Fri, Sat 4–11pm
Dinner Theatre: Thurs–Sat 6:30pm dinner, 8pm show
Sun Matinee 11:30am brunch, 1pm show;
5:30pm dinner, 7pm show

Web site:
http://www.sylvias.net

Capacity: Piazza Room, 80 people; Dinner Theatre, 100 people (limited evenings)
Price Range: $9 and up (including room)
Catering: off premise up to 5,000
Types of Events: sit-down, buffet, and cocktails and hors d'oeuvres; meetings, wedding receptions, rehearsal dinners, family feasts

Availability and Terms
Sylvia's can be reserved on an as-available basis, with a minimum $100 nonrefundable deposit. We request a minimum of two-weeks notice for cancellations.

Description of Facility and Services
Seating: tables and chairs provided
Servers: staff included if you use in-house banquet facilities; 16% gratuity added
Bar facilities: full bar
Dance floor: available on request; extra charge
Linens and napkins: burgundy cloth linens and napkins at no charge; other colors available for extra charge
China and glassware: white dinnerware and restaurant glassware available for in-house banquets
Decorations: brass lanterns provided; table decorations provided for a charge; early decorating welcomed; please no confetti
Cleanup: provided by Sylvia's
Audiovisual: equipment available upon request; extra charge
Equipment: podium and easel available
Parking: parking available at no additional cost
ADA: fully accessible

Dinner Theatre
Treat your guests to the best Portland has to offer in food and entertainment with Sylvia's Class Act Dinner Theatre. Group rates are available for parties of 15 or more on Thursday and Sunday nights only. Price includes salad, choice of entree, nonalcoholic beverage, dessert, and show. A deposit is due one week from day you make your reservation. Full payment is due two weeks prior to your reservation date. Please call for additional information.

TIFFANY CENTER

1410 S.W. Morrison
Portland, Oregon 97205
(503) 222-0703 or (503) 248-9305
Office Hours: Monday–Friday 9am-5pm.
Appointments recommended; after hours and
Saturday appointments available

Capacity: from 10 to 1,200 people; seven rooms and two elegant grand ballrooms ranging from 200 to 6,918 square feet

Price Range: call for price schedule

Catering: exclusively by Rafati's Elegance in Catering, prepared on-site in their commercially licensed kitchen. Rafati's full-service catering can assist you with your selection of the perfect menu for your corporate event. From continental breakfasts to casual or formal reception services, all events are customized to reflect the needs of your organization. Rafati's offers personalized menu planning in all price ranges.

Types of Events: corporate meetings, seminars, conferences, receptions, dinners, private parties, holiday parties, dances, concerts, theater productions, exhibits and fund-raising events

Availability and Terms

The Tiffany Center has three ballrooms with dance floors and stages as well as several smaller meeting and conference rooms. Early reservations are suggested, but short notice reservations will be accommodated with space availability. A refundable deposit is required at the time of booking. Client must provide liability insurance.

Description of Facility and Services

Seating: table and chair setup included in room rental
Servers: provided by Rafati's Elegance in Catering
Bar facilities: provided by Rafati's Elegance in Catering; fully licensed
Dance floor: accommodates up to 700 people
Parking: convenient street and commercial lot parking; located on MAX line
ADA: all event rooms are fully ADA accessible
- Central air conditioning in second floor Ballroom; spot cooling available in fourth floor Ballroom

Special Services

The Tiffany Center's expert staff can provide you with complete meeting and event planning services. From audiovisual needs, theme decor and decorated ice carvings to candle and floral centerpieces, balloons and musicians and much more.

PORTLAND'S PREMIER EVENT FACILITY

The Tiffany Center features traditional charm and elegance in a centrally located historic downtown building. The Tiffany Center offers your organization a variety of meeting spaces that will fulfill all your corporate requirements. From large ballrooms to breakout rooms, the Tiffany Center is the perfect facility for your corporate functions.

See page 337 under Caterers & Ice Carvings.

TIMBERLINE LODGE

Timberline, Oregon 97028
Sales Office: (503) 219-3192; Fax 295-1855
Business Hours:
Mon–Fri 8am-5pm or by appointment
http://www.timberlinelodge.com
E-mail: sales@timberlinelodge.com

Capacity: up to 250 banquet, 400 reception or theater-style; 4 meeting/banquet rooms, outdoor patio and day lodge facilities plus Silcox Hut accommodates 24
Price Range: price is determined by the event and specific menu selection
Catering: in-house only
Types of Events: meetings, conferences, seminars, retreats, social gatherings, buffet, sit-down, cocktails, overnight lodging, ski events

Availability and Terms
The Raven's Nest (1,400 square feet), complete with soaring ceilings and large picture windows with views of Mt. Hood and Mt. Jefferson, is perfect for social functions as well as informal meetings. Ideal for meetings or meals, Ullman Hall (2,300 square feet), is divisible into two sections and features windows with spectacular views, a dance floor and recessed screen. An adjacent patio allows for winter ski-in meetings and summer outdoor festivities. The historic Barlow Room (1,600 square feet), with its unique, original decor, offers state-of-the-art projection capabilities and is versatile for all uses. The Day Lodge is also available seasonally for trade shows and as additional breakout space. For a truly uncommon experience, the newly restored Silcox Hut is available for overnight lodging, meetings and group retreats. This exclusive retreat, located 1,000 feet above the Lodge, offers bunkroom accommodations, hearty mountain-style meals and a Great Room with a massive stone fireplace perfect for any gathering. Please contact the Portland Sales Office for a complete Conference Packet.

Description of Facility and Services
Seating: rooms can be arranged in any style to meet your event requirements
Servers: friendly service staff included
Bar facilities: full-service bars available
Audiovisual: full selection of audiovisual services available; please inquire for pricing
Parking: ample parking available; Sno-Park permit required during the winter months
ADA: yes, within the limitations of a historical building

Special Services
Timberline, a National Historical Landmark, has 70 guest rooms that accommodate up to 150 guests. Amenities include a sauna, hydro-spa, and seasonal outdoor swimming pool. Timberline is also home to a full-service ski area with the longest ski season in North America. Nearby activities include championship golf, hiking, horseback riding, windsurfing and mountain biking. Our microbrewery, the Mt. Hood Brewing Company, offers tours, tastings and pub-style fare.

TIMBERLINE—HALFWAY UP THE HILL TOWARD HEAVEN
This spectacular alpine resort, nestled midway to the summit of Mt. Hood, is a favorite destination for skiers and non-skiers alike from around the world. Unique lodging, gourmet dining, excellent skiing and panoramic views of the Cascade Mountain Range welcome guests year-round. Located 65 miles from Portland, Oregon.

Tuality Health Education Center
Facilities for your special events.
A member of the Tuality Healthcare family.

334 S.E. Eighth Avenue
Hillsboro, Oregon 97123
(503) 681-1700
Business Hours: Mon–Fri 9am–5pm

Capacity: rooms range in size from 27–3,100 square feet and can accommodate up to 400 people, or 250 in banquet/seating format
Price Range: price varies according to event
Catering: choose from one of our preferred caterers
Types of Events: meetings, seminars, banquets, parties, receptions

Availability and Terms
A 50% rental deposit and signed license agreement reserves your space up to one year in advance. Day, evening and weekend space is available. Minimal kitchen fee per person.

Description of Facility and Services
Seating: tables and chairs provided and set up to your specification
Servers: provided by caterer
Bar facilities: provided by caterer
Dance floor: dance floor available up to 18' x 18'
Linens: provided by caterer
China and glassware: white Wedgwood china, variety of glassware available
Decorations: no rice, birdseed or confetti; enclosed dripless candles only
Audiovisual: video/data projector (rear or front), 35mm slide dissolvers, wireless microphones, sound system, satellite receivers
Equipment: podium, 12' x 13' stage
Cleanup: handled by caterer
Parking: ample free parking
ADA: fully accessible

PERFECT FOR SMALL OR LARGE EVENTS
The Tuality Health Education Center features a beautiful sunlit foyer area that is perfect for cake and buffet service tables. The combination of skylights and foliage in our lobby is a perfect setting for your guests to mingle. A selection of different sizes of classrooms and conference rooms with moveable walls allow for creating a space that is just the right size for your event. Our variety of microphones and the large screen audiovisual projection system assures that all of your guests will see and hear whatever is presented.

ULTRAZONE
"Portland's Best Laser Tag"®

16074 S.E. McLoughlin Boulevard
Milwaukie, Oregon 97267
Contact: Teresa Toole
(503) 652-1122;
Fax (503) 652-5204

Capacity: up to 150
Price Range: a variety of complete packages are available; please call for current prices
Catering: full-service catering available
Types of Events: business meetings, office parties, team-building events, birthday parties, morale boosting, sales meetings, performance reward

Availability and Terms
Please make your reservations as early as possible. Visa and MasterCard accepted.

Description of Facility and Services
Seating: tables and chairs provided for up to 60
Servers: provided by Ultrazone
Dance floor: LaserTag arena can be used a 5,000-square-foot, two-level dance floor
Audiovisual: provided on request
Cleanup: provided by Ultrazone
Parking: ample free parking
ADA: fully accessible

ULTRAZONE—THE FUN BUSINESS MEETING

Break the routine and inject a dose of fun and excitement into your business meeting! Ultrazone is a high-tech laser game played in a themed arena where special effects and other players create an exciting adventure. Simply put, it is a futuristic entertainment facility that is fun and safe for all ages. Action takes place in a multi-level arena with 5,000 square feet of fog-filled mazes, electronic wizardry, and computerized obstacles. Teamwork and strategy are key as you locate other teams and score points using our state of the art laser tag system.

Join the list of Portland's leading companies that have taken the Ultrazone challenge.

- Hewlett Packard
- Horizon Airlines
- Tektronix
- American Honda
- Burger King
- Commercial Credit
- AT&T Cellular
- Civil Air Patrol
- Boyd Coffee
- Safeco Insurance
- Intel
- Red Lion Hotels
- Shari's Restaurants
- Home Depot
- Sprint
- Adventist Medical
- Ikon
- The Good Guys
- Voicestream Wireless
- Zellerbach
- U.S. Bank
- Western Wireless
- Mentor Graphics
- Standard Insurance
- Phoenix Inn
- Burgerville
- Prestige Care
- Electric Lightwave
- Louisiana Pacific
- Kaiser Permanente

The Uptown Billiard Club

120 N.W. 23rd Avenue • Portland, Oregon 97210
Contact: Jennifer Saucy (503) 226-8980
The Uptown Billiard Club (503) 226-6909
Web site: http://www.uptownbilliards.com

Capacity: 10 to 200 for parties; seated dinners up to 80
Catering: in-house chef; updated menu available on the Internet
Types of Events: specializing in office parties, client entertaining, holiday events, wedding receptions, teambuilding and sales-team functions; we have billiards and casino equipment for parties up to 200 on-premise; 1,500 off-premise—**See Uptown Casino Events, page 242 under Audience Participation & Games**

Availability and Terms
The Club's unique attraction are its 10 mahogany pool tables, two of which are located in the private setting of the Parlor, a room perfect for parties of up to 40 people. Adjacent to the library is our dining room, and the heavy tapestry curtains between the two rooms can be tied back to create an intimate setting for parties of 40 to 80.

Description of Facility and Services
Seating: 10 to 200 for parties; seated dinners up to 80
Servers: the finest in Portland at 15% of service charge on food and beverage
Bar facilities: full-service by cocktail staff or from our turn-of-the-century bar
Dance floor: 70-person capacity, expandable
Linens: included in the "no nickel-and-diming" policy
China and glassware: included in the "no nickel-and-diming" policy
Decorations: Uptown Billiards is decorated in the style of the "Old English Gentlemen's Club"; holiday decorations are up on Dec. 1; you are welcome to decorate for your party
Cleanup: included in the "no nickel-and-diming" policy
Meeting and audiovisual services: you name it, we will get it done
Additional services: parties can be arranged to feature a casino room at discounted rates, wine tastings by local experts, tournaments can be orchestrated for no charge, etc.
Parking: Pay & Park space for 60 cars within one block

HAVE SOME FUN THIS YEAR...IN STYLE!
Crafted in late 19th century tradition, The Uptown Billiard Club is Portland's architectural award-winning billiard room. Libraries and overstuffed couches, antiques and brass chandeliers complement our 10 mahogany pool tables, creating an unparalleled atmosphere in which to host the most memorable social and corporate affairs.

A WESTCOAST HOTEL

VALLEY RIVER INN
1000 Valley River Way
Eugene, Oregon 97401
Contact: Donna Earley-Theil
(541) 341-3461; Fax (541) 687-0289

Capacity: 15,000 square feet of unique meeting space comprised of three main ballrooms and four smaller riverview meeting rooms

Price Range: varies with size of event; room rental waived with minimum food and beverage purchase

Catering: full-service, in-house catering service specializing in fresh and creative Northwest cuisine

Types of Events: from small board meetings to large multi-day conventions, wedding receptions, and fundraisers

Availability and Terms
Reservations are highly recommended at your earliest notice. Our dedicated, professional staff will work with you to ensure a successful and memorable event. Please contact our sales/catering office for assistance with availability and terms.

Description of Facility and Services
Seating: 550 rounds; 800 theatre-style
Servers: all service staff provided by hotel
Bar facilities: full beverage/bar service provided by hotel
Dance floor: yes
China and glassware: fine china and glassware available at no additional charge
Linens and napkins: linens available to match your decor/theme
Decorations: contact our catering department to discuss decorations and early access
Audiovisual: complete AV equipment arranged by catering department; Essig Entertainment is hotel's supplier
Equipment: lecterns/risers at no charge
Cleanup: provided by staff
Parking: ample, free on-site parking and complimentary airport shuttle service
ADA: ADA compliant

Special Services
Our 257 deluxe guest rooms offer balconies and patios with views overlooking the scenic Willamette River, Owen Rose Garden, and our beautifully landscaped gardens and courtyards. All rooms are oversized, offering two vanities, large work areas, voicemail, modem hookup, in-room coffee service and a complimentary newspaper delivered to your door each morning.

ON THE BANKS OF THE SCENIC WILLAMETTE RIVER
Located on the banks of the scenic Willamette River, Valley River Inn offers a resort setting with landscaped grounds and gardens right in the heart of Eugene.

Please let this business know that you heard about them from the Bravo! Event Resource Guide.

Washington County Fair Complex

873 N.E. 34th Street • Hillsboro, Oregon 97124
Contact: Lisa DuPré (503) 648-1416; Fax (503) 648-7208
Business Hours: Mon–Fri 8am–5pm

Capacity: 40 to 2,500
Price Range: varies depending on event; please call
Catering: no in-house catering; can assist with selection of caterer, if requested
Types of Events: indoor and outdoor facilities for weddings and receptions, trade shows, seminars, business events, concerts, corporate picnics, livestock events, AND MUCH MORE!

Availability and Terms

All bookings are encouraged as early as possible. A deposit is required. The Fair Complex features a room small enough for a quiet gathering of 40, two meeting and reception halls that accommodate 300 (complete kitchens), a Main Exhibit Hall that hosts trade shows comfortably or a banquet of 1,500 (catering kitchen), many covered outdoor facilities (one with stage), and room in the amphitheater for 4,000. Public address systems available in two halls.

Description of Facility and Services

Seating: tables and seating provided for most facilities
Servers: caterer to provide
Bar facilities: you provide bartender and liquor liability; OLCC permit required for any sale of alcohol
Dance floors: sprung wooden dance floor in Square Dance Hall, with capacity of 300; polished concrete in other halls for 100 to 500 depending on the facility
Linens, china and glassware: available from caterer or you provide
Decorations: please inquire about restrictions
Cleanup: you provide or Fair Complex provides for a charge
Equipment: podium, easel, and risers available
Parking: free parking for up to 10,000
ADA: fully complied

Special Services

We provide event staff on site to make sure everything is taken care of. Staging, extra tables and chairs, and setup and take down can be provided.

A FACILITY FOR ALL NEEDS

The Washington County Fair Complex has a facility, or that special open space, to accommodate any type of event one can imagine. Metal detector hunts, car shows, trade shows, gymkhanas, and concerts all happen at the Fair Complex! Every Fair Complex employee is dedicated to making your event a success!

THE WESTIN
PORTLAND

750 S. W. Alder Street
Portland, Oregon 97205
Contact: Aaron R. Babbie (503) 294-9000; Fax (503) 241-9565
Office Hours: Mon–Fri 8am–6pm
E-mail: aaron.babbie@westin.com; Web site: www.westin.com

Capacity: Alder Ballroom: up to 120 (1,282 sq. ft.); **Park Room:** up to 50 (550 sq. ft.); The Boardroom: up to 8 (228 sq. ft.)
Price Range: price varies depending on room and catering
Catering: full-service, in-house catering available
Types of Events: banquets, private dining, meetings and other events

Availability and Terms
Banquet and private dining can be confirmed 30 days prior to the event. Cancellation and deposit requirements are based on the program details.

Description of Facility and Services
Seating: tables and chairs provided
Servers: staff is included in catering costs
Bar facilities: full beverage services available
Dance floor: may be provided
Linens and napkins: extra charge for specialty linens
China and glassware: available
Cleanup: provided
Equipment: podiums and easels provided
Parking: valet parking with in and out privileges for a charge
ADA: compliant; 7 ADA accessible rooms

Special Services
The Westin Portland's 205 guest rooms and suites incorporate new technology, convenience and welcoming surroundings. From high speed internet access, to The Heavenly Bed®, to CD players and CDs, to our spacious bathrooms, we provide the thoughtful extras that make every guest feel at home.

THE WESTIN PORTLAND
AS UNIQUE AS YOU
Your arrival is met with a friendly smile and a warm greeting. You're standing in the midst of the city's business, retail and cultural districts. You're staying at The Westin Portland. Experience the intimate ambiance of a European boutique hotel and the numerous services and upscale amenities synonymous with the Westin name.

THE WESTIN SALISHAN
LODGE & GOLF RESORT
Gleneden Beach, Oregon

7760 Highway 101 North • Gleneden Beach, Oregon 97388
Contact: Group Sales
(800) 890-9316; Fax (503) 764-3510
Web site: http://www.salishan.com

Capacity: 14,000 square feet of flexible meeting space for groups of 5 to 500
Price Range: price varies depending on event
Catering: full-service in-house catering
Types of Events: conferences, receptions, banquets, catered functions

Availability and Terms
Reservations are recommended six months to one year in advance.

Description of Facility and Services
Seating: tables and chairs provided for up to 600
Servers: one server per 25 guests
Bar facilities: full-service in-house bar
Dance floor: 400 sq. ft. dance floor available
Linens: a variety of colors are available at no charge
China and glassware: china and crystal available
Audiovisual: flipcharts, overhead projectors
Equipment: podiums, easels and risers available at no charge
Cleanup: provided at no charge
Parking: plenty of parking available
ADA: yes

Special Services
The Westin Salishan Lodge features 205 oversized guest rooms with fireplaces, private balconies, and ocean views; on-site massage, golf links, tennis courts, Westin Kids Club, putting course, and outward bound course.

EXPERIENCE YEAR-ROUND ATTRACTIONS OF THE OREGON COAST
The Westin Salishan Lodge and Golf Resort offers conference groups, individuals, couples and families a unique opportunity to experience the year round attractions and activities of the Oregon coast. Recreational activities include Oregon coast eco tours, hiking, beach combing, shopping at the local factory stores and marketplace, classic tours of the nationally renown wine cellar, wine tasting, horseback riding, tennis, golf, massages and storm watching. In addition to two unique on-site restaurants, Salishan is located within a seven mile radius of over 60 restaurants.

WILF'S
Restaurant and Piano Bar at Historic Union Station

N.W. 6th and Irving
Portland, Oregon 97209
(503) 223-0070;
Fax (503) 223-1386
Web site: www.wilfs.citysearch.com

Capacity: up to 160 reception-style; 150 seated; private rooms up to 40 people
Price Range: starting at $15 per person; room charge additional; menus available in varying price ranges
Catering: full-service in-house catering plus off-premise catering
Types of Events: sit-down, hors d'oeuvres, buffet; breakfast, lunch, or dinner meetings; corporate or personal; informal or silver service

Availability

Wilf's offers private rooms for up to 35 guests, or our main dining room that accommodates up to 130 guests, all decorated in rich, lush, comfortable colors to complement the historic decor of Union Station. Reserve early for your desired date. Last-minute reservations welcome, as space allows. Advance deposit required; cancellation terms vary.

Description of Facility and Services

Seating: tables and chairs for up to 175 on-site; off-premise, rentals available
Servers: wait-staff provided; off-premise at additional charge
Bar facilities: full-service bar on-site with liquor, wine, beer, nonalcoholic, bartender, and liquor liability; off-site Wilf's or host can provide liquor, liability to be discussed
Dance floor: 30- to 100-person capacity dance floor available at additional charge
Linens: cloth napkins and tablecloths in a variety of colors
China and glassware: ivory china; appropriate glassware
Decorations: special needs may be accommodated; please no tape or nails
Cleanup: included in rental charge
Audiovisual and meeting equipment: arrangements can be made
Parking: free parking at Union Station or valet parking offered
ADA: fully accessible

Special Services

When your business or personal life requires expert catering, with little work on your part, then *JUST LET US DO IT*. You can trust us down to the last detail for your business entertaining for associates, vendors, employees, or personal entertaining for friends and family. We will plan your event at the restaurant, at your business, or in your home. You can use our private rooms or rent the entire restaurant! We are a "one-stop" catering company offering full coordination of superb menus, beverages, wait-staff, entertainment, decorations, equipment rentals, guest gifts, photography and any other special needs you might have.

WILF'S CATERS TO YOU

Since 1975, the Portland area has enjoyed fine food, impeccable service and a warm, relaxed atmosphere at Wilf's. Classic steaks, seafood, seasonal creations, and our renowned jazz and Sinatra-style piano bar lend to make your event perfect! Intel, NIKE, Precision Castparts and PacifiCorp are just a few references who have enjoyed their experiences with Wilf's. Located at historic Union Station in the Pearl District.

In The Willamette Athletic Club
4949 S.W. Landing Drive • Portland, Oregon 97201
Contact: Catering (503) 225-1068

Capacity: from 2 to 250
Price Range: from $5–$20 per person
Catering: in-house only
Types of Events: conferences, board meetings, seminars, receptions and holiday parties

Availability and Terms
The Willamette Cafe located inside the Willamette Athletic Club offers two private meeting rooms each with a capacity of 18 for board meetings and 24 for seminars. Both rooms may be combined into one large room.

For meetings from 2–48 persons, please call for basic or deluxe rates. A deposit is required to secure the facility. Deposit is refundable with seven days advance cancellation (basic package) or one day in advance (deluxe package).

The full restaurant is available for larger groups. Room charges from $75 to $250 may apply. A $500 deposit is required to secure the facility. The deposit is refundable if written cancellation notice is given at least 90 days before the event.

Description of Facility and Services
Seating: tables and chairs provided
Servers: appropriate service staff provided; 15–20% gratuity on food and beverage
Bar facilities: beer and wine—full-service bar available (minimum sales of $300)
Dance floor: available for an additional charge
Linens: included with deluxe service or restaurant rental
Cleanup: provided by Willamette Cafe at no additional charge
Audiovisual: TV, VCR, overhead and slide projectors complimentary with deluxe packages; flip charts, dry erase boards and podium offered in both basic and deluxe packages; copier (10¢ per copy), fax (phone charges) also available
Outdoor facilities: a mahogany terrace with a view to the Willamette River is available.
Parking: ample free parking available
ADA: yes

CUSTOMIZED SERVICE
The Willamette Cafe offers white tablecloth service and excellent food, combined with years of experience catering for local businesses. All table arrangements, seating, A/V equipment and menus can be customized to suit your specifications. Your every need will be attended to by a staff that specializes in serving business executives on a daily basis. So if you're in search of meeting facilities removed from workplace distractions, give the Willamette Cafe a call today.

WILLAMETTE EVENTS CENTER AT THE LINN COUNTY FAIR AND EXPO

I-5 and Knox Butte Road • Albany, Oregon 97321
Contact: Jill Henderson
(541) 926-4314, (800) 858-2005; Fax (541) 926-8630
E-mail: fairexpo@co.linn.or.us
Office Hours: 8:30am–5pm; facility staffed 24 hours

Capacity: Willamette Events Center can accommodate up to 6,000 guests; conferences from 10 to 400 in 48,600 sq. ft.; three additional buildings totalling five acres under cover
Price Range: $40–$1,600
Catering: in-house catering available; contracted and flexible
Types of Events: conventions, conferences, workshops, training seminars, parties, board meetings, expositions, livestock show/sales, horse shows, and more

Availability and Terms
Currently booking into 2005. Please call for availability.

Description of Facility and Services
Seating: provided according to event; up to 3,000
Servers: provided; contracted
Bar facilities: contracted through caterer
Dance floor: available at market rate
Linens: available in a variety of colors
China and glassware: contracted
Decorations: some limitations apply
Audiovisual: slide projector, overhead, TV/VCR
Equipment: A/V carts, cords, podiums, sound; anything can be arranged
Parking: approximately 2,000 public parking spaces available; additional vendor/exhibitor parking; loading dock
ADA: fully accessible

Special Services
Service is extreme here! On-site assistance with local contacts and arrangements. The Linn County Fair and Expo Center is a full-service conference center, exhibit hall, and fairgrounds facility with a professional "can do" staff.

Located near restaurants, lodging, shopping and recreational opportunities. A 10,000 seat amphitheater is adjacent in a wooded park with a lake.

Willamette Gables

Riverside Estate

*10323 Schuler Road
Aurora, Oregon 97002
Contact: Laurel and Scott Cookman
(503) 678-2195
E-mail: w.gables@juno.com
Web site:
www.willamettegables.com*

Special events in an intimate country setting on the banks of the Willamette River

Willamette Gables is a five-acre country estate on the banks of the Willamette River, 30 minutes south of Portland and 30 minutes north of Salem. This beautiful southern plantation-style home provides the perfect backdrop for your special event or meeting.

The adjacent gardens and grounds overlook the meandering Willamette River, offering gorgeous views and solitude. Willamette Gables specializes in quality customer service and attention to detail.

Capacity: 200 outdoors; 10 to 50 seated indoors; 100 reception-style indoors
Price Range: please inquire; half-day and full day rates available
Catering: choose your own caterer (we reserve the right to approve your selection) or choose from our list
Types of Events: meetings, seminars, retreats, private parties, picnics, garden parties, teas, weddings, receptions, anniversaries

Availability and Terms

Indoor facility is available year round; outdoor setting is available June through September. All reservations must be accompanied by a 50% deposit; the balance is due 30 days prior to your scheduled event. Five bed & breakfast rooms are available for lodging.

Description of Facility and Services

Seating: indoor: tables and chairs provided for up to 50; **outdoor:** provided up to 200
Servers: provided by caterer
Bar facilities: caterer or renter provides licensed bartender and liability insurance; beer, wine and champagne only
Dance floor: inquire about availability
Linens and napkins: provided by caterer
China and glassware: provided for up to 50 at no charge
Setup and tear down: provided; caterers are expected to provide their own cleanup and trash removal
Decorations: many items are provided; little decoration needed; no rice, birdseed or confetti
Sound system: responsibility of client
Event coordination services: available for an additional fee
Covered Area: 40' x 40' canopy (upon request) available for an additional fee
Parking: ample parking; parking attendants included in the fee

Special Services
- **Five Bed and Breakfast rooms available, all with private baths**

"WILLAMETTE QUEEN" STERNWHEELER

Located at Riverfront Park—Salem, Oregon
Contact: Irene Solomon
Message phone: (541) 928-4090

WELCOME ABOARD THE 'WILLAMETTE QUEEN,' designed as a scaled down likeness of the former Mississippi and Yukon Territory Riverboats. Relive Oregon's historical past in an elegant dining experience as the ship leisurely glides along the Willamette River.

Capacity: Dining room: up to 92; during summer months an additional 15 can be accommodated on outer decks
Price Range: $10; excursions to $35 (dinner with two hour cruise)
Catering: daily lunches, Sunday brunches, dinners, hors d'oeuvres
Types of Events: birthdays, anniversaries, business meetings, banquets, weddings, class reunions, proms, fundraisers—both private and public

Availability and Terms
Reserve seating as soon as possible. Caterers require a 48 hour minimum notice for larger groups; smaller groups may be more flexible.

Description of Facility and Services
Seating: up to 115
Bar facilities: full-service bar
Dance floor: 12' x 12' dance floor available
Linens and napkins: available at no charge
China and glassware: available at no charge
Decorations: flowers, table decorations available, special decorations to be approved
Audiovisual: TV, VCR available at no charge
Equipment: podium, cordless microphone and punch bowels available at no charge
Cleanup: provided; fee for rearrangement of room setup
Parking: available at both Bowman and Salem Riverfront Park
ADA: ADA approved ramps at Bowman and Salem Riverfront Park

Special Services
The captain is a licensed minister and can perform weddings, renewal of vows, live music DJs, melodrama, talent nights and holiday events.

Sternwheeler Excursions, Inc.
P.O. Box 2228
Corvallis, Oregon 97339

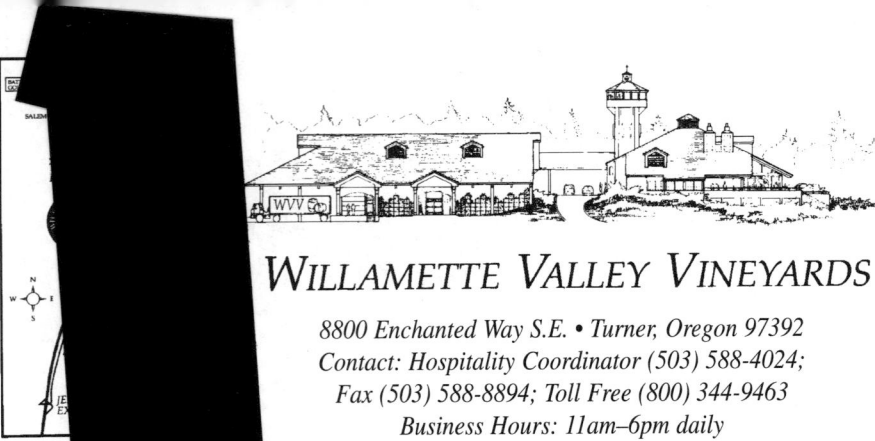

WILLAMETTE VALLEY VINEYARDS

8800 Enchanted Way S.E. • Turner, Oregon 97392
Contact: Hospitality Coordinator (503) 588-4024;
Fax (503) 588-8894; Toll Free (800) 344-9463
Business Hours: 11am–6pm daily

Capacity: up to 600 inside and outside
Price Range: $150 to $1,800
Catering: exclusively by Willaby's Catering, prepared on-site; Willaby's full-service catering can assist you with your selections of the perfect menu for your event; all events are customized to reflect each individual's taste; Willaby's offers personalized menu planning in all price ranges
Types of Events: indoor and outdoor meetings and events. The indoor facility and outdoor facility can be utilized together. Other rentals include holiday parties, business meetings, class reunions, all-day seminars, family gatherings, company barbecues and more.

Availability and Terms
Reservations should be made as soon as possible. We require a deposit of 50% of room charge at the time of rental.

Description of Facility and Services
Seating: tables and chairs are available
Licensed servers: Willamette Valley Vineyards arranges for wine servers for both indoor and outdoor events
Liquor liability: we are not licensed to serve any alcoholic beverages other than wine and beer on premise. Our award-winning wines are available for purchase in our tasting room.
Music and dance floor: amplified music is allowed, and dance floor areas are available both inside and outside the facility
Linens and glassware: available for rent
Decorations: please discuss decorating ideas with our staff
Cleanup: client or caterer to provide
Parking: free parking available to Willamette Valley Vineyards patrons
ADA: access to restrooms, tasting room, and event rooms

Special Services
Personalized neck labels attached to your choice of Willamette Valley Wines are available for purchase prior to your event. This personalized touch is a special remembrance for your guests. Special tours and wine tasting can be arranged for your group with prior notice.

PANORAMIC VIEW
Our newly built Visitor Center with panoramic view of the Willamette Valley and Coastal Range is the perfect location for any event.

WILSONVILLE FAMILY FUN CENTER AND BULLWINKLE'S RESTAURANT

29111 S.W. Town Center Loop W. • Wilsonville, Oregon 97070
(503) 685-5000, ext. 21; Fax (503) 685-9694
Web site: wffc.citysearch.com
Open year-round
Business Hours: winter: 11am–9pm; summer 9am–11pm

Capacity: amusement park, 2,000 people; Bullwinkle's dining room, 175 people
Price Range: $3–$28 per person
Catering: in-house
Types of Events: corporate picnics, holiday parties, graduation parties, employee incentives, birthday parties, family reunions

Availability and Terms
First come, first served. Reservations available during all operating hours. After-hour packages also are available. Deposits are required.

Description of Facility and Services
Seating: indoor, 175; outdoor, 250; weather protection provided
Servers: provided
Bar facilities: no
Linens: paper napkins available
China and glassware: paper cups and plates available
Decorations: no limitations
Audiovisual: not provided; arrangements for rental can be made on request
Equipment: not provided; arrangements for rental can be made on request
Cleanup: provided
Parking: 250 spaces
ADA: yes

ENTERTAINMENT FOR ALL AGES

This amazing 6-acre amusement park is located in the city of Wilsonville (I-5, exit 283). The Wilsonville Family Fun Center and Bullwinkle's Restaurant provide a fun and clean atmosphere, safe attractions, great food and entertainment for all ages. Attractions are miniature golf, go karts, bumper boats, batting cages, Lazer-Xtreme, Kidopolis (indoor, soft play) and a two-story arcade.

See page 99 under Attractions, Activities & Tours.

SKY ROOM AND TERRACE

Top Floor of the Holiday Inn
1021 N.E. Grand Avenue • Portland, Oregon 97232
Contact: Mary Baskerville at Catering Office
(503) 820-4160; Fax (503) 235-0396
Office Hours: Mon–Fri 8am–5pm; other times by appointment

Capacity: *Ballroom:* up to 250; *Sky Room:* up to 200; *Terrace:* up to 100
Price Range: prices vary with size and menu selection; we will work with you and your budget
Catering: provided by the hotel exclusively
Types of Events: dinners, cocktail receptions, themed events, retirement parties, holiday parties, luncheons, and much more

Availability and Terms

Grand Ballroom has four separate reception rooms that can be used individually or in combination to host as many as 250 guests. Windows Sky Room with floor-to-ceiling windows offers a spectacular view of downtown Portland. Also available for private functions is our open-air terrace. All banquet facilities are located on the top floor of the Holiday Inn Portland—Downtown. A deposit is required to reserve space with the deposit applied to the final bill.

Description of Facility and Services

Seating: tables and chairs provided
Bar facilities: full beverage service; hotel provides all alcoholic beverages
Dance floor: dance floor and electrical hookups available at an additional charge
Linens: linens and cloth napkins available in a variety of colors, complimentary basis with catering
Entertainment, props and decorations: can be provided at an additional charge
Cleanup: provided by Windows at no charge
Parking: complimentary parking; street and lot parking nearby

Special Services

Windows catering staff offers personalized attention to every detail of your event. We will customize a menu to fit your needs from a theme party to a formal sit-down dinner or elegant cocktail party on our terrace.

ELEGANCE AND SPECTACULAR CITY VIEW

Windows is a full-service banquet facility. In addition to our 4,000-square-foot ballroom, Windows Sky Room, with its panoramic view, is also available for private events. Our open-air terrace provides a fantastic view of downtown Portland and the Oregon Convention Center. Windows catering serves fine Northwest Cuisine highlighting fresh foods of the Pacific Northwest. Whether it be three persons or 250, your event is special to us! Call for more details.

WITTENBERG INN

5188 Wittenberg Lane
Keizer, Oregon 97303
Contact: Richard Andres (503) 390-4733; Fax (503) 390-1108
Business Hours: Open 24 hours
Web site: www.wittenberginn.com

Capacity: seven banquet rooms; three will seat up to 160, four will seat up to 450
Price Range: varies with menu selection
Catering: in-house catering; award-winning chef
Types of Events: meetings, banquets, receptions, weddings, conventions, seminars

Availability and Terms
Rooms are reserved based on availability. A deposit is required at the time of confirmation with the balance due 30 days prior to the event. Deposits are refundable if cancellation is received at least 30 days prior to the function.

Description of Facility and Services
Seating: tables and chairs provided as needed
Servers: provided
Bar facilities: full-service bar
Dance floor: available for a charge
China and glassware: china and glassware provided
Linens and napkins: white linens provided; other colors available for an additional fee
Audiovisual: overhead, screens, slide projector, etc. available to rent
Equipment: podium included in rental fee; risers and staging available for a charge
Cleanup: provided by Wittenberg Inn
Parking: ample free parking available
ADA: ADA compliant

Special Services
- 86 mini-suites with microwaves, refrigerators, and coffee makers
- Complimentary gourmet continental breakfast buffet
- 24-hour indoor heated pool, spa, and fitness center
- Free local phone calls plus two-line telephones with data port

GIVING NEW LIFE TO YOUR MEETING
The first impression is often the most important. Your next banquet, social affair or meeting will make a spectacular impression by scheduling it in one of our elegant banquet rooms. The Wittenberg Inn will make any event a grand affair.

WORLD FORESTRY CENTER

4033 S.W. Canyon Road
Portland, Oregon 97221
Contact: Facilities Coordinator
(503) 228-1367 ext. 101; Fax (503) 228-4608
Office Hours: Mon–Fri 9am–4pm
Web site: http://www.worldforest.org

Capacity: banquet, 40-250; classroom, 35-175; conference, 50-300; stand-up reception, inside—200–400, outside plaza—1,000
Price Range: price varies by type of facility and time; please call for specific pricing.
Catering: client or approved caterers, full kitchens available; caterer referral list on request
Types of Events: seminars, conferences, banquets, trade shows, board meetings, formal dinners and buffets, breakfast and luncheon meetings, workshops, receptions

Availability and Terms
Located in Portland's Washington Park, our three meeting halls and 10,000-sq.-ft. outdoor plaza are available year-round, seven days a week for day and evening events. Our 30,000-sq.-ft. museum is open after-hours for events, such as receptions. Three rustic cabins, a picnic area and a well-maintained meadow are available for day and overnight use at or Magness Memorial Tree Farm near Wilsonville, Oregon. A deposit is required for booking; deposit is nonrefundable unless date can be booked in same calendar year.

Description of Facility and Services
Seating: Miller Hall: 300 chairs, 25 eight-foot tables, 30 five-foot round tables; Cheatham Hall: 200 chairs, 25 eight-foot tables; David Douglas Room: 50 chairs
Servers: provided by caterer
Bar facilities: liquor allowed, OLCC regulations apply
Dance floor: Cheatham Hall, 18' x 18' dance floor available
Stage: Miller Hall, 12 sections, 3' x 4' portable stage, two sets of steps
Linens and napkins: provided by client or caterer
China and glassware: provided by client or caterer
Decorations: buildings are available three hours prior to event for decorating; please no confetti, glitter, mylar, rice or birdseed; candles are allowed only in hurricane shade or water base; no nails, push pins, tacks, staples or tape
Audiovisual: PA system, microphone, screen
Cleanup: client or cater to remove everything brought into facility
Parking: ample parking, shared lot with Oregon Zoo; on MAX line (easy access from hotels)
ADA: meets most ADA requirements; upgrades planned

A SERENE, SYLVAN SETTING
Escape to Portland's beautiful Washington Park, where the World Forestry Center offers a quiet sylvan setting for your business meetings or social events. Enjoy the natural warmth of wood tones in Miller and Cheatham Halls, which are inviting spaces with large, open ceilings. Select your favorite caterer and use our full kitchen facilities. The David Douglas Room is an ideal mid-week getaway for small group sessions, business retreats, planning meetings, or small classroom settings. When the season permits, gaze into a star-studded evening from our outdoor plaza, or escape to our 80-acre tree farm meadow and picnic area.

WORLD TRADE CENTER PORTLAND

Two World Trade Center Portland

25 S.W. Salmon Street
Portland, Oregon 97204
Reservations: (503) 464-8688
Office Hours: Mon–Fri 8am–5pm

Capacity: **inside:** 400 reception, 300 seated; **outside:** 800 reception, 500 seated; **Flags riverfront space:** 125 reception, 80 seated

Price Range: please call for specific price information

Catering: full in-house catering

Types of Events: banquets, conferences, seminars, trade shows, board meetings, formal dinners and buffets, breakfast and luncheon meetings, receptions

Availability and Terms

Over 14 rooms are available to meet your specific needs. Our riverfront banquet space offers a fantastic view of the river and Tom McCall Waterfront Park. Reservations at least six months in advance are suggested—particularly during spring and summer months. An advance deposit of 25% of the anticipated total expenses is required within seven days of confirmation.

Description of Facility and Services

Seating: seating capacity based on room(s) selected and chair arrangement
Bar facilities: full beverage service provided
Dance floor: dance floor upon request at standard rental rate; electrical hookup for bands or disc jockey available
Decorations: creative theme events may be arranged
Audiovisual: extensive audiovisual equipment available upon request; 1-800# conference calling, satellite receiving capabilities
Equipment: podium, easels, and risers available
Parking: underground daytime and evening parking available in building
ADA: all rooms are disabled accessible

Special Services

Our event coordinators will work closely with you to make sure all your arrangements are complete. Our facility includes an auditorium with seating for more than 200, simultaneous translation system, 14 conference and meeting rooms, and extensive exhibit space. We also have a covered open plaza for outdoor functions.

WHERE THE WORLD MEETS

Located in vibrant downtown Portland, with easy access from I-84 and I-5, the World Trade Center is an ideal location for seminars, conferences, receptions, parties, trade shows, art exhibits and weddings. The Conference Center can easily accommodate both indoor and outdoor functions. Unique to Portland is our 10,000-square-foot covered outdoor plaza, with potted trees and flowering plants. A part of the three-building World Trade Center, the Conference Center is located at Two World Trade Center on the block between Front and First Avenues, and Salmon and Taylor Streets. Please call for a tour and information packet.

Please let this business know that you heard about them from the Bravo! Event Resource Guide.

Notes

Portland Area Banquet & Event Sites

PORTLAND AREA BANQUET AND EVENT SITE LISTINGS

ADDRESS	CAPACITY	GUEST ROOMS	CONTACT
DOWNTOWN PORTLAND			
The Adrianna Hill Grand Ballroom 918 S.W. Yamhill, 2nd Fl. Portland, OR 97205 *See page 446*	Up to 300 R/B/S/M/C/		Philip Sword or Barbara Abalan (503) 227-6285
Arlene Schnitzer Concert Hall S.W. Broadway at Main Portland, OR 97205 *See page 533*	Grand Lobby: Sit-down: Up to 200 Reception: Up to 400 Theatre: Up to 2,776 R/B/S/M/C/		Booking & Sales (503) 248-4335 Fax (503) 274-7490
The Atrium 100 S.W. Market St. Portland, OR 97201 *See page 451*	Sit-down: Up to 150 Reception: Up to 300 R/B/S/M/		Catering Director (503) 220-3929
Atwater's Restaurant & Bar 111 S.W. 5th Ave., 30th fl. Portland, OR 97204 *See page 452*	Up to 300 R/B/S/M/		Hollie Stafford (503) 275-3662
The Benson Hotel 309 S.W. Broadway at Oak Portland, OR 97205 *See page 454*	Reception: Up to 600 Sit-down: Up to 350 R/B/S/M/C/	286	Sales (503) 295-4100 Fax (503) 226-2709
Berbati Restaurant 19 S.W. Ankiny Portland, OR 97204	Up to 350 R/B/S/M/		John (503) 226-2122
Cassidy's Restaurant 1331 S.W. Washington Portland, OR 97205 *See page 323*	Sit-down: Up to 50 Reception: Up to 300 R/B/S/M/		Christine, Bob or Mercedes (503) 223-0054
Central Library 801 S.W. 10th Ave. Portland, OR 97205 *See page 459*	Sit-down: Varies Reception: Up to 1,200 R/B/S/M/C/		Events Coordinator (503) 306-5578
City Hall 1120 S.W. 5th Ave. Portland, OR 97204 *See page 465*	Reception: Up to 4,000 R/B/S/M/C/		Faye Musselman (503) 823-6947 Fax (503) 823-6924
The Crown Ballroom 918 S.W. Yamhill, Fifth Floor Portland, OR 97205 *See page 469*	Sit-down: Up to 350 Reception: Up to 400 R/B/S/M/C/		Manager (503) 227-8440
Crystal Ballroom 132 W. Burnside Portland, OR 97209 *See page 472*	Sit-down: Up to 350 Reception: Up to 1,000 R/B/S/M/C/		Mary Hendrickx (503) 492-2777

P=Picnic   R=Reception   B=Banquet   S=Seminar   M=Meeting   C=Convention

Please let these businesses know that you heard about them from the Bravo! Event Resource Guide.

PORTLAND AREA
BANQUET AND EVENT SITE LISTINGS

ADDRESS	CAPACITY	GUEST ROOMS	CONTACT
Days Inn City Center 1414 S.W. Sixth Ave. Portland, OR 97201 *See page 473*	Up to 200 R/B/S/M/C/	173	Judy Kaski (503) 221-1611 (800) 899-0248 Fax (503) 226-0447
Demetri's Mediterranean Restaurant 1650 W. Burnside Portland, OR 97209	Up to 150 R/B/S/M/		Owner (503) 222-1507
DoubleTree Downtown 310 S.W. Lincoln Portland, OR 97201 *See page 475*	Up to 400 R/B/S/M/C/	235	Sales Office (503) 221-0450
Embassy Suites—Portland Downtown 319 S.W. Pine St. Portland, OR 97204 *See page 481*	Sit-down: Up to 220 Reception: Up to 300	276	Rich Kannapell (503) 279-9000 Fax (503) 497-9051
Fifth Avenue Suites Hotel/ Red Star Tavern & Roast House 506 S.W. Washington Portland, OR 97204 *See page 483*	Reception: Up to 200 R/B/S/M/C/	221	Phyllis Steers (503) 222-0001
Four Points Sheraton 50 S.W. Morrison St. Portland, OR 97204 *See page 356*	Sit-down: Up to 40 Reception: Up to 50 R/B/S/M/	140	Karol Norris (503) 221-0711 Fax (503) 274-0312
Georgian Room Restaurant Meier & Frank 621 S.W. 5th Ave., 10th Fl. Portland, OR 97204	Party Room: Up to 20 Grill: Up to 50 Tea Room: Up to 150 B/P/M/S/R/		Special Events (503) 223-0512
Jake's Catering at The Governor Hotel 611 S.W. 10th St. Portland, OR 97205 *See page 487*	Sit-down: Up to 450 Reception: Up to 600 R/B/S/M/P/	100	Catering Sales (503) 241-2125 Fax (503) 220-1849
Greek Cusina Minoan Room 404 S.W. Washington Portland, OR 97204 *See page 488*	Up to 500 R/B/S/M/		Ted Papas (503) 224-2288
The Heathman Hotel 1001 S.W. Broadway at Salmon St. Portland, OR 97205 *See page 491*	Reception: Up to 220 Sit-down: Up to 120 R/B/S/M/C/	75	Catering Manager (503) 790-7126

P=Picnic   R=Reception   B=Banquet   S=Seminar   M=Meeting   C=Convention

Please let these businesses know that you heard about them from the Bravo! Event Resource Guide.

PORTLAND AREA
BANQUET AND EVENT SITE LISTINGS

ADDRESS	CAPACITY	GUEST ROOMS	CONTACT
Portland Hilton 921 S.W. Sixth Ave. Portland, OR 97204 *See page 495*	Up to 1,200 R/B/S/M/C/	461	Catering (503) 226-1611 Fax (503) 220-2293
Huber's 411 S.W. Third Portland, OR 97204 *See page 437*	Sit-down: Up to 50 R/B/		James (503) 228-5686 Fax (503) 227-3922
Typhoon! **at The Imperial Hotel** 400 S.W. Broadway Portland, OR 97205 *See page 501*	Up to 150 R/B/S/M/	136	(503) 224-8285 Fax (503) 224-1894
Jake's Grill 611 S.W. 10th Portland, OR 97205	Up to 500 R/B/S/M/C/		Dorcas Popp (503) 241-2125
Jasmine Tree 401 S.W. Harrison Portland, OR 97201	Up to 150 R/B/S/M/		Manager (503) 223-7956
Kells Irish Restaurant **& Pub** 112 S.W. Second Ave. Portland, OR 97204 *See page 504*	Sit-down: Up to 150 Reception: Up to 300 R/B/S/M/		Banquet Manager (503) 227-4057
Kingstad Meeting Centers Pacific First Center Mezzanine Level 850 S.W. Broadway Ave. Portland, OR 97205 *See page 440*	Up to 200 R/B/S/M/		Eric Kingstad (503) 626-6338
Mallory Hotel 729 S.W. 15th Ave. Portland, OR 97205	Sit-down: Up to 100 Reception: Up to 125 R/B/S/M/	150	Food & Beverage Director (503) 223-631
Mandarin Cove 111 S.W. Columbia Portland, OR 97201	Sit-down: Up to 250 Reception: 250 R/B/S/M/		Jen Tsui Banquet Manager (503) 222-0006
Portland Marriott **City Center** 520 S.W. Broadway Portland, OR 97205 *See page 508*	Up to 120 R/B/S/M/	249	(503) 226-6300 Fax (503) 227-7515
Marriott Hotel—Portland 1401 S.W. Naito Parkway Portland, OR 97201 *See page 507*	Up to 1,000 R/B/S/M/C/	504	Sales & Catering (503) 499-6360
McCormick & Schmick's **Seafood Restaurant** 235 S.W. First Ave. Portland, OR 97204	Up to 40 R/B/S/M/		General Manager (503) 224-7522 Fax (503) 220-1881

P=Picnic   R=Reception   B=Banquet   S=Seminar   M=Meeting   C=Convention

Please let these businesses know that you heard about them from the Bravo! Event Resource Guide.

PORTLAND AREA
BANQUET AND EVENT SITE LISTINGS

ADDRESS	CAPACITY	GUEST ROOMS	CONTACT
Morton's Steakhouse 213 S.W. Clay St. Portland, OR 97201 *See page 441*	Up to 80 R/B/S/M/		T. Angelique Leonard (503) 238-2100 Fax (503) 248-2005
New Theatre Building at the Portland Center for the Performing Arts 1111 S.W. Broadway Portland, OR 97205 *See page 533*	Intermediate Theatre Theatre: Up to 880 Dolores Winningstad Theatre: Up to 292 Rotunda Lobby Sit-down: Up to 400 Reception: Up to 1,000 R/B/S/M/C/		Booking & Sales (503) 248-4335 Fax (503) 274-7490
The Old Church 1422 S.W. 11th Ave. Portland, OR 97201 *See page 519*	Auditorium: Up to 300 Reception: Up to 180 R/B/S/M/		Trish Augustin (503) 222-2031 Fax (503) 222-2981
Oregon Sports Hall of Fame 321 S.W. Salmon St. Portland, OR 97204 *See page 525*	Sit-down: Up to 150 Reception: Up to 300 P/R/B/S/M/		Operations Director (503) 227-7466 ext. 10 Fax (503) 227-6925
Pazzo Ristorante Hotel Vintage Plaza 422 S.W. Broadway Portland, OR 97205 *See page 528*	Sit-down: Up to 140 Reception: Up to 200 R/B/S/M/C/	107	Private Dining (503) 412-6316
Piatti on Broadway 319 S.W. Broadway Portland, OR 97205	Up to 110 R/B/S/M/		Ray Colvin (503) 525-0945
Portland Art Museum North Wing 1119 S.W. Park Ave. Portland, OR 97205 *See page 532*	Up to 1,500 R/B/S/M/		Food & Beverage Manager (503) 226-2811x4291
Portland Civic Auditorium S.W. Third & Clay St. Portland, OR 97201 *See page 533*	Sit-down: Up to 400 Reception: Up to 500 Theatre: Up to 3,000 R/S/M/C/B/		Booking & Sales (503) 248-4335 or (503) 274-6557
RiverPlace Hotel 1510 S.W. Harbor Way Portland, OR 97201 *See page 542*	Sit-down: Up to 200 Reception: Up to 400 R/B/S/M/C/	84	Sales & Catering (503) 423-3111
Rock Bottom Brewery 210 S.W. Morrison Portland, OR 97204 *See page 543*	Up to 100 R/B/S/M/		Banquet Coordinator (503) 796-2739
Scottish Rite Center 1512 S.W. Morrison Portland, OR 97205	Up to 400 R/B/S/M/C/		Building Manager (503) 226-7827 Fax (503) 823-3562

P=Picnic   R=Reception   B=Banquet   S=Seminar   M=Meeting   C=Convention

Please let these businesses know that you heard about them from the Bravo! Event Resource Guide.

PORTLAND AREA BANQUET AND EVENT SITE LISTINGS

ADDRESS	CAPACITY	GUEST ROOMS	CONTACT
Tiffany Center 1410 S.W. Morrison St. Portland, OR 97205 *See page 558*	Up to 1,300 Theatre: Up to 975 R/B/S/M/C/		Events Manager (503) 222-0703 or (503) 248-9305
Westin Portland 750 S.W. Alder Portland, OR 97205 *See page 565*	Up to 120 R/B/S/M		Aaron Babbie (503) 294-9000 Fax (503) 241-9565
Wilf's Restaurant & Piano Bar N.W. Sixth & Irving Portland, OR 97209 *See page 567*	Sit-down: Up to 150 Reception: Up to 160 R/B/S/M/		Manager (503) 223-0070 Fax (503) 223-1386
World Trade Center Two World Trade Center 25 S.W. Salmon St. Portland, OR 97204 *See page 577*	Indoor: Up to 300 Reception: Up to 400 Outdoor: Sit-down: Up to 500 Reception: Up to 800 R/B/S/M/C/		Reservations (503) 464-8688

NORTH PORTLAND

ADDRESS	CAPACITY	GUEST ROOMS	CONTACT
Best Western Inn At The Meadows 1215 N. Hayden Meadows Dr. Portland, OR 97217	Up to 75 R/B/S/M/C/	146	Director of Sales (503) 286-9600 Fax (503) 286-8020
Courtyard Marriott— Portland North Harbour 1231 N. Anchor Way Portland, OR 97217 *See page 468*	Indoor: Up to 100 Outdoor: Up to 250 R/B/S/M/		Christine Skarphol (503) 735-1818 Fax (503) 735-0888
Cucina! Cucina! One Center Court Portland, OR 97227	Up to 200 R/B/S/M/		Doreen Lowndes (503) 238-9800 Fax (206) 238-9749
Crown Vista Events 1341 N. Killingsworth St. Portland, OR 97217 *See page 470*	Indoor: Up to 150 Outdoor: Up to 350 P/R/B/S/M/		Wendy Daniels (503) 240-6057
DoubleTree Columbia River 1401 N. Hayden Island Dr. Portland, OR 97217 *See page 474*	Sit-down: Up to 500 Reception: Up to 900 R/B/S/M/C/	351	Sales Office (503) 283-2111
DoubleTree Jantzen Beach 909 N. Hayden Island Dr. Portland, OR 97217 *See page 477*	Sit-down: Up to 1,400 Reception: Up to 2,000 R/B/S/M/C/	320	Sales Office (503) 283-4466
Interstate Firehouse Cultural Center 5340 N. Interstate Ave. Portland, OR 97217	Up to 200 Theatre: Up to 110 R/M/S/		Rental Coordinator (503) 823-4322 Fax (503) 823-2061

P=Picnic   R=Reception   B=Banquet   S=Seminar   M=Meeting   C=Convention

PORTLAND AREA BANQUET AND EVENT SITE LISTINGS

ADDRESS	CAPACITY	GUEST ROOMS	CONTACT
Historic Kenton Firehouse Community Center 8105 N. Brandon Portland, OR 97217	Upstairs: Up to 20 Downstairs: Up to 100 R/B/S/M/		Coordinator (503) 285-7843
McMenamins St. Johns Pub 8203 N. Ivanhoe Portland, OR 97203	Sit-down: Up to 100 Reception: Up to 200 Entire facility: 300 P/B/S/M/		Jeff Bryant (503) 669-8610 Fax (503) 283-8609
Memorial Coliseum at the Rose Quarter One Center Court, Ste. 200 Portland, OR 97227 *See page 410*	Up to 1,800 R/B/S/M/C/		(503) 235-8771 Fax (503) 736-2192
North Star Ballroom 635 N. Killingsworth Court Portland, OR 97217 *See page 516*	Sit-down: Up to 150 Reception: Up to 250 R/B/S/M/		Harriet Fasenfest (503) 240-6088
The Overlook House 3839 N. Melrose Dr. Portland, OR 97227	Indoor: Up to 75 Outdoor: Up to 150 P/R/S/M/		Building Coordinator (503) 823-3188
Oxford Suites Hotel 12226 N. Jantzen Dr. Portland, OR 97217	Up to 120 R/S/M/	203	Sales (503) 283-3030 Fax (503) 735-1661
Portland Meadows 1001 N. Schmeer Rd. Portland, OR 97217	Up to 900 R/B/M/		Group Sales Dept. (503) 285-9144 Fax (503) 286-9763
Portland Metropolitan Exposition Center 2060 N. Marine Dr. Portland, OR 97217	Up to 6,000 P/R/S/M/C/		Sales Department (503) 736-5200 Fax (503) 736-5201
Queen Ann Victorian Mansion 1441 N. McClellan Portland, OR 97217	Indoor: Up to 60 Outdoor: 200 P/R/B/S/M/		Banquet Coordinator (503) 283-3224 Fax (503) 283-5605
Red Lion—Coliseum 1225 N. Thunderbird Way Portland, OR 97227	Sit-down: Up to 150 Reception: Up to 300 R/B/S/M/C/	212	Catering Office (503) 235-8311
Rose Garden arena One Center Court, Ste. 200 Portland, OR 97227 *See page 410*	Arena:Up to 21,000 Reception: Up to 300 R/B/		(503) 235-8771 Fax (503) 736-2192
Rose Quarter Commons One Center Court, Ste. 200 Portland, OR 97227 *See page 410*	Outdoor: Up to 3,000 P/R/B/S/M/C/		(503) 235-8771 Fax (503) 736-2192

P=Picnic   R=Reception   B=Banquet   S=Seminar   M=Meeting   C=Convention

Please let these businesses know that you heard about them from the Bravo! Event Resource Guide.

PORTLAND AREA BANQUET AND EVENT SITE LISTINGS

ADDRESS	CAPACITY	GUEST ROOMS	CONTACT
Shenanigans' **on the Willamette** 4575 N. Channel Portland, OR 97217 *See page 548*	Sit-down: Up to 400 Reception: Up to 800 P/R/B/S/M/		Michael Baker (503) 289-1597
University of Portland **Chiles Center** 5000 N. Willamette Blvd. Portland, OR 97203	Up to 5,000 R/B/S/M/C/		Director, University Events (503) 283-7523 Fax (503) 283-7451
University of Portland **Commons/Main Dining Rm** 5000 N. Willamette Blvd. Portland, OR 97203	Up to 600 R/B/S/M/C/ *Dining Room available summer break only		Director, University Events (503) 283-7330 Fax (503) 283-7544
Widmer Gasthaus 929 N. Russel Portland, OR 97227 *See page 444*	Up to 75 B/P/M/S/		Manager (503) 281-3333 Fax (503) 331-7242
YWCA St. Johns Center 8010 N. Charleston Portland, OR 97203	Large Hall: Up to 100 Meeting Room: Up to 30 R/B/S/M/		Rental Coordinator (503) 721-6777 Fax (503) 721-6751

NORTHEAST PORTLAND

ADDRESS	CAPACITY	GUEST ROOMS	CONTACT
Alberta Station Ballroom 1829 N.E. Alberta Portland, OR 97211	Up to 570 R/B/S/M/		Pat Goebel (503) 284-8666
Albertina's **at The Old Kerr Nursery** 424 N.E. 22nd Ave. Portland, OR 97232 *See page 447*	Up to 250 R/B/		Event Coordinator (503) 231-3909
Capers Café & Catering 12003 N.E. Ainsworth Cir., Ste. A Portland, OR 97220 *See page 322*	Up to 150 R/B/S/M/		Christian or Annette Joly (503) 252-1718 Fax (503) 252-0178
Colwood Nat'l Golf Course 7313 N.E. Columbia Blvd. Portland, OR 97218	Up to 200 R/B/S/M/		Club Manager (503) 254-2567 Fax (503) 255-0504
Courtyard by Marriot— **Lloyd Center** 435 N.E. Wasco St. Portland, OR 97232 *See page 352*	Up to 40 S/M/	202	Kathy Bayerkohler (503) 234-3200
Courtyard by Marriott— **Portland Airport** 11550 N.E. Airport Way Portland, OR 97220	Up to 125 R/B/S/M/C/	150	Dawna Anderson Catering (503) 252-3200 Fax (503) 252-8921

P=Picnic   R=Reception   B=Banquet   S=Seminar   M=Meeting   C=Convention

PORTLAND AREA
BANQUET AND EVENT SITE LISTINGS

ADDRESS	CAPACITY	GUEST ROOMS	CONTACT
DoubleTree Lloyd Center 1000 N.E. Multnomah Portland, OR 97232 *See page 478*	Up to 1100 R/B/S/M/C/	476	Catering (503) 249-3130
Embassy Suites Portland Airport 9700 N.E. 82nd Ave. Portland, OR 97220 *See page 480*	Up to 563 R/B/S/M/C/	251	Sales & Catering (503) 460-3000 Fax (503) 460-3030
Hilton Garden—Airport 12048 N.E. Airport Way Portland, OR 97220 *See page 494*	Up to 100 B/S/M/	121	Liz Charbonneau (503) 255-8600 Fax (503) 255-8998
Holiday Inn—Airport 8439 N.E. Columbia Blvd. Portland, OR 97220 *See page 496*	Up to 1,200 R/B/S/M/	303	Sales & Catering (503) 256-5000
Irvington Club 2131 N.E. Thompson Portland, OR 97212	Up to 175 R/B/S/M/		Heidi Kamm (503) 287-8749 Fax (503) 284-5308
J.J. North's Grand Buffet 10520 N.E. Halsey Portland, OR 97220	Up to 125 R/B/S/M/		Manager (503) 254-5555 Fax (503) 254-8411
Kingstad Meeting Centers 5933 N.E. Win Sievers Dr. Portland, OR 97220 *See page 505*	Sit-down: Up to 100 Reception: Up to 200 R/B/S/M/C/		Eric Kingstad (503) 626-6338
McMenamins Kennedy School 5736 N.E. 33rd Ave. Portland, OR 97211 *See page 390*	Reception: Up to 250 Sit-down: Up to 125 Theater: Up to 250	35	(503) 2288-3286
O'Callahan's at Ramada Inn 6221 N.E. 82nd Ave. Portland, OR 97220 *See page 517*	Sit-down: Up to 300 Reception: Up to 600 R/B/S/M/C/	202	Ann Conger (503) 253-2400 Fax (503) 253-1635
Oregon Convention Center 777 N.E. MLK Jr. Blvd. Portland, OR 97212 *See page 406*	Up to 2,500 R/B/S/M/C/		(503) 731-7851
Port of Portland 7000 N.E. Airport Way Portland, OR 97218 *See page 531*	Up to 100 6 rooms R/B/M/S/C/		Paula Sorensen (503) 460-4051
Portland Conference Center 300 N.E. Multnomah St. Portland, OR 97232 *See page 534*	Up to 700 12 rooms R/B/S/M/C/		Event Coordinator (503) 239-9921

P=Picnic   R=Reception   B=Banquet   S=Seminar   M=Meeting   C=Convention

Please let these businesses know that you heard about them from the Bravo! Event Resource Guide.

PORTLAND AREA
BANQUET AND EVENT SITE LISTINGS

ADDRESS	CAPACITY	GUEST ROOMS	CONTACT
Portland's White House 1914 N.E. 22nd Ave. Portland, OR 97212	Up to 100 R/S/M/	9	Owners Steve & Lanning (503) 287-7131 (800) 272-7131
Radisson Hotel Portland 1441 N.E. Second Ave. Portland, OR 97232 *See page 363*	Sit-down: Up to 200 R/B/S/M/C/	238	Michelle Long (503) 233-2401 Fax (503) 238-7016
The Refectory Restaurant 1618 N.E. 122nd Ave. Portland, OR 97230	Indoor: Up to 300 R/B/S/M/		Rita (503) 255-8545 Fax (503) 255-8230
The Ringside 14021 N.E. Glisan Portland, OR 97230	Up to 30 *Not weekends B/S/M/		Kathy/John (503) 255-0750
Rheinlander German Restaurant 5035 N.E. Sandy Blvd. Portland, OR 97213 *See page 541*	Sit-down: Up to 100 Reception: Up to 150 R/B/S/M/		Banquet Manager (503) 288-8410
Salty's on the Columbia 3839 N.E. Marine Dr. Portland, OR 97211 *See page 544*	Reception: Up to 200 Sit-down: Up to 100 R/B/S/M/		Dorothy Lane (503) 288-4444
Sheraton Portland Airport Hotel 8235 N.E. Airport Way Portland, OR 97220-1398 *See page 549*	Sit-down: Up to 700 Reception: Up to 750 R/B/S/M/	214	Janet Eichner (503) 249-7642 Fax (503) 249-7624
Shilo Inn Suites Hotel— Restaurant & Convention Center 11707 N.E. Airport Way Portland, OR 97220 *See page 550*	Sit-down: Up to 350 Reception: Up to 500 R/B/S/M/C/	200	Catering Office (503) 252-7500 ext. 270
Sylvia's Italian Restaurant 5115 N.E. Sandy Blvd. Portland, OR 97213 *See page 557*	Up to 80 Theatre: Up to 100 R/B/S/M/		Norm Stone (503) 288-6828
Windows Sky Room & Terrace at the Holiday Inn 1021 N.E. Grand Ave. Portland, OR 97232 *See page 574*	Reception: Up to 250 R/B/S/M/C/	160	(503) 820-4160 Fax (503) 235-0396
YWCA N.E. Center 5630 N.E. MLK Jr. Blvd. Portland, OR 97211	Meeting Room1: Up to 12 Meeting Room2: Up to 25 M/S/		Rental Coordinator (503) 721-1750 Fax (503) 721-1751

P=Picnic   R=Reception   B=Banquet   S=Seminar   M=Meeting   C=Convention

Please let these businesses know that you heard about them from the Bravo! Event Resource Guide.

PORTLAND AREA
BANQUET AND EVENT SITE LISTINGS

ADDRESS	CAPACITY	GUEST ROOMS	CONTACT
NORTHWEST PORTLAND			
BridgePort Brewing Co. 1313 N.W. Marshall Portland, OR 97209 *See page 456*	Sit-down: Up to 250 R/B/S/M/ *Non-smoking		Event Coordinator (503) 241-7179 Fax (503) 241-0625
Couch Street Fish House 105 N.W. 3rd Ave. Portland, OR 97209	Sit-down: Up to 20 R/B/M/		Manager (503) 223-6173 Fax (503) 721-0820
Friendly House 1737 N.W. 26th Portland, OR 97210	Up to 300 P/R/B/S/M/		Vaune Albanese (503) 228-4391 Fax (503) 228-0085
Gatelodge Restaurant at Pittock Mansion 3229 N.W. Pittock Dr. Portland, OR 97210	Sit-down: Up to 50 P/B/S/M/		Lisette Hollis (503) 823-3627
Il Fornaio 115 N.W. 22nd Ave. Portland, OR 97210 *See page 439*	Up to 130 R/B/S/M/		Faith Chhim (503) 248-4324 or (503) 248-9400 Fax (503) 248-5678
Montgomery Park 2701 N.W. Vaughn St. Portland, OR 97210 *See page 513*	Sit-down: Up to 400 Reception: Up to 1,200 R/B/S/M/		Event Coordinator (503) 228-7275
Northwest Neighborhood Cultural Center 1819 N.W. Everett St. Portland, OR 97209	Sit-down: Up to 200 Reception: Up to 200 Theatre: Up to 650 R/B/S/M/		Scheduling Coordinator (503) 228-6972 Fax (503) 228-8368
Paragon 1309 N.W. Hoyt Portland, OR 97209	Up to 150 R/B/S/M/		Joe Moreau (503) 833-5060
Pittock Mansion 3229 N.W. Pittock Drive Portland, OR 97210 *See page 530*	Sit-down: Up to 50 Reception: Up to 200 P/R/B/S/M/		(503) 823-3623
Rock Creek Country Club & Banquet Facility 5100 N.W. Neakahnie Ave. Portland, OR 97229-1964	Indoor: Up to 225 Outdoor: No limit P/R/B/S/M/		Manager (503) 690-4816
The Screening Room 925 N.W. 19th Portland, OR 97209 *See page 443*	Sit-down: Up to 40 Standing: Up to 60 Back lot: Up to 120 R/B/S/M/		(503) 294-7153
The Uptown Billiard Club 120 N.W. 23rd Ave. Portland, OR 97210 *See page 562*	Sit-down: Up to 80 Reception: Up to 200 R/B/M/		(503) 226-6909 or (503) 226-8980

P=Picnic   R=Reception   B=Banquet   S=Seminar   M=Meeting   C=Convention

Please let these businesses know that you heard about them from the Bravo! Event Resource Guide.

PORTLAND AREA
BANQUET AND EVENT SITE LISTINGS

ADDRESS	CAPACITY	GUEST ROOMS	CONTACT
SOUTHEAST PORTLAND			
The American Advertising Museum 5035 S.E. 24th Ave. Portland, OR 97202	Up to 100 R/S/M/		Catherine Coleman (503) 226-0000 Fax (503) 226-2635
Arnegards 1510 S.E. Ninth Portland, OR 97214 *See page 450*	Up to 450 R/B/S/M/C/		Robin Andersen (503) 236-2759
Bagdad Theatre & Pub 3702 S.E. Hawthorne Blvd. Portland, OR 97214	Theatre: Up to 500 B/S/M/C/		Ed Winter (503) 236-9234
Brentwood/ Darlington Center 7211 S.E. 62nd Ave. Portland, OR 97206	Up to 130 P/R/B/S/M/		Mary Davis (503) 306-5961 ext. 223
Chez Grill 2229 S.E. Hawthorne Portland, OR 97214	Private room: Up to 40 Restaurant: Up to 120 R/B/M/		Charlie Slate (503) 239-4002
Chief Obie Lodge Scouters Mountain 11300 S.E. 147th Ave. Portland, OR 97236	Up to 270 *No alcohol *P/R/B/S/M/C/	76	Sales Office (503) 225-5759
Chuck E. Cheese's 9120 S.E. Powell Blvd. Portland, OR 97226 *See page 464*	Up to 600 R/B/S/M/		Lynne Maginnis (503) 774-2992
Crystal Springs Rhododendron Garden S.E. 28th N. of Woodstock P.O. Box 86424 Portland, OR 97286	Indoor & Outdoor: Up to 150 P/R/B/S/M/		Event Coordinator (503) 256-2483
Eastmoreland Grill at the Eastmoreland Golf Course 2425 S.E. Bybee Blvd. Portland, OR 97202 *See page 479*	Sit-down: Up to 125 Reception: Up to 175 R/B/S/M/		Jerilyn Walker (503) 775-5910
The Fountains Ballroom 223 S.E. 122nd Ave. Portland, OR 97233 *See page 485*	Up to 300 P/B/M/S/		Denise or Becky (503) 261-9424 Fax (503) 261-2989
Lakeside Gardens 16211 S.E. Foster Rd. Portland, OR 97236	Indoor: Up to 180 Indoor/outdoor: Up to 300 P/R/B/S/M/		Consultant (503) 760-6044

P=Picnic   R=Reception   B=Banquet   S=Seminar   M=Meeting   C=Convention

PORTLAND AREA BANQUET AND EVENT SITE LISTINGS

ADDRESS	CAPACITY	GUEST ROOMS	CONTACT
Laurelhurst Club 3721 S.E. Ankeny St. Portland, OR 97214	Up to 200 R/B/S/M/P/		Manager (503) 235-0015
Lucky Labrador Brewing Company 915 S.E. Hawthorne Blvd. Portland, OR 97214	Up to 60 R/B/S/M/		Catering Manager (503) 236-3555
Melody Ballroom 615 S.E. Alder St. Portland, OR 97214 *See page 511*	Grand Ballroom: Sit-down: Up to 300 Reception: Up to 600 Lower Level: Sit-down: Up to 200 Reception: Up to 300 R/B/S/M/C/		Kathleen Kaad (503) 232-2759
Metro Police Club 618 S.E. Alder Portland, OR 97214	Up to 350 R/B/S/M/C/		Manager (503) 235-0202
Monte Carlo 1016 S.E. Belmont St. Portland, OR 97214	Up to 150 R/B/M/		Linda (503) 238-7627 Fax (503) 235-9171
Oaks Park Historic Dance Pavilion At Oaks Park (Sellwood) Portland, OR 97202 *See page 518*	Indoor: Sit-down: Up to 275 Reception: Up to 500 Outdoor: Up to 1,000 P/R/B/S/M/		Volanne Stephens (503) 233-5777
OMSI—Oregon Museum of Science & Industry 1945 S.E. Water Ave. Portland, OR 97214 *See page 524*	50–4,000 * after regular museum hours P/R/B/S/M/C/		Event Sales Office (503) 797-4671 Fax (503) 797-4566
Pantheon Banquet Hall 5942 S.E. 92nd Ave. Portland, OR 97266	Up to 500 R/B/S/M/		Banquet Coordinator (503) 775-7431 Fax (503) 775-3068
Persimmon Country Club 500 S.E. Butler Rd. Gresham, OR 97080 *See page 529*	Sit-down: Up to 300 Reception: Up to 500 R/B/S/M/		Mark Wallace (503) 667-7500
Sayler's Old Country Kitchen 10519 S.E. Stark Portland, OR 97216 *See page 545*	Reception: Up to 500 R/B/S/M/		Sally Kanan (503) 252-4171 or (503) 644-1492
Sellwood Community Center 1436 S.E. Spokane St. Portland, OR 97202	Sit-down: Up to 75 R/B/S/M/		Portland Parks & Recreation Building Director (503) 823-3195
The S.M.I.L.E. Station 8210 S.E. 13th Ave. Portland, OR 97202	Sit-down: Up to 80 Reception: Up to 100 R/B/S/M/		Booking Director (503) 234-3570

P=Picnic   R=Reception   B=Banquet   S=Seminar   M=Meeting   C=Convention

Please let these businesses know that you heard about them from the Bravo! Event Resource Guide.

PORTLAND AREA
BANQUET AND EVENT SITE LISTINGS

ADDRESS	CAPACITY	GUEST ROOMS	CONTACT
The Wedding House 2715 S.E. 39th St. Portland, OR 97202	Sit-down: Up to 100 Reception: Up to 150 R/B/S/M/		Owner (503) 236-7353

SOUTHWEST PORTLAND

ADDRESS	CAPACITY	GUEST ROOMS	CONTACT
Avalon Technology Group 0607 S.W. Idaho St. Portland, OR 97201 *See page 434*	Up to 9 students		David Mandel (503) 246-3630 Fax (503) 246-3124
Buffalo Gap & Eatery 6835 S.W. Macadam Ave. Portland, OR 97219 *See page 435*	Up to 50 R/B/S/M/		Events Coordinator (503) 244-7111 Fax (503) 246-8848
Chart House 5700 S.W. Terwilliger Blvd. Portland, OR 97201 *See page 462*	Up to 200 R/B/S/M/		Banquet Manager (503) 246-6963
Ernesto's 8544 S.W. Apple Way Portland, OR 97225 *See page 436*	Sit-down: Up to 150 R/B/S/M/		Gwen Tiemeyer (503) 292-0119 Fax (503) 292-6451
Four Points Sheraton 50 S.W. Morrison St. Portland, OR 97204 *See page 356*	Sit-down: Up to 40 Reception: Up to 50 R/B/S/M/	140	(503) 221-0711 Fax (503) 274-0312
Holiday Inn Select 25425 S.W. 95th Ave. Wilsonville, OR 97070	Sit-down: Up to 450 Reception: Up to 700 R/B/S/M/	170	Carrie Hayes Catering (503) 682-2211
Mandarin Cove Chinese Restaurant 111 S.W. Columbia Portland, OR 97201	Up to 250 R/B/S/M/		Jen Tsui (503) 222-0006
The Multnomah Center 7688 S.W. Capitol Hwy. Portland, OR 97219	Sit-down: Up to 180 Reception: Up to 400 R/B/S/M/		Rental Coordinator (503) 823-2787 Fax (503) 823-3161
Old Spaghetti Factory 0715 S.W. Bancroft Portland, OR 97201	Up to 150 B/M/		(503) 222-5375
Oregon Zoo 4001 S.W. Canyon Rd. Portland, OR 97221 *See page 526*	Indoor: Up to 800 Outdoor: Up to 6,000 P/R/B/S/M/		Gary Wilson or Lisa Schur (503) 220-2789 Fax (503) 220-3689
Plainfield's Mayur Cuisine of India 852 S.W. 21st Portland, OR 97205	Up to 160 R/B/S/M/		Richard Plainfield (503) 223-2995

P=Picnic   R=Reception   B=Banquet   S=Seminar   M=Meeting   C=Convention

PORTLAND AREA
BANQUET AND EVENT SITE LISTINGS

ADDRESS	CAPACITY	GUEST ROOMS	CONTACT
Sandoval's Food & Cantina 460 S.W. Miller Portland, OR 97204	Sit down: Up to 200 Reception: Up to 250 P/R/B/M/C/		(503) 223-7020 Fax (503) 223-6883
Shilo Inn— Portland/Beaverton 9900 S.W. Canyon Rd. Portland, OR 97225	Up to 160 R/B/S/M/C/	142	Catering Office (503) 297-1214
The Willamette Cafe (Willamette Athletic Club) 4949 S.W. Landing Dr. Portland, OR 97201 *See page 568*	Sit-down: Up to 75 Reception: Up to 250 R/B/S/M/		Catering Coordinator (503) 225-1068
World Forestry Center 4033 S.W. Canyon Rd. Portland, OR 97221 *See page 576*	Sit-down: Up to 250 Reception: Up to 400 Outdoor: Up to 1,000 P/R/B/S/M/		Facilities Coordinator (503) 228-1367 ext. 101

ALOHA

Aloha Odd Fellows Hall 3670 S.W. 185th Ave. Portland, OR 97007	Up to 100 R/B/S/M/		Estella (503) 292-3988
The Keg Restaurant 18875 S.W. TV Hwy. Aloha, OR 97006	Up to 30 R/B/S/M/		Manager (503) 649-2092
The Reserve Vineyards & Golf Club 4805 S.W. 229th Ave. Aloha, OR 97007 *See page 539*	Up to 175 R/B/S/M/		Nancy Marshall (503) 649-2345

AURORA

Aurora Colony Historical Society 21581 Main St., N.E. Aurora, OR 97002	Indoor/Outdoor: Up to 150 P/R/B/		Dan McElhinny (503) 678-5754
Willamette Gables 10323 Schuler Rd. Aurora, OR 97002 *See page 570*	Up to 200 P/R/S/M/		Laurel Cookman (503) 678-2195

BEAVERTON

All Seasons Indoor Golf Club 9665 S.W. Allen Blvd. Beaverton, OR 97005 *See page 448*	Up to 300 R/B/S/M/		Nick George (503) 644-7676 Fax (503) 646-3550

P=Picnic   R=Reception   B=Banquet   S=Seminar   M=Meeting   C=Convention

Please let these businesses know that you heard about them from the Bravo! Event Resource Guide.

PORTLAND AREA BANQUET AND EVENT SITE LISTINGS

ADDRESS	CAPACITY	GUEST ROOMS	CONTACT
Beaverton Community Center 12350 S.W. Fifth St. Beaverton, OR 97006	Vose: Up to 35 Comm. Room: Up to 140 P/R/B/M/S/		Neighborhood Office (503) 526-2648
Best Bet Sports Bar & Night Club 3720 S.W. Cedar Hills Blvd. Beaverton, OR 97005	Reception: Up to 250 Sit-down: Up to 100 R/B/S/M/C/		Sarina (503) 644-8075
Elsie J. Stuhr Adult Leisure Center 5550 S.W. Hall Blvd. Beaverton, OR 97005	Reception: Up to 200 Sit-down: Up to 150 R/B/S/M/ *No alcohol		Center Supervisor (503) 643-9434
The Greenwood Inn 10700 S.W. Allen Blvd. Beaverton, OR 97005 *See page 489*	Up to 800 R/B/S/M/C/	250	Catering Office (503) 643-7444 x 726 or x 727
Griffith Park Athletic Club 4925 S.W. Griffith Dr. Beaverton, OR 97005	Reception: Up to 300 R/		Carter (503) 644-3900
Hall Street Grill 3775 S.W. Hall Blvd. Beaverton, OR 97005	Up to 40 B/M/		Manager (503) 641-6161
Hilton Garden Inn 15520 N.W. Gateway Ct. Beaverton, OR 97006 *See page 493*	Up to 100 B/S/M/		Lisa Brown (503) 466-2604 Fax (503) 439-1818
Kingstad Meeting Centers 3800 S.W. Cedar Hills Blvd. Ste. 120 Beaverton, OR 97005 *See page 440*	Up to 200 R/B/S/M/		Eric Kingstad (503) 626-6338
LaserPort 10975 S.W. Canyon Rd. Beaverton, OR 97005 *See page 506*	Up to 150 S/M/B/R		Jamie Mondell (503) 526-9501 Fax (503) 626-6912
McCormick & Schmick's Fishhouse & Bar 9945 S.W. Beaverton-Hillsdale Hwy. Beaverton, OR 97005	Up to 34 R/B/S/M/		Stephanie McIntosh (503) 643-1322
McMenamins— Cedar Hills 2927 S.W. Cedar Hills Blvd. Beaverton, OR 97005	Sit-down: Up to 64 Patio: Up to 48 P/R/B/M/		Management Team (503) 641-0151
New Seoul Yakiniku Korean Restaurant 10860 S.W. Beav-Hills Hwy. Beaverton, OR 97005 *See page 515*	Up to 180 R/B/S/M/		Paul Rouse (503) 643-8818 Fax (503) 256-8800

P=Picnic   R=Reception   B=Banquet   S=Seminar   M=Meeting   C=Convention

Please let these businesses know that you heard about them from the Bravo! Event Resource Guide.

PORTLAND AREA BANQUET AND EVENT SITE LISTINGS

ADDRESS	CAPACITY	GUEST ROOMS	CONTACT
Phoenix Inn—Beaverton 15402 N.W. Cornell Rd. Beaverton, OR 97006	Up to 75 Classroom: Up to 65 M/S/		Jody Barnes (503) 614-8100 (888) 944-8100
Red Robin 4105 S.W. 117th Beaverton, OR 97005	Up to 75 R/B/S/M/		Manager (503) 641-3784 Fax (503) 626-1899
Sayler's Old Country Kitchen 4655 S.W. Griffith Dr. Beaverton, OR 97005 *See page 545*	Reception: Up to 500 R/B/M/		Sally Kanan (503) 644-1492 or (503) 242-4171
Shilo Inn— Portland/Beaverton 9900 S.W. Canyon Rd. Portland, OR 97225	Up to 160 R/B/S/M/C/	142	Catering Office (503) 297-1214 (800) 222-2244
Stockpot Restaurant 8200 S.W. Scholls Ferry Rd. Beaverton, OR 97005	Indoor: Up to 60 Outdoor: Up to 600 P/R/B/S/M/		Gary (503) 643-5451 Fax (503) 641-3265

CANBY

ADDRESS	CAPACITY	GUEST ROOMS	CONTACT
Pat's Acres Karting Complex 6255 Arndt Rd. Canby, OR 97013 *See page 94*	Indoor: Up to 100 Outdoor: Up to 1,500 P/B/S/M/		Chris Egger (503) 266-7287

CLACKAMAS

ADDRESS	CAPACITY	GUEST ROOMS	CONTACT
Clackamas Armory 10101 S.E. Clackamas Rd. Clackamas, OR 97015	Sit-down: Up to 450 R/B/S/M/		Facility Manager (503) 557-5368
Clackamas Community Club Dow Center 15711 S.E. 90th Ave. Clackamas, OR 97015	Sit-down: Up to 110 Reception: Up to 150 R/B/S/M/		Director (503) 653-7432
Clackamas County Fair & Event Center 694 N.E. Fourth Ave. Canby, OR 97013	Sit-down: Up to 450 Reception: Up to 500		Sherry Vita (503) 266-1136 Fax (503) 266-2833
Old Spaghetti Factory 12725 S.E. 93rd Ave. Clackamas, OR 97015	Up to 150		Manager (503) 653-7949
Tallina's Gardens & Conservatory 15790 S.E. Hwy. 224 Clackamas, OR 97015	Indoor: 160 Outdoor: Up to 300 P/R/B/M/		Tallina or Tina (503) 658-6148

P=Picnic   R=Reception   B=Banquet   S=Seminar   M=Meeting   C=Convention

Please let these businesses know that you heard about them from the Bravo! Event Resource Guide.

PORTLAND AREA
BANQUET AND EVENT SITE LISTINGS

ADDRESS	CAPACITY	GUEST ROOMS	CONTACT
COLUMBIA GORGE/HOOD RIVER			
Best Western Columbia River 735 Wanapa St. Cascade Locks, OR 97014 *See page 368*	Indoor: Up to 100 R/B/S/M/	63	Sales Department (800) 595-7108
Charburger Restaurant 4100 Westcliff Dr. Hood River, OR 97031	Sit-down: Up to 95 B/P/M/S/		Steve or Blanch (541) 386-3101
Cherry Hill Bed & Breakfast 1550 Carroll Rd. Mosier, OR 97040	Indoor: Up to 80 Outdoor: Up to 200 P/R/B/S/M/	3	Elizabeth Toscano (541) 478-4455
Columbia Gorge Hotel 4000 Westcliff Dr. Hood River, OR 97031 *See page 467*	Up to 290 P/R/B/S/M/	40	Director of Sales & Catering (800) 345-0931
Hood River Hotel & Pasquale's Ristorante 102 Oak Ave. Hood River, OR 97031 *See page 498*	Up to 250 R/B/S/M/	41	Sales Office (800) 386-1859
Hood River Inn 1108 E. Marina Way Hood River, OR 97031 *See page 499*	Sit-down: Up to 225 Reception: Up to 300 R/B/S/M/	149	Sales & Catering (541) 386-2200 (800) 828-7873
Maryhill Museum of Art 35 Maryhill Museum Dr. Goldendale, WA 98620	Indoor: Up to 175 Outdoor: Up to 1,500 P/R/B/S/M/		Elizabeth Toscano at Cherry Hill (541) 478-4455
Oregon Army National Guard Armory 1590 12th St. Hood River, OR 97031	Reception: Up to 450 B/S/		David Arnold (541) 386-3161
Skamania Lodge 1131 Skamania Lodge Way Stevenson, WA 98648 *See page 552*	Up to 500 P/R/B/S/M/	195	Sales Office (509) 427-2503 (800) 376-9116
CORBETT/BRIDAL VEIL			
Bridal Veil Lakes P.O. Box 5 Bridal Veil, OR 97010 *See page 428*	Indoor: Up to 150 Outdoor: Up to 1,000 P/R/B/S/M/		Jennifer Miller (503) 981-3695
The Viewpoint Inn 40301 E. Larch Mtn. Rd. Corbett, OR 97019	Sit-down: Up to 140 Reception: Up to 160 P/R/B/S/M/		Geoff Thompson (503) 695-3256

P=Picnic   R=Reception   B=Banquet   S=Seminar   M=Meeting   C=Convention

Please let these businesses know that you heard about them from the Bravo! Event Resource Guide.

PORTLAND AREA BANQUET AND EVENT SITE LISTINGS

ADDRESS	CAPACITY	GUEST ROOMS	CONTACT
CORNELIUS			
Pumpkin Ridge Golf Club 12930 Old Pumpkin Ridge Rd. Cornelius, OR 97113-6147 *See page 536*	Up to 250 P/R/B/S/M/C/		Event Coordinator (503) 647-4747
DUNDEE			
Alfie's Wayside Country Inn 1111 Hwy., 99W Dundee, OR 97115	Indoor: Up to 400 R/B/S/M/		Mickie Hoftiezer (503) 538-9407
FOREST GROVE			
Elk Cove Vineyards 27751 N.W. Olson Rd. Gaston, OR 97119	Up to 200 P/R/B/S/M/		Brett Butler (503) 985-7760
Laurel Ridge Winery 46350 N.W. David Hill Rd. Forest Grove, OR 97116	Sit-down: Up to 65 Reception: Up to 200 P/R/B/S/M/		David Teppola (503) 359-5436
Masonic Lodge 2019 Main St. Forest Grove, OR 97116	Reception: Up to 120 P/R/B/S/M/ *No alcohol		Harold Johnson (503) 357-6979
Oregon Nat'l Guard Armory 2950 Taylor Way Forest Grove, OR 97116	Reception: Up to 450 R/B/S/M/		Frank Wallace (503) 359-4632
Pacific University **University Center** 2043 College Way Forest Grove, OR 97116	Up to 50 R/B/S/M/		Owen Fox, Director of Conferences (503) 359-2133
GRESHAM/BORING			
Cascade Athletic Club 19201 S.E. Division St. Gresham, OR 97030	Up to 200 R/B/S/M/		Brian Ancheta (503) 665-4142 Fax (503) 667-4948
East Fork Country Estate 9875 S.E. 222nd Dr. Gresham, OR 97080	Indoor/Outdoor: Up to 250 P/R/B/S/M/		Owner (503) 667-7069
Gresham Armory 500 N.E. Division St. Gresham, OR 97030	Up to 379 R/B/S/M/		State Employee (503) 665-2511
The Keg Restaurant 3150 N.E. Division St. Gresham, OR 97030	Up to 100 R/B/S/M/		General Manager (503) 667-5114
Mt. Hood Community College 26000 S.E. Stark St. Gresham, OR 97030	Indoor: Up to 371 Outdoor: Up to 500		DeAnn Melland (503) 491-7449 Fax (503) 491-6011

P=Picnic   R=Reception   B=Banquet   S=Seminar   M=Meeting   C=Convention

Please let these businesses know that you heard about them from the Bravo! Event Resource Guide.

PORTLAND AREA
BANQUET AND EVENT SITE LISTINGS

ADDRESS	CAPACITY	GUEST ROOMS	CONTACT
Persimmon Country Club 500 S.E. Butler Rd. Gresham, OR 97080 *See page 529*	Sit-down: Up to 300 Reception: Up to 500 R/B/S/M/		Events Coordinator (503) 667-7500

HILLSBORO

ADDRESS	CAPACITY	GUEST ROOMS	CONTACT
McMenamins— Cornelius Pass Roadhouse 4045 N.W. Cornelius Pass Rd. Hillsboro, OR 97124	Indoor: Up to 65 P/R/B/S/M/		Dineen (503) 640-6174 or (503) 492-2777
Cavanaugh's Best Western Hotel 3500 N.E. Cornell Rd. Hillsboro, OR 97124 *See page 457*	Sit-down: Up to 150 Reception: Up to170 P/R/B/S/M/	124	Catering Office (503) 648-3500x507
Meriwether National Golf Club 5200 S.W. Rood Bridge Hillsboro, OR 97123	Up to 300 R/B/S/M/		John Derr (503) 693-8707
Old Spaghetti Factory 18925 N.W. Tanasbourne Dr. Hillsboro, OR 97124	Up to 150 B/M/		(503) 617-7614
Tuality Health Education Center 334 S.E. 8th Ave. Hillsboro, OR 97123 *See page 560*	Sit-down: Up to 250 Reception: Up to 400 R/B/S/M/		Secretary (503) 681-1700
Washington County Fair Complex 873 N.E. 28th St. Hillsboro, OR 97124 *See page 564*	40 to 2,500 P/R/B/S/M/C/		Lisa DuPré (503) 648-1416 Fax (503) 648-7208

JUNCTION CITY

ADDRESS	CAPACITY	GUEST ROOMS	CONTACT
Shadow Hills Country Club 92512 River Rd. Junction City, OR 97448	Up to 250 P/R/B/S/M/		Jennifer Brandt (541) 998-2365 Fax (541) 998-6779

LAKE OSWEGO

ADDRESS	CAPACITY	GUEST ROOMS	CONTACT
Amadeus 148 B. Ave. Lake Oswego, OR 97034	Up to 100 R/B/M/		General Manager (503) 636-7500
Big Horn Brewing Co. & Ram Restaurant 320 Oswego Point Blvd. Lake Oswego, OR 97034	Up to 70 P/B/S/M/		(503) 697-8818 Fax (503) 697-7743

P=Picnic   R=Reception   B=Banquet   S=Seminar   M=Meeting   C=Convention

Please let these businesses know that you heard about them from the Bravo! Event Resource Guide.

PORTLAND AREA
BANQUET AND EVENT SITE LISTINGS

ADDRESS	CAPACITY	GUEST ROOMS	CONTACT
Celebrate! Catering & Reception Facility 15555 S.W. Bangy Rd. Lake Oswego, OR 97035 *See page 458*	Sit-down: Up to 200 Reception: Up to 300 R/B/S/M/		Barb Chirgwin (503) 684-1880
Crowne Plaza 14811 Kruse Oaks Blvd. Lake Oswego, OR 97035 *See page 471*	Up to 300 R/B/S/M/C/	161	Crystal Harrell (503) 624-8400 ext. 253
Lacey's in Lake Oswego 500 S.W. 1st St. Lake Oswego, OR 97034	Sit-down: Up to 60 Reception: Up to 100 P/R/B/		Ed Lacey (503) 636-2024
Lakewood Center for the Arts 368 S. State St. Lake Oswego, OR 97034	Sit-down: Up to 150 Reception: Up to 225 Theatre: Up to 200 R/B/S/M/		Executive Director (503) 635-6338
Phoenix Inn—Lake Oswego 14905 S.W. Bangy Rd. Lake Oswego, OR 97034	Up to 75		Lori Johnson (800) 824-9992 (503) 624-7400
Sherwood Inn Best Western 15700 S.W. Upper Boones Ferry Rd. Lake Oswego, OR 97035	Sit-down: Up to 80 Reception: Up to 100 R/B/S/M/C/	101	Manager (503) 620-2980 Fax (503) 639-9010

MARYLHURST

ADDRESS	CAPACITY	GUEST ROOMS	CONTACT
Marylhurst University P.O. Box 261 Marylhurst, OR 97036 *See page 510*	Up to 200 P/R/B/S/M/C/	54	Conference Office (503) 699-6250

McMINNVILLE

ADDRESS	CAPACITY	GUEST ROOMS	CONTACT
McMenamins Hotel Oregon 310 N.E. Evens St. McMinnville, OR 97128 *See page 438*	Up to 80 R/B/S/M/	42	(503) 492-2777 or (877) 492-2777

MILWAUKIE

ADDRESS	CAPACITY	GUEST ROOMS	CONTACT
Amadeus at the Fernwood 2122 S.E. Sparrow St. Milwaukie, OR 97222 *See page 449*	Up to 300 R/B/S/M/		Kristina Poppmeier (503) 659-1735 or (503) 353-8948
Broetje House, Historic 3101 S.E. Courtney Milwaukie, OR 97222	Indoor: Up to 150 Indoor & Outdoor: Up to 150 P/R/B/S/M/	3	Lorraine or Lois (503) 659-8860
Gray Gables Inn 3009 S.E. Chestnut Milwaukie, OR 97267	Indoor: Up to 75 Indoor & Outdoor: Up to 300 P/R/B/S/M/	7	(503) 654-0470

P=Picnic   R=Reception   B=Banquet   S=Seminar   M=Meeting   C=Convention

Please let these businesses know that you heard about them from the Bravo! Event Resource Guide.

PORTLAND AREA
BANQUET AND EVENT SITE LISTINGS

ADDRESS	CAPACITY	GUEST ROOMS	CONTACT
The Milwaukie Center (in North Clackamas Park) 5440 Kellogg Creek Dr. Milwaukie, OR 97222	Sit-down: Up to 315 Reception: Up to 600 Three areas P/R/B/S/M/		Community Use Scheduler (503) 653-8100
The Milwaukie Grange P.O. Box 220071 Milwaukie, OR 97269	Up to 200 R/B/S/M/ *No alcohol		Carmelita Coats (503) 654-8771
Paradigm Conference Center 3009 S.E. Chestnut Milwaukie, Oregon 97207 *See page 527*	Up to 290		Clem or Mark (503) 654-6426 Fax (503) 654-3929
Ultrazone 16074 SE McLoughlin Blvd. Milwaukie, OR 97267 *See page 561*	Up to 150 R/B/M/		Lee Sturman (503) 652-1122 Fax (503) 652-5204

MOLALLA

Canterbury Falls & English Gardens P.O. Box 156 Molalla, OR 97038	Outdoor: Up to 400 P/R/B/S/M/		Judy Hall (503) 829-8821

MOUNT HOOD/SANDY

Cedar Springs Country Estate 12353 S.E. Lusted Rd. Sandy, OR 97055	Up to 300 P/R/B/S/M/		Sandy Poutala (503) 668-6911 Fax (503) 668-9023
Mt. Hood Skibowl Winter & Summer Resort P.O. Box 280 Government Camp, OR 97028 *See page 429*	Up to 6,000 P/R/M/S/C/		Karen Norton (503) 222-2695 ext. 0
Mt. Hood Meadows Ski Resort 1975 S.W. First Ave, Ste. M Portland, OR 97201 *See page 514*	Up to 400 P/R/B/S/M/C/		Karen Lite (503) 287-5438
The Resort at The Mountain 68010 E. Fairway Ave. Welches, OR 97067 *See page 540*	Up to 700 P/R/B/S/M/	160	Director of Sales (503) 622-2220 (800) 733-0800
Timberline Lodge Timberline, OR 97028 *See page 559*	Sit-down: Up to 250 Reception: Up to 400 P/R/B/S/M/C/	70	Portland Sales Office (503) 295-1828 Fax (503) 295-1855

P=Picnic   R=Reception   B=Banquet   S=Seminar   M=Meeting   C=Convention

Please let these businesses know that you heard about them from the Bravo! Event Resource Guide.

PORTLAND AREA BANQUET AND EVENT SITE LISTINGS

ADDRESS	CAPACITY	GUEST ROOMS	CONTACT
NEWBERG			
Chehalem Armory 620 N. Morton St. Newberg, OR 97132	Up to 350 R/B/S/M/		Anna (503) 538-7454
Chehalem Community Center 502 E. Second St. Newberg, OR 97132	Reception: Up to 200 R/B/		Anna (503) 538-7454
Chehalem Park & Recreation Senior Center 101 W. Foothills Dr. Newberg, OR 97132	Reception: Up to 200 P/R/B/S/M/ *No alcohol		Anna (503) 538-7454
George Fox University 414 N. Meridian St. Newberg, OR 97132	Heacock Commons: Sit-down: Up to 400 Cap & Gown Room: Up to100 B/P/M/S/		Lisa Leslie (503) 538-8383 ext. 2557 Fax (503) 537-3834
Shilo Inn 501 Sitka Ave. Newberg, OR 97132	Up to 49 B/P/S/		Manager (503) 537-0303
Tilikum Retreat Center 15321 N.E. North Valley Rd. Newberg, OR 97132	Outdoor: Up to 200 Indoor: Up to 60 P/S/M/C/	58 beds	Mo Hurbin (503) 538-2763 Fax (503) 538-7536
OREGON CITY			
Captain Ainsworth House Bed & Breakfast 19130 Lot Whitcomb Dr. Oregon City, OR 97045	Sit-down: Up to 70 Reception: Up to 100 P/R/B/S/M/	4	Claire Met (503) 655-5172
Carnegie Center 606 John Adams Oregon City, OR 97045	Sit-down: Up to 100 Reception: Up to 150 R/B/S/M/		Barb (503) 557-9199
Carpenter Hall 276 Warner Milne Rd. Oregon City, OR 97045	Up to 200 R/B/S/M/		Marcy Schram (503) 656-7716 Fax (503) 650-8051
End of the Oregon Trail Interpretive Center 1726 Washington St. Oregon City, OR 97045 *See page 482*	Indoor/Outdoor Up to 300 P/R/B/M/		(503) 657-9336
Environmental Learning Center at Clackamas Community College 19600 S. Molalla Ave. Oregon City, OR 97045	Lakeside Hall: Up to 110 *No alcohol P/R/B/		Dawn Todd (503) 657-6958 ext. 2351 Fax (503) 650-6669

P=Picnic   R=Reception   B=Banquet   S=Seminar   M=Meeting   C=Convention

Please let these businesses know that you heard about them from the Bravo! Event Resource Guide.

PORTLAND AREA BANQUET AND EVENT SITE LISTINGS

ADDRESS	CAPACITY	GUEST ROOMS	CONTACT
The Grand Oregon Lodge 600 Seventh St. Oregon City, OR 97045	Up to 299 R/B/S/M/C/		(503) 722-4190
Oregon City Golf Club 20124 S. Beavercreek Rd. Oregon City, OR 97045 *See page 520*	Sit-down: Up to 125 Reception: Up to 160 R/B/S/M/		Event Coordinator (503) 656-2846
TIGARD/TUALATIN/SHERWOOD			
Century Hotel 8185 S.W. Tualatin-Sherwood Rd. Tualatin, OR 97062	Up to 200 R/B/S/M/	40	Manager (503) 692-3600 Fax (503) 691-9142
ClubSport 18120 S.W. Lower Boones Ferry Rd. Tigard, OR 97224 *See page 466*	130,000 sq. ft. Up to 400 B/P/M/C/		Holly Jensen (503) 968-4519
Cucina! Cucina! Italian Cafe 10205 S.W. Washington Sq. Rd. Tigard, OR 97223	Sit-down: Up to 30 R/B/S/M/		Banquet Manager (503) 968-2000 Fax (503) 968-2079
Embassy Suites Hotel 9000 S.W. Washington Sq. Rd. Tigard, OR 97223 *See page353*	Indoor: Up to 1,200 R/B/S/M/C/	354	Sales (503) 644-4000
Majorie Stewart Senior Community Center 855 N. Sherwood Blvd. Sherwood OR 97140	Sit-down: Up to 225 B/P/M/S/		Peggi Federspiel (503) 625-5644
Phoenix Inn—Tigard 9575 S.W. Locust Tigard, OR 97223	Up to 75 M/S		(503) 624-9000 (800) 624-6884
Rich's Restaurant 18810 S.W. Boones Ferry Rd. Tualatin, OR 97062	Up to 50 R/B/S/M/		Banquet Manager (503) 692-1460
The Sweetbrier Inn 7125 S.W. Nyberg Rd. Tualatin, OR 97062 *See page 556*	Sit-down: Up to 250 Reception: Up to 300 R/B/S/M/	131	Catering Office (503) 692-5800 (800) 551-9167 Fax (503) 691-2894
Tualatin/Durham Senior Center 8513 S.W. Tualatin Rd. Tualatin, OR 97062	Sit-down: Up to 160 P/R/B/S/M/		(503) 692-6767

P=Picnic   R=Reception   B=Banquet   S=Seminar   M=Meeting   C=Convention

Please let these businesses know that you heard about them from the Bravo! Event Resource Guide.

PORTLAND AREA
BANQUET AND EVENT SITE LISTINGS

ADDRESS	CAPACITY	GUEST ROOMS	CONTACT
TROUTDALE			
The Lake House at Blue Lake Park 21160 N.E. Blue Lake Rd. Troutdale, OR 97060	Indoor: Up to 175 Outdoor: Up to 400 P/R/S/B/M/C/		Colette/Deanna (503) 667-3483
McMenamins Edgefield 2126 S.W. Halsey Troutdale, OR 97060 *See page 389*	Sit-down: Up to 200 Reception: Up to 250 Theatre: Up to 125 R/B/S/M/	103	Sales Office (503) 492-2777
Multnomah Falls Lodge P.O. Box 367 Troutdale, OR 97060	Up to 100 R/B/S/M/		Restaurant Manager (503) 695-2376 Fax (503) 695-2338
Phoenix Inn—Troutdale 477 N.W. Phoenix Dr. Troutdale, OR 97060	Up to 75 M/		(503) 669-6500 (800) 824-6824
WEST LINN			
McLean House & Park 5350 River St. West Linn, OR 97068	Indoor & Outdoor: Up to 100 P/R/B/S/M/		(503) 655-4268
The Oregon Golf Club 25700 S.W. Pete's Mtn Rd. West Linn, OR 97068 *See page 523*	Up to 500 R/B/S/M/		Catering Department (503) 650-6900
WILSONVILLE			
Charboneau On The Green 32050 S.W. Charbonneau Dr. Wilsonville, OR 97070 *See page 461*	Up to 200 R/B/S/M/		Bob Russell (503) 694-5234 Fax (503) 694-6385
Holiday Inn Select 25425 S.W. 95th Ave. Wilsonville, OR 97070 *See page 497*	Sit-down: Up to 600 Reception: Up to 900 R/B/S/M/C/	169	Catering Department (503) 682-2211
Hunter Creek Farm 14441 S.W. Wilsonville Rd. Wilsonville, OR 97070 *See page 500*	Indoor: Up to 125 Outdoor: 400+		Angela or Marilyn (503) 625-3424
Namasté Retreat & Conference Center 29500 S.W. Grahams Ferry Wilsonville, OR 97070 *See page 391*	Up to 1,000 P/R/B/S/M/C/	158	C. Diane Ragsdale (503) 682-5683 (800) 893-1000 Fax (503) 682-4275
Phoenix Inn—Wilsonville 29769 S.W. Boones Ferry Rd. Wilsonville, OR 97070	Up to 75 M/		(503) 570-9700 (888) 336-9700

P=Picnic   R=Reception   B=Banquet   S=Seminar   M=Meeting   C=Convention

Please let these businesses know that you heard about them from the Bravo! Event Resource Guide.

PORTLAND AREA
BANQUET AND EVENT SITE LISTINGS

ADDRESS	CAPACITY	GUEST ROOMS	CONTACT
Wilsonville Family Fun Center & Bullwinkle's Restaurant 29111 S.W. Town Center Loop Wilsonville, OR 97070 *See page 573*	Sit-down: Up to 175 Amusement Park: Up to 2,000 P/R/B/S/M/		(503) 685-5000 ext. 21 Fax (503) 685-9694
WOODBURN			
Holiday Inn Express 2887 Newberg Hwy. Woodburn, OR 97071	Up to 50 R/S/M/	81	(503) 982-6515 (800) 766-6433
YAMHILL			
Flying M Ranch 23029 N.W. Flying M Rd. Yamhill, OR 97148	Indoor: Up to 200 Outdoor: Up to 1,500 P/R/B/S/M/C/	36	Barbara Ann (503) 662-3222 Fax (503) 662-3202

P=Picnic   R=Reception   B=Banquet   S=Seminar   M=Meeting   C=Convention

PORTLAND AREA
BOATS & YACHTS, TRAINS AND TROLLEY SITE LISTINGS

ADDRESS	CAPACITY	CONTACT
BOATS & YACHTS		
Sternwheeler "Columbia Gorge" P.O. Box 307 Cascade Locks, OR 97014 *See page 554*	Columbia Gorge: Up to 599 Cascade Queen Up to 149 P/R/B/S/M/	Sales Department (503) 223-3928
Portland Spirit 842 S.W. First Ave. Portland, OR 97204 *See page 419*	Sit-down: Up to 350 Reception: Up to 540 P/R/B/S/M/	(503) 224-3900 (800) 224-3901 Fax (503) 286-7673
Sternwheeler Excursions 6211 N. Ensign Portland, OR 97217 *See page 421*	Up to 130 P/R/B/S/M/	Judy (503) 286-7673
Willamette Jetboats 1945 S.E. Water Ave. Portland, OR 97214 *See page 104*	Up to 83 per jetboat Board on S.E. Water Ave. in Portland	Manager (503) 231-1532 (888) 538-2628
Willamette Star 842 S.W. First Ave. Portland, OR 97204 *See page 419*	Sit-down: Up to 80 Reception: Up to 120 P/R/B/S/M/	Jan Lake (503) 224-3900 (800) 224-3901
Willamette Queen 1109 N.W. Ninth St. Corvallis, OR 97330 *See page 422*	Up to 107 R/B/S/M/	Irene Salomon (541) 928-4090
Yachts-O-Fun Cruises, Inc. Foot of S.E. Marion St. Portland, OR 97202 *See page 423*	Sit-down: Up to 48 B/P/M/S/R/P/C/	Vikki Collie (503) 234-6665
TRAINS		
Mount Hood Railroad & Dinner Train 110 Railroad Ave. Hood River, OR 97031 *See page 424*	Up to 332 R/S/M/	Passenger Service (541) 386-3556 (800) 872-4661
TROLLEY		
Vintage Trolley 115 N.W. First, Ste. 200 Portland, OR 97209 *See page 425*	Up to 68 R/M/	Sarah Fuller (503) 323-7363

P=Picnic   R=Reception   B=Banquet   S=Seminar   M=Meeting   C=Convention

Please let these businesses know that you heard about them from the Bravo! Event Resource Guide.

PORTLAND AREA PARK EVENT SITE LISTINGS

ADDRESS	CAPACITY	CONTACT
CASCADE LOCKS		
Marine Park & Thunder Island P.O. Box 307 Cascade Locks, OR 97014 *See page 432*	Outdoor: Up to 4,000 Indoor: Up to 400 P/R/B/M/	The Cascade Sternwheelers (503) 223-3928
CORBETT		
Columbia Gorge/ Rooster Rock I-84 Exit 25 Corbett, OR 97019 *See page 431*	Up to 2,000 B/P/	Reservations Northwest (800) 452-5687 Information Line (503) 695-2261
ESTACADA		
McIver State Park 24101 S. Entrance Rd. Estacada, OR 97023 *See page 431*	Outdoor: Up to 1,000 P/R/S/M/	Reservations Northwest (503) 636-9886 (800) 452-5687
GRESHAM		
Oxbow Park 3010 S.E. Oxbow Park Way Gresham, OR 97080	Outdoor shelters: (4) Up to 350 P/R/B/S/M/ * No electricity	Metro Regional Parks (503) 797-1834
MILWAUKIE		
North Clackamas Park The Milwaukie Center 5440 S.E. Kellogg Creek Milwaukie, OR 97222	Indoor: Up to 600 Outdoor: Up to 1,200 (shelters) 2 rooms R/B/S/M/	Lynn (503) 653-8100
PORTLAND		
Council Crest Park S.W. Council Crest Dr. Portland, OR 97201	Outdoor (no shelter): Up to 150 R/	Parks Permit Center (503) 823-2525 (503) 823-2514
Crystal Springs Rhododendron Garden S.E. 28th N. of Woodstock 7215 S.E. Hawthorne Portland, OR 97215	Indoor (shelter): Up to 150 Outdoor: 3 Sites Up to 200 P/R/M/S/	Rita Knapp (503) 256-2483
Howell Territorial Park 13901 N.W. Howell Rd. Sauvie Island, OR	Outdoor: Up to 300 P/R/B/S/M/	Metro Parks & Greenspaces (503) 797-1834
Hoyt Arboretum 4000 S.W. Fairview Blvd. Portland, OR 97221	Outdoor (shelter): Up to 140 P/R/	Parks Permit Center (503) 823-2514

P=Picnic   R=Reception   B=Banquet   S=Seminar   M=Meeting   C=Convention

Please let these businesses know that you heard about them from the Bravo! Event Resource Guide.

PORTLAND AREA PARK EVENT SITE LISTINGS

ADDRESS	CAPACITY	CONTACT
Laurelhurst Park S.E. 39th & Oak Portland, OR 97214	Outdoor (no shelter): 100+ P/R/	Parks Permit Center (503) 823-2525
Leach Botanical Gardens 6704 S.E. 122nd Ave. Portland, OR 97236	Indoor: Up to 70 Outdoor: Up to 85 P/R/B/S/M/	Barbara Ham (503) 761-9503 (503) 761-2165
Mt. Tabor Park S.E. 60th & Salmon Portland, OR 97214	Outdoor (shelter): 100+ P/R/	Parks Permit Center (503) 823-2525 Coordinator (503) 823-2514
Oaks Park S.E. Portland (Sellwood area) Portland, OR 97202 *See page 430*	Up to 1,000 P/R/B/S/	(503) 233-5777
The Overlook House 3839 N. Melrose Dr. Portland, OR 97227	Indoor: Up to 75 Outdoor: Up to 150 P/R/S/M/	Building Coordinator (503) 823-3188
Peninsula Park Rose Garden N. Albina & Portland Blvd. Portland, OR 97217	Outdoor (shelter):Up to 70 P/R/	Parks Permit Center (503) 823-2525 Coordinator (503) 823-2514
Pier Park N. Seneca & St. John's Portland, OR 97203	Outdoor (shelter): 200+ P/R/	Parks Permit Center (503) 823-2525
Pioneer Courthouse Square 701 S.W. Sixth Portland, OR 97204	Outdoor: Up to 15,000 P/R/B/M/C/	Program Director (503) 223-1613 Fax (503) 222-7425
Washington Park **Rose Garden Amphitheater** 400 S.W. Kingston Blvd. Portland, OR 97201	Outdoor: Up to 3,000 P/R/	Parks Permit Center (503) 823-2525
Washington Park **Rose Garden** **Gold Medal Garden** 400 S.W. Kingston Blvd. Portland, OR 97201	Outdoor (small gazebo): Up to 100	Parks Permit Center (503) 823-2525
Washington Park **Rose Garden** **Shakespearean Garden** 400 S.W. Kingston Blvd. Portland, OR 97201	Outdoor (no shelter): Up to 100	Parks Permit Center (503) 823-2525

ST. PAUL

ADDRESS	CAPACITY	CONTACT
Champoeg Park 8239 Champoeg Rd. N.E. St. Paul, OR 97137-9709 *See page 431*	Indoor: Up to 49 Outdoor: Up to 200 P/R/	Reservation Information: (800) 452-5687 (503) 678-1251

P=Picnic   R=Reception   B=Banquet   S=Seminar   M=Meeting   C=Convention

Please let these businesses know that you heard about them from the Bravo! Event Resource Guide.

PORTLAND AREA PARK EVENT SITE LISTINGS

ADDRESS	CAPACITY	CONTACT
TROUTDALE/FAIRVIEW		
Blue Lake Park 20500 N.E. Marine Dr. Fairview, OR 97024	Outdoor: Up to 7,000 Covered shelters: (10) Varies: 50–125 people Lake House: Up to 175 P/R/B/S/M/	Metro Regional Parks (503) 797-1834
Glenn Otto Community Park & Sam Cox Bldg. 1120 E. Historical Columbia River Hwy. Troutdale, OR 97060	Indoor: Up to 250 Outdoor: Up to 1,000 P/R/B/S/M/	Samantha (503) 665-5175 ext. 254 Fax (503) 665-1137
WASHINGTON COUNTY		
Cedar Hills Park Cedar Hills Blvd. & Walker Rd. Beaverton, OR 97005	Outdoor only: Up to 100 P/R/	Tualatin Hills Park & Recreation (503) 645-3539 Fax (503) 614-9514
Jenkins Estate Grabhorn Rd. at S.W. 209th & Farmington Aloha, OR 97006	Indoor: Up to 125 Outdoor: Up to 175 Stable: Up to 250 P/R/B/S/M/	Program Supervisor (503) 642-3855 Fax (503) 591-1028
Metzger Park Hall 8400 S.W. Hemlock St. Portland, OR 97223	Indoor Facility Reception: Up to 200 P/R/B/S/M/	Administrative Asst. (503) 246-0998
Raleigh Park 3500 S.W. 78th Ave. Portland, OR 97225	Outdoor only: Up to 100 P/R/	Tualatin Hills Park & Recreation (503) 645-3539
Scoggins Valley Park/ Henry Hagg Lake 111 S.E. Washington Hillsboro, OR 97124	"C" Ramp Pavilion: Up to 700 Sain Pavilion: Up to 300 2 additional sites: Up to 125 P/R/	Administrative Asst. (503) 648-8715
WEST LINN		
McLean House & Park 5350 River St. West Linn, OR 97068	Indoor & Outdoor: Up to 100 P/R/B/S/M/	(503) 655-4268
Willamette Park 12th & Volpp St. West Linn, OR 97068	Gazebo: Up to 35 Willamette Shelter: Up to 64 Entire area, including park: Up to 150 P/R/	Parks Dept. (503) 557-4700 Fax (503) 657-3237

P=Picnic   R=Reception   B=Banquet   S=Seminar   M=Meeting   C=Convention

OREGON WINERY SITE LISTINGS

ADDRESS	CAPACITY	CONTACT
Airlie Winery 15305 Dunn Forest Rd. Monmouth, OR 97361	Outdoor: Up to 200 P/R/	Owner (503) 838-6013
BeckenRidge Vineyard 300 Ruben-Boise Rd. Dallas, OR 97338 *See page 453*	Up to 120; more if using covered patio P/R/B/S/M/	(503) 831-3652
Champoeg Wine Cellar 10375 Champoeg Rd. N.E. Aurora, OR 97002	Indoor: Up to 20 Outdoor: Up to 100 P/R/M/	John Killian (503) 678-2144 Fax (503) 678-1024
Chateau Benoit 6580 N.E. Mineral Springs Rd. Carlton, OR 97111	Indoor: Up to 100 Indoor-Outdoor: Up to 150 P/B/S/M/	(503) 864-2991
Chateau Lorane 27415 Siuslaw River Rd. Lorane, OR 97451	Outdoor: 40 Indoor: Up to 125 P/R/B/	(541) 942-8028 (541) 942-5830
Chehalem Winery 31190 N.E. Veritas Newberg, OR 97132	Indoor: Up to 150 Outdoor: Up to 150 Bed & Breakfast 4 Guest Rooms B/P/M/S/R/P/	Judy Peterson-Nedry (503) 538-0317 Fax (503) 537-0850
Cristom Vineyards 6905 Spring Valley Rd. N.W. Salem, OR 97304	Indoor: Up to 75 Outdoor: Up to 125 P/R/B/M/	Eileen Gerrie (503) 375-3068
Elk Cove Vineyards 27751 N.W. Olson Rd. Gaston, OR 97119	Indoor: Up to 150 Outdoor: limited P/R/B/S/M/	Hospitality Director (503) 985-7760
Eola Hills Wine Cellars 501 S. Pacific Hwy. Rickreall, OR 97371	Indoor: Up to 250 Outdoor: Up 450 P/R/B/S/M/	L.J. Gunderson (503) 623-2405 Fax (503) 623-0350
Erath Vineyards 9009 N.E. Worden Hill Rd. Dundee, OR 97115	Indoor: Up to 25 Outdoor: Up to 50 B/P/M/S/P/	Sherri Rowman (800) 539-9463 Fax (503) 538-1074
Evesham Wood Vineyard & Winery 3795 Wallace Rd. N.W. Salem, OR 97304	Indoor: Up to 40 R/B/M/S/	(503) 371-8478
Honeywood Winery 1350 Hines St. S.E. Salem, OR 97302	Indoor: Up to 150 P/R/B/S/M/	Marlene Gallick (503) 362-4111 Fax (503) 362-4112
Inn at Otter Crest Winery 301 Otter Crest Loop Otter Rock, OR 97369 *See page 502*	Up to 300 P/R/B/S/M/C/	Ginny Whiffen (800) 326-5806

P=Picnic   R=Reception   B=Banquet   S=Seminar   M=Meeting   C=Convention

Please let these businesses know that you heard about them from the Bravo! Event Resource Guide.

OREGON WINERY SITE LISTINGS

ADDRESS	CAPACITY	CONTACT
Kramer Vineyards 26830 N.W. Olson Rd. Gaston, OR 97119	Outdoor: 50 to 100 Indoor: 30 P/R/S/M/	Trudy Kramer (503) 662-4545
Laurel Ridge Winery 46350 N.W. David Hill Rd. P.O. Box 456 Forest Grove, OR 97116	Sit-down: Up to 65 P/R/B/S/M/	David Teppola (503) 359-5436
Marquam Hill Vineyards 35803 S. Hwy. 213 Molalla, OR 97038	Indoor: Up to 20 Outdoor: Up to 2,000 P/R/M/	Marylee or Joe Dobbes (503) 829-6677
Oak Grove Orchards 6090 Crowley Road Rickreall, OR 97371	Winter: Up to 30 Summer: Up to 200 P/B/R/M	(503) 364-7052
Rex Hill Winery 30835 N. Hwy. 99W Newberg, OR 97132	Indoor: Up to 150 Outdoor: Up to 200 Amphitheater: Up to 300	Hospitality Manager (503) 538-0666
Stangeland Vineyards & Winery 8500 Hopewell Rd. N.W. Salem, OR 97304	Indoor: Up to 50 Outdoor: Up to 200 P/R/B/S/M/	Kinsley Miller (503) 581-0355
St. Josef's Wine Cellars 28836 S. Barlow Rd. Canby, OR 97013	Indoor: Up to 125 Indoor-outdoor: Up to 250 P/R/B/S/M/	Lilly Fleischmann (503) 651-3190 Fax (503) 651-3190
Torii Mor Wine 18325 N.E. Fairview Dr. McMinnville, OR 97128	Outdoor: Up to 25 B/P/	Patty Green (503) 434-1439 Fax (503) 434-5733
Tualatin Vineyards 10850 N.W. Seavey Rd. Forest Grove, OR 97116	Indoor: Up to 32 Indoor/Outdoor: Up to 120 P/R/B/S/M/	(503) 357-5005 Fax (503) 357-1702
Willamette Valley Vineyard 8800 Enchanted Way S.E. Turner, OR 97392 *See page 572*	Indoor/Outdoor: Up to 600 P/R/B/S/M/	Hospitality Coordinator (503) 588-9463 (800) 344-9463
Wine Country Farm 6855 Breyman Orchard Rd. Dayton, OR 97114	Indoor: Up to 80 Outdoors: Up to 250 7 Guest Rooms	Joan Davenport (503) 864-3446 Fax (503) 864-3446
Youngberg Hill Vineyard 10660 S.W. Youngberg Hill Rd. McMinnville, OR 97128	Small Conference Room: Up to 30 Outdoor: Up to 120 B/M/S/R/	(503) 472-2727 Fax (503) 472-1313

P=Picnic   R=Reception   B=Banquet   S=Seminar   M=Meeting   C=Convention

Please let these businesses know that you heard about them from the Bravo! Event Resource Guide.

Vancouver Area Banquet & Event Sites

VANCOUVER AREA BANQUET AND EVENT SITE LISTINGS

ADDRESS	CAPACITY	GUEST ROOMS	CONTACT
BATTLE GROUND			
Battle Ground Senior Center 113 N.E. Third Ave. Battle Ground, WA 98604	Up to 100 *No alcohol B/S/M/		Battle Ground City Hall (360) 342-5000
The Burdoin Mansion 18609 N.E. Cramer Rd. Battle Ground, WA 98604	Indoor: Up to 80 Outdoor: Up to 200 P/R/B/S/M/		Rob & Becky Neuschwander (360) 666-4828
BRUSH PRAIRIE			
Alderbrook Park Corp. Brush Prairie, WA 98606 *See page 527*	Up to 10,000 P/B/		Peter Hessler (503) 283-5152
The Cedars Golf Club 15001 N.E. 181st St. Brush Prairie, WA 98606	Sit-down: Up to 175 Reception: Up to 250 R/B/S/M/		Vickie Hernandez (360) 687-6092 (503) 285-7548
CAMAS			
Camas Community Center 1718 S.E. 7th Camas, WA 98607	Up to 300 R/B/S/M/		Camas Parks & Recreation Dept. (360) 834-7092
Crown Park N.E. 15th Ave. & Everett St. Camas, WA 98607	20'x20' Picnic Shelter *No alcohol P/		Parks & Recreation Dept. (360) 834-7092
Rocket City Neon Advertising Museum & Reception Hall 1554 N.E. Third Ave., Ste. 2 Camas, WA 98607	Up to 300 R/B/S/M/		Kirsten Benko (360) 834-9467
GOLDENDALE			
Maryhill Museum of Art 35 Maryhill Museum Dr. Goldendale, WA 98620	Indoor: Up to 75 Outdoor: Up to 1,500 P/R/B/		Elizabeth Toscano at Cherry Hill (541) 478-4455
KALAMA			
Columbia Inn Restaurant 698 Frontage Rd. Kalama, WA 98625	Up to 100 R/B/S/M/		General Manager (360) 673-2800

P=Picnic   R=Reception   B=Banquet   S=Seminar   M=Meeting   C=Convention

Please let these businesses know that you heard about them from the Bravo! Event Resource Guide.

VANCOUVER AREA
BANQUET AND EVENT SITE LISTINGS

ADDRESS	CAPACITY	GUEST ROOMS	CONTACT
RIDGEFIELD			
Clark County Fair Association 17402 N.E. Delfel Rd. Ridgefield, WA 98642	Indoor: Up to 200 Outdoor: 100+ Grandstand: Up to 7,200 P/R/B/S/M/	RV	Tomi Mosby Event Coordinator (360) 737-6180
STEVENSON			
Columbia Gorge Interpretive Center 990 SW Rock Creek Dr Stevenson, WA 98648	Reception: Up to 400 Theatre: 45 P/R/B/S/M/		Pamela Robinson (509) 427-8211 Fax (509) 427-7429
Skamania Lodge (in Columbia River Gorge) 1131 Skamania Lodge Way Stevenson, WA 98648 *See page 552*	Up to 500 P/R/B/S/M/	195	Sales Office (509) 427-2503 (800) 376-9116
VANCOUVER			
The Academy Reception Rooms 400 E. Evergreen Blvd. Vancouver, WA 98660	Sit-down: Up to 250 Reception: Up to 300 R/B/S/M/		Windsor Consultant (360) 696-4884
American Legion/Post 14 710 Esther St. Vancouver, WA 98660	Up to 350 R/B/S/M/		Les Scott (360) 696-2579
American Legion/Post 176 14011 N.E. 20th Ave. Vancouver, WA 98686	Up to 200 R/B/S/M/		Karen (360) 573-2331 Fax (360) 573-1475
Bagley Center 4100 Plomondon Vancouver, WA 98661	Sit-down: Up to 300 Reception: Up to 350 *No alcohol R/B/S/M/		Facilities Coordinator (360) 696-8219
The Best Inn & Suites 221 N.E. Chkalov Dr. Vancouver, WA 98684	Sit-down: Up to 200 R/B/S/M/C/	116	Sales Office (360) 256-7044 (800) 426-5110
Best Western Ferryman's Inn 7901 N.E. 6th Ave. Vancouver, WA 98665	Up to 200 R/B/S/M/C/	134	Tonya Kelly Manager (360) 574-2151
Chart House 101 E. Columbia Wy. Vancouver, WA 98661 *See page 562*	Up to 200 Meeting: Up to 45 R/B/S/M/		General Manager (360) 693-9211

P=Picnic   R=Reception   B=Banquet   S=Seminar   M=Meeting   C=Convention

Please let these businesses know that you heard about them from the Bravo! Event Resource Guide.

VANCOUVER AREA BANQUET AND EVENT SITE LISTINGS

ADDRESS	CAPACITY	GUEST ROOMS	CONTACT
City Grill—N.E. 605 N.E. 78th St. Vancouver, WA 98683 *See page 326*	Up to 125 R/B/S/M/		Leslie Walls (360) 574-2270
City Grill—S.E. 916 S.E. 164th Ave. Vancouver, WA 98683 *See page 326*	Up to 125 R/B/S/M/		Dave Walls (360) 253-5399
Clark County Square Dance Center 10713 N.E. 117th Ave. Vancouver, WA 98662	Up to 500 R/B/S/M/C/		Rental Coordinator (360) 256-5049
Club Green Meadows 7703 N.E. 72nd Ave. Vancouver, WA 98661	Indoor: Up to 275 P/R/B/S/M/		Ray Weldon (360) 256-1510
Covington House 4201 Main St. Vancouver, WA 98660	Up to 75 R/B/S/M/		Owner (360) 695-6750
Fruit Valley Community Center 3203 Unander St. Vancouver, WA 98660	Up to 100 *No alcohol R/B/		Irene Ells (360) 694-5450
The Heathman Lodge 7801 N.E. Greenwood Dr. Vancouver, WA 98662 *See page 492*	Up to 300 R/B/M/S/	143	Catering Office (360) 254-3100 (888) 475-3100
Hidden House Restaurant 100 W. 13th St. Vancouver, WA 98660	Indoor: Up to 80 Indoor-outdoor: Up to 125 R/B/S/M/		Susan Courtney Manager (360) 696-2847
The Holland Restaurant 1708 Main St. Vancouver, WA 98660	Up to 50 R/B/S/M/		Manager (360) 694-7842
The Hostess House Reception Center 10017 N.E. Sixth Ave. Vancouver, WA 98685	Sit-down: Up to 175 Reception: Up to 300 R/B/S/M/		Julie or Tom (360) 574-3284
Leverich Park 39th & Main St. Vancouver, WA	Sit-down: Up to 100 P/R/B/S/M/		Facilities Coordinator (360) 696-8236
LeSlam Sports Cafe 11808 NE Fourth Plain Vancouver, WA 98682	Skyroom: Up to 25 VIP Room: Up to 25		Manager (360) 944-5510
Luepke Senior Center 1009 E. McLoughlin Blvd. Vancouver, WA 98663	Up to 300 *No alcohol R/B/S/M/		Facilities Coordinator (360) 696-8219

P=Picnic   R=Reception   B=Banquet   S=Seminar   M=Meeting   C=Convention

VANCOUVER AREA
BANQUET AND EVENT SITE LISTINGS

ADDRESS	CAPACITY	GUEST ROOMS	CONTACT
Marshall Center 1009 E. McLoughlin Blvd. Vancouver, WA 98663	Up to 125 *No alcohol R/B/S/M/		Facility Coordinator (360) 696-8236
The Marshall House 1301 Officers Row Vancouver, WA 98661 *See page 509*	Indoor: Up to 225 More if using gardens P/R/S/M/		Frances Anderson (360) 693-3103
My Sister & I 116 E. Evergreen Blvd. Vancouver, WA 98660	Up to 50 R/B/S/M/		Owner (360) 695-2164
Norris Road Recreation Center 2000 Norris Road Vancouver, WA 98661	Up to 50 * No alcohol		(360) 696-8219
Pearson Air Museum 1115 E. Fifth St. Vancouver, WA 98661	Up to 500 Single Day Events B/P/T		John Nold (360) 694-7026 Pearson@Pacifier.com
Phoenix Inn—Vancouver 12712 S.E. Second Circle Vancouver, WA 98684	Up to 80		(360) 891-9777 (888) 988-8100
The Pythian Retirement Center 3409 Main St. Vancouver, WA 98663	Up to 200 R/B/M/		Douglas James Director of Food Service (360) 694-1370
Red Lion 100 Columbia St. Vancouver, WA 98660 *See page 537*	Theatre style: Up to 700 R/B/S/M/C/	163	Sales & Catering Office (360) 694-8341
Regal Hall Ballroom at A Night in Shining Amour 115 W. Ninth St. Vancouver, WA, 98660 *See page 538*	Up to 175 R/B/S/M/		Joe or Pam (360) 750-7891 Fax (360) 750-1956
Sheldon's Cafe at the Grant House 1101 Officers' Row Vancouver, WA 98661 *See page 547*	Indoor: Up to 115 Outdoor: Up to 125		Gary or Barbara Sheldon (360) 699-1213
Shilo Inn—Vancouver 401 E. 13th St. Vancouver, WA 98660	Up to 25 S/M/	120	Manager (360) 696-0411
Water Resource Education Center P.O. Box 1995 4600 S.E. Columbia Way Vancouver, WA 98668	Community Room: Up to 180 B/P/M/S/		(360) 696-8478

P=Picnic   R=Reception   B=Banquet   S=Seminar   M=Meeting   C=Convention

Please let these businesses know that you heard about them from the Bravo! Event Resource Guide.

VANCOUVER AREA BANQUET AND EVENT SITE LISTINGS

ADDRESS	CAPACITY	GUEST ROOMS	CONTACT
Water Works Park on Reserve behind Clark College Vancouver, WA	No maximum Outdoor amphitheater		Facilities Coordinator (360) 696-8219
Who-Song & Larry's 111 E. Columbia River Wy. Vancouver, WA 98661	Up to 70 R/B/S/M/		Manager (360) 695-1198
WASHOUGAL			
Hathaway Park G St. & 24th Washougal, WA 98671	Outdoor (shelter): Up to 50 P/R/B/		Brenda Snell (360) 835-8501
Washougal Community Center 1681 C St. Washougal, WA 98671	Banquet Room: Up to 100 Auditorium: 120 R/B/S/M/		City of Washougal (360) 835-8113

P=Picnic   R=Reception   B=Banquet   S=Seminar   M=Meeting   C=Convention

Please let these businesses know that you heard about them from the Bravo! Event Resource Guide.

Salem Area Banquet & Event Sites

SALEM AREA BANQUET AND EVENT SITE LISTINGS

ADDRESS	CAPACITY	GUEST ROOMS	CONTACT
DOWNTOWN SALEM			
Historic Reed Opera House 189 Liberty St., N.E. Salem, OR 97301	Reception: Up to 300 R/B/S/M/		Manager (503) 391-4481
NORTHEAST SALEM			
Best Western New Kings Inn 1600 Motor Court, N.E. Salem, OR 97301	Reception: Up to 150 R/B/S/M/C/		Sales Manager (503) 581-2756
Best Western Pacific Highway Inn 4646 Portland Rd., N.E. Salem, OR 97305	2 banquet rooms Up to 65 M/S/	52	Sales Office (503) 390-3200 Fax (503) 393-7989
Canton Garden Restaurant 3225 Market St. N.E. Salem, OR 97301	Up to 150 R/B/S/M/		Mary or Simon (503) 588-1125
Heritage Tree Restaurant 574 Cottage N.E. Salem, OR 97301	Up to 90 R/B/S/M/		Owner (503) 399-7075
Izzy's Pizza Restaurant 2205 Lancaster Dr. N.E. Salem, OR 97305	Up to 35 R/B/S/M/		Manager (503) 399-0915
O'Callahans at Quality Inn 3301 Market St. N.E. Salem, OR 97301	Up to 450 R/B/S/M/C/	150	Catering (503) 370-7835 or (503) 370-7997
Oregon National Guard Armory Auditorium 2320 17th St. N.E. Salem, OR 97303	Auditorium: Sit-down: Up to 700 Stage: Sit-down Up to 200 Concerts & Dances: Up to 4,000 B/P/M/S/C/		(503) 378-6923 Fax (503) 378-6413
Oregon State Fair & Expo Center 2330 17th St. N.E. Salem, OR 97310	50-4,000+ P/R/B/S/M/C/		Events Manager (503) 378-3247 Fax (503) 373-1788
Phoenix Inn—Salem North 1590 Weston Rd. Salem, OR 97301	Up to 75 S/M	80	(503) 581-7004 (888) 239-9593
Salem Inn 1775 Freeway Court, N.E. Salem, OR 97303 *See page 442*	Up to 50	63	(503) 588-0515 (888) 305-0515

P=Picnic   R=Reception   B=Banquet   S=Seminar   M=Meeting   C=Convention

Please let these businesses know that you heard about them from the Bravo! Event Resource Guide.

SALEM AREA
BANQUET AND EVENT SITE LISTINGS

ADDRESS	CAPACITY	GUEST ROOMS	CONTACT
Salem Senior Center 1055 Erixon St. N.E. Salem, OR 97303	Up to 300 R/S/M/C/		Chris (503) 588-6303 Fax (503) 588-6377
Shilo Inn Salem Suites Motel 3304 Market St., N.E. Salem, OR 97301	Reception: Up to 85 R/B/S/M/	98	Reservationist (503) 581-4001 (800) 222-2244

NORTHWEST SALEM

ADDRESS	CAPACITY	GUEST ROOMS	CONTACT
La Estrellita 1111 Edgewater St., N.W. Salem, OR 97304	Up to 80 R/B/S/M/		Manager (503) 362-0522
McGrath's Public Fish House 350 Chemeketa St., N.W. Salem, OR 97301	Up to 30 R/B/M/		Manager (503) 362-0736
Roth's Hospitality Meeting Center 1130 Wallace Rd., N.W. Salem, OR 97304	5 banquet rooms Up to 150 R/B/P/M/S/C/		Catering Dept. (503) 370-3790 Fax (503) 581-4762
Sundance Farm 3247 Orchard Heights Rd., N.W. Salem, OR 97304	Up to 60 P/R/S/M/		Owner (503) 585-7023

SOUTH SALEM

ADDRESS	CAPACITY	GUEST ROOMS	CONTACT
Phoenix Inn—Salem South 4370 Commercial St. S. Salem, OR 97302	2 banquet rooms Up to 50 B/P/M/S/	89	Sales Dept. (503) 588-9220 Fax (503) 585-3616
Rudy's at at Salem Golf Club 2025 Golf Course Rd. S. Salem, OR 97302	Sit-down: Up to 80 Reception: Up to 150 R/B/S/M/		Owner (503) 399-0449

SOUTHEAST SALEM

ADDRESS	CAPACITY	GUEST ROOMS	CONTACT
Alessandro's Park Plaza Restaurant 325 High St. S.E. Salem, OR 97301	Up to 300 R/B/S/M/ 2 rooms: up to 125		Phil (503) 370-9951
Big Horn Brewing Co. 515 12th St., S.E. Salem, OR 97302	Sit-down: Up to 40 Reception: Up to 75 R/B/		Wes Foulger (503) 363-1940
Comfort Suites 630 Hawthorne S.E. Salem, OR 97301	Indoor: Up to 225 P/R/B/S/M/C/	85	Banquet Coordinator (503) 585-9705
Creekside Golf Club 6250 Clubhouse Dr., S.E. Salem, OR 97306	Up to 220 R/B/S/M/		Linda Little (503) 363-4653

P=Picnic   R=Reception   B=Banquet   S=Seminar   M=Meeting   C=Convention

Please let these businesses know that you heard about them from the Bravo! Event Resource Guide.

SALEM AREA
BANQUET AND EVENT SITE LISTINGS

		GUEST ROOMS	
Historic Deepwood Estate 1116 Mission St. S.E. Salem, OR 97302	Indoor: Up to 50 Outdoor: Up to 150 P/R/B/S/M/		Staff Director (503) 363-1825
Historic Elsinore Theatre 170 High St. S.E. Salem, OR 97301	Sit-down: Up to 150 Theater: Up to 1,340 P/R/B/S/M/		Jean Deems (503) 375-3574 Fax (503) 375-0284
Izzy's Pizza Restaurant 2990 Commercial St. S.E. Salem, OR 97302	Up to 45 R/B/		Manager (503) 581-9831 Fax (503) 316-3909
Mill Creek Inn— **Best Western** 3125 Ryan Dr., S.E. Salem, OR 97301	Up to 200 B/S/M/C/	109	Sales & Catering (503) 585-3332 Fax (503) 375-9618
Mission Mill Village 1313 Mill St. S.E. Salem, OR 97301 *See page 512*	Inside: Up to 500 R/B/S/M/P/		Cheryl Clark (503) 585-7012 Fax (503) 588-9902
Salem Public Library 585 Liberty St. S.E. Salem, OR 97301	Loucks Lecture Hall: Up to 250 Anderson Auditorium: Up to 100 P/R/B/S/M/C/		Library Business Office (503) 588-6071 Fax (503) 589-2011
Scottish Rite Masonic Center 4090 Commercial St. S.E. Salem, OR 97302	Sit-down: Up to 250 *No alcohol R/B/S/M/		Building Manager (503) 363-9240 Fax (503) 363-2018
ALBANY			
Willamette Events Center at **Linn County Fair & Expo** 3700 Knox Butte Road Albany, OR *See page 569*	Up to 6,000 R/B/S/M/C/		(541) 926-4314 (800) 858-2005
CORVALLIS			
Bell Fountain Cellars 25041 Llewellyn Rd. Corvallis, OR 97333	Outdoor: Up to 100 Indoor: Up to 50 P/R/B/S/M/		Jeanne Mommsen (541) 929-3162
Benton County Fairgrounds 110 S.W. 53rd Corvallis, OR 97330 *See page 455*	Indoor: Up to 400 Outdoor: Up to 1,500 R/B/S/M/C/		(541) 757-1521
CH2M Hill Alumni **Center at OSU** 204 CH2M Hill Alumni Center Corvallis, OR 97330 *See page 460*	Up to 1,000 R/B/S/M/C		Lisa Templeton (541) 737-2351 Fax (541) 737-3481

P=Picnic   R=Reception   B=Banquet   S=Seminar   M=Meeting   C=Convention

SALEM AREA
BANQUET AND EVENT SITE LISTINGS

ADDRESS	CAPACITY	GUEST ROOMS	CONTACT
Salbasgeon Suites 1430 N.W. Ninth St. Corvallis, OR 97330	2 Banquet Rooms Up to 340 People R/B/S/M/C/	105	Virginia Gillespie (541) 753-4320 (800) 965-8808
Willamette Queen 1109 N.W. Ninth St. Corvallis, OR 97330 *See page 571*	Up to 107 R/B/S/M/		Irene Salomon (541) 929-4090

DALLAS/RICKREALL

ADDRESS	CAPACITY	GUEST ROOMS	CONTACT
BeckenRidge Vineyard 300 Ruben-Boise Rd. Dallas, OR 97338 *See page 453*	Up to 120; more if using covered patio P/R/B/S/M/		Becky Jacroux (503) 831-3652
Eola Hills Wine Cellars 501 S. Pacific Hwy 99W Rickreall, OR 97371	Up to 250 More if outdoor P/R/B/S/M/		(503) 623-2405
Polk County Fairgrounds 520 S. Pacific Hwy. W. Rickreall, OR 97371	1 to 600 Multiple bldgs. available P/R/B/S/M/C/		Manager (503) 623-3048 or (503) 745-7256

EUGENE/SPRINGFIELD

ADDRESS	CAPACITY	GUEST ROOMS	CONTACT
DoubleTree Hotel 3280 Gateway Road Springfield, OR 97477 *See page 476*	Up to 2,000 R/B/S/M/C	234	Kim Barbisan (541) 988-4019
Valley River Inn 1000 Valley River Way Eugene, OR 97401 See page 563	Up to 800 R/B/S/M/C/	257	Donna Earley-Thiel (541) 341-3461 Fax (541) 689-0289

GRAND RONDE

ADDRESS	CAPACITY	GUEST ROOMS	CONTACT
Spirit Mountain Casino 27100 Salmon River Hwy. Grand Ronde, OR 97347 *See page 543*	Up to 200 Theatre: Up to 300 R/B/S/M/C/		Group Sales (800) 760-7977

INDEPENDENCE

ADDRESS	CAPACITY	GUEST ROOMS	CONTACT
Amador Alley Restaurant 870 N. Main St. Independence, OR 97351	Up to 75 B/M/		Owner (503) 838-0170
Inn at Oak Knoll Restaurant 6345 Salem-Dallas Hwy. Independence, OR 97351	Up to 50 R/B/M/		(503) 378-0102 Fax (503) 399-0348

KEIZER

ADDRESS	CAPACITY	GUEST ROOMS	CONTACT
Izzy's Pizza Restaurant 3400 River Rd. Keizer, OR 97303	Up to 50 R/B/M/		Manager (503) 390-5002

P=Picnic   R=Reception   B=Banquet   S=Seminar   M=Meeting   C=Convention

Please let these businesses know that you heard about them from the Bravo! Event Resource Guide.

SALEM AREA
BANQUET AND EVENT SITE LISTINGS

ADDRESS	CAPACITY	GUEST ROOMS	CONTACT
Wittenberg Inn 5188 Wittenberg Lane Keizer, OR 97303 *See page 575*	Up to 450 R/B/S/M/	86	Richard Andres (503) 390-4733

MONMOUTH

Gentle House 855 N. Monmouth Ave. Monmouth, OR 97361 *See page 486*	Indoor: Up to 200 Outdoor: Up to 500 P/R/B/S/M/		Program Coordinator (503) 838-8673 Fax (503) 838-8289

SILVERTON

Oregon Garden 879 W. Main Street Silverton, OR 97381 *See page 522*	Indoor: Up to 1,200 Outdoor: Up to 2,000 P/R/B/S/M/C/		Tamara Muldoon (503) 874-8100 Fax (503) 874-8200

SUBLIMITY

Silver Falls Conference Center 20022 Silver Falls Hwy. S.E. Sublimity, OR 97385 *See page 551*	Indoor: Up to 86 P/R/B/S/M/		Dayna Rich (503) 873-8875 Fax (503) 873-2937

TURNER

Aldersgate Conference Center P.O. Box 16 7790 Marion Rd. S.E. Turner, OR 97392	Meetings: 10–1,600 Lodging: 10–450 P/R/B/S/M/C/ * Lodging and use of facility for non-profit or agency groups only * No alcohol	400	Guest Services (503) 743-2494 Fax (503) 743-4858
Willamette Valley Vineyards 8800 Enchanted Way S.E. Turner, OR 97392 *See page 572*	Indoor/Outdoor: Up to 600 R/B/S/M/C/		Hospitality Coordinator (503) 588-9463 (800) 344-9463

WOODBURN

Holiday Inn Express 2887 Newberg Hwy. Woodburn, OR 97071	Up to 60	81	(503) 982-6515 (800) 766-6433
Settlemeier Mansion 355 N. Settlemeier Ave. Woodburn, OR 97071	Indoor/Outdoor: Up to 30 P/R/B/S/M/		(503) 982-1897

P=Picnic   R=Reception   B=Banquet   S=Seminar   M=Meeting   C=Convention

SALEM AREA
BANQUET AND EVENT SITE LISTINGS

ADDRESS	CAPACITY	GUEST ROOMS	CONTACT
SALEM PARKS			
Bush Pasture Park **Rose Garden** 600 Mission St., S.E. Salem, OR 97301	Outdoor: Up to 100 *No tables or chairs * No alcohol P/R/		Bruce Bolton (503) 588-6261
Cascade Gateway Park 2100 Turner Rd. S.E. Salem, OR 97302	2 Uncovered: Up to 150 Covered: Up to 300 P/R/M/		Bruce Bolton (503) 588-6261
Minto Brown Island 2200 Minto Island Rd. (Off South River Rd.) Salem, OR 97302	Outdoor (shelter): Up to 150 P/R/M/		Bruce Bolton (503) 588-6261
Spongs Landing **Marion County Parks** 2500 Niagra St., N. Salem, OR 97303	Up to 300 guests 2 shelter areas P/R/M/		Denise Clark (503) 588-5036 Fax (503) 588-7970
Willamette Mission **State Park** 10991 Wheatland Rd., N.E. Gervais, OR 97026 *See page 431*	Up to 15,000		(503) 393-1172 ext. 23 Reservations: (800) 452-5687

P=Picnic   R=Reception   B=Banquet   S=Seminar   M=Meeting   C=Convention

Please let these businesses know that you heard about them from the Bravo! Event Resource Guide.   **623**

Notes

Coastal, Central & Southern Oregon Area Sites

COASTAL AREA
BANQUET AND EVENT SITE LISTINGS

ADDRESS	CAPACITY	GUEST ROOMS	CONTACT
COASTAL AREA			
The Adobe Resort 1555 Hwy 101 N. Yachats, OR 97498	Up to 100 R/B/S/M/	97 10 suites	Deana or Gary (800) 522-3623
Best Western OceanView Resort 414 N. Prom Seaside, OR 97138 *See page 369*	Up to 300 R/B/S/M/	104	Leslie Peterson (800) 234-8439 Fax (503) 738-3264
Chinook Winds Convention Center 1777 N.W. 44th St. Lincoln City, OR 97367 *See page 463*	Indoor: Up to 1,500 R/B/M/S/C/		Sales Staff (888) CHINOOK
Driftwood Shores 88416 First Ave. Florence, OR 97439	Up to 150 R/B/S/M/	136	Jennifer Fox (800) 422-5091
Embarcadero Resort Hotel 1000 S.E. Bay Blvd. Newport, OR 97365 *See page 371*	Up to 150 R/B/S/M/	75	(541) 265-8521 (800) 547-4779
Florence Events Center 715 Quince Florence, OR 97439 *See page 484*	Up to 500 R/B/S/M/C/		Barbara Gulias (541) 997-1994 Fax (541) 902-0991
Hallmark Inns & Resorts— Cannon Beach 1400 S. Hemlock Cannon Beach, OR 97110 *See page 372*	Up to 150 W/R/B/M/	128	Sales Department (888) 448-4449
Hallmark Inns & Resorts— Newport 744 S.W. Elizabeth Newport, OR 97365 *See page 372*	Up to 200 R/B/S/M/	158	Sales Department (888) 448-4449
Holiday Inn Newport at Agate Beach 3019 N. Coast Hwy. Newport, OR 97365 *See page 373*	Up to 500 R/B/S/M/	146	Sales Office (800) 546-5010
The Inn at Otter Crest 301 Otter Crest Lp. Otter Rock, OR 97369 *See page 376*	Up to 250 4 rooms R/B/S/M/	120	Marilyn Ebe (800) 326-5806

P=Picnic   R=Reception   B=Banquet   S=Seminar   M=Meeting   C=Convention

Please let these businesses know that you heard about them from the Bravo! Event Resource Guide.

COASTAL AREA
BANQUET AND EVENT SITE LISTINGS

ADDRESS	CAPACITY	GUEST ROOMS	CONTACT
Inn at Spanish Head 4009 S.W. Hwy 101 Lincoln City, OR 97367 *See page 377*	Reception: Up to 200 Sit-down: Up to 150 R/B/S/M/	120	Jeanne Schneider (541) 996-2161 (800) 452-8127 Fax (541) 996-4089
Oregon Coast Aquarium 2820 S.E. Ferry Slip Rd. Newport, OR 97365 *See page 521*	Sit-down: Up to 100 Reception: Up to 500 R/B/S/M/C/		Events Office (541) 867-3474 ext. 5221 Fax (541) 867-6846
Seaside Civic & Convention Center 415 First Ave. Seaside, OR 97138 *See page 414*	Up to 2,500 R/B/S/M/C/		Gretchen Darnell (503) 738-8585 (800) 394-3303 Fax (503) 738-0198
Shilo Inn—Lincoln City 1501 N.W. 40th St. Lincoln City, OR 97367 *See page 382*	Sit-down: Up to 500 Reception: Up to 642 R/B/S/M/	247	Group Sales (541) 994-6275 (800) 222-2244
Shilo Inn—Newport 536 S.W. Elizabeth St. Newport, OR 97365 *See page 383*	Sit-down: Up to 350 Reception: Up to 600 R/B/S/M/	179	Group Sales (541) 265-7701 (800) 222-2244
Shilo Inn—Seaside 30 N. Prom Seaside, OR 97138 *See page 384*	Up to 400 R/B/S/M/	112	Group Sales (503) 738-9571 (800) 222-2244
Stephanie Inn P.O. Box 219 Cannon Beach, OR 97110	Up to 15 R/B/S/M/	46	Group Sales (800) 797-4666
Surfsand Resort P.O. Box 219 Cannon Beach, OR 97110 *See page 386*	Up to 50 Outdoor: Unlimited R/B/S/M/	82	Jesse Remer Henderson (800) 797-4666 Fax (503) 436-9116
The Westin Salishan Lodge & Golf Resort Hwy 101 Gleneden Beach, OR 97388 *See page 566*	Up to 500 R/B/S/M/C/	205	Group Sales (800) 890-9316 Fax (503) 764-3510

P=Picnic   R=Reception   B=Banquet   S=Seminar   M=Meeting   C=Convention

Please let these businesses know that you heard about them from the Bravo! Event Resource Guide.

CENTRAL & SOUTHERN OREGON AREA BANQUET AND EVENT SITE LISTINGS

ADDRESS	CAPACITY	GUEST ROOMS	CONTACT
CENTRAL OREGON			
Big K Guest Ranch & Conference Center 20029 Hwy 138 W. Elkton, OR 97436 *See page 388*	P/R/B/S/M/C/	80	Kathie Williamson (800) 390-2445
Black Butte Ranch P.O. Box 8000 Black Butte Ranch, OR 97759	Indoor: Up to 40 Outdoor: Up to 300 R/B/M/		Reservations (800) 452-7455
Eagle Crest Resort 1522 Cline Falls Rd. Redmond, OR 97756 *See page 370*	Indoor: Up to 350 R/B/S/M/C/	100	Robbin Murray (541) 923-2453 (800) 682-4786
Kah-Nee-Ta Resort P. O. Box K Warm Springs, OR 97761 *See page 378*	Indoor: Up to 700 P/R/B/S/M/C/	170	Sales Department (503) 768-9830
Shilo Inn Bend 3105 O.B. Riley Rd. Bend, OR 97701 *See page 381*	Up to 250 R/B/S/M/C	151	(800) 222-2244
Mount Bachelor Village 19717 Mt. Bachelor Drive Bend, Oregon 97702 *See page 379*	Up to 150 R/B/S/M/C/	130	Sales Department (800) 452-9846 Fax (541) 388-7820
Rock Springs Guest Ranch & Conference Center 64201 Tyler Rd. Bend, OR 97701 *See page 392*	Up to 70 R/B/S/M/	20–50 people	Carole Springer or John Gill (800) 225-3833 Fax (541) 382-7774
Sunriver Resort P.O. Box 3609 Sunriver, OR 97707 *See page 385*	Up to 500 R/B/S/M/C/		Catering Office (541) 593-4605 Fax (541) 593-2742
SOUTHERN OREGON			
The Running Y Ranch Resort 5115 Running Y Rd. Running Y, OR 97601 *See page 380*	R/B/S/M/	83	(888) 850-0275
Seven Feathers Casino 146 Chief Milwaleta Lane Canyonville, OR 97417 *See page 546*	Up to 1,500 R/B/S/M/C/	147	Sales & Catering Department (800) 548-8461 Fax (541) 839-4222
Windmill Inn of Ashland 2525 Ashland St. Ashland, OR 97520	Sit-down: Up to 750 R/B/S/M/	230	(541) 482-3010 (800) 333-8310

P=Picnic   R=Reception   B=Banquet   S=Seminar   M=Meeting   C=Convention

Please let these businesses know that you heard about them from the Bravo! Event Resource Guide.

INDEX BY NAME & SUBJECT

Symbols

1847 Williams Holmes House 117

A

A Dancing Penguin
  Music Live Music & DJ 286
A Little Pony & A Little Petting Zoo 243
A Taste of Holland Bakeries & Catering 312
A to Z Party Rental 187
A.C. Gilbert's Discovery Museum 116
AA Two's Company DJ Service 285
ACEP—Association of Catering & Event
  Professionals 64
ARAMARK—GPL 406, 587
The Academy Reception Rooms 613
Accent Event Management 50
Accent on Events 313
Accommodations—
  Hotels 349–366
  Resorts 367–386
  Retreats 387–394
Adams & Faith Photography 140
Adelman Peony Gardens 117
Aden, Keith—
  Photography & Video Productions 141
The Adobe Resort 626
The Adrianna Hill Grand Ballroom 446, 580
Advertising 129–136
Airlie Winery 106, 609
Alameda Brew House 105
Alberta Station Ballroom 586
Albertina's at The Old Kerr Nursery 447, 586
Alderbrook Park Corp 427, 612
Aldersgate Conference Center 622
Alessandro's Park Plaza Restaurant 619
Alfie's Wayside Country Inn 597
All About Music DJ Co 287
All Events & Entertainment Agency 245
All Seasons Indoor Golf Club 448, 593
All-Wright Music Co 288
Aloha Odd Fellows Hall 593
Always Perfect Catering 314
Amadeus 598
Amadeus at the Fernwood 449, 599
Amador Alley Restaurant 621
American Advertising Museum 116, 590
American Legion/Post 14 613
American Legion/Post 176 613
Amity Vineyards 106

Amtrak 112
Amusement Centers 108–109
Amusement Parks 94, 96–99
An Elegant Affair 315
Anthony Lakes 110
Anthony Wedin Productions, Inc 289
Aquatic Park 96
Argyle Winery 106
Arlene Schnitzer Concert Hall 580
Arnegards 450, 590
Association & Conference
  Services (A&CS) 396
Association of Catering &
  Event Professionals (ACEP) 64
The Atrium 451, 580
Atwater's Restaurant & Bar 452, 580
Audience Participation 237–256
Audiovisual Services 167–178
Aurora Colony Historical Society 593
Authentic Texas BBQ 316
Autumn Wind Vineyard 106
Avalon Technology Group 434, 592

B

Bagdad Theatre & Pub 590
Bagley Center 613
Baja Grill Restaurant & Catering 317
Bakeries 299–302, 312
Balloon Decor 207–209
Bands 263–276
Banquet Sites 417–578
Barbur Blvd. Rentals, Inc 169, 188
Barton Productions Catering 318
Baskin Robbins Ice Cream & Yogurt 300
Battle Ground Senior Center 612
Beaverton Community Center 594
Beaverton Mall 111
BeckenRidge Vineyard 106, 453, 609, 621
Bell Fountain Cellars 106, 620
Bell, Da Verne 225
The Benson Hotel 351, 454, 580
Benton County Fairgrounds 455, 620
Berbati Restaurant 580
Best Bet Sports Bar & Night Club 594
The Best Inn & Suites 613
Best Western
  Columbia River Inn 368, 596
  Ferryman's Inn 613
  Hood River Inn 375, 499, 596
  Inn at the Meadows 584

629

Best Westerns continued...
Mill Creek Inn 620
New Kings Inn. 618
Oceanview Resort 369, 626
Pacific Highway Inn 618
Sherwood Inn 599
Bethel Heights Vineyard. 106
Big Horn Brewing Co. &
   Ram Restaurant 105, 599
Big Horn Brewing Co.—Salem 106, 619
Big Horse Brewery & Pub 105
The Big K Guest Ranch &
   Conference Center. 388, 628
Black Butte Ranch 628
Blimpie. 319
Blue Lake Park 608
Boats & Yachts Listings 605
Boats—Event Sites 113, 419–423
Bob Miller's Almost All-Star Band 265
Bouquets & Balloons 207
Brainwaves Improvisational Comedy 234
Brentwood/Darlington Center 590
Breweries............................ 105
Brewery Tours......................... 93
Bridal Veil Lakes 428, 596
BridgePort Brewing Co. 105, 456, 589
Bridgetown Coffee Co. 304
Broadmoor Golf Course 114
Broetje House, Historic 599
Bruce Goldberg & Co. 320
Buffalo Gap Saloon & Eatery. 435, 592
Bullwinkle's Restaurant &
   Wilsonville Family Fun Center 99, 573
The Burdoin Mansion. 612
Burns-Miller, Jo Anna 280
Bus Rentals 85–86
Buses.............................. 112–113
Bush Pasture Park Gardens 117, 623
The Business Journal 131
Buster's Texas-Style Barbecue. 321
Butterfly Magic. 182, 204
Byll Davis & Friends 266
B•O•E•K Mfg — Banners Of Every Kind.... 125

C

CH2M Hill Alumni Center at OSU 460, 621
CRGVA — Columbia River Gorge Visitors
   Association 65
CVALCO — Convention & Visitors Association
   of Lane County, Oregon 66
Calendar Of Events 119–122
Camas Community Center 612
Canterbury Falls & English Gardens 600
Canton Garden Restaurant 618

Capers Cafe & Catering Co. 322, 586
Captain Ainsworth House Bed & Breakfast... 601
Caribiner Audio Visual................... 170
Caricatures by Philip O'Neil 229
Carnegie Center 601
Carpenter Hall 601
Cascade Athletic Club 597
Cascade Gateway Park.................. 623
Cascade Soaring 108
Casino Games & Parties 241–242
Cassidy's Restaurant & Catering 323, 580
Catering........................... 307–348
Catering At Its Best 324
Cavanaughs Hillsboro Hotel 457, 598
Cedar Hills Park 608
Cedar Springs Country Estate 600
The Cedars Golf Club. 114, 612
Celebrate! Catering &
   Reception Facility 458, 599
Celebration Music & Events 258
Celebration! Gift Basket Co. 162
Central Library 459, 580
Central Oregon Area Banquet &
**   Event Site Listings................... 628**
Century Hotel 602
Chair Covers...................... 183, 206
Chambers of Commerce 62–63
Champoeg Park 607
Champoeg Wine Cellar 106, 609
Charbonneau On The Green. 461, 603
   Charbonneau Golf Club............... 114
Charburger Restaurant 596
Chart House 462, 592, 613
Chateau Benoit 106, 609
Chateau Lorane. 106, 609
Chef du Jour 325
Chehalem Armory 601
Chehalem Community Center 601
Chehalem Park & Recreation Senior Center .. 601
Chehalem Winery................... 106, 609
Cherry Hill Bed & Breakfast 596
Chez Grill 590
Chief Obie Lodge 590
Childcare............................ 76
Chinook Winds Casino &
   Convention Center............. 110, 463, 626
Chocolate Logos 301
Chuck E. Cheese's 98, 464, 590
City Grill Catering 326, 614
City Hall—Portland 465, 580
Clackamas Armory..................... 595
Clackamas Co. Historical Museum 116

INDEX

Clackamas Community Club Dow Center 595
Clackamas County Fair & Event Center 595
Clackamas Promenade 111
Clackamas Town Center 111
Claremont Golf Course................... 114
Clark County Fair Association 613
Clark County Historical Museum.......... 116
Clark County Square Dance Center 614
Class Act Event Coordinators............... 51
Club Green Meadows.................... 614
ClubSport 108, 466, 602
Coach Rentals....................... 85–86
Coaches 112
**Coastal Area Banquet &
Event Site Listings............... 626–627**
Columbia Crossroads Tours 52
Columbia Gorge Factory Stores 111
Columbia Gorge Hotel 467, 596
The Columbia Gorge Interpretive
Center 117, 613
Columbia Gorge/Rooster Rock 606
Columbia Inn Restaurant 612
Columbia River Gorge Visitors Association
(CRGVA)............................. 65
Columbia River Inn—Best Western..... 368, 596
Colwood National Golf Course 114, 586
Comedian 232
ComedySportz 235
Comfort Suites 619
Communication Rentals............ 177, 185
Communication Services 167–178
Complete Music Disc Jockey Service 290
Computer Classroom 434
Connor's Events & Catering, Inc. 327
**Convention & Visitor Information
Bureaus............................ 61**
Convention & Visitors Association of Lane
County, Oregon 66
Convention & Visitors Bureau of Washington
County, Oregon 73
Convention Facilities 403–416
Convention Services 395–402
Cooley's Gardens, Inc. 117
Copying 128
Cornelius Pass Roadhouse &
Brewery....................... 105, 598
Corporate Gifts.................... 155–166
Couch Street Fish House 589
Council Crest Park 606
The Country Basket 163
Courtyard Marriott—
Portland North Harbour........... 468, 584

Courtyard by Marriott—
Lloyd Center 352, 586
Portland Airport...................... 586
Covington House 614
Creative Childcare Solutions, Inc. 76
Creekside Golf Club................. 114, 620
Crimson & Clover Florist................. 210
Cristom Vineyards 106, 609
The Crown Ballroom &
Garden Court.................. 469, 580
Crown Park........................... 612
Crown Vista Events 470, 584
Crowne Plaza 471, 599
Crystal Ball Productions.................. 228
Crystal Ballroom 472, 580
Crystal Dolphin 113, 419, 535
Crystal Lilies Exquisite Floral Artistry....... 211
Crystal Mountain Resort.................. 110
Crystal Springs Rhododendron
Garden.................. 117, 590, 606
Cucina! Cucina! Italian Cafe 584, 602
Custom Chair Covers 183, 206
Cúl an Tí............................. 267

D

DWA Trade Show & Exposition Services 399
Da Verne Bell 225
Dale's Catering Service 328
Data Base Services 396–398
Davis, Byll & Friends.................... 266
Days Inn City Center 473, 581
DeAngelo's Catering & Events 329
Decades Mobile Music................... 291
Decorations 201–214
DeeJay Entertainment.................... 292
Delilah's Catering....................... 330
Demetri's Mediterranean Restaurant 581
Desktop Publishing................ 123–128
Desserts 299–302
Developing an Exhibit 405
Digitype Imaging & Design, Inc............ 126
Disc Jockeys 283–298
DoubleTree
Columbia River 474, 584
Hotel Eugene-Springfield 476, 621
Hotel Jantzen Beach 477, 584
Hotel Portland • Lloyd Center....... 478, 587
Hotel • Portland Downtown 475, 581
Dove Release 182, 204
Driftwood Shores 626
Duck Pond Cellars 106
Duo con Brio 280

E

ESI—Event Solutions Inc. 53, 397
EWE-ME & Co. 55
Eagle Crest Resort 370, 628
   Golf Course 114
East Fork Country Estate 597
Eastmoreland Grill at the
   Eastmoreland Golf Course 479, 590
   Golf Course 114, 479
Eastport Plaza 111
Eddie May Murder Mysteries. 239
Edgefield Brewery & Power Station—
   McMenamins. 105, 106, 389, 603
Edmund Keene Photographers 142
Electronic Polling 184, 255
Elk Cove Vineyards 106, 597, 609
Elk Rock Garden of the Bishops Close 117
Ellen Lindquist 279
Elsie J. Stuhr Adult Leisure Center 594
Elway Research, Inc. 184, 255
Embarcadero Resort Hotel & Marina. . . . 371, 626
Embassy Suites Hotel
   Portland—Downtown 354, 481, 581
   Portland—Washington Square 353, 602
   Portland Airport. 480, 587
Embroidery. 160
Emerald Employment. 80
Employment Services. 79–82
Enchanted Forest 108
Encore Studios
   Disc Jockeys 293
   Photography. 143
   Video 152
End of the Oregon Trail
   Interpretive Center. 116–117, 482, 601
Entertainers 227–236, 263–298
Entertainment Consultants 257–262
Environmental Learning Center 601
Eola Hills Wine Cellars 106, 609, 621
Erath Vineyards 106, 609
Ernesto's Italian Restaurant 436, 592
Espresso Catering. 303–306
Espresso Volare! Espresso Catering 305
The Essentials. 268
Essig Entertainment 171
Event Insurance 78
Event Planners 49–58
Event Planning Organizations 59–74
Event Rental Communications, Inc. 177, 185
Event Sites. 417–578
Event Solutions Inc. (ESI) 53, 397
Events Etcetera 54
Evesham Wood Vineyard & Winery 609

Exhibition Facilities 403–416
Exhibition Services. 395–402

F

Fairway Village Golf Club 114
Family Fun Centers 96–99
Ferryman's Inn—Best Western 613
Fifth Avenue Suites Hotel. 338, 355, 483, 581
The Final Touch Floral Design &
   Balloon Decor 208
Five Star Limousine Service 112
Flerchinger Vineyards 106
Fletcher, Jerry. 225
Florence Events Center 484, 626
Florists. 207–208, 210–213
Flowers Tommy Luke. 213
Flowers by Jacobsen's 212
Flying Dutchman Restaurant & Winery. 502
Flying M Ranch 108, 604
Food in Bloom Catering. 331
Forest Hills Golf Course. 114
Forest Park 117
Formal Wear. 215–218
Fort Vancouver National Historic Site 117
Fortune Teller 228
Foster Rentals. 189
The Fountains Ballroom. 485, 590
Four Points Hotel Sheraton 356, 581, 592
Frey's Dahlias. 117
Friendly House. 589
Fruit Valley Community Center 614
Fun-Mobile Adventures, Inc. 87, 108, 112

G

GO-SGMP—Greater Oregon Society of
   Government Meeting Professionals 72
Gales Creek Insurance Services 78
The Galleria 111
Game Shows 241
Games 237–256
Games-To-Go Rentals &
   MiniGolf-On-Wheels 246
Gaming Centers 110
The Gatelodge Restaurant at
   Pittock Mansion. 530, 589
Gentle House 486, 622
George Fox University 601
Georgian Room Restaurant 581
Gift Baskets. 162–166
Gifts 164, 222
Gingiss Formalwear 217

Glendoveer Golf Club—East 114
Glenn Otto Community Park 608
Goldberg, Bruce & Co. 320
Golden Valley Brewery & Pub 105
Golf Courses 114
Golf Discounters 161
The Governor Hotel—
 Jake's Catering 332, 357, 487, 581
The Grand Oregon Lodge. 602
Grant, Tom 281
Graphic Design 123–128
Gray Gables Inn 600
Gray Line of Portland 85, 112
Grayland, Vicki—Photographer 144
Greater Newport Chamber of Commerce 68
Greater Oregon Society of Government
 Meeting Professionals—GO-SGMP 72
Greek Cusina—Minoan Room 488, 581
The Greenwood Inn 489, 594
Greep, Linda 225
Gresham Armory 597
Gresham Golf Course 114
Griffith Park Athletic Club 594
The Grotto 117

H

H.O.R.S.E.S., Ltd. 108
Hall Street Bar & Grill 594
Hallmark Inns & Resorts, Inc.—
 Cannon Beach 372, 490, 626
 Newport 372, 490, 626
Harrison, Michael Allen 278
Hathaway Park 616
The Heathman Hotel 491, 581
The Heathman Lodge 492, 614
Heffernan's Corporate Catering 343
Helpful Hints—
 Ad Specialties & Promotions 156
 Attractions, Activities & Tours 92
 Audience Participation & Themes 238
 Audiovisual Services 168
 Bands 264
 Banquet, Meeting & Event Sites 418
 Corporate & Specialty Gifts 157
 Decorations & Party Supplies 202
 Desktop Publishing & Signage 124
 Developing an Exhibit 405
 Disc Jockeys 284
 Event Catering 308
 Event Liquor 309
 Florists 203
 Formal Wear & Tuxedos 216
 Hotel Accommodations 350
 How to Write a Press Release 130
 Invitations & Paper Supplies 220
 Meeting Planning Organizations 60

Helpful Hints continued...
 Photography & Video Services 138
 Planning a Picnic 426
 Questions to Ask Your Facility 404
 Rental Services 180
 Specialty Services 181
 Themes & Props 196
 Transportation 84
Heritage Tree Restaurant 618
Heron Lakes Golf Course (Gray Blue) 114
Hidden House Restaurant 614
High Desert Museum 116
Hilton Garden Inn—
 Portland Airport 494, 587
 Portland/Beaverton 493, 594
Hilton Portland 495, 582
Historic Deepwood Gardens 117, 620
The Historic Elsinore Theatre 117, 620
Historic Gentle House 486, 622
Historic Hawthorne District 111
Historic Kenton Firehouse
 Community Center 585
Historic Portland City Hall 465
Historic Reed Opera House 618
Holiday Inn—
 Airport 587
 Express 604, 622
 Newport at Agate Beach 373, 626
 Portland Airport Hotel & Trade Center 496
 Select 497, 592, 603
 Windows Restaurant & Terrace 588
The Holland Restaurant 614
Holland Studios
 Special Occasion Photography 145
Hollywood Lights, Inc. 172
Homestead Village 358
Honeywood Winery 106, 609
Hood River Hotel 374, 498, 596
Hood River Inn 375, 499, 596
Hoodoo 110
The Hoop 108
The Hostess House 614
Hotel Accommodations 349–366
Hotel Oregon—McMenamins 105, 438
Hotel Vintage Plaza &
 Pazzo Ristorante 359, 528, 583
Howell Territorial Park 606
Hoyt Arboretum 606
Huber's 437, 582
Hunter Creek Farm 500, 603
Hut Airport Shuttle 112
Hybrid Moon Video Productions 153

I

Ice Carvings 205, 310
Ice Cream 300

idesign —
    graphic design & print production 127
Il Fornaio 439, 589
Imperial Hotel—
    Typhoon! on Broadway 501, 582
Improvisational Comedy 227–236
Incentive Marketing 158
Indian Creek Golf Course 114
Indian Head Gaming Center 110
Inn Crowd 81
Inn at Oak Knoll Restaurant 621
The Inn at Otter Crest 106, 376, 502, 609, 626
Inn at Spanish Head 377, 503, 627
Instant Digital Photography 139
Interactive Games 237–256
International Discount Golf 161
Interstate Firehouse Cultural Center 584
Interstate Special Events 173, 190
Invitations 219–222
Irvington Club 587
It's a Mystery 240
Izzy's Pizza Restaurant 618, 620, 622

J

J.J. North's Grand Buffet 587
JaCiva's Bakery & Chocolatier 301
Jak Tanenbaum Photography Associates 146
Jake's Catering at
    The Governor Hotel 332, 357, 487, 581
Jake's Grill 582
Jantzen Beach Center 111
Japanese Garden 117
Jasmine Tree 582
Jenkins Estate 608
Jerry Fletcher 225
Jetboat/Tours 104
Jo Anna Burns-Miller 280
John BarleyCorns Brewery 105
John, Michael 233
Jordan, Pamela 281

K

Kah-Nee-Ta Resort 378, 628
    Golf Course 114
Kart Racing 94, 253
Keene, Edmund—Photographers 142
The Keg Restaurant 593, 597
Keith Aden Photography &
    Video Productions 141
Kells—
    Portland's Irish Restaurant & Pub 504, 582
Kennedy School—McMenamins . . . 105, 390, 587

Kilarney West Golf Course 114
Kim Ralphs & Co 269
King City Golf Course 114
Kingstad
    Meeting Centers 440, 505, 582, 587, 594
Kramer Vineyards 106, 610

L

LYNMAR enterprises, inc. 159
La Estrellita 619
Labyrinth 56
Lacey's in Lake Oswego 599
The Lake House at Blue Lake Park 603
Lake Oswego Golf Course 114
Lakeside Gardens 591
Lakeside Golf & Racquet Club 114
Lakewood Center for the Arts 599
Lamb, Patrick 274
Lancaster Mall 111
Lane County, Oregon—
    Convention & Visitors Association 66
Langdon Farms Golf Club 114
Lange Winery 107
Laser Tag 251–252
LaserPort 108, 251, 506, 594
Laurel Ridge Winery 106, 597, 610
Laurelhurst Club 591
Laurelhurst Park 607
LeSlam Sports Cafe 614
Leach Botanical Gardens 607
Legendtelling 230
Leo Commercial Photography 147
Leverich Park 614
Lewis & Clark Railroad Co. 112
Lewis River Golf Course 115
Limousines 88–89, 112
Linda Greep 225
Lindquist, Ellen 279
Linn County Fair & Expo—
    Willamette Events Center 416, 569, 620
Listings—Banquet & Event Sites
    Boats & Yachts 605
    Central Oregon Area 628
    Coastal Area 626
    Oregon Winery Sites 609
    Park Sites 606
    Portland Area 579
    Salem Area 617
    Southern Oregon Area 628
    Trains 605
    Trolley 605
    Vancouver Area 611
Livery 112
Lloyd Center 111

London Catering. 333
Lone Oak Racing, Inc. 108
Loose Cannons 270
Lucky Labrador Brewing Co.. . . . . 105, 591
Luepke Senior Center. 614
Luminos 271

M

M & M Balloon Co. 209
MPI—Meeting Professionals International 67
Made In Oregon 164
Magazines 135
Mainlight Media, Inc.. 148
Majorie Stewart Senior Community Center. . . 602
Malibu Grand Prix 108
Mall 205 111
Mallory Hotel 582
Mandarin Cove Chinese Restaurant. 582, 592
Marine Park 113, 420, 432, 554, 606
Marion Country Historical Society Museum . . 116
Market Street Catering 334
Marquam Hill Vineyards 107, 610
Marriott, Courtyard by—
    Portland North Harbour. 468
    Lloyd Center 352
Marriott Hotel—
    Downtown Portland. 507, 582
    Portland City Center 508
Marshall Center 615
The Marshall House 509, 615
Maryhill Museum of Art. 116, 596, 612
Marylhurst University Conference &
    Retreat Center 510, 599
Masonic Lodge. 597
McCormack, Tom—Legendtelling. 230
McCormick & Schmick's
    Fishouse & Bar 594
    Jake's Catering 332, 487, 581
    Seafood Restaurant 582
McGrath's Public Fish House. 619
McIver State Park. 606
McLean House & Park. 603, 608
McLoughlin House National Historical Site . . 117
McMenamins—
    Cedar Hills. 105, 594
    Cornelius Pass Roadhouse &
    Brewery. 105, 598
    Edgefield Brewery &
    Power Station 105, 389, 603
    Hotel Oregon. 105, 438, 599
    Kennedy School 105, 390, 587
    St. Johns Pub. 585
McQueen 272
Media 129–136

Meeting Planners 49–58
Meeting Planning Organizations 59–74
Meeting Professionals International (MPI) 67
Meeting Sites. 417–578
Meetings in the West 132
Meier & Frank 581
The Melody Ballroom 511, 591
Memorial Coliseum 410, 585
    Floor Map 411
Meriwether National Golf Club 115, 598
Metro Police Club 591
Metzger Park Hall 608
Michael Allen Harrison 278
Michael John 233
Mill Creek Inn—Best Western 620
The Mill Gaming Center & Resort. 110
Miller's, Bob—Almost All-Star Band 265
The Milwaukie Center 600
The Milwaukie Grange. 600
MiniGolf-On-Wheels &
    Games-To-Go Rentals 246
Mint Valley Golf Course. 115
Minto Brown Island 623
Mission Mill Museum 512
Mission Mill Village. 116–117, 620
The Moes 273
Moments In Time Photography 149
Monte Carlo 591
Montgomery Park. 513, 589
Montinore Vineyards 107
Morton's of Chicago—
    The Steakhouse 441, 583
Motivational Speakers 223–226
Mt. Angel Brewing Co. 105
Mt. Ashland Ski Area 110
Mt. Bachelor Ski Resort 110
Mount Bachelor Village Resort 379, 628
Mt. Hood Community College. 598
Mount Hood Golf Club 115
Mt. Hood Meadows
    Ski Resort 95, 110, 514, 600
Mt. Hood Railroad 112
Mount Hood Railroad & Dinner Train. . . 424, 605
Mt. Hood Skibowl Winter &
    Summer Resort 110, 429, 600
Mount St. Helens
    Coldwater Ridge Visitors Center. 117
Mountain View Golf Club 115
Mr. Formal 218
Mt. Tabor Park 607
The Multnomah Center 592
Multnomah Falls Lodge 603

Multnomah Greyhound Park 108
Multnomah Village 111
Murder Mysteries 239–241
The Museum at Warm Springs 116
Museum of Natural History 116
Museums 116
Music Express
  Mobile Disc Jockey Service 294
Musical Comedian 233
Musicians 257–282
My Sister & I 615

Orchard Heights Winery 107
Oregon Army National Guard Armory 596
Oregon City Golf Club 115, 520, 602
Oregon Coast Aquarium 117, 521, 627
Oregon Convention Center 406, 587
  Calendar of Events 120
  Floor Map 407
Oregon Electric Railway Museum 116
Oregon Garden 118, 522, 622
The Oregon Golf Club 523, 603
Oregon History Center 116
Oregon Maritime Center & Museum 116
Oregon Museum of Science &
  Industry—OMSI. 408, 524, 591
  Floor Map 409
Oregon National Guard Armory 597
Oregon National Guard Armory Auditorium . . 618
Oregon Screen Impressions 160
Oregon Speakers Association 224
Oregon Sports Hall of Fame
  Museum 116, 525, 583
Oregon State Capitol & Grounds 118
Oregon State Fair & Expo Center 618
Oregon State Parks—
  Portland/Columbia Gorge 431
Oregon Winery Site Listings 609–610
Oregon Zoo 109, 526, 592
Orenco Woods Golf Course 115
The Overlook House 585, 607
Oxbow Park 606
Oxford Suites Hotel 585
O'Callahan's Restaurant & Catering at
  Ramada Inn Portland Airport 517, 587
Quality Inn Hotel &
  Convention Center 362, 618
O'Neil, Philip—Caricatures by 229

N

NIKETOWN 111
NW Expo Services 400
Namasté Retreat & Conference Center . . 391, 603
The Networking Ninja 225
New Kings Inn—Best Western 618
New Seoul Garden &
  Salt & Pepper Club 515, 594
New Theatre Building 583
Newport Chamber of Commerce 68
Newspapers 134
Nob Hill Shopping District 111
Nonstop Entertainment 259
Norris Road Recreation Center 615
North Clackamas Aquatic Park 96, 108
North Clackamas Park—
  The Milwaukie Center 606
North Star Ballroom 516, 585
Northwest Artist Management 260
Northwest Neighborhood Cultural Center 589

O

OMSI—Oregon Museum of
  Science & Industry . . . 100, 116, 408, 524, 591
  Floor Map 409
OSU—CH2M Hill Alumni Center 460, 621
Oak Grove Orchards 610
Oak Knoll Winery 107
Oaks Amusement
  Park 97, 108, 430, 518, 591, 607
Oaks Park Historic
  Dance Pavilion 430, 518, 591, 607
OceanView Resort—Best Western 626
Officers' Row
  The Marshall House 509
  Sheldon's Cafe at the Grant House . . . 547, 615
The Old Church Society, Inc. 519, 583
Old Market Pub & Brewery 105
Old Sellwood Antique Row 111
Old Spaghetti Factory 592, 595, 598

P

PDX Conference Center 531
POVA—Portland Oregon Visitors
  Association 70
Pacific Executive Services, Inc. 88, 112
Pacific Talent, Inc. 261
Pacific University—University Center 597
Paintball Island 94, 108, 253, 595
Pamela Jordan 281
Pantheon Banquet Hall 591
Paper Supplies 221–222
PaperPlus® 221
Paradigm Conference Center 527, 600
Paradym Events 197
Paragon Restaurant & Bar 589
The Paramount Hotel 360

Park Site Listings 606–608	**Pony Rides** 243–244
Parks 426–432	Ponzi Vineyards 107
Parties Inc. — A Tommy's Toys Co. 247	Port of Portland—
Party Outfitters Interactive Games 248	Portland International Airport
The Party Place 191	(PDX) Conference Center 531, 587
The Party Pro's 189	Porter's Catering & Woodsmoke Barbecue ... 336
Partyworks Interactive 249	**Portland Area Banquet &**
Pasquale's Ristorante 374, 498, 596	**Event Site Listings** 579–604
Pat's Acres Karting Complex ... 94, 108, 253, 595	Portland Art Museum 116
Patrick Lamb Productions 274	North Wing 532, 583
Pazzo Ristorante 359, 528, 583	Portland BrewBus 93, 105, 108
Pearson Air Museum 116, 615	Portland Brewing Co 105
Peninsula Park Rose Garden 607	Portland Center Stage 102
Performers 227–236	Portland Center for the
Performing Arts 101–102	Performing Arts 101, 533, 583
Persimmon Country Club 115, 529, 591, 598	Calendar of Events 121
Petting Zoos 243–244	Portland Children's Museum 116
Phoenix Inn—	Portland Civic Auditorium 583
Beaverton 595	Portland Conference Center 534, 588
Lake Oswego 599	Portland Forest Dragons (AFL) 109
Salem North 618	Portland Limousine Co. 89, 112
Salem South 619	Portland Marriott—
Tigard 602	City Center 361, 508, 582
Troutdale 603	Downtown 507, 582
Vancouver 615	Portland Meadows 108, 585
Wilsonville 603	Portland Metropolitan Chamber of
Photo Promotions 139	Commerce 69
Photography Services 137–150	Portland Metropolitan Exposition Center 585
Piatti on Broadway 583	Portland Oregon Visitors
Pier Park 607	Association (POVA) 70
Pioneer Courthouse Square 118, 607	Portland Pythons (PSA) 109
Pioneer Place 111	Portland Saturday Market 111
Pioneer Place II 111	Portland Spirit 113, 419, 535, 605
Pittock Mansion 118, 530, 589	Portland Trail Blazers (NBA) 109
Pizzicato Catering & Delivery 335	Portland Winter Hawks (WHL) 109
Plainfield's Mayur Cuisine of India 592	Portland's White House 588
Planning A Meeting Or Event—	Powell's City of Books 118
Administration Needs 38	Premiere Valet Service, LLC 112
Budget 33	**Presentations** 223–226
Checklist, Profile & Scheduling 32	**Printing** 123–128
Negotiation & Vendor Selection 37	Professional Ice Carving 205, 310
On-site & Meeting Survival Supplies 40	Progress Downs Municipal Golf Course 115
Organizing A Golf Tournament 44	**Promotional Items** 155–160
The Planning & Timeline Process 34–35	The Prop Shop 198
Planning A Class Reunion 47	**Props** 195–200
Planning A Company Picnic 46	Pumpkin Ridge Golf Club 115, 536, 597
Planning A Ski Day 45	The Pythian Retirement Center 615
Post Meeting Or Event 42	
Promotion & Press Releases 39	**Q**
Site Selection & Negotiation 36	
Sponsorship 43	Quail Run Golf Club 115
Types Of Events & Where To Start 30	Quality Inn Hotel &
Why, What & Who 31	Convention Center 362, 618
Plans & Action 57, 398	Queen Ann Victorian Mansion 585
Platinum Records Lights & Sound 174	
Polk County Fairgrounds 621	

Queen Bee Gift Baskets 165
Questions to Ask Your Facility 404

R

Radio Stations 133
Radisson Hotel Portland 363, 588
Rafati's Elegance in Catering 337, 558
Raleigh Park 608
Ralphs, Kim & Co. 269
Ramada Inn Portland Airport—
 O'Callahan's Restaurant &
 Catering 517, 587
Ramona's Baskets Bearing Gifts 166
Raz Transportation & Tours 86, 112
Recreation 108–109
Red Hawk Vineyard 107
Red Lion Hotel at the Quay 537
Red Lion—Coliseum 585
Red Robin 595
Red Star Tavern &
 Roast House 338, 355, 483, 581
The Refectory Restaurant 588
Regal Hall Ballroom at
 A Night in Shining Amour 538, 615
Registration Services 396–398
Rental Services 179–194
The Reserve Vineyards &
 Golf Club 115, 539, 593
Resort Accommodations 367–386
The Resort at The Mountain 115, 540, 600
Retreat Accommodations 387–394
Rex Hill Winery 107, 610
Rheinlander German Restaurant . . . 339, 541, 588
Rice, Susan—Comedian 232
Rich's Restaurant 602
The Ringside 588
RiverPlace Hotel 364, 542, 583
Rock Bottom Restaurant &
 Brewery 105, 543, 583
Rock Creek Country Club &
 Banquet Facility 589
Rock Springs Guest Ranch &
 Conference Center 392, 628
Rocket City Neon Advertising Museum &
 Reception Hall 612
Rose City Golf Club 115
Rose City Sound & Lighting 175
Rose Garden 410
Rose Garden arena 585
Rose Quarter 122, 410
Rose Quarter Commons 410, 585
 Calendar of Events 122
 Campus Map 413

Rose's Tea Room 311
Roth's Hospitality Meeting Center 619
Rudy's at Salem Golf Club 619
The Running Y Ranch Resort 380, 393, 628

S

S.A.L.E.M. Treks Llama Tours 109
The S.M.I.L.E. Station 592
SCVA—Salem Convention & Visitors
 Association 71
SK Watercraft Rentals, Inc. 103, 109, 186
Salbasgeon Suites 621
**Salem Area Banquet &
 Event Site Listings 617–623**
Salem Area Transit—Cherriots 112
Salem Center 111
Salem Convention & Visitors
 Association (SCVA) 71
Salem Inn 442, 618–619
Salem Public Library 620
Salem Senior Center 619
Salem/Keizer Volcanoes (NWLPB) 109
Salty's on the Columbia 544, 588
Salvador Molly's Catering Co. 340
Samtrak 112
Sandoval's Food & Cantina 593
Sandwich Depot Deli 341
Saxer Brewing Co. 105
Sayler's Old Country Kitchen 545, 591, 595
Scenic Sites 117
Schreiner's Iris Gardens 118
Scoggins Valley Park/Henry Hagg Lake 608
Scottish Rite Center 583
Scottish Rite Masonic Center 620
The Screening Room 176, 443, 589
Screenprinting 160
Sea Lion Caves 118
Seaside Civic & Convention Center 414, 627
 Floor Map 415
Sellwood Community Center 591
Serendipity Cellars Winery 107
Settlemeier Mansion 623
Seven Feathers Hotel &
 Casino Resort 110, 546, 628
Shadow Hills Country Club 598
Shafer Vineyard Cellars 107
Sheldon's Cafe at the Grant House—
 Officers' Row 547, 615
Shenanigans' on the Willamette 548, 586
Sheraton Portland Airport Hotel 549, 588
Sherwood Inn Best Western 599

Shilo Inn—
  Suites Hotel Bend 381, 628
  Lincoln City Oceanfront Resort &
    Conference Center................ 382, 627
  Newberg 601
  Newport Oceanfront Resort......... 383, 627
  Suites Hotel & Conference Center
    Portland Airport/I-205......... 365, 550, 588
  Portland/Beaverton 593, 595
  Salem Suites Motel 619
  Seaside Oceanfront Resort 384, 627
  Vancouver 615

Shopping **111**
Signage.......................... **123–128**
Signature Sound Mobile DJ Service 295
Silver Falls Conference Center..... 394, 551, 622
Silver Falls State Park 118
Sir Speedy................................ 128
Skamania Lodge................ 552, 596, 613
  Golf Course 115
Skate Palace 109
Ski Resorts............................. **110**
Smaller Venues **433–444**
Snead's Party Time Rentals & Decorations ... 192
Soirée 58
Sokol Blosser Winery.................... 107
Sonsational Activities, Events &
  Atmosphere....................... 250
Sound Express Multi Entertainment Inc...... 296
Southern Oregon Area Banquet &
  Event Site Listings.................... **628**
Speakers **223–226**
Special Events Co........................ 193
Spirit Mountain Casino........... 110, 553, 621
Spongs Landing 623
Sports 245
Sports Teams......................... **109**
Spring Hill Cellars 107
St. Innocent............................. 107
St. Johns Pub—McMenamins 585
St. Josef's Wine Cellars 107, 610
Staffing Services **79–82**
Stangeland Vineyards & Winery 107, 610
Stationery **221–222**
Stephanie Inn 627
Sternwheeler
  "Columbia Gorge".... 113, 420, 432, 554, 605
Sternwheeler Excursions 605
The Sternwheeler Rose................. 113, 421
Sternwheeler "Willamette Queen" 113, 422
The Stockpot Restaurant 595
Strong Photography 150
Summerfield Golf Course................. 115
Summit Ski Area........................ 110

Sundance Farm......................... 619
Sunrise Entertainment Services—
  Mobile DJs & Lighting 297
Sunriver Resort................ 385, 555, 628
Surfsand Resort 386, 627
Susan Rice—Comedian 232
Susy Wolfson 282
The Sweetbrier Inn............. 366, 556, 602
Swingline Cubs.......................... 275
Sylvia's Italian Restaurant &
  Class Act Dinner Theatre........... 557, 588
System 99.............................. 282

T

Tallina's Gardens & Conservatory 595
Tanenbaum, Jak—Photography Associates ... 146
Tanger Factory Outlet..................... 111
Tea Catering **311**
Television Stations **134**
Themes......................... **195–200**
Three Rivers Golf Course................. 115
Thrill-Ville U.S.A., Inc................... 108
Tiffany Center.................. 337, 558, 584
Tilikum Retreat Center................... 601
Timberline Lodge 110, 559, 600
Tir na Nog............................. 267
Tom Grant............................. 281
Tom McCall Waterfront Park 118
Tom McCormack's Legendtelling 230
Tommy's Toys Co — Parties Inc........... 247
Tommy Yo-Yo 231
Tony Roma's Famous for Ribs............. 342
Top O'Scott Course 115
Torii Mor Wine..................... 107, 610
Towncars.......................... **88–89**
Towne Papers.......................... 222
Trains........................ **112, 424–425**
Train Listings **605**
Transportation **112**
Transportation **83–90**
Tri-Met MAX Light Rail 112
Trolley Listing........................ **605**
Tualatin Vineyards 610
Tualatin/Durham Senior Center 602
Tuality Health Education Center 560, 598
Tubby's Deli 343
Tuxedos **215–218**
Tyee Wine Cellars...................... 107
Typhoon! on Broadway at
  Imperial Hotel 501, 582

U

Ultimate Entertainment
  Mobile Disc Jockey Service 298
Ultrazone 109, 252, 561, 600
University of Portland Chiles Center 586
University of Portland Commons/
  Main Dining Room 586
The Uptown Billiard Club 562, 590
Uptown Casino Events............... 109, 242

V

Valet Service 112
Valley River Inn 563, 621
Valley Shuttle 112
Van Rentals........................ 85–89
**Vancouver Area Banquet &
  Event Site Listings............... 611–616**
Vancouver Mall 111
Vancouver-Clark Parks & Recreation 109
Vans................................. 112
Vicki Grayland Photographer.............. 144
Video Services..................... 151–154
The Viewpoint Inn 596
Vintage Trolley 112, 425, 605
Virtual Promotions 254
Virtual Reality Entertainment 254
Visitor & Convention Information 61

W

Wallace Sports Complex, Inc. 109
Washington County Fair Complex 564, 598
Washington County, Oregon—
  Convention & Visitors Bureau 73
Washington Park Rose Garden............. 118
  Amphitheater........................ 607
  Gold Medal Garden................... 607
  Shakespearean Garden 607
Washington Square & Square Too 111
Washougal Community Center............. 616
Water Resource Education Center 615
The Water Tower at John's Landing 111
Water Works Park....................... 616
Watercraft Rentals.................. 103, 186
The Wedding House 592
Wedin, Anthony 289
West Coast Event
  Productions, Inc............. 194, 199, 401
West Hills Catering Co. 344
The Westin Portland 565, 584
The Westin Salishan Lodge &
  Golf Resort 566, 627
  Golf Course 115

Who-Song & Larry's 616
Widmer Gasthaus 105, 444, 586
Wild Bill's 241
Wild Horse Gaming Casino & Resort 110
Wildlife Safari 108
Wildwood Golf Course................... 115
Wilf's Restaurant & Piano Bar..... 345, 567, 584
Willaby's Catering 346
Willamette Athletic Club—
  Willamette Cafe................. 568, 593
Willamette Events Center at
  Linn County Fair & Expo 416, 569, 620
Willamette Gables Riverside Estate..... 570, 593
Willamette Jetboat
  Excursions 104, 109, 113, 605
Willamette Mission State Park............. 623
Willamette Park 608
"Willamette Queen"
  Sternwheeler 422, 571, 605, 621
Willamette Star............. 113, 419, 535, 605
Willamette University Gardens 118
Willamette Valley Vineyards .. 107, 572, 610, 622
Wilsonville Family Fun Center &
  Bullwinkle's Restaurant 99, 108, 573, 604
Windmill Inn of Ashland 628
Windows Sky Room & Terrace 574, 588
Wine Country Farm 107, 610
Wineries.................. 106–107, 609–610
Wish Upon A Pony...................... 244
Witness Tree Vineyard 107
Wittenberg Inn 575, 622
Wolfson, Susy.......................... 282
Woodburn Company Stores 111
The Wooden Nickel Catering.............. 347
World Forestry Center 116, 576, 593
World Trade Center Portland 577, 584

Y

YWCA—
  N.E. Center 589
  St. Johns Center..................... 586
Yachts............................... 113
Yachts-O-Fun Cruises, Inc......... 113, 423, 605
Yamhill Valley Vineyards................. 107
Yo-Yo Entertainer..................... 231
Yogurt Treats........................ 300
Youngberg Hill Vineyard 107, 610

Z

Zoo—Oregon 526, 592